Colored Glassware of the Depression Era 2

**is the second book of a two-part set
compiled by Hazel Marie Weatherman
for the use and pleasure of
fellow glass collectors.**

Colored Glassware of the Depression Era 1

is the book that charted your way through the 80 most basic Depression Glass patterns.

It's the book that put Depression Glass on the map as "the nation's most popular new collectible."

It's the book that went on to become one of the best-loved books in the collectible field.

**Book 1 stands as firm today
as the day it first made history.
It will not be redone.**

Colored Glassware of the Depression Era 2

does not repeat Book 1, but is the continuation of those harder-to-find patterns only now identified for the advanced collector.

Book 2 may not be for everyone. But if you have items in colored glass not identified in any other book, your chances of finding them here – among 1000 more patterns pictured, named, and dated – is excellent.

After four years of research, Hazel Marie Weatherman features 43 glass companies in these 400 pages. Not another fact, not another picture, would fit in.

**With Book 1 and now Book 2,
you will have all the best research
of Hazel Marie Weatherman.**

To order Book 2, see back page.

COLORED GLASSWARE of the DEPRESSION ERA 2

Published by Weatherman Glassbooks, Rt. 1, Box 357A, Ozark, Missouri 65721

HAZEL MARIE WEATHERMAN

EDITOR
ART DIRECTOR

Annette Weatherman

B & W PHOTOGRAPHY

Vernon Weatherman

GRAPHIC ARTS
PHOTOGRAPHY

Sue Weatherman

COLOR PHOTOGRAPHY

Robert Johnson
& Glassbooks Staff

A Glassbooks Production

For the Families . . .

Fourth Printing
Printed in the United States of America 1991

Photos pages 1, 7, 9, and endsheets courtesy of Library of Congress
Photos pages 3, 4 courtesy of Carnegie Library of Pittsburgh
Photos pages 2, 3 from Brown family album; photo this page courtesy 'our gang'

ISBN 0913074-04-7

To begin with...

... let me thank just a few of the people who helped me most. I've got lots of things to tell you about this book to make it better understood and more easily used—so stay with me!—but right now I want to bring these names up front where they belong.

Of the 43 glass companies featured in this book, half are still in existence today and I've researched almost every one of them personally in my numerous trips to 'glass country'. At every company I found interested people who wanted to help collectors collect their glass or wanted to help me record glass history—and some, I think, who just wanted me to get this book together at last! Anyway, in almost every case all catalogs and past files were open to me and many loaned for the months it took to publish. I am sure I speak for the entire glass-collecting community when I express appreciation for this great trust and concern.

Of many, the Brainards at Westmoreland, the Dalzells at Fostoria, the Bartletts at Bartlett-Collins, Arthur Harshman at Indiana, Gene Miller at New Martinsville, Lucille Kennedy at Imperial, Francis Hanse at Lotus, Frank Fenton at Fenton, William Otto of Hazel-Atlas, George Wood and Vernon Nicholson at Federal, Paul Sailer and John Delison at Jeannette, C. L. Spence at L. E. Smith, Harry Kammerer at Seneca, Bill Carlson at Tiffin, and the folks at Anchor-Hocking, were very special.

The companies now defunct were difficult to research, as you might imagine, but none the less fascinating. I visited the areas where these companies had been located and sought out—often door-to-door—folks who had once worked in the old factories. From their stories and feelings I gained a wonderful insight into the glass industry of that time of so many changes. I made friends, too; and, I think, brought happiness to many who now know of the great personal interest we have in the glass they made with their own hands. I kept a list of everyone who helped me here—and it is too long to print. But I know they will find themselves in these pages.

William Huntley of the Library of Congress has given so much to these glassbooks over the years and especially to this one, I cannot begin to thank him. Louise Johns and the Carnegie Library of Pittsburgh, and Virginia Wright and the Corning Museum Library were marvelous too. And every library in every glasstown was hit for as many facts as we could dust out of the stacks. Many librarians were helpful beyond their duty; some names I kept but others I never even knew so copies of this book will be sent to their libraries in appreciation of their extra interest in us glass collectors.

Speaking of *glass collectors* . . . so many fine and fun folks, friends all, helped out by sending me a piece or a photograph. Jo Ann Sausley, Mary Underhill, Ann Thomas, Jackie Stockwell, Austin and Shirley Hartsock, Phil Bee, Ed and Blanche McKinney, George and Helen DeNeen, Julian Toulouse, Landrum and Jody Cox, Barbara Shaeffer, Bob and Verlyn

Ernst, Charlie and Joyce Mefford, Pat and Sue McGrain, Fred and Dee Ray, Clyde Brugh, Chuck and Ruth Crawford, Jim and Sophia Papapanu, Hazel Easter, Jim and Catherine Boles, Jerry and Connie Monarch, Mrs. Wayne Livesay, Mr. and Mrs. Joe Reese, Virginia Hart, Ruby Hall, Alice Wilson, Dorothy Dupes, Pat Shope, Chuck Smith, Dick Beadles, Doug Lucas, Holly Millard, Bonnie Day, Dave Bennett, JoAnn Zak, James Christopher, Dorothy Rookstool, Barbara Hamilton, all the clubs and show promotors who invited me so I could keep up my homework,—and of course, Nora Koch—you are all precious. I can't begin to credit many of my dearest collector friends who write me information, but you can be sure I'll never forget what you've done for me. At least, as you read this book, you'll be able to say "I contributed *that*".

Here at home I must tribute typesetter Donna Bowman with an incredible nerve, and Larry Bangle whose artwork graces so many of the pages to come. Annette wants to thank R. Hunter Caffee for telling her what a halftone is and Loren Foltz for teaching her and Sue how to shoot them. —I don't have to thank my family. They *know*. I wouldn't know how to anyway. That's them over on the 'credit page' and no family could ever be prouder of what we accomplished working together.

Now, about Book 2. *Why did I do it?* So you would have all this information—in the simplest, quickest, and clearest form possible—at your right hand always. And so I would, too! How much longer do you think I could've dug through 11 file cabinets and 17 stacks of catalogs and 2,001 piles of letters to answer one little question? "Let's just get it between two covers", I've been saying for years now.

What is its purpose? To help you collect glass and better enjoy the glass you have collected. This question may seem rhetorical, but it's important because it excludes those reasons I didn't do it for. I *didn't* write it for historians of the glass industry, for instance. Accuracy must be impeccable for that, whereas our accuracy here is merely admirable. Our facts are only as good as our sources, which were journalistic ones. Annette and I chased those company-history facts through newspaper accounts, trade journals, county histories and old city directories. Sometimes the facts contradicted—even in the glass companies' own literature!—but we took our best hold and tied one down. In the absence of 'fact' we didn't guess, and we didn't publish anything that wasn't already in print—someplace. (Really, I don't think you'll find that much amiss. We're sticklers for the truth, when we can find it at all. I just don't want you to be alarmed if you do find a wayward name or date.)

I'm proud to say there were *very* few errors about the glassware in Book 1 and there should be a minimum in Book 2, too. My facts are taken straight from original ads, trade journal reports, and company records (they can be wrong, of course) and from my own personal observation. I don't speculate. When I can't be specific I make the most helpful generalization I can, and when I can't even do that I use the space for something else.

How complete are the chapters? Not complete—never complete. But practically speaking many of them can be considered 'complete', meaning this: I had access to all available information on that company and it is all published here. And this sort of 'completeness' was certainly my goal for every chapter possible; if it looked like I was close to getting it 'all' then I went all the way until I got it. I want you to know I did everything I could. In other cases I didn't have

access to it all; I say so, and give what I have. And in a few chapters I simply try to represent a company's wares—when other books have been done on them, for instance—by giving examples. I do this because I think it important we collectors are exposed to the whole range of our subject. The better for perspective.

What exactly is our subject here? What companies do I cover and why? The subject is all popular colored glassware made during the 20s and 30s and I try to cover as many companies who made it as possible. Some companies on which I had extremely limited information are briefly represented in the "XYZ" chapter; others—but these are few—are not mentioned at all.

The whole of my study has always been concerned with all colored glassware of that era. I know a hand-made piece from one made by machine, certainly and I also know the pressed from the blown and so on. But my greater interest is not in the various techniques of manufacture but in the remarkable trend of color which overwhelmed the glass industry from about 1920 to 1940. I collect this glass all together, I study it all together, and I believe history will be most interested in it as a color trend which actually became a part—a meaningful, significant part—of the sociology and culture of the 20s and 30s. And if you ask me, it's a lot less complicated to collect this way. When I look out there I see a great field of glassware all dressed in the same colors and all belonging to the same generation (mine!) and I just want to get out there and frolic with all of it.

Okay. *What did I exclude from Book 2 and why?* I had to leave out quite a bit, I'll tell you right now. I picture each pattern at least once, of course, and as many different pieces as possible, but too often I simply couldn't show—or even list—all the pieces to each pattern. There just wasn't the room, for one thing; and for another I didn't always *have* all the pieces. Future PRICE TRENDS will carry the lists I have and the lists we can put together with the evidence of our collecting and observing. Naturally—as ever—your help will be needed here. Other exclusions are most crystal patterns when they did not also come in color and most pre-and post-Depression era items *unless* they are significantly important to collectors. There was much in these categories I'd liked to have put in, knowing you were interested in it, but— *400 pages!*

The book has a sort of jumbled-up appearance to me and I regret this, but I know it was inevitable. When you must coordinate so many hundreds of different items from so many different sources—ads, trade journals, xerox copies (you'll recognize those when you see them!), line sketches, photographs—you just can't make them fit into as neat a layout as you'd like. Especially when you try to get as much on every page you possibly can. But the layout follows a logical order, at least, and after a few days with the book you should have no trouble finding or following any part of it.

You know, I just about worked myself to death on this book. (I'll laugh at this statement five years from now. Well, maybe ten.) We all did, put everything we had into it. We wanted it to be so much. Here at the last I can only say, I hope you like it very, very much.

Happy Collecting!

—H.M.W. 1974

In using this book, know that...

Companies are featured as chapters, in alphabetical order. The size of a chapter, or the length of a company's history, does not necessarily reflect the relative size of a company, or its importance.

Within each chapter, glassware lines are presented in the approximate order they were originally introduced. Every attempt is made to show a pattern in the earliest year it was made or advertised. Most patterns were made on past the years given.

Original advertisements are indicated by lines drawn square around them. While parts of the original ad may have been deleted, all text WITHIN the ad is reprinted directly from the original. All captions OUTSIDE the lines of the ad, *usually in this italics*, are supplied by me and provide additional information known by me.

Sometimes trade journal briefs are reprinted exactly as they originally appeared; these captions are identified as such by me.

In the catalog reprints, due to short space, my notes—names, years, colors, etc.—are superimposed on the originals and must be recognized by the characteristic type-style and headline-style used throughout this book.

Official names like *SHARON, BLACK FOREST* and *AMERICAN PIONEER* are without quotation marks. Unofficial names are enclosed in quotation marks: *"STRAWBERRY", "PEACOCK AND ROSE"* and *"AUNT POLLY"*. The more significant lines, as a rule, are named in the larger headline type.

Where no date is given, I don't know that date. Where color information is incomplete, I have given all the colors I know. (As additional colors are found, they will be listed in PRICE TRENDS.) Colors are listed in the order they were issued when possible.

Lists of pieces are given where possible. Many more lists of pieces will be given in PRICE TRENDS, and lists will be updated in that publication as additional pieces are found and reported.

The most important patterns made by several companies have already been fully pictured and discussed in Book 1. These patterns will not be covered again, but many are updated as needed in a special section called *BOOK 1 UPDATE* which begins these companies' chapters. *BOOK 2 PATTERNS*, then, presents more patterns made by these companies. Often, the numbered items in the last section of Book 1 are amplified as Book 2 patterns.

1

The Farm, 1925

She is five years old and already a part of the working-together that makes the farm. From the time she awakens her small doings at her mother's side are strokes in the rhythm of this farm, and though these small doings vary and grow as she does, the rhythm of the farm is always the same.

In the mornings now she cuts the biscuit, sets the table, dries the dishes from her stool-top; then runs to the pantry or the cellar-house for this or that—whatever she can do for her mother who will not stop working so long as it is daylight and not Sunday. Next year she will do more and by the year after that she'll have her part in working the garden, preparing and cooking the food, milking cows and churning butter and cleaning the cream separator (she would hate that the most; you *couldn't* get it clean enough that it wouldn't smell sour by night-time) and all the things you do for the farm. But just now she is only five and it is summer and haying season and soon she and her mother will start getting dinner for the 15-man crew.

The farm is not a large one, but pocketed as it is in the hilly landscape of the Ozarks it requires more than one life's work to live off it. It takes Farmer Brown and all three of his sons and sometimes the neighbors too to plant and harvest, raise and slaughter, build and mend. A work-day on the farm is as many hours long as there is light in the sky, and then some.

Whistle blows from the lumber yard in town—you could hear it the two miles away, easy—and it is time. She runs to the front porch to watch distant hat-brims swim up the valley; first they swim, then they bob as they come closer to the edge of the field; they are crossing the road and she ducks back inside. In a few moments her father makes his entrance, always the first, red, body like wood, bristling and grinning and sometimes hollering *"Pa and Ma were Methodists, and all us children too"*—one of the old rhymes, you know, just for fun. It is his household. Then the men come in off the porch and as

they fill Mother Brown's kitchen so do the sweat and smells and a great exhalation of energy. Moments before these were discharged into the vastness of the work, the field and the open sky; now, compressed into one room, these things confound the air and charge it with the day's greatest intensity.

In the midst of hard work, dinner is the great pleasure for everyone. Haying time, like the hog-butchering or herding many head of cattle, is a special time of the year; strong men and men's sons come from neighbor farms sometimes five miles away to help with this work. And dinnertime is the only break in a back-breaking 12-hour day. When you start the hay, of course, you cannot stop until it is all cut, so for two weeks they will retire at dusk and rise at dawn and this dinnertime is the only society they will know. And when Farmer Brown's hay is cut he will be part of the crew that moves on to Speaker's field, then Johnson's, and so on until all the area hay is cut.

The buzz of dinner over, dishes done, the little girl will play out under the trees for the rest of the afternoon. But Mother Brown will go on working—the house, the big garden, the washing on the wash-board, and the canning, week-in and week-out through this season; the sewing, the quilting, and the mending through the next. And she worked in the field when she was needed, when it was spring and time to plant. If the farmer's body is of wood, Mother Brown's is of some wondrous fibre quite unknown to most of the modern world.

Hard work is so much a way of life on the farm that you don't spend much time thinking about it; it wasn't so hard then—you learn that before you're old enough to think, really. Another thing you learn like instinct: you always do for others, whether it's fixing a well-pump or felling a tree or sitting with someone's sick; and others will always do for you. All these things go without saying; it is making a good life and a good community; they are the rhythms of the farm and they are always the same.

On Saturday afternoon Grandad Brown would drive them over the clay/dust road into the little railroad town of Birch Tree; its only street is cut through by the tracks and the train-whistle that gives it much of its character and just about its only excitement. Here they would stock up on salt or sugar or whatever else they were needing and hear the latest talk. Farmer Brown would do a little politicking; he was Justice of the Peace sometimes and sometimes he was sheriff. And maybe the new plow had come in; or the new dress she'd ordered out of Ward's catalog. When her mother came along they picked out material for dresses or aprons and maybe a new piece of oil-cloth for the kitchen table. Besides the Farmers Exchange there's the bank and post office and Doc Davis' Drugstore; in Doc's window are all the latest city-things Birch Tree will get to see and inside are pills, syrups, penny candy and the amazing doctor himself.

There wasn't a whole lot more to Birch Tree than this, and the little town along old Highway 60 was almost transparent to the highway travelers or Frisco passengers flying by it on their way to Atlanta or Denver, Salt Lake City or Los Angeles. Such big cities—you'd have to go a long way in either direction before you got to one and since the little girl never drove any further than Mountain View and never rode the train at all she didn't get to see any of the conniptions being cut there in the middle of these scandalous 20s. She knew nothing of the rapidly inflating society with its scads of new products and new notions of instant prosperity; knew nothing of people's mad dashes to invest the cash they had and speculate with cash they didn't have to the tune of Stock Values Rising Again, Hurrah! She knew nothing of the party-crashing and fashion-splashing and ticker-taping that was all the rage there; saw no flappers, speakeasies; heard no brassy saxophones. She sensed none of those heady spices that gave the age its outrageous flavor, the flavor that, thanks to an equally capricious wind of history, was to linger so long in the memories of Americans.

Farmer Brown knew something of all this and smelled a

little something in it, too. He understood that people would want to forget the war, but he hadn't realized how much else they wanted to forget along with it, and with disappointment he watched the idealism of WWI, with its promise of a genuine democracy, melt away as postwar inflation waxed warmer. He saw the visions of such men as Woodrow Wilson and the young Franklin Roosevelt, with their progressive ideas for social and economic reforms to help all men, moved aside for the corrupt government of Harding and the cold, business-oriented governments of Coolidge and Hoover. Moved aside, by this generation of city-folks who for a decade were indifferent to any social or political issue except whether they had a right to drink whiskey or not.

He whose way of life kept him in constant touch with human values might well have felt they were being lost in the scramble for the quick buck, the easy success, in those times that were the 20s.

By the time the girl could read the *Saturday Evening Post*, and *Collier's*, and *Liberty* at Doc's she began to know something of it. She saw incredible fashions in those pages, and advertisements for the most magical new gadgets and decorations. At the movie theatre in Mountain View she saw Joan Crawford in an open touring car carrying on like nobody ever saw. Yes, by that time even from Birch Tree you caught sight sometimes of the glittering excesses, like the sparks let fly from a new Stutz Bearcat breezing through town on its way to Kansas City or Memphis.

But such things were far from her mind this Saturday on her way back from town when she was five. Today the road made her think of school, which she would start this fall; the schoolhouse was two miles from her house, if you cut across the Pierce place, and she and her brothers would walk it every day, through falling leaves and winter snows and spring wet, until she was 11; then the schoolbus would come. And she thought about tomorrow because the preacher was coming. Preacher always came to someone's house for Sunday dinner and tomorrow it was their time.

Back on the farm, after supper, in the reflective moments that would end the day for them all, the kerosene lamps would be lit. Papers would be read, a couple hands of Rook played, or maybe a neighbor would stop by. Mother Brown might crochet or finish up a letter by this final light, but for the most part night-time brings the day to a sure close.

In the rhythm of the farm, sun-up is highest pitch; you work through and finally spend out each day's light as you descend toward night. The fireflies take their last dusky turns; the household closes, folds up; the lamps go out.

The City, 1925

Switch on the electric lights, swing open the double doors to the first great room and the Pittsburgh Glass Exhibit breaks in another new year for the glass industry.

Enter the Pittsburgh Exhibit: mirror to an image of the world of American glassware; the single biggest event of the year and one which will shape the nation's vases, goblets and fishbowls for the years to come.

The floor fills with glass manufacturers and glass buyers and in moments comes to life with argument, comment, speculation, and more argument. Pittsburgh is the spiritual center of 'glass country'; glassmakers have come chiefly from Ohio, Indiana, Pennsylvania, and West Virginia—but from as far as New Jersey and Oklahoma—to display their new lines and notions to the buyers who have come even further to see them, choose among them, and buy what they hope will be 'hot' this year for the stores they represent.

The Exhibit is huge and grand: room after brilliant room fairly winks and glints its glass toward these buyers. Wannamaker's from New York is there; Stix, Baer & Fuller from St. Louis; Miami, Chicago, El Paso, San Francisco. But this year talk seems to outshine even the glassware and after quick

turns around the tables the buyers and sellers, having seen what they came to see, now bunch in groups to say what they came to say. Conversations are excited, determined—and, quite often, inflated.

Companies want to talk about Success: *What a boom time for the trade! Housewives are buying more glass than ever before; why at this rate glass tableware is going to replace all pottery and china—and now, with the new all-glass dinnerware coming on—We've arrived! And those stocks and dividends and prices just keep going up—Life's a big glass bowl full of cherries, Gentlemen!* And they brag on their factory's expansion; everyone, it seems, who hasn't already, is building new plants, creating design departments and special color labs, developing color control measures, and adding more decorating facilities. *Why we're going to have the biggest this— and the fanciest that— and the latest—! Far cry from yesterday, eh, when the old factory foreman did everything by himself! —Say, what're you going to invest in next?*

But the buyers want to know about this Automation buzz. Look how many companies—respected companies, too!—have been directing all this research and expansion of the past several years toward mechanization of entire plants for completely automatic production. Why even today the first machine-made tumblers are rolling off assembly lines—and by next year, or the year after, they're saying complete dinner services! How radical, really; how progressive; how crude; how impressive; how presumptuous; how . . . frightening, in a sense. Is it really going to work? Will the people buy it? And what will it mean to the industry? On this question you can take only one of two sides, it seems,—but here, let's drop in on these two gentlemen . . .

"Excuse me, young man, but I must ask—have you no interest in preserving the tradition, the honor, the very essence of your product? Glass-making is no less than an art, my dear sir; it has been for 2000 years now and always, always wrought by the long-trained hands of fine artisans. Do you not consider your—fabrication—a final departure from all that is true glass-making technique? Can you really—with any pride at all—offer to the public one of these-these *fakes?*"

"Bosh-bosh, sir,—with all due respect I mean sir;—but what an incredible weight you are pulling on the invigorating, and *inevitable*, march of progress! Surely you acknowledge that your entirely hand-crafted piece will eventually be obsolete, both time-wise and price-wise, as we continue to undergo such rapid growth of consumer demand—a demand which can only be met by a ware made faster and more economically than tedious hand techniques can ever be. And our glass will be the same, sir; element for every one of your essential elements, only assembled by a brand new, very exciting,—very *20th Century*, if you will, sir—concept. A brilliant step forward, if I may say so—and the ladies are going to love it, you can be sure of that!"

"If your sense of respect will not serve you, my dear sir (and when I think of what your father—) let me simply say that I hope for your stockholders' sake your business sense will. You cannot really believe that any such product will be acceptable to a single soul. The machine cannot be conceived—much less built—that begins to approach the delicate quality of a handmade piece—the purity, the beauty. Why think of that monstrous piece of metal you have sitting out there—oh, yes, I've seen them! *Ka-chunka, chunka, chunka*—think of the seams! Think of the burps. The poor balance, the rough edges that no seeing-eye contraption could ever detect or remove. Why think of the *cracks*! One-fourth your 'glass' will be broken by the time your gristmills get through with it; and the rest will be in pieces when it arrives at your customer's door. Good heavens, man, if good taste cannot appeal to you—at best mightn't good sense?"

"I must— I can only laugh, sir; I am almost without words. Maybe others—but you have not seen our new presses; we invented them and no one else has anything like them—the design is supurb—but let me beg off, sir; may I simply say that

although YOU might see the differences in your glass and ours, no housewife will be able to tell one from the other—except by the price tag!—and much less would they care if they could see the difference!"

"And you, sir? What will you see?"

"I, sir, will see absolutely no comparison at all between a 100% Modern American Wonder and a hopelessly doomed anachronism!"

Curtain falls, along with heaps of scorn from both parties; but the debate goes on in every corner.

Moving on down the aisle we find ourselves in the middle of another conversational ballgame—this time, this notion of National Advertising is being batted about. Here in the 20s advertising is just finding itself out, and as the incredible power is discovered and developed by the bigger corporations, progressive smaller ones are beginning to ask, Why not? *—Because it's just plain vulgar, that's why; you don't sell fine glassware from the pages of a ten-cent rag next to Dr. Dumafudgit's Soothing Salve or 'You Too can be a Motion Picture Actress in just 12 Easy Lessons!'* Well, they've sold a lot of Fords that way, and vacuum cleaners too. Ask me, it stands a damn good chance. Most of the population never see a fancy downtown window, and people's got to see a thing before they want it. Besides, there's something deeper to this advertising thing. Theory is, the more times a person sees a product—specially in a sharp-looking ad—the more he wants it. It instills a desire, they say; creates a market where there wasn't one before . . . you know, Fostoria is starting it and probably some others, too. In the best magazines—and have you heard what it's costing them? *—Glad it's them and not us; let them spend up all their profits. Mark my words, the whole idea will fall flat and set 'em back five years!*

By this time, however, it is apparent that we are surrounded by discussions of still another subject, one which is obviously of greatest interest to this Exhibit. It is impossible not to overhear that one word which is being repeated so often it almost flows from table to table, in one aisle and out the other. That word is 'color' and starting just about now it will dominate glass talk and glass activity for the next decade.

Despite the fact that crystal glass—with decorations, the current trend—is in clear majority at the 1925 Exhibit, this is nonetheless the crucial year on the color question. For three or four years now several companies—some leaders, some adventurers—have been trying out short lines of ornamental glassware in colors, first in opaques and most recently in transparent shades quite new to the American industry. To everyone's surprise the colorful lines went over with quite a bang, and last year the color theme had been expanded into the area of tableware. So everyone has come to this Exhibit to find how this important venture fared. Glass-makers look to glass-buyers for the answers that will determine who will cast their lot and go the way of all color: Did it go? Will they buy it for another year?

And the buyers bring the word: Yes, yes, they loved it and bought it all and couldn't get enough! Refreshment sets, liquor sets, bridge sets—all sorts of those 'leisure time' specialty items are catching on like crazy and color suits them perfectly. What colors? All of them! Canary, blue, amber, green, amethyst—and we can't wait to see that bold new rosy-pale pink shade in the works for fall. And this new colored dinnerware—it's going to be the berries! (One leading house, Fostoria, has just brought out daring new all-glass dinnerware—an original concept in itself—but in colors to boot. Other houses were already planning to follow suit.) Yes, sir, here in 1925 any glassman who doesn't sense that color will absolutely bloom this next year isn't worth his silica.

Still and all, a good many are yet to be convinced that the public could actually prefer their glassware in color for any length of time, and some companies continue to hold out against the new trend. "Just a short-lived fad, that's all" intones one man with the air of centuries. "Look across this room: every display predominantly crystal, just as every decade of American glassware has been. You see spots of color on maybe half these tables: one spots fewer colors than this through all of glassware history. No, you'll never replace crystal as the only proper ware. Especially for the *table*." But those who stuck to their guns lost their stirrups this time, and fell behind; the houses who knew a good horse when they saw one gave the trend full rein and it was through this color race that the 'name' houses established their great leads. One leader sends this general letter to the trade in 1928:

"As a keen merchandiser you have watched the current craving for color in everything. Not only in automobiles and wallpaper but refrigerators, stoves, kettles, sinks, and bathtubs are being regaled in tints that rival the flowers in grandmother's garden. When people want color, sell it to them. Feature glassware in colors. Play it up strong this spring and summer. Make displays. Show it in your windows. Bring it home to your customers" exhorts an exuberant A. H. Heisey.

Who started the trend? You can trace color in glass back as far as you'd like to go, but most recently the fantastic color creations of Frederick Carder of Steuben and other individuals experimenting with limited art-wares since 1900 were, in some way, prototypes. Decoratively colored imports about this time, such as those from Venice, may have had their influence, and probably the relative commercial success of Fenton and Imperial with vibrant iridescent effects in the 'teens. But popularly-sold glassware was almost completely crystal before color sprouted in the start of the 20s, and it would be difficult to trace who planted the first seeds. Certainly Cambridge was showing opaque giftwares before other major companies, but the transparents seemed to come out concurrently each season. Word got around fast among the leading color houses, and nobody really scooped anybody by more than a few months.

Even so, the same leaders who had introduced color had in mind a short reign for it. Let the country have its fling, sure, but that "only fine crystal can represent the highest achievement in glassware" was their personal conviction to a man (still is, you will find). Besides, glass fashion must change as does any other fashion, else who would buy more of it? And these companies, seeing themselves as trend-setters, felt it their responsibility to lead the public back home to the true elegance of crystal in a very few years. And indeed crystal was back on the drawing boards by 1929.

But few companies were thinking crystal as they left the 1925 Exhibit. They were thinking color, and what else could possibly be done with it. Next year they would etch fanciful designs on it, and these patterns would become a major new trend. And their wheels were turning, What can we do that's more exciting and more daring than anyone else? What new color can we come up with; what wild new piece? What embellishment might be crazy enough to suit the extravagant mood of these roaring, soaring 20s?

Before we take our leave of all this glitter we might stop a moment for the thoughts of a curious, Dapper Little Man who is standing very quietly by the doorway. If we have not noticed him earlier it is because he has said very little, perferring to watch and listen. His appearance doesn't tell us much either; he might be the editor of a glass journal or the manager of the show itself, I don't know, but he has been around for many years and if we can edge in on his thoughts we might round out our impression of the Exhibit, for the vision of the Dapper Little Man is a far-reaching one.

We find him reviewing the history of popular glassware in this country, and considering how the events of today will fit into this picture. He remembers how glassware in the 19th Century had been a luxury destined for wealthy homes (and later, museums). But by 1900, while brilliant-cut crystal wares of famed companies were at peak popularity with the privileged few, scores of new factories were offering simpler, utilitarian pieces to a growing market. It was only logical, really, that glass—such a flexible, sanitary, and attractive product, with so many uses—would eventually find its place in the average home, and this is what happened. Through increased exposure and promotion, glass for table and kitchen use gained favor and by the 20s caught on in a big way among those who could afford it.

Considering the potential demand for glass among those who could not afford handmade pieces, it also seemed logical that new methods be devised to accommodate this market. The Dapper Little Man could not see that there'd be that much competition between the low-priced machine-made glass and the higher-priced ware of the hand-houses, especially if advertising worked like it was supposed to and established the 'quality' ware of the name-companies as the prestigious glass to own. And if advertising worked, the existing hand factories with their slower methods of production could not begin to fill the coming demand. He saw no reason, in fact, why both kinds of factories could not co-exist and be prosperous together; indeed, the future seemed to him most promising. Broaden the broom, and the sweep would be even wider. Of course, as automation became more and more refined and increasingly important to modern society, the day might come when the majority of glassware was made by machines. But these last were thoughts in the back of his mind, and the Dapper Little Man was very careful to keep them there.

As for color—more power to it! People wanted change, and change was most always good if it fostered creativity. People wanted their lives more colorful—so surround them with color. Let them express themselves with it! Certainly people needed to spend some of this excitement being generated by this swirling age. At the moment even the Dapper Little Man feels excited, sort of like things are on the brink of something big happening. Well, with all these new elements promising to break things open for the glass industry, there's surely enough to be excited about. And our friend cannot help being a bit chagrined at the glassmen on these floors who always seem to be too intent on their own particular points, to the exclusion of other elements which could prove important one day soon. They shouldn't shove matters so far to one side or another . . . this was just not the day to be short-sighted, with so much storm in the air.

The Farm, 1935

She is fifteen and should you ask her if her life has changed much in the last few years, she wouldn't know how to answer. So much on the farm is always the same. But recently, yes, there's been some changes. She knows, of course, that the nation has been disturbed for several years; the economy is still very bad, they say, and she believes it because where she and her friends used to have only a little money to spend, now they have none at all. Oh, and you couldn't order from the catalog any more, but Grandad brought her a store-bought dress from Springfield that year and lots of other girls she knew didn't get even one. Like the others, she makes her dresses now out of some old ones of Auntie's and her mother makes hers out of feed and flour sacks—just for everyday, you know. And they make the family underwear out of the sacks, too.

Farming is no harder than it's ever been but the lack of cash leaves the edges so sharp. Just last fall for the first time Farmer Brown lost to the bank—a whole herd of cattle—and since then the Browns were the poorest they'd ever been. There'd been droughts in Missouri, too, but it was lots worse for the others, he told them. Those farmers out on the Plains, the ones who'd managed to keep their farms from the bank, lost them now when their crops were blown away by the terrible dust of drought.

Her father seems more preoccupied, she thinks; his '*Dark*

and dreary was the night, a storm was drawing near' sounds more serious than silly these days. He is more determined than ever in his farming; more vociferous and more Democrat than ever; and he listens to his radio all the time for the news of the nation. Right now he is excited about these strikes. One after another—auto workers, coal miners, jobless garment-working mothers being beaten and shot; it was incredible. The sound of such violence coming over the radio made Farmer Brown think some kind of war was about to start right here in America. At first these strikes had all been broken, the points lost; but now it seemed the workers were gaining a little ground, ground on which a new labor strength would gradually be built. This labor union thing is a strange giant to him, but God knows something has got to be done for the men on the bottom.

There'd been some pretty bad hurt right here in Birch Tree recently, for that matter, like the Evanses losing their feed store and having to move back East to their folks. She'd known the Evanses long as she could remember. And Margo Walker's father coming down with the consumption like that; they had to take him away; that left Margo with all the kids. Next thing anybody knew, Margo'd packed 'em all up and left, no one knows where. And there were worse stories . . . .

Still and all, it seems like much is the same. If there's been more work than ever before, she hasn't noticed so much, growing into it like she did, and in between times is the same fun for most of the kids she knows. The fair is still the fair and they always get to go see it—never used to spend much money there anyhow. Baseball and basketball and band concerts and ice cream socials were all free and these were the only places you could go to anyway—and Sunday School, of course. There was almost never any gas so you didn't get to drive over to Mountain View very often to see the talking pictures but you could steal a kiss behind the bleachers right here in Birch Tree (a very recent discovery on her part, you may be sure) and that was even better than the movies.

Above all else, there is the same sustenance from the farm. You give to the land and it provides. The rhythms of the farm are always the same, and caught up as she is in these rhythms, rocked by them, an essential part of them, she lives out this most dramatic period in American history. If there are nothing but oranges for Christmas, one orange in the toe of a long red stocking, she thinks that is pretty great. If that's the way it is then that's the way it should be.

Still she sees more than she knows and knows more than she thinks about, though these pictures come in parts. But her own rhythms are changing, and as her mind grows restless and then reflective—and as a fractured country begins to pull itself together—so do the perceptions of her youth begin to form a consciousness that will fit these parts into a whole.

On this day at noon-time she walks from school into town to help Ethel Hendricks spend her nickel; Ethel always had a nickel to spend when no one else did, her father was a schoolteacher and made $40 a month regular. Today our girl feels a strange resentment toward that nickel; she thinks of the Wallace kids who never bring any lunch to school at all and don't wear any shoes, either. Billie Wallace was quitting school, she said; going to the city where there was work.

The town looks the same as it always has, near as she can tell. The cafe is still there, only it's changed hands three or four times and you can't get a chocolate soda there anymore. Doc Davis' Drugstore is there on the corner as usual and so is Doc, naturally. He's still everybody's remedy for everything and he still takes eggs for pay, if people had eggs.

But there were changes in the mood of the town; drifts the girl could not quite catch hold of. A wariness in people; a shiftiness in the eyes of men on corners.—A resentment.

Train's whistling into town—she watches the big Frisco choo up the tracks towards California. She knows where it's going, now; she knows people who've gone there. Her brother used to tell her about a camp of men settled up the track a ways; twenty, thirty men, maybe more, with tin plates, and

dark faces. Dressed the most curious you ever saw, he said, suit-clothes, but all ragged. They rode in there on the freights, but where they slept or how they got food for their stew-pots, he didn't know, unless the train brought it to them somehow. The girl wouldn't have believed this except she heard on the radio that a jungle had been broken up, the men getting 90 days labor, and her father said that was the one. They were back in there now, though. Her brother used to scare her with these stories but today she thinks she might like to be on the train so she could see this thing. Who were these men?

She didn't remember a newsreel she'd seen a year ago at the picture-show; it showed a Hooverville where whole families were living in rusted-out shells of old cars and even orange crates, with sick children, and worn-out faces. She might have remembered those faces, so startling were they, but she didn't; the screen flashed so many strange scenes in that 10 minutes, captions blazing across the screen in rapid order, read in loud and ominous tones by the faceless announcer, that she understood none of it.

She had more time with the magazines, with their unsettling photographs in black-and-white and easy captions: 'William Randolph Hearst organizes free bread and soup stations in New York City; indigent line up blocks long for giveaway': 'Banks foreclose hundreds in Kansas; angry land-owners pack what they can and leave the rest behind'. But it was another world to her, really; besides, the magazines were otherwise filled with such things as movie stars, romantic little tales and the most delightful color advertisements for Maxwell House Coffee, DeSoto Motor Cars, Camels and Wrigley's Spearmint Gum. This too was another world, but a much more pleasant one. Still, the black-and-white images stuck in her mind and pricked the budding consciousness.

She sits down on Doc's steps and reads the headlines of the Springfield newspaper. 'Roosevelt Bill Passes; Wall Street Negative.' She thought about Roosevelt and then about her father who had campaigned so hard for him in 1932 and had-n't yet stopped campaigning, seemed like. —What a President, what a man. He brought us confidence; he'll pull this country out! She would have to ask her father tonight where this Wall Street was; he'd been to Springfield many times.

The headlines stared blackly back at her and she realized that the closest she ever came to the rest of the world were these headlines; the closest she ever came to reality were these black strings of words or the black words of announcers. Headlines and more headlines; radio, newsreel, magazine and newspaper headlines. Headlines written hundreds of miles away from her; and written, in turn, hundreds of miles from the fact. Headlines terse, quick—and often, though she did not know it, false. Headlines strung together overnight, fragments of today's truths to make tomorrow's lies. Sometimes this was done intentionally, for political reasons, but often the truth could not be told because it was not known; still headlines had to be set for the next day. The lie is at least short-lived, thanks to the transiency of headlines; today's top banner may hold an entire nation at its beck and call, but it is king for only one day; tomorrow's first broadcast will become instant ruler. Nothing is faster forgotten than yesterday's news. Thus there is the daily chance of replenishing the truth; but in these dark days the odds for seeing the truth were not good, and too often day-old lies were replaced by fresh ones. Perhaps it mattered little, but the aspect of people being misled through their darkness sits uncomfortably with us today.

The reality which was the Great Depression came to most people, like it did to the different folks of Birch Tree, in degrees; sooner or later, to one extent or another, sometimes bringing a lot of damage and sometimes none at all. Emanating from one source—the Crash itself—these waves of effect formed patterns, domino-like, as they spread over the entire nation. These patterns were not visible then as they are now; had they been, the tragic progression might have been better stayed.

From the pattern we draw now, we can trace the path the Depression took to families like the Browns or the migrant Wallaces. Even more interesting, perhaps, against such a pattern we can clearly see the irregularities in this supposedly inevitable series of waves: the men and the corporations who, through the ugly quirks of Fortunes, slipped through the decades quite unhurt by the Depression—and generally unnoticed by the public.

Naturally those nearest the thunderclap when it struck tended to be hit the quickest and hardest; the higher one's office overlooked Wall Street the further one had to fall. Many did, and their biggest clients, tied so closely to these offices by telephone and telegraph wires, fell with them. But this is speaking figuratively; one of the prevailing Depression-myths is that many such people threw themselves out of windows. Actually there were few documented cases of suicide in 1929, and some historians think there were none.

We also still tend to believe that the great Fall took its toll evenly on all the wealthy and their brokers, that they were all ruined by it, and this is not so. Many large corporations, and many individual wizards as well, were crafty enough to turn the hard times into quick cash and ready profit for themselves. Many companies whose names are household words today recovered almost overnight—while the effects of their original financial overplays and irresponsible financial leadership reverberated through the land for years, striking blow after blow upon the people who could least recover.

Others, of course—the rich and the not-so-rich—who had rashly, ignorantly, or simply unluckily, overinvested or speculated in "securities" which were not secure, suddenly found themselves in the ranks of the unemployed. But it is also true that many people who owned their businesses or farms, or even their homes—if they were not heavily invested or if they had some productive resource—managed to make it through the time without great hardship. These survivors might have had to cut back a little, but it was dollars they were pinching and not pennies, and they continued to buy products and support other businesses. Many people continued to buy fine glassware, for instance, and thus several glass companies lost money one or two years at the most. But other businesses, of course, with a weaker financial structure to begin with, or managerial inadequacies or other short-comings, were forced to surrender.

There were casualties among the workers in either case, be they those laid off by companies so its business could survive or those left without a job when their boss's business failed. To some it happened quickly and to others it came later, but when it did happen most of these blue-and white-collar workers and tradesmen—unskilled, semi-skilled or having skills shared by too many—were unable to find work again. These were the people who joined the relief rolls, the bread lines, and, to some extent, the lost: the men became the hoboes, the migrants, the back-door beggars and philosophers. The women and children—those who knew the worst of it, and these were many—mainly stayed in the cisterns of the cities; through suffocating summers and freezing winters they existed in tenement rooms, six in a filthy bed, eyes open and stomachs empty.—*Open up the window, and let me breathe*—but even the air was thin and held no answers for the thousands of helpless ones.

Then there were the small farmers whose lands were all they had, or thought they had, until the banks came and foreclosed their land away. Men and women who had, starting with nothing, put every dime and every effort into

making their place what it was, spent their lives on it, only to be left with nothing again. These people were no poorer, often, than those out of work in the cities, but it might be said that they were the poorer in spirit. The experience of making, having, then losing this great thing they had—their *land*—was totally demoralizing. The laborer in the city may have lost his job but he hadn't lost his resource for making a living—his skills—completely, and he could look forward to regaining his job again one day and with it the life-style he had formerly known. But most farmers could not regain their land, their life's work, their only means of livelihood, again. These became the hopeless ones. With no place else to turn, they headed into the Western sun to be blinded by the promise of dying in an orange grove or other fruited plain. Blinded, humiliated, their deaths were almost always ignoble, and their deserted farms and transient camps and sanitation centers form the skull and bones of our images of the worst that was the Depression.

These were the real suicides. Many corporations had regained their profits by the time the first Okie farm was stolen back again, or by the time the first migrant died of a broken heart. Businesses of all kinds were thriving again while fruit was being picked at 5c a bushel and the camps of death were still allowed to live.

The fate of still another people—the sharecroppers of the south—can hardly be measured on the graph we have drawn. Their existences were sub-normal before the holocaust; now, they ate roots and weeds and died only a little faster than they had died before. If the times reached them at all, it was perhaps in the form of Roosevelt's Farm Security workers who entered their lives at this point and began the reforms that would eventually alleviate the worst of these conditions.

So distant was Farmer Brown from the initial explosion, the only waves he felt were those urgent sounding ones that came across his radio in the form of the newscaster's voice—insistent, presidential—and for weeks, years, almost unceasing. The headlines. He owned his farm, if little else, and so for a long time these sound-waves and headlines were the strongest effect the Depression had on him. They moved him, though, and kept him in motion; he talked politics to whoever would listen and campaigned for Roosevelt and championed his reforms. If Roosevelt and his new policies could not end the Depression—the stimulation of a pre-war economy would finally do that—Farmer Brown, like so many others, *believed* that he could, and that is really what counted through the roughest of it.

Our girl is still sitting on the steps with the headlines in front of her. She would ask her father about these things, who read and heard everything there was to hear and seemed to understand so much of what lay behind it all. He didn't know, really, any more than most did, but his instincts were good and his knowledge of human nature sound and his body and will-power were strong. And his heart was with the people who needed it most. He stood with the little man,—a giant.

But she wants to forget the headlines now and think about something pleasant once again. Good, Ethel is back from the post office with something obviously on her mind. *—Look here, I want you to see something.*—Oh, she's got the new Sears & Roebuck catalog, that'll be fun.—*You remember that set of dishes Doc had in his window for so long—the green ones, with the little dancing girl? Old Widow Perkins's got it now. Well look at these—this page, the pink ones. Sorta like the Widow's, but it's got blossoms all over it—and pink! Well, my Momma's getting the whole set. Daddy promised her—*

But our girl's initial envy has already dissolved into the beautiful memory of an event that happened earlier that year. She'll never forget it . . . She's at the county fair in Eminence and she's standing under the swirling carnival lights, watching people toss pennies into a maze of pink, green, yellow, red and blue glassware . . . she can't resist; she takes one of the

pennies her Grandad has given her—it isn't possible of course but—she closes her eyes and tosses. The barker's voice booms out, *A winner*! There, that big amber bowl with the pattern of tiny roses—yes, that one; he hands it to her. She is held spellbound by the glittering thing; in its glassy collage of lights and colors she catches a glimpse of her own plain face. Suddenly she is ready to go home and it's not even dinnertime yet. *Wait 'til Mother sees what I've brought her*!

The City, 1935

It's still Ready Set, Strike up the Band and Here they Come in Pittsburgh as this year's Exhibit marches on with all the pomp it has ever shown. And if circumstances are any different here in 1935 than they were, say, 10 years ago, the business-like thing to do is ignore them and watch the parade go by. Certainly the glass itself, dressed in its new styles, turned out in all new shapes, and fresh with the new ideas you came to expect from each new Exhibit, has never shown off more brilliantly.

We who visited the 1925 Exhibit might notice changes on these floors, but to listen to the table-talk, laced with the usual aspirations for success, nothing seems amiss. The show goes on, and Optimism, that fine key of business, is still the note everyone is tuned to. If the drum roll seems less insistent or the bugle more subdued, so much better does it compliment the tone of this year's Exhibit—don't you think? After all, the ol' bugle is calling fewer glassmakers to the floors this year; this recent bout of financial troubles, which put everyone in something of a bad way for a while, put quite a few companies under for good. Most unfortunate. Of course, these were mainly your smaller companies, those who hadn't really got their feet on the ground before the going got so rough. But some were companies you wouldn't have thought, true; a few of the big ones—respected old companies—whose tables would not be set up here again. Privately these absences might be felt as losses, but publicly they are regarded as inevitable and explained in terms of progress.

These attitudes are the professionally sound ones; if they have been forced and reinforced by certain events of the last few years, no one lets on. The trade journals led the way to this 'blind' optimism: no headline ever even acknowledged that there'd been a Crash, and none so much as hinted at any backsliding in the business, even through the worst of it. "1930 Exhibit Promises Biggest Year Yet"; "More Buyers Throng to Pittsburgh in 1932 than Ever Before!" Reading on down these articles you found that 'there were some reports of depressed sales, but a booming fall season is expected to make up the slow start'. Finishing off the columns would be the briefest of briefs noting the passings of companies who did not recover as predicted. This was no time for rhapsodies in blue—it was a time for the green light of faith.

You had to think of these things as progress. Consider the huge changes you see in the glass on these tables here today—more than half of it made automatically, more than half of it in colors—and consider at the same time the continued popularity of glass tableware through all this. Still selling astonishingly well to all markets—the thin crust of rich, the filling of middle class, and—in pieces anyway—to the great spreading bottom of poor folks. You had to think of it as progress good for the industry.

As these disparate tables co-exist here on the floors of the Exhibit, side by side, so do all makers and buyers enjoy a peaceful co-existence. There is really no room for argument these days; buyers come representing different markets, and they will leave having bought just enough glass to satisfy the demands of these different markets. These are sort of unusual times, you know. Them's that's got, shall get the expensive glassware they want anyway, those that don't—well, if the machine ware pleases them whose days have not been so bright here recently, good enough. It's certainly kept the glass industry visible, that's for sure.

If there's no longer a thirst for argument, there is still some hunger for speculation. The feeling is strong that something significant has occurred within the trade, though no one knows why, and the glassmen can't help interjecting a little wonder into the marvel at whatever it is that's been happening. —*Really something, isn't it, the way that colored glass is holding in there. Can't really understand it; it's more than a trend, you know,—it's a regular fad; and just when you'd expect a cutback in such things. Other industries are floundering, and we're holding on!* Holding on—why most of us are making good, and have been right along. *Sure, the machine houses—* No sir, I'm talking about your big hand houses as well. Course, they had to get down with it a little bit—come up with some lower-priced stuff, that sort of thing—to help keep their better lines alive through it all. But with the name and image they created for themselves with that advertising business— and you know they don't have the imports to compete with like they did in the 20s, thanks to Hoover's Tariff Bill. I will say this, when Uncle Sam lets that cheaply-produced hand-made foreign glass back into the country, you'll see some more hand houses take the fall. They've survived the automation thing—most of 'em, so far—but no way they can beat that low-cost glass coming from Europe, Japan, who knows where else. *Oh well, long as everybody keeps liking us this well . . . Really, who would have predicted that all-glass dinnerware—breakfast sets, of all things—would just take over like that? I tell you, we've become the biggest trend for the American home. I mean it, there's not another home product as universally popular as glass has been for years now.*

Most everyone knows that machine-made glass, with its widespread availability and low prices, had much to do with keeping the industry alive. But curiously enough, very few realize how great a role color has played; what color has actually meant for the industry—and society as well. Few theorized about it at all beyond a strictly business viewpoint; most of those factories who poured out the colors after 1930 looked no further than their last sales sheet for their answers. —Color still selling? Keep the tanks bright, boys.

Those who did theorize about it theorized wrong—and it just about rankled them to death. Leading this pack were the big-name hand houses who felt it their responsibility to shape the tastes of consumers as the time befitted such a change. And the time had clearly been calling for a change since 1930, when the machine houses were just starting to land carloads of that 'instant dinnerware' in department stores all across the country. All-glass dinnerware, in the very same colors, and with the same fanciful designs (only now etched in the molds by automatic methods) as the delicately etched colors and patterns they themselves had introduced to the public in the latter 20s. So that year, with the sure optimism that so befits such men of business, the leaders brought announcements and offerings of a New Crystal Age to the Exhibit—and when it was over, they packed up crystal, proclamations and optimism and left rather quietly. Confidence undaunted, they had presented newer and better crystal fronts to equally undaunted buyers at every Exhibit since. By now they've managed to get just about one foot in the door; this particular year, they are *sure*, the forces will shift for good. —But here, I've found a man whose optimism has worn a bit thin; let's hear him out.

"I just can't understand what makes people tick these days," he complains over a tableful of new crystal lines. "Why we've tried everything we could think of to get this color thing back where it belongs. We started phasing out our color tanks five years ago, brought out the most elegant crystal dinnerware you ever saw. Useful crystal, too; should've been just what they wanted. But no go, Joe. All we heard was 'color, color, color. The public wants more color'. Well, when you can buy stacks of pink and green and yellow in store basements, why come up to the first floor for ours? So we came up with the ruby, the dark blues and dark greens. But what we really wanted was to see crystal back in again—the machine houses could *never* beat us there. So we just kept the crystal coming. Why, you'll never see finer lines of crystal than what you see

in front of you right now. The trade journals have supported us all the way, too. They write up our crystal lines on the front pages, and barely mention color anything, even though you still see it everyplace.

"No sir, I just don't understand it. People believed us when we brought 'em color in the first place. It was our advertising did it, you know; we told them color was right for their tables and they believed us. Our word became gold through those ads. Quality, prestige. Well, our ads read crystal now. Our image says crystal is right for now—been saying so for five years at least. We can't even get anybody's *attention*. If the ads worked once, you'd think they'd work again, wouldn't you? What's happening in this industry, anyway?"

There is no one around who, in 1935, can answer him completely—except, perhaps, the Dapper Little Man who is still standing over in the doorway to the great Exhibit. The problem with these gentlemen, thinks he, is that they're still too close to their subject. They see their product as merely that—a product, when it has actually become something more. More than a trend, more even than a fad; colored glassware has become something with a far greater meaning to society than that usually earned by any mere product.

That these men are not aware of this greater significance does not surprise the Dapper Little Man. Goodness knows it has taken their All to bring about—then adjust to!—the revolution within their industry, much less pay attention to that which has taken place without. Most all businesses had to undergo mighty changes in the industrial age, certainly, but the utter transformation of the glass trade—from a hand-craft and an art, with essentially no changes in technique for 2000 years, to a machine-dominated, mass-producing industry *almost overnight* had been a particularly unsettling one for these men. It would be years before they would attain the perspective we enjoy now—we, and this Dapper Little Man. From whatever vantage point he has been able to gain by his gateway watch over the years, be he reporter, businessman, or doorman, his remarkable vision extends in two directions—into the rooms of the glass industry, and also out into the far

greater world of men and events that surrounds these rooms. And only he seems to know how much this greater world has affected the one inside.

The events of the tumultuous years since we saw him last appear to have taken a great toll, so deepfelt were his perceptions and so intent were his efforts to comprehend all he had seen. He has waited a long time for his vision to become complete, and now—perhaps because this is his last year at his doorway post, perhaps because the import of what he has seen weighs too heavily on him, I don't know—he seems almost eager to develop this picture which is only now beginning to reveal itself to him.

In recent years he has seen the eventful changes within the glass industry in dramatic fusion with the eventful history transforming the society around it, a fusion made possible by astonishing coincidences in timing. And in the light of this historical phenomena, the full significance of colored glassware of the Depression Era emerges.

So we can better share this vision, let's go back with the Dapper Little Man to when products and consumerism were at a peak—the 20s, when colored glass was still just a product, and a popular one. It so happened that 'color' in glassware was delivered to society's door at just the right time to suit everyone; not only that, it arrived just in time to team up with National Advertising, also in its first appearance to the industry. If color was the key, advertising turned it, and what might have remained a minor trend among advantaged consumers was turned into the pie-plate in the sky for every housewife's dream-table. To those who could afford it, the fancifully etched colored dinnerware became one of the brightest personal hallmarks of the age, glowing with the promised prosperity of the 20s.

And so the promise had not been kept. For many, the lights seemed to die out of everything—everything, that is, but that lovely glassware, its transparent beauty still a perfect symbol of the irony of that incredible age. No wonder those who had some money continued to buy colored glass well into the 30s. They weren't ready to let it go. They wanted to stay with it awhile longer, as if the blossoms of the 20s could be kept fresh forever.

And colored glassware might have remained simply that, a symbol for the privileged few who had known a little of Paradise, who could point to the colorful crystal dinnerware and say, *'that's* what it was like'. But by another series of incredible coincidences it was to become one more.

The hand-made glass of the 20s had not sold to everybody, of course, but the *idea* of it had, and the machine companies in 1929 were just getting set to reach out for those millions of people who so far had only dreamed of owning colored glass. When the Depression brought its terrible reality crashing down on them, it looked like their dream would be ended forever. But instead, this perfectly-timed new development in the glass industry not only kept it alive—in the midst of everything, it made the dream come true as well.

1929 was the very year that the machine houses came on with the first great loads of dinnerware in the same colors which had radiated from the pages of magazines and in the same fancifully etched patterns they had seen in the big store windows. Patterns etched by automatic methods, true, but still the prettiest thing many people ever hoped to own. And for so little! It sold for nickels, dimes—even less than it was originally supposed to—and you could even collect it free, as premiums for buying this or that. So as people slowly awoke from their nightmare, they glimpsed an old sweet dream shining in the darkness just ahead of them. And the dream could actually be theirs, if they just stayed together, pulled together. For many, many families it became something they could focus on, group around, work towards, in its own small way. For some, simply owning a piece of it was enough; it afforded a bit of brightness they would never forget.

So before the industry knew what had hit it, this new kind of colored glass became another kind of symbol for another age and another people. If the 20s liked color because it was new, the 30s liked it because it was familiar. If for the affluent it reflected the memories of the 20s and the reality that never came to be, for the rest it became the memories of the 30s and the reality that came to them only too well.

If in the 20s it seemed the ultimate product, in the 30s it actually brought the concept of 'product' back closer to its original meaning: an item made for a purpose, a human purpose, arising from very real social needs rather than those induced by business and advertising.

And in the end it became far more than just a product. It became social history, a part of its culture, a piece of its time. Because of a crazy juxtaposition of forces—scientific, economic, social, historical—this product became a force in itself. The people wanted it, and through their collective will gave it a life of its own. No wonder the businessmen have been so bewildered, thinks the Dapper Little Man. Their product has been beyond their control, and the time wrong for new ideas and 'returns to elegance'.

Yet he knew that color was passing—that it had to pass. Color in glassware found its highest expression in the 20s and its greatest meaning in the 30s; now color must be stilled, that its place in history be well-defined. It is his guess that 1935 will be something of a fulcrum year for the color-balance of the glass industry, just as 1925 was an eon ago, and he is right. As the slow mend of 'normalcy' begins to take hold of the ragged edges of society, so does crystal glass begin to find its ground again. By Depression's end, so too will its characteristic colors be ended.

But what a reign. Surely, thinks our friend, it will be among the best-remembered of all such trends. Not only was colored glassware linked to an important and dramatic period of history—it was actively and effectively involved in that history. It truly affected society, meant something to people. Can the same be said for any other 'product' of the day? Can the same be said for any other period of glass history? He couldn't think of one. But then, maybe even the Dapper Little Man might admit to a little prejudice!

Afterthought

In the minds of some historians and in the recollections of many who actually lived it, the struggle that was the Depression was not a great or noble one. They see the time pitted by deep caverns of suffering, humans reduced to the lowest kind of existence; they remember too many people bowed to indignities and too many suffused with shame for reasons they knew not. Certainly as I have read and heard the different stories I have been struck by the sheer brutality of the details; many were so gruesome I didn't feel I could write them here.

And this is why, I suppose, the fact that people 'love' Depression Glass has been something of a wonder to me. I can see collecting it, sure: it's so pretty, and fun to watch the pieces of the many patterns fall into place. But it is also particularly reminiscent of very bad times. The colored ware was indelibly etched into daily lives; through this glass today people surely see details they would just as soon forget. Yet they love it still, and with a depth of feeling unequalled for any other bit of nostalgia from the time. Why do people build monumental collections of the glassware that provides them a perpetual looking-glass to these roughest of images?

Why have we remembered it so long? Why so well?

The pieces of this puzzle—my pattern, you might say—have fallen into place for me now. To begin with, I collected as many pieces of history as I could, and tales of reality from my folks, and through them I've reached a conclusion that is shared, I am sure, by many. To me the Depression Era provides a proud statement of man's strength, a parable of human endurance and transcendence at a time it seemed impossible. I see people not on their knees but on their feet, working to right whatever nameless thing it was that had gone wrong. Perhaps my feeling is born, at least in part, of my mother's experiences, so strongly positive in the midst of such negativism, or the even more amazing experiences of my father, the son of a musician who turned migrant worker when people could no longer afford to pay the fiddler. His story of survival and finally success is even more profound.

And now, through my study of the development of the glass industry at this time I finally understand just how intimately Depression Glass was involved in the better part of this valor. The whole story of colored glassware looms up before me as a metaphor for so much that was happening then —a thread so intricately woven in the pattern of the time that the whole fabric can be felt through it, from the 20s when color was bursting out all over and glassware did its part to advance that mood, to the 30s when even one piece of it in the poorest of homes did its part to revive whatever bright mood it could.

Doubtless some will say that through any such particular can be found the universal, that this same tracing can be drawn from other industries or occupations of the era, but let me be bold and say that I think colored glassware was a very special baby. Why? For one thing, because of the essential closeness of one's tableware to one's family. Especially during the

Depression, what bit of colored glassware there was, was dinner-time, family-together time, respites in each day's struggle whatever that struggle may have been for that family. It was the yellow pitcher of ice water in the center of the table and the pink plate under Mom's apple pie and no American who ever lived with that bright spot of color through those blackest of times will ever be able to wash it out of his memory.

Because it was so close, and because it was a symbol for what was yet so far away. It was a goal. While fathers were out doing piece-work jobs so their families could eat, mothers who could afford little else could save her dimes for the set of dishes her whole family could eat on, and enjoy together. Housewives pieced together that glassware just like they all pieced their lives back together. Each piece acquired was a little step won.

Indeed, for many, garnering a set of the glassware then was remarkably like the collecting of it now. It was the first time such glassware was widely available in large dinner services and the first time it was inexpensive enough to obtain. And collecting as an activity was then as now a joy and a restoration. When an extra dime or quarter turned up, you could all go down to the store and pick out another piece of the pattern you had chosen. Undoubtedly too, the large number and variation of patterns had the same intrigue then that they do for us now. Families who were able couldn't resist picking up pieces of Princess and Madrid and Royal Lace or other of the scores of new motifs that kept coming out, each more desirable than the one before.

And the etched designs were, of course, amazingly fine, delightfully fresh and utterly fascinating to people who had, naturally, never seen anything like them before. People may not regard our favorite glassware as very artistic now, but *then* —if we may be allowed to define art in its most basic and useful application, as giving pleasure and uplift to society— it was one of the few arts created accessible to the troubled many. In many a tenement and shanty, it was the only beautiful thing.

And because even then for so many it was such a *prize*. It was the tumbler you were given at the movies and the water set you got with a purchase of $3 or more and the nappy you found in the box of soap-powder—better than cracker-jacks, even! And you could send off any number of coupons for mail-order treasure, if you had a little extra money hidden away. It was a fun thing.

Because so many people everywhere came to have it

it became a fad, something people could identify with and communicate through because it was so familiar. In the conformity people found a certain security; it sort of went to prove they were all in this thing together.

The closer I looked into those times, the more important places I found colored glassware and I always found it close to the hearts of the people who used it. So I don't wonder about Depression Glass any more—I marvel at it, and at the people to whom it meant something. The people who with their sweat and strength of heart made it mean something; tough, gentle people who bore the hardest of times with a stoicism that seems remarkable today. Some had barely enough to see it through, but all had some measure of strength, purpose, will to live and to transcend; a desire to construct and when that failed to reconstruct again and again.

They strike me hard, these great virtues of the Depression Era. If you are about my age—25, at this writing—you may be struck too. In our too too 'comfortable' society the kind of *blood* and *bone* and *heart* displayed in our parents' day seems without place: *blood* finds no purpose for which to flow, *bone* finds no structure sure enough to build, and *heart* finds no kindred heart in which to come home. Ours is a complex age, and confusion often clouds our existence.

Our problems sometimes sound the same as our parents', but they are not the same problems at all. We, too, feel lost— not because we have no work or home to go to, but because our work and our home seem to have less and less meaning in the growing impersonality of our society. We feel we have nowhere to go—not because someone has taken our land away but because there is no longer land enough for us all to have. And we do not merely think there will be no tomorrow—we *know* there will not be, unless we can solve the new moral dilemmas that face our age and our age alone. From many examples let's draw just one: no single generation has ever solved the problem of war between men, but we must, or we will be the generation to annihilate all men.

Where in the long history of man can we look for the answers to our particular problems? To what age, to what group of people, can we look to recover our goals? Or must our answers be new ones, as yet undreamed of by man . . . .

Our problems are not our parents' problems, and our virtues are not our parents' virtues. Perhaps we are already in the midst of the severest test ever to try the intelligence and morale of men's souls. Perhaps our best is yet to come. None of us know, but we may know soon.

I believe that in the experiences of our parents during that era-gone-by are strengths that can still give us strength. And even if the victories won and the lessons learned in that time cannot provide us everything we need to meet the challenges of our own time, they can help provide us the faith in humankind that we must find and hold on to if we are to make it through.

The story of the little girl is my mother's, but the stories of your parents, though differing in particulars, will carry the same theme, the same truths, and the same inspiration. I hope you will hear their stories and, to the extent you can, make their experiences a part of you and your children. Depression Glass can be one small way of doing this. When we hold a piece of colored glassware in our hands we should feel the weight of a portentous history. When we see it sitting, shining in its place of honor in our homes we should see infinite reflections of time-pictures, to be reflected upon in our own time; and we should see our own times, our own selves, reflected.

And when we commit Depression Era Glassware to our family's treasure, to be given to children in turn, we should also commit, as well as we are able, the real treasure born of the Depression years: the human values of courage, hope, generosity, determination and love that can never be lost so long as our families live—and remember.

—Annette Weatherman

1st ROW: "TOP PRIZE" punch set (unknown).

2nd ROW: "RING OF RINGS" decanter & tumbler (unknown); Cambridge's ice bucket; McKee's Seville yellow reamer; New Martinsville's cigaret holder; "STANDING RIB" cocktail set (unknown).

3rd ROW: Paden City's "PARTY LINE" cocktail shaker & tumbler; L.E. Smith's "WIG-WAM" console bowl & pink candle-holder; Westmoreland's "WOOLWORTH" nappies; Imperial's pink nappy; Houze lamp; burgundy "PRIME RIB" bowl (unknown); Hocking's ruby SANDWICH nappy; Westmoreland's cobalt "JAUNTY ROOSTER" cup; Hocking's HOBNAIL wine set; L.E. Smith's jardiniere; "MR. BLUE" jug (unknown).

4th ROW: Jeannette's FLORAL ice tub sitting on "COPE" cake stand (unknown); canary CLARK'S TEABERRY GUM stand (unknown); L.E. Smith's pink satin bowl; Hocking's ruby SANDWICH bowl; L.E. Smith's "MT. PLEASANT" cobalt bowl; Duncan & Miller's SWAN; McKee's pink BROCADE bowl; U.S. Glass' "PEEP-HOLE" bowl; green "FAVE" vase (unknown); "AUNT POLLY" nappies and sherbet plates (unknown); New Martinsville's ruby "MOONDROPS" bowl; L.E. Smith's pink "DRIPPLE" console set; Hocking's HOBNAIL water set; Jeannette's ultra-marine DORIC AND PANSY 7" plate; U.S. Glass' green "FLOWER GARDEN with BUTTERFLIES" plate; "BIRCH TREE" cream & sugar (unknown); Duncan & Miller's 6" ruby plates.

TOP: Westmoreland's satin DOLPHIN lamp; Heisey's CHERUB candleholder.

1st ROW: Paden City's "LELA BIRD" jug: Co-Operative's ELEPHANT: U.S. Glass' "FLOWER GARDEN with BUTTER-FLIES" vase; Westmoreland's basket; New Martinsville's "GENEVA" and "JUDY" dresser sets and "WISE OWL" jug; Paden City's "LELA BIRD" vase; Heisey goblets.

2nd ROW: Cambridge's flower holder, dolphin candlestick and swan; Federal's SYLVAN jug, footed tumbler, butterdish and thin sherbet; Fostoria's VESPER candy dish; Westmoreland's #185 lamp.

3rd ROW: Imperial's EARLY AMERICAN HOBNAIL toilet set; U.S. Glass' STIPPLE candy dish and "FLOWER GARDEN with BUTTERFLIES" console set; Westmoreland's ENGLISH HOBNAIL toilet bottle and egg cup; Westmoreland's DOLPHIN console set.

1st ROW: Jeannette's ultra-marine "JENNY WARE" shakers, reamer, refrigerator bowl; SWIRL butterdish and candy dish; DORIC AND PANSY cream, sugar, and shaker. Westmoreland's ENGLISH HOBNAIL jug; Jeannette's DORIC cream soup. Federal's "INDIAN" tumbler. Westmoreland's ENGLISH HOBNAIL demitasse and cocktails.

2nd ROW: Westmoreland's ENGLISH HOBNAIL lamps; Macbeth's fat "DOGWOOD" jug; Jeannette's CHANTILLY jug and tumbler; Cambridge's WEATHERFORD bowl & serving plate; Imperial's EARLY AMERICAN HOBNAIL cupped vase; Dunbar's RAMBLER ROSE cream & sugar; Imperial's pressed glass bowl; U.S. Glass' "FLOWER GARDEN with BUTTERFLIES" dresser set.

3rd ROW: "AUNT POLLY" collection (unknown); Hazel Atlas' CLOVERLEAF shaker, ashtray, and sherbet; U.S. Glass-Tiffin's black satin "MEFFORD" comport; Fostoria's #2395½ black candlestick; L.E. Smith's "MT. PLEASANT" cream/sugar, salt/pepper on tray; McKee's Jade green "SARAH" vase, 3-foot jardiniere, Chaline blue reamer; Jade green and Old Rose (tan) BOTTOMS UP; Jeannette's Delfite match holder.

4th ROW: L. E. Smith's #433 vase; Fry's pearl-glass reamer; ruby cocktails with metal bases (unknown); ruby "STORMY" ice bucket (unknown); punch set with Macbeth's ruby ROLY POLY tumblers; New Martinsville's "MOONDROPS" ruby butter & cover, miniature cream & sugar, and amethyst decanter; Macbeth's green satin all-over pattern 10¼" light shade; Cambridge's keg set.

Jeannette's FLORAL jug and footed comport; Macbeth's "AMERICAN SWEETHEART" lampshade; Jeannette's CAMEO sandwich server; McKee's ruby ROCK CRYSTAL FLOWER lamp; Hocking's PACHYDERMs; Fostoria's azure ORLEANS pieces.

FRONT ROW: Jeannette's FLORAL vase; Liberty Works' AMERICAN PIONEER jugs and covers, dresser set, green and pink lamps, ice bucket, & coaster; U.S. Glass' "GALLEON" ashtray; "OLLIE MAY" dresser set (unknown); Indiana's #612 candy dish; Imperial's FANCY COLONIAL handled salt dip; Akro Agate's Lemonade & Oxblood child's pieces; Federal's MADRID gravy boat & tray; Hazel Atlas' FLORENTINE candy dish; Federal's TRUMP BRIDGE SET pieces.

BACK ROW: Aladdin's alacite CUPID lamp and G-22 lamp; Jeannette's "DAISY J" candy dish; McKee's AZTEC punch bowl; Westmoreland's DELLA ROBBIA candleholder; Lancaster's oil lamp; McKee's TAMBOUR ART clock; Indiana's TEA ROOM lamp; McKee's INNOVATION vase; Duncan & Miller's CARIBBEAN punch set.

Akro Agate

The Akro Agate Company incorporated in Clarksburg, West Virginia in 1914 and for the next forty years manufactured the nation's most famous glass marbles. Through their early (and exclusive) marble production a distinctive glass was developed, and by 1932 the company was molding its characteristic colors into lines of flowerpots, ashtrays, child's dishes, and other small novelties which are readily recognized by collectors today.

The Akro styles were born of the Depression years, but were carried on into the post-30s period (the factory closed in 1951). As it is not known which lines were made early and which later, collectors tend to group them all under the umbrella for colored glassware of the Depression era.

Identification of Akro Agate items can usually be ascertained by the presence of the fetching company trademark, "A-kro" with marbles in its beak and claws. The mark was not always used, but on pieces where it is missing the Akro colors speak for themselves. Besides the special marblized effects were opaques and transparent colors just as distinctive.

Some items have been remade from the same molds, but without the trademark, by other parties since 1951, but Dr. Appleton* has fingered most of these recent items in his book and believes the new to be distinguishable from the original.

So many colors and novelty lines were made through the years they cannot all be covered here. We'll take a peek at the lines probably most interesting to us collectors; for further insight you might look to the publications listed below.

Much has yet to be cataloged, but Budd Appleton's AKRO AGATE (1972, privately published) shows many novelty lines in color. Sophia Papapanu's 1973 booklet (privately published) has the CHILDREN'S LINEs in color.

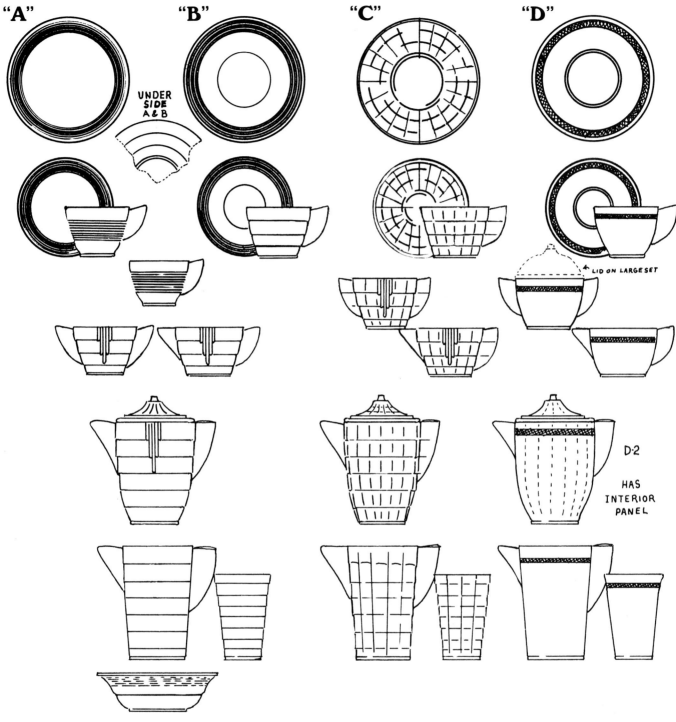

"A" STYLE
small and large plates
"A" COLORS:
mixed opaques—green, white, pink, yellow, blue, orange (pumpkin)
concentric rings on underside of plates and saucers

"B" STYLE
small and large plates
"B" COLORS:
mixed opaques—green, white, pink, yellow, blue, orange (pumpkin)
concentric rings on underside of plates and saucers

"C" STYLE
small and large sets
"C" COLORS:
transparent blue and green and opaque colors

"D" and "D-2" STYLE
small and large sets
"D" COLORS:
transparent green, amber, light blue
"D-2" COLORS:
transparent green and amber

The Akro mark as it appears (and in approximately this size) in the bottom of the pieces.

On these two pages are illustrated the Akro Agate child's sets. These came in large or small sizes as indicated, and in a variety of colorations. Because they came in transparent colors, they are included in this book. Most have the Akro mark in the bottom.

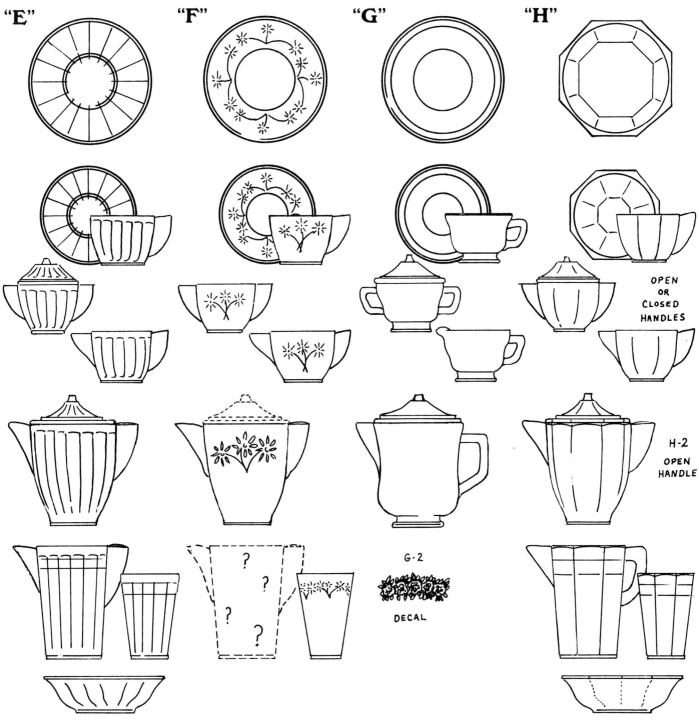

"E"   **"F"**   **"G"**   **"H"**

OPEN OR CLOSED HANDLES

H-2 OPEN HANDLE

G-2

DECAL

"E" STYLE
small and large sets
"E" COLORS:
transparent amber and green;
opaque marbled red, blue or
green with white

"F" STYLE
small sets
"F" COLORS:
opaque yellow, blue,
and green

"G" and "G-2" STYLE
large sets
"G" COLORS:
opaque white
"G-2" COLORS:
opaque white with decal

"H" and "H-2" STYLE
small and large sets
"H" and "H-2" COLORS:
mixed opaques—green, white, blue,
yellow, orange (pumpkin)
"H" also in lemonade (translucent
dull yellow-green) and oxblood
(lemonade with dark red, see
color section)

*LARGE SIZE: plate 4¼", cup 2-1/8" or 2-3/8" diam.;
saucer 3¼" or 3-3/8"; teapot 2-5/8"
high, 2-5/8" diam.; cream & sugar
2-1/8" or 2-3/8" diam.; lid 2¼";
cereal 3-3/8" (largest sets only)*

*SMALL SIZE: plate 3¼"; cup 1-7/8" diam.; saucer
2¾"; teapot 2-3/8" high, 2¼" diam.;
cream & sugar 1-7/8" diam.*

*WATER SETS: pitcher 2-7/8" high, 2-3/8" diam.;
tumbler 2" high ("D" pattern 1¾")*

Aladdin

So magic was the trade-name used by the Mantle Lamp Company of America that we will do best to consider Aladdin lamps under this familiar heading!

Starting in 1908 with its "mantle" concept and brass bases, the company moved its champion kerosene-burners through the 20s and into the 30s with bases made of colored glass. Mantle began making electric lamps in 1932, but it was the kerosene type, still so essential to millions of Americans, that dominated production until the 40s.

The glass Aladdin lamps so zealously collected today were made at Alexandria, Indiana, where Mantle acquired a glass factory in 1926. In 1953 operations were moved to Nashville, Tennessee, but no lamps have been made by Aladdin Industries (as the firm is now incorporated) in this country since 1968.

Of chief interest here are the lamps made in Crystal Art Glass (transparent amber, green, ruby, and cobalt blue); Moonstone Art Glass (the luminous opaque green, jade, rose or 'flesh', peach, yellow, and white, sometimes with black base); and the special Alacite developed for Aladdin in 1938 by the man who created Crown Tuscan and other famous colors for the Cambridge Glass Company and marbled effects for Akro Agate. Early Alacite is always ivory in tone, translucent with 'fire', while the later is more opaque.

The Aladdin story as told by J. W. Courter in "ALADDIN—THE MAGIC NAME IN LAMPS" (Rt. 2, Simpson IL) is a fascinating one. Mr. Courter supplied the photographs here and collectors with a greater interest in this subject should obtain his book.

VENETIAN
1932-33; pink, green, tan (peach), white satin

"COLONIAL"
1933; green, amber, crystal

"CATHEDRAL"
1934-35; green, amber, crystal; 1935 moonstone white, green, jade, rose

"CORINTHIAN"
1935-36; green, amber, crystal; 1936 crystal bowl w/ black, green, amber base; moonstone white, jade, green, rose, white w/ black, jade, rose base

"MAJESTIC"
1935-36; moonstone white or rose w/ gold-plated base, moonstone green w/ silver-plated base

"ORIENTALE"
1935-36; metal lamp w/ ivory or green lacquer and trims; bronze-, rose gold-, or silver-plate

"BEEHIVE"
1937-38; green, amber, ruby, crystal

"DIAMOND QUILT"
1937; moonstone white w/black or rose base; jade

QUEEN
    1937-39, moonstone white, jade w/ bronze-
    or silver-plated base, moonstone rose
    w/ silver-plate base

"TREASURE"
    Metal lamp; 1937-38 chromium-plated;
    1937-53 bronze-, nickel-plated

"VERTIQUE"
    1938; moonstone rose, yellow, jade, white

"SOLITAIRE"
    1938; moonstone white

"WASHINGTON DRAPE"
    1939; green, amber, crystal

"SHORT LINCOLN DRAPE"
    1939; amber, ruby; alacite

"TALL LINCOLN DRAPE"
    1940 cobalt blue; 1941 ruby; 1940-49
    alacite

"WASHINGTON DRAPE"
    B-style pedestal; c. 1940-41; amber, green,
    crystal

"WASHINGTON DRAPE"
    Bell-shaped pedestal; c. 1940-41; amber,
    green, crystal

"WASHINGTON DRAPE"
    Plain pedestal; 1941-42 amber, green;
    1941-53 crystal

VICTORIA
    1947; porcelain china w/ white glaze,
    floral design w/ gold trim

"SIMPLICITY"
    1948 alacite, plain & decorated; 1949-53
    rose, green, decorated crystal, white

*From 1938 to 1945 lines
of miscellaneous ware
—most commonly ashtrays—
were also made in
Alacite, but not many.
Most carry the mark
"Alacite by Aladdin".
You will find many more
Alacite lamps from the
40s illustrated in
Mr. Courter's book.*

21

Bartlett-Collins

Oklahoma oil man Bartlett teamed up with East Coast glass man Collins in 1914 to found the Sapulpa, Oklahoma glass house which was still in 1931 "the only independent glass plant making tableware west of the Mississippi". So far west—and south—was it that several of the Depression-era catalogs are subtitled in Spanish!

The company began as a hand house, making utilitarian pressed table items and lampshades in crystal and opal glass. The firm attained a gradual success; in the 20s production was chiefly hand-pressed and blown table-and stemware, kitchenware, light cut ware, decorated water sets and other items in crystal glass. By the 30s lines of tableware were being made—still by hand—in color, and these patterns are collectible today. A wide variety of occasional pieces were offered in those years as well. It was not until 1941 that hand operations were stopped in favor of machines.

Bartlett-Collins may well be best-known for its production of kitchen lamps, which began in earnest when the company did and continues to the present day. Tableware is still being made, too.

COLOR

Color is showing here by 1927—rose lustre, amber lustre, and crystal iridescent. The factory's only Depression colors were its Nu-green and Nu-rose, and some special enameled and silk-screened decorations were done.

BARTLETT-COLLINS COMPANY

Large 1-Piece Lamps, Special Insert Collars

Patented March 17, 1925

Lamparas Grandes de una sola pieza con cuello Insertado Especial

Patentado
el 17 de Marzo, 1925

No. 300—Library Lamp Complete
No. 300—Lampara de Biblioteca

Fount only made in Nu-Green
1 dozen Lamps and Burners in carton
Weight 41 lbs.

Completa con quemandor y Bombilla
Altura 17½-in.
Capacidad 41-onzas
300 F. Fuente Solamente
Verde Tambien

No. 260—Capacity 31-oz.
1 dozen in carton, weight 40 lbs.
(Also Nu-Rose and Nu-Green
½ dozen each in carton)

1 dna. en carton, peso 40 lbs.
Rosado y Verde Tambien

22

No. 261—D Lamp
31 oz. capacity
1 dozen in carton
Weight 45 lbs.

CATALOG REPRINTS

The following catalog pages are selected for reprint to show Bartlett-Collins' characteristic colored ware from 1927 through the 30s.

No. 2—Phoenix Engraved Chimney

SAPULPA, OKLAHOMA, U.S.A.

Water and Ice Tea Sets—Decorated
Scale, One-fourth Size
esala de una cuarta parte del tamano

JUEGOS PARA AGUA—Decorados
Consistiendo de 1 jarro, y 6-9 oz. vasos —empaquetados 6 juegos en un carton. Peso 30 libras.

JUEGOS PARA TE HELADO— Decorados
Consistiendo de 1 jarro, y 6-13 oz. vasos —empaquetados 6 juegos en un carton. Peso 33 libras.

Packed 6 sets in carton
Made in Crystal, NuRose and Nu-Green
Hecho en Cristal, Rosado y Verde

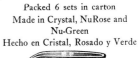

No. 416—9-oz.
Decorated 26
12 doz. in carton, wt. 46 lbs.

Decorado 26
12 dnas. en carton
Peso 46 lbs.

No. 416—13-oz.
Decorated 26
6 loz. in carton, wt. 35 lbs.

Decorado 26
6 dnas. en larton
Peso 35 lbs.

No. 821—Jug. Capacity 72-oz.
Decorated 36
1 doz. in carton, wt. 33 lbs.

No. 821—Jarro. 72-oz.
Decorado 36
1 dnas. en carton, peso 33 lbs.

No. 416—9-oz.
Decorated 36
12 doz. in carton
Weight 46 lbs.

Decorado 36
12 dnas. en carton
Peso 46 lbs.

No. 415—13-oz.
Decorated 36
6 doz. in carton
Weight 35 lbs.

Decorado 36
6 dnas. en carton
Peso 35 lbs.

No. 810—Jug
Decorated 36
1 doz. in carton
Weight 33 lbs.

No. 810—Jarra
Decorado 36
1 dna. en carton
Peso 33 lbs.

SAPULPA, OKLAHOMA, U. S. A.

Special Assortment, Decoration No. 26.
Fourteen pieces in assortment—two of each shown below in Nu-Rose Color
Surtido especial No. 26.
Escala ¼ del tamano natural
Catorce piezas surtidas—dos de cada una abajo dibujados en color de rosa

No. 87—Console Set Dec. 26
Num. 87—Florero con dos candileros, decorados 26

No. 88—Sandwich Tray Dec. 26
Num. 88—Charola, decorado 26

No. 87—Sandwich Tray Dec. 26
Num. 87—Charola, decorado 26

No. 87—Fruit Bowl Dec. 26
Num. 87—Compotera, decorado 26

No. 88—Frut Bowl Dec. 26
Num. 88—Compotera, decorado 26

No. 90—Mayonnaise Bowl Dec. 26
Num. 90—Juego de salsera con platon y cucharon, decorado 26

No. 416—9-oz., Tumbler
Decorated 26
Num. 416—Vaso de 9 oz. decorado 26

No. 423—Jug. 42-oz. Dec. 26
Num. 423—Jarro de 42 onzas, decorado 26

BARTLETT-COLLINS COMPANY

Assortment No. 40 Decoration

This assortment is not big, consists of only twelve pieces, six different items, one of each in Nu-Rose and Nu-Green, yet each piece is a big value.

Este surtimiento consiste de doce piezas solamente, 6 articulos diferentes en Nu-Rose y en Nu-Green cada una.

No. 88—11-in. Sandwich Tray
One each - Nu-Green and Nu-Rose
Decoration 40 - Decorado 40

No. 88—10-in., Cupped Bowl
One each - Nu-Green and Nu-Rose
Decoration 40 - Decorado 40

No. 90—11-in., Salver
One each - Nu-Green and Nu-Rose
Decoration 40 - Decorado 40

No. 87—10-in., Cupped Bowl
One each - Nu-Green and Nu-Rose
Decoration 40 - Decorado 40

Packed in Box
Weight 46 lbs.

Env en cajon,
Peso 46 lbs.

No. 90—9-in., Comport
One each - Nu-Green and Nu-Rose
Decoration 40 - Decorado 40

No. 820—Ice Bucket, 5½-in. Tall
One each - Nu-Green and Nu-Rose
Decoration 40 - Decorado 40

NO. 500—FT. SHERBET
22 doz. in bbl., weight 135 lbs.
½ doz. in carton, weight 30 lbs.

NO. 500—4-INCH NAPPY
40 doz. in bbl., weight 190 lbs.

NO. 500—7-INCH NAPPY
9 doz. in bbl., weight 180 lbs.

NO. 500—BUTTER AND COVER
5 doz. in bbl., weight 180 lbs.

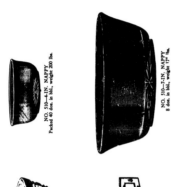

NO. 51—4-IN. NAPPY
40 doz. in bbl., weight 200 lbs.

NO. 511—7-IN. NAPPY
8 doz. in bbl., weight 175 lbs.

NO. 500—SUGAR AND COVER
10 doz. in bbl., weight 165 lbs.

NO. 510—4-IN. NAPPY
Packed 40 doz. in bbl., weight 200 lbs.

NO. 510—7-IN. NAPPY
8 doz. in bbl., weight 17? lbs.

SHERATON
NO. 550 LINE
Scale, One-half Size

BUTTER AND COVER
5 doz. in bbl., weight 145 lbs.

4½ IN. NAPPY
25 doz. in bbl., weight 185 lbs.

HD. CUSTARD
25 doz. in bbl., weight 155 lbs.

9 IN. NAPPY
5 doz. in bbl., weight 150 lbs.

12 IN. PUNCH BOWL
¾ doz. in bbl., weight 100 lbs.

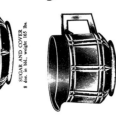

SUGAR AND COVER
8 doz. in bbl., weight 165 lbs.

CREAM
10 doz. in bbl., weight 145 lbs.

SPOON
10 doz. in bbl., weight 140 lbs.

Scale, One-half Size

NO. 851 JUG, SPIRAL OPTIC
Capacity,
1 doz. in carton, weight 40 lbs.

NO. 450—52 OZ. WATER TUMBLER
Packed 12 doz. , weight 48 lbs.

No. 800—Water Sets
Packed 4 in carton, weight 24 lbs.
No. 800—Ice Tea Sets
Packed 4 in carton, weight 25 lbs.
No. 850—Ice Tea Sets with Covered Jug
Packed 4 in carton, weight 28 lbs.
No. 807—Ice Tea Sets with Covered Jug
Packed 4 in carton, weight 28 lbs.

NO. 807—CRACKED JUG AND COVER
Packed 1 doz. in carton, weight 40 lbs.

NO. 800 OPTIC, 58-OZ.
1 doz. in carton, weight 38 lbs.

NO. 417 ICE TEA TUMBLER, 13-OZ.
Packed 4 in carton, weight 27 lbs.

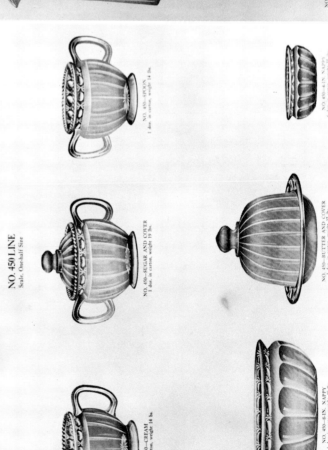

NO. 450 LINE
Scale, One-half Size

NO. 450—SPOON
1 doz. in carton, weight 14 lbs.

NO. 450—4-IN. NAPPY
6 doz. in carton, weight 27 lbs.

NO. 450—SUGAR AND COVER
1 doz. in carton, weight 19 lbs.

NO. 450—BUTTER AND COVER
1 doz. in carton, weight 27 lbs.

NO. 450—CREAM
1 doz. in carton, weight 14 lbs.

NO. 450—8-IN. NAPPY
1 doz. in carton, weight 40 lbs.

Hand Made Blown Stemware
Cut No. 52 Assortment—Nu-Rose or NuGreen

This line of stemware is new in design and has the tall graceful shape and long stem so much in demand at the present. It is daintily hand cut by experts

The goblet, high foot sherbet, low foot sherbets, plates, cocktails and wines can all be purchased separately— 3 dozen in a carton, and the creamer and sugar—1 dozen pair in a carton, at the same price per dozen pieces, package included.

No. 820—Goblet   No. 820—Hi-Footed Sherbet   No. 820—Low Footed Sherbet

Made in Nu-Rose or Nu-Green

The assortment consists of the following:

1½ Dozen low foot Sherbet
3   "   Goblets
1½ "   hi foot Sherbet
2   "   8-in. Plates
½   "   Wine
½   "   Cocktails
½   "   Creamers
½   "   Sugars

See next page for Plates, Sugars and Creamers.

No. 820—Cocktail   No. 820—Wine

BARTLETT-COLLINS COMPANY

Made in Nu-Rose or Nu-Green
All Items Cut No. 52

You have been waiting a long time for hand made, hand cut, colored glassware to sell at 25c each on which you can make a nice profit—here it is !

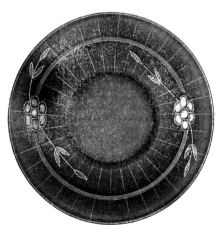

No. 91—8-in. Plate

No. 87—Sugar   No. 87—Cream

Blown Stemware
Scale, One-fourth size

Made in Crystal, Nu-Rose Optic and Nu-Green
Hecho en Cristal, Rosado Optico y Verde Optico

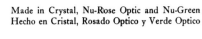

No. 1931—Goblet
3 doz. in carton
Weight 16 lbs.

No. 1931—Hi-Ft. Sherbet
3 doz. in carton
Weight 14 lbs.

No. 1931—L. Ft. Sherbet
3 doz. in carton
Weight 12 lbs.

No. 1931—Wine
3 doz. in carton
Weight 8 lbs.

No. 1931—Ft. Ice Tea
3 doz. in carton
Weight 16 lbs.

No. 1931—High Ball
3 doz. in carton
Weight 14 lbs.

No. 1931—Sherbet
Cut No. 50
3 doz. in carton
Weight 12 lbs.

BLOWN BEVERAGE TUMBLERS
Scale, One-half Size
Made in Crystal
Nu-Rose and Nu-Green

No. 201—1¼-oz., Sham Tumbler
Cut 185
12 doz. in carton, wt. 20 lbs.
12 dnas. en carton, peso 20 lbs.

No. 531—1½-oz., Sham Tumbler
Cut 54
12 doz. in carton, wt. 27 lbs.
12 dnas. en carton, peso 27 lbs.

Blown Bud Vases
Scale, One-fourth Size

Made in Nu-Rose and Nu-Green

No. 385—10-in., Cut 210
10-in. Blown Bud Vase
2 doz. in carton, wt. 12 lbs.

No. 385—Jarron, Carte 210
2 dnas. en carton, peso 12 lbs.

No. 252—Cut 238
2 doz. in carton, wt. 12 lbs.

Carte 210
2 dnas. en carton, peso 12 lbs.

No. 375—10-in., Cut 260
10-in. Blown Bud Vase
2 doz. in carton, wt. 12 lbs.

No. 375—Jarron, Carte 260
2 dnas. en carton, peso 12 lbs.

No. 380—Cut 9
2 doz. in carton, wt. 12 lbs.

Carte 9
2 dnas. en carton, peso 12 lbs.

NU-GREEN AND NU-ROSE
Hecho en Rosado y Cristal Optico

Juegos para agua—
Consistiendo de 1 jarro, y 6-9 oz. vasos
6 en canton, Peso 34 lbs.

Juegos para te helado—
Consistiendo de 1 jarro, y 6-13 oz. vasos,
6 en carton, Peso 36 bs.

No. 826—Jug, Capacity 66-oz.
1 doz. in carton, weight 35 lbs.

Num. 826—Jarro,
capacidad 66 onzas, empacados
1 dna. en carton, peso 35 lbs.

No. 426—13-oz., Ice Tea
6 doz. in carton
Weight 35 lbs.

Num. 426—Te helado de 13 onzas,
6 dnas. en carton, peso 35 lbs.

No. 426—9-oz., Tumbler
12 doz. in carton
Weight 46 lbs.

Num. 426—Vaso de 9 onzas,
12 dnas. en carton, peso 46 lbs.

No. 828—Jug and Cover
1 doz. in carton, weight 38 lbs.

Num. 828—Jarro y Tapa,
1 dna. en carton, peso 38 lbs.

No. 820—Ice Bucket
1 doz. in carton, weight 26 lbs.

Cubo para hielo con asa
1 dna. en carton, peso 26 lbs.

No. 820—Cookie Jar
1 doz. in carton, weight 36 lbs.

No. 820—Galletero
1 dna. en carton, peso 36 lbs.

Water and Ice Tea Sets
Made in Crystal and Nu-Rose
All Tumblers on this page made also in Green

Juegos para agua y te helado
Hecho en Cristal y Rosado
Todas vasos hecho en verde tambien

No. 824—Jug, Capacity 72-oz.
1 doz. in carton, weight 35 lbs.

No. 824—Jarro
1 dnas. en carton, peso 35 lbs.

No. 415—13-oz.
6 doz. in carton
Weight 35 lbs.

No. 415—9-oz.
12 doz. in carton
Weight 46 lbs.

No. 415—5-oz.
12 doz. in carton
Weight 41 lbs.

No. 415—13-oz.
6 dnas. en carton
Peso 35 lbs.

No. 415—9-oz.
12 dnas en carton
Peso 46 lbs.

No. 415—5-oz.
12 dnas. en carton
Peso 41 lbs.

WATER SETS—1 Jug and 6 9-oz. Tumblers
Packed 6 sets in carton, weight 30 lbs.

ICE TEA SETS—1 Jug and 6 9-oz. Tumblers
Packed 6 sets in carton, weight 33 lbs.

Juegos para agua—Un Jarro y 6 vasos de
9 onzas empacados 6 juegos en carton,
peso 30 lbs.

Juegos para te helado—Un Jarro y seis vasos
de 9 onzas empacados 6 juegos en carton,
peso 30 lbs.

No. 823—Jug, 72-oz.
1 doz. en carton, weight 33 lbs.

No. 823—Jarro, 72-oz.
1 dna. en carton, peso 33 lbs.

Spiral Optic
No. 416—13-oz.
6 doz. in carton
Weight 35 lbs.

Spiral Optic
No. 416—9-oz.
Water Tumbler
12 doz. in carton
Weight 46 lbs.

Spiral Optic
No. 416—5-oz.
12 doz. in carton
Weight 41 lbs.

No. 416—13-oz.
6 dnas. en carton
Peso 35 lbs.

No. 416—9-oz.
12 dnas. en carton
Peso 46 lbs.

No. 416—5-oz.
12 dnas. en carton
Peso 41 lbs.

Crystal and Nu-Rose Glassware
Hand Blown Stemware in Crystal and Nu-Rose, the latter a delicate shade of pink, the color that has been
increasing in popularity since colors have been the vogue.
The No. 25 and No. 26 lines are made in six pieces in Crystal and Nu-Rose.

Cristaleria en Cristal y Rosado
Copas, sopladas a mana en cristal y Nueva Rosa—el segundo un rosado delicado, el color que he ha aumentado
en popularidad desde que cristaleria en color ha sido la mado.
Los numeros 25 y 26 se hacen en 6 piecas en Cristal y Nu-Rose

No. 25—Goblet
3 doz. in carton
Weight 14 lbs.

3 dnas. en carton
Peso 14 lbs.

No. 25—Champagne
3 doz. in carton
Weight 14 lbs.

3 dnas. en carton
Peso 14 lbs.

No. 25—Sherbet
3 doz. in carton
Weight 12 lbs.

3 dnas. en carton
Peso 12 lbs.

No. 25—Cocktail
3 doz. in carton
Weight 7 lbs.

3 dnas. en carton
Peso 7 lbs.

No. 25—Wine
3 doz. in carton
Weight 7 lbs.

3 dnas. en carton
Peso 7 lbs.

No. 26—Goblet
3 doz. in carton
Weight 14 lbs.

3 dnas. en carton
Peso 14 lbs.

No. 26—Champagne
3 doz. in carton
Wt. 14 lbs.

3 dnas. en carton
Peso 14 lbs.

No. 26—Sherbet
3 doz. in carton
Weight 12 lbs.

3 dnas. en carton
Peso 12 lbs.

No. 26—Cocktail
3 doz. in carton
Weight 7 lbs.

3 dnas. en carton
Peso 7 lbs.

No. 26—Wine
3 doz. in carton
Weight 7 lbs.

3 dnas. en carton
Peso 7 lbs.

No. 26
Footed Tumbler
3 doz. in carton
Weight 16 lbs.

3 dnas. en carton
Peso 16 lbs.

No. 25-Oyster
Cocktail
3 doz. in carton
Wt. 10 lbs.

3 dnas en carton
Peso 10 lbs.

No. 25
Footed Tumbler
3 doz. in carton
Weight 16 lbs.

3 dnas. en carton
Peso 16 lbs.

Blown Water and Ice Tea Sets
Scale, One-fourth Size
escala de una cuarta parte del tamano
Packed 6 sets in carton

JUEGOS SOPLADOS PARA AGUA—
Consistiendo de 1 jarro, y 6-9 oz. vasos
—empaquetados 6 juegos en un carton.
Peso 32 libras.

JUEGOS SOPLADOS
PARA TE HELADO—
Consistiendo de 1 jarro, y 6-13 oz. vasos
—empaquetados 6 juegos en un carton.
Peso 35 libras.

No. 820—Jug with Ice Lip
Capacity 72 oz.
1 doz. in carton, weight 35 lbs.
Nu-Rose and Nu-Green

I dna. en carton, peso 35 lbs.
Rosado y Verde

No. 820—13-oz., Ice Tea
1 doz. in carton, weight 35 lbs.
Nu-Rose and Nu-Green

1 dnas en carton, peso 35 lbs.
Rosado y Verde

No. 820—9-oz., Water Tumbler
12 doz. in carton, weight 46 lbs.
Nu-Rose and Nu-Green

12 dnas. en carton, peso 46 lbs.
Rosado y Verde

No. 820—Jug, Capacity 72-oz.
1 doz. in carton, weight 33 lbs.
Nu-Rose Only

1 dna. en carton, peso 33 lbs.
Rosado Solamente

Spiral Optic
No. 416—13-oz.
6 doz. in carton
Weight 35 lbs.

Spiral Optic
No. 416—9-oz.
12 doz. in carton
Weight 46 lbs.

Spiral Optic
No. 416—5-oz.
12 doz. in carton
Weight 41 lbs.

Crystal, Nu-Rose and Nu-Green

No. 416—13-oz.
6 dnas. en carton
Peso 35 lbs.

No. 416—9-oz.
12 dnas. en carton
Peso 46 lbs.

No. 416—5-oz.
12 dnas. en carton
Peso 41 lbs.

Cristal, Rosado y Verde

Enamel No. 66 Assortment
Made in Nu-Rose and Nu-Green Colors - Decorated White and Green

Surtido No. 66
12 piezas 2 de cada uno de los estilos ilustrados.
1 en Nu-Rose y 1 en Nu-Green - Decoradas a mano

No. 90—Decorated 66
8-in. Two Handled Deep Nappy
Nu-Green and Nu-Rose

No. 90—Decorated 66
9-in. Large Deep Footed Comport
Nu-Green and Nu-Rose

No. 90—Decorated 66
11-in. Two Handled Cake Plate or Plaque
Nu-Green and Nu-Rose

No. 88—Decorated 66
11-in. Handled Sandwich Tray
Nu-Green and Nu-Rose

No. 820—Decorated 66
Cookie Jar and Cover, 76-oz.
Height 9-in.
Nu-Green and Nu-Rose

No. 90—Decorated 66
11-in. Footed Salver
Nu-Green and Nu-Rose

Special 210 Assortment
Cut 210
12 Pieces—all good sellers
Nu-Rose and Nu-Green
Weight 49 lbs.

Surtido especial No. 210
12 piezas atractivas
que se venden por si
Colores Rosa y Verde

No. 90—8-in. Handled Deep Bowl

Num. 90—Plato hondo color de
rosa, 8 pulgadas

No. 90—11-in. Handled Cake Plate
Num. 90—Platon verde con asas,
11 pulgadas

No. 88—10-in. Handled Fruit Bowl

Num 88—Compotera verde con asa,
10 pulgadas

No. 90—11-in. Footed Salver
or Cake Stand
Num. 90—Charola con pie color de
rosa, 11 pulgadas

No. 90—9-in. Footed Bowl
or Comport

Num. 90—Compotera con pie color
de rosa, 9 pulgadas

No. 88—11-in. Handled
Sandwich Tray
Num. 88—Charola verde con asa,
11 pulgadas

Two of each item, one Nu-Rose
and one Nu-Green in assortment

Miscellaneous
Miscelanea
Scale, One-fourth Size

Made in Nu-Rose and Nu-Green only
Hecho en Rosado y Verde Solamente

No. 89—Cupped Fruit Bowl, 10-in.
1 doz. in carton, wt. 31 lbs.

No. 89—Compotera para fruta
1 dna. en carton, peso 31 lbs.

No. 90—Mayonnaise Dish Plate
and Ladle
1 doz. in carton, wt. 30 lbs.

NO. 90—Juego de salsera ; con
cucharon y platon
1 dna. en carton, peso 30 lbs.

No. 90—8-in. Nappy
1 doz. in carton, wt. 26 lbs.

No. 90—Foutina
1 dna. en carton, peso 26 lbs.

No. 90—Salver, 10-in.
1 doz. in carton, wt. 31 lbs.

No. 90—Compotera
1 dna. en carton, peso 31 lbs.

No. 90—10-in., Plaque
1 doz. in carton, wt. 26 lbs.

No. 90—Plato para pasteles, de 10″
1 dna. en carton, peso 26 lbs.

No. 90—Comport
1 doz. in carton, wt. 31 lbs.

No. 90—Compotera
1 dna. en carton, peso 31 lbs.

No. 88—Cupped Fruit, 10-in.
1 doz. in carton, wt. 32 lbs.

No. 88—Compotera para fruta
1 dna. en carton, peso 32 lbs.

No. 821—Cookie Jar
capacity 2/3 gallon
1 doz. in carton, wt. 38 lbs.

Num. 821 Guarda dulces
capacidad 3 litros.
1 dna. en carton, peso 38 lbs.

No. 521—Cookie Jar
Capacity 1 gallon
1 doz. in carton, wt. 40 lbs.

Num. 521 Guarda dulces
capacidad 4 litros
1 dna. en carton, peso 40 lbs.

No. 16
Beverage Tumbler
capacity 1 oz. sham.
12 doz. in carton
Wt. 40 lbs.

Num. 16 Vaso
para licores
capacidad 1 oz.
12 dnas. en carton
peso 40 lbs.

No. 531
Beverage Tumbler
capacity 1½ oz.
12 doz. in carton
Wt. 27 lbs.

Num 531 Vaso para
Licores
capacidad 1½ oz
12 dnas. en carton
Peso 27 lbs.

No. 201
Beverage Sham
capacity 1¼ oz.
12 doz. in carton
Wt. 20 lbs.

Num. 201 Para
Licores
capacidad 1¼ oz.
12 dnas. en carton
Pesos 20 lbs.

27

No. 820—Blown Stemware
Scale, One-fourth Size—Nu-Rose and Nu-Green

No. 820—Goblet
3 doz. in carton, wt. 14 lbs.
3 dnas. en carton, peso 14 lbs.

No. 820—Champagne
3 doz. in carton, wt. 14 lbs.
3 dnas. en carton, peso 14 lbs.

No. 820—Sherbet
3 doz. in carton, wt. 12 lbs.
3 dnas. en carton, wt. 12 lbs.

No. 820—Ftd. Ice Tea
3 doz. in carton
Weight 16 lbs.

3 dnas. en carton
Peso 16 lbs.

No. 820—Wine
3 doz. in carton
Weight 8 lbs.

3 dnas. en carton
Peso 8 lbs.

No. 820—Cocktail
3 doz. in carton
Weight 8 lbs.

3 dnas. en carton
Peso 8 lbs.

No. 25—Parfait
3 doz. in carton
Weight 12 lbs.
Nu-Rose Only
3 dnas. en carton
Peso 12 lbs.
Rosado Solamente

Blown Sham Beverage Tumblers
Scale, One-half Size

No. 201—1¼ oz.
12 doz. in carton, wt. 20 lbs.

12 dnas. en carton, peso 20 lbs.

No. 531—1½-oz.
12 doz. in carton wt. 27 lbs.

12 dnas. en carton, peso 27 lbs.

Miscellaneous
Miscelanea

Made in Nu-Rose, Nu-Green and Crystal

No. 600—Footed Sherbets
3½-in.
6 doz. in carton
Weight 40 lbs.
Crystal Only

No. 600—Copa para
Sorbetes—3½-in.
6 dnas. en carton
Peso 40 lbs.
Cristal Solamente

No. 610—Footed Sherbets
3¾-in.
6 doz. in carton
Weight 52 lbs.
Crystal and Nu-Green Only

No. 610—Copa para
Sorbetes—3¾-in.
6 dnas. en carton
Peso 52 lbs.
Cristal y Verde Solamente

No. 300—Mollasses Can. 12-oz.
2 doz. in carton, wt. 23 lbs.

No. 300—Vasija Senitaria con Tapa
removible, 12-oz.
2 dnas. en carton, peso 23 lbs.

No. 632—19-oz.
4 doz. in carton
Weight 60 lbs.

No. 632—19-oz.
4 dnas. en carton
Peso 60 lbs.

No. 91—Plate, 8-in.
6 doz. in box, wt. 82 lbs.
Nu-Rose and Nu-Green Only

6 dnas. en cajon, peso 82 lbs.
Rosado y Verde Solamente

No. 260—Capacity, 31 oz.
Patented Insert Collar
Scale, One-fourth Size
½doz. Nu-Rose, ½ doz. Nu-Green
in carton
1 doz. in carton, wt. 40 lbs.

1 dnas. en carton, peso 40 lbs.

SAPULPA OKLAHOMA USA

Miscellaneous
Miscelanea

Scale One-fourth Size

No. 820—Ice Bucket
1 dozen in carton
Weight 26 lbs.

Num. 820
Cubo para hielo con asa
1 dna. en carton
Peso 26 lbs.

No. 91—Card Case and Cover
3 dozen in carton
Weight 56 lbs.

Num. 91—Tarjeteros con Tapa
3 dnas. en carton
Peso 56 lbs.

No. 90—Coaster and Tray
Scale, One-half Size
6 dozen in carton, weight 30 lbs.
Num. 90—Bandeja y cenizera
empacados, 6 dnas. en carton
Peso 30 lbs.

No. 16—Sham, 1-oz.
128 dozen in barrel
Weight 270 lbs.

12 dozen in carton
Weight 30 lbs.

Num. 16—1-oz.
128 dnas. en barril
Peso 270 lbs.

No. 91—Plate, 8-in.
6 dozen in box
Weight 93 lbs.
Nu-Rose and Nu-Green Only

No. 820—Decorated 66
Cookie Jar and Cover, 76-oz.
Height 9-in.
1 dozen in carton
Weight 36 lbs.
Nu-Green and Nu-Rose

SAPULPA, OKLAHOMA, U. S. A.

Miscellaneous
Miscelanea

Made in Nu-Rose and Nu-Green only
Hecho en Rosado y Verde Solamente

No. 87—Candle Holder
3 doz. in carton, wt. 11 lbs.

No. 87—Candelero
3 dnas. en carton, peso 11 lbs.

No. 87—11-in. Flower Bowl
1 doz. in carton, wt. 38 lbs.

No. 87—Florero, de 11 plgds.
1 dnas. en carton, peso 38 lbs.

No. 87—Cupped Fruit Bowl, 10-in.
1 doz. in carton, wt. 33 lbs.

No. 87—Compotera para fruta
1 dna. en carton, peso 33 lbs.

No. 87—Cream and Sugar
Packed assorted 1 doz. each in carton
Weight 15 lbs.

Juego de Servicio. Azucarera y jarra
de crema. Empacados surtidos;
1 docena en un carton
Peso 15 lbs.

No. 87—Sugar
No. 87—Azucarera

No. 87—Cream
No. 87 Jarrito para crema

No. 87—11-in. Sandwich Tray
1 doz. in carton, wt. 33 lbs.

No. 87—Charola, 11-in.
1 dna. en carton, peso 33 lbs.

No. 820—Candy Box
2 doz. in carton, wt. 51 lbs.

No. 820—Dulcera
2 dnas. en carton, peso 51 lbs.

Miscellaneous
Miscelanea

Scale ¼ size except Percolator Tops ½ size and Awning Rings full size

2⅛-in., Percolator Top
12 doz. in carton, wt. 21 lbs.

Tapa de Percolator
12 dnas. en carton, peso 21 lbs.

Puritan 5-in. High Foot Bowl
6 doz. in bbl., wt. 105 lbs.

Tazón de 5-in. con pie Alto
6 dnas. en barril, peso 105 lbs.

Oklahoma Ice Tub, 6½-in.
3½ doz. in bbl., wt. 140 lbs.

Helera Oklahoma, 6½-in.
3½ dnas. en barril, peso 140 lbs.

2⅛-in. Colonial Percolator Top
12 doz. in carton, wt. 20 lbs.

Also Nu-Green

12 dnas. en carton, peso 20 lbs.
Verde Tambien

No. 65—5-in. Nappy
6 doz. in carton, wt. 40 lbs.

6 dnas. en carton, peso 40 lbs.

No. 65—Berry Cream
2 doz. in carton, wt. 25 lbs.
Also Nu-Green
Jarros para Crema
2 dnas. en carton, peso 25 lbs.
Verde Tambien

No. 65—Berry Sugar
2 doz. in carton, wt. 25 lbs.
Also Nu-Green
Azucareras para Frutas
2 dnas. en carton, peso 25 lbs.
Verde Tambien

Awning Rings
Small
Medium
Large

No. 60—Basket
Scale, One-fourth Size
2 doz. in carton, wt. 41 lbs.
No. 60—Cesta
2 dnas. en carton, peso 41 lbs.

8-in. Puritan Nappy
1 doz. in carton, wt. 25 lbs.
Puritan Frutero, 8-in.
1 dnas. en carton, peso 25 lbs.

NO. 92 LINE—GREEN
ILLUSTRATIONS ONE-FOURTH SIZE

"TWITCH"

No. 92-5 oz. TUMBLER, GREEN
12 dozen in Carton
Weight 48 lbs.

No. 92-9 TUMBLER, GREEN
12 dozen in Carton
Weight 65 lbs.

No. 92-12 oz. ICE TEA, GREEN
8 dozen in Carton
Weight 65 lbs.

No. 92-25 oz. JUG, GREEN
2 dozen in Carton
Weight 45 lbs.

NO. 92 SUGAR, GREEN
2 dozen in Carton
Weight 15 lbs.

No. 92 CREAM, GREEN
2 dozen in Carton
Weight 15 lbs.

No. 92 SHERBET, GREEN
6 dozen in Carton
Weight 29 lbs.

No. 92 SUGAR AND CREAM, GREEN
1 dozen Pair in Carton
Weight 15 lbs.

No. 92 CUP AND SAUCER, GREEN
No. 92 CUP, GREEN
6 dozen in Carton, Weight 31 lbs.
NO. 92 SAUCER, GREEN
6 dozen in Carton, Weight 38 lbs.

No. 92-8½" PLATE, GREEN
4 dozen in Carton
Weight 55 lbs.

BLOWN TUMBLERS, JUGS AND SETS
ILLUSTRATIONS ONE-HALF SIZE

No. 842/422—9 oz. Seven Piece Set
One No. 842 Jug and
six No. 422—9 oz. Tumblers
Packed 1set in carton, weight 6 lbs.

Sets also packed with Ice Lip Jug.
Order not less than 6 sets.

No. 422—5 oz. Tumbler
12 dozen in carton
Weight 30 lbs.

No. 422—9 oz. Water Tumbler
12 dozen in carton
Weight 42 lbs.

No. 842—76 oz. Jug
1 dozen in carton, weight 33 lbs.

No. 842/422—13 oz. Seven Piece Ice Lip Set
One No. 842 Ice Lip Jug and
six No. 422—13 oz. Ice Tea Tumblers
Packed 1set in carton, weight 6 lbs.

Sets also packed with Plain Lip Jug.
Order not less than 6 sets.

No. 422—13 oz. Ice Tea Tumbler
6 dozen in carton, weight 30 lbs.

No. 842—76 oz. Ice Lip Jug
1 dozen in carton, weight 34 lbs.

Puritan Line
Renglon Puritan

Sugar and Cover
1 doz. in carton, wt. 20 lbs.

Azucarera con tapa
1 dnas. en carton, peso 20 lbs.

Cream
1 doz. in carton, wt. 15 lbs.

Jarrito para Crema
1 dnas. en carton, peso 15 lbs.

4½-in., Nappy
6 doz. in carton, wt. 40 lbs.

Dulcera 4½-in.
6 dnas. en carton, peso 40 lbs.

Puritan 4-Piece Set
2 doz. in bbl., wt. 125 lbs.

Servicios de 4 piezas Puritan
2 dnas. en barril, peso 125 lbs.

Puritan Oil Bottle
2 doz. in carton, wt. 26 lbs.

Botella Puritana para Aceite
2 dnas. en carton, peso 26 lbs.

9-in., Nappy

Butter and Cover

COVERED REFRIGERATOR JARS—GREEN
ILLUSTRATIONS ONE-HALF SIZE

ROLLED EDGE BOWLS—GREEN
ILLUSTRATIONS ONE-HALF SIZE

6 in. Refrigerator Jar and Cover, Green
2 dozen in carton, weight 29 lbs.

No. 6—6 in. Rolled Edge Bowl, Green
2 dozen in carton, weight 21 lbs.

7 in. Refrigerator Jar and Cover, Green
2 dozen in carton, weight 53 lbs.

No. 8—8 in. Rolled Edge Bowl, Green
2 dozen in carton, weight 44 lbs.

8 in. Refrigerator Jar and Cover, Green
1 dozen in carton, weight 40 lbs.

No. 10—10 in. Rolled Edge Bowl, Green
1 dozen in carton, weight 36 lbs.

MISCELLANEOUS — GREEN
ILLUSTRATIONS ONE-HALF SIZE

MISCELLANEOUS — GREEN

No. 500—Footed Sherbet, Green
6 dozen in carton, weight 34 lbs.

No. 1—Lemon Reamer, Green
3 dozen in carton, weight 30 lbs
Made in Green only

Small Caster Cup, Green
12 dozen in carton, weight 27 lbs.
Illustration full size

Colonial Percolator Top, Green
2⅛ in. Fitter
12 dozen in carton, weight 20 lbs.
Illustration half size

No. 15—Salt and Pepper, Green
12 dozen in carton, weight 34 lbs.
4 dozen in carton, weight 12 lbs.

Medium Caster Cup, Green
12 dozen in carton, weight 38 lbs.
Illustration full size

No. 20—Ice Tea Coaster, Green
12 dozen in carton, weight 34 lbs.
Illustration full size

No. 2—Orange Reamer, Green
2 dozen in carton, weight 38 lbs.

No. 3—Measuring Cup, Green
2 dozen in carton, weight 17 lbs.

Large Caster Cup, Green
12 dozen in carton, weight 42 lbs.
Illustration full size

No. 63—Ash Tray, Green
3 dozen in carton, weight 27 lbs.
Illustration half size

Belmont

Many facts about this Bellaire, Ohio company are not known; a fire blazed through the old factory in 1952 and few clues remain.

A very early Belmont Tumbler advertisement bears the slogan "Nothing but hand blown tumblers in all sizes and desirable shapes for all purposes from one ounce up"—which pretty well sums up its pre-Depression activity! In the 20s automation was acquired and more tumblers made than ever before, ranging from the simple utilitarian to the ornately etched or enamel decorated. Then the company branched into color and mold-etched wares; it was Belmont's designer who in 1931 created our "Rose Cameo".

Advertisements show that pink, green, a frosted green, and a sprayed-on iridescent were made before this company, like so many others, went under with the Depression.

BOOK 1 UPDATE

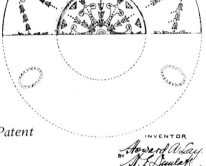

Dec. 1, 1931.

H. A. LAY
PLATE OR SIMILAR ARTICLE
Filed Aug. 25, 1931

"ROSE CAMEO"

Happily we can now acknowledge the creator of one of our very familiar patterns. Shown are the 5" tumbler and the 5" nappy.

—*United States Patent*

INVENTOR

BOOK 2 PATTERNS

"ABC-STORK" CHILD'S PLATE
is 7½" in green and crystal

BELMONT SHIP PLATE
*8", green, crystal, amber,
and iridescent amber. You may find
this ship w/checkerboard outer rim*

Bryce

This company's celebrated roots can be traced back to the mid-1800's to its initial site in Pittsburgh and through a series of well-known glass names and managements. But the Bryce Brothers Company of Mt. Pleasant, Pennsylvania was incorporated in 1896, its modern tradition of hand-blown stemware for home, hotel and restaurant use beginning at this time.

Bryce continued to specialize in cut, etched, engraved, and decorated stemware through this century (sidelining in vases, baskets, and other accessory pieces), and earned one of the finest names in American glassware before becoming a part of the Lenox Corporation (under the new label, Lenox Crystal) in 1965.

From the earliest 20s Bryce began introducing color into its lines—listing in company catalogs amber, ruby, green, canary, blue, amberosa, amethyst, and iridescents. Later in the 20s came pink, dark blue and light blue; in the 30s black was often featured as was Aurene, a gold tint. Indeed most all the popular colors of the times were used—usually in combination with crystal—in the hundreds of patterns and blanks made. The examples shown here can only begin to give you an idea of Bryce's repertoire.

—1928 patent

—1929 patent

Following are reprints from a Bryce catalog showing some of the stemware shapes made in the company colors through the years.

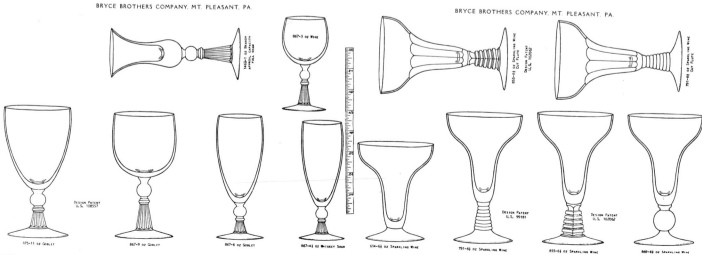

32

Cambridge

Out of the fallen National Glass Company combine, this Cambridge Ohio factory picked itself up and went on to become one of the all time greatest makers of American glass in this century.

The young (built 1901) but incredible Cambridge, under private management, began turning heads within a decade. Tableware and imaginative occasional pieces of all kinds were made first in crystal, then—certainly as early as anywhere else—in fantastic color creations. Unquestionably this factory was a source and an inspiration for the colored glass trend which was to last two decades. Excellent glass quality, design and workmanship ranked Cambridge table and dinnerware of this period with the best being made. And taking together the extent and sheer virtuosity displayed in the decorative (yet popularly priced) art lines each year, the company may well be without peer.

An effective national publicity campaign beginning in the 20s brought the Cambridge name—and the notion of color—before the public and linked it with ideas of elegance and prosperity. So many of the Cambridge lines became best-sellers that the factory was expanded to accommodate the tremendous demand, and the company became probably the largest producer of handmade glass in the 20s and 30s era.

So much was its colored glass contribution during this time it all cannot be covered here. Several books have already been compiled on Cambridge glass, highly collectible since the firm's demise in 1958, and though none are comprehensive the interested collector will do well to refer to them.* Many details of date and color do not appear in these publications, however, and for this reason I want to add here all the data my own research has brought to light on the important color years of Cambridge Glass.

After the company's close the molds went to the Imperial Glass Corporation, and some are in use today in crystal and new colors.

COLOR

Cambridge—champion of color from the earliest 20s. Each new year brought new shades; each new shade brought much todo from the trade press, which generally gives the company credit for pioneering the popular use of opaque color (and some transparents, most notably pink) for a national market.

*Harold and Judy Bennett's THE CAMBRIDGE GLASS BOOK (Wallace-Homestead, 1970) in color; the Welkers' catalog reprints and Virginia McLean's 1949 catalog reprint (both privately published in 1970).

'Juice Extractor', 1922, and undraped girl figure from large, varied, and colorful line, 1931

Here is a resume of Cambridge's color activity—including the many opaques—during the span of our interest, compiled from the trade journal reports of each year. These reports were not always complete. Descriptions are given verbatim. Colors were often in production for several years after their introduction date.

1921   Gold encrustations

1922   Introduced: Ebony, Azurite (a lovely bright blue)

1923   Introduced: Primrose yellow (a yellow of warmth and volume, but not extreme); Helio (of the purple family, with a delicate tone); Carrara (a brilliant white); topaz; light green; Mulberry

1924   Introduced: Amber; Ivory; Jade

1925   Introduced: Rubina (a combination of red, green, and blue transparent glass, each tone diverging into the other); Onyx (a light tan); Emerald; Cobalt blue; Black trims

1926   Introduced: Peach-Blo; Amber-Glo; crackled glass in several colors; Blue Willow treatments, in which a famous Indian Tree design, duplicated from a china pattern, is etched on crystal and 1) filled in with blue and lines of gold, 2) filled in with Nankin green or Old purple, 3) etched onto ivory glass, and 4) encrusted in gold on amber or Emerald pieces

1927   Introduced: First all-glass dinnerware, in transparent colors; Golden Showers (a true golden); stemware with pink bowls and green feet

1928   Introduced: Swans in six sizes in Peach-Blo, Emerald, Ebony and crystal

1929   Introduced: Gold Krystal, (a deep yellow gold rather than amber gold) especially in stemware with gold bowl and crystal feet; Willow blue

1930   Introduced: Madiera (golden amber); Mystic blue; Rose du Barry; Cinnamon; Jade

1931   Introduced: Carmen (a bright ruby); Burgundy (a deep amethyst); Royal blue; Forest green; Royal purple; Wine

1932   Introduced: Heatherbloom

1933   Introduced: Eleanor blue; amethyst

SWANS

Glass Swans from CAMBRIDGE are distinctive table accessories. They are offered in a variety of sizes, from three to 13 inch, and in choice of Ebony, Peach-Blo, Crystal and Emerald.   Swan candle holders, used with the large swan flower holder, make an attractive center piece. Our line of decorated swans includes acid-etched treatments.

*The Cambridge Swans
1928 advertisement*

The annual trade journal write-ups of each company's new colors are not comprehensive after this date; from advertisements we know that LaRosa pink, Moonlight blue (light), ruby, and Coral ("Crown Tuscan" later) were brought on in the next years.

The Cambridge frog, dog, squirrel, moth, butterflies, birds, and turkey from 1930 trade journal features.

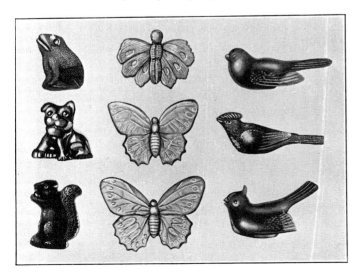

Two new patterns in deep plate etchings. At left ETTA and right BORDEAUX on optic shapes.

ONE PINT DECANTER
Unusual small glasses and decanter, all on a tray. In colored glass, plain or decorated.

A refreshment set in the new Cambridge BLOCK OPTIC in amber, emerald, mulberry, plain or with gold hair-line edge, scalloped or straight rims.

VANITY SET in crystal, amber, emerald, mulberry, blue.

WINE SET UNIQUE is a decanter with footed glasses on a round tray. Amber, emerald, mulberry, blue; tray is ebony.

#705 FLOWER POT & SAUCER
in all Cambridge colors.

Cambridge Glass Co. has for three years sent out a very extensive line of colored glass and their 1924 offerings in art glass take front rank among the wares now before the public. Above, the comport and candlestick are ebony stippled with silver or gold. The footed vase is jade green with gold encrustation; the vase basket is ivory, its enameled decoration is in natural colors.

A compilation of Cambridge wares, with official names & colors, from 1924-25 ads or trade reports.

FLOWER BLOCK
small, large sizes in Rock
Crystal, Emerald, Peach-blo.

CONSOLE SET
Jar is decorated with gold, DANCING GIRL
design. Candlesticks, DOLPHIN design. In Amber-
glo or Emerald.

Two new
patterns
in deep plate
etchings:
MARJORIE, left, and CLEO right.

GEISHA GIRL
flower holder in Emerald,
Amber-glo, Peach-blo, crystal;
she is 12" high.

ROSE BUD Candy Box
This is only one shape for this box
with Rose Bud knob. Amber-glo,
Peach-blo, or Emerald with knob in
constrasting colors.

WEATHERFORD DESIGN
shown is the 8½" bowl. Comes plain or engraved
in Emerald, Amber-glo, Peach-blo.

#596 SALAD PLATE
is the 8" size and can be
had in Emerald or Amber-glo.

#620 SUGAR & CREAM SET
on seperate handled tray. Made in
crystal, Emerald, and Amber-glo.

#618 is an ashtray with holders for
cigarets, cigars, paper and box matches.

COMPACT #680 is one of the
popular new items in the 1926 line.
In all the popular Cambridge transparent colors.

A compilation of items, with official names & colors, from 1926 advertisements.

A triumph in CAMBRIDGE Art Glass is this gold-encrusted Night Set composed of small, covered jug, oval tray and tumbler. Supplied in Amber-Glo, Peach-Blo or Emerald.

An attractive and substantial pair of book ends in CAMBRIDGE colors of Amber-Glo, Peach-Blo and Emerald.

A DESK SET IN GLASS

The all-glass desk set is a most attractive number. It includes ridged holder for pens and pencils, a paper rack, ink bottle and stopper and pin holder. Can be had in Amber-Glo, Peach-Blo and Emerald, both plain and decorated.

3-FOOT BOWL & CANDLESTICKS
in Peach-blo, Amber-glo, Emerald

Square dishes for brick ice cream and other confections. The larger plate for cake or serving. In Amber-Glo, Peach-Blo, Emerald, plain, decorated.

QUALITY DINNERWARE

A complete glass dinner service is available in Amber-glo, Peach-blo, and Emerald. Can be had plain, in etchings or in gold band and gold spray decorations.

COMPARTMENT RELISH
dish is seven compartments in one piece of glass. Amber-glo, Peach-blo, and Emerald with gold encrusted band.

The Cambridge Glass Company

Demand for aquaria has become almost a staple thing in the glassware store or section and as an aid for dealers to meet that demand, the Cambridge Glass Co., of Cambridge,

Ohio, has brought out recently the two items illustrated. These can be had in the Cambridge transparent colors of Peach-Blo, Amber-Glo and emerald.

Item No. 787 is designed to meet the demand for a small table aquaria. It has a wide foot and ample space for a small number of fish. The piece also can be used as a footed vase, so that it has a two-fold utility. The design of the No. 787 aquarium is new. It is eight inches tall. The other aquaria is known as No. 791 and is 11 by 7 inches at the top and six inches deep. It is smooth finished at the bottom and makes a very competent article.

In blown stemware in colored glass, CAMBRIDGE wares rightfully have a high place. The shape illustrated is new and graceful. Shown are the goblet, tumbler and sundae. This is especially attractive in bowl of Peach-Blo and foot of Emerald. Also procurable in other combinations.

Salteers and Pepperettes of distinction. Best design on the market in three sizes. In colored glass with silver tops. Ask for Nos. 396, 397 and 398.

A compilation of items, with official names & colors, from 1927-28 advertisements or trade journal reports.

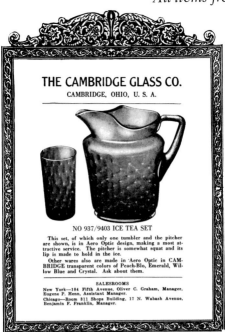

THE CAMBRIDGE GLASS CO.
CAMBRIDGE, OHIO, U. S. A.

NO 937/9403 ICE TEA SET

This set, of which only one tumbler and the pitcher are shown, is in Aero Optic design, making a most attractive service. The pitcher is somewhat squat and its lip is made to hold in the ice.

Other wares also are made in Aero Optic in CAMBRIDGE transparent colors of Peach-Blo, Emerald, Willow Blue and Crystal. Ask about them.

SALESROOMS
New York—184 Fifth Avenue, Oliver C. Graham, Manager, Eugene P. Henn, Assistant Manager.
Chicago—Room 311 Shops Building, 17 N. Wabash Avenue, Benjamin F. Franklin, Manager.

HANDY CONDIMENT SERVICE
green, peach, amber, blue

AERO OPTIC
ice tea set

Candy Box and
Salad Set (below)
in #731 etching

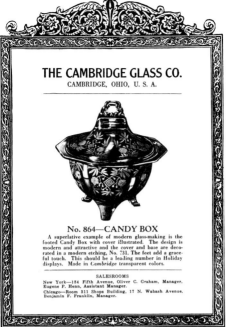

THE CAMBRIDGE GLASS CO.
CAMBRIDGE, OHIO, U. S. A.

No. 864—CANDY BOX

A superlative example of modern glass-making is the footed Candy Box with cover illustrated. The design is modern and attractive and the cover and base are decorated in a modern etching, No. 731. The feet add a graceful touch. This should be a leading number in Holiday displays. Made in *Cambridge* transparent colors.

SALESROOMS
New York—184 Fifth Avenue, Oliver C. Graham, Manager, Eugene P. Henn, Assistant Manager.
Chicago—Room 311 Shops Building, 17 N. Wabash Avenue, Benjamin F. Franklin, Manager.

TABLE GLASSWARE

Utility in the modern manner is typified in the No. 3300 line of *Cambridge* glassware. The design is new and the several pieces make an attractive setting. Illustrated are the regular 9-ounce table tumbler, the 8-ounce goblet, the tall sherbet and the footed 10-ounce soda goblet.

Made in attractive transparent shades, including Madeira (golden amber), Peach-Blo, Emerald and Crystal.

No. 971/972/698 SALAD SET

Just the thing for Summer featuring are salad, bridge, relish and refreshment sets in CAMBRIDGE colors of Peach-Blo, Emerald, Amber-Glo and Willow Blue. Attractive patterns in etchings, the decorative mode of the day, are available. The salad set has eight pieces providing service for six. The etching is No. 731.

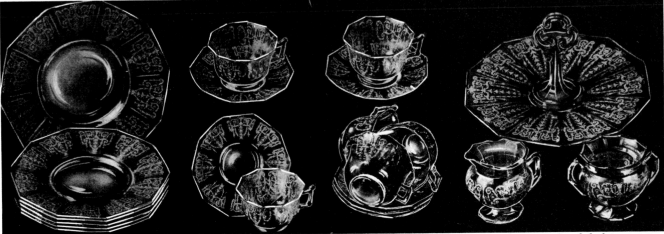

The CLEO etching is shown above in a 21-piece luncheon set on the popular DECAGON line. Six cups and saucers, six salad plates, sugar, creamer, and handled cake or sandwich tray in Willow blue, Peach-blo, Emerald. Most suitable for June!

GOLDEN, AMBER TRANSPARENT COLOR
ADDED TO CAMBRIDGE GLASS CO. LINE

This unusual aquarium has a bird in prominent position. It is etching No. 736 and is a product of the Cambridge Glass Co., Cambridge, Ohio. Made in various colors.

In this piece, the figure of a hunting dog in the field is used to decorate a cigarette case. This decoration is brought out in strong etched relief. This is a product of the Cambridge Glass Co., Cambridge, Ohio.

A DDING to its variety of transparent colors, the Cambridge Glass Co., Cambridge, Ohio, recently has introduced a light golden amber shade which it has named "Madeira." This new color is in addition to the attractive Willow Blue, Peach-Blo and Emerald which have been the leading transparent colors with the Cambridge Glass Co.

The "Madeira" is neither a canary yellow nor a deep amber, but what might be described as a half-way shade between the two. It is a clear, entrancing color and keeps its tone effect in both blown and pressed ware.

Many of the new items brought out in the past few weeks

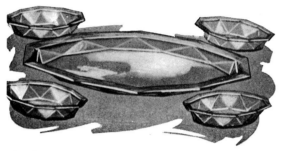

by the Cambridge Glass Co. are being offered in "Madeira" or in combinations, especially in stemware, of "Madeira" bowl and crystal stem and foot. Among the new items available in "Madeira" is the relish set illustrated. The set is in five pieces, including four individual dishes and one large serving dish. The design of the dishes is new and is Early American in spirit.

PINCH DECANTER SET

Ultra-modern and quite attractive is the Pinch Decanter set consisting of pinch decanter with stopper and six glasses, all in Aero Optic. The design makes decoration unnecessary.

Made in superlative transparent colors of Peach-Blo, Emerald and Willow Blue. A stock of these should be on hand in every store.

The New LORNA · · · · ·

T HE beauty of the brilliant DECAGON line is now enhanced by the introducion of this new etching. The LORNA is truly a brilliantly attractive etching. It should be immensely popular.

Available in complete lines, including Stemware, Dinnerware, Individual Decorative Pieces and Novelty Items. Made in the CAMBRIDGE colors: Gold Krystol, Amber, Emerald, Peach Blo and Crystal.

The Cambridge Glass Company

FOUR PLATES showing the CLEO etching (upper left); the APPLE BLOSSOM etching (u.r.); the #732 etching (l.l.) and the GLORIA.

SWEET POTATO VASE
—1932 advertisement

BEAUTIFUL RICH GREEN FOLIAGE in the Home may be had by the ordinary SWEET POTATO

...PRACTICAL...
..INEXPENSIVE..

INSTRUCTIONS FOR GROWING SWEET POTATO VINE

Cut Sweet Potato at one end to fit top rim of Vase. Fill vase with water, covering half of the potato and keep at this height. Put near window so potato will get plenty of sunlight or daylight, in two or three weeks you will grow a Sweet Potato Vine like the illustration, that will last for months.

These beautiful vines are more desirable than ivy, as the foliage is equally attractive and grows in much less time and is much less expensive.

FURNISHED IN

Forest Green ... Ruby
Amethyst .. Royal Blue

MARTHA WASHINGTON
—1932 advertisement

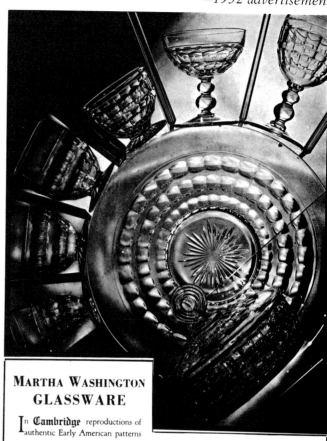

MARTHA WASHINGTON GLASSWARE

In **Cambridge** reproductions of authentic Early American patterns

A full and complete line obtainable in sparkling crystal, the antique colors of amber, royal blue, forest green and ruby and in the modern colorings. Heatherbloom and Gold Krystol.

The MOUNT VERNON pattern above is by the Cambridge Glass Co. and is being shown at their display room, 184 Fifth Avenue. It is brilliant crystal. MOUNT VERNON is made in the finest Cambridge antique colors of amber, Royal blue, Forest green, Carmen and crystal.

MOUNT VERNON *from 1933 trade journal*

The IMPERIAL HUNT etching by the Cambridge Glass Co. on their new Tally Ho patented line is pictured above. It is made in a complete pressed stemware line ranging from the 18-oz goblet to a 1-oz cordial and also in fancy tableware and novelty pieces in a range of the Cambridge colors and crystal.

IMPERIAL HUNT *from 1932 trade journal*

The No. 3078 stemware line of the Cambridge Glass Co. at the right illustrates four sizes of half sham beverage tumblers. In capacity these are 15, 12, 5 and 2½ oz. The jug and decanter shown are supplementary pieces to a full stemware line. This line is in colors of crystal, forest green, royal blue, amber and amethyst. The tumblers illustrated may also be had in ruby.

EVERGLADES

One of the new lines to be brought out this Fall by the Cambridge Glass Co. is their Everglades. The few pieces of this which we illustrate will give an idea of its attractiveness. In addition to the items pictured this line also consists of three or four types of candlesticks, high, low and double candelabra, various bowls of different types and shapes and four different types of vases. It is to be had in colors of crystal, Eleanor blue, Forest green, and amber with a few pieces made in Carmen (ruby).

*Four trade journal excerpts
from 1933-1934.*

The No. 3122 patented shape in stemware shown at the left has just been introduced by the Cambridge Glass Co., 184 Fifth avenue. A feature of it is the brilliance of the stem, due to a mitre effect. It may be had in Forest green, Royal blue, amber, Carmine (ruby), gold krystol, peach, emerald, heatherbloom and crystal. The line is made either plain, etched, or in rock crystal.

OCTOBER, 1934

DISTINCTIVE WARES FOR PROFIT

—By Cambridge

For the Holiday Gift Season, the CAMBRIDGE line includes hundreds of attractive items. Make your selections early. Write us today about the wares shown and other outstanding designs in hand-made quality table and decorative glassware.

The Narcissus Bulb Vase, above, sells readily and profitably because it is attractive. Designed to hold four bulbs, it is useful for other bulbs, such as Hyacinth and Lily-of-the-Valley, as well as Narcissus. Done in the wide selection of masterful CAMBRIDGE colors.

Quite appealing is the Floating Rose Bowl, for use as a centerpiece or on the occasional table. Beautifully blown, it has a design which increases the beauty of the rose floating on the water as illustrated. The bowls also may be used as vases.

Hand Made Quality Glassware Exclusively

The Nautilus design is an outstanding creation. Wine sets are especially attractive because of the striking decanter and the handsome glasses. Done in Crystal, Amber, Royal Blue, Forest Green, Amethyst and Carmen and combinations of crystal and color. Protected by Design Patents 84482 and 89828.

The Cambridge Glass Company

Shown above is the No. 1402 Tally Ho line by the Cambridge Glass Co. that shows a beer mug set complete with pitcher that is a very timely item. This plain ring decoration is fully covered by patent and the line may be had in the full range of Cambridge colors as well as in crystal. Incidently the mugs or jugs can be purchased separately if desired.

Cambridge
Advertising Features America's Most Popular Pattern

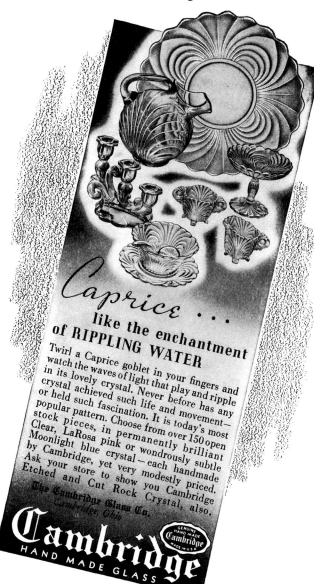

The Cambridge Glass Co.
CAMBRIDGE, OHIO

CAPRICE

Cambridge billed its biggest selling line as the country's favorite pattern in 1936 advertising. A trade journal the same year stated that over 200 pieces comprised the line.

In addition to the crystal, LaRosa (pink) and Moonlight blue, it was also advertised satin finish and called ALPINE CAPRICE. The salad set (right) and jugs (below) were featured in the trade report, which noted that the jugs

also came with "etched crystal decoration."

—1935 ad

SEA SHELL
A Cambridge Creation

■ As refreshing as a May breeze is this new and delightful "Sea Shell" line decorated with the modeled figure of a sea maid. Embracing such items as compotes, candlesticks, centerpieces, sea-food cocktails, bowls, plates, vases and relishes, its colors of Amber, Carmen, Royal Blue, Coral, Amethyst and Forest Green present a variety of the widest range. Shells, dolphins and sea maid motifs have inspired these shapes. You will be delighted to sell them.

The Cambridge Glass Company
Cambridge, Ohio

Central

The Central Glass Works was a large, well-known and respected Wheeling, West Virginia factory at the time of our interest. The original establishment dates back to the 1860s and the name Central Glass Company, when bottles, lamps, and eventually pressed and blown tableware were its products. The Works (so called in 1896) centered production around crystal and decorated tableware, bar goods, tumblers and stemware for homes and famous hotels, and cut and etched colored glass in the 20s and 30s. Besides creating its own extensive lines Central did a big business in supplying blanks to other companies for finishing.

Over the years this firm manufactured a tremendous volume of glass for world-wide sale as well as domestic use. But the hand house never really recovered from the blow of the Depression, and finally closed in 1939 leaving behind an excellent reputation for quality goods.

COLOR

Central was another influential factory making profuse—and original—use of color in the early 20s. By 1924, shades of green, blue, canary, black, amethyst, and amber are advertised. In 1925 there was purple, amber, and white opalescent; in 1926 light blue and pink. Black, dark blue and ruby appeared sometime after this, and later trade notices show that Central's topaz, Golden Sapphire, was introduced in 1931. These colors—and probably there were more—stayed in production for several years and were often combined with crystal. Satin finishes, iridescents, gold encrustations, and many other decorations were done through the entire era.

It is unfortunate that no catalogs have yet come to light, for this firm made hundreds of shapes and etchings during the Depression Era and many unidentified collectible patterns could doubtless be attributed here.

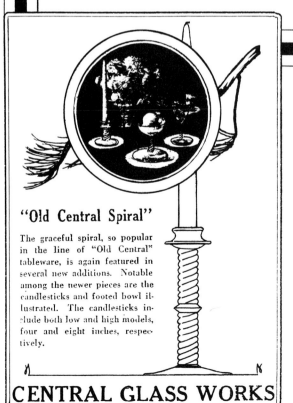

"Old Central Spiral"

The graceful spiral, so popular in the line of "Old Central" tableware, is again featured in several new additions. Notable among the newer pieces are the candlesticks and footed bowl illustrated. The candlesticks include both low and high models, four and eight inches, respectively.

CENTRAL GLASS WORKS
WHEELING, W. VA.

—1925 advertisement

"MEMPHIS" CONSOLE SET
satin finish blue, black, canary, green, amethyst; also came etched; 1923 ad

45

Consolidated

Consolidated Lamp and Glass Company of Coraopolis, Pennsylvania, began in 1894. Illuminating wares, globes and shades were foremost in its lines for many years, but pressed and blown tableware patterns and arty occasional pieces—most notably vases—are also part of Consolidated history.

The famous lamps were made in all styles and sizes, colored and fancy-decorated according to the best fashion of the time, and ranged from the simple to the elaborate. Among the many varieties over the years were those with shades of white or creamy glass with hand-applied nature scenes in beautiful colors (mid-20s) and colored glass shades of Jade, Honey, Rose, and French crystal like the one shown here (late 20s).

From the "Art Glass Division" of the factory came the vases and Consolidated's Depression-era tableware, made mainly by hand. Its patterns were few, but those few were memorable. A production of black satin glass starting in 1925 attracted much attention from the trade. Martele, the big line of 1926, was made from molds, but so well crafted it was "the closest thing in this country to the productions of Lalique, the well-known French artificers" according to a glass journal report of that year. Fruits, flowers, love birds, and dancing girls were some of the different motifs used, and colors were orchid, red, two shades of green, and brown.

In 1927 the Catalonian line was created, in reproduction of glass from 17th Century Spain. No two pieces of the hand-finished ware were the same, ran the advertisements. Colors were Spanish Rose, Honey, Emerald, Jade, and amethyst.

The Lighting Glassware Division of the Consolidated Lamp & Glass Co., of Coraopolis, Pa., has just brought out a most attractive line of lighting units designed in the modern effects. The Martele Modernizer illustrated can be had in two sizes, 11 and 17 inches, and in a range of colors including jade, honey, rose, and French crystal. For the exclusive shop this new line has an especial appeal, producing a beautiful lighting effect as well as efficient light.

—1929 trade report

In 1928 Consolidated unveiled its incomparable Ruba Rombic in Smoky topaz, Jungle green, Silver grey, Honey, Jade, Lilac, and amethyst. Consolidated called it "an epic of Modern Art". The trade called it "bewildering", its colors "out of the ordinary".

Despite the relative success of these few lines the company went under in 1933, reopening in 1936 under new management. The Consolidated molds had been lent to Phoenix Glass Company of nearby Monaca, Pennsylvania, during this dormant period, and apparently Phoenix grew quite attached to these molds which were successful for them as well. Most of the molds were eventually recovered, however, and Consolidated production was resumed on Martele (then offered in crystal, green, pink, and blue) and Catalonian lines ("soft, rich tones of Honey, blue, crystal, amethyst, and green".)

Consolidated prospered in the 30s and 40s but slowed in its later years, changing hands and finally closing down in 1967.

Martelè

Hand Wrought Designs in Glass

As with every work of art, words do scant justice to the beauth of this new ware. It must be seen to be appreciated.

Different from anything else made in this country in glass, Martele has the appearance of being hand wrought.

The glass is semi-transparent; colors are orchid, russet, sepia and jade green. Fire polished, with tops and bottoms hand cut and polished.

Consolidated Lamp and Glass Company

Art Glass Division   *Coraopolis, Pennsylvania*

FRUIT & LEAF *Martele,* **BIRD & FLOWER** *Martele,* & **FLOWER** *Martele from 1927 ad.*

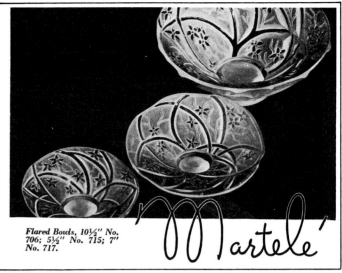

Flared Bowls, 10½" No. 706; 5½" No. 715; 7" No. 717.

Martelè

"FAIRY" *Martele from 1936 advertisement*

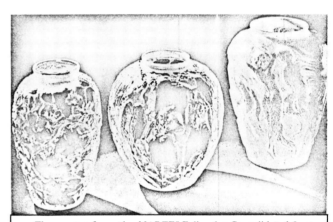

Three vases from the MARTELE line by Consolidated Lamp & Glass Co. include the Dogwood and Love Bird vase, both with French crystal finish, and the Dancing Girl vase with satin finish.

—1937 trade journal report

"DANCE OF THE NUDES"

Those closely associated with Consolidated remember making this pattern in pink and crystal in the late 20s. You may find more pieces besides these:

Nappy, 6½"
Cup & Saucer
Sherbet & Plate
Footed tumbler, 5½", 3½"
Plate, 8¼"
Berry Dish

The "Curve of Beauty" Becomes Angular
in
Ruba Rombic

Rubaiy
(meaning epic or poem)
Rombic
(meaning irregualr in shape)

Salad plate, bread & butter, sherbet, finger bowl, compote, candleholder, oval bowl, ashtray, powder box, vase, flared bowl, water jug, cigarette boxes, footed ice teas, cream and sugar

CONSOLIDATED
ART GLASSWARE DIVISION
LAMP & GLASS COMPANY · CORAOPOLIS, PA.

Hogarth, the painter, defined beauty in terms of curves—his "line of beauty" has made its impress throughout the entire world of art. But in our architecture today we find the curve supplanted by straight lines—because the modern architect has learned how to support masonry without the aid of the old arches, trusses and pilasters that once were necessary.

And when you come to think of it, there is no real reason why a vase should be spherical instead of angular, is there? Or a goblet rounded instead of cornered?

This glassware in cool greens, in soft warm browns, in lovely lavenders, is entirely new for the alert hostess. And, it is BLOWN glass!

CATALONIAN *from 1927 advertisement*

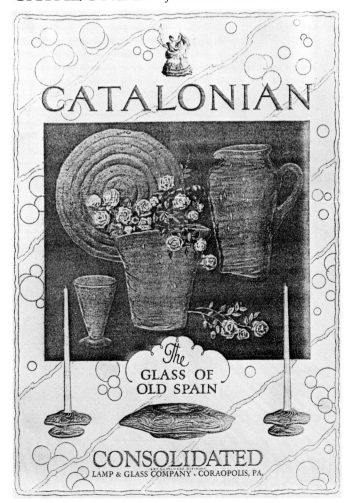

—1927 patent

Pinch bottle first made 1927; this ad 1936

Whiskey Set, No. 1162—
Cigarette Box, No. 1107
—Ash Tray, No. 1125.

This old pinch bottle of by-gone days is reproduced with all the added beauty of Catalonian Old Spanish

Co-Operative Flint

Co-Operative Flint Glass Company originated in 1879 in the Pennsylvania borough of Beaver Falls. It began as the Beaver Falls Co-Operative Glass Company; the name was changed in 1889.

For this company as for so many others of its time, pressed wares common to the crystal period evolved to fancifully colored lines of tableware and occasional pieces by the 20s. The Co-Operative lines were always extensive; in addition to gift items and novelties, which were often decorated, a considerable trade with restaurants, hotels, and soda fountains was maintained during the era. And all the while, the company sidelined in glass objects of all persuasions—including furniture knobs and mushroom covers, gazing balls and pipe rests, bird baths and seed cups!

The tough trial of the Depression was fought by Co-Operative, but not won, and the factory closed in 1934.

COLOR

The Co-Operative displays were suffused with color by the very first of the 20s. Transparent shades of amethyst, blue, canary, green, turquoise, and black glass were being done by 1923. The black was called midnight Glass and frequently came decorated with a gold or white band. Amber and cobalt blue were added in 1924— and so was ruby in an unusually early appearance. Clearly this factory was a pacesetter for color.

In 1925 Sunset was offered; this effect was deep red in the center thinning into lighter shades of yellow toward edges. Rose came out in 1926; aquamarine just after that. By 1929 the company was so securely immersed in colors they advertised simply "all lines available in all popular colors" of the day.

—1924 ad

NEW ITEMS IN CRYSTAL AND COLORS

The smaller bowl is #471 and comes in crystal, black, and a choice of several colors. The illustration shows a flower block in position. The candlestick is #449.

The larger bowl has a multiple base and a wide edge falling gracefully from the top. The Co-Operative factory will soon offer new shapes in baked apple servers and grapefruit bowls.

CO-OPERATIVE FLINT GLASS CO.
BEAVER FALLS, PENNSYLVANIA.

CO-OPERATIVE FLINT GLASS CO
BEAVER FALLS, PA.

*FOREST tableware line
(cream & sugar; nappies; bowls, some covered) in green, blue, pink & other colors; also satin finished; 1928 ad*

Animal Figures In Glass

ELEPHANT, *1927*
trade journal report;
holes in his back for
flowers; all colors

WHALE, *1927*
trade journal report;
used as container;
all colors

— 1928 ad

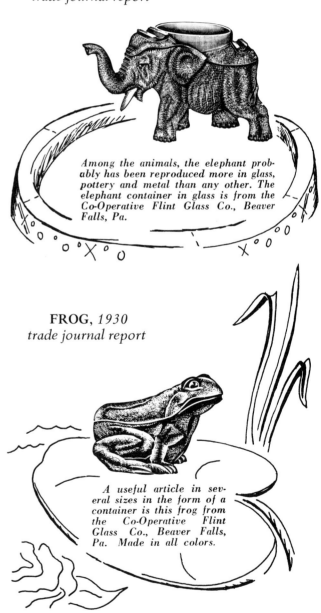

'NOTHER ELEPHANT, *1930*
trade journal report

Among the animals, the elephant probably has been reproduced more in glass, pottery and metal than any other. The elephant container in glass is from the Co-Operative Flint Glass Co., Beaver Falls, Pa.

FROG, *1930*
trade journal report

A useful article in several sizes in the form of a container is this frog from the Co-Operative Flint Glass Co., Beaver Falls, Pa. Made in all colors.

These are only a few of the animals from Co-Operative's glass menagerie. Unfortunately no catalogs have turned up so that we might identify more of this company's wares!

Early American Glassware

Refectory items in our Early American pattern No. 587. This pattern available in Crystal, Green, Amber, Rose, Cobalt-bue, Topaz and Ruby.

EARLY AMERICAN

*tableware line
from 1932 advertisement*

"POOKIE" SET
*in colors
1931 ad*

USEFUL WARES
IN
COLORED GLASS

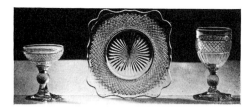
Our No. 387 Puff Box

Novelties and Useful Wares in full array of transparent colors are plentiful in our interesting line.

Every display can use Co-Operative Flint novelties and we shall be glad to know your requirements.

Just out. Plates and dinner sets in black glass. The dinner sets have 40 pieces. Black glass is very popular. Our black is good.

CO-OPERATIVE
FLINT GLASS CO
BEAVER FALLS, PA.

The No. 566 handled 8-inch bowl is only one of a great variety of useful and unique wares made in all the popular colors as well as black and crystal. Let us know your needs.

— 1929 ads

STURDY
TABLE
GLASS

No. 557—Goblet

No. 557—Ice Tea

In all popular colors and black. Glass dinner sets of 40 pieces also in black.

No. 557—Footed Tumbler

Co-Operative Flint Glass Company
Beaver Falls, Pa.

Manufacturers of

Ivy Balls in Colors with Black Glass Bases, Gazing Balls, Ruby Glassware, Cobalt Blue Glassware, Glass Novelties in popular colors, Soda Fountain Glass ware, Crystal and Green, Cake Covers, Cake Stands, Cake Trays, Animal Novelties, Dinner Ware, etc.

No. 574—Ivy Ball

REPRESENTATIVES—
New York—Messers H. C. Gray Co., 200 Fifth Avenue.
Chicago—T. M. Schollenberger Co., 17 N. Wabash Avenue.
Baltimore—John A. Dobson Co., 110 Hopkins Place.
Dallas, Texas—Fred Kline, 718 Santa Fe Terminal Building.
Philadelphia—U. S. Crockery & Glass Exchange, 922 Chestnut St.
Los Angeles and San Francisco—Shaw-Newell Co., 212 Lissner Building, Los Angeles.

No. 573—Flower Pot and Block

Diamond

In Indiana, Pennsylvania a factory first known as Indiana Glass Company got underway in 1891, only to change form three more times (becoming the Northwood Company for a while and then the Dugan Glass Company) before it finally emerged as the Diamond Glass-Ware Company.

But three was still no charm for this factory—despite many marketing successes in the 20s, it was brought to the ground by fire in 1931 and never rebuilt.

In its brief career as Diamond Glass a high grade of handmade glass was manufactured in light cut and decorated tableware, and arty novelties with special effects. The firm even developed a considerable foreign as well as domestic trade, and it's certainly unfortunate no more of Diamond's patterns have been identified.

Colors abounded in Diamond's last decade—green, blue, and gold were brilliantly iridized, satin finished or decorated in the early 20s, and the popular transparent colors followed. Diamond anticipated the ruby period by bringing on its deep red glass in 1924, and an Antique Ivory was shown in 1926. Further trade journal reports indicate that pink, amethyst and Ritz blue were on hand by 1929.

In the end, though, black was perhaps Diamond's foremost color. Appearing as early as 1926, it was made in many items with various gold and silver trims every year until the company's demise.

One of the most interesting new items shown at the Pittsburgh Exhibit was a glass epergne in transparent colors from the Diamond Glass-Ware Company of Indiana, Pa. The epergne is a table center piece in the form of a flower holder. In the new Diamond production there are four small vases all attached to the center stem, one in the center and three of shorter length. All are joined to the base with the use of a metal band inside a glass band. The base is round with a raised edge. Each of the smaller vases has a crimped top with a glass thread wound about the center. The new epergenes can be had in "Even Glow," a pink glass; in green, and in amber.

—1928 trade journal write-up and 1929 advertisement

VICTORY

was one of Diamond's best-known tableware lines. It is shown here in a 1929 advertisement; it also comes in Ritz blue and amethyst.

A partial listing:

Plate 7", 8", 9"
Cup
Saucer
Cream
Sugar
Bowl 6½"
Platter
Sandwich Server 11"
Bon Bon 5½" hi-footed

#99 LINE

was being advertised in 1930; it was only one of several black lines made popular by Diamond.

Dunbar

In 1913 the Dunbar Flint Glass Corporation of Dunbar, West Virginia, began in a very small way—making lamp chimneys from one small tank—but by the Depression era had greatly expanded its production and achieved a wide success with pressed and blown tableware of many kinds. In 1930 the "Flint" was dropped from the corporate title, and in 1953 the company closed for good.

Throughout the Depression period color was the emphasis here as it was at glasshouses everywhere. In the 20s the principal colors were Rose pink and Bermuda green; in the 30s, Steigel green, cobalt blue and ruby. A special line came out in 1936 in topaz-, amethyst-, ruby-, and blue-lustres. Gold encrustations were a big feature in all colors.

Many of the lines were downright fancy, but Dunbar's specialty through the years was always the refreshment set, usually thin-blown and with a light cutting. Many liquor services and cocktail sets with shakers were also made.

5 Piece Servette Set
Consists of tray and handle and four 12 oz. tumblers with gold encrustation in rambler rose design. Comes in rose pink or plain.

12 Piece Service Set
Consists of quart size cocktail shaker, ice tube and tongs, six tumblers, and tray. Either rose pink or green glass. Shaker top, tongs and detachable handle of ice tub are genuine silver-plated.

—1928 advertisements

No. 4016—Iced Tea Set with band of gold encrusted in rambler rose design.
Color: Rose pink.

THANKSGIVING
NOVEMBER

CHRISTMAS
DECEMBER

NEW YEARS
1929
JANUARY

Gifts
of COLORED GLASSWARE

No. 6350—Water Set, six 9-oz. tumblers and jug.
Color: Rose pink.

12″ Optic Vase
No. 4072, Gold encrusted in rambler rose design. Comes in rose pink only.

Mayonnaise Set
No. 1223/4/4 Three piece. cut 100. Comes in rose or green.

No. 4089—Cheese and Cracker with gold inlaid design. The latest art treatment in glassware.
Color: Rose pink or Green.

Bridge Set

No. 4071—Footed cake stand with gold inlaid design. The latest treatment in glassware.
Color: Rose pink or Green.

6½ *inch*
trumpet vase.

Checo Vase
No. 4077, Gold encrusted in rambler design. Comes in rose pink only.

Servette Set
No. 1247, Line 412. Cut 17. five-piece. Comes in rose pink only.

Nite Set
No. 4082, Gold encrusted in rambler rose design. Comes in rose pink only.

7-inch candy box

No. 4091—Three partition candy box and cover with gold inlaid design. The latest art treatment in glassware.
Color: Rose pink or Green.

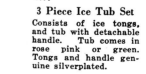

3 Piece Ice Tub Set
Consists of ice tongs, and tub with detachable handle. Tub comes in rose pink or green. Tongs and handle genuine silverplated.

Dunbar items this page from 1928 & 1929 ads

This is Station DFGC
broadcasting BIG NEWS

3-Piece Mayonnaise Set. Bowl, Plate and Ladle richly gold encrusted with the new one-inch bands in the Rambler Rose design. No. 4179.

Handled Sandwich Tray. Smart simplicity. The new, generously wide band, gold encrusted, Rambler Rose pattern, make this a particularly handsome piece. No. 4177.

IT'S news about the new Dunbar Glassware shown here! Introducing the new one-inch wide gold encrusted Rambler Rose border! These wider bands are the latest of the Dunbar innovations. They lend new smartness and beauty to the pieces. And—more news—they are obtainable also in Cheese-and-Cracker, Seven-piece Relish, Console Sets, Footed Salvers, Candy Jars and Footed Fruit Bowls. "Broadcast" sales over your counter by stocking this newest Dunbar Glassware now!

DUNBAR FLINT GLASS CORP., DUNBAR, W. VA.

3-Partition Covered Bon-Bon box. In rose pink or Bermuda green, with the new inch gold embossed bands. Rambler Rose design No. 4192.

Footed Relish Stand with five compartments, in rose-pink or green glass. 11 in. diam. The novel 12-sided outline sets off the rich gold rambler-rose border.—No. 4093.

A five-compartment flat Relish. 10 in. diam. Rose-pink or green glass. The rolled border with rambler rose design in gold gives special smartness to this design.—No. 4081.

Six assembled compartments make this 13¼ in. Dunbar Relish a very popular seller. Convenient to use and refill. Rose-pink or green glass. In addition to the rambler rose border in gold, each compartment is edged with gold—No. 4033.

DUNBAR GLASS
New Designs at Popular Prices

RAMBLER ROSE *from 1929 ads*

—1928 ad

THE YEAR'S GREATEST NOVELTY IN GLASSWARE
Fancy Glassware Adorned With Decalcomania Decorations

HERE is something really new and worthwhile. A wide variety of decals specially adapted for use on glassware are obtainable. The Mayonnaise Set illustrated is merely one of a large number of tableware items to which the treatments are applied. They include Sandwich Trays, Cracker and Cheese Dishes, Salad Plates, Sugars and Creamers, etc.

"BARBRA"
pink beverage set, 1928 ad

No. 4114—New Bell Vase with gold encrusted rim in rambler rose design. Comes in rose pink only.

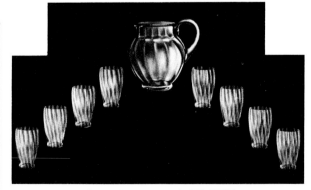

#5116 BEVERAGE SET
rose pink or Bermuda green, 1930 ad

—1929 ad

NEW!
DUNBAR 1929 BEVERAGE SETS

No. 5022
New Iced Tea Set.
Comes in pink or
green.

No. 5023
New Iced Tea Set.
Comes in pink or
green.

No. 5024
New Iced Tea Set.
Comes in pink or
green.

No. 5025
New Water Set.
Comes in pink or
green.

No. 5026
New Water Set.
Comes in pink or
green.

. . . Now on display at the
Pittsburgh Show are these 1929 Dunbar Beverage
Sets. Room 718, Fort Pitt Hotel. Mr. F. F. Hyre
and Mr. H. F. Phillips in charge. Don't miss the
Dunbar Exhibit.

DUNBAR
DUNBAR FLINT GLASS CORP. . . DUNBAR, W. VA.

DUNBAR GLASS CORP.

New York Office: 1107 Broadway, Room 916

| Assorted colored stripes | Cut Silver Rose | Six assorted lusters | Six assorted lusters |
| To retail for $1 | To retail for $1.95 | To retail for $1.95 | To retail for $1.79 |

No. 6248—New Fancy Shaped Vase with floral cut design. Comes in rose pink only.

—1932 ad

"ATHOS", "PORTHOS", "ARAMIS", *and* "D'ARTAGNAN"; *1936 ad*

DUNBAR MODERNISTIC CUTTING

MODERNIST *and* POINSETTIA
*cuttings in colors
from 1932 ad*

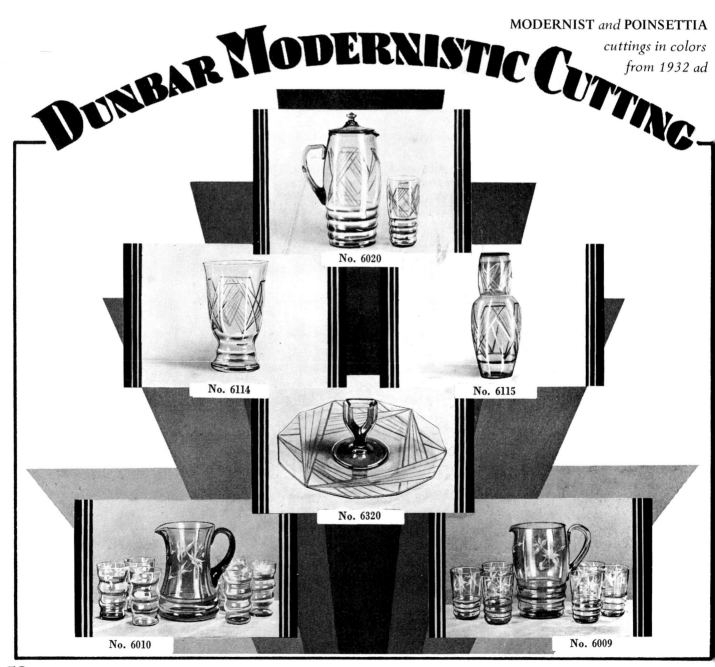

No. 6020

No. 6114

No. 6115

No. 6320

No. 6010

No. 6009

58

Duncan & Miller

The origins of Duncan and Miller Glass Company can be traced back through some fascinating glass history to its first Pittsburgh site in 1865, but the factory we remember best was built in 1893 in Washington, Pennsylvania.

Here the Duncan achievement found its highest expression. Designs in crystal, created around the turn of the century by J. E. Miller and honored even in his own time, have long been prizes in pattern glass collections along with other very early pressed wares by this company.

We who collect from the next era of glass history will want to look back to the 20s when color first spread into the Duncan displays. Dinnerware, table pieces, and imaginative giftwares—cut or etched, sometimes decorated and always handmade—appeared, turning heads in the trade. In particular it was the color reproductions of Early American pressed glass patterns that won the Depression-era reputation for Duncan and Miller. A trade journal credits the company with the first re-creation of the Sandwich pattern, which was evidently as popular then as it is with collectors now. "Here is real art in mould making and glass pressing and it evidently pleases the public fancy very much" says another article about the Sandwich lace work design of 1926. Hobnail was another important reproduction line about that time.

New designs in colors were also created in the 20s, of course, and always drew attention. As early as 1934, though, the company ushered in another crystal era with such large lines as Tear Drop and Caribbean in 1936. While spots of color remained in the Duncan displays through the later 30s, crystal predominated until the War years. It was about this time, too, the famous swans were begun, though most were made, in many sizes and colors, after the war.

In 1955 Duncan and Miller was sold to United States Glass Company, and the operation of its molds transferred to Tiffin, Ohio. A few of the popular molds were later sold—Sandwich #41 went to Indiana Glass, for example—but some are still being used by Tiffin today.

Duncan and Miller was another of the fine hand houses celebrating color in the 20s. Starting with green in 1924, the factory worked in colors for the next decade: amber in 1925, Carmen in 1926, Rose pink in 1926, ebony, ruby and Royal blue (dark) in 1931, Sapphire blue (light) in 1936. Most of these lasted out the 30s, though in limited use. Many times color was put in combination with crystal.

In 1940 a series of opalescents was developed for the Sanibel line—sea shells and the like—as well as many of the tableware lines. These opalescents were Cranberry pink, Cape Cod blue, and a Jasmine yellow. The yellow-green, Chartreuse, was not made until 1948.

Color was given a hearty revival after the War, with ruby, dark blue and such new shades as Teakwood, Avocado, and Biscayne green lasting into the 50s when Duncan became a division of U. S. Glass.

Most lines from the color era will be found in this chapter; Frances Bones' BOOK OF DUNCAN GLASS (Wallace-Homestead, 1973) includes some earlier lines.

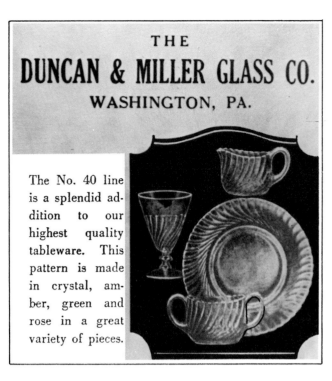
"SPIRAL FLUTES"

Introduced in 1924, "SPIRAL FLUTES" was a large and popular line to which a variety of pieces were added in subsequent years. It was first issued in crystal, green, and amber, then in pink in 1926. Besides the pieces pictured on this page, the pattern includes baskets, finger bowls, flower bowls, vases, and more.

Plate, dinner, 10½"	Cream & Sugar
Plate, Luncheon, 9-3/8"	Sherbet, 5" tall
Plate, Salad, 7-3/8"	Tumbler, 4-7/8"
Plate, Sandwich, 14"	Tumbler, ftd., 9 oz, 5¼"
Cup & Saucer	Goblet, 6¼"
Bowl, round, 10", flared, 12"	Almond, Ftd., 2¼" tall
Bowl, nappy, 5"	Parfait 5-3/8"
Bowl, Oval vegetable, 10¼"	Celery, 11-1/8"
Bowl, Cream soup, 3-7/8"	Candlestick, 3½" tall
Platter 12¾"	Compote

"FULL SAIL"
This design was pressed into the underside of plates in 1925 in amber and green.

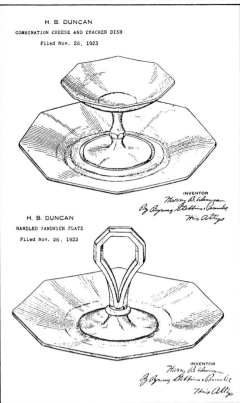

H. B. DUNCAN
COMBINATION CHEESE AND CRACKER DISH
Filed Nov. 26, 1923

INVENTOR

H. B. DUNCAN
HANDLED SANDWICH PLATE
Filed Nov. 26, 1923

INVENTOR

"RITA" *(top) and* **"TERI"**
from 1924 patents

Early American Lace Glass In Ruby

RICH in the traditions of Sandwich, that famous old Cape Cod factory which kept alive the Early American spirit in glass for many years, this stately lace design presents an unusual appeal in this period of wide interest in Colonial types. While the design is not new, it is timed to the moment by being produced in a sparkling ruby (red) glass of extraordinary merit. This "Early American Lace Glass" in ruby is really new. It is made of the purest pot-glass by skilled craftsmen in the Duncan & Miller Glass Co. factory, at Washington, Pa. In addition to ruby, it is produced also in all the needed tableware pieces in crystal, green, amber and rose.

Ruby glass, it might be pointed out, is more expensive to make than crystal and transparent colors. In the first place, the materials are more costly and are more wearing on the melting pots and moulds. Further, in order to bring out the rich coloring, such as this Duncan glass possesses, more care is needed in shaping and the glass must be re-heated oftener.

—1932 ad

SANDWICH
(Duncan and Miller's)

Continued next page . . .

**UNIQUE COASTER PLATE IS NEW ITEM
IN EARLY AMERICAN LACE GLASS LINE**

QUITE useful is the new four-inch coaster plate added to its line of Eary American lace glass by the Duncan & Miller Glass Co., of Washington, Pa. The Early American lace glass, as made by Duncan & Miller, takes its inspiration from Sandwich productions of 100 years ago and takes its place as a Colonial type along with the hob-nail and similar designs.

This Early American lace glass is known as the No. 41 pattern of the Duncan & Miller Glass Co. In addition to the new coaster plate, a nine-ounce footed tumbler and a footed cocktail have been added to the line. The additions bring the total of items to 24, including goblets, plates in four sizes, nappies, comportes, finger bowls, fruit salad, grape fruit dish, tea cup and saucer and footed ice cream and sundae dishes. The line is made in ruby, green, amber and crystal.

The illustration shows the new four-inch coaster plate. This is not an ordinary coaster, because it has many other uses. The plate is reminiscent of a fine lace doily and it has as many uses and attractions. For use as a coaster or as a holder for tumblers, sundaes and other glassware, it is admirable. Almost invisible raised ribs cross the center of the plate. The piece is wide enough so that a spoon can be placed or rested on its shoulder. So many coasters are made to fit one particular size of tumbler or glass. This new design is not so restricted. It also may be used as an individual bread and butter plate and for other forms of individual service. It is large enough, too, to serve as an ash tray.

SANDWICH
(Continued from preceding page)

Duncan and Miller brought out its fantastic re-creation of Sandwich glass in 1925. The initial colors were crystal, green, amber; then rose; then ruby and finally in 1949, chartreuse (a yellow green).

So well and widely received was it that a score of additional pieces were made during its run, which lasted as long as the company did. The pattern continued, in fact, through the life of the Duncan and Miller Division of U. S. Glass Co., and even now these same molds are in production for Indiana Glass who bought them in the 60s.

In recent years Indiana has made pieces in new colors such as a Sandwich Gold (deep amber), Sunset (red-yellow blend), a contemporary green, and blue.

The reprints on the coming pages should bring further elucidation.

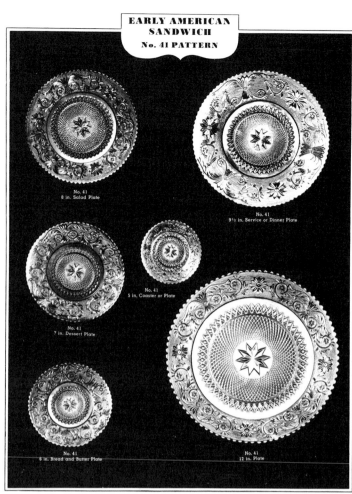

EARLY AMERICAN SANDWICH
No. 41 PATTERN

No. 41 8 in. Salad Plate

No. 41 9½ in. Service or Dinner Plate

No. 41 7 in. Dessert Plate

No. 41 5 in. Coaster or Plate

No. 41 6 in. Bread and Butter Plate

No. 41 12 in. Plate

EARLY AMERICAN SANDWICH
No. 41 PATTERN

No. 41 9 oz. Goblet Height—6"

No. 41 5 oz. Saucer Champagne Height—5½"

No. 41 3 oz. Wine Height—4½"

No. 41 3 oz. Cocktail Height—4½"

No. 41 5 oz. Ice Cream Height—4¼"

No. 41 5 oz. Flared Sundae Height—3½"

No. 41 3 in. Ind. Jelly

No. 41 6 oz. Fruit Cup or Jello Height—2½"

No. 41 5 oz. Oyster Cocktail Height—2¾"

No. 41 13 oz. Ice Tea Tumbler—Straight Height—5¼"

No. 41 ½ gal. Ice Lip Jug Height—8"

No. 41 12 oz. Ft'd. Ice Tea Height—5½"

No. 41 9 oz. Ft'd. Tumbler Height—4½"

No. 41 5 oz. Ft'd. Orange Juice Height—3¼"

No. 41 4 oz. Parfait Height—5¼"

EARLY AMERICAN SANDWICH
No. 41 PATTERN

No. 41 Tea Cup and Saucer Teacup—6 oz. Saucer—6"

No. 41 2½ in. Salted Almond

No. 41 Finger Bowl and Plate Diameter Bowl—4" Diameter Plate—6½"

No. 41 8 in. Oval Tray Width—4¾"

No. 41 Small Salt—Glass Top Small Pepper—Glass Top Height—2½"

No. 41 5½ in. Grapefruit with 41 Fruit Cup Liner

41—5 Pc. Oil and Vinegar Condiment Set Consisting of 41—3 oz. Oil Bottle Height—5¼" 41—3 oz. Vinegar Bottle 41—Salt and Pepper—Glass Top 41—8 in. Oval Tray

41—3 Pc. 5 oz. Sugar and Cream Set Consisting of 41—5 oz. Sugar Height—2½" 41—5 oz. Cream Height—3" 41—8 in. Oval Tray

No. 41 8 in. Butter or Cheese and Cover Diameter Cover—4¼"

No. 41 9 oz. Sugar Height—3¼"

No. 41 7 oz. Cream Height—4"

**EARLY AMERICAN
SANDWICH
No. 41 PATTERN**

No. 41
5 in. Ftd. Mayonnaise
Height—2¾"

41—3 Pc. 13 in. Salad Dressing Set
Consisting of
41—5 in. Mayonnaise Bowl—Ladle
41—13 in. Plate W/Ring

41—3 Pc. Mayonnaise Set
Consisting of
41—5 in. Ftd. Mayonnaise
41—7 in. Plate W/Ring
41—Ladle

41—3 Pc. 6 in. 2 Compt. Salad Dressing Set
Consisting of
41—2 Compt. Salad Dressing Bowl
Height—4"
41—2 Glass Ladles

No. 41
12 in. Shallow Salad Bowl
Height—2½"

41—2 Pc. 6 in. Mayonnaise Set
Consisting of
41—6 in. Ftd. Mayonnaise Bowl
Height—4"
41—Glass Ladle

41—2 Pc. Salad Set
Consisting of
41—10 in. Salad Bowl
Height—4"
41—13 in. Plate

41—3 Pc. 6 in. Mayonnaise Set
Consisting of
41—6 in. Ftd. Mayonnaise Bowl
Height—4"
41—8 in. Plate with Ring
41—Glass Ladle

41—4 Pc. 6 in. 2 Compt. Salad Dressing Set
Consisting of
41—2 Compt. Salad Dressing Bowl
Height—4"
41—2 Plate with Ring
41—2 Glass Ladles

**EARLY AMERICAN
SANDWICH
No. 41 PATTERN**

41—12 in. 3 Pc. Midnight Supper Set
Consisting of
41—12 in. Devilled Egg Plate
41—5 in. Ftd. Mayonnaise—Ladle

No. 41
11½ in. Crimped Ftd. Fruit Bowl
Height—7½"

41—13 in. 2 Pc. Cheese and Cracker Set
Consisting of
41—13 in. Plate W/Ring
41—5½ in. Cheese Stand

No. 41
5½ in. Cheese Stand
Height—3"

No. 41
13 in. Ftd. Cake Salver, Flat Edge
Height—5"

No. 41
12 in. Ftd. Cake Salver, Rolled Edge
Height—5¼"

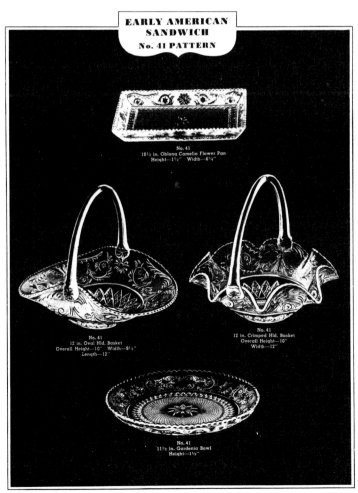

**EARLY AMERICAN
SANDWICH
No. 41 PATTERN**

No. 41
10½ in. Oblong Camelia Flower Pan
Height—1½"   Width—6¾"

No. 41
12 in. Oval Hld. Basket
Overall Height—10"   Width—9½"
Length—12"

No. 41
12 in. Crimped Hld. Basket
Overall Height—10"
Width—12"

No. 41
11½ in. Gardenia Bowl
Height—1½"

**EARLY AMERICAN
SANDWICH
No. 41 PATTERN**

No. 41
5½ in. Tall Compart
Height—4¼"

No. 41
6 in. Low Foot
Compart
Height—5"

No. 41
6 in. Low Foot
Flared Compart
Height—4½"

No. 41
4 in. Grape Fruit
Height—1½"

No. 41
5½ in. Grapefruit with Rim Liner
or Large Frozen Fruit Server

No. 41
6 in. Fruit Salad
Height—2"

No. 41
10 in. 3 Compt. Fruit Bowl
For serving three kinds of canned fruit
Height—3¾"

No. 41
12 in. Fruit Bowl, Flared
Height—2¾"

No. 41
6 in. Dessert Nappy

No. 41
5 in. Fruit Nappy

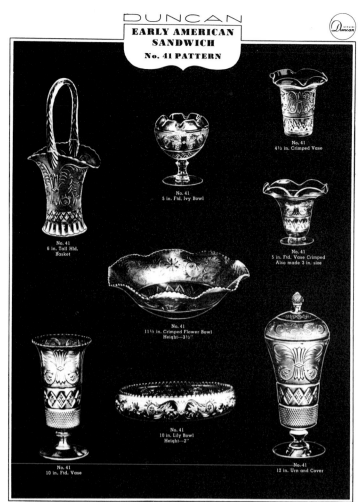

No. 41
6 in. Tall Hld.
Basket

No. 41
5 in. Ftd. Ivy Bowl

No. 41
4½ in. Crimped Vase

No. 41
5 in. Ftd. Vase Crimped
Also made 3 in. size

No. 41
11½ in. Crimped Flower Bowl
Height—3½"

No. 41
10 in. Lily Bowl
Height—2"

No. 41
10 in. Ftd. Vase

No. 41
12 in. Urn and Cover

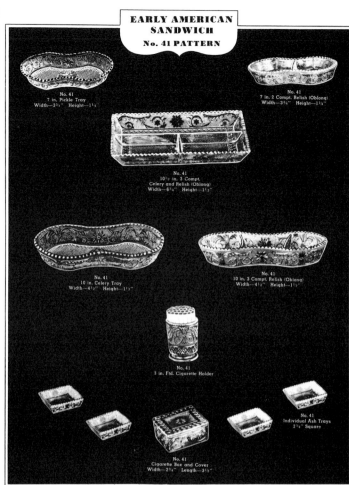

No. 41
7 in. Pickle Tray
Width—3¾" Height—1¼"

No. 41
7 in. 2 Compt. Relish (Oblong)
Width—3¾" Height—1¼"

No. 41
10½ in. 3 Compt.
Celery and Relish (Oblong)
Width—6¾" Height—1½"

No. 41
10 in. Celery Tray
Width—4½" Height—1½"

No. 41
10 in. 3 Compt. Relish (Oblong)
Width—4½" Height—1½"

No. 41
3 in. Ftd. Cigarette Holder

No. 41
Individual Ash Trays
2¾" Square

No. 41
Cigarette Box and Cover
Width—2¾" Length—3½"

No. 41
12 in. Ice Cream Tray
Height—1¼"

No. 41
12 in. Devilled Egg Plate

No. 41
12 in. 3 Compt. Relish

No. 41
11 in. Nut Bowl Cupped
Height—4"

No. 41
13 in. Plate, Flat Edge
Also made Rolled Edge

No. 41
5 in. 2 Light Candlestick
Height—5" Width—9"

No. 41
4 in. Candlestick

No. 41
12 in. Oblong Bowl
Height—3¾" Width—6¾"

No. 41
4 in. Candlestick

No. 41
5 in. 3 Light Candlestick
Height—7" Width—9"

DUNCAN

EARLY AMERICAN SANDWICH
No. 41 PATTERN

Duncan & Miller

EARLY AMERICAN SANDWICH
No. 41 PATTERN

No. 1-B-41—3 Light
Candelabrum W/U Prisms
Height—10" Width—13"
2 Bobeches

No. 1-41—1 Light
Candelabrum W/U Prisms
Height—10"

No. 1-41—1 Light
Hurricane Lamp Candelabrum
W/Prisms
Height—15"

No. 1-C-41—3 Light
Candelabrum W/U Prisms
Height—16" Width—13"
3 Bobeches

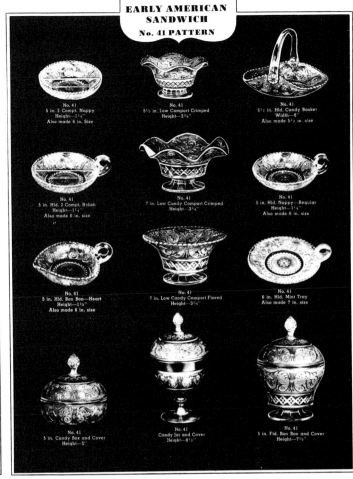

No. 41
5 in. 2 Compt. Nappy
Height—1¼"
Also made 6 in. Size

No. 41
5½ in. Low Comport Crimped
Height—2¾"

No. 41
5½ in. Hld. Candy Basket
Width—6"
Also made 5½ in. size

No. 41
5 in. Hld. 2 Compt. Relish
Height—1¼"
Also made 6 in. size

No. 41
7 in. Low Candy Comport Crimped
Height—3¼"

No. 41
5 in. Hld. Nappy—Regular
Height—1¼"
Also made 6 in. size

No. 41
5 in. Hld. Bon Bon—Heart
Height—1½"
Also made 6 in. size

No. 41
7 in. Low Candy Comport Flared
Height—3¼"

No. 41
6 in. Hld. Mint Tray
Also made 7 in. size

No. 41
5 in. Candy Box and Cover
Height—5"

No. 41
Candy Jar and Cover
Height—8½"

No. 41
5 in. Ftd. Bon Bon and Cover
Height—7½"

Small Pepper
(Metal Top)
Height: 2½"

Small Salt (Metal Top)
Height: 2½"

Large (Metal Top)
Salt: 3¾" H.
Large (Metal Top)
Pepper: 3¾" H.

Large Salt & Pepper
3 Pc. Set
(3¾" Salt & Pepper;
6" Tray)

Oil & Vinegar
3 Pc. Set
Vinegar & Oil: 5¾"
Tray: 8"

Condiment 5 Pc. Set
Vinegar & Oil: 5¾"
Large Salt &
Pepper: 3¾"
Tray: 8"

Epergne Garden
Height: 9"

3 oz. Oil
Height: 5¾"

Sugar or Grated
Cheese Shaker
13 oz.

Syrup Pitcher
13 oz.

THE
DUNCAN & MILLER GLASS CO.
WASHINGTON, PENNA.

No. 103—Georgian Pattern

Among the several lines of quality tableware, the Georgian Pattern is of timely interest. Can be had in Crystal, Green, Amber and Rose.

GEORGIAN

was a tableware line introduced in 1928.

THE
DUNCAN & MILLER GLASS CO.
WASHINGTON, PENNA.

PURITAN PATTERN

Glassware of real beauty in design and workmanship always has been the ideal of our factory. And the Puritan takes rank with the best.

Insist on Duncan & Miller if you want quality pressed glassware in your department. It will help.

PURITAN

was a tableware line introduced in 1929.

*—1932
trade journal*

Early American Hob Nail Glassware

Here are pictured a few items of an antique design as revived by Duncan & Miller. The many pieces in this extensive line are available in crystal, green, amber and rose.

—1930 ad

DUNCAN RUBY GLASS LINE NOW
INCLUDES VASES AND IVY BALLS

THE variety of wares being made in ruby glass has been extended constantly since last Spring by the Duncan & Miller Glass Co., of Washington, Pa. The demand for the ruby has been most gratifying and the company has been adding new items to the ruby line. Among the interesting new ruby wares are the attractive flower holders illustrated. To the left is the No. 1 violet vase. It is in hobnail finish and the top is crimped. While known as a violet vase, it also is useful for other short-stemmed flowers and for ivy. To the right is the footed ivy ball, also

in hobnail finish. It also may be used for flowers of many kinds.

The vase and footed ivy ball are made in two sizes, denoted as large and small. The vase illustrated shows the small size, while the footed ivy ball is the larger size. "Duncan" glass is well known for its purity of metal, excellent workmanship and attractive finish. The flower holders are made in amber, crystal, green, blue and rose glass in addition to ruby. The colors, of course, are in the glass. They are not applied.

EARLY AMERICAN HOB NAIL

CATALOG REPRINT

The initial tableware issue was brought out in 1930 (see trade journal feature preceding page); new pieces were added for several years. The catalog reprint here is the 1940 crystal issue, but many pieces had been made earlier in amber, green, Rose, and some in Ruby red and Sapphire blue.

HOBNAIL NO. 118 PATTERN

No. 118
Teacup and Saucer
6 oz. Teacup
5½" Saucer

118—3 Pc. Ind. Sugar and Cream Set
Consisting of
118—5 oz. Sugar   Height 2¾"
118—3 oz. Cream   Height—3"
118—8" Oval Tray

No. 118
Small Pepper—Glass Top
Small Salt—Glass Top
Height—3"

No. 118
4 in. Puff Box and Cover
8 oz. Cologne and Stopper
Puff Box Height—4"
Cologne and Stopper Height—6½"

No. 118
6 oz. Oil and Stopper
Height—7"

No. 118
12 oz. Decanter and Stopper
2 oz. Whiskey
Decanter Height—8¾"

No. 118
Low Mint Box and Cover
Height—2½" Diameter—4¾"

No. 118
½ Gal. Flip Jug
Height—8"

No. 118
3½ in. Cigarette Jar and Cover
Diameter—3"
3 in. Ash Tray
Diameter—3"

HOBNAIL NO. 118 PATTERN

No. 118
10 in. 2 Handled 3 Compt. Relish
Height—2½"

No. 118
12 in. 2 Hld. Oval Celery and Relish
Height—1½" Width—6¾"

118—3 Pc. Mayonnaise Set
Consisting of
118—5 in. 2 Hld. Flared Mayonnaise
Height—2½"
118—6 in. Mayonnaise Plate w/ring
Mayonnaise Ladle

No. 118
12 in. Shallow Salad Bowl
Height—2¾"

No. 118
9 in. Deep Salad Bowl
Height—4½"
Also made in 13 in. Size

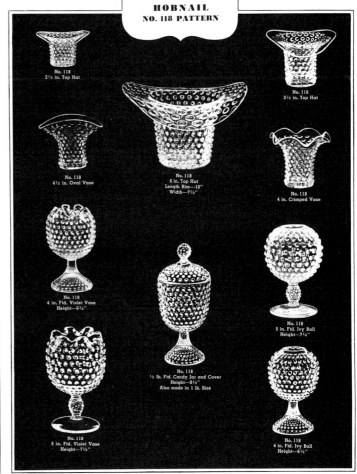

HOBNAIL NO. 118 PATTERN

No. 118
2½ in. Top Hat

No. 118
3½ in. Top Hat

No. 118
4½ in. Oval Vase

No. 118
6 in. Top Hat
Length Rim—10"
Width—7½"

No. 118
4 in. Crimped Vase

No. 118
4 in. Ftd. Violet Vase
Height—6¾"

No. 118
½ lb. Ftd. Candy Jar and Cover
Height—9½"
Also made in 1 lb. Size

No. 118
5 in. Ftd. Ivy Ball
Height—7¼"

No. 118
5 in. Ftd. Violet Vase
Height—7½"

No. 118
4 in. Ftd. Ivy Ball
Height—6½"

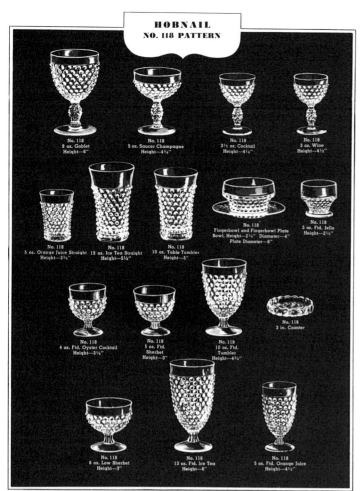

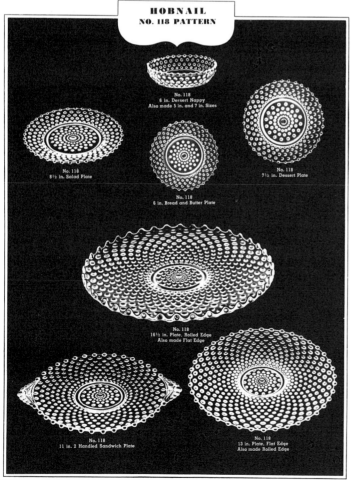

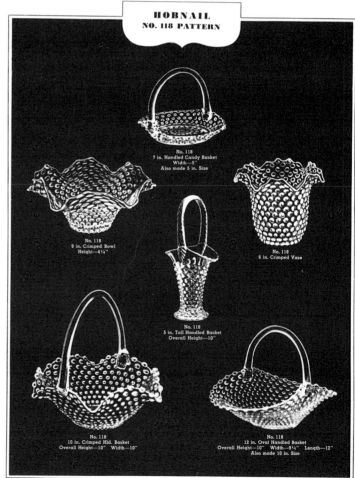

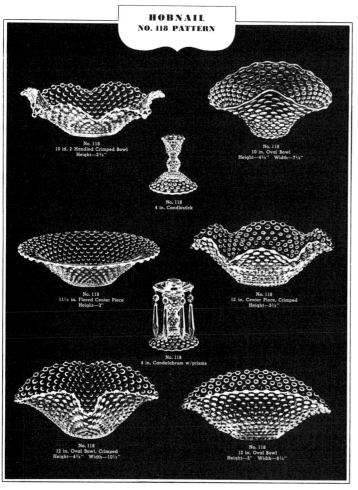

HOBNAIL NO. 118 PATTERN

No. 118
10 in. 2 Handled Crimped Bowl
Height—2¾"

No. 118
10 in. Oval Bowl
Height—4¾" Width—7¼"

No. 118
4 in. Candlestick

No. 118
11½ in. Flared Center Piece
Height—3"

No. 118
12 in. Center Piece, Crimped
Height—3½"

No. 118
4 in. Candelabrum w/prisms

No. 118
12 in. Oval Bowl, Crimped
Height—4¼" Width—10½"

No. 118
12 in. Oval Bowl
Height—5" Width—8½"

HOBNAIL NO. 118 PATTERN

No. 118
10 in. Footed Salver
Height—7½"

118½—15 Pc. Punch Set
Consisting of
118—One 10½" Punch Bowl
Height—5½" Capacity—1 Gal.
118—One 16½" Punch Tray, R.E.
118½—Twelve 5 oz. Hld. Punch Cups
118—One Punch Ladle

118—11 in. 2 Handled Cheese & Cracker Set
Consisting of
118—11" 2 Hld. Plate w/ring
118—Cheese Stand
Height—3½" Diameter—3¼"

HOBNAIL NO. 118 PATTERN

No. 118
6½ in. Low Comport, Crimped
Height—5"

No. 118
6 in. Crimped Comport
Height—5"

No. 118
6 in. Flared Comport
Height—4½"

No. 118
8 in. Low Comport, Crimped
Height—6"

No. 118
8 in. Flip Vase

No. 118
12 in. Flip Vase

No. 118
8 in. Flip Vase, Crimped

Duncan's
Flair
THE NO. 150 PATTERN

a late 40s line of occasional pieces.

SOMETHING NEW!

No. 21 Line—"Design Patent Pending."
Distinctive and attractive in crystal, green, amber or rose.
Available in an extensive line, including all stemware
pieces, footed tumblers, tumblers, jugs and plates.

THE
DUNCAN & MILLER GLASS CO.
WASHINGTON, PA.

"PUNTIES" *from 1931 advertisement*

Duncan's KIMBERLY

KIMBERLY

*This line, made in green, amber, rose, and
crystal in 1931, is a reproduction of an old
Waterford cutting combined with a band of
diamond shapes. When U. S. Glass used the
mold in crystal in the early 60s, it was called
DUNCAN'S KIMBERLY.*

—1931 ad

No. 12 Vase; No. 12 Crimped Bonbon; No. 106 Covered
Candy Box; No. 18 Cigarette Box; No. 18 Ash Tray;
No. 16 Ash Tray

Ebony Glassware

The Ebony Glassware made by Duncan & Miller is
absolutely jet black and has a superb brilliancy that
distinguishes it.

The pieces illustrated are but a few of the many
popular shapes in articles which combine utilitarian
and decorative properties that the line embraces.

The entire line may also be had in crystal, green and
rose glass.

Write for illustrations and prices.

The
Duncan & Miller Glass Co.
Washington, Pa.

REPRESENTATIVES:

Paul Joseph, 200 Fifth Avenue, New York.
Murt Wallace, 157 Summer St., Boston, Mass.
F. T. Renshaw, 58 E. Washington St., Chicago, Ill.
Wm. C. Byrnes, Burd Bldg., 9th and Chestnut Sts., Philadelphia
E. B. Hill, A. A. Graesser, Factory Representatives,
Washington, Pa.

VENETIAN

*as introduced in 1932 advertisement
and later illustrated
in #77 Duncan & Miller catalog, 1943.*

UNUSUAL AND SMART

Distinctive table pieces are offered in the new No. 5 Vase, the No. 126 Vase and the No. 28 Urn and cover, illustrated. In pairs, these pieces make a very attractive table decoration. Made in crystal, ruby and blue in quality glass.

THE

DUNCAN & MILLER GLASS CO.

WASHINGTON, PA.

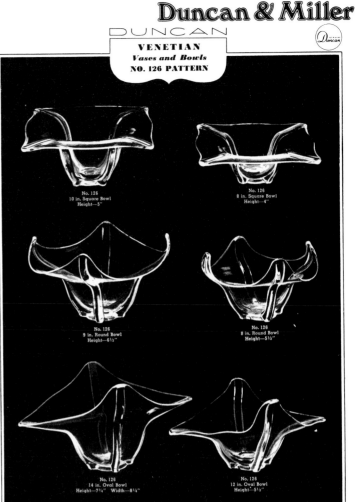

No. 126
10 in. Square Bowl
Height—5"

No. 126
8 in. Square Bowl
Height—4"

No. 126
9 in. Round Bowl
Height—6½"

No. 126
8 in. Round Bowl
Height—5½"

No. 126
14 in. Oval Bowl
Height—7¼" Width—8¼"

No. 126
12 in. Oval Bowl
Height—5½"

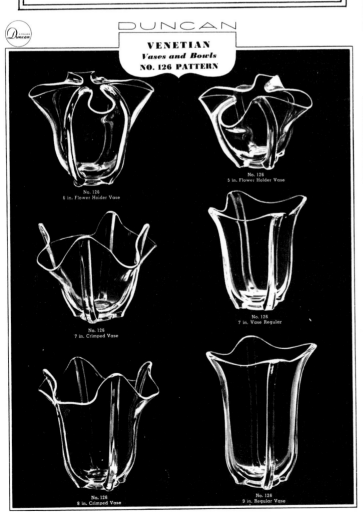

No. 126
6 in. Flower Holder Vase

No. 126
5 in. Flower Holder Vase

No. 126
7 in. Crimped Vase

No. 126
7 in. Vase Regular

No. 126
8 in. Crimped Vase

No. 126
9 in. Regular Vase

WHITNEY *from 1933 trade journal account.*

The Whitney 75 pattern. which is named after Harry B. Whitney, a veteran glass salesman, is made in a complete

Two unusual pieces in the new Whitney 75 Pattern. The flower vase is striking with its fine lines. The tall compote is made plain or with solid partitions as illustrated.

selection of table pieces. These include regular tumblers, footed tumblers, stemware, nappies, plates, sugars and creams, jugs, salts and peppers, compotes, cocktail glasses and mixers, finger bowls, candlesticks and bowls.

"GORDON" decanter service, 1933 trade journal.

CLUB and MASTERS
ashtrays from 1933 ad.

NEW ASH TRAYS SHOWN

Development of a fine line of ash trays is announced by the Duncan & Miller Glass Co., of Washington, Pa. Coming at a time when all the retail market is on the lookout for attractive gift items, the introduction of these pieces is of real news. Four numbers from this line are illustrated

and they present an aristocratic selection. In the second row is the large, No. 12, 5-inch "Club" ash tray; a tray with a capacity built for service. Next to it is the smaller No. 11, "Masters" ash tray. The foreground shows the square No. 17 tray with fluted base and the unusual triangular tray, No. 16. These are illustrated in crystal but may be had in green, amber, blue or black also.

"BEAUTY TWO TONE" line, 1933 advertisement.

ARLISS mug from 1933 advertisement.

73

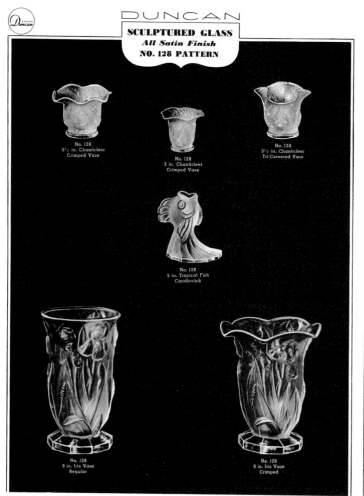

DUNCAN
SCULPTURED GLASS
All Satin Finish
NO. 128 PATTERN

No. 128
3½ in. Chanticleer
Crimped Vase

No. 128
3 in. Chanticleer
Crimped Vase

No. 128
3½ in. Chanticleer
Tri-Cornered Vase

No. 128
5 in. Tropical Fish
Candlestick

No. 128
9 in. Iris Vase
Regular

No. 128
9 in. Iris Vase
Crimped

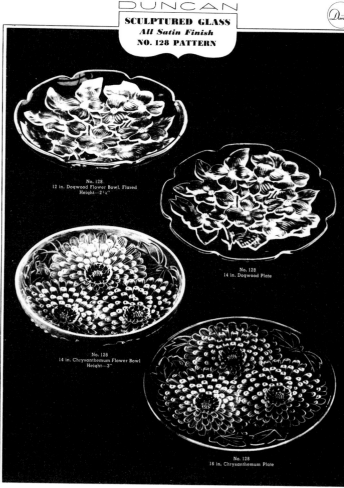

DUNCAN
SCULPTURED GLASS
All Satin Finish
NO. 128 PATTERN

No. 128
12 in. Dogwood Flower Bowl, Flared
Height—2¼"

No. 128
14 in. Dogwood Plate

No. 128
14 in. Chrysanthemum Flower Bowl
Height—3"

No. 128
16 in. Chrysanthemum Plate

SCULPTURED GLASS *line was introduced in 1934; this from 1943 catalog.*

113½—15 Pc. Punch Set
Consisting of
1—No. 113 —1½ Gal. Punch Bowl Height—6¼"
12—No. 113½—5 oz. Punch Cups (Pressed Handle)
1—No. 113 —18 in. Punch Bowl Tray R.E.
1—No. 113 —Ladle

"FESTIVAL" *Punch Bowl,
part of 1937 line in amber, Royal blue,
Sapphire blue, green, and crystal.
Additional pieces.*

MARDI GRAS *Punch Bowl
in crystal with Royal blue
or Ruby red trim; 1943 catalog.
Additional pieces to this line.*

No. 42
2 Gal. Punch Bowl and Foot
Height Overall—12"
Height Bowl Only—7½"
Width Bowl—13½"

TEAR DROP

*The next pages
carry reprints of
the large TEAR DROP
line, introduced in 1934.
For clear illustration
the 1943 catalog
showing is used.*

TEAR DROP
No. 301 PATTERN

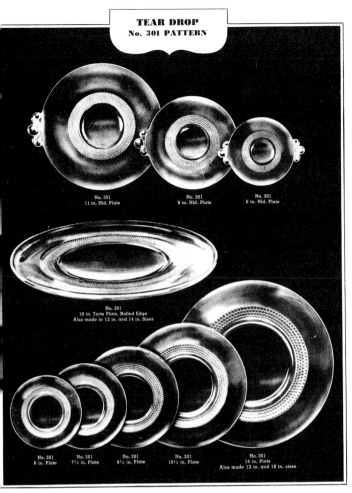

No. 301
11 in. Hld. Plate

No. 301
8 in. Hld. Plate

No. 301
6 in. Hld. Plate

No. 301
18 in. Torte Plate, Rolled Edge
Also made in 13 in. and 14 in. Sizes

No. 301
6 in. Plate

No. 301
7½ in. Plate

No. 301
8½ in. Plate

No. 301
10½ in. Plate

No. 301
14 in. Plate
Also made 13 in. and 18 in. sizes

TEAR DROP
No. 301 PATTERN

No. 301
2½ oz. Demi Tasse Cup & Saucer
Diameter Saucer—4½"
Height Cup—2¾"

No. 301
6 oz. Tea Cup & Saucer
Saucer Diameter—6"
Cup Height—2¾"

No. 301
3 in. Salt & Pepper
Glass Top

No. 301
6 oz. Cream
Height—4"

No. 301
8 oz. Sugar
Height—3¼"

No. 301
Mustard and Cover
Height—4¼"

No. 301
3 oz. Oil and Stopper
Height—4¾"

301—5 Pc. Oil & Vinegar Condiment Set
Consisting of
301—3 oz. Oil & 3 oz. Vinegar
301—3 in. Salt & 3 in. Pepper
8 in. Oval Tray

301—3 Pc. Marmalade Set
Consisting of
301—Marmalade and Cover Height—4"
301—6 in. Hld. Marmalade Plate

No. 301
5 in. Salt & Pepper
Glass Top

No. 301
Pint Pitcher (Stuck Hdl.)
Height—5"

TEAR DROPS
No. 5301 STEMWARE
No. 5300 TUMBLERS
(Lead Blown)

No. 5301—4½ oz. Ftd.
Orange Juice
Height—4"

No. 5301—3 oz. Ftd.
Whiskey or Cocktail
Height—3"

No. 5301—2 oz.
Ftd. Whiskey
Height—2¾"

No. 5301
½ Gal. Pitcher with Ice Guard Lip
Height—8½"

No. 5301—14 oz. Ftd.
Ice Tea or Hiball
Height—6"
Also made 12 oz.
Height—5½"

No. 5301
8 oz. Ftd. Split
or Party Glass
Height—5"

No. 5301—9 oz.
Ftd. Tumbler
Height—4½"

No. 5300—2 oz.
Whiskey
Height—2¼"

No. 5300—3½ oz.
Orange Juice
Height—3¼"

No. 5300—5 oz.
Orange Juice
Height—3½"

No. 5300
9 oz. Tumbler
Height—4¼"

No. 5300
10 oz. Hiball
Height—4¼"

No. 5300
14 oz. Hiball
Height—5¾"

No. 5300
12 oz. Ice Tea
Height—5¼"

No. 5300
8 oz. Split
Height—4½"

No. 5300
7 oz. Old Fashioned
Height—3¼"

TEAR DROP
Lead Blown Stemware
NO. 5301 PATTERN

No. 5301
9 oz. Goblet
Height—7"

No. 5301
5 oz. Saucer
Champagne
Height—5"

No. 5301
3½ oz.
Liquor Cocktail
Height—4½"

No. 5301
4 oz. Claret
Height—5½"

No. 5301
3 oz. Wine
Height—4¼"

No. 5301
1¾ oz. Sherry
Height—4½"

No. 5301
1 oz. Cordial
Height—4"

No. 5301
Finger Bowl
Height—2¼"
Diameter—4¼"

No. 5301
9 oz.
Luncheon Goblet
Height—5¾"

No. 5301
5 oz.
Ice Cream
Height—3½"

No. 5301
5 oz. Ftd.
Sherbet
Height—3½"

No. 5301
3½ oz. Ftd.
Oyster Cocktail
Height—2¾"

No. 5301
8 oz.
Ale Goblet
Height—6¼"

No. 301
10 in. Fruit Bowl, Flared
Height—3½"

No. 301
10 in. 2 Hld. Star Center Piece
Height—3"

No. 301
12 in. Oval Hld. Basket
Overall Height—10" Width—8½" Length—12"
Also made 11½ in. Crimped

No. 301
9 in. Vase Fan Shape
Length—6" Width—3¾"

No. 301
9 in. Vase Regular
5" Diameter

No. 301
12 in. Crimped Low Foot Bowl
Height—5"

No. 301
11½ in. Flared Flower Bowl
Height—3"

No. 301
13 in. Gardenia Bowl
Height—2"

No. 301
3 in. Individual Ash Tray

No. 301
3 in. Coaster or Ash Tray

No. 301
5 in. Ash Tray

No. 301
Bar Bottle & Stopper
Height—12"

No. 301
6 in. Canape Plate with Ring

No. 520½
4 oz. Ftd. Cocktail
Height, Cocktail—3½"

No. 301
6 in. Ice Bucket
Height—6½" Diameter—5½"

No. 301
6 in. Low Foot Comport
Height—4"

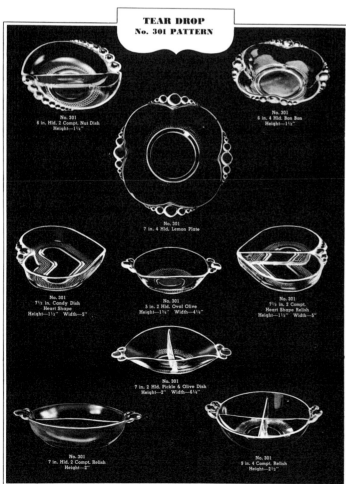

No. 301
6 in. Hld. 2 Compt. Nut Dish
Height—1¼"

No. 301
6 in. 4 Hld. Bon Bon
Height—1½"

No. 301
7 in. 4 Hld. Lemon Plate

No. 301
7½ in. Candy Dish
Heart Shape
Height—1½" Width—5"

No. 301
5 in. 2 Hld. Oval Olive
Height—1¾" Width—4½"

No. 301
7½ in. 2 Compt.
Heart Shape Relish
Height—1½" Width—5"

No. 301
7 in. 2 Hld. Pickle & Olive Dish
Height—2" Width—6¼"

No. 301
7 in. Hld. 2 Compt. Relish
Height—2"

No. 301
9 in. 4 Compt. Relish
Height—2½"

No. 301
6 in. Hld. 2 Compt. Olive
Height—1¼" Width—3"

No. 301
6 in. Hld. Pickle
Height—1¼" Width—3"

No. 301
11 in. Handled Celery
Height—1½" Width—3½"

No. 301
11 in. 2 Compt. Celery & Radish
Height—1½" Width—3½"

No. 301
11 in. Hld. 3 Compt. Relish
Height—1½" Width—3½"

No. 301
12 in. 3 Compt. Oblong Celery & Relish
Height—1½" Width—6"

No. 301½
12 in. 5 Compt. Relish
Height—1¼"
Also made 10 in.

No. 301
12 in. 6 Compt. Relish
Height—1¼"
Also made 10 in.

TEAR DROP
No. 301 PATTERN

No. 301
7 in. 2 Hld. Star Shape Sweetmeat
Height—2¼"

No. 301
6½ in. Hld. Sweetmeat

No. 301
7½ in. 2 Hld. Oval Candy Basket
Height—2¾" Width—5½"

No. 301
5½ in. 2 Hld. Star Shape Sweetmeat
Height—1¾"

No. 301
5½ in. 2 Hld. Oval Candy Basket
Height—2" Width—4¼"

No. 301
5 in. Hld. Nappy
Height—1½"

No. 301
7 in. 2 Compt. Candy Box & Cover
Height—4¼"

No. 301
5 in. Nappy

No. 301
7 in. Hld. Nappy
Height—2"

No. 301
6 in. Nappy

No. 301
9½ in. Hld. Nappy
Height—2½"

No. 301
7 in. Nappy

TEAR DROP
No. 301 PATTERN

No. 301
Cheese Stand
Height—3½"
Diameter—5¼"

301—11 in. 2 Pc. Cheese & Cracker Set
Consisting of
301—11 in. 2 Hld. Plate
301—Cheese Stand

No. 301
5 in. Ftd. Comport
Height—4¼"
Diameter—4¾"

No. 301
11 in. Hld. Plate w/Ring

No. 301
11 in. Salad Set

No. 301
2 Compt. Mayonnaise
Height—4" Diam.—6"

301—3 Pc. 4½ in. 2 Hld. Flared Mayonnaise Set
Consisting of
301—4½ in. Hld. Flared Mayonnaise
Height—3"
301—6 in. Plate w/ring—Ladle

No. 301
12 in. Shallow Salad Bowl
Height—2"

301—3 Pc. Mayonnaise Set
Consisting of
301—8 in. Hld. Plate—Ladle
301—4½ in. Hld. Flared Mayonnaise
Height—3"

301—2 Pc. Salad Set
Consisting of
301—9 in. Salad Bowl Height—4¼"
301—13 in. Plate, Rolled Edge
Also made Flat Edge

TEAR DROP
No. 301 PATTERN

No. 301
4 in. Candlestick

No. 301
12 in. Round Flower Bowl
Height—3¼"

No. 301
4 in. Candlestick

No. 301
4 in. Candlestick

No. 301
12 in. Oval Flower Bowl
Height—3½" Width—8"

No. 301
4 in. Candlestick

301—3 Pc. 2 Light Console Set
Consisting of
301—12 in. Oval Bowl
301—2 Light Candlestick

TEAR DROP
No. 301 PATTERN

No. 301
13 in. Ftd. Cake Salver
Height—3½"

No. 301
Mayonnaise
Height—4½"
Diameter—4¼"

301—3 Pc. Midnight or Buffet Supper Set
Consisting of
301—18 in. Plate
301—12 in. 6 Compt. Relish
301—Salad Dressing Bowl

301—15 Pc. Punch Set
Consisting of
301—21 qt. Punch Bowl Ht. 7½" Diam. 15½"
301—18 in. Punch Bowl Tray, R.E.
301—Punch Ladle
301—6 oz. Handled Punch Cups

TERRACE

was advertised in 1935 (pieces at right) in crystal, blue, ruby, and amber. Many more pieces are in this line, which was popularly made for several years.

awarded "high honors" at the Show

This latest Duncan creation stopped buyers and secured orders in a sensational fashion. Strikingly modern, the three graduated fluted "terraces" it features (patent pending) are best illustrated above on the Goblet. Also note how cleverly they circle the well of the nine inch Square Plate and the Saucer. Available in an unusually complete line of flatware and stemware—you'll find it profitable to stock all items of "Terrace." Write for prices.

THE DUNCAN & MILLER GLASS CO.
WASHINGTON, PA.

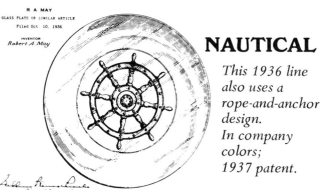

NAUTICAL

This 1936 line also uses a rope-and-anchor design. In company colors; 1937 patent.

CARIBBEAN (WAVE)

was a complete line brought out in 1936 in crystal and Sapphire blue. The crystal also came trimmed with ruby glass.

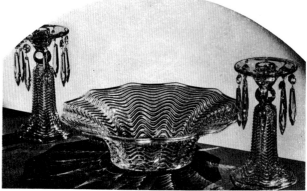

CATALOG REPRINT

The pages to come carry selected reprints from a 1943 catalog. All were being made in crystal, but most carry earlier mold numbers and had been made in the company colors.

Pieces in PALL MALL, CANTERBURY, MURANA, THREE FEATHERS, SWIRL, SYLVAN, GRECIAN, and SANIBEL were made in Cranberry pink, Cape Cod blue, and Jasmine yellow (later these colors were called simply opalescent pink and blue) as early as 1940. Ruby red and Chartreuse were made through the 40s. Duncan's swans were made in ruby, Biscayne green, Avocado, Teakwood, crystal and the opalescent colors, then U. S. Glass made them in opaque and other colors.

For your interest, some of the popular crystal etched lines being made in 1943 are included here, though not all pieces are shown.

MISCELLANEOUS TABLEWARE

No. 25
5 in. Candy Jar and Cover
Height—7¼"

No. 25
5 in. Nappy
Also made 3½, 4, 4½, 5 and 6 in. Sizes

No. 25
Footed Grape Fruit
Height—4¾"
Diameter—5¼"
5 oz. Footed
Grape Fruit Liner
Diameter—3½"

No. 26
3½ in. Coaster

25—11 in. Cheese & Cracker Set
Consisting of
25—11 in. Cheese Plate with ring
940—Cheese Stand Height—3"

No. 26
3 in. Nappy

No. 28
4 in. Candlestick

No. 28
3 Pc. Hospital or Breakfast Tray Set
(See Nested below)

No. 29
5½ in. Nappy

No. 28
6 in. Muffin Cover

28—3 Pc. Hospital Tray Set
Consisting of
28—5 oz. Hospital Sugar
28—4 oz. Hospital Cream
28—3 in. Hospital Butter
Height nested—3½"

No. 29
6 in. Grape Fruit
Also made 6½ in. Size

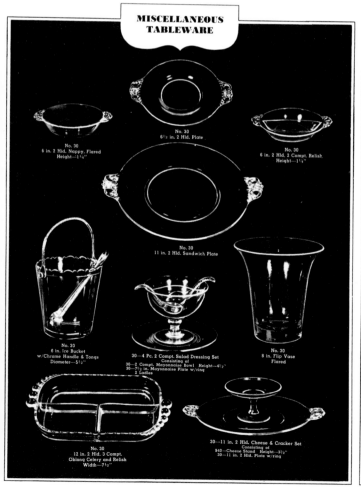

MISCELLANEOUS TABLEWARE

No. 30
6 in. 2 Hld. Nappy, Flared
Height—1¼"

No. 30
6½ in. 2 Hld. Plate

No. 30
6 in. 2 Hld. 2 Compt. Relish
Height—1¼"

No. 30
11 in. 2 Hld. Sandwich Plate

No. 30
6 in. Ice Bucket
w/Chrome Handle & Tongs
Diameter—5½"

30—4 Pc. 2 Compt. Salad Dressing Set
Consisting of
30—2 Compt. Mayonnaise Bowl Height—4½"
30—7½ in. Mayonnaise Plate w/ring
2 Ladles

No. 30
8 in. Flip Vase
Flared

No. 30
12 in. 2 Hld. 3 Compt.
Oblong Celery and Relish
Width—7½"

30—11 in. 2 Hld. Cheese & Cracker Set
Consisting of
940—Cheese Stand Height—3½"
30—11 in. 2 Hld. Plate w/ring

MISCELLANEOUS TABLEWARE

129—3 Pc. Perfume Set
Consisting of
1—No. 129—4 in. Puff Box & Cover   Height—5¾"
2—No. 129—Perfume Bottle & Stopper   Height—7"

No. 106
6 in. 3 Compt. Candy Box & Cover
Height—4"

No. 91
4½ in. Nappy
Height—1"

No. 91
5½ in. Nappy
Height—1¼"

101—Ice Cocktail & Liner
Consisting of
101—11 oz. Ice Cocktail Goblet
Height—5"
101—3 oz. Ice Cocktail Liner

No. 218
4 oz. Oyster Cocktail Center
Height—2¼"
Also made 2½ oz. Size No. 219

No. 91
8½ in. Pickle Tray
Height—2"   Width—3"

No. 220
3 oz. Oyster
Cocktail Center
Height—2½"

No. 91
11 in. Celery Tray
Height—1½"   Width—4½"

PALL MALL
No. 30 PATTERN

No. 30
32 oz. Decanter and Stopper
Height—10¾"

No. 30
12 in. Devilled Egg Plate

No. 30
30 oz. Hld.
Cocktail Mixer w/Spoon
Height—8¼"

No. 30½
14 in. Torte Plate, Flat Edge
Also made Rolled Edge

No. 30—12 in. Rd., 3 Compt.
Celery and Relish
Height—1"

No. 30—12 in. Pimlico
Celery and Relish, Flat Rim
Height—1" Width—5"

DUNCAN'S RUBY

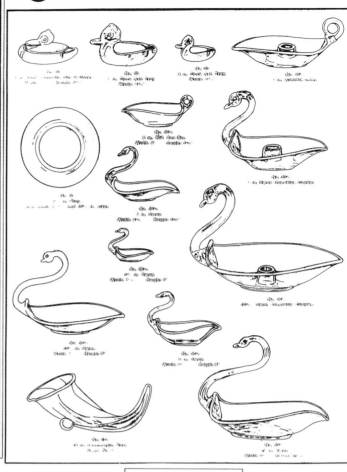

PALL MALL
No. 30 PATTERN

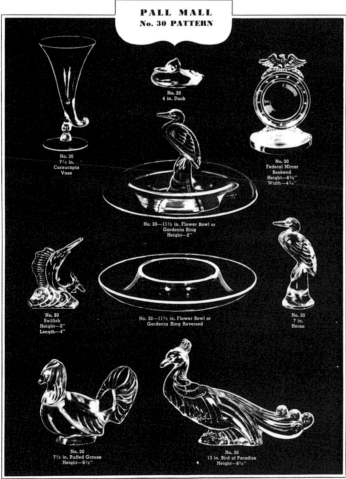

No. 30
7½ in.
Cornucopia
Vase

No. 30
4 in. Duck

No. 30
Federal Mirror
Bookend
Height—5¾"
Width—4¾"

No. 30—11½ in. Flower Bowl or
Gardenia Ring
Height—2"

No. 30
Sailfish
Height—5"
Length—4"

No. 30—11½ in. Flower Bowl or
Gardenia Ring Reversed

No. 30
7 in.
Heron

No. 30
7½ in. Ruffed Grouse
Height—6½"

No. 30
13 in. Bird of Paradise
Height—8½"

PALL MALL
No. 30 PATTERN

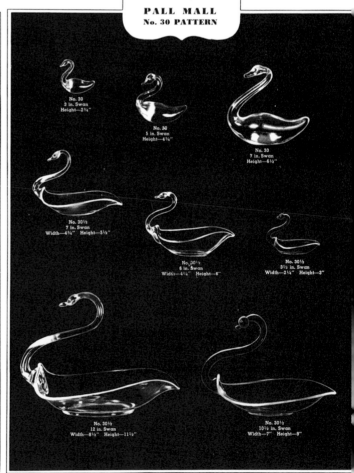

No. 30
3 in. Swan
Height—2¾"

No. 30
5 in. Swan
Height—4¾"

No. 30
7 in. Swan
Height—6½"

No. 30½
7 in. Swan
Width—4¾" Height—5½"

No. 30½
5 in. Swan
Width—4¼" Height—6"

No. 30½
3½ in. Swan
Width—2¼" Height—3"

No. 30½
12 in. Swan
Width—8½" Height—11½"

No. 30½
10½ in. Swan
Width—7" Height—9"

WATERFORD
NO. 102 PATTERN

No. 102
9 oz. Goblet
Height—6"

No. 102
6 oz. Saucer
Champagne
Height—4½"

No. 102
3 oz. Wine
Height—4¼"
Also made 5 oz.
Cocktail, Flared Edge

No. 102
6 oz. Ice Cream
Height—3¾"

No. 102
5 oz. Parfait
Height—5¼"

No. 102
14 oz. Ice Tea
Height—5½"

No. 102
12 oz. Ice Tea
Height—5¼"

No. 102
9 oz. Table Tumbler
Height—4¼"

No. 102
5 oz. Orange Juice
Height—4"

No. 102
7½ oz. Hi Ball
Height—5"

No. 102
8½ in. Plate
Also made 6 in. and 7½ in. Sizes

No. 102
2 oz. Tumbler
Height—2¾"

No. 102
Finger Bowl
Height—2½"
Diameter—4"

No. 102
½ gal. Jug
Height—8¼"

AMERICAN WAY
CRYSTAL
SATINTONE FINISH

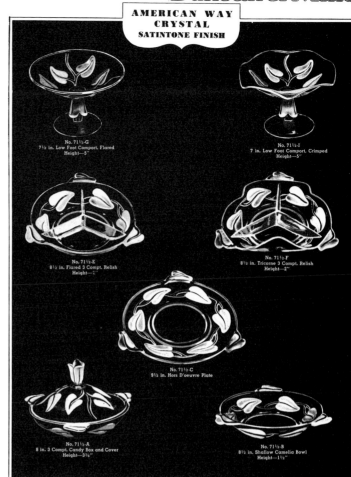

No. 71½-G
7½ in. Low Foot Comport, Flared
Height—5"

No. 71½-I
7 in. Low Foot Comport, Crimped
Height—5"

No. 71½-E
8½ in. Flared 3 Compt. Relish
Height—2"

No. 71½-F
8½ in. Tricorne 3 Compt. Relish
Height—2"

No. 71½-C
9½ in. Hors D'oeuvre Plate

No. 71½-A
8 in. 3 Compt. Candy Box and Cover
Height—3¾"

No. 71½-B
8½ in. Shallow Camelia Bowl
Height—1½"

AMERICAN WAY
CRYSTAL
SATINTONE FINISH

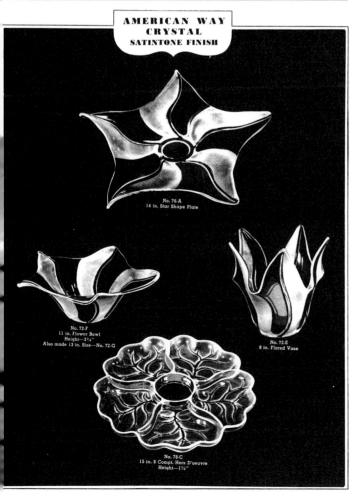

No. 76-A
14 in. Star Shape Plate

No. 72-F
11 in. Flower Bowl
Height—3¾"
Also made 13 in. Size—No. 72-G

No. 72-E
8 in. Flared Vase

No. 78-C
15 in. 6 Compt. Hors D'oeuvre
Height—1½"

AMERICAN WAY
CRYSTAL
SATINTONE FINISH

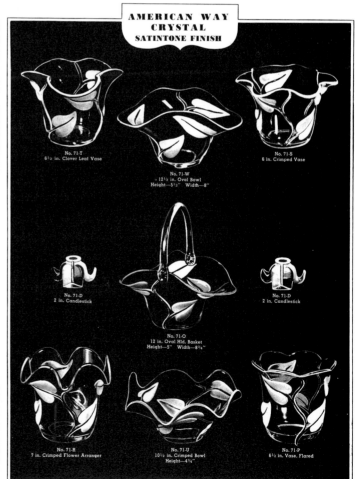

No. 71-T
6½ in. Clover Leaf Vase

No. 71-W
12½ in. Oval Bowl
Height—5½" Width—8"

No. 71-S
6 in. Crimped Vase

No. 71-D
2 in. Candlestick

No. 71-D
2 in. Candlestick

No. 71-O
12 in. Oval Hld. Basket
Height—5" Width—8¾"

No. 71-R
7 in. Crimped Flower Arranger

No. 71-U
10½ in. Crimped Bowl
Height—4¾"

No. 71-P
6½ in. Vase, Flared

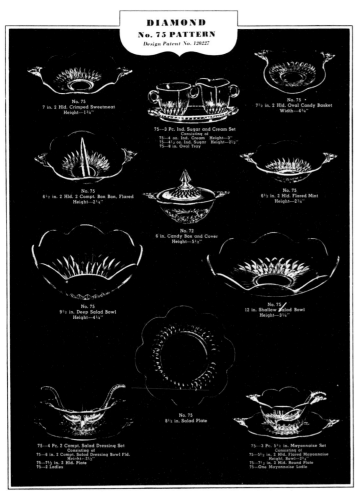

No. 75
7 in. 2 Hld. Crimped Sweetmeat
Height—1¾"

75—3 Pc. Ind. Sugar and Cream Set
Consisting of
75—4 oz. Ind. Cream Height—3"
75—4½ oz. Ind. Sugar Height—2½"
75—8 in. Oval Tray

No. 75
7½ in. 2 Hld. Oval Candy Basket
Width—4¾"

No. 75
6½ in. 2 Hld. 2 Compt. Bon Bon, Flared
Height—2¼"

No. 72
6 in. Candy Box and Cover
Height—5½"

No. 75
6½ in. 2 Hld. Flared Mint
Height—2¼"

No. 75
9½ in. Deep Salad Bowl
Height—4¼"

No. 75
12 in. Shallow Salad Bowl
Height—3¼"

No. 75
8½ in. Salad Plate

75—4 Pc. 2 Compt. Salad Dressing Set
Consisting of
75—6 in. 2 Compt. Salad Dressing Bowl Fld.
Height—2½"
75—7½ in. 2 Hld. Plate
75—2 Ladles

75—3 Pc. 5½ in. Mayonnaise Set
Consisting of
75—5½ in. 2 Hld. Flared Mayonnaise
Height, Bowl—2¼"
75—7½ in. 2 Hld. Round Plate
75—One Mayonnaise Ladle

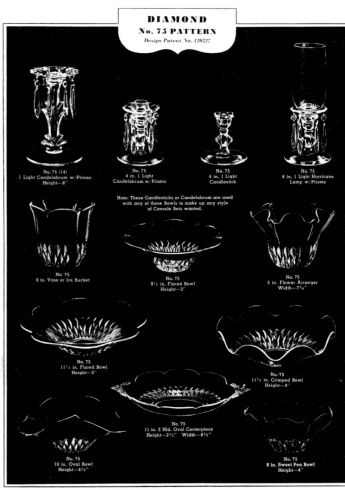

No. 75 (14)
1 Light Candelabrum w/Prisms
Height—8"

No. 75
4 in. 1 Light Candelabrum w/Prisms

No. 75
4 in. 1 Light Candlestick

No. 75
4 in. 1 Light Hurricane Lamp w/Prisms

Note: These Candlesticks or Candelabrum are used
with any of these Bowls to make up any style
of Console Sets wanted.

No. 75
6 in. Vase or Ice Bucket

No. 75
9½ in. Flared Bowl
Height—3"

No. 75
5 in. Flower Arranger
Width—7¾"

No. 75
11½ in. Flared Bowl
Height—3"

No. 75
11½ in. Crimped Bowl
Height—4"

No. 75
11 in. 2 Hld. Oval Centerpiece
Height—2½" Width—8½"

No. 75
10 in. Oval Bowl
Height—4½"

No. 75
8 in. Sweet Pea Bowl
Height—4"

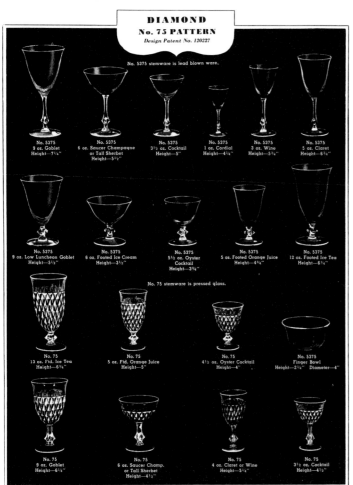

No. 5375 stemware is lead blown ware.

No. 5375
9 oz. Goblet
Height—7¼"

No. 5375
6 oz. Saucer Champagne
or Tall Sherbet
Height—5½"

No. 5375
3½ oz. Cocktail
Height—5"

No. 5375
1 oz. Cordial
Height—4¼"

No. 5375
3 oz. Wine
Height—5¾"

No. 5375
5 oz. Claret
Height—6¾"

No. 5375
9 oz. Low Luncheon Goblet
Height—5½"

No. 5375
6 oz. Footed Ice Cream
Height—3½"

No. 5375
5½ oz. Oyster Cocktail
Height—3¾"

No. 5375
5 oz. Footed Orange Juice
Height—4¾"

No. 5375
12 oz. Footed Ice Tea
Height—6¾"

No. 75 stemware is pressed glass.

No. 75
13 oz. Fld. Ice Tea
Height—6¾"

No. 75
5 oz. Fld. Orange Juice
Height—5"

No. 75
4½ oz. Oyster Cocktail
Height—4"

No. 5375
Finger Bowl
Height—2¼" Diameter—4"

No. 75
9 oz. Goblet
Height—6¼"

No. 75
6 oz. Saucer Champ.
or Tall Sherbet
Height—4½"

No. 75
4 oz. Claret or Wine
Height—5¼"

No. 75
3½ oz. Cocktail
Height—4½"

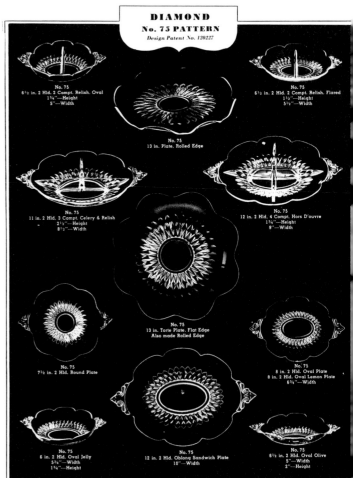

No. 75
6½ in. 2 Hld. 2 Compt. Relish, Oval
1¾"—Height
5"—Width

No. 75
6½ in. 2 Hld. 2 Compt. Relish. Flared
1½"—Height
5½"—Width

No. 75
13 in. Plate, Rolled Edge

No. 75
11 in. 2 Hld. 3 Compt. Celery & Relish
2½"—Height
8½"—Width

No. 75
12 in. 2 Hld. 4 Compt. Hors D'ouvre
1¾"—Height
9"—Width

No. 75
13 in. Torte Plate, Flat Edge
Also made Rolled Edge

No. 75
7½ in. 2 Hld. Round Plate

No. 75
8 in. 2 Hld. Oval Plate
8 in. 2 Hld. Oval Lemon Plate
6¾"—Width

No. 75
6 in. 2 Hld. Oval Jelly
5¾"—Width
1¾"—Height

No. 75
12 in. 2 Hld. Oblong Sandwich Plate
10"—Width

No. 75
6½ in. 2 Hld. Oval Olive
5"—Width
2"—Height

CANTERBURY
NO. 115 PATTERN

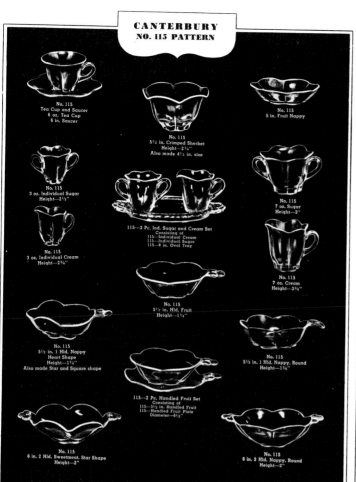

No. 115
Tea Cup and Saucer
6 oz. Tea Cup
6 in. Saucer

No. 115
3 oz. Individual Sugar
Height—2½"

No. 115
3 oz. Individual Cream
Height—2¾"

No. 115
5½ in. Crimped Sherbet
Height—2¾"
Also made 4½ in. size

115—3 Pc. Ind. Sugar and Cream Set
Consisting of
115—Individual Cream
115—Individual Sugar
115—8 in. Oval Tray

No. 115
5 in. Fruit Nappy

No. 115
7 oz. Sugar
Height—3"

No. 115
7 oz. Cream
Height—3¾"

No. 115
5½ in. Hld. Fruit
Height—1¾"

No. 115
5½ in. 1 Hld. Nappy
Heart Shape
Height—1¾"
Also made Star and Square shape

115—2 Pc. Handled Fruit Set
Consisting of
115—5½ in. Handled Fruit
115—Handled Fruit Plate
Diameter—6½"

No. 115
5½ in. 1 Hld. Nappy, Round
Height—1¾"

No. 115
6 in. 2 Hld. Sweetmeat, Star Shape
Height—2"

No. 115
6 in. 2 Hld. Nappy, Round
Height—2"

CANTERBURY
NO. 115 PATTERN

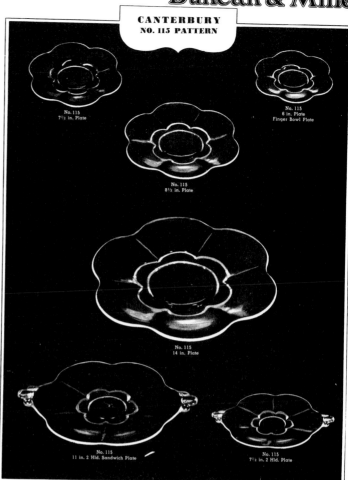

No. 115
7½ in. Plate

No. 115
6 in. Plate
Finger Bowl Plate

No. 115
8½ in. Plate

No. 115
14 in. Plate

No. 115
11 in. 2 Hld. Sandwich Plate

No. 115
7½ in. 2 Hld. Plate

CANTERBURY
NO. 115 PATTERN

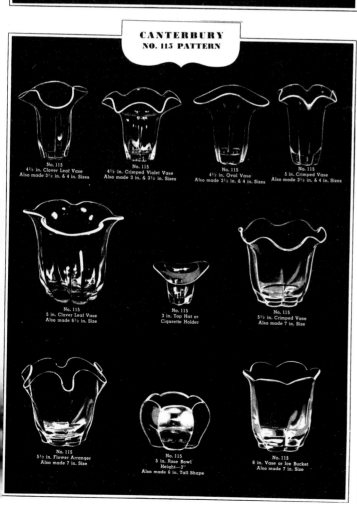

No. 115
4½ in. Clover Leaf Vase
Also made 3½ in. & 4 in. Sizes

No. 115
4½ in. Crimped Violet Vase
Also made 3 in. & 3½ in. Sizes

No. 115
4½ in. Oval Vase
Also made 3½ in. & 4 in. Sizes

No. 115
5 in. Crimped Vase
Also made 3½ in. & 4 in. Sizes

No. 115
5 in. Clover Leaf Vase
Also made 6½ in. Size

No. 115
3 in. Top Hat or
Cigarette Holder

No. 115
5½ in. Crimped Vase
Also made 7 in. Size

No. 115
5½ in. Flower Arranger
Also made 7 in. Size

No. 115
5 in. Rose Bowl
Height—3"
Also made 6 in. Tall Shape

No. 115
6 in. Vase or Ice Bucket
Also made 7 in. Size

CANTERBURY
NO. 115 PATTERN

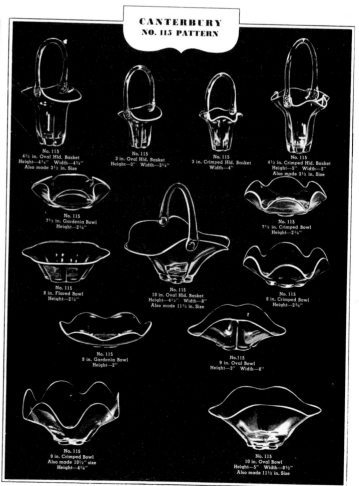

No. 115
4½ in. Oval Hld. Basket
Height—4¾"   Width—4¼"
Also made 3½ in. Size

No. 115
3 in. Oval Hld. Basket
Height—3"   Width—3¼"

No. 115
3 in. Crimped Hld. Basket
Width—4"

No. 115
4½ in. Crimped Hld. Basket
Height—5"   Width—5"
Also made 3½ in. Size

No. 115
7½ in. Gardenia Bowl
Height—2¼"

No. 115
7½ in. Crimped Bowl
Height—2¼"

No. 115
8 in. Flared Bowl
Height—2½"

No. 115
10 in. Oval Hld. Basket
Height—4½"   Width—8"
Also made 11½ in. Size

No. 115
8 in. Crimped Bowl
Height—2¾"

No. 115
9 in. Gardenia Bowl
Height—2"

No. 115
9 in. Oval Bowl
Height—3"   Width—6"

No. 115
9 in. Crimped Bowl
Also made 10½" size
Height—4¼"

No. 115
10 in. Oval Bowl
Height—5"   Width—8½"
Also made 11½ in. Size

CANTERBURY
NO. 115 PATTERN

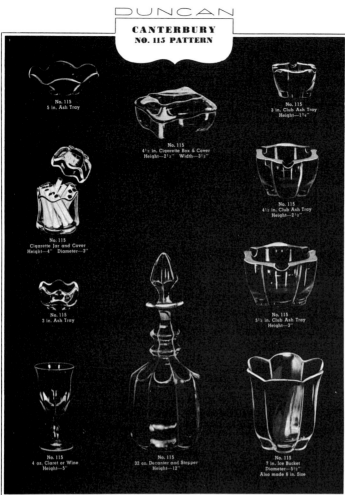

No. 115
5 in. Ash Tray

No. 115
3 in. Club Ash Tray
Height—1¾"

No. 115
4½ in. Cigarette Box & Cover
Height—2½" Width—3½"

No. 115
Cigarette Jar and Cover
Height—4" Diameter—3"

No. 115
4½ in. Club Ash Tray
Height—2½"

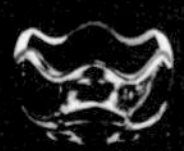
No. 115
3 in. Ash Tray

No. 115
5½ in. Club Ash Tray
Height—3"

No. 115
4 oz. Claret or Wine
Height—5"

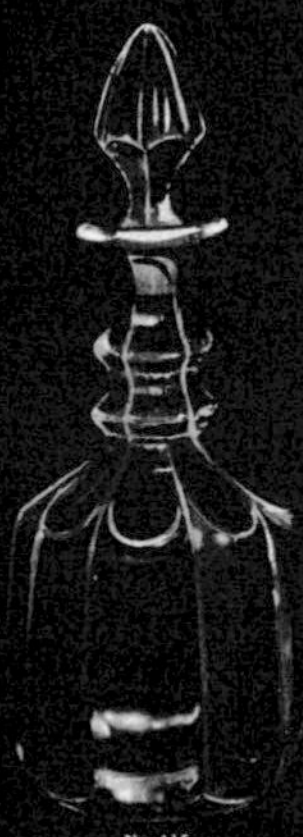
No. 115
32 oz. Decanter and Stopper
Height—12"

No. 115
7 in. Ice Bucket
Diameter—5½"
Also made 6 in. Size

CANTERBURY
NO. 115 PATTERN

No. 115
9 oz. Goblet
Height—6"

No. 115
6 oz. Saucer Champ.
or Tall Sherbet
Height—4½"

No. 115
4 oz. Claret or Wine
Height—5"

No. 115
3½ oz. Cocktail
Height—4¼"

No. 115
4½ oz. Oyster
Cocktail
Height—4"

No. 115
6 oz. Ice Cream
Height—3¾"

No. 115
5 oz. Ftd.
Orange Juice
Height—4¼"

No. 115
9 oz. Luncheon
Goblet
Height—5½"

No. 115
13 oz. Ftd.
Ice Tea
Height—6¼"

No. 5321
13 oz. Footed Ice Tea
Height—6¼"

No. 115
9 oz. Table Tumbler Straight
Height—4½"

No. 115
5 oz. Orange Juice
Height—3¾"

CANTERBURY
NO. 115 PATTERN

No. 115
8 in. 3 Hld. 3 Compt.
Candy Box and Cover
Height—3½"

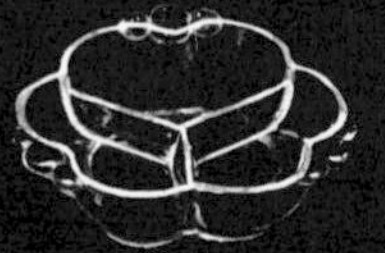
No. 115
8 in. 3 Hld. 3 Compt. Relish
Height—1¾"

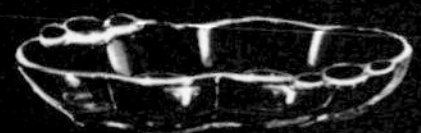
No. 115
9 in. 2 Hld. Celery Tray
Height—1¼" Width—4"

No. 115
9 in. 2 Compt. Pickle and Olive Tray
Height—1¼" Width—4"

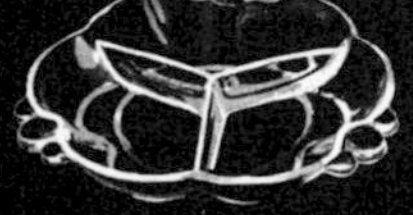
No. 115
9 in. 3 Hld. 3 Compt. Relish
Height—1½"

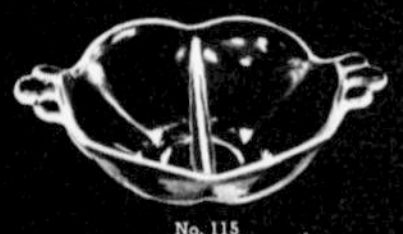
No. 115
6 in. 2 Hld. 2 Compt Round Relish
Height—2"
Also made Star shape

No. 115
7 in. 2 Hld. 2 Compt. Oval Relish
Height—2¼" Width—5¼"

No. 115
6 in. Oval Olive
Height—2¼" Width—5¼"

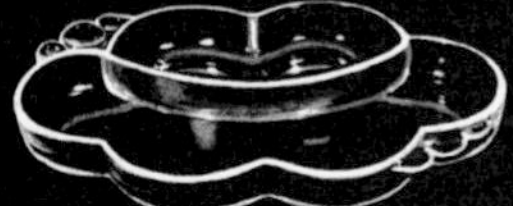
No. 115
10½ in. 2 Hld. 2 Compt. Celery and Relish
Height—1¼" Width—6¾"

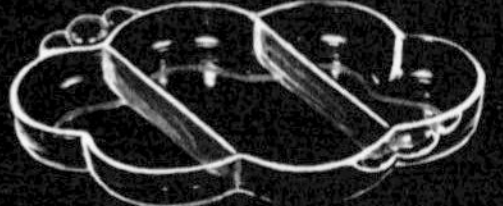
No. 115
10½ in. 2 Hld. 3 Compt. Celery and Relish
Height—1¼" Width—6¾"

CANTERBURY
Lead Blown Stemware
NO. 5115 PATTERN

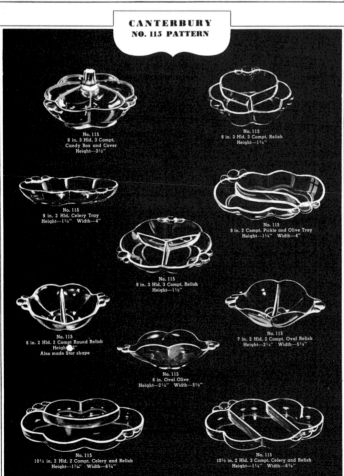

No. 5115
10 oz. Goblet
Height—7¼"

No. 5115
5 oz. Saucer Champ.
Height—5½"

No. 5115
1 oz. Cordial
Height—4¼"

No. 5115
3½ oz. Wine
Height—6"

No. 5115
5 oz. Claret
Height—6¾"

No. 115
32 oz. Hld. Martini
Mixer w/Spoon
Height—9¼"

No. 5115—3 oz.
Liquor Cocktail
Height—5¼"

No. 115
Finger Bowl
Height—2"
Diameter—4¼"

No. 115
32 oz. Martini
Mixer w/Spoon
Height—9¼"

No. 5115
12 oz. Ftd. Ice Tea
Height—5¾"

No. 5115
10 oz. Ftd. Tumbler
Height—4½"

No. 5115
5 oz. Ftd. Orange Juice
Height—4¼"

No. 5115
5 oz. Ftd. Ice Cream
Height—2½"

No. 5115
4 oz. Ftd. Oyster Cockta[il]
Height—3¼"

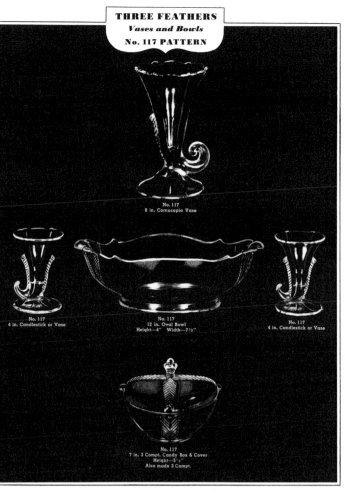

THREE FEATHERS
Vases and Bowls
No. 117 PATTERN

No. 117
8 in. Cornucopia Vase

No. 117
4 in. Candlestick or Vase

No. 117
12 in. Oval Bowl
Height—4" Width—7½"

No. 117
4 in. Candlestick or Vase

No. 117
7 in. 3 Compt. Candy Box & Cover
Height—5½"
Also made 3 Compt.

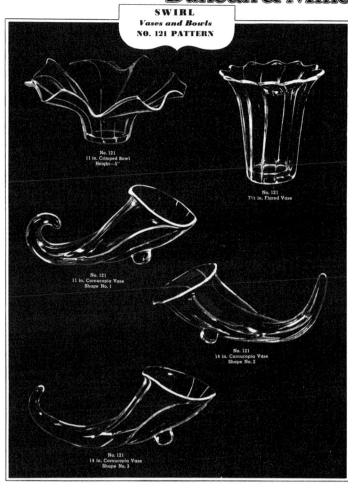

SWIRL
Vases and Bowls
NO. 121 PATTERN

No. 121
11 in. Crimped Bowl
Height—5"

No. 121
7½ in. Flared Vase

No. 121
11 in. Cornucopia Vase
Shape No. 1

No. 121
14 in. Cornucopia Vase
Shape No. 2

No. 121
14 in. Cornucopia Vase
Shape No. 3

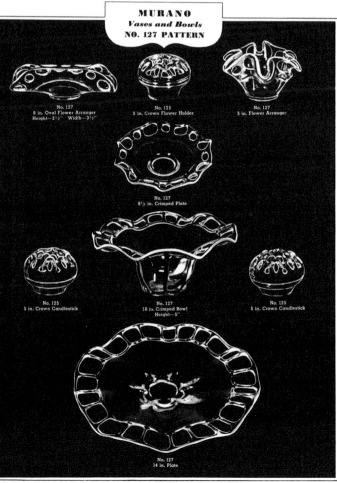

MURANO
Vases and Bowls
NO. 127 PATTERN

No. 127
8 in. Oval Flower Arranger
Height—2½" Width—3½"

No. 125
5 in. Crown Flower Holder

No. 127
5 in. Flower Arranger

No. 127
8½ in. Crimped Plate

No. 125
5 in. Crown Candlestick

No. 127
10 in. Crimped Bowl
Height—5"

No. 125
5 in. Crown Candlestick

No. 127
14 in. Plate

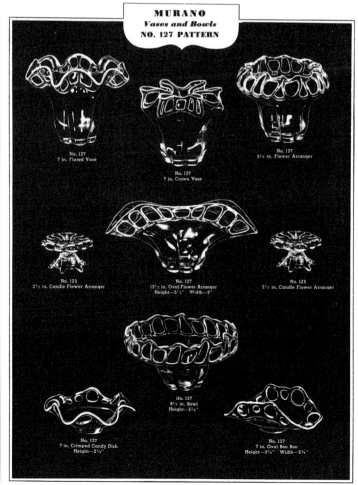

MURANO
Vases and Bowls
NO. 127 PATTERN

No. 127
7 in. Flared Vase

No. 127
7 in. Crown Vase

No. 127
5½ in. Flower Arranger

No. 125
2½ in. Candle Flower Arranger

No. 127
12½ in. Oval Flower Arranger
Height—5½" Width—5"

No. 125
2½ in. Candle Flower Arranger

No. 127
9½ in. Bowl
Height—5¼"

No. 127
7 in. Crimped Candy Dish
Height—2½"

No. 127
7 in. Oval Bon Bon
Height—3¾" Width—5¾"

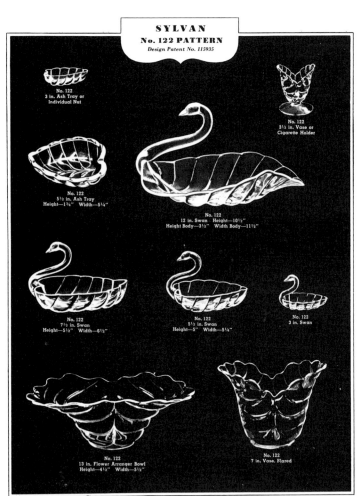

No. 122
3 in. Ash Tray or
Individual Nut

No. 122
3½ in. Vase or
Cigarette Holder

No. 122
5½ in. Ash Tray
Height—1¾" Width—5¼"

No. 122
12 in. Swan Height—10½"
Height Body—3½" Width Body—11½"

No. 122
7½ in. Swan
Height—5½" Width—6½"

No. 122
5½ in. Swan
Height—5" Width—5¼"

No. 122
3 in. Swan

No. 122
13 in. Flower Arranger Bowl
Height—4½" Width—5½"

No. 122
7 in. Vase, Flared

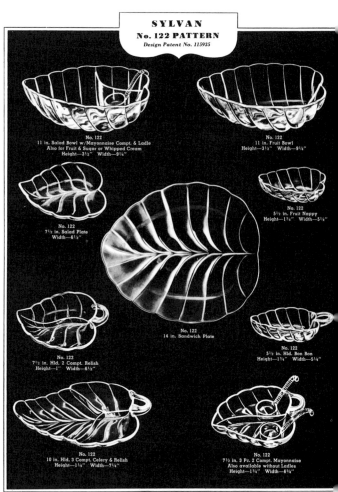

No. 122
11 in. Salad Bowl w/Mayonnaise Compt. & Ladle
Also for Fruit & Sugar or Whipped Cream
Height—3½" Width—9¼"

No. 122
11 in. Fruit Bowl
Height—3½" Width—9¼"

No. 122
7½ in. Salad Plate
Width—6½"

No. 122
5½ in. Fruit Nappy
Height—1¾" Width—5¼"

No. 122
14 in. Sandwich Plate

No. 122
7½ in. Hld. 2 Compt. Relish
Height—1" Width—6½"

No. 122
5½ in. Hld. Bon Bon
Height—1¾" Width—5¼"

No. 122
10 in. Hld. 3 Compt. Celery & Relish
Height—1¼" Width—7¼"

No. 122
7½ in. 3 Pc. 2 Compt. Mayonnaise
Also available without Ladles
Height—1¾" Width—6¾"

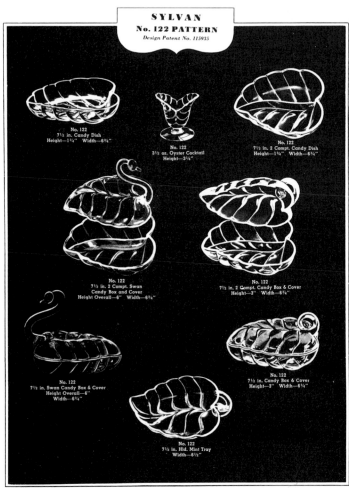

No. 122
7½ in. Candy Dish
Height—1¾" Width—6¾"

No. 122
3½ oz. Oyster Cocktail
Height—3¼"

No. 122
7½ in. 2 Compt. Candy Dish
Height—1¾" Width—6¾"

No. 122
7½ in. 2 Compt. Swan
Candy Box and Cover
Height Overall—6" Width—6¾"

No. 122
7½ in. 2 Compt. Candy Box & Cover
Height—3" Width—6¾"

No. 122
7½ in. Swan Candy Box & Cover
Height Overall—6"
Width—6¾"

No. 122
7½ in. Candy Box & Cover
Height—3" Width—6¾"

No. 122
7½ in. Hld. Mint Tray
Width—6½"

No. 122
3 in. 1 Light Candlestick

No. 122
3 in. 1 Light Candlestick

No. 122
12 in. Oval Flower Bowl, Shallow
Height—3¾" Width—8¼"

No. 122
5 in. Ftd. 2 Light Epergne
Width—7"

No. 122
12½ in. Oval Fruit Bowl Deep
Height—4¼" Width—6¾"

No. 122
5 in. Ftd. 2 Light Epergne
Width—7"

No. 122
12 in. Flared Flower Bowl
Height—2¾" Width—11"

No. 122
14 in. Flower Pan
Height—2" Width—11"

SANIBEL
NO. 130 PATTERN

No. 130
5½ in. Ftd. Oval Vase
Length—8" Width—5"

No. 130
Bookend Vase
Height—5¾" Width—4¼"
Length—7"

No. 130
5½ in. Crimped & Ftd. Vase
Length—7½" Width—4½"

No. 130
13 in. Oblong Floating Garden
Height—1" Width—9¾"

No. 130
14 in. Floating Garden
Height—3" Width—13"

No. 130
14 in. Crimped Flower Bowl
Height—2¾" Width—13"

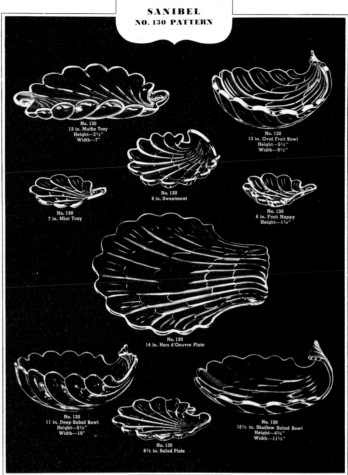

SANIBEL
NO. 130 PATTERN

No. 130
13 in. Muffin Tray
Height—2½"
Width—7"

No. 130
13 in. Oval Fruit Bowl
Height—5½"
Width—9½"

No. 130
8 in. Sweetmeat

No. 130
7 in. Mint Tray

No. 130
6 in. Fruit Nappy
Height—1¼"

No. 130
14 in. Hors d'Oeuvre Plate

No. 130
11 in. Deep Salad Bowl
Height—5½"
Width—10"

No. 130
8½ in. Salad Plate

No. 130
12½ in. Shallow Salad Bowl
Height—4¾"
Width—11¼"

SANIBEL
NO. 130 PATTERN

No. 130
9 in. Candy Jar and Cover
Diameter—4¾"

No. 130
5½ in. Cigarette Jar and Cover
Diameter—2¾"

No. 130
30 oz. Decanter
Height—9½"
Diameter—4¼"

No. 130
3½ in. Tropical Fish Ash Tray

No. 130
3 in. Life Preserver Ash Tray

No. 130
8½ in. 2 Compt. Relish
Height—1¼"

No. 130
9 in. Celery Tray
Height—2" Width—6"

No. 130
6 in. Life Preserver Ash Tray

No. 130
13 in. 3 Compt. Oblong Celery & Relish
Height—1¼" Width—9¾"

No. 130
13 in. Oblong Sandwich Plate
Width—9½"

GRECIAN
Urns, Vases and Bowls

No. 553
8½ in. Sq. Ftd. Sq. Hld. Bowl
Height—6"

N- 552
6 in. Sq. Ftd. Sq. Hld. Compor.
Height—4½"

No. 551
10 in. Scroll Hld. Urn
Square Foot

No. 547
9 in. Scroll Hld. Urn
Square Foot

No. 546
8 in. Swan Hld. Urn
Square Foot

No. 550
10 in. Swan Hld. Urn
Square Foot

No. 549
10 in. Square Hld. Urn
Square Foot

No. 534
9½ in. Square Hld. Urn
Square Foot

No. 545
8 in. Sq. Hld. Urn
Square Foot

No. 530
7 in. Square Hld. Urn
Square Foot

No. 115
8 in. 3 Compt. Candy Box & Cover
Height—3¼"

No. 5200
6 in. Candy Box & Cover
Height—5"
Also made 8" Size

No. 30
8 in. Rectangular Candy Box & Knob Cover
Height—3½"   Width—5"
Also made 2 Compt.

No. 117
8 in. Cornucopia Vase

No. 534
3½ in. Square 2 Hld. Urn

No. 506
12 in. Vase
Also made 10" Size

No. 30
2 in. Square
Candlestick

No. 30
12 in. Rectangular Floating Garden
Height—1¾"   Width—7½"

No. 30
2 in. Square
Candlestick

No. 115
9 in. Tall Vase

No. 126
14 in. Oval Bowl
Height—7½"   Width—8"

No. 30
8 in. Flip Vase
Flared

No. 30½
12½ in. Flared Flower Bowl
Height—3½"

No. 115
11½ in. Oval Bowl
Height—5"   Width—8¼"
Also made 10 in. Size

No. 115
10½ in. Crimped Bowl
Height—5"
Also made 9 in. Size

No. 1
1 Light Hurricane Lamp
w/prisms and
No. 505 Chimney
Height—15"

No. 30½
10½ in. Salad Bowl
Height—4½"

No. 115
14 in. Plate

No. 30
12 in. Devilled Egg Plate

No. 5321
10 oz. Goblet
Height—7½"

No. 5321
6 oz. Saucer Champagne
or Tall Sherbet
Height—6"

No. 5321
1 oz. Cordial
Height—4½"

No. 5321
3½ oz. Liquor Cocktail
Height—5½"

No. 5321
3 oz. Wine
Height—6¼"

No. 5321
13 oz. Footed Ice Tea
Height—6¼"

No. 5321
5 oz. Footed Orange Juice
Height—4½"

No. 5321
4½ oz. Oyster Cocktail
Height—3½"

No. 5321
6 oz. Ice Cream
Height—3½"

No. 38
8 oz. Sugar
Height—2¾"

No. 38
7 oz. Cream
Height—3½"

No. 30
11 in. 2 Hld. Sandwich Plate

No. 30½
8½ in. Salad Plate
(Also made in 7½" Dessert Size)
(Also made in 6½" Bread & Butter Plate)

No. 117
8 in. Cornucopia Vase
Diameter—4¾"

No. 115
9 in. 3 Hld. Flared Relish
Height—1½"

No. 30
6 in. 2 Hld. Nappy Flared
Width—3½"

No. 1
1 Light
Hurricane Lamp
Candelabra w/prisms
Height overall 15 inches

No. 30
5 in. 2 Light Candlestick
Height—6"   Width—7"

No. 8
12 in. Flower Bowl
Height—3½"
Also made crimped

No. 30
5 in. 2 Light Candlestick
Height—6"   Width—7"

No. 8—6 in. 3 Pc. Mayonnaise Set
Consisting of
1—No. 8—Mayonnaise Bowl   Height—3"
1—No. 8—Mayonnaise Plate
1—Ladle

No. 117
7 in. 3 Compt. Candy Box & Cover
Height—4½"

"FIRST LOVE"
ETCHING TO HARMONIZE WITH
1847 Rogers Bros.
"First Love" Silverplate

No. 30
4½ in. Rect. Cig. Box & Cover
Height—2½"   Width—3½"

No. 30
3½ in. Rect. Ash Tray
Width—2½"

No. 30
5 in. Rect. Ash Tray
Width—3¼"

No. 25
5 in. Ftd. Candy Jar & Cover
Height—7¼"

No. 106
6 in. 3 Compt. Candy Box & Cover
Height—3½"

No. 30
6½ in. Rect. Ash Tray
Width—4¼"

No. 115
8 in. 3 Hld. 3 Compt. Candy Box & Cover
Height—4"

No. 115
6 in. Low Comport
Height—4¼"

No. 30
12 in. Devilled Egg Plate

No. 115
High Foot Comport
Height—5½"

No. 30
6 in. Ice Bucket
w/Chrom. Hdl. & Tongs

No. 5200
32 oz. Cocktail Shaker
w/Metal Top
Height—9"
Also made
14 oz. and 18 oz. Sizes

No. 5202
80 oz. Jug Ice Lip
Height—9"

"FIRST LOVE"
ETCHING TO HARMONIZE WITH
1847 Rogers Bros.
"First Love" Silverplate

No. 529
7 in. Vase or Urn

No. 525
5 in. Vase or Urn

No. 117
8 in. Cornucopia Vase
Also made 4 in. Size

No. 117
4 in. Candlestick or Vase

No. 117
4 in. Candlestick or Vase

No. 117
12 in. Oval Flower Bowl
Height—4"   Width—7½"

No. 115
12 in. Flared Vase

No. 115
5 in. Crimped Vase

No. 111
10 in. Footed Vase

"FIRST LOVE"
ETCHING TO HARMONIZE WITH
1847 Rogers Bros.
"First Love" Silverplate

No. 5111½
10 oz. Tall Goblet
Height—6¾"

No. 5111½
5 oz. Saucer Champagne
Height—5"

No. 5111½
3½ oz. Liquor Cocktail
Height—4½"

No. 5111½
3 oz. Wine
Height—5¼"

No. 5111½
4½ oz. Claret
Height—6"

No. 5111½
1 oz. Cordial
Height—3¾"

No. 5111½
4½ oz. Oyster Cocktail
Height—3¾"

No. 5111½
12 oz. Ftd. Ice Tea
Height—6½"

No. 5111½
10 oz. Low Luncheon Goblet
Height—5¾"

No. 5111½
14 oz. Ftd. Ice Tea
Height—6¾"

No. 5111½
5 oz. Ice Cream
Height—4"

No. 5111½
5 oz. Ftd. Orange Juice
Height—5¼"

No. 5200
1½ oz. Whiskey or Cordial
Tumbler, Sham
Height—2"

No. 5200
3½ oz. Cocktail Tumbler,
Sham
Height—3"

No. 5200
14 oz. Tumbler, Sham
Height—4½"
Also made 12 oz. and 10 oz.

No. 5111½
Fingerbowl
Diameter—4¼"

"FIRST LOVE"
ETCHING TO HARMONIZE WITH
1847 Rogers Bros.
"First Love" Silverplate

No. 111
4 in. Low Candlestick

No. 111
4 in. Low Candlestick

No. 111
11 in. Flared Bowl
Height—3¼"   Width—11"

No. 30
2 Light Candlestick
Height—6"   Width—7"

No. 41
5 in. 2 Light Candlestick
Width—6½"

No. 6
12 in. Flower Bowl, Flared
Height—3½"

No. 126
14 in. Oval Bowl
Height—7½"   Width—6"

No. 30
2 Light Candelabrum
w/prisms
Height—6"   Width—8"

No. 30
2 Light Canledabrum
w/prisms
Height—6"   Width—8"

No. 28
3 Pc. Breakfast Set
Sugar, Cream and Butter Plate—nested
Height nested—3½"

No. 111
7½ in. Square Salad Plate
Also made 6 in. Size

No. 111
10 oz. Cream
Height—3"

No. 111
10 oz. Sugar
Height—3"
Also made w/Cover

No. 111
8½ in. Round Salad Plate
Also made 6 in. and 7 in. Sizes

No. 111
13 in. Torte Plate Flat Edge
Also made Rolled Edge

No. 111
6 in. 2 Hld. Lemon Plate

No. 111
11 in. 2 Hld. Sandwich Plate

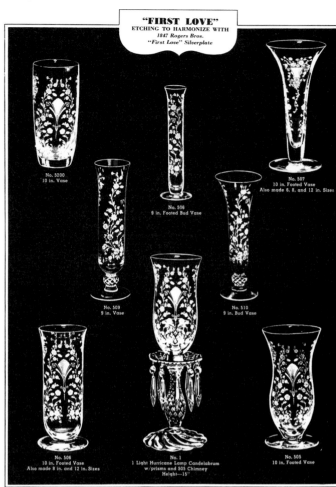

No. 5200
10 in. Vase

No. 506
9 in. Footed Bud Vase

No. 507
10 in. Footed Vase
Also made 6, 8, and 12 in. Sizes

No. 509
9 in. Vase

No. 510
9 in. Bud Vase

No. 506
10 in. Footed Vase
Also made 8 in. and 12 in. Sizes

No. 1
1 Light Hurricane Lamp Candelabrum
w/prisms and 505 Chimney
Height—15"

No. 505
10 in. Footed Vase

LANGUAGE OF FLOWERS
an etching in the
Kate Greenaway Tradition

No. 5331
10 oz. Goblet
Height—7½"

No. 5331
6 oz. Saucer Champagne
or Tall Sherbet
Height—4¾"

No. 5331
3 oz. Wine
Height—5¾"

No. 5331
3½ oz. Liquor Cocktail
Height—4½"

No. 5331
1 oz. Cordial
Height—4¼"

No. 5331
13 oz. Ftd. Ice Tea
Height—7½"

No. 5331
10 oz. Low Luncheon Goblet
Height—6¾"

No. 5331
5 oz. Ftd. Orange Juice
Height—5½"

No. 5031
5 oz. Ftd. Ice Cream
Height—6¾"

No. 5331
4½ oz. Oyster Cocktail
Height—4¾"

No. 115
7 oz. Sugar
Height—3"

No. 115
7 oz. Cream
Height—3¼"

No. 115
6 in. Low Comport
Height—4¾"

No. 115
Ind. Sugar
Height—2½"

No. 115
Ind. Cream
Height—2¼"

No. 115
7 in. 2 Hld. Oval Relish
Height—2"   Width—5¼"

115—3 Pc. 4½ in. Crimped Marmalade Set
Consisting of
1—No. 115—4½ in. Crimped Marmalade   Height—2½"
1—No. 115—6 in. Plate and Marmalade Spoon

No. 115
8 in. Sugar & Cream Tray
Width—4¾"

LANGUAGE OF FLOWERS
an etching in the
Kate Greenaway Tradition

No. 115
9 in. 3 Hld. 3 Compt. Relish
Height—1½"

No. 115
5½ in. Crimped Vase

No. 115
8 in. 3 Hld. 3 Compt.
Candy Box & Cover
Height—4"

No. 115
7½ in. 2 Hld. Plate

No. 115
14 in. Plate

No. 30½
8½ in. Plate
Also made 7½"

No. 115
3 in. Low Candlestick

No. 115
10 in. Oval Bowl
Height—3"   Width—7¼"

No. 30
2 Light Candlestick
Height—6"   Width—7"

INDIAN TREE DESIGN
Cameo Etching

No. 5326
9 oz. Goblet
Height—7¾"

No. 5326
6 oz. Saucer
Champagne or
Tall Sherbet
Height—6"

No. 5326
3½ oz.
Liquor Cocktail
Height—5¼"

No. 5326
3 oz. Wine
Height—6¼"

No. 5326
4½ oz. Claret
Height—6¾"

No. 5326
1 oz. Cordial
Height—5"

No. 5326
4½ oz.
Oyster Cocktail
Height—4¼"

No. 5326
5 oz. Ftd.
Orange Juice
Height—4¾"

No. 5326
9 oz. Luncheon
Goblet
Height—6"

No. 5326
13 oz. Ftd.
Ice Tea
Height—6¾"

No. 115
7 oz. Sugar
Height—3"

No. 115
7 oz. Cream
Height—3¾"

5326—Finger Bowl   Diameter—4¼"
5326—6 in. Finger Bowl Plate

No. 115
8½ in. Salad Plate
Also made 6 in. Size
and 7½ in. Size

115—3 Pc. Ind. Sugar & Cream Set
Consisting of
115—3 oz. Ind. Sugar Height—2½"
115—3 oz. Ind. Cream Height—2¾"
115—8 in. Oval Tray

INDIAN TREE DESIGN
Cameo Etching

No. 115
6 in. 2 Hld. Nappy, Round
Height—1¾"

No. 115
6 in. 2 Hld. Oval Olive
Height—2½"

No. 115
11 in. 2 Hld. Sandwich Plate

No. 115
11 in. 2 Hld. Sandwich Plate
115—3 Pc. 5½ in. Crimped Mayonnaise Set
Consisting of
115—5½ in. Crimped Mayonnaise Bowl & Ladle
Height—3½"
115—7½ in. Handled Plate

No. 115
9 in. 3 Hld. 3 Compt. Relish
Height—1½"

No. 115
12 in. Shallow Salad Bowl
Height—3½"

No. 115
7 in. High Foot Comport
Height—5½"

No. 115
14 in. Plate

INDIAN TREE DESIGN
Cameo Etching

No. 506
9 in. Ftd. Bud Vase

No. 115
8 in. 3 Compt. Candy Box & Cover
Height—4"

No. 117
8 in. Cornucopia Vase
Diameter—4¾"

No. 115
3 in. 1 Light Candlestick

No. 115
10 in. Oval Handled Basket
Height—4¼" Width—7"
Also made 11½ in. Size

No. 115
3 in. 1 Light Candlestick

No. 30
5 in. 2 Light Candlestick
Width—7"

No. 30
10½ in. Crimped Bowl
Height—5"

No. 30
5 in. 2 Light Candlestick
Width—7"

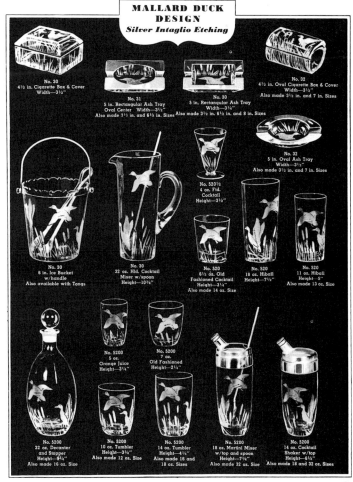

MALLARD DUCK DESIGN
Silver Intaglio Etching

No. 30
4½ in. Cigarette Box & Cover
Width—3½"

No. 31
5 in. Rectangular Ash Tray
Oval Center Width—3½"
Also made 3½ in. and 6½ in. Sizes

No. 30
5 in. Rectangular Ash Tray
Width—3½"
Also made 3½ in., 6½ in. and 8 in. Sizes

No. 32
4½ in. Oval Cigarette Box & Cover
Width—3½"
Also made 3½ in. and 7 in. Sizes

No. 32
5 in. Oval Ash Tray
Width—3½"
Also made 3½ in. and 7 in. Sizes

No. 520½
4 oz. Cocktail
Height—3½"

No. 30
6 in. Ice Bucket
w/handle
Also available with Tongs

No. 30
32 oz. Hld. Cocktail
Mixer w/spoon
Height—10¾"

No. 520
6½ oz. Old
Fashioned Cocktail
Height—3¼"
Also made 14 oz. Size

No. 520
18 oz. Hiball
Height—7½"

No. 520
11 oz. Hiball
Height—5"
Also made 13 oz. Size

No. 5200
5 oz.
Orange Juice
Height—3¼"

No. 5200
7 oz.
Old Fashioned
Height—2¼"

No. 5200
32 oz. Decanter
and Stopper
Height—9¾"
Also made 16 oz. Size

No. 5200
10 oz. Tumbler
Height—3¾"
Also made 12 oz. Size

No. 5200
14 oz. Tumbler
Height—4½"
Also made 16 and
18 oz. Sizes

No. 5200
18 oz. Martini Mixer
w/top and spoon
Height—7¾"
Also made 32 oz. Size

No. 5200
14 oz. Cocktail
Shaker w/top
Height—6½"
Also made 18 and 32 oz. Sizes

Federal

We take special note of the great Depression Glass heritage borne by Federal Glass Company, father to so many of our memorable patterns.

Columbus, Ohio has housed the plant since its origins in 1900. It began as a hand operation, making pressed crystal wares plain or with needle etchings, decorations, or crackled effects. But Federal was well attuned to its time and quick to sense the change in consumer need. Much early effort was directed to developing the methods which could produce large amounts of glass automatically for a country eager for an economical ware.

The switch to automation followed a direct line to success. By the 20s Federal had become one of the biggest suppliers of machine-made tumblers and jugs. In the 30s it was one of the leaders in making the machine-pressed, mold-etched dinnerware in colors which is so readily collectible today. The firm continued to expand tremendously, and in the 40s branched into the food service industry. Today it is still a major supplier to restaurants, motels, and institutions all over the world.

The glass company became a division of the Federal Paper Board Company in 1958 and at present continues to make its good quality, quantity product for the American home table and kitchen. You see Federal glassware in retail stores everywhere.

COLOR

Color began in the 20s with "iridescent and lustre treatments", fired-on and crystal-and-color applications in handmade stemware and refreshment sets. The company announced its first issue of colored glass, machine-made tumblers with optic design, in Springtime green in 1926. The idea of color in modestly-priced wares took strong hold, as we know, and throughout the 30s the major Depression-era hues were in production at Federal.

The green was phased out about 1936. The amber, Golden Glow, enjoyed a long life from (approximately) 1931 to 1942, as did the pink, Rose Glow, from 1933 to 1941. Dinnerware in Madonna blue, a medium shade, was made from 1933 to 1934, and in iridescent amber from 1934 to 1935.

You will find most of Federal's major Depression-era patterns covered in full in Book I. They are listed again briefly in this book, however, in order to update where necessary. These major patterns immediately follow, grouped according to date of introduction.

After this update, more Federal patterns I have researched since Book I are presented to you. These also are ordered by the year the pattern first appeared. Numbered items from the last section of Book I will fall in among the catalog reprints and illustrations.

Remember: The Federal trademark has been used intermittently through the years to the present. In the Depression Era you will most often see it in some pieces of "RAINDROPS", "THUMBPRINT", COLONIAL FLUTED and GEORGIAN.

COLONIAL FLUTED ("Rope")

Also made in crystal, and in the decorated Bridgette Set shown.

THE BRIDGETTE SET

Composed of 1 each covered sugar, cream, 6 each, cups, saucers, 8½ inch dinner plates and sherbets.

Each piece is deorated with Hearts and Diamonds in Red and Clubs and Spades in Black enamel.

—1930 advertisement

"RAINDROPS"

Advertised as a "pebble optic", tumblers in green were first issued in 1927 and other pieces followed. Shown below are the sherbet, the sugar and cover, and creamer.

"HONEYCOMB" (HEXAGON OPTIC)

Federal did make the small HEXAGON OPTIC tumbler pictured in Book I, but the rest of this set was made by Jeannette, and can be referred to under "Honeycomb" in that chapter! More of Federal's HEXAGON OPTIC tumblers are pictured here; they were made in pink and green in the 30s.

2½-oz, 9-oz, and 10-oz HEXAGON OPTIC tumblers. 5-oz not shown.

GEORGIAN ("Lovebirds")

The hot plate was also used as part of a wooden lazy susan measuring 18¼" across and standing on a 4¾" high pedestal. Seven indentations in the tray contain the 5" crystal or green hot plate dishes of GEORGIAN center design. Label on underside reads "Cold Cut Server".

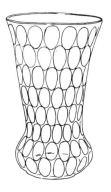

"THUMBPRINT"

One of those first green tumblers made in 1927 was this Pear Optic design which has since been called "THUMBPRINT" by collectors. Jugs and vases were issued the following year and a Hostess Set (plates, cups, saucers) was made in 1929. More pieces followed.

—"THUMBPRINT" vase and ice tea set, 1928 catalog

—"THUMBPRINT" water set, 1928 catalog

SYLVAN ("Parrot")

The earliest official record of this pattern is a 1931 advertisement introducing it by name, SYLVAN. It listed the 5" hot dish coaster, 9 oz tumbler, and the 5¾" footed tumbler, which are not in Book I. The ad did not list the 8½", 80 oz jug, the 4¼" tall thin sherbet or the 10¼" square grill plate (all new to our listing) but we find them.

SYLVAN 4½" tall thin sherbet, footed tumbler, jug, and butterdish.

MADRID

The rarely-found gravy boat was never listed in old catalogs and must have been made up specially.

Most cups have the ribbing on the outside, but some have ribbing on the inside. Two styles of lazy susan exist; made of wood, one uses plain hot dish coasters upside down for inserts, the other uses pieces with an off-center ring.

Correction: the footed shakers were part of the earliest issue. The straight sided ones were made as late as 1938.

Additional MADRID: the ashtray is the sherbet plate, 6" square, with 2 grooves for cigars and 2 for cigarets; gravy boat is two pieces, boat 4"x6½" and tray 6"x8¼"; and the coaster with ring.

PATRICIAN

The cream soup correctly measures 4¾".

NORMANDIE

A sugar cover exists in pink.

MAYFAIR

The 9½" grill plate is added to your list since Book I.

ROSEMARY

Slight variations in pattern exist in some cups, sugars, creamers, and tumblers. (For instance, the creamer pictured in Book I has more pattern in its lower half than the sugar.)

SHARON

Many variations of the crystal cake plate exist. One is plain; some have silver, red, blue, or other colors painted on underneath side; one has an indentation for a metal cover; others have different style cover and knob.

The cheese dish cover is identical to the butterdish cover. The cheese dish bottom is flattish, measures 7¼"x¾" with a rim for the cover to fit into. Butterdish bottom: like the 7½"x1½" low soup bowl, but with an indentation to hold the cover.

Several kinds of "mint errors" have turned up in the Depression Glass field: double imprints, squashed nappies and other disfigures, or one pattern over another. The two-spouted creamer pictured here is my favorite!

SHARON butterdish, cheese dish, two-spout creamer.

DIANA

Pictured here with the shaker are these pieces not listed in Book I: the 9 oz, 4½" tumbler; ash tray; and sherbet.

COLUMBIA

A small issue was made in pink. You may find satin-finished crystal pieces, a butterdish with metal cover, or gold-rimmed pieces.

HERITAGE

Small issues in pink and light blue were made.

Beginning this page are Federal patterns not already covered in Book 1, and some only briefly noted in the final section of that book.

"NEW MODE" etching
in Rose Lustre, Amber Glow or Amethyst Glow applied color; 1926 ad

No. 1510. 9 oz. Goblet. Needle Etched No. 1.

#1 NEEDLE ETCH
in crystal & green, 1926 company catalog

THE BIG THREE

DIAMOND OPTIC   PEAR SHAPE OPTIC   POLKA DOT OPTIC

PATENT APPLIED FOR

Federal has "done it" again. This time by perfecting a process by which it is now possible to manufacture Thin Blown Automatic Machine-Made Tumblers in the popular Fancy Optics; Pear Shape, Polka Dot and Diamond.

First "automatic machine-blown" tumblers in green & crystal; 1926 ad

—1926 ad

—1928 advertisement

THE BRIDGE SEASON STARTS AGAIN AND EVERY GLASS DISPLAY SHOULD HAVE THE

TRUMP BRIDGE LUNCHEON SET

ORDERS should be placed promptly to take advantage of Fall and Holiday demand for these attractive sets. Wonderful for prizes, useful and distinctive.

The Trump Bridge Luncheon Set is composed of four thin blown footed goblets, four thin blown footed sherbets, four octagon salad plates and one sandwich tray with detachable silver plated handle, all with color enamel decoration as shown. Packed in special display box.

THE FEDERAL GLASS CO.
COLUMBUS, OHIO

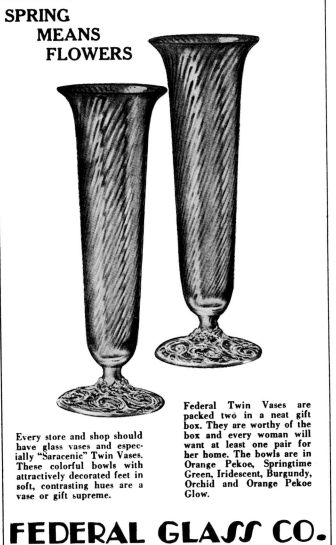

SPRING MEANS FLOWERS

Every store and shop should have glass vases and especially "Saracenic" Twin Vases. These colorful bowls with attractively decorated feet in soft, contrasting hues are a vase or gift supreme.

Federal Twin Vases are packed two in a neat gift box. They are worthy of the box and every woman will want at least one pair for her home. The bowls are in Orange Pekoe, Springtime Green, Iridescent, Burgundy, Orchid and Orange Pekoe Glow.

FEDERAL GLASS CO.

Two 1928 water sets in green & crystal.

No. 170-80/90 Tudor Ring Optic Water Set

TUDOR RING

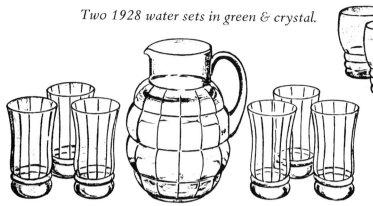

No. 20-85/115-R—10-oz. Water Sets

"MUTT N' JEFF"

*Two 1928 tumblers
in green & crystal*

No. 30—7½-oz. Goblet
TWISTED OPTIC
Manufactured by
THE FEDERAL GLASS CO.
COLUMBUS - - OHIO
Agents in Principal Cities.

—1930 advertisement

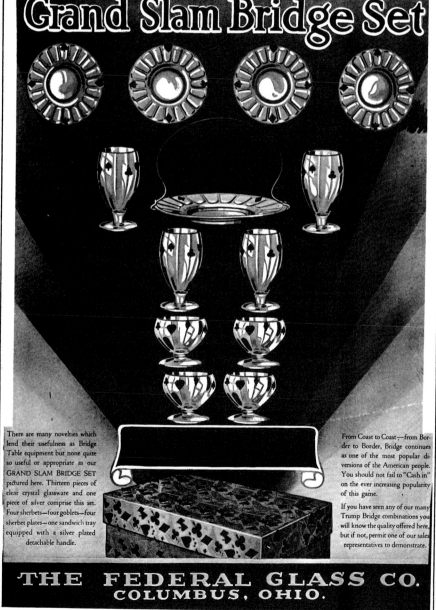

Grand Slam Bridge Set

There are many novelties which lend their usefulness as Bridge Table equipment but none quite so useful or appropriate as our GRAND SLAM BRIDGE SET pictured here. Thirteen pieces of clear crystal glassware and one piece of silver comprise this set. Four sherbets—four goblets—four sherbet plates—one sandwich tray equipped with a silver plated detachable handle.

From Coast to Coast,—from Border to Border, Bridge continues as one of the most popular diversions of the American people. You should not fail to "Cash in" on the ever increasing popularity of this game.

If you have seen any of our many Trump Bridge combinations you will know the quality offered here, but if not, permit one of our sales representatives to demonstrate.

**THE FEDERAL GLASS CO.
COLUMBUS, OHIO.**

CORDED OPTIC
THE FEDERAL GLASS COMPANY
COLUMBUS — — — OHIO

96

HOSTESS LINE

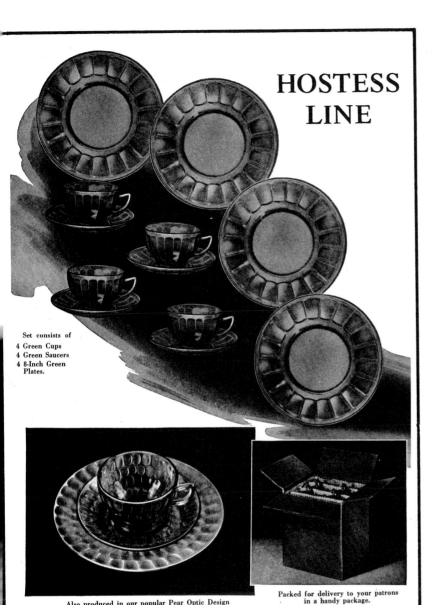

Set consists of
4 Green Cups
4 Green Saucers
4 8-Inch Green Plates.

Also produced in our popular Pear Optic Design

Packed for delivery to your patrons in a handy package.

HOSTESS line (#187 Book I)
from a 1930 advertisement

RED FLOWERS
GREEN LEAVES

PINK FLOWERS
GREEN LEAVES

WHITE FLOWERS
GREEN LEAVES

YELLOW FLOWERS
GREEN LEAVES

DECORATION No. 472.

"MARY ROSE" *decoration, 1928*
advertised with
Federal's ROSEMARY *dinnerware.*

Lemon Reamer.

Orange Reamer

"INDIAN" *tumbler*
Marked H A
green, c. 1930

LEMON AND ORANGE REAMERS
from 20s catalog

CORDED OPTIC *10-oz water set*
green, 1929 company catalog.

"TALL BOY" *10-oz or 12-oz ice tea sets,*
green, 1928 company catalog.

12-oz DIAMOND OPTIC ICE TEA SET

10-oz SQUAT OPTIC WATER SET

9-oz DIAMOND SQUAT WATER SET

Jack Frost Crackled Beverage Sets

JACK FROST CRACKLED WATER SET

JACK FROST CRACKLED ICED TEA SET

JACK FROST CRACKLED LEMONADE SET

146½R – 65 oz. Jug

146-R – 15 oz. Footed

Federal jugs and tumblers in Rose Glow, Golden Glow, crystal, and green from a mid-30s catalog.

ROWS 1 & 2: LIDO LINE (#114 Book I)
ROW 3: TUDOR RING

146R – 5 oz. Optic

146R – 9 oz. Optic

146R – 10 oz. Optic

146R – 12 oz. Optic

5 oz. Tudor Ring Optic

9 oz. Tudor Ring Optic

12 oz. Tudor Ring Optic

199½R – 80 oz. Jug

ROW 4: PYRAMID OPTIC *tumbler;* CROSSBAR *tumbler;* JOHN *jug and* MARY *jug.*

131M – 9 oz. Tall

177R – 9 oz. Optic

172½R – 80 oz. Jug

171R – 80 oz. Jug

B-10 – 4 pc. Kitchen Bowl Set

Federal kitchenware from 1938-1939 company catalogs

15 Piece Kitchenware Set – (BJ-3)
Crystal or Golden Glow
1 each 6½, 7½, 8½, 9½" Mixing Bowls
2 only 4 x 4" Jars and Covers — 1 only 8 x 4" Jar and Cover
1 each 2523 Covered Butter — Lipped Cooking Cup
2520 Lemon Reamer — 2521 Orange Reamer

CODE: C—CRYSTAL; GG—GOLDEN GLOW; RG—ROSE GLOW

14 pc. Kitchenware Set (BJ-6)
2 only 4 x 4", 1 only 8 x 4", 1 only 8 x 8" Jar and Cover
1 only No. 2528 Jar and Cover
1 only No. 2524 ¼ lb. Butter and Cover
1 only No. 2539 Handled Measuring Cup
1 only No. 2521 Orange Reamer
Pkd. Ind. R/S Carton — Wt. 18 lbs.
C — GG

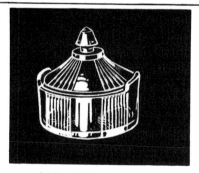

307 – Tub Butter and Cover

C — GG

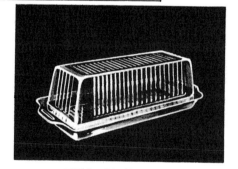

2524 – ¼ lb. Butter and Cover

C — GG — RG

2523 – 1 lb. Butter and Cover

C — GG — RG

2520 – Lemon Reamer

2521 – Orange Reamer

2539 – Handled Measuring Cup

Triple Lip Measuring Cup

100

PIONEER (#19 Book I)

Only the original issue, a short one, was in pink. In the 40s a crystal line was made, and this is the issue reprinted below. Federal has been making certain pieces of this line since then—at one point, some was decorated—and as late as 1973 the 11" fluted bowl and the 12" plate were still being manufactured in crystal.

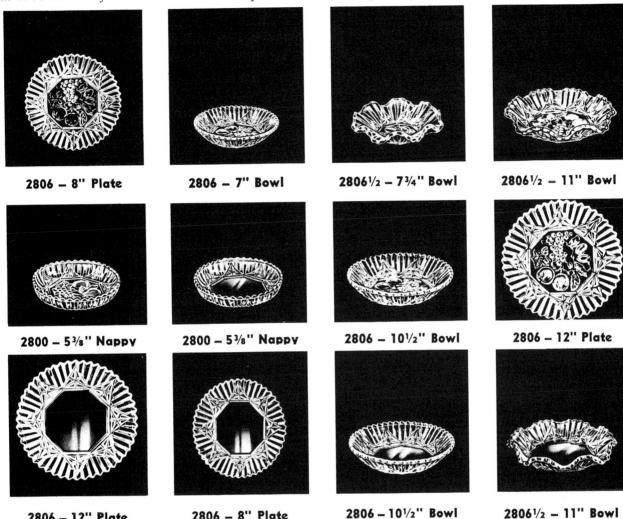

2806 – 8" Plate   2806 – 7" Bowl   2806½ – 7¾" Bowl   2806½ – 11" Bowl

2800 – 5⅜" Nappy   2800 – 5⅜" Nappy   2806 – 10½" Bowl   2806 – 12" Plate

2806 – 12" Plate   2806 – 8" Plate   2806 – 10½" Bowl   2806½ – 11" Bowl

MISCELLANEOUS ITEMS *in colors from 1936-1939 Federal catalogs.*

2804 – 4¼" Nappy   2804 – 7¼" Nappy   1914 – 9 oz. Etched   1914 – 9 oz. Etched

145-R – 14 oz.   2826 – Candlestick   186R – 9¼ oz.   2825 – Clover – C or RG

Fenton

The brothers Fenton took the first slender profits from an initial glass decorating enterprise and built a glassmaking plant in 1906 that would distinguish their name for decades.

Fenton's earliest achievements were some of its finest. The amazing color department is among other things credited with originating iridescent-colored ware not long after the company began—this is collected as Carnival glass today—and its art wares of the 20s are even more highly regarded by glass fanciers.

Amidst the gift lines in colors, combinations, and special effects too numerous to mention here, the transparent pink, green, blue and yellow of our interest were made, often in table- and dinnerware lines popular to the day. This chapter will concentrate on those collectible lines and pieces which are, in concept and color, most representative of the Depression Era.

Fenton Art Glass is still very active; visitors to Williamstown, West Virginia can watch glass made in the Fenton tradition yet today.

A good history, and examples in color of the art lines, are in Alan Linn's THE FENTON STORY OF GLASS MAKING (privately published, 1969).

FENTON ART GLASS CO., WILLIAMSTOWN, W. VA.
Supplement to Catalog.

232. 8¼" Candlestick.

231. 10" Footed Shallow Cup Bowl.

232. 8½" Candlestick.

891. 12" Vase.

888. 10" Vase.

887. 8" Paste Mold Vase.

886. 6" Paste Mold Vase.

885. 5" Paste Mold Vase.

231. 8" Deep Cupped Footed Bowl.

846. 8¾" Flared Cup Bowl and Base.

318. 7" Butter Ball.

847. 5" Footed Vase Shell Shaped.

No. 2 Sugar and Cream Set.

200. 2 Piece Guest Set.

847. Cupped Rose Bowl.

847. 6½" Nut Bowl.

635. ½ lb. Candy Jar.

56. Cologne Drip Stopper.

735. ½ lb. Candy Jar.

57. Powder Puff.

401. 2 Piece Night Set.

847. 7" Shallow Cup Footed Bowl.

847. 6" Footed Bulb Bowl.

847. 8" Shallow Footed Bowl.

403. 2 Piece Ice Cream Set.

1647. 2 Piece Sweet Meat Set.

15 PIECE WATER SET
6 handled tumblers, 10 oz; jug & cover, 76 oz;
6 tumbler coasters, 1 jug coaster.
Coasters & handles in Royal blue.

14 PIECE LEMONADE SET
6 handled tumblers, 12 oz; jug, 62 oz;
6 tumbler coasters; 1 jug coaster.
Coasters & handles in Royal blue

Items on the preceding page, and these sketched here, are selected examples of the many colored giftwares offered by Fenton throughout the 20s. They are taken from company catalogs which list such colors as topaz, Florentine green, iridescent and plain Wisteria, Celeste blue, ruby, Persian Pearl, Grecian gold, Jade yellow, turquoise, Rose, and ebony. Often bases and handles are ebony or Royal blue.

Here is a suggestion from the Fenton Art Glass Co.'s factory which is being featured by the Horace C. Gray Co. The new assortment of beverage glasses illustrated at the left may be had in a choice of amber, ruby or crystal. The four sizes pictured comprise the set, and consists of a highball, table tumbler, juice glass, and small whisky. Notice their extra-heavy bases, which act as a safeguard against tipping over and at the same time gives them a unique touch. A decanter also is available, if desired, to round out the set.

"FRANKLIN" *as described in a 1934 trade journal write-up.*

THE FENTON ART GLASS CO.
WILLIAMSTOWN, W. VA.
No. 1611 Georgian Tableware Line
Colors · Crystal · Green · Pink · Amber · Ruby · Royal Blue · Topaz · Black

No. 1611—2½ oz. Tumbler   No. 1611 Decanter   No. 1611—5 oz. Tumbler   No. 1611—10 oz. Tumbler   No. 1611—½ Gal. Jug

No. 1611 — 8" Salad Plate
No. 1611 — 6" Salad Plate   No. 1611 Sherbet   No. 1611 Goblet   No. 1611—12 oz. Ice Tea

GEORGIAN

*tableware line
from company catalog
dating c. 1930*

103

An advertisement to the trade in 1929 pictures the LINCOLN INN tableware line and describes other Fenton wares for that year like this:

"A beautiful line of Tableware, Flower Bowls, Baskets, Vases, Candlesticks, Nymph Sets, Vanity Sets, Guest Sets, Console Sets and Novelties in exclusive colors, designs, and decorations. Translucent Jade, rich Red Ruby, deep Royal Blue, Ebony Black, Victoria Blue and Green, Velva Rose and Aquamarine have proven fine selling colors and will add to your prestige and profit."

LINCOLN INN

This popular and varied dinner service was introduced in 1928 and continued for many years in pink, green, jade, ruby, Royal Blue and perhaps others. At left, 1928 ad; below and top of next page from company catalogs.

1700 Goblet	1700 Sherbet	1700S Oval	1700S Nut	1700S Mint

1700 Cream 1700 Sugar 1700 Cup and Saucer 1700 Cereal

1700 Hdl. Olive 1700-S Hdl. Bon Bon Square 1700-S Hdl. Bon Bon Oval 1700-C 6" Crimp

1700 12" Plate 1700 8" Plate 1700-G Comport Plate 1700-G Shallow Comport

104

No. 1700 Lincoln Inn Line

1700-5 oz. Tumbler Straight .
1700-9 oz. Tumbler Straight .
1700-12 oz. Ice Tea or
  Hi-Ball-Straight . . . .
1700-7 oz. Ftd Tumbler . . . . .
1700-12 oz. Ftd Ice Tea . . . . .
1700 Goblet . . . .
1700-5 oz. Fruit Juice
  Low Ftd . . . .
1700 Cocktail or Wine . . . . . .
1700 High Ftd Sherbet . . . . . .
1700-6″ Plate . . . .
1700-8″ Plate . . . .
1700-9¼″ Plate . . . .
1700-12″ Plate . . . .
1700 Sugar & Cream Set . . . .
1700 Cup & Saucer . . . .
1700 Finger Bowl & Plate . . .
1700-5″ Fruit Saucer . . . .
1700 Salt & Pepper . . . .
1700-9¼″ Fld Bowl . . . .
1700-10½″ Fld Bowl . . . . . .
1700-5 pc Ash Tray
1700-2 pc Snack Set . . . .
1700 Relish . . . .

The Fenton Art Glass Co., Williamstown, W. V.
No 1700 Lincoln Inn Line. Crystal
Hand Made - Highly Polished

Goblet — Sherbet — Wine or Cocktail — 4 oz Fruit Juice — 7 oz Footed Tumbler — 12 oz Footed Ice Tea

12 oz High Ball — 9 oz Tumbler — Finger Bowl & Plate — Cup & Saucer — Salt & Pepper

5″ Fruit Saucer — Sugar & Cream

6″ Bread & Butter — 12″ Plate — 8″ Salad Plate

PLYMOUTH

Another of Fenton's larger tableware lines, PLYMOUTH was being made in 1933 in ruby, Steigel green and amber. Goblets, sherbets, iced teas, 9-oz table tumblers; 5-oz orange juices, 2½-oz liquors, salad plates and bread & butter plates were among pieces offered. A "44 Piece Repeal Set", a complete liquor service, was advertised in 1933 also, consisting of decanter, cocktail shaker, ice bucket, pilsners, wines, old fashioneds, hiballs, and jigger.

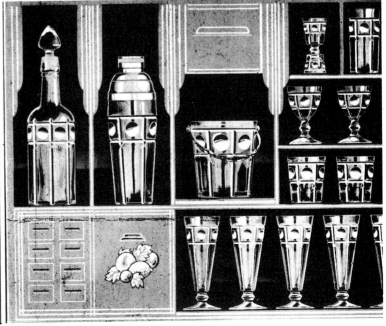

SHEFFIELD LINE

This mid-30s pattern was made in crystal and mermaid blue, gold, and ruby. From company catalogs.

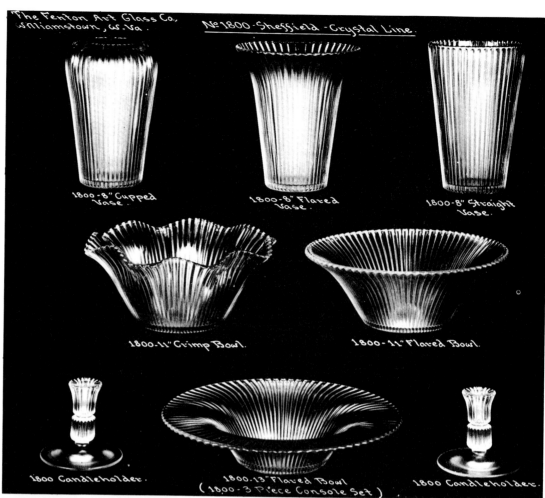

The Fenton Art Glass Co., Williamstown, W. Va.

No 1800 - Sheffield - Crystal Line.

1800 - 8" Cupped Vase.

1800 - 8" Flared Vase.

1800 - 8" Straight Vase.

1800 - 11" Crimp Bowl.

1800 - 11" Flared Bowl.

1800 Candleholder.

1800 - 13" Flared Bowl
(1800 - 3 Piece Console Set)

1800 Candleholder.

The Fenton Art Glass Co., Williamstown, W. Va.

No 1800 Crystal -
12 Piece Assortment - Sheffield

No. 1800 - 3 Ftd. 7½ in. Shallow Bon Bon.

No. 1800 6½ in. Reg. Vase.

No. 1800 - 3 Ftd. 7 in. Flared Bowl

No. 1800 - 6½ in. Flared Vase.

No. 1800 - 6½ in. Tulip Vase.

No. 1800 - 3 Ftd. Covered Bon Bon.

No. 1800 - 6½ in. Cupped Vase.

No. 1800 - 3 Ftd. Triangular Bon Bon

No. 1800 - 3 Ftd. Cupped Bon Bon.

No. 1800 - 6½ in. Club Bon Bon.

No. 1800 - 3 Ftd. 8½ in. Plate.

No. 1800 - 6½ in. Crimped Vase.

AT THE PITTSBURGH SHOW—ROOM 643—FORT PITT HOTEL

THE FENTON ART GLASS COMPANY
Williamstown, West Virginia

PEACOCK
BOOK-ENDS

An excellent item for Fall and Holiday turn-over, these Book-ends in famous Fenton Art glass will provide a fast-moving profit number for your department. Made in crystal, rose, green, matt etched, and black glass. Be among the first to offer these.

FENTON ART GLASS CO.
WILLIAMSTOWN — W. VA.

FENTON for every occasion

MING CRYSTAL

AT THE PITTSBURGH SHOW—ROOMS 552-554, WM. PENN

THE FENTON ART GLASS COMPANY
Williamstown, West Virginia

MING
*was made of
crystal, pink, or green glass*
—1935 advertisement

Fostoria

Among the numerous distinctions held by Fostoria Glass Company, one is outstanding. Of the major hand houses of the 20s and 30s era, only Fostoria has survived to the present day—the oldest, largest, and best-known American glass house still in operation.

The company began in Fostoria, Ohio in 1887 but when the fuel supply ran short at that site, the Fostoria name was brought to Moundsville, West Virginia, and made famous there.

Pressed crystal wares were the first products, but Fostoria's specialty in its early decades was the oil-burning lamp. All kinds were made, including the hand painted, blown globe type collected as "Gone with the Wind" lamps today. Hundreds of different patterns were made.

In the 'teens the company began to concentrate on glassware for home use and in no time at all had made success of this venture. The glass itself became brilliant with improved chemistry and technique. The craftsmen became experts at shaping, finishing, and decorating. And the designers came up with concepts that helped shape the industry. By the 20s Fostoria ranked with the very best hand houses making glass for the popular market.

In 1924 the company came on with its first colors and a plan to advertise widely in major national magazines. Then in 1925 Fostoria became the first glasshouse to introduce all-glass dinnerware in color. These elements fused beautifully and in no time the Fostoria name was known to brides and homemakers everywhere—and a new trend in glassware was firmly set. All Fostoria patterns are collectible today, but these colorful patterns from the Depression era are special treasure.

Through the years the factory was expanded and expanded again to keep up with its great market. Probably about 1940 Fostoria passed even Cambridge to become the largest producer of quality glassware for home use. The factory, under the same management and at the same site—and even with many of the same shapes and patterns from earlier days—has continued its fine production to the present. Echoes of a great tradition sound when today's bride, like her mother before her, considers making Fostoria crystal her own.

By giving examples, this chapter will simply try to characterize Fostoria ware since it can't begin to cover everything here. If you have a greater interest in Fostoria you may wish to refer to my book on the subject.

COLOR

When Fostoria decided to bring on the color it did so in a big way—and if its colors were not fast or fancy, they were sure, most running years longer than average. While this company did not make the opaque colors in decorative occasional pieces that some others did, we find more colored dinnerware by Fostoria than by any other hand house in this era.

The iridescent Mother of Pearl and gold band treatments were begun very early and have continued since.

Five important colors were introduced in 1924 and some had extremely long lives: Canary lasted until 1927, green until 1941, amber until 1941, blue until 1928, and ebony which has continued since. Orchid dates from 1927 to 1929 and Azure, the lighter blue, from 1928 to 1943. Fostoria's pink, which was called Rose or Dawn, started in 1928 and ran to 1941. Topaz color came on in 1929; its name was changed to Gold Tint in 1938 and made for several more years. Wisteria was made from 1931 to 1938. The last of this company's colors for this era were Empire green, Regal blue, and Burgundy appearing in 1933 (these were often put in combination with crystal) and ruby in 1935. These colors lasted out the era.

FOSTORIA: ITS FIRST FIFTY YEARS by Hazel Marie Weatherman (Glassbooks, 1972) covers comprehensively over 450 crystal and colored patterns; FOSTORIA PRICE WATCH gives complete lists of pieces with suggested prices.

—1930 article

New Fokker Cabin Plane Equipped With Fostoria Glass

ONE of the newest lines manufactured by the Fostoria Glass Co., of Moundsville, W. Va., has finally been selected by the Fokker Aircraft Corporation for the glassware to be used in equipping the dining sections of its new gigantic 32-passenger cabin monoplane. This plane, which is reported to be one of the largest and most luxuriously appointed of its kind in the world, has been outfitted with the greatest care and every selection has been made after detailed investigation of the market.

Further evidence of the popularity of black glass is given

ebony lines. This line is considered one of the smartest on the market today, and it is the creation of George Sakier, consulting designer for the Fostoria company.

The cups and saucers and the square plates are of solid ebony and they are enriched with gold bands placed on the outer edges. The ice bucket is of polished rock crystal with exquisite cuttings, while etched ebony bordered with rich gold characterizes the cake plate.

This huge air cruiser, which may be seen in the accompanying illustration, has aroused a great deal of interest,

32-Passenger Fokker Monoplane

in the choice made by the aircraft corporation, which selected either plain ebony or combined with crystal or gold. The glasses decided upon consist of 16-ounce and two-ounce tumblers in Decoration 605; cups and saucers and square plates in Decoration 604; an ice bucket in Cutting 192; and a cake plate in Decoration 501.

The tumblers in Decoration 605 have square black bases, and crystal bowls, the bowls being encircled with enameled

both on account of its size and lavishness of its appointments. It will shortly leave the Fokker airport at Hasbrouck Heights, N. J., for Detroit, where it will be placed on public exhibition at the air show which soon is to be staged in that city. It is understood that the plane has been purchased, completely outfitted, by a high official of the General Motors Corp., at a price which, because of its deluxe and special equipment, is close to the $150,000 mark.

*Four pattern groupings selected from Fostoria's many
large dinnerware lines in color.*

JUNE

*Introduced 1928; discontinued 1952.
Made in Rose, Azure, green 1928-44;
crystal 1928-1952; topaz 1929-1938;
Gold Tint 1938-1944; colors with
crystal bases 1931-1944.*

TROJAN

*Introduced in 1929; discontinued 1944.
Made in Rose, 1929-1935; topaz 1929
-1938; Gold Tint 1938-1944; colors with
crystal bases 1931-1944.*

VERSAILLES

*Introduced in 1928, discontinued 1944.
Made in Rose, Azure, & green 1928-44;
topaz 1929-1938; Gold Tint 1938-1944;
colors with crystal bases 1931-1944.*

MANOR

*Introduced in 1931; discontinued 1944;
Made in green 1931-1935; topaz 1931-
1938; green bowl/crystal base 1931-
1935; topaz bowl/crystal base 1931-38;
Crystal bowl/Wisteria base 1931-1938.*

Fry

Henry Fry, one of the great deans of the glass industry, established his own company in Rochester, Pennsylvania in 1901. For many years the firm held a reputation for excellency in heavy cut glass wares; when the popularity of such styles waned Fry, like other fine companies of its time, turned to making more competitively-priced lines for home use. In addition to colorful artistic and occasional pieces Fry turned in 1922 to the making of oven glass. The Pearl Glass opalescent color developed for this varied bake line, which was carried and added to for several years, was also tapped to make some special lines of artistic wares which are highly collectible today.

When Mr. Fry died in 1929 his firm went into receivership. It continued to make quality lines of tableware, etchings and occasional pieces, however, until 1933 when the factory was bought by Libbey Glass.

Fry used color often and imaginatively through the 20s, frequently associating it with crystal and Pearl Glass or even other shades for two-tone effects. Emerald and Golden Glow were advertised in 1925; Delft blue and Jade green trim in 1926; blue in 1928; black in 1929; Fuchsia (a deep wine) in 1930; and cobalt blue in 1931. More besides these were probably made.

James Lafferty's FRY INSIGHTS (privately published, 1968) shows more lines.

Some Rose, Emerald, blue, Canary, and Golden Glow items from a late 20s Fry brochure. The #7542 stemware included many sizes and came in rose/green/crystal combinations.

#40007
Sugar & Cream

Spice Tray

Fruit Reamer

#7542 Line

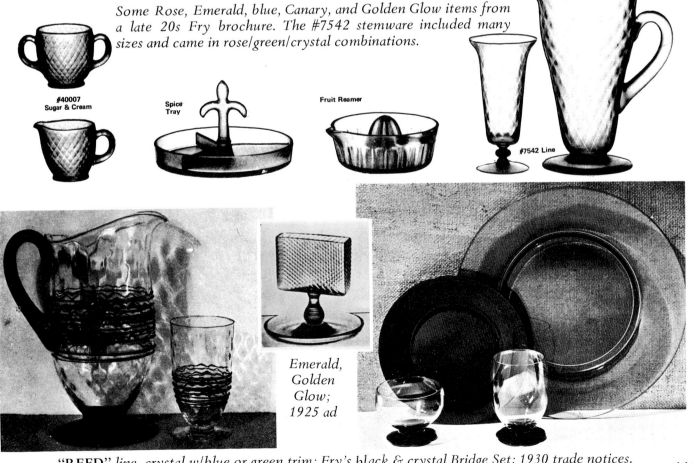

Emerald, Golden Glow; 1925 ad

"REED" *line, crystal w/blue or green trim; Fry's black & crystal Bridge Set; 1930 trade notices.*

Hazel-Atlas

Another great name in the Depression Glass legend was born of the union of two Washington, Pennsylvania container firms in 1902. Hazel Glass Company and the factory-next-door, Atlas Glass and Metal Company, became one Hazel-Atlas Glass Company and set up main offices at Wheeling, West Virginia.

The marriage was successful from the start and expansion was swift. The two Washington factories continued to make containers and before long new facilities were being raised in several cities to break into other glass markets. The day automation dawned upon the industry most Hazel-Atlas operations were geared to assembly-line production, and the company realized great leads in the fields it entered.

The Clarksburg, West Virginia plant specialized in pressed homewares, pouring out so many tumblers during the 20s that a trade journal called it the "World's Largest Tumbler Factory" in 1928. It was by this time one of the most automated factories in the country—and it was here so many of our favorite mold-etched, machine-made patterns were created in the early years of the 30s.

Two more factories in Zanesville, Ohio made thin-blown tumblers and other blown ware, and containers. Additional plants at Washington and Wheeling made tableware and still more kinds of containers.

Through the years Hazel-Atlas has continued its significant production of glassware both for the home and service industries. Continental Can took ownership in 1956 and sold glass under the Hazelware label; Brockway Glass Company bought out in 1964, and operates the organization today.

COLOR

Hazel-Atlas did not plant color into its lines until 1929, but the green tumblers and mixing bowl sets of that year took immediate hold, and verdant kitchenware and table items soon proliferated. Luncheon sets came out the next season and dinnerware after that; it was then the pink and topaz were added. Black glass was being made during this time also.

In 1933 Killarney green, Sunset pink, and topaz were advertised. A deep blue Hazel-Atlas called Ritz blue was developed for 1936. Next the factory tried to come up with a red glass to compete for this popular color market. But red is perhaps the hardest color to make, and falling short of its goal (the story goes) the company conceded to Burgundy, a dark amethyst, instead!

Dinnerware sets in an opaque white glass Hazel-Atlas called Platonite were brought out in the 30s. The earliest Platonite ware shows an opalescence around edges; later it is fully opaque.

You will find that the majority of Hazel-Atlas' important lines were covered fully in Book 1. We will re-trace those patterns here only to bring them up-to-date, and to give this chapter its best perspective. This time they are considered in the order they were originally made.

Patterns from the numbered section of Book 1, plus many other patterns not previously identified, will follow this update.

REMEMBER: The Hazel-Atlas trademark was used chiefly in kitchenware and tumblers from early years to 1956. Many lines, and in particular the mold-etched dinnerware, were not marked.

"NEW CENTURY"

This mold was used for other Hazel Atlas lines, such as "Floral Sterling" shown later in these pages. The shakers to this set are the same mold as "Cloverleaf" and are also found in black and yellow. Other pieces are seen in black and sometimes in pink and sometimes with fired-on red, green, yellow, or blue.

"LYDIA RAY"

At one time this pattern was advertised under the name "New Century," but since another pattern by Hazel-Atlas is widely known by that name we retain the collector's conventional name, "LYDIA RAY", here. It was made in the late 20s and early 30s, and pieces are being found in pink.

NOTE: not all pieces were made in all colors. Refer to PRICE TRENDS.

—Earliest "LYDIA RAY" tumblers, 12 oz, 10 oz, 9 oz, 5 oz, 1½ oz, from 1930 catalog.

"RIBBON"

Pieces in this pattern were made in pink. Add the 6½" tumbler to the list, and the salt-and-pepper which was pictured but not listed in Book I.

OLD FLORENTINE #1

This is the hexagonally-shaped FLORENTINE. The 54-oz straight-sided jug, pictured with "Florentine #2" in the first book, rightly belongs on this list. Add also 3¾" and 5½" ashtrays.

Listed as "Table Novelties" in 1935-38 were the ruffled cream and sugar, ruffled comport (sherbet size) and ruffled handled nut bowl (cream soup type).

An unusual item has turned up, and is shown here. It's a crystal cream & sugar with metal cover, along with the salt & pepper, all on a metal tray.

9-oz tumbler, 2½-oz footed wine, and 3¼-oz cocktail

FLORENTINE #2

You may find a fired-on blue on some pieces, and crystal occasionally comes with a platinum or gold rim. The 10" long relish dish comes in three different styles, no less, and the dinner plate is correctly 10" and not 9½" as listed in Book 1.

Listed since the first book are the 6¼" plate with center indention for a jello or custard cup; 80-oz, 8½" jug, 30-oz, 6¼" jug; and 5¼" nappy. We now know that the 54-oz straight jug belongs to "Florentine #1" above, and that some of the tumblers come ribbed while others are plain. Shown here also is the candy dish, 3½" high and 4¾" across.

Two 60-oz blown "LYDIA RAY" pitchers, with & w/o ice lip. Also came 80-oz.

FLORENTINE #2 jello or custard cup and candy dish

"LYDIA RAY" covered casserole, decanter, cream soup.

CLOVERLEAF

Curiously, the shakers have the CLOVERLEAF design mold-etched on them. So far the 9" dinner plate has not been seen in pink or green. Officially, the pieces made in black are:

Plate, 8" salad
Plate, 6" sherbet
Cup
Saucer
Salt & Pepper

Sherbet
Sugar
Creamer
Ash Trays, 4" and 5¾"

CLOVERLEAF: ashtray, salt shake, sherbet, and straight-sided tumbler.

MODERNTONE

At some point pieces in crystal MODERNTONE were made.

Platonite MODERNTONE was first made in the early 30s and continued until 1940. In the later 30s it was cast in several opaque colors and color combinations:

1938—"Carnivalware", which was fired-on solid orange, blue, yellow or green.
1938—Platonite white with red, blue, yellow or green stripes.
1939—"Carnivalware", this time fired-on solid red, blue, yellow or green.
1940—"Pastel MODERNTONE", fired-on pink, green, blue or yellow.
1940—"Gold Banded MODERNTONE", Platonite white with gold band.

About 1937 Hazel-Atlas made jello cups in blue along with the 9½" mixing bowl. These were made special order for a metal company that made this punch bowl pictured here, and I believe the sugar bowls and butterdishes with metal covers came from metal companies too.

MODERNTONE punch set, butterdish with metal cover.

5½" ashtray and 5-oz, 3¾" fruit juice tumbler (also 12-oz, 5½" ice tea and 9-oz, 4-1/8" table tumblers, not shown) shown with blue MODERNTONE in company catalogs.

MODERNTONE sugar with metal cover, ruffled nut bowl, and cream soup.

MODERNTONE "Little Hostess Party Set", made in late 40s.

ROYAL LACE

The ROYAL LACE cookie jar was sold on special order to various companies and used in various ways:

With metal stand and ladle (knob is wooden) and 8 roly poly punch cups, it's a "Hot Apple Cider Set" (below). In Burgundy, Ritz blue. Comes in another style also.

As a "tobacco jar", usually in crystal (above).

Finally, it was used by a cheese company who fitted it with a metal lid with "Creamed Cottage Cheese, Golden State Co. Oakland, Glendale, and Los Angeles" embossed in the metal.

As far as I know, there is no ashtray in ROYAL LACE as listed in Book I.

STARLIGHT

Additional pieces are the 4¾" nappy, and (shown below) the 7½-oz low sherbet and relish dish.

O-2015-2015½
SQUARE REFRIGERATOR BOWL

O-3060-1742
DRIPPING BOWL

O-3153-3160
ROUND REFRIGERATOR BOWL

O-759-759½
ROUND REFRIGERATOR BOWL

O-3127
ROUND KITCHEN SET

O-3027
MILK PITCHER

**PLATONITE
KITCHENWARE**
—1929 advertisement

Kitchenware from 1929 company catalog

PLATONITE KITCHENWARE *as advertised in 1929.*

G-1818 At left, Blown Pitcher with capacity of 80 ounces.

G-1488 At right, Pressed Ice-Lip Pitcher with capacity of 54 ounces.

G-1819 At right, Blown Pitcher with capacity of 80 ounces.

G-1489 At left, Pressed Ice-Lip Pitcher with capacity of 54 ounces.

Green kitchenware from 1930 company catalog

G-3025 At right, Pressed Pitcher with capacity of 44 ounces.

G-3026 At left, Pressed Pitcher with capacity of 41 ounces.

G-13025 At left, Pressed Pitcher with capacity of 44 ounces.

G-1933 At right, Pressed Ice-Lip Pitcher with capacity of 44 ounces.

G-1816 Blown Pitcher with a capacity of 80 ounces.

1821 Above, Wine Decanter, capacity 32 ounces. Shown with 1881 Stopper at the side.

1820 Right, Wine Decanter, capacity 16 ounces. Shown with 1881 Stopper at the side.

Green kitchenware from 1930 catalog

G-1049 Coaster, 3⅞ inches; scalloped edge adds to its attractions and the ridges in the bottom prevent the drinking glass from clinging to it. This coaster also makes an ideal ash tray.

G-1155 5-inch three-compartment candy tray.

G-703 Coaster, 3⅜ inches, made with ridges to prevent glass from clinging to it.

G-K-865 Wine Decanter, capacity 32 ounces. Shown with G-K-945 Stopper at the side.

G-3036 At left, 4 ounce Sherbet.

G-1883 Above, 3¾ ounce Sherbet.

G-3051 At right, 5½ ounce Sherbet.

1 G-766 Above at left, a 7 inch Nappy.

2 G-767 Above at right, an 8 inch Nappy.

3 G-765 Right, top of column, 6 inch Nappy.

4 G-764 Right, second from top, 5 inch Nappy.

5 G-763 Right, bottom of column, 4 inch Nappy.

REST-WELL—Mixing Bowl Set, embodying the new rolled edge and self-balancing features. From top to bottom the numbers and sizes are as follows:

G-1573	diameter 5½ inches
G-1574	diameter 6½ inches
G-1575	diameter 7½ inches
G-1576	diameter 8½ inches
G-1577	diameter 9½ inches

Kitchenware from 1930 company catalog

G-751 At right, Beater Bowl. An ideal Beater and Measuring Bowl, with accurate graduations in ounces, fractional cups, and pint.

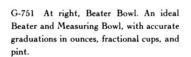

G-2013—G-2013½ At left, Oblong Covered Butter, with two handy grips.

G-759—G-759½ At left, Round Refrigerator Bowl with Knob Cover. Diameter 5¾ inches. Made so it can be used individually or in sets.

G-780—G-752½ At right, High Refrigerator Bowl with Flat Cover. Diameter 5¾ inches. Made to be used individually or in sets.

G-759—G-752½ At right, Round Refrigerator Bowl with Flat Cover. Diameter 5¾ inches. Made so it can be used individually or in sets.

G-2015—G-2015½ Oblong Refrigerator Bowl with Handy Grips and Flat Cover, 4½ inches wide by 5 inches long. Made to be used individually or in sets.

GREEN OR CRYSTAL GLASS.

Kitchenware from 1930 company catalog

G-K-345—G-796½ Utility Jar, complete with glass cover. Capacity 32 ounces.

G-K-802 Oil Bottle or Vinegar Cruet, capacity 8 ounces. Fancy peg stopper in crystal glass.

G-1095 Mixing Bowl with Lip. The diameter is 7 inches.

G-K-866 Syrup Pitcher complete with tin top. Capacity is 11 ounces.

G-3043 At left, Measuring Pitcher with 32 ounce capacity. Raised outstanding graduations in cups, ounces and fractional pints.

G-175 At right, Lemon Reamer. This is a solid reamer, without perforations. Made with protector to withhold seeds, and also handy-grip handle.

G-2954 left, Perforated Reamer.

G-3043—G-2954 right, Reamer Set. Raised outstanding graduations in cups, ounces and fractional pints. The reamer is perforated.

G-72 At left, Orange Reamer. A solid reamer, without perforations. Made with protector to withhold seeds, and also handy-grip handle.

Kitchenware from 1930 company catalog

G-1491 Salt and G-1491 Pepper. Each is 4½ inches high.

G-1102 At left, Crimped Top Vase, 6¾ inches high.

G-1950 Below, left, 5½ ounce Egg Cup.

G-3027 Below, right, Pitcher, capacity 19½ ounces.

G-1491 Sugar and G-1491 Flour. Each is 4½ inches high.

9778-9778½—¼ lb. Butter & Cover—**C-G-P**

9781-9781½—1 lb. Butter & Cover—**C-G-P**

9781½-9782—Ref. Jar & Cover **C-G-P**

9779-9779½—4 x 4 in. Sq. Ref. Jar & Cover—**C-G-P**

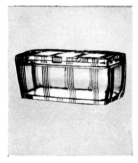

9780-9780½—4 x 8 in. Oblong Ref. Jar & Cover—**C-G-P**

9783-9783½—8 x 8 in. Sq. Ref. Jar & Cover—**C-G-P**

9835-9835½—5⅛ in. Round Ref. Bowl & Cover—**C-G**

9837—32 oz. 1-qt. bottle with dbl. shell black metal top—**C-G**

9838—64 oz. 2-qt. bottle with dbl. shell black metal top—**C-G**

9839—Lemon Reamer **C-G**

9840—Orange Reamer **C-G**

9855—Creamer **C-G**

9856-9856½—Sugar & Cover **C-G**

9836—54 oz. Jug—Ice Lip **C**

9889—9 oz. Tumbler **C**

9873—6½ in. Mixing Bowl **C-G**

COLOR CODE: C-CRYSTAL; G-GREEN; P-PINK; B-BLUE

CRISSCROSS *(#287 Book 1); some pieces also made in Ritz blue; 1938 catalog.*

1709—9 oz. Table Tumbler
Light Weight—**C-P**

1876—54 oz. Pressed Water
Pitcher—Ice Lip—**C-G-P**

372—9 oz. Table Tumbler
Light Weight—**C-P**

9526—9 oz. Table Tumbler
Light Weight—**C-P**

9937—80 oz. Blown Water
Pitcher—Tilt Style—**C-P**

485—40 oz. Blown Water
Pitcher—Tilt Style—**C-P**

486—80 oz. Blown Water
Pitcher—Tilt Style—**C-P**

367—70 oz. Blown Water

9939—9 oz. Table Tumbler
Light Weight—**C-P**

9869—9 oz. Table Tumbler
Light Weight—**C-P**

9870—80 oz. Blown Water
Pitcher—Ice Lip—**C-P**

9908—80 oz. Blown Water
Pitcher—Ice Lip—**C**

*Hazel-Atlas items this page, made variously in pink, green,
Ritz blue, or crystal, are reprinted from company catalogs
dating from 1936 to 1939.*

9878—¾ oz. Salt & Pepper
Molded Ruby Tops—**C**

311—12 oz. Ice Tea
Heavy Weight—**C-P**

9891—20 oz. Milk Pitcher
C-P

Hazel-Atlas items this page selected for reprint from 1936-1939 company catalogs. Most were made in pink, green, and crystal; some in Ritz blue.

9776—12 oz. Bulged Tumbler Beaded Edge—**C**

9585—5 oz. Georgian Tumbler **C-P**

1877—9 oz. Georgian Tumbler **J-P**

9820—9 oz. Georgian Tumbler **C-P**

1564—9 oz. Table Tumbler

1552—9 oz. Table Tumbler

232—6½ in. Round Divided Dish—**C-P**

248—6¼ in. Square Candy Dish—**C-P**

254—8 in. Handled Olive Dish—**C-P**

259—7 in. 3 sided Bon-bon **C-P**

1533—¾ oz. Salt & Pepper Shkrs. Nickel Pltd. Brass Tops—**C-G-P**

K-966/S—¾ oz. Salt & Pepper Shakers—Cast Metal Tops—**C**

K-477/8—⅞ oz. Salt & Pepper Shkrs.-Ch. Pltd. Brass Tops—**C-G**

3530—1 oz. Salt & Pepper Sh Nickel Pltd. Brass Tops—**G**

263—7 in. Mint Tray **C-P**

264—7 in. Fan-shaped Nut Dish—**C-P**

572—7 in. Three Partition Dish—**C-P**

573—6¾ in. Round Divided Dish—**C-P**

1875—1¼ oz. Salt & Pepper Shakers—Cast Metal Tops—**C**

K-491/2—1⅝ oz. Salt & Pepper Shakers—Alum. Tops—**C-G**

K-468/2—2 oz. Salt & Pepper Shakers—Alum. Tops—**C-G**

K-474/2—2 oz. Salt & Pepper Shakers—Alum. Tops—**C**

574—6 in. Square Candy Dish—**C-P**

575—7 in. Round Tray **C-P**

576—8½ in. Handled Olive Dish—**C-P**

577—6 in. Handled Preserve Tray—**C-P**

K-488/2—2½ oz. Salt & Pepper Shakers—Alum. Tops—**C**

9629—2¼ oz. Salt & Pepper Shakers—Alum. Tops—**C-G**

K-472/5—2½ oz. Salt & Pepper Shakers—Cast Metal Tops—**C**

9833—1 oz. Salt & Pepper Shakers, Black Molded Cap—

757½—4 in. Ash Tray **C-G**

9785—4¼ in. Ash Tray **C-B**

9786—4¼ in. Ash Tray **C**

788—5 in. Ash Tray **C-G**

K-422—4 oz. Oval Nurser—

K-410—8 oz. Oval Nurser—

K-413—8 oz. Round Nurser—

K-970—8 oz. Round Nurser

EWPORT

his pattern was being made in the mid-30s in Platonite, pink, Ritz blue, and Burgundy. Later colors such as pink, lue, green, yellow and orange were fired-on to opaque white NEWPORT. Photographed at right: 8¼" bowl; ¼" nappy; cup & saucer; ugar & creamer; sherbet ream soup; 4½" tumbler; ½" luncheon plate; salt pepper; 11¾" platter. Other pieces not shown: " sherbet plate; 11½" andwich plate; 5½" nappy.

WHITE SHIP DECORATED BLUE TUMBLERS AND JUGS

Light pressed blue glass

5 OUNCE FRUIT JUICE
52X-9591B—Dec. 420—12   Doz.
doz. in carton, 55 lbs......... .35

9 OZ. TABLE TUMBLERS
52X-9596B—Dec. 420—12   Doz.
doz. in carton, 62 lbs......... .37

10 OUNCE TALL TABLE TUMBLERS
52X-1568B—Dec. 420—6 doz.   Doz.
in carton, 37 lbs............. .40

12 OUNCE ICED TEAS
52X-1569B—Dec. 420—8 doz.   Doz.
in carton, 54 lbs............. .52

80 OZ. ICE-LIPPED JUGS
52X-1818B—Dec. 420—1 doz.   Doz.
in carton, 42 lbs........... 2.00

"X DESIGN" (#165 Book 1) *butterdish and candy jar;* COLONY 4½" *tumbler,* 6½" *jug; plain salt & pepper marked HA in bottom.*

WHITE SHIP
DECORATIONS ON BLUE
from 1938 catalog
(#203 Book 1)

TOP ROW PHOTO AT RIGHT: *WHITE SHIP cocktail mixer & stirrer;* ROLY POLY *tumbler;* WHITE SHIP *whiskey tumbler; ashtray w/metal sail; ice tub;* AFGHAN & SCOTTIE DOG

tumbler; POLO *tumbler.* **BOTTOM ROW:** *WHITE SHIP cocktail shaker and plate;* ANGEL FISH *cocktail shaker;* WINDMILL *cocktail shaker and tumbler; ice bowl in metal holder w/tongs (#196 Book I).*

"FLORAL STERLING"

This black luncheon set, signed "Sterling" on flower leaf, was made early 30s. Includes 8" plate, cup & saucer, cream & sugar, salt & pepper, candlesticks, sherbet, and sherbet plate.

JINGLE BELLS *Punch Set, 9" bowl and punch cups, red and green trim.* "WINTER SCENE" *Mug.* "INDIAN" *Mug, fired-on mulberry color.* HOPALONG CASSIDY *Mugs, green, red, and black trim.* TOM & JERRY *Set, 9" bowl and punch cups, red and green trim. Made in opaque white in 40s; all marked HA.*

"DUTCH" *Cookie Jar, 7½" high, fired-on white and blue.* "DUTCH" *Kitchen shakers.* EGG NOG *Set, 9¾" bowl and punch cups, red and green trim. This group not marked, but strongly believed to be Hazel-Atlas.*

126

Forget-Me-Not
FLORAL PATTERN

Pure white, hard-bodied glass of even texture, made under a new formula. Exceptionally strong and tough . . . will not craze . . . will withstand severe temperature changes.

Dutch Design

MIXING BOWLS
5, 6, 7, 8, 9 inch

OVIDE CUPS AND SAUCERS

VEGETABLE BOWLS

ST. DENIS CUPS AND SAUCERS

PLATTERS

6" COVERED REFRIGERATOR JARS

5" COVERED UTILITY BOWLS

SHAKERS

"LOONEY TUNES" *Infant's Ware*

9 IN. DINNER PLATES

CREAMERS

0-3211—Deep Plate

0-3421—Divided Plate

0-3404—Milk Mug

7 IN. SALAD PLATES

SUGARS

PLATONITE *from 1938 catalog*
All comes decorated red or blue

0-3422—Cereal Bowl

NAPPIES

Heisey

After many years in the trade A. H. Heisey in 1893 finally struck up furnaces of his own, and the august name has resounded ever since.

The factory was built in Newark, Ohio and here over a span of fifty years a body of handmade glassware among the most popular ever known in this country was put together.

It wasn't the kinds of wares made by Heisey—blown and pressed tableware, stemware, then dinnerware; plain, cut or etched—that made it remarkable, or even its color, which came to be emphasized at Heisey as it did at all houses during that period, and in essentially the same hues. In fact, to all outward appearances it would be difficult to tell a Heisey piece from a row of other high grade pieces of its day, so well does the Heisey concept fit into its time.

Yet the differences are there—in the quality of the glass metal itself, purer in composition than most others, and in the workmanship of the better designers and craftsmen. And that is where the finished piece stands: in company with a very few other hand houses, and above the rest.

Production is limited at a hand factory compared to factories with automatic methods, and handmade glassware is necessarily more expensive. But because of a highly successful advertising in major magazines during the 20s Heisey became one of the best-known of the hand houses, and consequently one of the largest. Much glass was sold during the era, and collectors find a great deal of it today compared to the incidence of most other hand wares.

The Heisey doors closed in 1956, and since that year its wares have been hunted and prized by thousands of admirers. The molds went to Imperial Glass Corporation and some are being used today.

We are lucky to have had several fine researchers in this field in past years, and your attention is drawn to these publications.[*] In them most all Heisey patterns, dates and colors are catalogued, and this chapter here, with its examples of colored Heisey only, primarily serves to fit this company's color era into the greater glass history of which it is so vital a part.

COLOR

Though not first, or even particularly foremost, with color during this era, Heisey must certainly be honored here as one who brought color so vividly to bear on the glass consciousness of the American consumer. Through early and prominent national advertising homemakers were exposed to the Heisey idea of glass fashion—elegant, often fancifully etched,—and colorful. The finest shop windows of the 20s displayed such Heisey colors as green, pink, and light amber in 1926 (later called Moon Gleam, Flamingo and Marigold respectively); the amethyst tint Hawthorne in 1928 and another amethyst called Alexandrite in 1930; and Sahara (yellow or topaz) in 1930. In 1937 Zircon (a light, soft blue-green) was made, and a similar shade Limelight in 1939. A dark blue called Steigel blue was also made in the 30s.

*Clarence Vogel's fine series, especially HEISEY'S ART AND COLORED GLASS (Heisey Publications, 1970); the Yeakleys' HEISEY GLASS IN COLOR (privately published, 1970); L-W Promotions' catalog reprint and price guide (1973); and Virginia McLean's HEISEY GLASSWARE (privately published, 1967) are some.

More than a dozen full-page, color ads like this appeared in prominant national magazines 1928-2:

GLASS SECRETS

A gift esteemed since Imperial Rome

DECEMBER in Rome when the gods held sway. It is the festival of Saturn, the time of gift-giving. A patrician youth seeks to speak his devotion with a gift of rare esteem . . . a beautifully wrought bottle, delicate in shape . . . with a heart and a message of love engraved on its tinted surface. A gift of glass, a triumph of the glassworker's art!

·◄ ▷·

Across the sea and over toilsome mountain roads went the Ancient Romans in search of the wondrous secret of molding glass. This secret Roman craftsmen carried to such heights that they were heralded by antiquity as the great masters of their art. They discovered many new forms and uses for glass.

Their surprising accomplishments were rewarded by a far-flung vogue of glassware. Nero exulted in a vast collection of it. The banquet tables of the wealthy gleamed and sparkled with it. Imperial Rome thought of glass as worthy of the finest uses; as a gift of rare excellence.

·◄ ▷·

This rich heritage is yours. In America today thousands turn to glassware as the gift supreme . . . to them it whispers a message deep with affection.

And from the glowing furnaces at Newark there come exquisite creations that you can be proud to give . . . that you would rejoice to receive.

Delightful in enchanting colors, is this glassware by Heisey. There are resplendent offerings in Moon Gleam, the glorious green . . . in the elusive, rosy tints of Flamingo . . . as well as in the clear, brilliant crystal.

Goblets, glasses, plates, vases, comports, bowls, candlesticks . . . complete table services . . . what an array of magic beauty there is in Heisey's Glassware for those who wish to choose gifts fittingly expressive of sentiment! They can be found at leading stores. By the ◈ symbol of quality you will know them.

A GIFT SET IN HEISEY'S MOON GLEAM. ODD PIECES, OR COMPLETE TABLE SERVICES, IN DAINTY COLORS, MAKE DELIGHTFUL YULETIDE REMEMBRANCES. YOU GIVE THE BEST WHEN YOU GIVE HEISEY'S GLASSWARE.

A beautiful booklet in colors, "Gifts of Glassware," is gladly sent on request. You will welcome it for its many wise gift suggestions.

A. H. HEISEY & COMPANY
301 Oakwood Ave., Newark, Ohio

HEISEY'S
GLASSWARE ◆ *for your Table*

*Reprinted here are trade journal reports
on new Heisey lines for 1929.*

 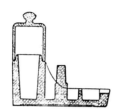

Patent design for combination cigarette holder and ashtray granted to Robert C. Irwin, Kansas City, Mo., assignor to A. H. Heisey & Co., Newark O., for a term of 14 years. Design filed November 19, 1928.

A. H. Heisey & Co., Newark, O., presents to the trade among its new items for 1929, this interesting study in art moderne. The new pattern is characterized by the utmost simplicity and is modeled along the pyramidial lines so alluring to the designer of the modernistic.

Summer weather turns the attention of housewives to table glassware and a pattern as attractive as this is sure to give them that "urge to buy." The pieces illustrated, an optic

On display in the New York salesrooms of A. H. Heisey & Co., 200 Fifth avenue, is to be found a full line of diamond optic tableware as is illustrated here. The eight-inch plate, cup

goblet, saucer champagne, sherbert, and eight-inch plate are part of a full line in this pattern, to be seen in the display rooms of A. H. Heisey & Co., 200 Fifth avenue, New York. The pieces may be had in crystal, green or rose.

and saucer and cream soup are shown here, and the line is known as No. 1182. This line may be had in the beautiful shades of rose or green, and also is to be had in crystal.

A full line in this attractive diamond optic table glassware and stemware pattern is to be found in the display rooms of

The middle vase is No. 4204 and the tall vase is No. 3359. The pieces may be had in green, rose or crystal. These items,

A. H. Heisey & Co. in New York. The pattern is known as No. 3362. Illustrated are the goblet, parfait, saucer champagne and jug. The line comes in rose, green or crystal.

as well as others in the same pattern, may be seen in the New York display rooms of the company at 200 Fifth ave.

People are thinking *Early American*

THUMB PRINT

Fashion has swung back to Early American glass . . . people are thinking of it . . . the Washington celebrations will increase its popularity . . . the vogue for Colonial interiors creates a demand for it.

To be in the current of the times, it will pay you to feature the outstanding Early American designs achieved by Heisey, the Thumb Print and Scroll patterns. A wide assortment of items is available in both, and your customers will quickly be attracted to them, in clear crystal, Moon Gleam green, Flamingo rose or Sahara golden yellow.

Show this glass with whatever Washington displays you will have during the year. Arrange attractive tables or other exhibits with it. We will gladly assist you in any way we can.

A. H. HEISEY & COMPANY
NEWARK, OHIO

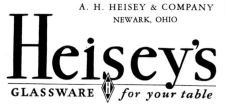

Heisey's
GLASSWARE *for your table*

Heisey's Early American No. 1404 Thumb Print design, adapted from Sandwich glass, of which we own many original models. The items shown are, Plate, Footed Tumbler, Goblet, Soda and Footed Ice Tea. A variety of other pieces supplied.

**EARLY
AMERICAN
SCROLL**

Here is the interesting No. 1405 Early American Scroll design by Heisey. Illustrated are the following items . . . Sherbet, *Saucer Champagne, Goblet, Plate, 10-Ounce Soda, 8-Ounce Soda, 5-Ounce Soda. A small part only of this line.*

from 1932 advertisement

The trademark was often, but not always, used in the colored glass of this era.

More THUMB PRINT pieces from a 1931 trade journal feature

Striking  the Chord

of customer response

T HE desire for beauty, and the impulse to admire and to possess that which is artistically pleasing, is the human chord which Heisey's Glassware so surely strikes. The customer's decision to own is a response to design that is born of leadership and high artistry. It is a response to the brilliance of exquisite crystal or delicate coloring and to the fine quality so evident in Heisey creations. Because Heisey's Glassware is a happy interpretation of the public's desires and because magazines are carrying the story of it into millions of homes, you are assured of popular demand for the Heisey's Glassware on your shelves.

A. H. HEISEY & COMPANY
Newark, Ohio

—1929 advertisement

ACHIEVEMENT

W/HEN the new colors and the new designs brought out by Heisey meet with such enthusiastic reception by the trade and your customers, we are led to believe achievement is again written large on our efforts. The new No. 1401 pattern, seen in the plates and bowls illustrated here, is an achievement in high quality pressed ware. With its lily petal motif and charming shapes, it fulfills public demand for gracious glass at a modest price. It is especially distinctive in the amethyst glow of the new Alexandrite color (the only amethyst tint which is brilliant under artificial light) and it is a beautiful line in the new Sahara golden yellow, as well as in the popular Flamingo and Moon Gleam tints. Complete table services are offered in these colors and crystal.

A. H. HEISEY & CO.,
Newark, Ohio.

At the left, the items illustrated are: No. 1401 plates and celery tray, No. 4164 jug, No. 3381 footed sodas. Below are these items in the new 1401 design: Flower bowl, salt, mint, mayonnaise and individual nut.

Patent applied for No. 1401 pattern.

MAY, 1930

—1930 advertisement

SATURN
—1937 trade feature

The salad bowl and platter shown directly above are in A. H. Heisey & Co.'s "Saturn" design, and it is available either in crystal or in Heisey's newest color—the soft pale green of the sea on a cloudy day. This color has been named "Zircon," and it is being brought out in all of the many items in the "Saturn" design—vases, bubble balls, plates, platters, both pressed and blown stemware, liquor glassware, and a full line of buffet pieces.

Hocking / Anchor Hocking

Hocking Glass Company left a stellar string of collectible patterns throughout the Depression Era, and is today one of the most eminent names in machine-pressed, mold-etched colored glassware of this period.

The company began at Lancaster Ohio in 1905 making small wares largely by hand, and by the mid-20s were advertising "tableware, plain and decorated; tumblers, jellies, lamp chimneys and lantern globes, opal ware, specialties and novelties". About this time too the enterprising firm was perfecting its own mechanics for making masses of low-priced tableware to meet the growing national demand, and soon "two-for-a-nickle" tumblers (half the pre-automation cost) were being marched off assembly lines. In 1928 the first automatic pressed tableware line was made in green, and the great mold-etched dinnerware lines so familiar to collectors today were soon to follow in quantity.

In the 20s the company acquired interests in other glass firms and entered the lucrative new container business; Hocking subsidiaries claim the first glass baby food jars and no deposit, no return beer bottles in the early 30s. By the time it merged with the Anchor Cap and Closure Corporation of Long Island City, New York (a major manufacturer of containers) in 1937 it was one of the country's leaders in machine-made glass tableware and containers.

Among the numerous glass houses assumed by Hocking in the early years were the Lancaster Glass Company, Standard Glass Company, and Monongah Glass Company. Wares by these firms can be seen in respective chapters of this book.

After the merger, the now Anchor Hocking Glass Corporation continued to expand its interests and ideas. New glass products were developed and even the plastics field was broached. In 1969 the name was modified to Anchor Hocking Corporation to allow its more diversified status.

At present the company operates some twenty plants, exports glass to a huge foreign market, and bills itself as "the world's largest manufacturer of glass tableware".

COLOR

Hocking was distinguished among machine houses for its color. Green, amber, blue and canary were being shown in occasional pieces in the mid-20s, and in 1926 trade journals find remarkable "this new shade 'Rose' in pressed glass, one of the sensations of the Pittsburgh Exhibit!" (Pink was first called Rose, then Flamingo, and sometimes Cerise until the color was discontinued in 1942.)

Topaz first appeared in 1928. Another blue, the blue of Mayfair, was apparently developed about 1930; medium in color, it was called simply 'blue'. The opaque white, which Hocking called Vitrock, was shown in a tableware line and kitchen items in 1932 and continued for several years.

By 1939 the passion for red glass was blooming, and the just-formed Anchor Hocking introduced as its first color its own Royal Ruby, the name referring to color only. This red, one of the most popular on the glass market of this time, was made on into the 40s, 50s, and even 60s. It was the largest production of automatic tableware in ruby by any company. In the 50s, many of the molds used for Royal Ruby were also used to make Anchor Hocking's Forest Green.

Still another blue was developed in 1940 for the Fire King line of kitchen and tableware, and this was also the first year Ivory was made. In 1942 the opalescent hobnail called Moonstone was introduced. Most other Hocking colors had faded out of the lines by 1940.

BOOK 1 UPDATE

The most important Hocking patterns from the Depression Era have already been presented in full in Book I, and are listed here again only to update where necessary. This update begins immediately below; the order of the listing is based on original date of issuance.

In the second part of this chapter, then, Hocking patterns not already covered in Book I (or perhaps only mentioned in the numbered section of that book) will be introduced to you.

REMEMBER: The Hocking trademark was rarely used in glass, and the trademark born of the 1938 Anchor-Hocking union appears only somewhat more frequently.

BLOCK OPTIC

The green with gold rim reprinted here was made about 1929. What we called a 10½" platter in Book I is actually a 10" sandwich plate. There is no record of a round BLOCK OPTIC butterdish, only the oblong one.

SPIRAL

Early blown water sets in green and crystal are pictured below. Also, in the center of the Block Optic reprint at right is the SPIRAL candy dish. (This same piece with a hole in its lid was sold as a preserve.)

THE HOCKING GLASS CO., LANCASTER, OHIO

GREEN AND GOLD LINE

G 904/11   G 905/11   G 903/11   G 901/11   G 906/11   G 909/11

G 930/11 Wine   G 934/11 Sundae   G 942/11 Goblet   G 940/11-8 in. Salad Plate

G 999/11 Cup   G 980/11 Ftd. Wine   G 981/11 Ftd. Tumbler   G 988/11 Ftd. Ice Tea   G 933/11 Sherbet
G 929/11-6 in. Plate   G 929/11-6 in. Plate

GREEN WARE

G 947 S Sugar   G 947 C Cream   G 999/1 Cup   G 920/3 Sherbet
                                G 999/2-6 in. Plate   G 999/2-6 in. Plate
                                (G 999/1/2 Cup & Saucer)   (G 920/3/2 Sherbet & Plate Set)

G 993 Candy Jar & Cover   G 90 Candy Jar & Cover   G 990 Candy Jar & Cover

G 82 R.T. Shaker   G 82 R.T. Caster Set   G 929-6 in. Salad Plate   G 940-8 in. Salad Plate

OUR "HOSTESS" ICED TEA SET

for serving

WATER, LEMONADE or ICED TEA

We offer in this iced tea set a most outstanding value. There are six ten ounce iced tea glasses and one 54-ounce pitcher in the set.

BLOCK OPTIC water set in green as shown in early brochure.

THE "IDEAL" FRUIT JUICE SET

A PRACTICAL HOUSEHOLD ARTICLE

OUR Fruit Juice Set is an item that can be used daily in the household. It consists of:

One 32-ounce Graduated Measuring Pitcher equipped with a Fruit Juice Reamer which also serves as a cover. This Reamer is especially constructed so as to permit the fruit juice to pass thru into the Pitcher but it very effectively holds back the pulp and seeds. Six Fruit Juice Glasses of 5-oz. capacity, just the right size for serving orange, sauer-kraut or tomato juice complete the set.

shipment 24 sets--100 lbs.

THE **HOCKING**
GLASS CO.
LANCASTER, OHIO

BLOCK OPTIC juice set in green as shown in early brochure.

PRINCESS

You may find green with gold rim, jugs with rope borders, and more pieces in topaz (9" octagonal bowl, 9½" orange or flower bowl). New to the listing is the 7½" relish without partitions (shown below with the ashtray and coaster). A few blue pieces have been found.

RING

Records show this early pattern still being made in 1933. Pieces have been found in pink, blue, crystal with different combinations of black, orange, red, yellow, blue or green stripes. See reprint for additional pieces.

1304 - 1½ OZ. 1362 - 3 OZ. 1303 - 5 OZ. 1301 - 9 OZ. 1306 - 10 OZ.

1382 - 3 OZ. 1381 - 10 OZ. 1388 - 14 OZ. 1334 HIGH SHERBET 1342 FTD. GOBLET

1379 CUP 1329 SAUCER 1353 SUGAR 1353 CREAMER 1329 - 6" PLATE

1372 - ICE BUCKET 1354 - 54 OZ. JUG 1302 DECANTER WITH GRD. STOPPER *1352 COCKTAIL SHAKER AL. TOP

1350 - 11" SANDWICH PLATE 1321 VASE 1340 - 8" PLATE

1380/1 - 9 PIECE
REFRESHMENT SET

COMPOSITION

ONE 80 OZ. JUG
EIGHT 10 OZ. TUMBLERS

EACH SET PACKED IN AN INDIVIDUAL CARTON
WEIGHT 8 LBS.

1300/13 - 10 PIECE
COCKTAIL SET

COMPOSITION

EIGHT COCKTAIL GLASSES
ONE COCKTAIL SHAKER
ONE ICE BUCKET

PACKED INDIVIDUALLY - WEIGHT 5 LBS. EACH

No. 1300/211—10 piece Cocktail Set

STYLISH PATTERN . . .

Our famous "Ring" design, known and appreciated everywhere for its extraordinary brilliance and sparkle. Each piece is artistic and graceful in shape. The footed cocktails have "Plain Feet", a notable improvement over the old style footed glasses.

No. 1300/211-10 Pce. Cocktail Set

Eight No. 1332 — 3½ Oz. Ftd. Cocktails
One No. 1349 — 32 Oz. Cocktail Shaker
One No. 1350 — 11 In. Plate

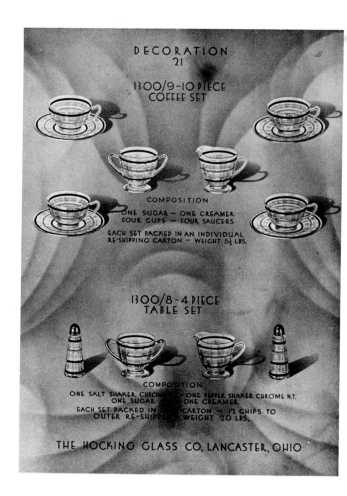

DECORATION 21

1300/9-10 PIECE COFFEE SET

COMPOSITION

ONE SUGAR — ONE CREAMER
FOUR CUPS — FOUR SAUCERS

EACH SET PACKED IN AN INDIVIDUAL
RE-SHIPPING CARTON — WEIGHT 5¼ LBS.

1300/8-4 PIECE TABLE SET

COMPOSITION

ONE SALT SHAKER CHROME N.T. — ONE PEPPER SHAKER CHROME N.T.
ONE SUGAR — ONE CREAMER
EACH SET PACKED IN ONE CARTON — 12 CHIPS TO
OUTER RE-SHIPPER — WEIGHT 20 LBS.

THE HOCKING GLASS CO., LANCASTER, OHIO

More RING pieces from early 30s catalog.

DECORATION 21

1300/15-11 PIECE ICE TEA and SANDWICH SET

COMPOSITION

EIGHT FOOTED ICE TEAS — ONE 80 OZ. JUG
ONE ICE BUCKET — ONE SANDWICH TRAY
PACKED INDIVIDUALLY — WEIGHT 14½ LBS.

THE HOCKING GLASS CO., LANCASTER OHIO

1300/6-17 PIECE LUNCHEON SET

DECOR 2

COMPOSITION

FOUR 8" PLATES
FOUR HIGH SHERBETS
FOUR FOOTED TUMBLERS
FOUR SHERBET PLATES
ONE SANDWICH TRAY

PACKED INDIVIDUALLY — WEIGHT 12½ LBS.

CAMEO

Additional pieces in green are: milk pitcher 5¾", vase 5¾", domino tray 7" with ring (found in pink without ring), sandwich server with center handle. In crystal, additional pieces are: 4½" nappy, 7" plate, cocktail shaker.

The 3¼" footed juice holds 3 oz, not 5. Two styles sherbet exist; they look the same size but one is thick with mold-etched design, 3" tall (this is the more common) and the other is 3¼" tall and thin blown like the tall sherbet.

The CAMEO second-style cup and indented saucer; domino tray; lid to ?, square plate; milk pitcher; and 5¾" vase.

"ROULETTE"

Also made in crystal.

MAYFAIR

Experimental colors: several different pieces have been found in topaz, and cups, saucers, plates, jugs, tumblers, bowls, relishes, and creams and sugars have been found in green. Obviously a small issue was made at some point!

Lamp shades have been discovered in pink and crystal, usually frosted; made of the 12" flared-out bowl with a hole.

In Hocking's "morgue"—the sample room for old wares—are stored away such pieces as the 8" footed vase in green (its rim is a 1" outward crimp); a second-style pink salt shake (it's round, footed, 4" tall); a 5¼" pink claret; and a 3¾" pink wine. A 9", 3-legged console bowl was also made.

Other pieces in addition to Book I are shown here.

The MAYFAIR jug; sugar and cover; and whiskey.

LACE EDGE

We sometimes call the preserve and cover a butterdish, but it isn't. The platter and relish platter actually measure 12¾" and not 13¾". Shown is the fish bowl as originally advertised in sizes of ½-, 1- and 2-gallons in crystal only.

MISS AMERICA

Old records list the cereal or fruit bowl as 5½", but when I measure it I get 6¼" every time! The butterdish, remember, is this same piece exactly. And the same bowl in crystal was once advertised and sold with a metal cover (shown); it was called a "Glass Candy Dish", not a butter and cover.

The shakers are 4¼" and not 5". Coasters are exactly like the 5¾" sherbet plate except with six raised spokes over the center motif to hold the tumbler up off the plate.

Originally catalogued only in pink, green, and crystal, pieces very occasionally turn up in Royal Ruby, Ritz Blue, light blue, and amber.

QUEEN MARY

Pictured here is the berry set (8" bowl, 4½" fruit), then the square ashtray and the QUEEN MARY punch set.

COLONIAL

The saucer and the 6½" plate are the same. Additional listings: 3-7/8" nappy; opaque white cups and saucers (saucer has a somewhat different motif).

HOBNAIL

Also comes decorated in red rims and red or black on base.

WATERFORD

A second-style sherbet, 3¾'' tall, has a scalloped top and scalloped base.

The 13½'' round sandwich tray mold was used again after 1940. It was made up into a relish set: in crystal with Royal Ruby inserts; and in Forest green with ivory inserts and with a little sauce dish in the center in 1956 (shown). The tray can also be found in satin finish. Still later, in 1959, the 10-oz, 5¼'' high goblet was issued in crystal.

—WATERFORD relish set

ROYAL RUBY

Following are shown additional pieces: punch bowl and cups, salad bowl and big plate. More ruby red pieces on page 147-148.

MANHATTAN

We find the crystal with metal trims, handles, bails, etc. Shown is the candleholder.

"FORTUNE"

Additions: Bowl, 5½'' nappy with rolled edge; tumbler, 5 oz 3½''.

"OYSTER AND PEARL"

Candlesticks with etching on base have been found.

"OLD CAFE"

Ruby cups were sold with crystal saucers.

"BUBBLE"

The Forest Green "BUBBLE" issue was in 1954, not 1937 as in Book I, and consisted of plates, cups, saucers, cereal bowls, the sugar and creamer. In 1963 pieces were made in Royal Ruby, including the pitcher and tumblers shown here. The complete set is the 64-oz lip pitcher, 16-oz ice tea, 12-oz tumbler, 9-oz old fashioned, and 6-oz fruit juice.

SANDWICH

Hocking made its first SANDWICH DESIGN berry sets in pink, and the Royal Ruby bowls, in 1939 and 1940. Because it was made in Depression-era colors, it is included here.

I find no more SANDWICH DESIGN catalogued until 1953, '54, and '55 when the company issued a complete line in crystal only. This is the showing you will find illustrated here. In 1956 all pieces were dropped except the 8½'' oval vegetable, cream and sugar (no cover) and 3-piece serving bowl set (6'', 7'', 8'') which they continued until 1959.

Then a small issue of Forest Green was made in the mid-50s. The opaque punch sets (see below) were made in 1956 (in plain Ivory or with 22 K gold trim) and again in '57 and '58. Five pieces of Forest Green and crystal (5 oz tumbler, 9 oz tumbler, 4-7/8'' nappy, custard cup and 4½'' plate) were made in the early 60s to go into cereal boxes.

In 1963 and '64 the Desert Gold line (a dark amber) was made in nine pieces, and this was the last issue made from Anchor Hocking's molds.

27 Pce. Punch Set – 22 K. Gold Trim

Anchorglass
Sandwich Design
GLASSWARE

Our Sandwich Design has been received so well during the past year that we have enlarged it to the extent shown in this folder. Homemakers all over America are intrigued with this type of glassware, doubtless because of their knowledge of the early American product in this pattern, called Sandwich Glass. This glassware was made in the town of Sandwich, Massachusetts from 1825 to 1888.

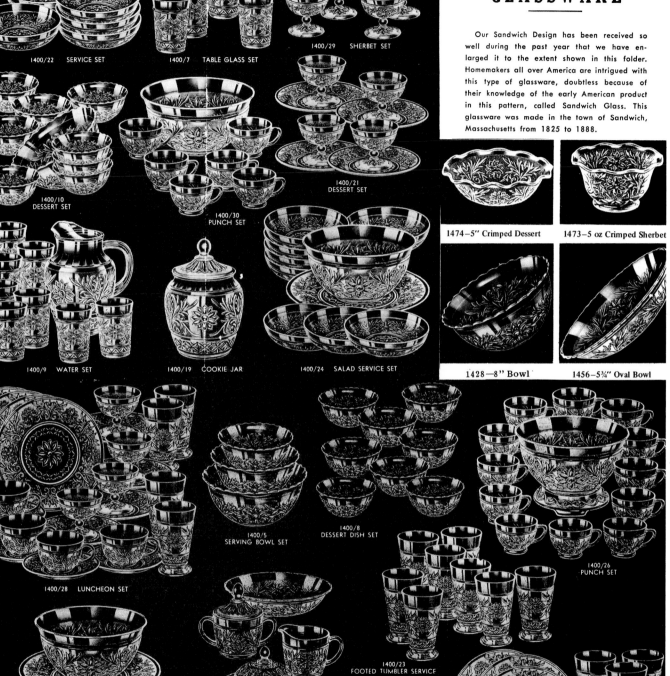

1400/22 SERVICE SET

1400/7 TABLE GLASS SET

1400/29 SHERBET SET

1400/10 DESSERT SET

1400/30 PUNCH SET

1400/21 DESSERT SET

1400/9 WATER SET

1400/19 COOKIE JAR

1400/24 SALAD SERVICE SET

1474—5" Crimped Dessert

1473—5 oz Crimped Sherbet

1428—8" Bowl

1456—5¾" Oval Bowl

1400/28 LUNCHEON SET

1400/5 SERVING BOWL SET

1400/8 DESSERT DISH SET

1400/26 PUNCH SET

1400/18 SALAD BOWL AND PLATE SET

1400/20 TABLE SET

1400/23 FOOTED TUMBLER SERVICE

1400/14 SNACK SET

1400/11 ICE LIP PITCHER

1400/27 LUNCHEON SET

Anchor Hocking's crystal SANDWICH DESIGN as shown in a company brochure.

CIRCLE

(#218 Book 1) *Jug and tumblers (below) and decanter and tumblers (right) in crystal and green; 1929 catalog.*

Miscellaneous catalog page, 1929.

Hocking's GEORGIAN

(#215 Book I) *Crystal, green; 1930 catalog.*

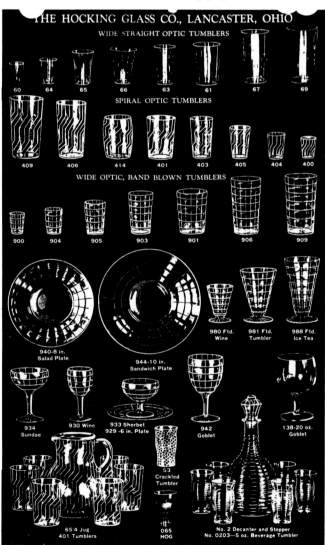

ALL PROVEN SELLERS

KITCHEN GLASSWARE

Pages from 1932 company brochure showing wares in green.

G600/12 8-PIECE BEER AND PRETZEL SET

COMPOSITION

ONE G695 - 130 OZ. PRETZEL JAR & COVER
ONE G680 - 80 OZ. JUG
SIX G636 - 12 OZ. BEER MUGS

NEW PINCH LINE

G124—1½ OZ.
BEVERAGE

G125—2½ OZ.
WINE

G123—5 OZ.
FRUIT JUICE

G126—10 OZ.
TALL TUMBLER

G128—13 OZ.
ICE TEA

G180—75 OZ. JUG

G151 COCKTAIL SHAKER
WITH ALUMINUM TOP

G102 DECANTER
WITH DROP STOPPER

THE HOCKING GLASS COMPANY, LANCASTER, OHIO

STRIPE
Applied bands of red and white

ATTRACTIVELY STRIPED GLASSWARE

ARCTIC, POLAR BEAR, CHARIOT
Applied decorations in red and white

BEVERAGE SETS IN FROSTED EFFECTS

1932 decorations on crystal from company catalog

"RING-DING"
Yellow, orange, green, red painted bands

DECORATION 88

3511-6 OZ.   3512-7 OZ.   3514-10 OZ.   3516-14 OZ.   3517-16 OZ.   92-18½ OZ.
3513-8 OZ.   3515-12 OZ.

465-7½ OZ.   64-½ OZ.   4304 1½ OZ.   4305 2½ OZ.   4302 4½ OZ.   4301 9 OZ.   4306-10 OZ.   4308-12 OZ.

33 - SHERBET   32-COCKTAIL   30 WINE   34-SAUCER   142- GOBLET
729-6" PLATE   CHAMPAGNE

182-3 OZ. COCKTAIL   181-10 OZ. TUMBLER   188- 15 OZ. ICED TEA   40-8½ PLATE

170-MIXER   7OZ. DECANTER WITH GRD. STOPPER   752-32 OZ. SHAKER   780-80 OZ.JUG-754-60 OZ.JUG

THE HOCKING GLASS CO.- LANCASTER, OHIO

"PANELLED RING-DING"
Red, yellow, black, orange, green painted bands

63-5 oz.   61-9 oz.   68-12 oz.
Fruit Juice   Tumbler   Ice Tea

181 Ftd. Tumbler   729-6 in. Plate   134 High Sherbet

188 Ftd. Ice Tea   740-8 in. Plate   142 Goblet

SHAKERS
in green and crystal

"WREN"
Shaker

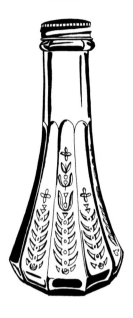

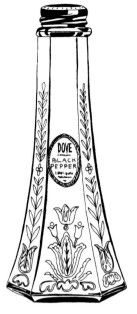

DOVE
*black pepper
from 1935 catalog*

"QUAIL"
Shaker

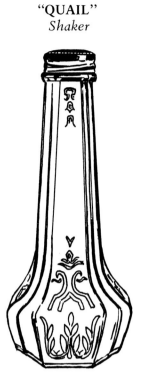

"CROW"
*Vinegar w/
cork stopper*

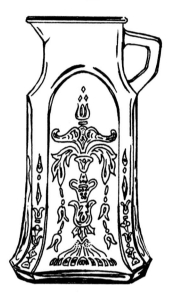

LAKE COMO

Delphinium blue decoration on Vitrock white dinnerware. Original 1935 issue included two styles of cup, saucer; 9¼" dinner plate; 7¼" bread and butter or salad plate; creamer and sugar; 9½" vegetable; 11" meat platter; salt and pepper. From 1935 catalog.

VITROCK
Tableware

(#237 Book 1)
*is "a handsome adaptation
of embossed China"
according to a
1935 catalog.*

	Cup
	Saucer
6″	Fruits
7½″	Cereal
9½″	Vegetable Bowls
11½″	Meat Platter
7¼″	Bread or Cream Soup Plate
8¾″	Luncheon Plates
9″	Soup Plates
10″	Dinner Plates
	Cream Soups
	Sugar
	Creamer
4″	Dessert

VITROCK
Kitchenware

from 1935 catalog

6½″	Mixing Bowls
7½″	" "
8½″	" "
9½″	" "
10½″	" "
11½″	" "
	Orange Reamers
	Left-over Jar and Cover
	Salt-Pepper-Sugar
	Flour and Spice
	Dripping Jar and Cover
	Egg Cups
	Ash Trays

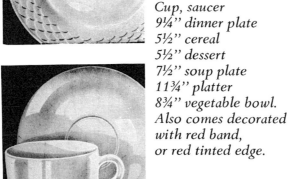

IVORY

"FISHCALE" Line
Cup, saucer
9¼" dinner plate
5½" cereal
5½" dessert
7½" soup plate
11¾" platter
8¾" vegetable bowl.
Also comes decorated
with red band,
or red tinted edge.

LEAF AND BLOSSOM DESSERT SET

FOR DESSERTS
Ice Cream, Sherbets, Puddings

FOR PLANTS
Cactus—Bulbs

Peach, yellow, green,
or blue applied color.

ST. DENIS
tableware line
comes in ivory;
undecorated, or
with red and black lines.

INFANTS' DECORATED TABLEWARE

LITTLE BO-PEEP
INFANTS WARE
decorated orange and green
on ivory: 7¾" divided plate;
5½" cereal; mug

Salt, pepper shakers
and range jar
are decorated with
black and red.

Items this page from 1940 catalog.

145

"FIRE-KING"

ROASTER

For the first time—a large double roaster, to retail at a popular low price.

B3449—10¾"x5½"
LARGE DOUBLE ROASTER
Each Roaster in Individual carton, 6 to a reshipping carton—35 lbs.
Retail—$1.00 Each

CASSEROLES KNOB COVERS

OPEN BAKERS

B3405—1 PINT
Pkd. 2 doz.—30 lbs.
Retail—25c Ea.
B3406—1 QUART
Pkd. 2 doz.—38 lbs.
Retail—35c Ea.

B3407—1½ QUART
Pkd. 2 doz.—65 lbs.
Retail—50c Ea.
B3408—2 QUART
Pkd. 2 doz.—28 lbs.
Retail—60c Ea.

B3445—1 PINT
Pkd. 2 doz.—15 lbs.
Retail—25c Ea.
B3446—1 QUART
Pkd. 2 doz.—28 lbs.
Retail—35c Ea.

B3447—1½ QUART
Pkd. 1 doz.—35 lbs.
Retail—35c Ea.
B3448—2 QUART
Pkd. 1 doz.—21 lbs.
Retail—40c Ea.

CASSEROLES PIE PLATE COVERS

PIE PLATES

B3497—1½ QUART
Pkd. 2 doz.—62 lbs.
Retail—50c Ea.

B3498—2 QUART
Pkd. 1 doz.—36 lbs.
Retail—60c Ea.

B3459—8¼"
Pkd. 4 doz.—42 lbs.
Retail—10c Ea.

B3460—9"
Pkd. 3 doz.—40 lbs.
Retail—15c Ea.

B3461—9¾"
Pkd. 2 doz.—32 lbs.
Retail—20c Ea.

CAKE PAN

A multiple-sales item! Offer to retail as a cake pan and as an outstanding small double roaster (one cake pan as a cover, one bottom), at an unheard of low price. You buy in only one packing, as Cake Pans.

For layer cakes, ginger bread, corn bread, biscuits, cobblers; an open baker for beans, macaroni and other dishes.

B3450—8¼" DEEP CAKE PAN
Pkd. 1 doz.—18 lbs.
Retail—25c per piece

DEEP LOAF PAN

UTILITY PAN

B3409—9⅛" DEEP LOAF PAN
Pkd. 2 doz.—38 lbs.
Retail—35c Ea.

B3410—10½" UTILITY PAN
Pkd. 2 doz.—44 lbs.
Retail—40c Ea.

REFRIGERATOR JARS AND COVERS

B3444—1 PINT SQUARE BAKER
B3494—4½"x5" JAR & COVER
B3499—5¼"x9¼" JAR AND COVER

FIRE-KING

Catalog reprints showing pieces of Hocking's large FIRE KING Oven Glass line in blue which was in production from 1942 to 1945. The crystal FIRE KING came later.

"FIRE-KING"

INDIVIDUAL CASSEROLE AND COVER   **DEEP PIE DISH**

B3402—10 OUNCE
Retail—10c Ea.

B3465—5¾"
Retail—10c Ea.

NURSING BOTTLES

B3464—4 OUNCE
Retail—10c Ea.
B3468—8 OUNCE
Retail—10c Ea.

PERCOLATOR TOP   **CUSTARD CUPS—INDIVIDUAL BAKERS**   **MEASURING CUP**

B5—2⅛"
Retail—5c Ea.

B3420—5 OZ. SHALLOW
Retail—5c Ea.
B3413—6 OUNCE DEEP
Retail—5c Ea.

B97—8 OUNCE
Retail—10c Ea.

"PHILBE"

A dinnerware line issued in 1940 in pink, blue, and blue with platinum trim.

8" Plate
10½" Plate
10½" Grill Plate
11-5/8" Service Plate
9" Oval Bowl
7¼" Soup
5½" Cereal
Creamer
Sugar
6½" Footed Tumbler

5½" Footed Tumbler
3½" Footed Juice
4" Tumbler
5" Tumbler

ROYAL RUBY – FOREST GREEN

Most items this page were made in both these colors, often in combination with crystal. Royal Ruby dinnerware was made in the 40s; Forest Green dinnerware in the 50s. But accessory pieces—vases, ashtrays, punch cups, etc.—in both colors were carried in Anchor-Hocking catalogs until 1967. More Forest Green items were made than are shown here.

Royal Ruby Anchorglass *
Trade-Mark

SERVA-SNACK SETS

OBLONG Serva-Snack Set • "DEMON" Cigarette Set • FAN Serva-Snack Set

★ E2200/11

★ E2279 — ★ E2229   ★ E2275 — E2267

E2237 — ★ E2241   E2277

E2247   E2253 — E2254

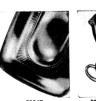

DESCRIPTION

FOREST GREEN
Anchorglass*

16 PCE. LUNCHEON SET

★ **E2200/11—16 PCE. LUNCHEON SET**
Each Set Pkd. in Ind. R/S Ctn.
—wt. 10 lbs.
COMPOSITION:
Four E2279 Cups
Four E2229 Saucers
Four E2275 Desserts
Four E2241 Plates

OPEN STOCK

★ **E2279—CUP**
Pkd. 6 doz.—wt. 29 lbs.

★ **E2229—SAUCER**
Pkd. 6 doz.—wt. 30 lbs.

★ **E2275—4¾″ DESSERT OR CEREAL**
Pkd. 6 doz.—wt. 35 lbs.

E2267—6″ SOUP
Pkd. 3 doz.—wt. 26 lbs.

E2237—6⅞″ SALAD PLATE
Pkd. 3 doz.—wt. 21 lbs.

★ **E2241—8⅜″ LUNCHEON PLATE**
Pkd. 3 doz.—wt. 39 lbs.

E2277—7⅜″ BOWL
Pkd. 2 doz.—wt. 39 lbs.

E2247—11″ PLATTER
Pkd. 1 doz.—wt. 19 lbs.

E2253—SUGAR
Pkd. 3 doz.—wt. 15 lbs.

E2254—CREAMER
Pkd. 3 doz.—wt. 14 lbs.

20 PCE. LUNCHEON SET

E2200/15—20 PCE. LUNCHEON SET
Each Set Pkd. in Ind. R/S Ctn.
—wt. 13 lbs.
COMPOSITION:
Four E2279 Cup
Four E2229 Saucer
Four E2275 Dessert
Four E2241 Plate
One E2277 Bowl
One E2247 Platter
One E2253 Sugar
One E2254 Creamer

"BOOPIE" Tumblers
9-oz, 4-oz, 3½-oz, 6-oz

WHIRLY-TWIRLY Sets
5-oz, 9-oz, 12-oz tumblers
3-qt water pitcher

"BURPLE" Dessert Set
4-5/8″, 8½″ bowls

"BIBI" 6½″ Bonbon

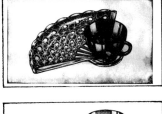

SQUARE Serva-Snack Set

FLORAL GLASSWARE
ROYAL RUBY AND FOREST GREEN

"WILSON" 4″ Ivy Ball

"HARDING" 6-3/8″ Vase

"COOLIDGE" 6-3/8″ Vase

"HOOVER" 9″ Vase

"ROOSEVELT" 3-3/4″ Vase
with 2 gold bands

15 HR. CANDLE TUMBLER

147

MORE
ANCHOR HOCKING

ROYAL RUBY

ROW 1:
"RACHAEL" *Bowl, 11"*
"MONARCH" *Tumbler,*
5-3/8"
ROYAL RUBY *Sugar &*
Cover w/hole
ROYAL RUBY *Creamer*

ROW 2: *7-oz Bottle inscribed* ROYAL RUBY ANCHOR GLASS, *3 sizes.* HOCKING HOBNAIL *Water Set, 8½" jug, 4¼" tumbler (AH's early red glass, late 30s).* HIGH POINT *Water Set, 8½", 80-oz jug, 5-, 9-, and 12-oz tumblers.*

"JANE-RAY"

Jade-ite Fire King Dinnerware was introduced in 1945, the year Jade-ite was first made, and carried until 1963. 1949 catalog.

"ALICE"

Kitchenware (see detail)
This short line (8½" plate, cup & saucer) was brought out briefly in the 40s in Jade-ite and in opaque white with blue or pink border.

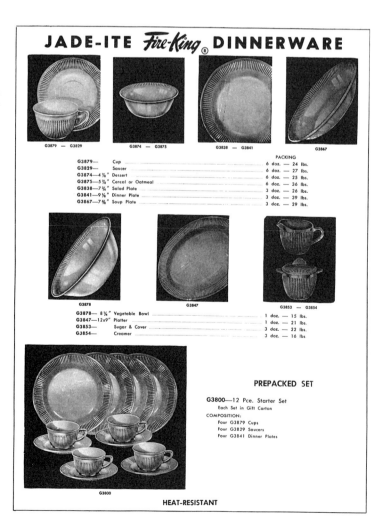

JADE-ITE *Fire-King* ® DINNERWARE

G3879 — G3829	G3874 — G3875	G3838 — G3841		G3867

		PACKING	
G3879—	Cup	6 doz. — 24 lbs.
G3829—	Saucer	6 doz. — 27 lbs.
G3874—4⅞"	Dessert	6 doz. — 25 lbs.
G3875—5⅜"	Cereal or Oatmeal	6 doz. — 36 lbs.
G3838—7¾"	Salad Plate	3 doz. — 26 lbs.
G3841—9⅛"	Dinner Plate	3 doz. — 39 lbs.
G3867—7⅝"	Soup Plate	3 doz. — 29 lbs.

G3878	G3847	G3853 — G3854

		PACKING	
G3878— 8¼"	Vegetable Bowl	1 doz. — 15 lbs.
G3847—12x9"	Platter	1 doz. — 21 lbs.
G3853—	Sugar & Cover	3 doz. — 22 lbs.
G3854—	Creamer	3 doz. — 16 lbs

PREPACKED SET

G3800—12 Pce. Starter Set
Each Set in Gift Carton
COMPOSITION:
Four G3879 Cups
Four G3829 Saucers
Four G3841 Dinner Plates

G3800

HEAT-RESISTANT

148

Huntington

Under this heading is space only to say that this Huntington, West Virginia company made lines and lines of stemware—plain, optic'ed, cut, and etched—during our era of interest. Small tableware pieces and novelties were also made. From 1928 to 1932 we find advertised green, rose, amber, amethyst, Ritz blue, topaz, black, ruby and combinations of these colors with crystal. After this date Huntington's trade journal reportage ceased, so in all probability this was another company sent by the Depression to its happy Hunting ground.

SHAPES AND DESIGNS OF MODERN APPEAL

High Grade Lead Blown Glassware, including Tumblers, Stemware, Refreshment Sets, Novelties, Vases, etc. Decorated, Cut, Etched and Iridescent ware in Crystal, Green, Amber and Rose.

SAMPLES ON DISPLAY AT

LEWIS H. SIMPSON & CO.,
17 N. Wabash Ave., Chicago, Ill.

COX & COMPANY,
120 Fifth Ave., New York, N. Y.

WILLIAM H. BUSH,
734 State St., Springfield, Mass.

E. B. HILL,
Mid-West Ter., Washington, Pa.

A. A. GRAESER,
Southern Ter., Washington, Pa.

BAKER-SMITH COMPANY,
222 Chronicle Building,
San Francisco, Calif.

BAKER-SMITH COMPANY,
608 Mutual Life Building,
Seattle, Wash.

BAKER-SMITH COMPANY,
1109 Broadway, Denver, Colo.

BAKER-SMITH COMPANY,
443 S. San Pedro St., Calo Bldg.,
Los Angeles, Calif.

HUNTINGTON TUMBLER CO.
HUNTINGTON, W. VA.

"NOVA" —1928 ad

"AVON" —1925 ad

A Happy Huntington New Year to All

Appreciative of 1929, we send our thanks and hope that 1930 will be a year of progress and prosperity for all.

For 1930, Huntington has many items of interest.

CUTTINGS, ETCHINGS, DECORATIONS
Color combinations, including
Black and Crystal
and many new things in
Green, Rose, Amber, and Crystal

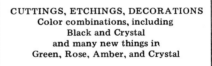

HUNTINGTON TUMBLER CO.
HUNTINGTON, W. VA.

"GRACIOUS" —1930 ad

The real test of popularity is not in claims but in how it sells. Stock the new things that the public wants and sales take care of themselves. Our new numbers are proving their selling appeal by quick turnover and continuous re-orders. A well selected assortment will prove the right move to

STIMULATE THE ENTIRE GLASSWARE SECTION

Full line of low square footed tumblers in Crystal and Colors. We Specialize in High Grade Rock Crystal Stemware, Tumblers, etc., on First Quality Lead Blanks. Full lines of Stemware, Tumblers, Jugs, Nappies, Beverage Sets, Novelties, etc., in solid colors or in combinations, Crystal, Green, Amber, Rose, Ritz Blue, Amethyst, Black and Topaz. Plain, Cut, Etched, Decorated and Engraved.

Illustrating five orange juice or tomato juice cocktail glasses. Crystal with colored decorations of lines and dots in black, blue, red, green and yellow combinations. Beverage Sets and Tumblers in the new decorations.

HUNTINGTON TUMBLER COMPANY
MANUFACTURERS
HUNTINGTON, W. VA.

LOW SQUARE FOOTED
NO. 2701—12-OUNCE

SALES REPRESENTATIVES
Cox & Co., 120 Fifth Avenue, New York, N. Y.
Martin M. Simpson & Co., Merchandise Mart, Chicago.
Baker-Smith Co., 222 Chronicle Building, San Francisco, Calif.
Baker-Smith Co., 608 Mutual Life Building, Seattle, Wash.
Baker-Smith Co., Commonwealth Building, Denver, Colo.
Baker-Smith Co., 515 Transportation Building, Los Angeles, Calif.

For the Fall and Holiday season, HUNTINGTON takes pride in presenting a most attractive new stemware design, featuring a most attractive new stem.

This is furnished for Rock Crystal or for two-tone effect in choice of two bowls, as shown. It is a complete line in lead Crystal or two-tone combinations of Green, Rose, Amber, Amethyst, Reitz Blue or Topaz with Crystal.

"DING" & **"DONG"** —1929 ad

"LIL' RASCALS"

Cocktail Sets: "SPANKY", "FARINA", "ALFALFA", "BULLSEYE", "BUCKWHEAT"

Imperial

To this day one of the country's best known hand houses, Imperial Glass Company organized in 1901 and first produced glass at the Bellaire, Ohio plant in 1904.

The firm began inconspicuously enough—early products were utilitarian wares such as hotel tumblers, jelly glasses, and pressed table items for five-and-dimes—but soon made its own distinctive mark. Imperial's big splash was color and special color effects. The brilliant "Iridescent Glass" of 1910-1920, the smash hit of teenage America, is our Carnival glass today. The "Imperial Jewels" collection started in 1916 is today's stretch glass. And the "Free Hand Ware", made from 1923-1928 by skilled artisans without molds of any kind, is collected today as art glass.

In the 20s Imperial also made "imitation cut glass" (called "Nu-Cut") in crystal and transparent colors. The lines of tableware were many and varied, with cuttings, etchings, gold trims and decorations. The luncheon set was a popular idea at the time of the Depression, and this company turned out thousands of them. Eventually, however, the competition from the machine houses during these lean years proved too much for such hand-pressed lines. Imperial went under in 1931, though it soon resurfaced as the Imperial Glass Corporation. The new management resumed production of the pressed colored lines, added some popular new patterns in anticipation of the return to crystal, and managed to rekindle its earlier prosperity.

In 1940 the company acquired Central Glass Works of Wheeling, and in 1958 the molds of both the great Cambridge Glass and A. H. Heisey Companies. In recent years Imperial has traded on its precious bank by re-issuing many of the famous old molds of these companies, some in crystal and some in modern colors. It has also re-issued many of its own original Carnival molds in new, marked, Carnival colors, to much national success. Imperial was sold to Lenox, Inc., in 1973, and continues to make attractive lines of largely hand-pressed gift and housewares for the glassbuyer of today.

COLOR

Imperial's principal Depression-era colors, pink (first called Rose Marie, then Rose), green, and amber, were on the scene by the mid-20s and prevailed right up to the 'second coming' of crystal in the 30s. Golden green, the color called "vaseline" by collectors, was advertised as early but did not last so long. Blue came out in 1926 and blue-green in 1927. Many of the etched or cut colored lines bore gold bands or decorations, and in 1929 a small assortment was offered in ivory, orchid or green glass embellished with floral decals.

In 1931 ruby and topaz were being advertised, and it was about this time too that Ritz blue and black were developed. These colors continued to make appearances throughout the 30s. Also in 1931 a new color treatment, Sea Foam, was brought to the line. This semi-transparent glass, in colors Harding blue, Moss green, and Burnt Almond, was edged with an opal effect.

Richard and Wilma Ross' IMPERIAL GLASS (Wallace-Homestead, 1971) focuses on the earlier art wares in color.

The trademarks were sometimes used in the glass during the 20s.

"TWISTED OPTIC"

Imperial's swirl was also made in Golden Green. The full line is reprinted in the catalog reprint to follow.

"DIAMOND QUILTED"

Imperial did make this pattern, listing it in Rose Marie, green, and crystal in the late 20s. Pieces in black and a medium blue were also made. The full line is reprinted in the catalog reprint to follow.

BOOK 2 PATTERNS

VIKING

A 1929 advertisement describes this cutting as VIKING by Imperial, 13 piece salad set in rose and green.

EARLY AMERICAN HOBNAIL

Imperial's hobnail as described in a 1931 advertisement. The complete line follows in catalog reprint.

A FEW NEW ITEMS IN EARLY AMERICAN

742 Flip Vase, 742 Tumbler, 742 Pitcher, 742 10" Salver, 742 Toilet Water Bottle, 742 Puff or Vanity Box and Cover.

A GAMUT OF COLORS

CRYSTAL, AMBER, BLUE, GOLDEN OPHIR, GREEN, ROSE, RUBY and BLACK. Also SEA FOAM in HARDING BLUE, MOSS GREEN, and BURNT ALMOND TINTS.

IMPERIAL GLASS CO.
BELLAIRE, OHIO

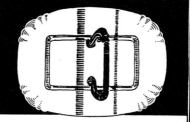
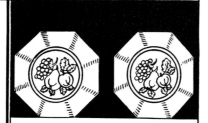

March 29, 1932.

E. W. NEWTON

BOWL OR SIMILAR ARTICLE

Original Filed Aug. 17, 1931

Fig.1

*Inventor
Earl W. Newton
By Gibson, Mann & Cot Attys.*

CAPE COD

as patented in 1932; shown in catalog reprint

1935.

E. W. NEWTON

PITCHER OR SIMILAR ARTICLE

Filed July 11, 1935

Fig.2.

Fig.1.

INVENTOR
Earl W. Newton
BY *H. G. Doolie*
ATTORNEY

"SPUN"

A later Imperial pattern, this line was made in dark red, blue-green, fired-on orange, various pastel colors and in crystal. Photographed here are the 8" plate, 2½", 5" tumblers, and the 8" jug. You may find other "SPUN" pieces, however. Note the 1935 patent at left.

152

CATALOG REPRINTS

Beginning here are selected reprints of colored glassware lines taken from Imperial catalogs dating from 1925 to 1935. Official pattern names and colors appear on the original; in some cases, names have been superimposed by me. You may find colors other than those listed.

Two major patterns from Book 1 fall in the reprint order, "TWISTED OPTIC" and "DIA-MOND QUILTED". Two numbered lines, #32 "BEADED BLOCK" and #34 "DIAMOND BLOCK", are here; others are presented for the first time.

The reprint includes some primarily crystal lines—MOUNT VERNON, MONTICELLO, CANDLEWICK, and CAPE COD—which were rarely made in color. This is the original issue shown here, so remember that these patterns were made on for many years with additional pieces added.

Open stock table glass—NO. 678 PART-CUT

Furnished in—ROSE MARIE GLASS, color 91
—IMPERIAL GREEN GLASS, color 81
—CRYSTAL GLASS

Each of the three colors is sold in open stock in quantities to suit yourself

The petals of the flowers and the centers of the hobnails in this 678 pattern are cut by hand, and in the gray finish, left by the cutter's wheel.

"D'ANGELO"

678 — 11 inch Oval Orange Bowl
678 — Candy Jar and Cover

NO. 678 PART-CUT GLASS
made in
CRYSTAL, IMPERIAL GREEN
and
ROSE MARIE GLASS

678 — 7-piece Water Set
consists of 1 pitcher and 6 table
tumblers

678 — Table Tumbler

678 — Pitcher

678 — Oval Sugar

678 — Oval Cream

678 — 7-piece Berry Set
consists of one 8¾ inch deep
salad and six 4¼ inch
berries

678 — 8¾ inch Deep Salad

678 — 4¼ inch Berry

NO. 678 PART-CUT open stock table glass
made in CRYSTAL, GREEN and ROSE MARIE

678 — 6 inch two handled Nappy

678 — 10 inch Celery Tray

678 — 10 inch Oval Vase

678 — 6 inch Tall Footed Bowl

678 — 5¾ inch one-handled Bon-Bon

678 — 6 inch Pickle Boat

153

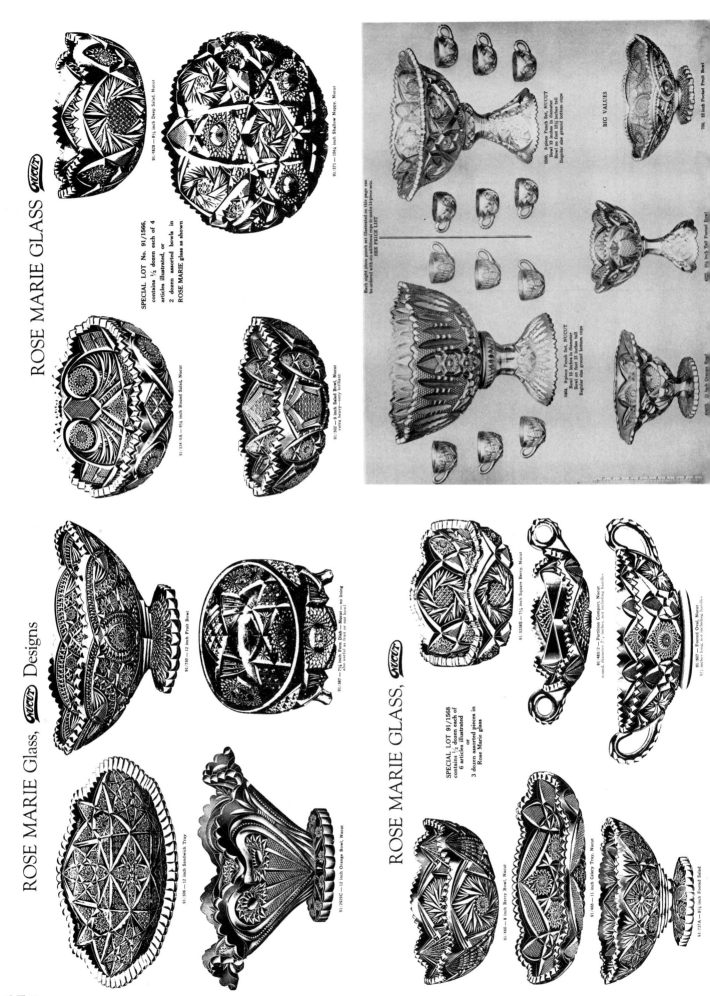

ROSE MARIE GLASS NUCUT

91/1828 — 8½ inch Deep Salad, Nucut

91/571 — 10¾ inch Shallow Nappy, Nucut

SPECIAL LOT No. 91/1566, contains ½ dozen each of 4 articles illustrated, or 2 dozen assorted bowls in ROSE MARIE glass as shown

91/534 9A — 9⅝ inch Round Salad, Nucut extra heavy—very brilliant

91/502 — 9 inch Salad Bowl, Nucut extra heavy—very brilliant

ROSE MARIE Glass, NUCUT Designs

91/587 — 7½ inch Fern Dish — Nucut — no lining also useful as fruit or nut bowl

91/730 — 12 inch Fruit Bowl

91/506 — 12 inch Sandwich Tray

91/2929C — 12 inch Orange Bowl, Nucut

ROSE MARIE GLASS, NUCUT

91/533MS — 7½ inch Square Berry, Nucut

91/407 — Partition Comport, Nucut round, diameter 7½ inches, not including handle

91/465/2 — Footed Oval, Nucut 9½ inches long, not including handle

SPECIAL LOT 91/1568 contains ½ dozen each of 6 articles illustrated or 3 dozen assorted pieces in Rose Marie glass

91/460 — 8 inch Berry Bowl, Nucut

91/466 — 11 inch Celery Tray, Nucut

91/737A — 8½ inch Footed Salad

Each eight piece punch set illustrated on this page can be ordered with its additional cups to make 16-piece sets.
SEE PRICE LIST

0590, 3-piece Punch Set, NUCUT
Bowl 12 inches in diameter
Bowl on foot 13½ inches tall
Regular size ground bottom cups

068A, 8-piece Punch Set, NUCUT
Bowl 15 inches in diameter
Bowl on foot 15 inches tall
Regular size ground bottom cups

BIG VALUES

700, 12 inch Footed Fruit Bowl

Designs in ROSE MARIE GLASS

SPECIAL LOT 91/1567
contains ³/₄ dozen each of 1
articles illustrated or
9 dozen assorted pieces in
Rose Marie glass,
packed in one barrel

91/564 — 8 inch Pickle Boat, Nucut

91/452B — 7 inch Footed Bowl
Nucut

91/538 — 7½ inch Oval Dish, Nucut

91/555 — Berry Sugar, Nucut

91/555 — Berry Cream, Nucut

91/555 — 6¾ inch Vase,
Nucut

91/555 — Oval Mayonnaise and Plate Set, Nucut
2 pieces

91/555 — 5½ inch Handled Bon-Bon, round
Nucut

91/555A — 6½ inch Round Nappy, Nucut

91/511 — 4½ inch Footed Jelly
Nucut

91/5316A — 6½ inch Round Nappy, Nucut

ROSE MARIE GLASS in open stock

91/460D — 10½ inch Plate, Nucut

91/555 — 7¾ inch Pickle, Nucut

91/360C — 13 inch Oval Fruit Bowl

91/537 — 4½ inch Footed Jelly, Nucut

91/485/1 — two-handled Nappy, 7¼ inches

91/498 — 5½ inch Handled Berry, Nucut

91/4742 — 9 inch Square Salad, Nucut

91/4826 — 6½ inch Deep Berry, Nucut

Berry Sets in ROSE MARIE glass

91/466 — 9 inch Berry Bowl, Nucut

91/4048 — 8½ inch Deep Berry, Nucut
ground bottom

91/484 — 5 inch Berry, Nucut

91/466 — 5 inch Berry, Nucut

91/475 — 5 inch Berry, Nucut
melon shape

91/4044 — 4½ inch Berry, Nucut
ground bottom

91/484 — 8 inch Berry, Nucut

91/475 — 8 inch Berry, Nucut
melon shape

91/497 — 6 inch Ice Cream Plate, Nucut

91/497 — 10½ inch Ice Cream Tray, Nucut

ROSE MARIE!

No. 91 color

91/4821 — 6½ inch Footed Bowl, Nucut

91/4047 — 13 inch Bouquet

91/4743 — 12 inch Vase

91/482 — 8½ inch heavy Footed Bowl, Nucut

91/404 — 9 inch Bouquet

91/387 — 7 inch Bouquet

155

FANCY COLONIAL

5825 — 5½ inch Handled Bon-Bon
12 dozen in barrel

5824 — 5 inch Handled Olive
17 dozen in barrel

Packed 1 dozen Salts or
Peppers in paper box
* * *
With heavy silver tops only

05821 — 5¼ inch Table Butter and
Cover
9 dozen in barrel

5823D — 5¾ inch Plate
fits custard cups
25 dozen in barrel

582 — Salt and Pepper Shaker
33 dozen in barrel

582 — 5 inch two-handled Footed Bowl
5½ dozen in barrel

582 — Custard
30 dozen in barrel

5822A — Punch Cup
28 dozen in barrel

582 — Handled Table Salt
50 dozen in barrel

582 — 12 inch Celery Tray
5 dozen in barrel

05823 — 3½ inch Nappy
ground bottom
55 dozen in barrel

05824 — 4½ inch Nappy
ground bottom
30 dozen in barrel

05824½ — 5 inch Nappy
ground bottom
25 dozen in barrel

05825 — 6 inch Nappy
ground bottom
16 dozen in barrel

05826 — 7 inch Nappy
ground bottom
10 dozen in barrel

05827 — 8 inch Nappy
ground bottom
6 dozen in barrel

05825 — 5 inch Mayonnaise and Plate
8 dozen sets in barrel

05826 — 8 inch Salad and Plate
2½ dozen sets in barrel

582 — 8 inch Pickle Tray, oval
14 dozen in barrel

5821 — 8 inch Spoon Tray, oval
12½ dozen in barrel

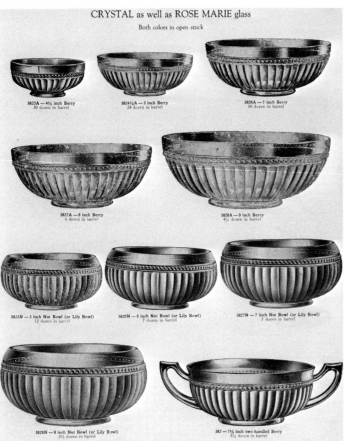

5823A — 4½ inch Berry
30 dozen in barrel

5824½A — 5 inch Berry
24 dozen in barrel

5826A — 7 inch Berry
10 dozen in barrel

5827A — 8 inch Berry
6 dozen in barrel

5828A — 9 inch Berry
4½ dozen in barrel

5825N — 5 inch Nut Bowl (or Lily Bowl)
12 dozen in barrel

5826N — 6 inch Nut Bowl (or Lily Bowl)
7 dozen in barrel

5827N — 7 inch Nut Bowl (or Lily Bowl)
5 dozen in barrel

5828N — 8 inch Nut Bowl (or Lily Bowl)
3½ dozen in barrel

582 — 7½ inch two-handled Berry
3½ dozen in barrel

ALL STEM WARE IN No. 582 DESIGN
HAVE HIGHLY POLISHED BOWLS
AND FEET

5822 — 3 oz. Cocktail
27 dozen in barrel

5822 — 4½ oz. Cocktail
(or tall ice cream)
16 dozen in barrel

5822 — 6 oz. Saucer Champagne
(or tall ice cream)
10½ dozen in barrel

5823 — Cafe Parfait
(or ice cream)
25 dozen in barrel

ALL THESE
TUMBLERS
HAVE GROUND
BOTTOMS

0582 — 2 oz. Whiskey
60 dozen in barrel

0582 — 4 oz. Tumbler
38 dozen in barrel

0582 — 5 oz. Tumbler
33 dozen in barrel

0582 — 6 oz. Tumbler
28 dozen in barrel

0582 — 8 oz. Tumbler
22 dozen in barrel

0582 — 10 oz. Tumbler
18 dozen in barrel

0582 — 12 oz. Ice Tea
16 dozen in barrel

0582 — 14 oz. Ice Tea
13 dozen in barrel

05821 — 8 oz. Bell Tumbler
19 dozen in barrel

156

All made in CRYSTAL as well as ROSE MARIE glass

5824A — 4 inch Footed Bowl
9 dozen in barrel

5825A — 5¼ inch Footed Bowl
3½ dozen in barrel

5826A — 6¼ inch Footed Bowl
2½ dozen in barrel

½ size cuts

582 — 7½ inch Salad Plate
15 dozen in barrel

5822D — 10¼ inch Cake Plate
6 dozen in barrel

CRYSTAL as well as ROSE MARIE glass

In open stock

5822 — 6¼ oz. Oil Bottle
14 dozen in barrel

5821 — 5¼ oz. Oil Bottle
13 dozen in barrel

582 — 8 inch Vase
6½ dozen in barrel

5822/3 — 10 inch Rose Vase
varies from 9 in. to 11 in. in height
about 3¼ dozen in barrel

5822 — Pressed Water Bottle
3 dozen in barrel

0582 — Table Tumbler
16 dozen in barrel

5821 — 3-pint Jug, large size
2¼ dozen in barrel

THE ENTIRE 582 LINE, SHOWN ON PAGES 27 TO 35, IS MADE IN
CRYSTAL as well as ROSE MARIE glass

5821 — 1 oz. Cordial
66 dozen in barrel

5821 — 2 oz. Wine
40 dozen in barrel

5821 — 3 oz. Port
30 dozen in barrel

5821 — 4 oz. Burgundy
24 dozen in barrel

5821 — 5 oz. Claret
18 dozen in barrel

BOTH COLORS -IN- OPEN STOCK

5821 — 6 oz. Champagne
15 dozen in barrel

5821 — 8 oz. Goblet
12½ dozen in barrel

5821 — 10 oz. Goblet
10 dozen in barrel

582 — Egg Cup
20 dozen in barrel

When ordering this open stock pattern in ROSE MARIE prefix these numbers by 91

5820 — Sherbet
diameter, 3¾ inches
22 dozen in barrel

5821 — Sherbet
diameter, 3½ inches
17 dozen in barrel

5822 — Sherbet
diameter, 4¼ inches
11 dozen in barrel

582 — 4½ inch Footed Jelly
height, 5½ inches
7 dozen in barrel

All made in CRYSTAL as well as ROSE MARIE glass

582 — Spoon
9 dozen in barrel

582 — Cream
9 dozen in barrel

582 — Butter and Cover
4 dozen in barrel

582 — Sugar and Cover
6 dozen in barrel

No. 582 — 6-piece Tea Set consists of 1 each of above 4 articles
packed 1½ dozen sets in barrel

5821 — Footed Sugar
9½ dozen in barrel

5821 — Footed Cream
9½ dozen in barrel

No. 5821 — Footed Sugar and Cream Set
packed 4¾ dozen sets in barrel

PACKED TWO 44 PIECE SETS IN BARREL.

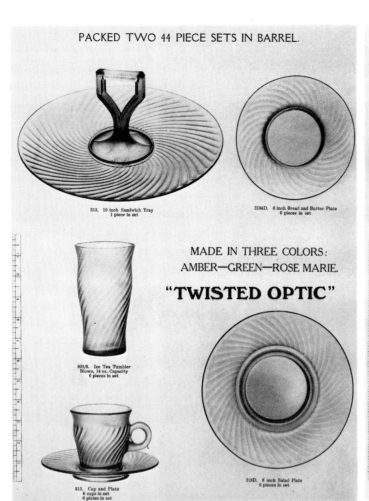

313. 10 inch Sandwich Tray
1 piece in set

3134D. 6 inch Bread and Butter Plate
6 pieces in set

MADE IN THREE COLORS:
AMBER—GREEN—ROSE MARIE.

"TWISTED OPTIC"

803/3. Ice Tea Tumbler
Blown, 14 oz. Capacity
6 pieces in set

313. Cup and Plate
6 cups in set
6 plates in set

313D. 8 inch Salad Plate
6 pieces in set

AMBER, GREEN and ROSE MARIE

313. Covered Powder Box
12 dozen in barrel

3122. Covered Comport
5 dozen in barrel

313. Covered Candy Jar
6 dozen in barrel

148/1. Covered Candy Box
7 dozen in barrel

645/3. Covered Candy Box
6 dozen in barrel

CAN BE ORDERED IN
ASSORTED BARRELS.

615/3. Sugar

615/3. Cream

Packed 11 dozen Sugar and Cream sets in barrel.

685/1. Covered Candy Jar
4 dozen in barrel

MADE IN THREE COLORS: AMBER, GREEN, ROSE MARIE.

PREFIX NUMBERS BY: 40 81 91

"PACKARD"

320. 3 PIECE OVAL CONSOLE SET, AS SHOWN
1½ dozen sets in barrel.

320. 8½ inch Candlestick
Oval Base
6½ dozen in barrel

320. 10½ inch Oval Bowl
2½ dozen in barrel

320. 8½ inch Candlestick
Oval Base
6½ dozen in barrel

3130/715/3. 3 PIECE OVAL CONSOLE SET, AS SHOWN BELOW
1¾ dozen sets in barrel.

715/3. 3½ inch Candlestick

3130. 10½ inch Oval Bowl

715/3. 3½ inch Candlestick

SPECIAL LOT 1584 contains ⅔ dozen each of 3 shapes, shown below in 313 pattern each in Green and Rose Marie or 4 dozen assorted in one barrel.

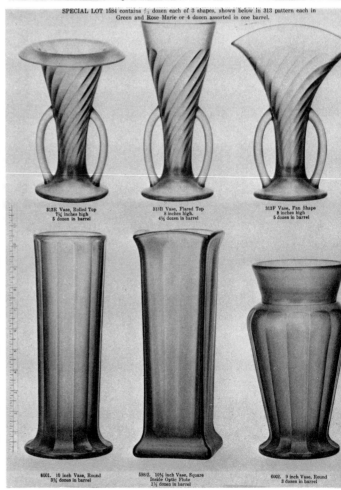

313R. Vase, Rolled Top
7¼ inches high
5 dozen in barrel

313B. Vase, Flared Top
8 inches high
4½ dozen in barrel

312F. Vase, Fan Shape
8 inches high
5 dozen in barrel

6001. 10 inch Vase, Round
3½ dozen in barrel

598/2. 10½ inch Vase, Square
Inside Optic Fluto
1½ dozen in barrel

6002. 9 inch Vase, Round
3 dozen in barrel

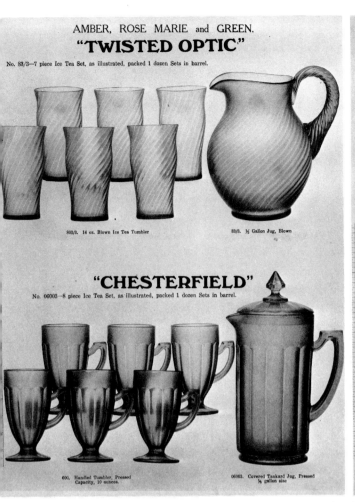

AMBER, ROSE MARIE and GREEN.
"TWISTED OPTIC"

No. 83/3—7 piece Ice Tea Set, as illustrated, packed 1 dozen Sets in barrel.

803/3. 14 oz. Blown Ice Tea Tumbler

83/3. ½ Gallon Jug, Blown

"CHESTERFIELD"

No. 06003—8 piece Ice Tea Set, as illustrated, packed 1 dozen Sets in barrel.

690. Handled Tumbler, Pressed
Capacity, 10 ounces.

06003. Covered Tankard Jug, Pressed
½ gallon size

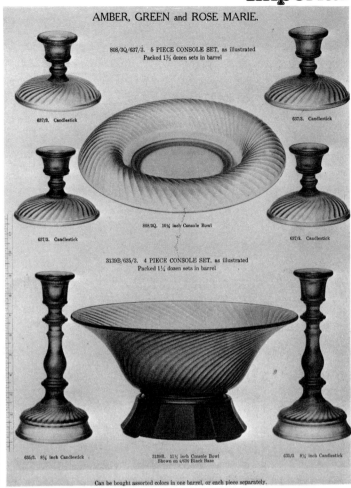

AMBER, GREEN and ROSE MARIE.

808/3Q/637/3. 5 PIECE CONSOLE SET, as illustrated
Packed 1⅓ dozen sets in barrel

637/3. Candlestick

637/3. Candlestick

637/3. Candlestick

637/3. Candlestick

808/3Q. 10½ inch Console Bowl

3139B/635/3. 4 PIECE CONSOLE SET, as illustrated
Packed 1¼ dozen sets in barrel

635/3. 8½ inch Candlestick

3139B. 11½ inch Console Bowl
Shown on 4/639 Black Base

635/3. 8½ inch Candlestick

Can be bought assorted colors in one barrel, or each piece separately.

AMBER—GREEN—ROSE MARIE.

675R. 5 PIECE CONSOLE SET, as illustrated
Packed 2 dozen sets in barrel

675. Candlestick

675. Candlestick

675. Candlestick

675. Candlestick

675R. 9½ inch Console Bowl

6567/2B/635. 4 PIECE CONSOLE SET, as illustrated
Packed 1¾ dozen sets in barrel

635. 8½ inch Candlestick

6567/2B. 9½ inch Console Bowl
Shown on 4/634 Black Base

635. 8½ inch Candlestick

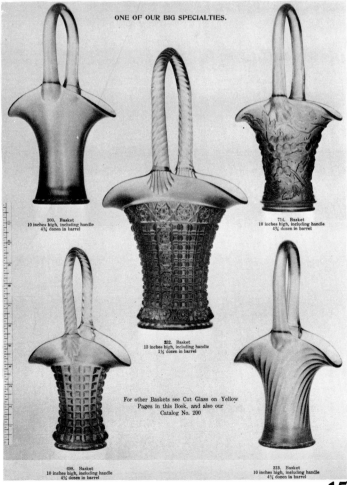

ONE OF OUR BIG SPECIALTIES.

300. Basket
10 inches high, including handle
4¾ dozen in barrel

714. Basket
10 inches high, including handle
4½ dozen in barrel

252. Basket
13 inches high, including handle
1½ dozen in barrel

698. Basket
10 inches high, including handle
4½ dozen in barrel

For other Baskets see Cut Glass on Yellow
Pages in this Book, and also our
Catalog No. 200

313. Basket
10 inches high, including handle
4½ dozen in barrel

MADE IN AMBER—GREEN—ROSE MARIE.

PREFIX NUMBERS BY: 40   81   91

ALSO MADE IN CRYSTAL.

"STRAWFLOWER"

629D. 7¼ inch Salad Plate, Round
Footed bottom
12 dozen in barrel

682D. 7¼ inch Square Plate
Footed bottom
12 dozen in barrel

"WOODBURY"

"BLAISE"

704. 8 inch Salad Plate, Round

705. 8 inch Salad Plate, Octagon

MADE IN THREE COLORS: AMBER, GREEN, ROSE MARIE.

WHEN ORDERING, PREFIX NUMBERS BY: 40   81   91

The two Casters come each set
in a paper box.

200. Tall Caster Set
3 pieces in set
6 dozen sets in barrel

428. Basket Caster Set
3 pieces in set
12 dozen sets in barrel

313R. 3 Piece Mayonnaise Set
3½ dozen sets in barrel

629B. 3 Piece Mayonnaise Set
6 dozen sets in barrel

682. 3 Piece Mayonnaise Set, Square
4 dozen sets in barrel

602. 3 Piece Mayonnaise Set
7 dozen sets in barrel

602/5. 3 Piece Mayonnaise Set
7 dozen sets in barrel

PREFIX NUMBERS BY: 40   81   91

"ZAK"

"ROXY"

No. 12. 3 Piece Guest Room Set
Consisting of Pint Pitcher, 6 oz. Tumbler and Oval Plate
3 dozen sets in barrel

600. 9 Piece Wine Set, including Tray, (as shown)
The Wine bottle is blown, the other pieces are pressed
2 dozen sets in barrel

505. 9 Piece Wine Set, including Tray, (as shown)
The Wine bottle is blown, the other pieces are pressed

650. 2 Piece Guest Room Set
Blown pitcher with pressed tumbler
3½ dozen sets in barrel

GREEN (color 81) AND ROSE MARIE (color 91)

SPECIAL LOT 1580 contains 1 dozen each 294,
6924, 304 Bud Vases each in Green and Rose
Marie, or 6 dozen assorted Bud Vases.

SPECIAL LOT 1581 contains 2 dozen each 6922
Wide and 6923 Tall Vases each in Green and
Rose Marie or 8 dozen assorted Vases.

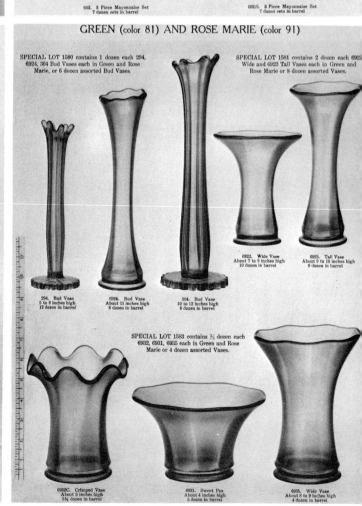

6922. Wide Vase
About 7 to 9 inches high
10 dozen in barrel

6923. Tall Vase
About 9 to 10 inches high
9 dozen in barrel

294. Bud Vase
5 to 8 inches high
12 dozen in barrel

6924. Bud Vase
About 11 inches high
8 dozen in barrel

304. Bud Vase
10 to 12 inches high
6 dozen in barrel

SPECIAL LOT 1583 contains ⅔ dozen each
6932, 6931, 6935 each in Green and Rose
Marie or 4 dozen assorted Vases.

6932C. Crimped Vase
About 5 inches high
5½ dozen in barrel

6931. Sweet Pea
About 4 inches high
5 dozen in barrel

6935. Wide Vase
About 8 to 9 inches high
4 dozen in barrel

160

MADE IN THREE COLORS: AMBER, GREEN, ROSE MARIE.

PREFIX NUMBERS BY: 40   81   91

313. 2 Piece Cup and Plate Set
12 dozen sets in barrel

313. 2 Piece Sherbet and Plate Set
9 dozen sets in barrel

THIS PUNCH SET IS MADE ONLY IN ROSE MARIE

91/615/5. Punch Cup

91/625/5. 8 Piece Punch Set
Consisting of One Bowl, One Foot and Six Cups

91/615/5. Punch Cup

AMBER—GREEN—ROSE MARIE.
"DIAMOND QUILTED"

4142R. 7¾ inch Footed Bowl
3 dozen in barrel

4146D. 8¼ inch Salver
2 dozen in barrel

4146F. 7½ inch Footed Bowl
2½ dozen in barrel

4146A. 6½ inch Covered Footed Bowl
2½ dozen in barrel

WHEN ORDERING, PREFIX NUMBERS BY: 81   91

6067/5X. 9 inch Footed Bowl
1½ dozen in barrel

6067/5W. 9 inch Footed Bowl
1½ dozen in barrel

6067/5R. 8¾ inch Footed Bowl
1½ dozen in barrel

6067/5D. 10 inch Salver
1½ dozen in barrel

MADE IN THREE COLORS: AMBER, GREEN, ROSE MARIE.

PREFIX NUMBERS BY: 40   81   91

414. 7 PIECE WATER SET, (as shown)
1 dozen sets in barrel

414. Table Tumbler, Blown
9 oz. capacity
15 dozen in barrel

414. ½ Gallon Jug, Blown
Capacity about 79 oz.
Hand made handle
2 dozen in barrel

698. 9½ oz. Table Tumbler

6983. 7 Piece Water Set

6983. ½ Gallon Pitcher

161

"OMERO"

6155NC/25. 5 inch Lily Bowl
609/25. Two Handled Sugar
609/25. Cream
6152/25. Two Handled Berry
6674/25. One Handled Berry
6155A/25. 5¼ inch Berry
615/25. Two Handled Pickle
099/25. Footed Jelly
692/25. 7½ inch Vase
692/25. 5 inch Vase
499H/25. Sherbet
499/25. Sherbet Plate

SPECIAL LOT 1933 contains ½ dozen each of 8 items illustrated, or 4 dozen assorted cut pieces.

6150/25. Two Handled Celery Tray
6156A/25. 7 inch Berry
646B/25. 8 inch Nappy
6253/25. Two Handled Footed Bon Bon
6153/25. Two Handled Berry
6934/25. 12 inch Tall Vase
6935/25. 7½ inch Sweet Pea
456/25. Tall Celery

AMBER (color 40) ROSE MARIE (color 91) GREEN (color 81)

SPECIAL LOT No. 1572
Contains 7 pieces each of 6 hand cut novelties, as illustrated, or 3½ dozen assorted.
FURNISHED IN EITHER AMBER or ROSE MARIE or GREEN.

"FLORA"

6253/Cut 205. 5¼ inch Footed Bowl

606 Cut 205. Open Sugar
606 Cut 205. Cream

STATE COLOR WANTED CLEARLY.

771 Cut 205. 6 inch Rose Bowl, Blown
6985 Cut 205. Wide Vase 8 to 10 inches high
648B Cut 205. Salad Bowl 10 inches Diameter

AMBER (color 40), ROSE MARIE (color 91) and GREEN (color 81)

SPECIAL LOT No. 1573
Contains ½ dozen each of six hand cut items, as illustrated, or 3 dozen assorted cut articles.

169R Cut 206. 3 Piece Mayonnaise Set

BE SURE TO STATE COLOR WANTED.

"ELIZABETH"

664 Cut 206. 10 inch Sandwich Tray
6567R Cut 206. Salad Bowl 8½ inch diameter
645 Cut 206. Candy Box and Cover
300 Cut 206. Basket 10 inches high, including handle
223 Cut 206. Blown Vase 9½ inches high

162

CRYSTAL—GREEN—ROSE MARIE.

CAN BE PACKED ASSORTED COLORS IN ONE BARREL.

300 Cut 2. Basket
4 dozen in barrel

805 Cut 217. 2 Piece Night Set
5 dozen sets in barrel

650 Cut 2. 2 Piece Guest Room Set
3½ dozen sets in barrel

VERY HIGH GRADE SQUARE CANDLE-
STICKS, IN HIGHLY POLISHED
THREE COLORS.

6247 Cut 61. Square Candlestick
7 inch high
10 dozen in barrel

6249 Cut 63. Square Candlestick
9 inch high
5½ dozen in barrel

62412 Cut 66. Square Candlestick
12 inch high
4 dozen in barrel

AMBER—GREEN—ROSE MARIE.

"ROMA"

715 Cut 200. Oval Candlestick

320 Cut 200. 10½ inch Oval Bowl

715 Cut 200. Oval Candlestick

320/715 Cut 200. 3 Piece Oval Console Set, as shown
Packed 1 dozen 3 piece sets in barrel.

VERY BRILLIANT HAND CUTTINGS.

"ITALIA"

718R Cut 201. Candlestick

718R Cut 201. Candlestick

6569Q Cut 201. 13½ inch Bowl

6569Q/718R Cut 201. 5 Piece Console Set,
as shown, packed 1 dozen 5 piece
sets in barrel.

718R Cut 201. Candlestick

718R Cut 201. Candlestick

VERY FINE HAND CUTTINGS

ON THREE COLORS

AMBER, GREEN, ROSE MARIE.

"SUSIE"

320 Cut 15. 8½ inch Candlestick
Oval

320 Cut 15. 8½ inch Candlestick
Oval

320 Cut 15. 3 Piece Console Set
Consisting of one 10½ inch Oval Bowl with two
8½ inch Candlesticks as shown

718R Cut 19. Candlestick

718R Cut 19. Candlestick

"APPIANO"

718R Cut 19. 5 Piece Console Set (or Center Set)
Consisting of one 11 inch Round Bowl with four
low Candlesticks as shown

718R Cut 19. Candlestick

718R Cut 19. Candlestick

ARE FURNISHED ON THREE COLORS OF GLASS

AMBER, GREEN, ROSE MARIE.

"MONACO"

637 Cut 16. Candlestick

637 Cut 16. Candlestick

637 Cut 16. Candlestick

637 Cut 16. Candlestick

6569R/637 Cut 16. 5 Piece Console Set
(or Center Set)
Consisting of one 11½ inch Round Bowl with four
low Candlesticks as shown

"Mt. MARIA"

718R Cut 202. Candlestick

718R Cut 202. Candlestick

75Q/718R Cut 202. 5 Piece Console Set
(or Center Set)
Consisting of one 12½ inch Round Bowl with four
low Candlesticks as shown

718R Cut 202. Candlestick

718R Cut 202. Candlestick

No. 16. HAND CUTTING, VERY FINE, FURNISHED ON 3 COLORS
AMBER—GREEN—ROSE MARIE.

"MONACO"

118 Cut 16.   8 inch Bowl, Blown

641 Cut 16.   Cheese and Cracker, 10 inches
2 pieces

664 Cut 16.   10 inch Sandwich Tray

169R Cut 16.   3 Piece Mayonnaise Set

717 Cut 16.   Candy Box and Cover

770 Cut 16.   8 inch Rose Bowl, Blown

79F Cut 16.   7½ inch Footed Bowl

AMBER—GREEN—ROSE MARIE.

170 Cut 16.   Footed Comport and Cover

790 Cut 16.   Oval Cake and Sherbet Set
2 pieces

615 Cut 16.   Cup and Plate

645 Cut 16.   Candy Box and Cover

79 Cut 16.   Sherbet and Plate

2428 Cut 16.   8 inch Salad Plate

169 Cut 16.   5 Piece My Lady Set

FINE HAND CUT, AS ILLUSTRATED.
MADE IN ROSE MARIE ONLY.

(See page 110 for additional pieces in same design, not included in 57 piece set)

"NAVONA"

91/6569R Cut 207.   11¼ inch Bowl
1 piece in dinner set

91/657 Cut 207.   Candlestick
4 pieces in dinner set

91/803 Cut 207.   4¾ inch Berry Saucer
Pressed
6 pieces in dinner set

91/664 Cut 207.   10 inch Sandwich Tray
1 piece in dinner set

91/615 Cut 207.   Cup and Plate
6 cups in dinner set
6 plates in dinner set

91/902 Cut 207.   Table Tumbler
Blown
6 pieces in dinner set

91/84 Cut 207.   ½ Gallon Pitcher
Blown
1 piece in dinner set

FINE HAND CUT ON ROSE MARIE GLASS ONLY.

91/6567R Cut 207.   9 inch Bowl
Rolled Edge
1 piece in dinner set

91/169R Cut 207.   3 Piece Mayonnaise Set
Counts 3 pieces in dinner set

91/609 Cut 207.   Open Sugar
1 piece in dinner set

91/609 Cut 207.   Cream
1 piece in dinner set

91/79 Cut 207.   Sherbet and Plate
6 sherbets in dinner set
6 plates in dinner set

91/641 Cut 207.   2 Piece Cheese and Cracker
Counts 2 pieces in dinner set

91/77 Cut 207.   8¼ inch Salad Plate
6 pieces in dinner set

THIS PATTERN IS MADE IN ROSE MARIE ONLY, (color 91)

"FRANCESCO"

91/718R Cut 204. Candlestick

91/75X Cut 204. 12½ inch Center Bowl

91/602 Cut 204. 3 Piece Mayonnaise Set

91/6567B Cut 204. 9½ inch Salad Bowl

91/45B Cut 204. Fruit Salad and Plate
Diameter of Fruit Salad 5 inches
Diameter of Plate 6½ inches

91/6567Q Cut 204. 10 inch Bowl, Rolled Edge

91/664 Cut 204. 10 inch Sandwich Tray

91/84B Cut 204. 7½ inch Preserve Dish
3 feet

91/6253 Cut 204. 5½ inch Footed Bon Bon

91/6150 Cut 204. Celery Tray
10¼ inches long, including handles

ROSE MARIE ONLY
(COLOR 91)

91/169 Cut 204. Candy Jar and Cover
Height including cover 9 inches

91/641 Cut 204. 10 inch Cheese and Cracker

This cutting, shown on pages 103, 104 and 105 is sold entirely in open stock, in quantities to suit yourself.

ROSE MARIE ONLY
(COLOR 91)

91/242 Cut 204. 12 inch Plate

Diameter, 9 inches   Height, 8 inches

91/6067R Cut 204. High Footed Bowl

91/77 Cut 204. 8½ inch Salad Plate

ROSE MARIE (color 91), AMBER (color 40) and GREEN (color 81)

SPECIAL LOT 1574, contains 8 each of 5 articles illustrated, all in any one of above 3 colors, or 3⅓ dozen assorted cut articles in one color.

"ANDREA"

5737B Cut 9. 9½ inch Salad Bowl

169 Cut 9. Footed Candy Jar and Cover

169R Cut 9. 3 Piece Mayonnaise Set

360 Cut 9. Basket

664 Cut 9. 10 inch Sandwich Tray

VERY FINE HAND CUTTINGS ON SATIN IRIDESCENT GLASS.

SPECIAL LOT 1676 contains ¼ dozen each of 4 articles illustrated, each in 2 Satin Iridescent Colors: ROSE ICE and BLUE ICE, or 2 dozen assorted Hand Cut SATIN NOVELTIES.

664 Cut 12. 10 inch Sandwich Tray

6641 Cut 20. 9 inch Handled Fruit Bowl

169R Cut 165. Compact and Plate

641 Cut 160. 10 inch Cracker and Cheese Set

FINE HAND CUTTING ON HIGHLY POLISHED CRYSTAL—GREEN—ROSE MARIE.

SPECIAL LOT 2060 contains ½ dozen each of 4 articles, illustrated, or 1 dozen assorted Sandwich Trays and 1 dozen assorted Cheese and Cracker Sets, all in one barrel.

"JULIANA"

664 Cut 13. 10 inch Sandwich Tray

"ROSETTA"

664 Cut 20. 10 inch Sandwich Tray

MADE IN EITHER CRYSTAL ROSE MARIE OR GREEN.

REAL HAND CUTTING ON HIGHLY POLISHED CRYSTAL—GREEN—ROSE MARIE.

SPECIAL LOT 2061 contains ½ dozen each of 4 articles, illustrated, or 1 dozen assorted Sandwich Trays and 1 dozen assorted Cheese and Cracker Sets, all in one barrel.

"KAROLA"

664 Cut 10. 10 inch Sandwich Tray

641 Cut 10. 10 inch Cheese and Cracker Set

"NANCY"

664 Cut 7. 10 inch Sandwich Tray

641 Cut 7. 10 inch Cheese and Cracker Set

MADE IN EITHER CRYSTAL, ROSE MARIE OR GREEN.

MADE ONLY IN GREEN—ROSE MARIE AND CRYSTAL.

Always state clearly which color is wanted.

SPECIAL LOT 2046

Consists of 6 pairs Hand Cut Crystal Vases, all different, or ½ dozen each of two shapes illustrated, each in the three cuttings shown, or 1 dozen assorted vases packed in one barrel.

The same assortment, but in Green Glass in place of Crystal Glass, is called SPECIAL LOT 81/2046

The same assortment, but in Rose Marie Glass in place of Crystal Glass, is called SPECIAL LOT 91/2046.

6944 Cut 98. Wide Vase 4 to 15 inches high.

6946 Cut 99. Tall Vase 11 to 14 inches high.

6946 Cut 99. Wide Vase

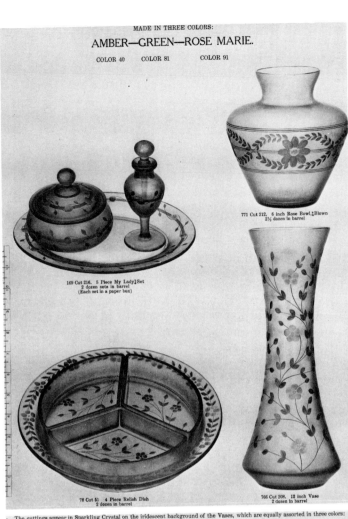

MADE IN THREE COLORS:

MADE IN THREE COLORS:
AMBER—GREEN—ROSE MARIE.

COLOR 40   COLOR 81   COLOR 91

771 Cut 212.   6 inch Rose Bowl, Blown
2½ dozen in barrel

169 Cut 216.   5 Piece My Lady Set
2 dozen sets in barrel
(Each set in a paper box)

78 Cut 51   4 Piece Relish Dish
2 dozen in barrel

766 Cut 208.   12 inch Vase
2 dozen in barrel

LOW PRICED, AS WELL AS FINE HAND CUTTING ON
CRYSTAL—AMBER—GREEN AND ROSE MARIE.

2428 Cut 2.   8 inch Plate

2428 Cut 18.   8 inch Plate

ALL THE PLATES ON
PAGES 118 AND 119
HAVE WELL
POLISHED BOTTOMS.

BE SURE TO STATE
WHICH OF ABOVE
FOUR COLORS
ARE WANTED.

77 Cut 9
8¼ inch Plate

2428 Cut 30.   8 inch Plate

2428 Cut 20.   8 inch Plate

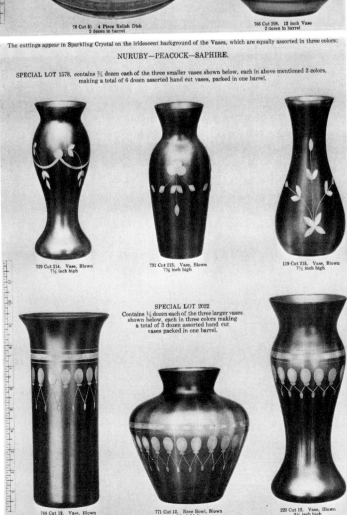

The cuttings appear in Sparkling Crystal on the iridescent background of the Vases, which are equally assorted in three colors:

NURUBY—PEACOCK—SAPHIRE.

SPECIAL LOT 1578, contains ⅔ dozen each of the three smaller vases shown below, each in above mentioned 3 colors, making a total of 6 dozen assorted hand cut vases, packed in one barrel.

729 Cut 214.   Vase, Blown
7½ inch high

731 Cut 213.   Vase, Blown
7½ inch high

119 Cut 215.   Vase, Blown
7½ inch high

SPECIAL LOT 2022
Contains ⅓ dozen each of the three larger vases
shown below, each in three colors making
a total of 3 dozen assorted hand cut
vases packed in one barrel.

768 Cut 12.   Vase, Blown
9 inch high

771 Cut 12.   Rose Bowl, Blown
6 inch high

223 Cut 12.   Vase, Blown
9½ inch high

STUDY THIS OFFER CAREFULLY.

A. B. C. GIFTS No. 1
Contains 6 each Vases in Class A—E—C
assorted Lead Lustre Colors
½ Plain, ½ Decorated or 18 different vases
Assorted in Shapes, Colors and Decorations.
SEE PRICE LIST.

CLASS C
Assorted shapes, colors and decorations

CLASS C
Assorted shapes, colors and decorations

CLASS A
Assorted shapes, colors and decorations

CLASS B
Assorted shapes, colors and decorations

CLASS B
Assorted shapes, colors and decorations

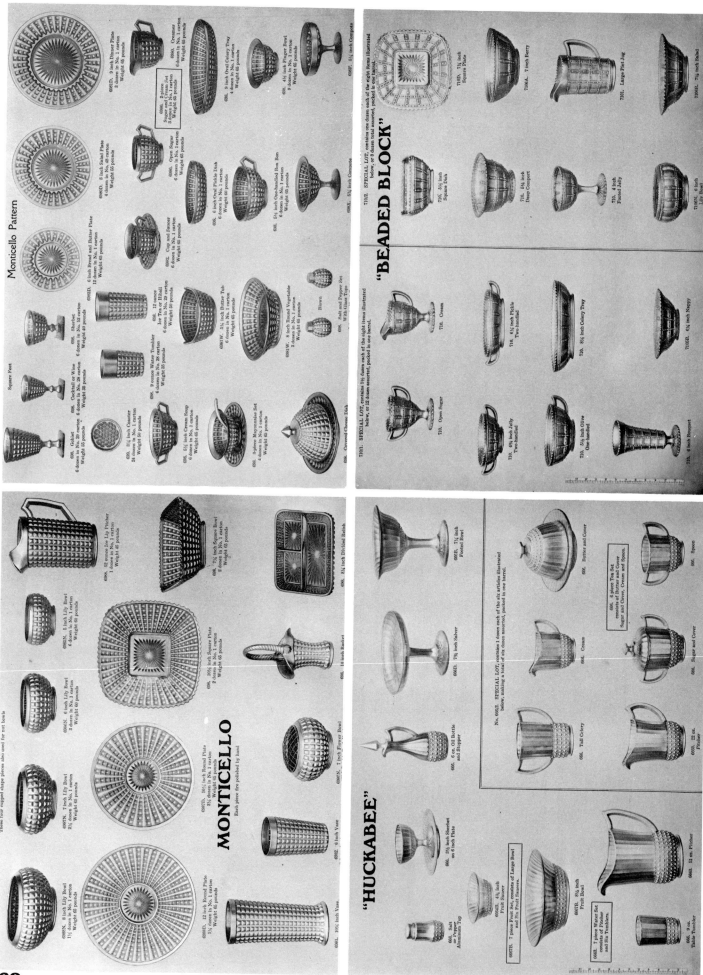

Monticello Pattern

Square Feet

These four cupped shape pieces also used for nut bowls

MONTICELLO

Each piece fire polished by hand

"HUCKABEE"

"BEADED BLOCK"

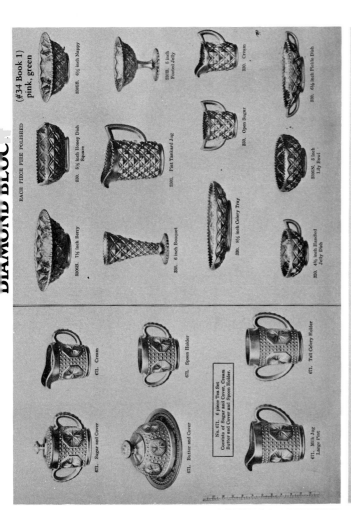

DIAMOND BLOCK

EACH PIECE FIRE POLISHED

(#34 Book 1)
pink, green

320N. 6½ inch Nappy
330B. 6 inch Footed Jelly
330. Cream
320. 6½ inch Pickle Dish

330. 8½ inch Honey Dish Square
330J. Pint Tankard Jug
330. Open Sugar
330N. 5 inch Lily Bowl

330B. 7½ inch Berry
330. 6 inch Bouquet
330. 8½ inch Celery Tray
330. 4½ inch Handled Jelly Dish

671. Cream
671. Spoon Holder
671. Tall Celery Holder

671. Sugar and Cover
671. Butter and Cover
671. Milk Jug Large Pint

No. 671. 6 piece Tea Set
Consists of Sugar and Cover, Cream, Butter and Cover and Spoon Holder.

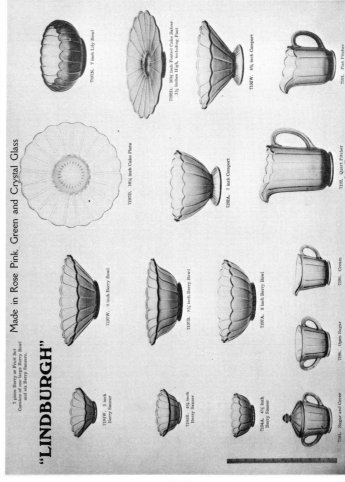

Made in Rose Pink, Green and Crystal Glass

719/N. 7 inch Lily Bowl
719D. 10½ inch Footed Cake Salver 13½ inches High, including Foot
7192W. 8½ inch Comport
719J. Pint Pitcher Large Size

719D. 10½ inch Cake Plate
7192C. 7 inch Comport
7192. Quart Pitcher Large Size

7197W. 9 inch Berry Bowl
7197B. 8½ inch Berry Bowl
7197A. 8 inch Berry Bowl
719C. Cream

7194W. 5 inch Berry Saucer
7194B. 4½ inch Berry Saucer
7194A. 4¼ inch Berry Saucer
719W. Open Sugar
719B. Sugar and Cover

7 piece Berry or Fruit Set
Consists of one large Berry Bowl and six Berry Saucers.

"LINDBURGH"

"AMELIA"

671. 6½ inch Compott Deep
671. 7 inch Oval Dish
671B. 5 inch Preserve
671. 8 inch Celery Tray

671. 8½ inch Square Dish
6716F. 8½ inch Shallow Nappy
671AB. 7½ inch Salad Bowl
671. 6 inch Bouquet

671. Custard Cup
671. 9 oz. Table Tumbler
671. 12 oz. Ice Tea Tumbler
671. 8 oz. Goblet

671. 6½ inch Oval Pickle
671. 6 inch Handled Nappy
671. 7 inch Candlestick
671C. 5¾ inch Jelly, Crimped

671. 5 inch Lily Bowl
671B. 6½ inch Nappy
671. 6 oz. Tall Ice Cream
671. 6 inch Plate

The 6 inch Plate fits under Tall Ice Cream, Ice Tea Tumbler, Table Tumbler, Goblet or Footed Jelly.

A LINE OF PRESSED STEMWARE WITH POLISHED FEET.

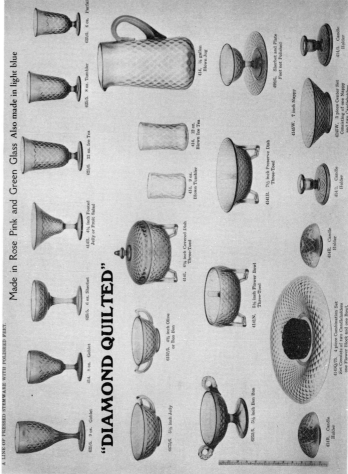

Made in Rose Pink and Green Glass Also made in light blue

625/S. 6 oz. Parfait
414. ½ gallon Blown Jug
499/S. Sherbet and Plate Foot not Polished
414/1. Candle Holder

625/S. 8 oz. Tumbler
414. 12 oz. Ice Tea
414. 12 oz. Blown Ice Tea
416W. 7 inch Nappy
416W. 3 piece Center Set Consisting of one Nappy and two Candleholders

625/S. 12 oz. Ice Tea
414. 9 oz. Blown Tumbler
414IR. 7½ inch Preserve Dish Three-Toed
414/1. Candle Holder

414N. 4¾ inch Footed Jelly or Fruit Salad
414IL. 6¼ inch Covered Dish Three-Toed
414R. Candle Holder

625/S. 9 oz. Goblet
414. 8 oz. Goblet
414I. 4¾ inch Olive or Bon Bon
414IN. 5¼ inch Flower Bowl Three-Toed
414Q/S. 4 piece Combination Set Set Consists of two Candleholders one Flower Block and one Bowl.

625/S. 6½ inch Jelly
625/S. 5½ inch Bon Bon
614R. Candle Holder

"DIAMOND QUILTED"

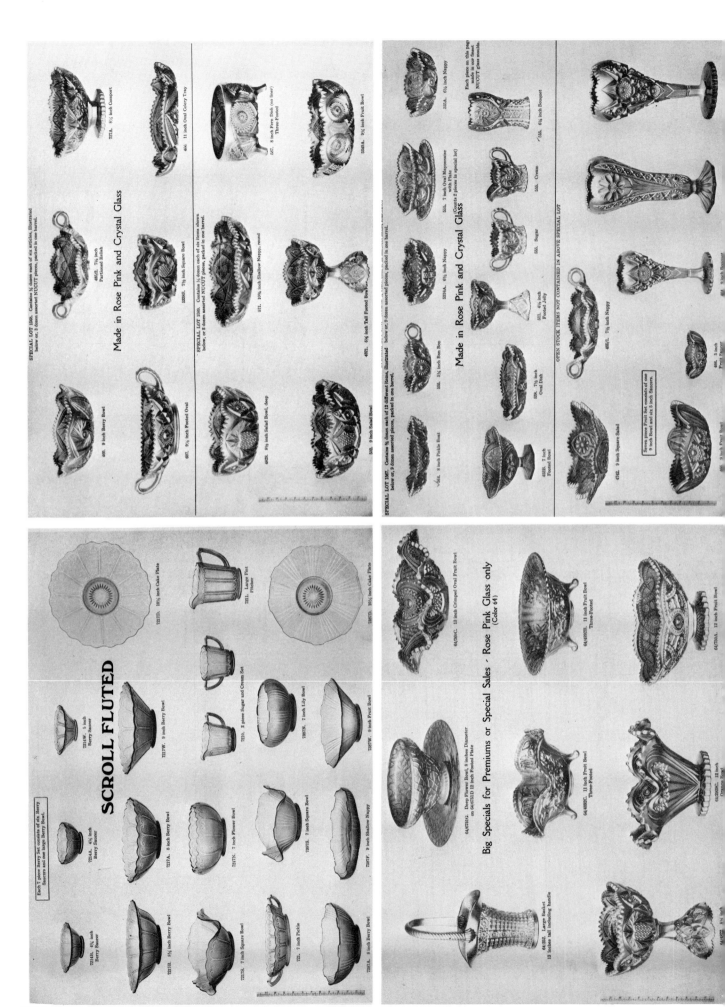

SPECIAL. LOT 1568. Contains ½ dozen each of six articles, illustrated below or, 3 dozen assorted NUCUT pieces, packed in one barrel.

Made in Rose Pink and Crystal Glass

707A. 8½ inch Compert

460. 11 inch Oval Celery Tray

485/2. 7½ inch Partioned Relish

535RS. 7½ inch Square Bowl

607. 9½ inch Footed Oval

482R. 8½ inch Salad Bowl, deep

SPECIAL. LOT 1569. Contains ½ dozen each of six items shown below or, 2 dozen assorted NUCUT pieces, packed in one barrel.

671. 10½ inch Shallow Nappy, round

607. 8 inch Fern Dish (no liner) Three-Footed

482I. 6½ inch Tall Footed Bowl

502. 9 inch Salad Bowl

542A. 9½ inch Fruit Bowl

Each piece on this page made in our finest NUCUT glass moulds.

555A. 6½ inch Nappy

550. 6 inch Oval Mayonnaise with Plate

555. Cream

55K. 6½ inch Bouquet

SPECIAL. LOT 1567. Contains ½ dozen each of 12 different items, illustrated below or, 9 dozen assorted pieces, packed in one barrel.

555. 5½ inch Bon Bon

551A. 6½ inch Nappy

555. Sugar

Made in Rose Pink and Crystal Glass

564. 8 inch Pickle Boat

52H6A. 6½ inch Nappy

58R. 7½ inch Oval Dish

511. 4½ inch Footed Jelly

OPEN STOCK ITEMS NOT CONTAINED IN ABOVE SPECIAL LOT

452I. 7½ inch Footed Bowl

742. 7 inch Footed Bowl

482I. 9 inch Square Salad

485/0. 7½ inch Nappy

496. 5 inch Fruit Saucer

Seven piece Fruit Set consists of one 9 inch Bowl and six 5 inch Saucers.

Each 7 piece Berry Set consists of six Berry Saucers and one large Berry Bowl.

SCROLL FLUTED

7214D. 4½ inch Berry Saucer

7216W. 5 inch Berry Saucer

721TD. 10½ inch Cake Plate

7211. Large Pint Pitcher

7285TD. 10½ inch Cake Plate

7214B. 4½ inch Berry Saucer

7217B. 8½ inch Berry Bowl

721TW. 9 inch Berry Bowl

7217A. 8 inch Berry Bowl

7210. 2 piece Sugar and Cream Set

7285TN. 7 inch Lily Bowl

7285TD. 9 inch Fruit Bowl

7217N. 7 inch Flower Bowl

7285TS. 7 inch Square Bowl

7285TW. 9 inch Fruit Bowl

7287A. 8 inch Berry Bowl

7217S. 7 inch Square Bowl

721. 7 inch Pickle

7285TF. 9 inch Shallow Nappy

Big Specials for Premiums or Special Sales - Rose Pink Glass only
(Color 64)

64/256/C. 13 inch Crimped Oval Fruit Bowl

64/673/G. Deep Flower Bowl, 8 inches Diameter on 64/675/D 12 inch Footed Plate

64/492H. 11 inch Fruit Bowl Three-Footed

64/780A. 12 inch Fruit Bowl

64/492C. 11 inch Fruit Bowl Three-Footed

64/252. Large Basket 13 inches tall including handle

64/220/C. 12 inch

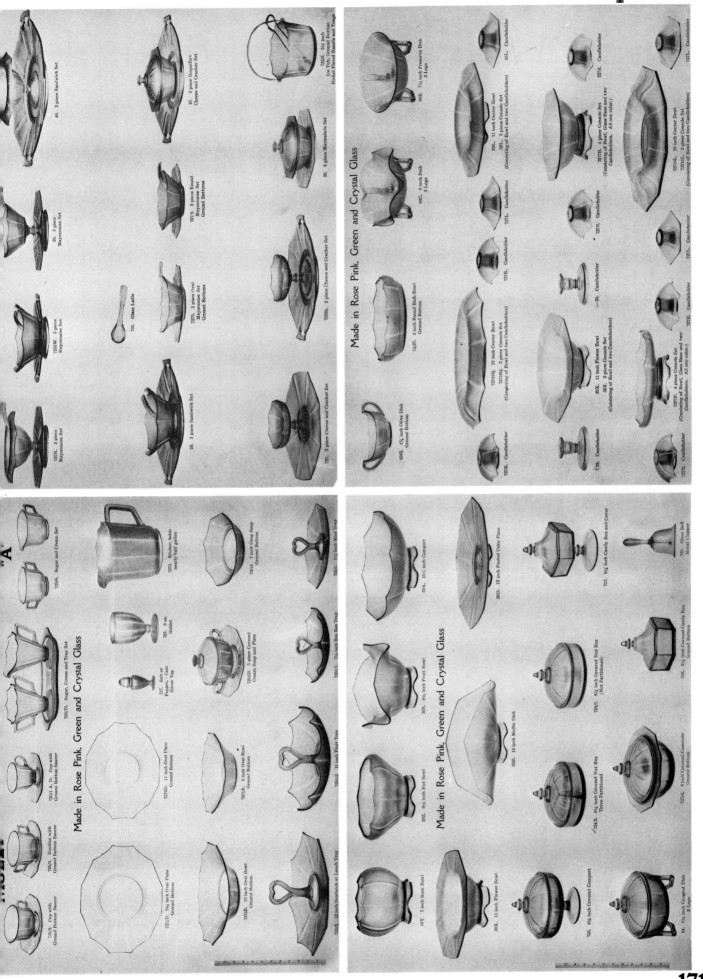

Made in Rose Pink, Green and Crystal Glass

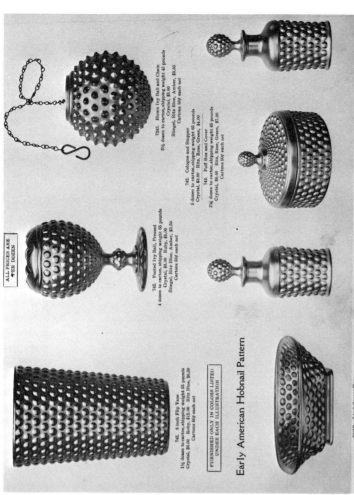

Early American Hobnail Pattern

ALL PRICES ARE PER DOZEN

741. Blown Ivy Ball and Chain
3½ dozen to carton, shipping weight 45 pounds
Crystal, $3.10
Stiegel, Ritz Blue, Amber, $3.50
Cartons 50¢ each set

742. Footed Ivy Ball, Pressed
4 dozen to carton, shipping weight 50 pounds
Crystal, $2.50, Ruby, $6.00
Stiegel, Ritz Blue, Amber, $3.50
Cartons 50¢ each set

742. Cologne and Stopper
6 dozen to carton, shipping weight 65 pounds
Crystal, $3.50, Ritz, Rose, Green, $7.00
Cartons 50¢ each set

742. Puff Box and Cover
2½ dozen to carton, shipping weight 65 pounds
Crystal, $6.00, Ritz, Rose, Green, $7.00
Cartons 50¢ each set

742. 8 inch Flip Vase
1½ dozen to carton, shipping weight 55 pounds
Crystal, $3.50, Ruby, $12.00, Ritz Blue, $6.50
Cartons 50¢ each set

FURNISHED ONLY IN COLORS LISTED UNDER EACH ILLUSTRATION

Early American Hobnail Pattern

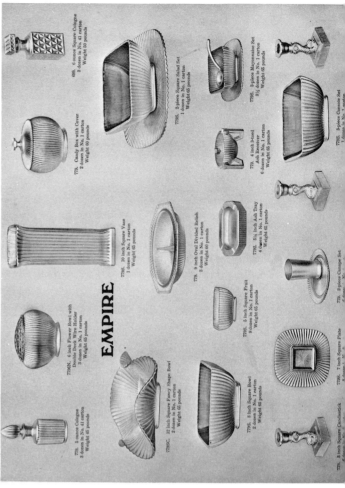

090. 9 ounce Square Cologne
3 dozen in No. 41 carton
Weight 60 pounds

779. Candy Box with Cover
2 dozen in No. 1 carton
Weight 60 pounds

779. 3-piece Mayonnaise Set
1 dozen in No. 1 carton
Weight 65 pounds

779. 3-piece Square Salad Set
1 dozen in No. 1 carton
Weight 65 pounds

779. 4 inch 3-toed Ash Receiver
6 dozen in No. 1 carton
Weight 60 pounds

779. 3-piece Console Set

779. 10 inch Square Vase
1 dozen in No. 41 carton
Weight 65 pounds

779. 5½ inch Ash Tray
4 dozen in No. 1 carton
Weight 65 pounds

779. 9 inch Oval Divided Relish
2 dozen in No. 1 carton
Weight 60 pounds

779. 3-piece Orange Set

EMPIRE

779. 6 inch Flower Bowl with Double Deck Wire Holder
3 dozen in No. 1 carton
Weight 65 pounds

779. 5 inch Square Fruit
8 dozen in No. 1 carton
Weight 65 pounds

779. 8 inch Square Plate

779. 5 ounce Cologne
3 dozen in No. 41 carton
Weight 60 pounds

779. 12 inch Square Fancy Shape Bowl
1 dozen in No. 1 carton
Weight 65 pounds

779. 8 inch Square Bowl
2 dozen in No. 1 carton
Weight 65 pounds

779. 7 inch Square Nappy

749B. 6-piece Toilet, Dresser or Bath Room Set (as shown)

749B. 7 inch Square Nappy

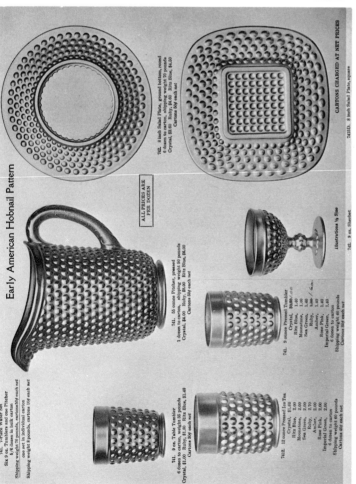

Early American Hobnail Pattern

Six 9 oz. Tumblers and one Pitcher
6/6 dozen in bulk carton
Shipping weight 70 pounds, cartons 50¢ each set
one set in individual carton
Shipping weight 8 pounds, cartons 10¢ each set

741. 7-Piece Water Set

ALL PRICES ARE PER DOZEN

742. 8 inch Salad Plate, ground bottom, round
6 dozen to carton, shipping weight 70 pounds
Crystal, $2.80, Ruby, $6.00, Ritz Blue, $4.50
Cartons 50¢ each set

741D. 8 inch Salad Plate, square

CARTONS CHARGED AT NET PRICES

741. 50 ounce Pitcher, pressed
1 dozen to carton, shipping weight 50 pounds
Crystal, $4.00, Ruby, $6.00, Ritz Blue, $6.00
Cartons 50¢ each set

741. 9 oz. Table Tumbler
6 dozen to carton, weight 35 pounds
Crystal, $1.00, Ruby, $1.30, Ritz Blue, $1.40
Cartons 50¢ each set

741. 9 ounce Sherbet

Illustrations ½ Size

741. 12 ounce Pressed Tumbler
Crystal $1.00
Ritz Blue 1.00
Moonstone 2.00
Sea Green 2.00
Ruby 2.70
Amber 1.40
Rose Pink 1.40
Imperial Green 2.00
6 dozen to carton
Shipping weight 40 pounds
Cartons 50¢ each set

741. 9 ounce Pressed Ice-Tea
Crystal $1.00
Ritz Blue 1.00
Moonstone 2.00
Sea Green 2.00
Ruby 2.70
Amber 1.40
Rose Pink 1.40
Imperial Green 2.00
6 dozen to carton
Shipping weight 40 pounds
Cartons 50¢ each set

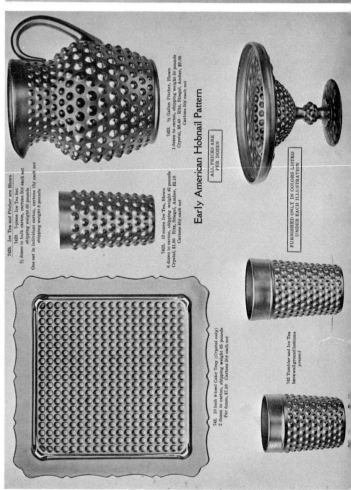

Early American Hobnail Pattern

742. Ice Tea and Pitcher are Blown
742. 7-piece Ice Tea Set
½ dozen in bulk carton, cartons 50¢ each set
shipping weight 60 pounds
One set in individual carton, cartons 10¢ each set
shipping weight 8 pounds

742. ½ Gallon Pitcher, Blown
1 dozen to carton, shipping weight 50 pounds
Crystal, $8.40, Ritz, Stiegel, Amber, $9.00
Cartons 50¢ each set

742. 10 ounce Ice Tea, Blown
6 dozen to carton, shipping weight 35 pounds
Crystal, $1.90, Ritz, Stiegel, Amber, $2.10
Cartons 50¢ each set

ALL PRICES ARE PER DOZEN

FURNISHED ONLY IN COLORS LISTED UNDER EACH ILLUSTRATION

742. 10 inch 4-toed Cake Tray (Crystal only)
2 dozen to carton, shipping weight 65 pounds
Per dozen, $7.50
Cartons 50¢ each set

742. Tumbler and Ice Tea have well ground bottoms pressed

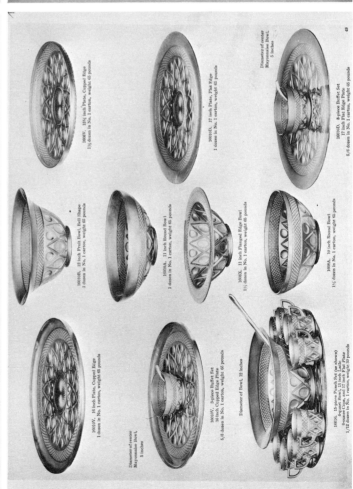

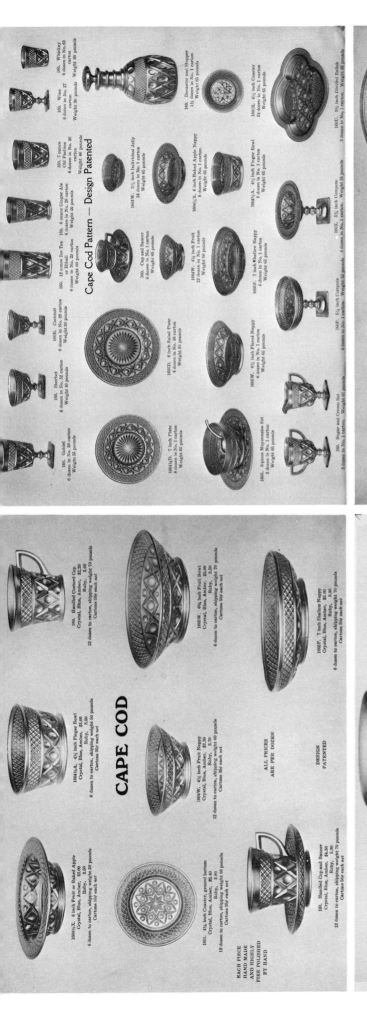

Imperial

Cape Cod Pattern — Design Patented

160. Whiskey. Weight 30 pounds

160. Wine. 6 dozen in No. 27 carton. Weight 30 pounds

160. 7 ounce Old Fashion. 6 dozen in No. 26 carton. Weight 40 pounds

160. Decanter and Stopper. 1½ dozen in No. 1 carton. Weight 60 pounds

1601L. 4½ inch Coaster. 3¼ dozen in No. 1 carton. Weight 65 pounds

160. Cocktail. 6 dozen in No. 28 carton. Weight 30 pounds

160. 6 ounce Ginger Ale or Hiball. 6 dozen in No. 26 carton. Weight 40 pounds

1601W. 3½ inch Individual Jelly. 2¼ dozen in No. 1 carton. Weight 60 pounds

1604½X. 6 inch Baked Apple Nappy. 8 dozen in No. 1 carton. Weight 65 pounds

1604½W. 4½ inch Finger Bowl. 12 dozen in No. 1 carton. Weight 60 pounds

1604½X. 4½ inch Finger Bowl. 6 dozen in No. 1 carton. Weight 65 pounds

160. Sherbet. 6 dozen in No. 52 carton. Weight 40 pounds

160. 12 ounce Ice Tea or Hiball. 6 dozen in No. 29 carton. Weight 60 pounds

160. Cup and Saucer. 6 dozen in No. 1 carton. Weight 65 pounds

1604. 4½ inch Fruit. 12 dozen in No. 1 carton. Weight 60 pounds

160F. 7 inch Shallow Nappy. 6 dozen in No. 1 carton. Weight 65 pounds

160. Goblet. 6 dozen in No. 29 carton. Weight 55 pounds

1601D. 8 inch Salad Plate. 4 dozen in No. 48 carton. Weight 55 pounds

1604½D. 7 inch Plate. 8 dozen in No. 1 carton. Weight 65 pounds

160L. 3-piece Mayonnaise Set. 3 dozen in No. 1 carton. Weight 65 pounds

160C. 5¼ inch Compote. 6 dozen in No. 1 carton. Weight 55 pounds

160. Sugar and Cream Set. 3 dozen in No. 1 carton. Weight 50 pounds

160F. 5½ inch Flared Nappy. 6 dozen in No. 1 carton. Weight 60 pounds

160G. 9¼ inch Turto Plate. 1½ dozen in No. 1 carton. Weight 65 pounds

165. Ice Pitcher. 1 dozen in No. 4 carton. Weight 45 pounds

160. 36 ounce Refrigerator Jug. 1½ dozen in No. 1 carton. Weight 60 pounds

1608P. 13½ inch Turto Plate. 1½ dozen in No. 1 carton. Weight 65 pounds

1608A. 11 inch Salad Bowl. 1 dozen in No. 1 carton. weight 55 pounds

1608X. 11¼ inch Fruit Bowl. 1 dozen in No. 1 carton. weight 55 pounds

160. 5-piece Whiskey Set

160. 5-piece Wine Set

160. 5-piece Whiskey Set

CAPE COD

160. Handled Custard Cup. Crystal, Blue, Amber, $3.00. Ruby, $3.50. 12 dozen to carton, shipping weight 70 pounds. Cartons 50¢ each net

1604½A. 4½ inch Finger Bowl. Crystal, Blue, Amber, $3.00. Ruby, 3.50. 12 dozen to carton, shipping weight 60 pounds. Cartons 50¢ each net

1605W. 6¾ inch Fruit Bowl. Crystal, Blue, Amber, $2.30. Ruby, 3.75. 6 dozen to carton, shipping weight 70 pounds. Cartons 50¢ each net

1604½X. 6 inch Fruit or Baked Apple. Crystal, Blue, Amber, $3.00. Ruby, 3.50. 6 dozen to carton, shipping weight 60 pounds. Cartons 50¢ each net

1601. 4½ inch Coaster, ground bottom. Crystal, Blue, Amber, $2.30. Ruby, 2.80. 12 dozen to carton, shipping weight 65 pounds. Cartons 50¢ each net

1604W. 4½ inch Fruit Nappy. Crystal, Blue, Amber, $2.30. Ruby, 2.80. 12 dozen to carton, shipping weight 60 pounds. Cartons 50¢ each net

160. Handled Cup and Saucer. Crystal, Blue, Amber, $4.50. Ruby, 5.30. 12 dozen to carton, shipping weight 70 pounds. Cartons 50¢ each net

ALL PRICES ARE PER DOZEN

DESIGN PATENTED

EACH PIECE HAND MADE AND HIGHLY FIRE POLISHED BY HAND

160V. 13½ inch Plate, Cupped Edge. 1½ dozen in No. 1 carton. weight 65 pounds

1601X. 17 inch Plate, Flat Edge. 1 dozen in No. 1 carton. weight 65 pounds

1601D. 3-piece Buffet Set. 17 inch Flat Edge Plate. 6/4 dozen in No. 1 carton. weight 65 pounds

1601D. 12 inch Fruit Bowl, Bell Shape. 1 dozen in No. 1 carton. weight 65 pounds

1608A. 11 inch Round Bowl. 1 dozen in No. 1 carton. weight 65 pounds

1608X. 11 inch Flanged Edge Bowl. 1½ dozen in No. 1 carton. weight 65 pounds

1608A. 10 inch Round Bowl. 1½ dozen in No. 1 carton. weight 65 pounds

160V. 16 inch Plate, Cupped Edge. 1 dozen in No. 1 carton. weight 65 pounds

1608V. 3-piece Buffet Set. 16 inch Cupped Edge Plate. 6/8 dozen in No. 1 carton. weight 65 pounds

160L. 15-piece Punch Set (as above). 7/12 dozen in No. 1 carton. weight 80 pounds

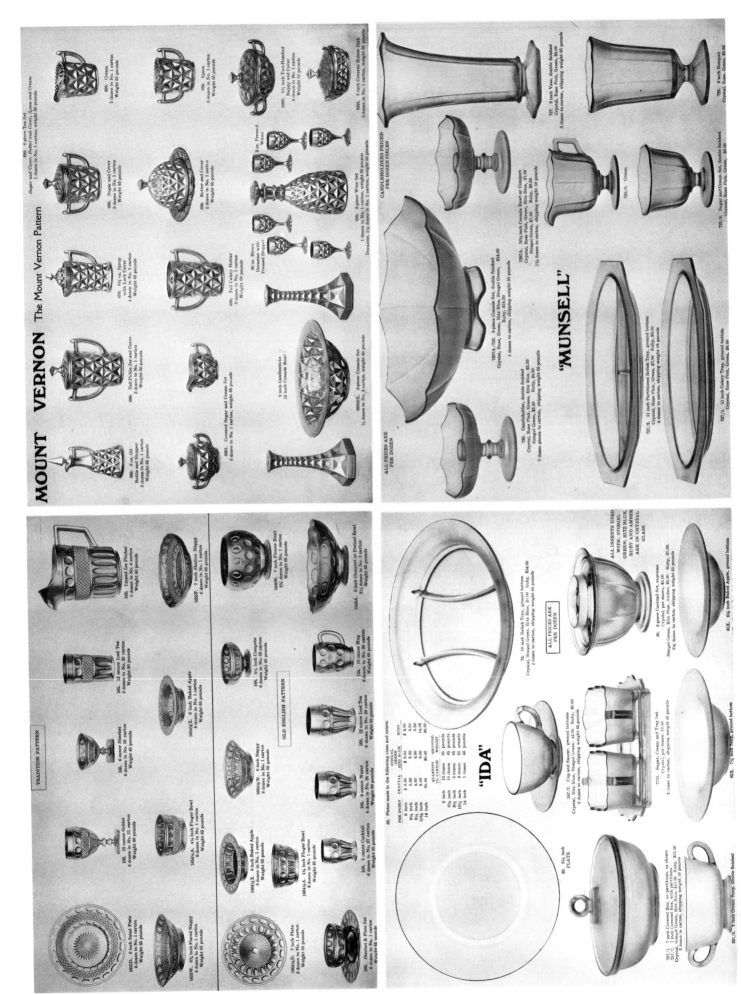

MOUNT VERNON   The Mount Vernon Pattern

600. 6-piece Tea Set
Sugar and Cover, Butter and Cover, Spoon and Cream
1 dozen in No. 1 carton, weight 60 pounds

600. Cream
5 dozen in No. 1 carton
Weight 65 pounds

650. Spoon
6 dozen in No. 1 carton
Weight 65 pounds

699E. 5½ inch Two-Handled Nappy
3 dozen in No. 1 carton
Weight 65 pounds

699. Sugar and Cover
3 dozen in No. 1 carton
Weight 65 pounds

699. Tall Pickle Jar and Cover
2 dozen in No. 1 carton
Weight 65 pounds

699. Butter and Cover
2 dozen in No. 1 carton
Weight 65 pounds

6991. 5 inch Covered Butter Dish
3 dozen in No. 1 carton, weight 65 pounds

690. 8¾ oz. Syrup with Lock Cover
4 dozen in No. 1 carton
Weight 65 pounds

2 oz. Pressed Wine

690. Tall Celery Holder
3 dozen in No. 1 carton
Weight 50 pounds

690. 6-piece Wine Set
1 dozen in No. 1 carton, weight 60 pounds
Decanter, 1½ dozen in No. 1 carton, weight 50 pounds

690. 6 oz. Oil Bottle and Stopper
5 dozen in No. 1 carton
Weight 65 pounds

6991. Covered Sugar and Cream Set
3 dozen in No. 1 carton, weight 65 pounds

9 inch Candlesticks

26 oz. Blown Decanter with Pressed Stopper

690. 3-piece Console Set
½ dozen in No. 1 carton, weight 60 pounds
12 inch Console Bowl

699MX. 3-piece Console Set

TRADITION PATTERN

16L. Lipped Ice Pitcher
1 dozen in No. 4 carton
Weight 45 pounds

165EF. 7 inch Shallow Nappy
6 dozen in No. 1 carton
Weight 65 pounds

1346N. 7 inch Flower Bowl
3¾ dozen in No. 1 carton
Weight 65 pounds

1346A. 9 inch Comport or Pretzel Bowl
2½ dozen in No. 1 carton
Weight 65 pounds

165. 12 ounce Iced Tea
6 dozen in No. 32 carton
Weight 60 pounds

1655D. 8 inch Salad Plate
6 dozen in No. 1 carton
Weight 60 pounds

165VW. 6½ inch Flared Nappy
6 dozen in No. 1 carton
Weight 65 pounds

16L. 10 ounce Goblet
6 dozen in No. 61 carton
Weight 60 pounds

16L. 6 ounce Sherbet
6 dozen in No. 32 carton
Weight 45 pounds

1664½X. 6 inch Baked Apple
6 dozen in No. 1 carton
Weight 65 pounds

16L. 5 ounce Cocktail
6 dozen in No. 27 carton
Weight 35 pounds

16L. 4½ inch Flared Finger Bowl
8 dozen in No. 1 carton
Weight 65 pounds

18L. Sherbet & Plate Set
6 dozen in No. 1 carton
Weight 65 pounds

1664½W. 8 inch Compote
8 dozen in No. 1 carton
Weight 45 pounds

OLD ENGLISH PATTERN

16L. 6 inch Nappy
8 dozen in No. 1 carton
Weight 65 pounds

16L. 4½ inch Compote
6 dozen in No. 32 carton
Weight 45 pounds

32L. 10 ounce Mug
6 dozen in No. 1 carton
Weight 60 pounds

1664½X.A. 4½ inch Finger Bowl
8 dozen in No. 1 carton
Weight 65 pounds

16L. 9 ounce Water
6 dozen in No. 26 carton
Weight 60 pounds

16L. 12 ounce Iced Tea
6 dozen in No. 29 carton
Weight 60 pounds

18L. 7 inch Plate
3 dozen in No. 1 carton
Weight 50 pounds

CANDLEHOLDERS PRICED PER DOZEN PIECES

728TA, 722. 3-piece Console Set, double finished
Crystal, Rose, Green, Ritz Blue, Stiegel Green, $14.00
1 dozen to carton, shipping weight 50 pounds

728TA. 16½ inch Console Bowl or Comport
Crystal, Rose Pink, Green, Ritz Blue, $5.00
Stiegel Green, $7.00
1½ dozen to carton, shipping weight 50 pounds

727. 8 inch Vase, double finished
Crystal, Rose Pink, Green, $6.40
3 dozen to carton, shipping weight 65 pounds

722. 6 inch Bouquet
Crystal, Rose, Green, $2.50

728. Candleholder, double finished
Crystal, Rose Pink, Green, Ritz Blue, $5.50
Ruby, $4.00
Stiegel Green, $3.50

725/8. Sugar and Cream Set, double finished
Crystal, Rose Pink, Green, $6.40

725/6. Cream

"MUNSELL"

ALL PRICES ARE PER DOZEN

722/2. 11 inch Partitioned Relish Tray, ground bottom
Crystal, Rose Pink, Green, Ritz Blue
4 dozen to carton, shipping weight 65 pounds

727/1. 11 inch Celery Tray, ground bottom
Crystal, Rose Pink, Green, $3.50

7S. 10 inch Relish Tray, ground bottom
Crystal, Stiegel Green, Ritz Blue, $5.00, Ruby, $14.00
2 dozen to carton, shipping weight 65 pounds

ALL INSERTS USED WITH STIEGEL GREEN, RITZ BLUE, RUBY AND AMBER ARE CRYSTAL GLASS

46. 2-piece Cocktail Set, supreme
Crystal, per dozen, $5.00
Stiegel Green, Ritz Blue, Amber, $5.50, Ruby, $7.00
3½ dozen to carton, shipping weight 65 pounds

83X. 6½ inch Baked Apple, ground bottom

"IDA"

ALL PRICES ARE PER DOZEN

86. Plates made in the following sizes and colors:

PER DOZEN	CRYSTAL	STIEGEL GREEN, RITZ BLUE	RUBY	QUANTITY PER CARTON	SHIPPING WEIGHT
6 inch	$3.00	$3.50	$4.00	12 dozen	60 pounds
6½ inch	3.30	3.80	4.50	10 dozen	65 pounds
8½ inch	4.60	4.90	6.50	6 dozen	65 pounds
10½ inch	6.00	6.90	14.00	3 dozen	65 pounds
14 inch	30.00	36.00	48.00	1 dozen	65 pounds

85. 8½ inch PLATE

722R. Sugar, Cream and Tray Set
Crystal, per dozen, $8.00
3 dozen to carton, shipping weight 65 pounds

767/7. Cup and Saucer, ground bottoms
Crystal, Ritz Blue, Stiegel Green, $6.60, Ruby, $6.60
6 dozen to carton, shipping weight 65 pounds

767/1. 7 inch Covered Box, no partitions, as shown
Crystal, with pattern lid
767. 7 inch Covered Box, with partitions
Crystal, Stiegel Green, Ritz Blue, Stiegel Green, $10.00 Ruby, $15.00
3 dozen to carton, shipping weight 65 pounds

83X. 7½ inch SOUP, ground bottom

231/6. 7 inch Cream Soup, double finished

Pillar Flute Pattern

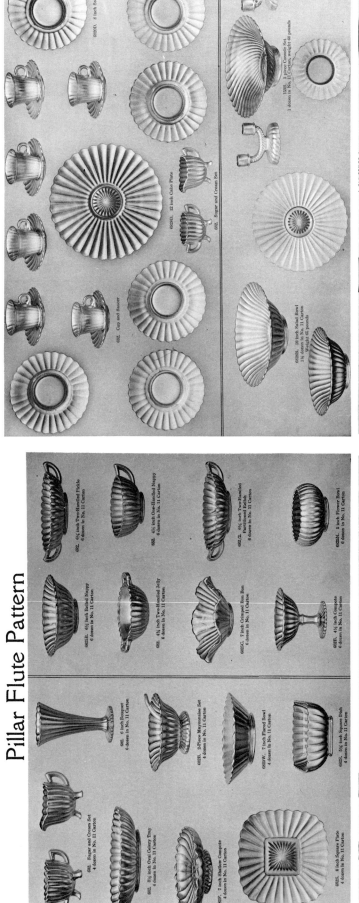

682. 8 inch Salad Plate

682SQ. 10 inch Salad Bowl
1½ dozen in No. 11 Carton
shipping weight 60 pounds

682. 12 inch Color Plate

682. Sugar and Cream Set

682. Cup and Saucer

132SL. 3 piece Console Set
1 dozen in No. 11 Carton, weight 60 pounds

682. 6½ inch Two-Handled Pickle
6 dozen in No. 11 Carton

682. 4½ inch One-Handled Nappy
6 dozen in No. 11 Carton

682SL. 6½ inch Salad Nappy
6 dozen in No. 11 Carton

682. 4½ inch Two-Handled Jelly
6 dozen in No. 11 Carton

682.Z. 6½ inch Two-Handled Partitioned Relish
6 dozen in No. 11 Carton

682. 7 inch Crimped Bon Bon
6 dozen in No. 11 Carton

682SN. 5 inch Flower Bowl
6 dozen in No. 11 Carton

682. 6 inch Bouquet
6 dozen in No. 11 Carton

682. 5-Piece Mayonnaise Set
4 dozen in No. 11 Carton

682SC. 7 inch Flared Bowl
4 dozen in No. 11 Carton

682R. 4½ inch Compote
6 dozen in No. 11 Carton

682. Sugar and Cream Set
4 dozen in No. 11 Carton

682. 8½ inch Oval Celery Tray
4 dozen in No. 11 Carton

682P. 7 inch Shallow Compote
4 dozen in No. 11 Carton

682S. 5¼ inch Square Dish
4 dozen in No. 11 Carton

682S. 8 inch Square Plate
4 dozen in No. 11 Carton

"SHAEFFER"

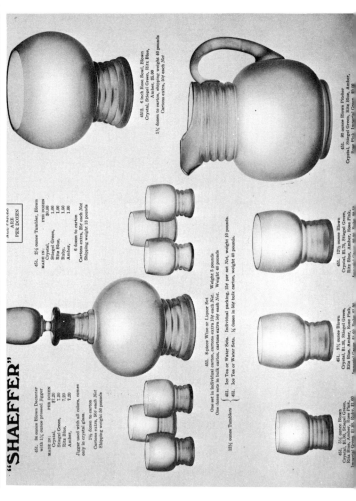

451. 34 ounce Blown Decanter
with 1½ ounce pressed Jigger

MADE IN:	PER DOZEN
Crystal,	$7.20
Stiegel Green,	7.20
Ritz Blue,	7.20
Amber,	7.20

Jigger used with all colors, comes only in crystal glass.

Cartons extra, 26c each Net
Shipping weight 50 pounds

451. 3½ ounce Tumbler, Blown

MADE IN:	PER DOZEN
Crystal,	$0.80
Stiegel Green,	1.00
Ritz Blue,	1.00
Ruby,	1.50
Amber,	1.00

6 dozen to carton
Cartons extra, 25c each Net
Shipping weight 18 pounds

451. 8-piece Wine or Liquor Set   Weight 5 pounds
One set in individual carton, cartons extra 10c each Net.
One dozen sets in bulk carton, cartons extra 50c each Net.

453. Ice Tea or Water Sets. Individual packing, 15c per set Net, weight 10 pounds
453. Ice Tea or Water Sets. ⅓ dozen in 50c bulk carton, weight 40 pounds

13½ ounce Tumblers

9¼ ounce Blown

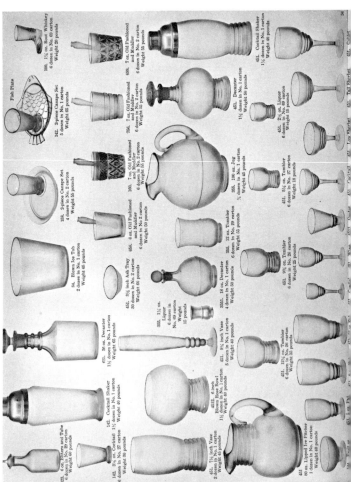

329. 6 oz. Fillers and Tube
6 dozen in No. 1 carton
Weight 40 pounds

142. 3¼ oz. Cocktail
6 dozen in No. 27 carton
Weight 30 pounds

143. Cocktail Shaker
1¼ dozen in No. 1 carton
Weight 40 pounds

612. 20 oz. Decanter
1½ dozen in No. 1 carton
Weight 60 pounds

60L. 1½ oz.
Liquor
6 dozen in No. 1
carton
Weight
10 pounds

451. 9½ inch Vase
2 dozen in No. 1 carton
Weight 40 pounds

6512. 6 inch
Blown Rose Bowl
1½ dozen in No. 1 carton
Weight 40 pounds

451. 3½ inch Ash Tray
30 dozen in No. 2 carton
Weight 60 pounds

64. Blown Ice Tub
2 dozen in No. 2 carton
Weight 65 pounds

142. 2-piece Canape Set
5 dozen in No. 1 carton
Weight 65 pounds

18K. 2-piece Canape Set
4 dozen in No. 1 carton
Weight 50 pounds

10G. 7 oz. Old Fashioned
and Muddler
6 dozen in No. 2 carton
Weight 50 pounds

6 oz. Old Fashioned
and Muddler
6 dozen in No. 2 carton
Weight 50 pounds

68K. 3½ inch Nappy
6 dozen in No. 2 carton
Weight 55 pounds

38SH. 18 oz. Decanter
4 dozen in No. 1 carton
Weight 40 pounds

305. 200 oz. Jug
¾ dozen in No. 1 carton
Weight 65 pounds

Fish Plate

100. 1½ oz. Boot Whiskey
6 dozen in No. 40 carton
Weight 20 pounds

60R. 7 oz. Old Fashioned
and Muddler
6 dozen in No. 2 carton
Weight 60 pounds

451. Decanter
1½ dozen in No. 1 carton
Weight 50 pounds

451. Cocktail Shaker
1½ dozen in No. 1 carton
Weight 40 pounds

305. 12 oz. Tumbler
6 dozen in No. 1 carton
Weight 55 pounds

451. 9½ oz. Tumbler
6 dozen in No. 1 carton
Weight 65 pounds

451. 13½ oz. Tumbler
6 dozen in No. 1 carton
Weight 35 pounds

451. 2½ oz. Liquor
6 dozen in No. 69 carton
Weight 18 pounds

451. Lipped Tee Pitcher
1 dozen in No. 1 carton
Weight 40 pounds

Top Left Panel

400/9833L. 3-piece Console Set
1 dozen in No. 1 Carton
Weight 60 pounds

400/3930B. 3-piece Console Set
1 dozen in No. 1 Carton, weight 60 Pounds

400/42E. 5½ inch two-handled Tray
9 dozen in No. 1 Carton
Weight 60 pounds

400/42B. 4½ inch two-handled Fruit
12 dozen in No. 1 Carton
Weight 55 pounds

400/52E. 7 inch two-handled Tray
Weight 45 pounds

400/52B. 6½ inch two-handled Nappy
4 dozen in No. 1 Carton
Weight 65 pounds

400/62E. 7 inch two-handled Tray
3½ dozen in No. 1 Carton
Weight 55 pounds

400/62B. 7 inch two-handled Bowl
4 dozen in No. 1 Carton
Weight 65 pounds

400/72E. 10 inch two-handled Tray
2 dozen in No. 1 Carton
Weight 60 pounds

400/72B. 8½ inch two-handled Bowl
3½ dozen in No. 1 Carton
Weight 65 pounds

400/42D. 8½ inch two-handled Plate
4 dozen in No. 1 Carton
Weight 55 pounds

400/72D. 10 inch two-handled Plate
2½ dozen in No. 1 Carton

400/52D. 7 inch two-handled Plate
7 dozen in No. 1 Carton
Weight 60 pounds

400/42D. 6½ inch two-handled Plate
12 dozen in No. 1 Carton
Weight 50 pounds

Top Right Panel

Pressed

7880/2. 3-piece Cigarette Set
1 dozen in No. 1 Carton
Weight 65 pounds

550/1. Candleholder
6 dozen in No. 1 carton
Weight 45 pounds

701/8. Candleholder
8 dozen in No. 1 Carton
Weight 55 pounds

701/9. 7 inch Footed Ball
4 dozen in No. 1 Carton
Weight 50 pounds

Blown

701/1D. 4 inch Footed Ball
4 dozen in No. 1 carton
Weight 40 pounds

701/2. 3½ inch Footed Ball
6 dozen in No. 1 carton
Weight 35 pounds

701/7. 6 inch Footed Ball
1½ dozen in No. 1 carton
Weight 45 pounds

Blown and cast feet

550/2. 3½ inch Footed Ball
6 dozen in No. 1 carton
Weight 25 pounds

550/3. 7 inch Footed Ball
¾ dozen in No. 1 carton
Weight 40 pounds

Chrome Top

36 ounce Shaker

550/1B. 3-piece Console Set
¾ dozen in No. 1 carton
Weight 45 pounds

7012. 7-piece Cocktail Set
1 dozen in 1 bulk carton, weight 56 pounds
Individual packing, set in No. 78 carton
Weight 6 pounds

701/2. 3½ ounce Cocktail
6 dozen in No. 1 carton
Weight 20 pounds

Blown and cast feet

701/2B. 3-piece Console Set
1 dozen in No. 1 carton
Weight 50 pounds

Blown and cast feet

Blown

13S. 8 ounce Jug
1 dozen in No. 1 Carton
Weight 45 pounds

13S. 16 ounce
1 dozen in No. 48 carton
Weight 18 pounds

13S. 13 ounce
6 dozen in No. 1 carton
Weight 20 pounds

13S. 10 ounce
6 dozen in No. 1 carton
Weight 20 pounds

13S. 6 ounce
6 dozen in No. 1 carton
Weight 15 pounds

Bottom Left Panel (CANDLEWICK)

CANDLEWICK

400/68B. 2-piece Canapé Set
6 dozen in No. 1 Carton
Weight 60 pounds

400/74B. 8½ inch 4-toed Nappy
3 dozen in No. 1 Carton
Weight 60 pounds

400/74J. 7 inch 4-toed Lily Bowl
3 dozen in No. 1 Carton
Weight 65 pounds

400/67B. 9 inch Footed Bowl
1½ dozen in No. 1 Carton
Weight 60 pounds

400/88. 10 inch Cheese and Cracker
2 dozen in No. 1 Carton
Weight 60 pounds

400/4L. 5-piece Mayonnaise Set
3 dozen in No. 1 Carton
Weight 60 pounds

400/745C. 9 inch 4-toed Dish
Fancy Square Shape
3 dozen in No. 1 Carton
Weight 65 pounds

400/33B. 11 inch Centerbowl
1½ dozen in No. 1 Carton
Weight 60 pounds

400/80. 5½ inch Compart
6 dozen in No. 1 Carton
Weight 80 pounds

400/68B. 4½ inch Compart
6 dozen in No. 1 Carton
Weight 50 pounds

400/87F. 8 inch Vase, Fan Shape
2½ dozen in No. 1 Carton
Weight 60 pounds

400/87B. 7 inch Vase
2½ dozen in No. 1 Carton
Weight 60 pounds

400/34. 4½ inch Ash Tray
24 dozen in No. 1 Carton
Weight 60 pounds

400/152. 10 inch Cake Stand
1½ dozen in No. 1 Carton
Weight 50 pounds

400/90. 3½ inch Candleholder
6 dozen in No. 1 Carton
Weight 80 pounds

400/80. Candleholder
6 dozen in No. 1 Carton
Weight 80 pounds

400/81. 3½ inch Candleholder
6 dozen in No. 1 Carton
Weight 60 pounds

Bottom Right Panel

All plates and bowls on this page have pressed and polished bottoms

400/1D. 9 inch Plate
4 dozen in No. 1 Carton
Weight 55 pounds

400/7D. 9 inch Plate
4 dozen in No. 1 Carton
Weight 55 pounds

400/5D. 8 inch Plate
4 dozen in No. 48 Carton
Weight 50 pounds

400/30. Sugar and Cream Set
6 dozen in No. 1 Carton
Weight 65 pounds

400/15D. 12 inch Plate
1½ dozen in No. 1 Carton
Weight 50 pounds

400/3D. 7 inch Plate
6 dozen in No. 1 Carton
Weight 55 pounds

400/17D. 14 inch Plate
1 dozen in No. 1 Carton
Weight 50 pounds

400/77. Cup and Saucer
6 dozen in No. 1 Carton
Weight 65 pounds

400/1F. 6 inch Plate
12 dozen in No. 1 Carton
Weight 65 pounds

400/3F. 6 inch Nappy
6 dozen in No. 1 Carton
Weight 60 pounds

400/5F. 7 inch Nappy
6 dozen in No. 1 Carton
Weight 65 pounds

400/7F. 8 inch Nappy
5 dozen in No. 1 Carton
Weight 65 pounds

400/17F. 12 inch Nappy
1 dozen in No. 1 Carton
Weight 55 pounds

400/34. 4½ inch Coaster
24 dozen in No. 1 Carton
Weight 65 pounds

400/52. 4 inch Individual Jelly
24 dozen in No. 1 Carton
Weight 60 pounds

400/1F. 5 inch Nappy
12 dozen in No. 1 Carton
Weight 65 pounds

400/51. 6 inch Handled Nappy
8 dozen in No. 1 Carton
Weight 50 pounds

400/13F. 10 inch Nappy
1 dozen in No. 1 Carton
Weight 55 pounds

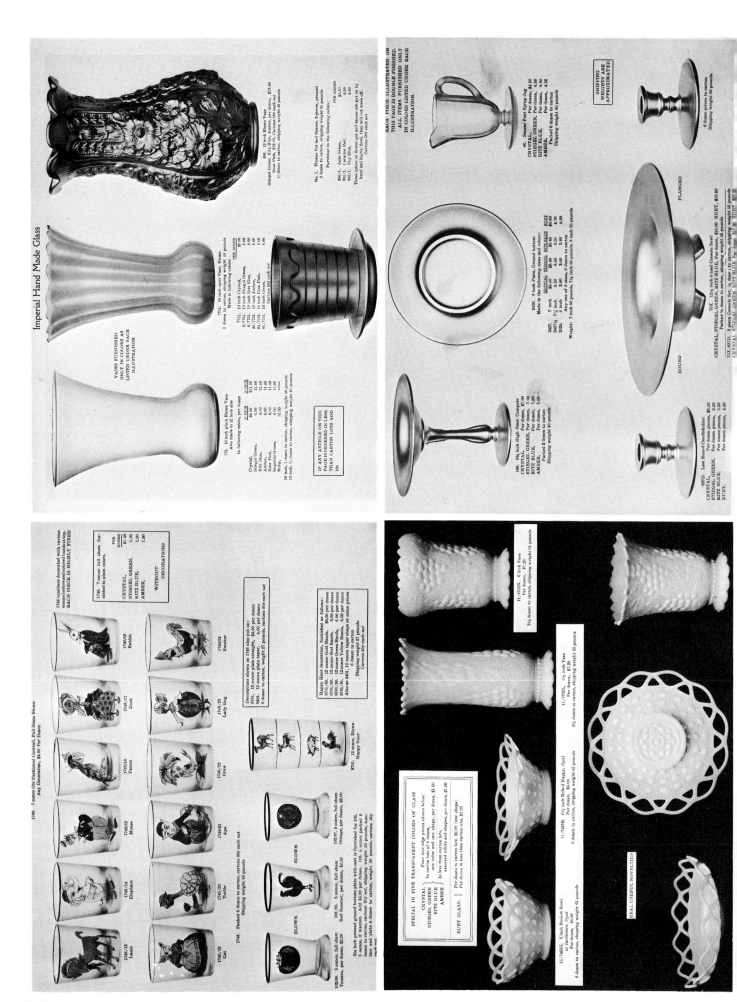

Imperial Hand Made Glass

VASES FURNISHED ONLY IN COLORS AS LISTED UNDER EACH ILLUSTRATION

IF ANY ARTICLE ON THIS PAGE IS ORDERED IN LESS THAN CARTON LOTS ADD 10%

488. 12 inch Blown Vase

Stiegel Green, Ritz Blue, Amber, Rose Pink. Cartons 50¢ each net.
½ dozen to carton, shipping weight 60 pounds

	PER DOZEN
Stiegel Green, Ritz Blue, Amber, Rose Pink	$12.00

77b. 10 inch plain Blown Vase
Also made in 12 inch size

In following colors, per dozen:

	10 INCH	12 INCH
Crystal	$6.00	$11.00
Stiegel Green	6.00	11.00
Ritz Blue	6.00	11.00
Amber	6.00	11.00
Rose Pink	6.00	11.00
Imperial Green	6.00	11.00
Ruby	12.00	

10 inch, 1 dozen to carton, shipping weight 40 pounds
12 inch, ½ dozen to carton, shipping weight 40 pounds

775l. 10 inch optic Vase, Blown

1 dozen to carton, shipping weight 40 pounds
Furnished in the following colors:

	PER DOZEN
775l. 10 inch Crystal	$8.00
8/775l. 10 inch Stiegel Green	8.00
6/775l. 10 inch Ritz Blue	8.00
40/775l. 10 inch Amber	8.00
64/775l. 10 inch Rose Pink	8.10
81/775l. 10 inch Green	8.00

No. 1. Flower Pot and Saucer, 2 pieces, pressed
2 pieces to carton, shipping weight 65 pounds
Furnished in the following colors:

	PER DOZEN
800/1. Jade Green	
801/1. Carmine Red	
802/1. Sky Blue	

Three colors on flower pot and saucer are put on by hand and highly fired, they will not wash off. Cartons 50¢ each net

---

EACH PIECE ILLUSTRATED ON THIS PAGE IS DOUBLE FINISHED.
ALL ITEMS FURNISHED ONLY IN COLORS LISTED UNDER EACH ILLUSTRATION.

SHIPPING WEIGHTS ARE APPROXIMATED

46. Saucer Foot Syrup Jug

	PER DOZEN
CRYSTAL, Per dozen,	$4.50
STIEGEL GREEN, RITZ BLUE, Per dozen,	4.50
AMBER, Per dozen,	4.50

Packed 6 dozen to carton
Shipping weight 60 pounds

160. 6¼ inch High Stem Compote

	CRYSTAL	STIEGEL GREEN	RITZ BLUE	RUBY
160. Per dozen	$2.50	$3.50	$4.50

STIEGEL GREEN, RITZ BLUE, AMBER, Per dozen
Packed 3 dozen to carton
Shipping weight 60 pounds

8 inch Plate, Ground bottom
Made in the following sizes and colors:

	CRYSTAL	STIEGEL GREEN	RITZ BLUE	RUBY
242Z. 7 inch	$2.40	$3.40	$3.40	$4.60
242½Z. 7½ inch	2.50	3.50	3.50	4.70
242B. 8 inch	2.60	3.60	3.60	4.80

Any one of 3 sizes, 6 dozen to carton
Weight: 7 inch 50 pounds, 7½ inch 60 pounds, 8 inch 65 pounds

FLANGED

ROUND

75X. 12½ inch 4 tool Console Bowl

CRYSTAL, STIEGEL, GREEN, RITZ BLUE. Per dozen, $10.00 RUBY, $12.50

Packed ¾ dozen to carton, shipping weight 45 pounds

75X/65TD. 3 piece Console Set, ½ dozen to carton, shipping weight 65 pounds

68TD. Low Round Candleholder

CRYSTAL, Per dozen pieces,	$2.50
STIEGEL, GREEN, Per dozen pieces,	3.50
RITZ, BLUE, Per dozen pieces,	3.50
RUBY, Per dozen pieces,	3.50

6 dozen pieces to carton
Shipping weight 60 pounds

1746. 7 ounce Old Fashioned Cocktail, Full Sham Blown
Any Decoration, $4.00 Per Dozen

1748. 7 ounce full sham furnished in plain colors.
EACH PIECE IS HIGHLY FIRED

1748. 7 ounce full sham, furnished in plain colors.

	PER DOZEN
CRYSTAL, STIEGEL, GREEN, RITZ BLUE, AMBER	$1.48
WITHOUT DECORATIONS	1.20
	1.20

1748/13 Lamb
1748/18 Rabbit
1748/14 Elephant
1748/17 Duck
1748/15 Mouse
1748/16 Parrot
1748/19 Cat
1748/20 Turtle
1748/21 Ape
1748/22 Crow
1748/23 Lady Bug
1748/24 Rooster

BLOWN
BLOWN

Decorations shown on 1746 also put on:
8701. 12 ounce plain straight, $4.00 per dozen
8401. 12 ounce plain taper, 4.00 per dozen
6 dozen to carton, weight 27 pounds, cartons 50¢ each net

Happy Hour decoration, furnished as follows:
8701/88. 12 ounce Gold Bands, $6.00 per dozen
8701/89. 12 ounce Red Bands, 6.00 per dozen
8701/90. 12 ounce Green Bands, 6.00 per dozen
8701/91. 12 ounce Yellow Bands, 6.00 per dozen
Also 8401, 12 ounce taper shape at same prices
6 dozen to carton
Shipping weight 27 pounds
Cartons 50¢ each net

Shipping weight 40 pounds

109. 5 ounce, full sham
Red Rooster, per dozen, $2.00

108/87. 5 ounce, full sham
Orange, per dozen, $2.00

8701. 12 ounce, Blown
Happy Hour

102/86. 5 ounce, full sham
Tomato, per dozen, $2.00

Six inch pressed ground bottom plate with nest is furnished for 168.
6 nested, if wanted. 168, 4 ounce packed 6 dozen to carton, cartons 25¢ net, shipping weight 30 pounds, tumbler and plate 4 dozen to carton, weight 50 pounds, cartons 36¢ each net.

REAL USEFUL NOVELTIES

11/4732N. 6 inch Vase
3½ dozen to carton, shipping weight 65 pounds

11/4732L. 7½ inch Vase
Per dozen, $7.20
3½ dozen to carton, shipping weight 65 pounds

SPECIAL IN FIVE TRANSPARENT COLORS OF GLASS

CRYSTAL, STIEGEL, GREEN, RITZ BLUE, AMBER
Floor lace edge pieces shown below:
In carton lots of 6 dozen,
one color and one shape, per dozen, $1.50
In less than carton lots,
assorted colors and shapes, per dozen, $1.89

RUBY GLASS
Per dozen in carton lots, $2.00 (one shape)
Per dozen in less than carton lots, $2.20

11/4745B. 5 inch Basket Bowl
or Jardiniere, Opal
Per dozen, $4.00
6 dozen to carton, shipping weight 65 pounds

11/745B. 6¼ inch Rolled Nappy, Opal
Per dozen, $1.20
6 dozen to carton, shipping weight 60 pounds

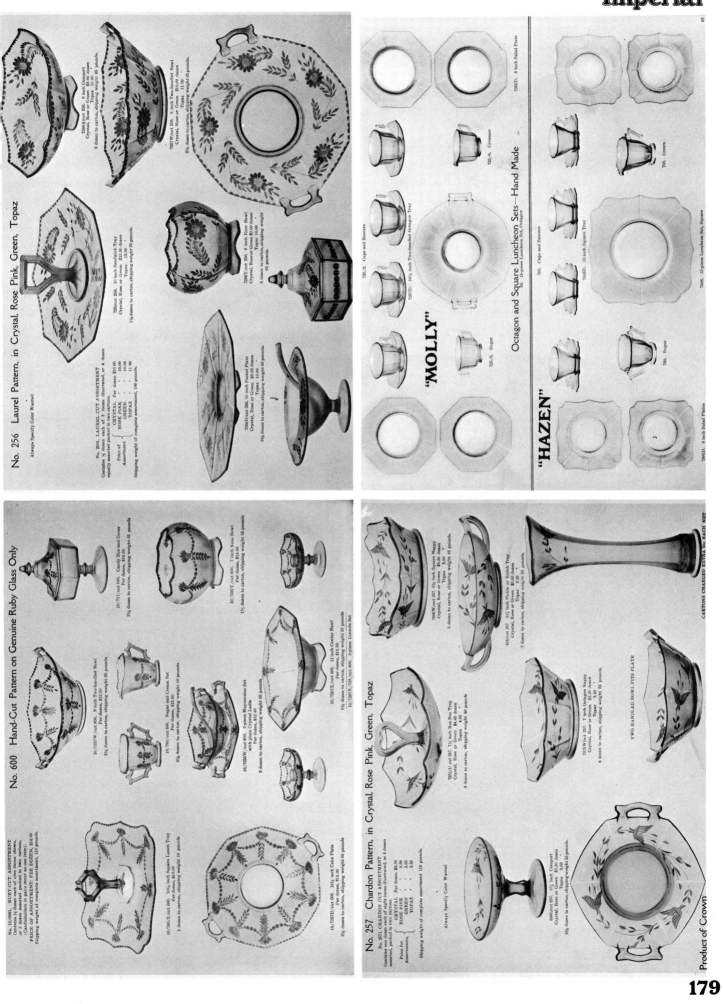

No. 256 Laurel Pattern, in Crystal, Rose Pink, Green, Topaz

Always Specify Color Wanted

Octagon and Square Luncheon Sets—Hand Made

"MOLLY"

"HAZEN"

No. 600 Hand-Cut Pattern on Genuine Ruby Glass Only

No. 257 Chardon Pattern, in Crystal, Rose Pink, Green, Topaz

Always Specify Color Wanted

CARTONS CHARGED EXTRA 50c EACH NET

TWO HANDLED BOWL FITS PLATE

Product of Crown

Indiana

The name Indiana Glass will ring special bells with collectors today. This Dunkirk, Indiana factory gave much to our Depression Glass house, and many of its patterns will never be forgotten.

Sometime in the late 19th Century a glass factory was devised in buildings originally intended for the railroad. Called Ohio Flint Glass Company, manufacturers of pressed tumblers and tableware, for a time, it later sold to the National Glass Company combine. Management finally stabilized in 1907 with the incorporation of the Indiana Glass Company which has maintained continuous operations since.

Indiana began with the usual hand-pressed lines of servicable crystal ware. Several lines were started expressly for "tea rooms and soda fountains" and were so well-received they were continued on into the 20s and eventually into color. These lines were always made by hand, as were several other pressed dinnerware lines introduced in the 20s and popularized through the 30s.

With the advent of the assembly line, though, some of the factory production was redesigned around machines, and when the ideas of automation, color, and mold-etched dinnerware fused in the late 20s much patterned ware by Indiana saw the market front. Today all these patterns—some hand-made and some machine-made—are favorites once again.

Indiana's most interesting sideline through the years started up with the automobile. The company made lenses and other necessary glass items for tin lizzies, and became a chief supplier to the industry over the next three decades.

A general line of tableware is still being made at Indiana Glass, now a subsidiary of the Lancaster Colony Corporation. Among its favorite lines are the reissues of old pressed patterns—most notably Sandwich, Avocado, and "Pyramid"—in new colors, and its "carnival glass", 70s-style.

COLOR

Indiana's Depression-era shades were the classic ones—green and amber beginning in 1925, Rose in 1926 and topaz about 1930. Yet with the exception of amber these colors were comparatively short-lived, passing out of production even before the mid-30s. An opaque ivory dinnerware was brought out in 1933. This company's blue-green, incidently, was not made until the 50s.

SANDWICH (Indiana's)

The original issue of Indiana's old #170 pattern is reprinted from a 20s catalog on the following page, and early accessory pieces are shown below. All the #170 you find in Depression-era pink, green and amber was made in the 20s, but the crystal was continued in various open-stock pieces through 1970. The blue-green was made in the 50s, and it was in the 40s when the #170 diamond-shaped cream, sugar, and tray were designed from the Pineapple and Floral mold. Pieces in milk glass were made in the 50s and 60s.

Indiana has discontinued the crystal, but is using some #170 molds for its exclusive (not sold in stores) "Tiara Home Plan" party line. In 1969 these pieces of #170 were made in Ruby Red:

Jug, 68-oz, 8"   Serving Platter, 13"
Goblet, 9-oz, 5¼"   Wine Decanter, 10" with wine goblets
Plate, 10½" dinner   Cream & Sugar
Plate, 8-3/8" salad   Sandwich Server (center handle
Cup & Saucer   not same as old #170)

The "Tiara" line also includes a Sandwich piece made from an old Duncan and Miller mold, the candy jar & cover, 8½" tall.

In 1970 "Tiara" offered Sandwich Gold (amber) and added new pieces for a few years; at the present time this is that listing:

Candlesticks, 3½" low   Ashtray (same as butter base)
Butterdish & Cover, 6" tall   Plate, 10" dinner
Console Bowl, 11½"   Berry, 8"; Nappy 4"
Handled Basket, 10" tall   Salt & Pepper, 4¾"
Snack Set, 8½"x6¾"   Tiered Ensemble
   oval plate and cup   Puff Box & Cover

But Indiana has made another line of SANDWICH from old Duncan and Miller molds now in Indiana's possession. These are the same molds Duncan and Miller used in the 30s to make pink, green, amber and ruby; the same molds next used by United States Glass (Tiffin) to make crystal in the 50s and 60s.

In 1972 and 1973 Indiana has used them to make Sunset (yellow-red), a new medium green, and medium blue for Montgomery Ward. You can see the pieces in the Duncan and Miller Chapter. This is the 1972 listing:

Torte Plate, 16"   Fruit or Salad Bowl, 10"
Luncheon Plate, 8"   Candlesticks
Deviled Egg Plate, 12"   Sugar & Creamer
Footed Cake Salver, 13"   Cup & Saucer
Relish Dish, 5", 2-part,   Goblet, 9-oz, 6"
   handle   Wine, 3-oz, 4½"
Candy Dish, 8½"   Sherbet—Champagne, 5-oz, 5¼"

"TEA ROOM"

Also made in amber. The lamp is in the color section; the rest of the line (except 9", 11" ruffled vases) is in the catalog reprint to follow.

NUMBER 612

Rare pieces have turned up and are pictured below: the butterdish & cover, and the candy dish & cover which sometimes is found in a metal holder. An additional piece not shown is the 9-oz, 4½" tumbler, not footed.

#612 candy dish & cover and butterdish & cover

LORAIN

Snack trays were made in the late 40s in crystal with fired-on red, blue, yellow, and green. The set uses the 11½" platter with an indention for a cup.

"PINEAPPLE AND FLORAL"

Also made with fired-on colors. Pieces listed since Book 1 are the 10½" grill plate, 9-3/8" and 11½" plates (both found with extra ridge around center), cream soup, and the flower vase on metal stand. Shown is the 12" high spike vase, 4½" ashtray, and the plate with center indent.

More items from the early #170 SANDWICH line.

#170 SANDWICH from 1925 advertisement.

ABOVE: Close-up of 6" hexagon nappy. RIGHT: The bridge set was made in Depression pink and green, but has been made in crystal through the years and most recently in an olive green and dark amber.

More #170 SANDWICH on next page.

No. 170 Pattern

No 170—Spade

No. 170—Diamond

No. 170—Heart

No. 170—Club

68-oz. Jug

9-oz. Goblet

Mayonnaise Ladle

Mayonnaise Bowl

11" Handled Sandwich

8-piece Wine Set

3-oz. Cocktail

8-oz. Footed Tumbler

12-oz. Footed Tumbler

Low Candlestick

11½" Console Bowl — Rolled Edge

Low Candlestick

13" Cake Tray

Tall Candlestick

9" Console Bowl — Deep
Also made Crimped or Flat Top

Tall Candlestick

Covered Butter

Covered Sugar

Cream

Covered Puff Box

6" Hexagon Nappy

Berry Cream

Berry Sugar

Cup and Saucer

6-oz. Oil

6" Deep Nappy

10½" Celery Tray

Footed Sherbet

8" Oval Plate

4¾" Berry

8½" Berry

10½" Plate

8⅜" Plate

7" Plate

6" Plate

No. 172—OLD ENGLISH WATER SET
Made in either Crystal or Colored.

INDIANA GLASS COMPANY
DUNKIRK, INDIANA
MANUFACTURERS OF

PRESSED AND BLOWN GLASSWARE
CRYSTAL—COLORED—DECORATED

No. 172—ONE-HALF POUND COVERED CANDY JAR
Crystal, Amber or Green

OLD ENGLISH

This line was introduced in crystal, amber, and green; later it was made in pink. The water set and the covered candy jar are shown from 1926 advertisements. You may find more pieces than these; not pictured, for instance, is the sandwich server with center handle.

OLD ENGLISH pieces photographed below are: Comport; 4" Candlestick; Sugar & Cover; Creamer; 4½", 5½" Footed Tumblers; Jug & Cover; 11" Fruit Bowl.

CATALOG REPRINTS

On the pages to come are Indiana's colored lines in the order they were made, reprinted from catalogs dating from 1926 to the mid-30s. Official names and colors appear as on the original; other names are superimposed by me.

Tea Room and Soda Fountain Special
NO. 304 PATTERN
Design Patent No. 76985   Made in Green or Pink

6 oz. Tumbler
Packs 24 doz. to bbl.   Weight 175 lbs.

8½ oz. Tumbler
Packs 18 doz. to bbl.   Weight 165 lbs.

Low Footed Sundae
Packs 16 doz. to bbl.   Weight 135 lbs.

Tall Footed Sundae
Packs 12 doz. to bbl.   Weight 120 lbs.

Goblet
Packs 10 doz. to bbl.
Weight 130 lbs.

6 oz. Footed Coca Cola
Packs 17 doz. to bbl.
Weight 165 lbs.

8 oz. Footed Service Tumbler
Packs 14 doz. to bbl.
Weight 150 lbs.

10 oz. Footed Ice Tea
Packs 11 doz. to bbl.
Weight 125 lbs.

12 oz. Footed Malted Milk
Packs 8 doz. to bbl.
Weight 150 lbs.

"SODA FOUNTAIN"

Berry Cream
Packs 14 doz. to bbl.   Weight 160 lbs.

4 oz. Oil
Packs 18 doz. to bbl.   Weight 130 lbs.

Berry Sugar
Packs 14 doz. to bbl.   Weight 175 lbs.

4⅞ in. Relish Dish
Packs 16 doz. to bbl.   Weight 145 lbs.

Finger Bowl
Packs 16 doz. to bbl.   Weight 135 lbs.

Footed Banana Split
Packs 10 doz. to bbl.   Weight 135 lbs.

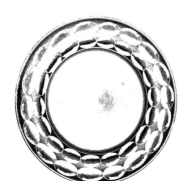

6 in. Plate
Packs 20 doz. to bbl.   Weight 145 lbs.

Shaker Salt and Pepper
Packs 75 doz. to bbl.   Weight 300 lbs.

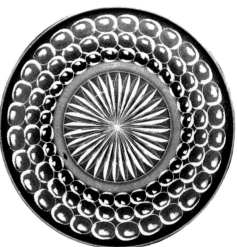

8½ in. Plate
Packs 15 doz. to bbl.   Weight 225 lbs.

184

No. 600 Tea Room and Soda Fountain Special
Design Patent No. 76986

SALT AND PEPPER
Nickel Plated Top

FINGER BOWL
Packs 18 doz. to bbl.
Weight 160 lbs.

9 oz. GOBLET
Packs 10 doz. to bbl.
Weight 130 lbs.

8½ oz. TABLE TUMBLER
Packs 20 doz. to bbl.
Weight 130 lbs.

½ gal. JUG. Packs 2 doz. to small tierce. Weight 140 lbs.

Water Set Above Packs 1 doz. Sets to bbl. Weight 120 lbs.

8 oz. FOOTED TUMBLER
Packs 14 doz. to bbl.
Weight 140 lbs.

HANDLED ICE BUCKET
Packs 3½ doz. to bbl. **Weight 120 lbs.**

"TEA ROOM"
See UPDATE

11 oz. FOOTED ICE TEA
Packs 9 doz. to bbl. Weight 140 lbs.
Packs 3 doz. to ctn. Weight 36 lbs.

LOW FOOTED SUNDAE
Packs 16 doz. to bbl. Weight 140 lbs.
Packs 6 doz. to ctn. Weight 50 lbs.

TALL FOOTED SUNDAE
Packs 12 doz. to bbl. Weight 130 lbs.
Packs 3 doz. to ctn. Weight 50 lbs.

FOOTED BANANA SPLIT
Packs 10 doz. to bbl. Weight 125 lbs.
Packs 3 doz. to ctn. Weight 30 lbs.

12 oz. FOOTED MALTED MILK
Packs 8 doz. to bbl. Weight 140 lbs.
Packs 3 doz. to ctn. Weight 42 lbs.

FOOTED ICE CREAM
Packs 14 doz. to bbl. Weight 130 lbs.
Packs 4 doz. to ctn. Weight 34 lbs.

8 oz. FOOTED SERVICE TUMBLER
Packs 14 doz. to bbl. Weight 140 lbs.
Packs 3 doz. to ctn. Weight 33 lbs.

6 oz. FOOTED COCA COLA
Packs 17 doz. to bbl. Weight 140 lbs
Packs 6 doz. to ctn. Weight 47 lbs.

COVERED MUSTARD
Plain or Slotted Cover
Packs 20 doz. to bbl.

COVERED SUGAR
Plain or Slotted Cover
Packs 14 doz. to bbl.

7½" FLAT BANANA SPLIT
Packs 30 doz. to bbl.

PARFAIT
Packs 18 doz. to bbl.

"TEA ROOM"

7 oz. GLACE
Also made 6½ oz. No. 600½
Packs 8½ doz. to bbl.

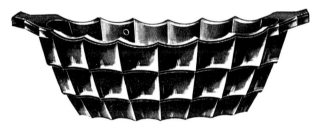

9¼ in. Deep Oval. Packs 3½ doz. to bbl. Weight 125 lbs.

3 piece
Console Set
Packs
2 doz Sets
to bbl
Weight
140 lbs.

Low Candlestick
Packs 12 doz. to bbl. Weight 150 lbs.

Sugar and
Cream
Packs 4½ doz.
pair to bbl.
Weight
140 lbs.

Handled Cream
Packs 10 doz. to bbl. Weight 130 lbs.

Handled Sugar
Packs 8 doz. to bbl. Weight 140 lbs.

Handled Berry Sugar
Packs 14 doz. to bbl. Weight 140 lbs.
3 pc. Sugar and Cream Set with Handled Tray.

Handled Berry Cream
Packs 14 doz. to bbl. Weight 140 lbs.
Packs 3¼ doz. sets to bbl. Weight 140 lbs.

11 in. Vase
Packs 1½ doz. to small tierce. Weight 160 lbs.

No. 600.   Tea Room and Soda Fountain Special
Design Patent No. 76986

Cup and Saucer
Packs 15 doz. sets to bbl.   Weight 150 lbs.

6 ½ in. Plate
Packs 30 doz. to bbl.   Weight 180 lbs.

10½ in. Plate
Packs 6 doz. to bbl.   Weight 150 lbs.

8¼ in. Plate
Packs 15 doz. to bbl.   Weight 160 lbs.

No. 600 PATTERN

Design Patent No. 76986
Made in Green and Pink

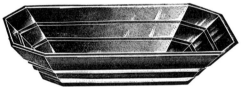

No. 600 - 8½ inch Pickle
Packs 12 Doz. to bbl.   Weight 160 lbs.

No. 600 - 8½ inch 2 Part Relish.
Packs 12 Doz. to bbl.   Weight 160 lbs.

No. 600 - 10½ inch Handled Sandwich
Packs 2½ Doz. to bbl. Weight 140 lbs.

No. 600 - Glace
Packs 9 Doz. to bbl.   Weight 140 lbs.

No. 600 - 3 Piece Oval Sugar and Cream Set.
Packs 4 Doz. Sets to bbl.   Weight 150 lbs.

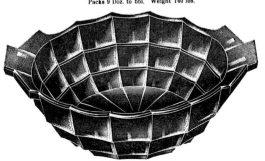

No. 600 - 8½ inch Deep Berry
Packs 3½ Doz. to bbl.   Weight 150 lbs.

No. 601 LINE
Green or Pink

Handled Berry Cream

7 in. Hld. Jelly

Handled Berry Sugar

AVOCADO

(#88 Book 1)
*Pieces made in
milk glass, 50s.*
See NOTE page 190

9 in. Salad Bowl

Footed Sundae and Plate

No. 6-5½ in. Plate

Cup and Saucer

No. 601 LINE
Green or Pink

No. 601—8¼" Salad Plate

No. 601—8" 2-Hld. Pickle

No. 601—½ gal. Jug

No. 601—6" Footed Relish

No. 601—10" 2-Hld. Plate

No. 601—5¼" 2-Hld. Olive

No. 601—6½" Cheese Plate

No. 601—7¼" Shallow Preserve

No. 601
Footed Sundae

No. 601
Tumbler

188

No. 605—Handled Cream

"LILY PONS"

No. 605—Handled Sugar

No. 605—8½" 2 Hld. Pickle

No. 605—Fruit Cocktail and Plate Set

No. 605— 6 in. Plate

No. 605—7 in. Nappy

No. 605—6½" Footed Bon Bon

No. 605—8½" Salad Plate

No. 606-7 in. Footed Bon Bon
Packs 12 doz. to bbl.-Weight 160 lbs.

606 "LOGANBERRY"

Made in Green or Pink

No. 607-8¼ in. Salad Plate
Packs 15 doz. to bbl.-Weight 165 lbs.

No. 605-Fruit Cocktail-Packs 25 doz.-Wt. 150 lbs.
No. 605-6 in. Plate-Packs 30 doz.-Wt. 160 lbs.

No. 605-6 in. Plate
Packs 30 doz. to bbl.-Weight 160 lbs.

607 "DUNKIRK"

No. 605-7 in. Preserve
Packs 16 doz. to bbl.-Weight 150 lbs.

No. 606-9 in. Service Plate
Packs 10 doz. to bbl.-Weight 165 lbs.

No. 605-7 in. Nappy
Packs 10 doz. to bbl.-Weight 150 lbs.

No. 608 PATTERN
Crystal, Green or Pink
Plain or Decorated

Cup and Saucer

Bridge or Luncheon Sets
Packed 1 Set to Carton
15 Piece Set for 4 Persons
21 " " " 6 "
27 " " " 8 "

Handled Cream

"ARTURA"

Footed Tumbler

Handled Sugar

Handled Sandwich

7½ in. Salad Plate

NOTE: INDIANA'S RECENT REISSUES

Besides the SANDWICH pattern, Indiana has to date reissued two other of its old patterns for exclusive sale under its "Tiara Home Plan." In the early 70s "PYRAMID" was offered in black glass in these pieces: 8- and 12-oz tumblers, 8½" and 4¾" berry, 8½" 4-part relish, and 3-piece sugar, cream & tray set. The AVOCADO ½-gal jug and tumblers were made in new pink in 1973 and sold under the name Sweet Pear.

"TWIGGY" 8" jelly, pink, green (pieces not shown: 8", 10" two-part relish, 8" plate, 4½", 8" nappy, 10" snack plate); made in 50s-60s in crystal with punch set. "JOYCE" 6" nut dish and 3" individual nuts, green. "CHARLIE" 7" candy dish, pink, green.

11 oz.   Footed Ser Tea

No. 610 Pattern
Design Patent Applied For   Made in Green or Pink

Berry Sugar
and Cream Set
Packs 6 doz. sets to bbl.

Handled Berry Cream
Packs 12 doz. to bbl.

Handled Berry Sugar
Packs 12 doz to bbl.

Ice Tub with Handle
Packs 3½ doz. to bbl.

8 oz. Footed Service Tumbler
Packs 13 doz. to bbl.

7 Pce.
Water Sets
Packs
1 doz sets
to barrel

Half Gallon Jug   Packs 2 doz to bbl.

No. 610 Pattern
Design Patent
Applied For
Made in Green or Pink

9½"   Oval
Packs 6½ doz. to bbl.

9½"   Pickle
Packs 8 doz to bbl.

4¾"   Berry
Packs 22 doz. to bbl.

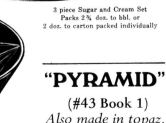

3 piece Sugar and Cream Set
Packs 2¾ doz. to bbl. or
2 doz. to carton packed individually

8½"   Berry
Packs 5 doz. to bbl.

"PYRAMID"
(#43 Book 1)
*Also made in topaz,
& pieces in milk
glass in 50s & 60s.
See NOTE page 190*

8½"   4 Part Relish
Packs 3 doz. to bbl.

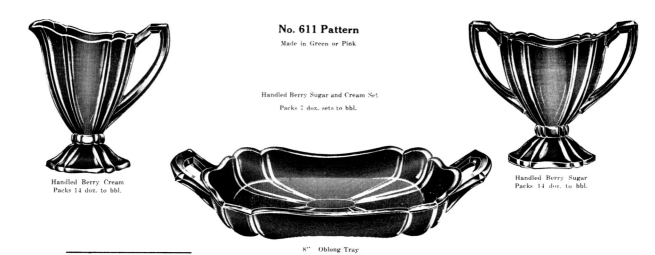

No. 611 Pattern
Made in Green or Pink

Handled Berry Sugar and Cream Set
Packs 7 doz. sets to bbl.

Handled Berry Cream
Packs 14 doz. to bbl.

8" Oblong Tray

Handled Berry Sugar
Packs 14 doz. to bbl.

"BANANAS"

6 oz. Footed Coca Cola
Packs 17 doz. to bbl.

8 oz. Footed Service Tumbler
Packs 14 doz. to bbl.

11 oz. Footed Ser Tea
Packs 8 doz. to bbl.

12 oz. Footed Malted Milk
Packs 8 doz. to bbl.

No. 613 Pattern
Made in Green or Pink

6⅝" Plate
Also
7" Plate

11" Meat Platter

"KING ARTHUR"

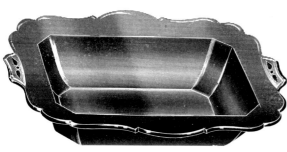

5" Oblong or Vegetable Dish

9" Meat Platter

192

"INDIANA CUSTARD"

(#239 Book 1)
*This line in ivory-color opaque was made from 1933 to 1935
in these pieces:*

Plate 9", 9¾"	Platter 12"	Bowl, 5½, 6, 9" nappy
Plate, salad 7½"	Cream	Bowl, oval veg. 9½"
Plate, sherbet 6"	Sugar and Cover	Bowl, 7½" soup
Cup and saucer	Sherbet	Butterdish and cover

*In 1957 the design was changed somewhat (compare original
patent at right) and made in milk glass under the name
ORANGE BLOSSOM (catalog page below).*

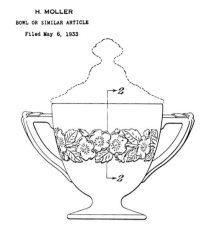

H. MOLLER
BOWL OR SIMILAR ARTICLE
Filed May 6, 1933

Inventor
Herbert Moller
Owen & Owen
Attorneys

ORANGE BLOSSOM

A company sales catalog of 1957 shows ORANGE BLOSSOM, a variation of the above, in milk glass.

Orange Blossom
LUNCHEON SET
in Indiana Milk Glass

Item	
#619	Plates
#619	Cups
#619	Saucers
#619	Desserts
#619	Sugars
#619	Creamers

Pattern No. 622
MACHINE MADE
Design Patent Number D-104618—D-104619

Handled Cream
4 doz. ctn. 31 lbs.

Cup
6 doz. ctn. 31 lbs.
Saucer
6 doz. ctn. 25 lbs.

Handled Sugar
4 doz. ctn. 35 lbs.

7½" Coupe Soup
4 doz. ctn. 47 lbs.

9⅜" Berry
2 doz. ctn. 42 lbs.

9⅜" Berry with 11½" Plate makes 2-piece Salad Set

11½" Sandwich or Cake Plate
2 doz. ctn. 43 lbs.

9⅜" Dinner Plate
4 doz. ctn. 47 lbs.

8⅜" Salad Plate
4 doz. ctn. 37 lbs.

6" Plate
6 doz. ctn. 25 lbs.

"PRETZEL"
(#153 Book 1)
This is original 30s crystal issue; such pieces as 10¼" celery, 7" nappy, 8½" pickle, and 7" olive were made in the 70s

Pattern No. 622
MACHINE MADE
Design Patent Number D-104618—D-104619

FRUIT CUP
6 Doz. Ctn—31 lbs.

7" HANDLED OLIVE
6 Doz. Ctn.—48 lbs.

**FRUIT CUP PLATE OR
CHEESE PLATE**
6 Doz. Ctn.—40 lbs.

8½" 2-HANDLE PICKLE
6 Doz. Ctn.—40 lbs.

10¼" CELERY TRAY
3½ Doz. Ctn.—56 lbs.

5-OZ. TUMBLER
6 Doz. Ctn.—36 lbs.

9-OZ. TUMBLER
6 Doz. Ctn.—50 lbs.

12-OZ. TUMBLER
6 Doz. Ctn.—65 lbs.

39 OZ. JUG
1 Doz. Ctn.—38 lbs.

194

GARLAND

"GARLAND" was shown in this 1935 ad, but Indiana made it in crystal with painted vari-colored decoration, and in milk glass, as late as the 50s. You will find more tableware pieces than these.

INTAGLIO

(#68 Book I)
Popular in the 30s, Indiana's crystal INTAGLIO has been reissued in crystal and some colors through 1970.

248—Relish Dish—7¼-inch, 3-part, etched.

248—Relish Dish—10-inch, 5-part, etched.

"CRACKED ICE"

This pattern was made by Indiana in the 30s in pink and green. You may find other pieces besides this 5" Footed Tumbler, Sugar & Cover, Sherbet, Creamer, and 6½" Plate.

Jeannette

Among glass houses of the 20s Jeannette Glass Company was looked to as a pioneer in bringing automation together with color. Today we look back upon it as one of the great contributors to the Depression Glass estate.

The organization began as a bottle plant in Jeannette, Pennsylvania at the turn of the century, but by the second decade it had turned almost entirely to the making of table items. Early and progressive use of automatic machines brought the company out in front in the production of tableware, kitchenware, and other specialties. As early as 1924 Jeannette is described by the trade as "one of the most complete automatic factories in the country"; in 1927 the management announced the cessation of all hand operations in favor of mechanical ones.

Short lines of colored tableware were being pressed in 1925, and in 1928 the first complete tableware lines in colors made automatically were introduced to the market. From this Jeannette went into the 30s with many of the most beautiful mold-etched patterns of the day. It would be hard to say when these patterns meant more—yesterday, when they lifted the suppertime spirits of many a Depression family, or today, when we look back at that supper table through the years of time—and remember.

In 1961 the company bought and the next year moved to the old McKee factory in Jeannette, where it continues to make a good percentage of this country's domestic glassware today. You see it being sold in stores everywhere.

COLOR

Jeannette has made iridescent ware off and on from 1920 to the present. In 1925, it introduced a color "somewhat like a brilliant apple green but different", which for a time was billed Jeannette green, in a hand-pressed, "mold-crackled" glass. A 27-piece bridge set was offered that same year in a "warm, rich amber" color called topaz; in 1926 lines in a shade called amber were brought out. Much green kitchenware was being advertised in 1926 as well.

In 1927, pink (which was sometimes called Wild Rose) joined the production, and a 1928 trade journal article hailed Jeannette "the first to our knowledge to make pink and green glass automatically in a continuous tank." For several years these were the two primary colors for this factory.

Jadite (the opaque jade green) was the next to come in 1932, then Delfite (the opaque blue) in 1936. Used chiefly for kitchenware, these color creations were also briefly tried in some of the popular tableware molds. This experimentation resulted in some of today's more uniquely collectible items.

Ultramarine was the big news of 1937 and 1938, and in the period from 1947 to 1949 the firm decided, unconventionally enough, to revive its pink for Holiday and Anniversary. In 1958 the pink opaque called Shell pink was issued.

Most of Jeannette's major patterns from the Depression Era were pictured and discussed in detail in Book I. Here these patterns are briefly noted again, solely to update that information. This time they are listed following the approximate order of original issuance.

More patterns by Jeannette not previously shown (or those from the final numbered section of Book I) follow the update.

REMEMBER: Very occasionally a tableware piece is found with the early trademark, the J-in-triangle. Otherwise, items were not marked.

Like all companies Jeannette ran occasional color trials from time to time and you may find isolated pieces in a color uncommon to it.

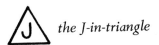 the J-in-triangle

"HONEYCOMB"

Jeannette's first machine-made tableware was made in 1928 in pink, green, iridescent and crystal and called "Hexagon Optic". The collectors' conventional name is preferred here since other companies also used the term Hexagon Optic to describe optic designs.

Most of the pieces pictured under HONEYCOMB in Book I were in fact made by Jeannette, but the small tumbler belongs to Federal and may be referred to in that chapter under 'Honeycomb', "Hexagon Optic".

Here are reprinted more pieces as originally advertised (1930). Besides the ones shown below, Jeannette also made a 10½" HONEYCOMB jug and tumblers similar in shape to the "Floral" lemonade jug.

CUBIST

Add to your listing the 8¾" jug. Pieces have also been found in Ultramarine. Shown here is a water set from a 1930 advertisement.

ADAM

Cups, saucers, and plates, all round in shape, are found very occasionally in topaz. You may find mold numbers on some pieces. The tall "Floral" shaker has the ADAM motif combined with the "Floral", and we sometimes find a butterdish with the ADAM bottom and combined ADAM and "Sierra" motif on the cover. These pieces are being found only in pink.

A variation exists in the base of ADAM pitchers. This one is round while the one in Book I is square.

FLORAL

First advertised in 1930, its earlier mold number dates it prior to "Cherry Blossom". The original listing shows an ice tub (not listed in Book I), but doesn't show the juice or milk jug, 20 oz, 5½"; the low footed comport 9" (both can be seen in the color pages); or the 2¾" cone-shaped footed tumbler which have all since been found. A small issue of FLORAL in Delfite was made in 1937, and a piece or two in topaz have shown up. Also in color section: the 7" footed green vase.

Additions to FLORAL: round shaker in pink; and ice tub and refrigerator dish in green.

DORIC

Items not in Book I: square relish dishes in a metal holder; a different style tumbler, 10 oz and 13 oz; candy dish in metal holder; and 5" cream soup (all shown); and the 7", 48 oz jug in Delfite. Several pieces have been found in topaz.

WINDSOR

Pieces made in a later crystal issue are: second-style sugar with pointed finial on cover; second-style creamer with same and pointed edges on bottom; comport 5½" high, 6" across; one-handled nappy 4¾". Relish trays have been found with the same metal holders as shown with "Doric".

CHERRY BLOSSOM

Shakers have been found, but are extremely rare. A small issue in Jadite was made; pieces are listed in PRICE TRENDS. You may chance upon a piece in blue, amber, or topaz—experiments in color only.

The straight-sided, 42-oz jug measures 7" tall, not 8" as claimed in Book I.

The CHERRY BLOSSOM shaker!

SWIRL

Plates and saucers may be ruffled or plain. A second-style Delfite candleholder was made in the same shaped mold as the "Floral" candleholder, and the Delfite round-handled tray 10½" (shown here) with concentric circles on bottom is a new addition.

The SWIRL butterdish, tray, candy dish and lug soup.

SIERRA

It appears there is no 6" sherbet plate after all. Pictured is the tumbler to this set.

198

DORIC
AND PANSY

These additional pieces have been found since Book I in Ultramarine or crystal only: salt and pepper; salad plate 7"; bowl, 9" handled; butter-dish; cream and sugar.

A few pieces were made in green. The child's plate is the same as the 6" sherbet plate (or bread and butter).

DORIC AND PANSY butterdish

HOMESPUN

Also made in crystal. New pieces are the 15-oz, 6½" footed tumbler and the cover for the child's teapot.

2900/4—4 Pc. TABLE SET

2948—9" PICKLE DISH   2960—8" RELISH DISH

2965—12½" CAKE PLATE   2982—7⅜" SOUP OR CEREAL BOWL

—*ANNIVERSARY as shown in pink and crystal in a 1949 catalog.*

HOLIDAY

There are two styles of cup and saucer that aren't interchangeable; one cup is plain-bottomed and one is rayed. A variation exists in the sherbet also. The 10½" cake plate is not listed in Book I.

ANNIVERSARY

This pattern was made in crystal and iridescent up to 1972. Reprinted below are several additional pieces.

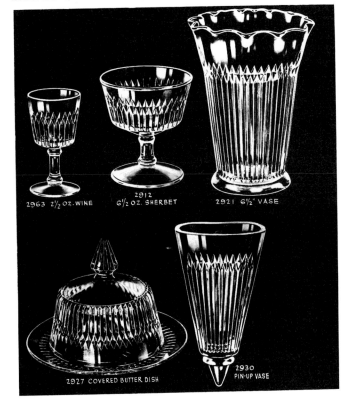

2963 2½ OZ. WINE
2912 6½ OZ. SHERBET
2921 6½" VASE
2927 COVERED BUTTER DISH
2930 PIN-UP VASE

"SUNFLOWER"

A company spokesman is sure Jeannette made our SUNFLOWER. The 5" and 8" nappy listed in Book 1 have never been found. Shown here is the 7" hot plate (or utility plate).

IRIS

An IRIS light fixture is the 12" bowl, satin finished in pink, light blue, or crystal. The nut dish is photographed below; the candy dish/cover, sherbet and coupe soup plate are reprinted from a 1950 catalog.

On the pages to come are Jeannette items not already covered in Book 1, or only briefly noted in the final numerical section of that book.

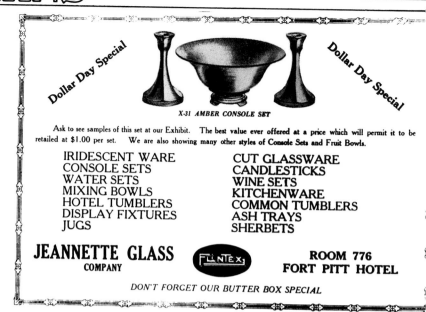

X-31 AMBER CONSOLE SET

Dollar Day Special   *Dollar Day Special*

No. 26/49—CONSOLE SET

—1924 advertisement

—1924 advertisement

—1925 catalog

JEANNETTE GLASS COMPANY

AUTOMOBILE VASES

No. 5155

No. 5265

Cut Crystal Automobile Vase.
With nickel plated holder.

Amber Iridescent Auto Vase.
With nickel plated holder.

SUGAR AND CREAM SETS

No. X-35
One—No. 5236 Sugar Bowl.
One—No. 5237 Cream Pitcher.

No. X-50
One—No. 5206 Sugar Bowl.
One—No. 5207 Cream Pitcher.

FLINTEX

"BRIDGET" *from 1925 advertisement*

The New

Jeannette
BRIDGE SET
[27 Pieces]
Truly Something New!

HAS an abundance of appeal—CONSIDER QUALITY—made of the best of glass and highly polished. Craftsmanship is asserted in the appearance.

THE COLOR alone is of note (made in Green and Topaz). The green is delicate, somewhat like a brilliant apple green but still so different and distinct we've named it JEANNETTE GREEN. The other color is a warm, rich amber color called TOPAZ.

JEANNETTE GLASS COMPANY

CRYSTAL WINE SET

No. X-33
Ringed Design

One — No. 5240 Three Pint Decanter and Stopper.

Six — No. 5242 Two Ounce Footed Wine Glasses.

One—No. 5036 Tray.

CRYSTAL WATER SET

No. X-32
Fluted Design

One—No. 5221 Three pint Jug.
Six —No. 5109 Eight ounce Tumblers.

FLiNTEX

1925 catalog

*Console sets in green
and amber, 1926 ad*

DAISY J" *tableware line in green and amber, 1926 advertisement*

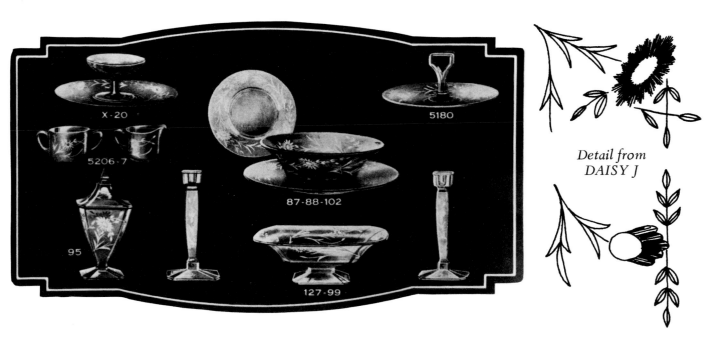

*Detail from
DAISY J*

Colored Glass Kitchenware

We have illustrated below the best staple items in Kitchenware.
These are absolutely necessary to complete your stock.
The entire line is made in both GREEN and PINK.

2051
KITCHEN SALT OR SUGAR SHAKER
Fluted Design with Aluminum Top

A Real Good Value

5019
LEMON REAMER

293
JUG

FOUR-PIECE MIXING BOWL SET

5015
TWO-POUND BUTTER BOX

5034—40 oz. Utility Crock with Cover

10
SALT BOX
With White Metal Holder

29
ORANGE REAMER

This is the newest line of opaque glass kitchenware. Marked by unusual pieces, as exemplified in the round salt and pepper, the twisted-screw reamer and handled measuring cup, the line is called "Jadite" and is made by the Jeannette Glass Company.

Kitchenware this page from late 20s ads, except for Jadite advertisement dating 1936.

Catalog c. 1934

Jeannette

Jeannette Glass Company ◆ Jeannette, Pa
KITCHENWARE & MISCELLANEOUS GLASSWARE

Jeannette Glass Company ◆ Jeannette, Pa.
KITCHENWARE & MISCELLANEOUS GLASSWARE

253 Ash Tray Green and Pink
Packed 6 doz. to the carton
Shipping weight 35 lbs.

254 Ash Tray Green and Pink
Packed 6 doz. to the carton
Shipping weight 40 lbs.

287—35 oz. Jug Green
Packed 2 doz. to the carton
Shipping weight 40 lbs.

289—9 oz. Tumbler Green
Packed 6 doz. to the carton
Shipping weight 35 lbs.

1102 Ash Tray Green
Packed 6 doz. to the carton
Shipping weight 56 lbs.

352 Refrigerator Tray and Cover
Green
Packed 2 doz. to the carton
Shipping weight 45 lbs.

393/4 Relish Dish with Nickel Plated
Band Green and Pink
Packed 4 doz. to 2 cartons
Shipping weight 72 lbs.

68—8½ oz. Tumbler Green and Pink
Packed 6 doz. to the carton
Shipping weight 35 lbs.

5175 Butter and Cover Green
Packed 2 doz. to the carton

379 Orange Reamer Green
Packed 3 doz. to the carton

37—Cigarette Jar
Pink and Green
Packed 12 doz.
to the carton
Shipping Weight
59 lbs.

207—Cigarette Jar
Pink and Green
Packed 6 doz. to the carton
Shipping Weight 48 lbs.

2051—Salt or Sugar Shaker
With Aluminum Top
Pink and Green
Packed 6 doz. to the box
Shipping Weight 55 lbs.

516—16 oz. Mug
Pink and Green
Packed 3 doz. to the carton
Shipping Weight 42 lbs.

300—Sugar
Dispenser
With Patented
Aluminum Top
Pink and Green
Packed 6 doz.
to the box
Shipping Weight
85 lbs.

517—16 oz. Measuring Cup
Green
Packed 3 doz. to the carton
Shipping Weight 42 lbs.

780/735 Cocktail Set
Pink and Green
Packed 1 set to carton
and 12 sets to master carton
Shipping Weight 34 lbs.

69—Puff Box
Pink and Green
Packed 8 doz. to the carton
Shipping Weight 57 lbs.

353—Large Refrigerator Tray and Cover
Green
Packed 1 doz. to the carton
Shipping Weight 42 lbs.

THE JEANNETTE GLASS CO., JEANNETTE, PA.

Crystal, Ultra-Marine or Pink

455

454

456

No. 400/6—REFRIGERATOR SET
Packed 1 set to carton
Shipping weight 6 lbs.

OPEN STOCK

No. 454—16-OZ. REFRIGERATOR JAR AND COVER
Packed 2 doz. to carton
Shipping weight 22 lbs.

No. 455—32-OZ. REFRIGERATOR JAR AND COVER
Packed 2 doz. to carton
Shipping weight 41 lbs.

No. 456—70-OZ. REFRIGERATOR JAR AND COVER
Packed 1 doz. to carton
Shipping weight 36 lbs.

459

458

457

No. 400/3—MIXING BOWL SET
Packed 1 set to carton
Shipping weight 7 lbs.

OPEN STOCK

No. 459—120-OZ. MIXING BOWL
Packed 1 doz. to carton
Shipping weight 41 lbs.

No. 457—26-OZ. MIXING BOWL
Packed 4 doz. to carton
Shipping weight 48 lbs.

THE JEANNETTE GLASS CO., JEANNETTE, PA.

Crystal, Ultra-Marine or Pink

442

441

No. 442—4½" x 9" REFRIGERATOR JAR AND COVER
Packed 2 doz. to carton
Shipping weight 48 lbs.

No. 441—4½" x 4½" REFRIGERATOR JAR AND COVER
Packed 4 doz. to carton
Shipping weight 55 lbs.

No. 445 REFRIGERATOR SET
Consisting of:
2—Square Jar & Cover No. 441
1—Oblong Jar & Cover No. 442
Packed 1 set to carton
Shipping weight 5 lbs.

No. 475—BUTTER BOX AND COVER
Packed 2 doz. to carton
Shipping weight 40 lbs.

No. 446—MEASURING CUP SET
Consisting of:
1—¼ Cup
1—⅓ Cup
1—½ Cup
1—Full Cup

THE JEANNETTE GLASS CO., JEANNETTE, PA.

Crystal, Ultra-Marine or Pink

No. 487—37-OZ. JUG
Packed 2 doz. to carton
Shipping weight 44 lbs.

No. 489—8-OZ. TUMBLER
Packed 12 doz. to carton
Shipping weight 65 lbs.

No. 420—LEMON REAMER
Packed 3 doz. to carton
Shipping weight 41 lbs.

No. 490—SHAKERS
SALT
Packed 2 doz. to carton
Shipping weight 14 lbs.
PEPPER

No. 400/4 RANGE SET
Consisting of:
1—Salt Shaker No. 490
1—Pepper Shaker No. 490
1—16 oz. Utility Bowl
& Cover No. 454
Packed 1 set to carton
12 sets to master carton
Shipping weight 30 lbs.

No. X-35 - 5 PC. BATH ROOM SET

Consists of

1 — No. 590 Boric Acid Bottle
1 — No. 590 Bicarbonate of Soda Bottle
1 — No. 590 Mouthwash Bottle } With Bakelite Caps.
1 — No. 590 Epsom Salts Bottle
1 — No. 528 10 oz. Tumbler

Packed one set to carton, 12 sets to master carton.   Shipping Weight 47 lbs.

No. 430 BEATER BOWL
Packed 4 doz. to carton
Shipping Weight 60 lbs.

No. 519 BUD VASE
Packed 3 doz. to carton
Shipping Weight 20 lbs.

No. 289 - 8 oz. TUMBLER
Packed 6 doz. to carton
Shipping Weight 35 lbs.

No. 530 ASH TRAY
Packed 3 doz. to carton
Shipping Weight 20 lbs.

No. 540 - 32 oz. ROUND JAR & COVER

No. 543 - 29 oz. SQUARE JAR & COVER

No. X-46 MEASURING CUP SET

Consists of

1 — ¼ Cup
1 — ⅓ Cup
1 — ½ Cup
1 — Full Cup

Packed one set to carton, 24 sets to master carton.
Shipping Weight 35 lbs.

No. 245 REAMER
Packed 3 doz. to carton
Shipping Weight 35 lbs.

No. X-45 REFRIGERATOR SET

Consists of

2 — No. 541 Small Refrigerator Tray & Cover
1 — No. 542 Large Refrigerator Tray & Cover
Packed one set to carton
Shipping Weight 7 lbs.

No. X-20 CEREAL SET
Consists of
1 — No. 543 Coffee Jar & Cover
1 — No. 543 Tea Jar & Cover
1 — No. 543 Sugar Jar & Cover
1 — No. 543 Cereal Jar & Cover
Packed one set to carton
Shipping Weight 9 lbs.

No. X7 REFRIGERATOR SET
Consists of:
3 — No. 541 Refrigerator Tray & Cover

Packed 1 set to carton and 12 sets to master carton.

Shipping Weight 54 lbs.

No. X6 REFRIGERATOR SET
Consists of:
2 — No. 352 Small Refrigerator Tray & Cover
1 — No. 353 Large Refrigerator Tray & Cover
Packed 1 set to carton
Shipping Weight 7½ lbs.

No. 5034 Round Crock & Cover
Packed 1 doz. to carton
Shipping Weight 30 lbs.

No. 5175 Butter Box & Cover
Packed 2 doz. to carton
Shipping Weight 42 lbs.

No. 370 Ice Box Jug & Cover
Packed 1 doz. to carton
Shipping Weight 60 lbs.

No. 379 Orange Reamer
Packed 3 doz. to carton
Shipping Weight 55 lbs.

No. 287—33 oz. Jug
Packed 2 doz. to carton
Shipping Weight 40 lbs.

No. 5170 Egg Cup
Packed 6 doz. to carton
Shipping Weight 35 lbs.

No. 5114 Salt Box with Wooden Cover
Packed 1 doz. to carton

No. X5 ROUND RANGE SET — 5 Pieces
Consists of:
1 — No. 544 Drippings Bowl & Cover
1 — No. 590 Salt Shaker } with polished Dome
1 — No. 590 Pepper Shaker } Aluminum Caps
1 — No. 590 Sugar Shaker
1 — No. 590 Flour Shaker
Packed 1 set to carton and 12 sets to master carton.   Shipping Weight 50 lbs.

No. X8 SQUARE RANGE SET 4 Pieces
Consists of:
1 — No. 580 Salt Shaker } with polished
1 — No. 580 Pepper Shaker } Dome
1 — No. 580 Sugar Shaker } Aluminum
1 — No. 580 Flour Shaker } Caps
Packed 1 set to carton and 24 sets to master carton.   Shipping Weight 60 lbs.

No. X11 SPICE SET
Consists of:
1 — No. 5162 Allspice Jar & Cover
1 — No. 5162 Pepper Jar & Cover
1 — No. 5162 Nutmeg Jar & Cover
1 — No. 5162 Ginger Jar & Cover
Packed 1 set to carton and 24 sets to master carton.   Shipping Weight 65 lbs.

No. X10 CEREAL SET
Consists of:
1 — No. 5161 Coffee Jar & Cover
1 — No. 5161 Tea Jar & Cover
1 — No. 5161 Sugar Jar & Cover
1 — No. 5161 Cereal Jar & Cover

Most items made in Delfite as well as Jadite; 1938 brochure.

500 Pattern
CRYSTAL OR WILD ROSE

Waffle Pattern

539—9-Oz. FOOTED TUMBLER

599—80-Oz. ICE LIP TILT JUG

513—14-Oz. FOOTED TUMBLER

52X-2105—5" CRIMPED NAPPY
Packed 12 Doz. to Carton.
Weight 60 lbs.   Doz. .20

52X-2106—9 Oz. TUMBLER
Packed 12 Doz. to Carton.
Weight 65 lbs.   Doz. .24

52X-2109—9" CRIMPED NAPPY
Packed 2 Doz. to Carton.
Weight 40 lbs.   Doz. .75

500/G—7-Pc. WATER SET
Consists of: 1—599 Ice Lip Tilt Jug   6—539 9-Oz. Footed Tumblers

500/H—7-Pc. ICED TEA SET
Consists of: 1—599 Ice Lip Tilt Jug   6—513 14-Oz. Footed Tumblers

52X-2111—CREAMER
Packed 2 Doz. to Carton.
Weight 11 lbs.   Doz. .40

52X-2110—SUGAR
Packed 2 Doz. to Carton.
Weight 12 lbs.   Doz. .40

52X-2112—12½ Oz. TUMBLER
Packed 6 Doz. to Carton.
Weight 45 lbs.   Doz. .36

52X-2115—COVERED BUTTER
Packed 4 Doz. to Carton.
Weight 38 lbs.   Doz. .72

500/S—13-Pc. REFRESHMENT SET
Consists of: 1—599 Ice Lip Tilt Jug   6—539 9-Oz. Footed Tumblers
6—513 14-Oz. Footed Tumblers

52X-2100 4—4 Pc. TOAST & JAM SET
Packed 1 Set to Carton.

52X-2109-5—7 Pc. BERRY SET
Packed 1 Set to Carton.   Weight 4 lbs.   Set .20

Crystal lines from 1939 catalog.

"HARP"

This line is being collected today, but it was made in the 50s. Shown is the 7" plate, cup & saucer, and set of 4¾x3¼" coaster ashtrays. You will find other pieces, such as the footed cake plate (9" high). Made in crystal and light blue.

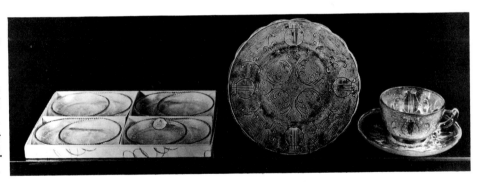

DEWDROP

Jeannette made this crystal line in 1954 and 1955, but it's being collected today.

Pieces are:

Cup, sugar & cover, creamer, butter & cover, 8" Maple Leaf dish, 7" candy jar & cover, 9-oz tumbler, 15-oz ice tea, 4¾" nappy, 8½" nappy, 60-oz and 64-oz jugs, 10-3/8" bowl, 13½" lazy susan tray, 11½" plate, 6-qt punch bowl w/o base, snack plate and cup.

CHANTILLY

The refreshment set pictured is pink; the tumbler line is shown in Jeannette catalogs of the 60s in crystal under the name CHANTILLY. Jug is 9"; tumblers 2½", 3½", 5", and 5¼".

CAMELLIA

This large gift ware line was made in crystal from 1947 to 1951.

NATIONAL

Crystal line from 1947 catalog.

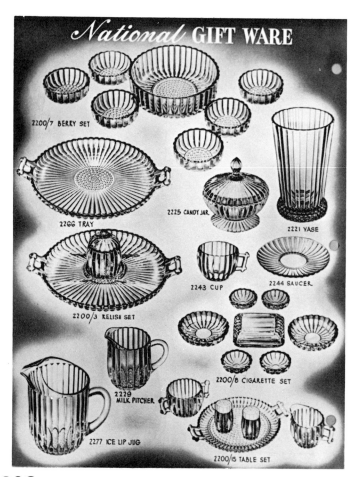

COSMOS

This water set comes in crystal, golden iridescent, and with decorations. From 1950 catalog.

DECORATION No. 58
ALL WHITE COSMOS

2100/7	7-Pc. WATER SET	1 Set	7 lbs.
2177	60 oz. Ice Lipped Water Jug	1 Doz.	44 lbs.
2142	11½ oz. Tumbler	6 Doz.	36 lbs.

Jeannette

EXCLUSIVE
SHELL PINK MILK GLASS *by Jeannette*

LOVELY COLOR AND DESIGN MAKE WOMEN ADMIRE IT — AND BUY IT!

/P—Cookie Jar and Cover
½" high, 5¾" diameter
One to a gift box
ton one-half dozen—33 lbs.
$1.10 each

3323/P—Footed Nut - Candy Dish
5¼" long, 3½" wide
Carton one dozen—8 lbs.
$3.00 dozen

125/P—Sq. Candy Jar and Cover
5½" square, 6½" high
One to a gift box
Carton one-half dozen—18 lbs.
$1.00 each

2400/5/P—5-piece Juice Set
One 24 oz. Juice Pitcher
Four 5 oz. Juice Glasses
Each set in a carton
Master carton six sets—24 lbs.
$1.25 set

2412/P—5 oz. Sherbet
Thumb-print design
Carton two dozen—14 lbs.
$3.60 dozen

2428/P—8 oz. Thumb Print Goblet
Height 6½"
Carton two dozen—20 lbs.
$3.60 dozen

2845/P—Florentine Footed Dish
10" long, 7⅜" wide
One to a gift box
Carton one-half dozen—16 lbs.
$.65 each

275/P—Gondola Fruit Bowl - Planter
17½" long, 5" wide, 4⅛" high
One to a gift box
Carton one-half dozen—28 lbs.
$1.10 each

291/P
15¾" long Oval Tray with Partitions
Carton ½ dozen—28 lbs.
$1.00 each

3710/P—10 oz. Sugar and Cover
Baltimore Pear design
6¾" high, 5¾" wide
Carton one dozen—12 lbs.
$.35 each

3711/P—6½ oz. Creamer
Baltimore Pear design 5¼" high
Carton one dozen—8 lbs.
$.25 each

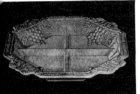

268/P—Octagonal Vineyard Dish with Partitions
12" wide, 2" deep
One to a gift box
Carton one-half dozen—32 lbs.
$1.20 each

100/1/P—Lazy Susan
One 13½" tray, base and ball bearing
One to a gift box
Carton one-half dozen—34 lbs.
$2.00 each

3423/P—Eagle Candle Holder
Carton two dozen—20 lbs.
3" high
$.30 each

3435/P—4 Toe Lombardi Bowl
10⅝" wide, 5¼" high
Carton ½ dozen—19 lbs.
$1.10 each

387/P—Two Light Candlestick
5" high, 6" wide
Carton one dozen—10 lbs.
$.50 each

3200/P—Punch Set—Feather Design
One 7½ qt. Punch Bowl; One Base—height 3½";
Twelve 5 oz. Punch Cups; One 12" Pink Ladle;
Twelve Nickel Plated Hooks
Carton one set—15 lbs.
$4.00 set

3203/P—Extra Punch Cups; Six doz. to a carton—25 lbs.; **$1.25 doz.**

Hostess Set
Eight Piece Set
4 CUPS 4 PLATES

3200/8/P—Snack Set—8 pieces
Four trays—7¾" x 10"
Four cups—5 oz.
Each set in a display box
Master carton six sets—42 lbs.
$1.75 set

3401/P—8" Wedding Bowl & Cover
Carton one dozen—28 lbs.
$.85 each

3412/P—6½" Wedding Bowl & Cover
Carton one dozen—15 lbs.
$.60 each

3525/P—½ lb. Candy Jar and Cover
5¼" high, 4½" wide
Carton one dozen—17 lbs.
$.55 each

265/P—10" Footed Cake Salver
Carton ½ dozen—19 lbs.
$.85 each

SHELL PINK MILK GLASS containers have a delicate coloring that blends perfectly with all kinds of flowers. Its smooth satiny finish goes all the way through the glass—is **not** a spray or surface coating.

3624/P—8" Pheasant Bowl
Carton ½ dozen—10 lbs.
$.75 each

2880/P—10½" Footed Bowl
Carton one dozen—35 lbs.
$.75 each

3479/P—9" Footed Fruit Bowl
Carton ½ dozen—20 lbs.
$1.00 each

3498/P—12½" x 9¾" Beverage Tray
Carton ½ dozen—22 lbs.
$1.00 each

628/P—Powder Jar and Cover
3¾" high, 4¾" wide
Carton one dozen—17 lbs.
$.55 each

3400/4/P—Butterfly Cigarette Set
One Cigarette Box and Cover
Two Ash Trays
Each set in a carton
Master carton six sets—18 lbs.
$1.00 set

7/P—Bee Hive Jar and Cover
4¼" high—Carton one doz.—15 lbs.
$.40 each

298/P—Venetian Tray—16½" long
Carton ½ dozen—27 lbs.
$1.00 each

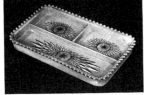

12/P—Celery and Relish Dish
12½" x 7¾"
Carton ½ dozen—16 lbs.

1324/P—6" Compote

2221/P—Heavy Bottom Vase
9" High

3621/P—7" Vase—5½" wide

2021/P—Cornucopia Vase—5" high

Jenkins

Our interest in this company begins in 1901, the year D. C. Jenkins became the president of the Kokomo Glass Manufacturing Company of Kokomo, Indiana. He so shaped this company's success that it was eventually named for him, and the business folded in 1932 not long after his death.

A second plant was started in 1913 in Arcadia, Indiana also by Mr. Jenkins, and molds were traded back and forth between the two facilities. Jenkins glass was often a heavy ware compared to other glass of the period, and proved useful for hotels and soda fountains. A great many tumblers were made, as were occasional pieces and novelties such as fishbowls. Kitchenware and several pressed dinnerware patterns were manufactured in crystal during the 20s.

Color was late to this house; surviving production records show only that green glass was ever made, that not until 1929 and then not very much. Jenkins' only other color activity during its later years was in producing "doped ware", in which pieces of crystal glass were given a golden iridescent bath to yield a carnival-like effect.

The dinnerware lines in green and the sandwich-design plates shown below are the most interesting Jenkins wares for collectors today.

"SEA-SIDE"

Jenkins'
SANDWICH
PLATES

8" Salad Plates
Crystal, Green, Iridescent Amber

"TWIN DOLPHIN"

"JENKINS' BASKET"

"FIELDCREST"

The following reprints are from company catalogs dating 1927 to 1931. Some lines were made in green and some in crystal only. You may find some items in the "doped ware" as well.

Jenkins'
"HOB"

in green

D. C. JENKINS GLASS CO., KOKOMO, IND. U. S. A.
G 250 TABLEWARE LINE

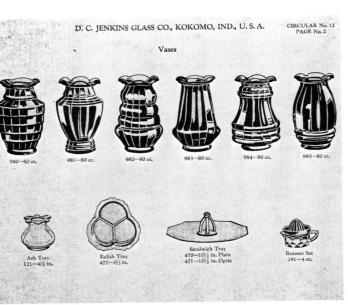

D. C. JENKINS GLASS CO., KOKOMO, IND., U. S. A.   CIRCULAR No. 12 PAGE No. 2
Vases

D. C. JENKINS GLASS CO., KOKOMO, IND., U. S. A.   CIRCULAR No. 11 PAGE No. 4
Water and Beverage Sets

All jugs listed on this page are blown with stuck handles. Tumblers and Ice Teas are blown. Supplied in crystal and green.

D. C. JENKINS GLASS CO., KOKOMO, IND. U. S. A.   CIRCULAR No. 5 PAGE No. 1
FISH GLOBES

D. C. JENKINS GLASS CO., KOKOMO, IND., U. S. A.   CIRCULAR No. PAGE No. 1
JUGS OR PITCHERS

DESIGN PATENT APPLIED FOR

Illustrations One-Half Size

OCEAN WAVE
("Ripple" #183 Book I)

No. 190—5 IN. TALL FOOTED PLATE

No. 190—8 IN. SALAD PLATE

No. 190—CUP AND SAUCER

No. 190—11 IN. SERVICE PLATE
Also supplied with recess to fit footed plates or sundaes

No. 190—3 PINT JUG

No. 190—9 OZ. WATER TUMBLER

No. 190—HANDLED BERRY SUGAR

No. 190—5 IN. LOW FOOTED PLATE

No. 190B—LOW SUNDAE

No. 190A—LOW SUNDAE

No. 190B—TALL SUNDAE

No. 190A—TALL SUNDAE

No. 190—BERRY CREAM

No. 190—4 IN. BERRY NAPPY

No. 190—6 OZ. BEVERAGE
OR WATER TUMBLER

No. 190—3 OZ. PARFAIT

No. 190—6 OZ. FOOTED SODA
OR BEVERAGE TUMBLER
No. 190—8 OZ. FOOTED SODA
OR BEVERAGE TUMBLER
(Illustration 6 Oz. Size)

No. 190—10 OZ. FOOTED SODA
OR LEMONADE

No. 190—12 OZ. FOOTED SODA
OR MALTED MILK

No. 190 A—8 IN. BERRY DISH

No. 190 C—8 IN. BERRY DISH

No. 202 LINE TABLEWARE

No. 202—WINE

No. 202—3 PT. JUG

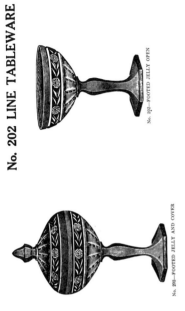

No. 202—FOOTED JELLY OPEN

No. 202—TABLE TUMBLER

No. 202—12-oz. ICE TEA

(ILLUSTRATIONS HALF SIZE)

No. 202—FOOTED JELLY AND COVER

No. 202—TALL CELERY

No. 202—5-Inch HANDLE NAPPY

No. 202—10-Inch CUPPED VASE

No. 202—6-Inch CUPPED VASE

No. 202—6-Inch FLARED VASE

No. 202—BON-BON AND COVER

(ILLUSTRATIONS HALF SIZE)

No. 202—10-Inch FLARED VASE

No. 202—8-Inch PICKLE

No. 202 "C"—8 IN FLARED NAPPY

No. 202—6 IN PLATE

No. 202 "B"—4 IN CUPPED NAPPY

"ARCADIA LACE"

No. 202—CREAM

No. 202 "B"—8 IN CUPPED NAPPY

No. 202—11 IN PLATE

(ILLUSTRATIONS HALF SIZE)

No. 202—SPOON

No. 202—BUTTER AND COVER

(ILLUSTRATIONS HALF SIZE)

No. 202—SUGAR AND COVER

No. 202 "A"—8 IN STRAIGHT NAPPY

No. 202 "C"—4 IN FLARED NAPPY

No. 202 "A"—4 IN STRAIGHT NAPPY

No. 286-C—FLARED 8-INCH NAPPY

No. 286-C—FLARED 4-INCH NAPPY

No. 286—Flared Sundae or Footed Mayonnaise

No. 285-B—CUPPED 8-INCH NAPPY

No. 286-B—CUPPED 4-INCH NAPPY

No. 286—Mayonnaise Bowl

No. 286—Mayonnaise Plate

No. 286-A—STRAIGHT 8-INCH NAPPY

No. 286-A—STRAIGHT 4-INCH NAPPY

No. 286-A—Straight Sundae or Footed Mayonnaise

No. 286—CREAM

"DAHLIA"

No. 286—3 PINT JUG

No. 286-C—FOOTED JELLY

No. 286—SUGAR

No. 286 4-piece Set

No. 286—SPOON

ILLUSTRATIONS HALF SIZE

No. 286—TUMBLER

No. 286-B—FOOTED JELLY

No. 286—BUTTER AND COVER

No. 286-A—FOOTED JELLY

No. 286—6 INCH VASE

No. 286—10 INCH VASE

No. 400 LINE TABLEWARE

No. 400 LINE TABLEWARE

"KOKOMO"

No. 336 LINE TABLEWARE

"LATTICE"

No. 400 LINE TABLEWARE

No. 400—TABLE TUMBLER

No. 400—5 IN. FOOTED JELLY BOWL AND COVER

No. 400—5 IN. HANDLED NAPPY

No. 400—3 PINT JUG

No. 400—8 IN. PICKLE TRAY

No. 400—5 IN. FOOTED JELLY BOWL

No. 400—SPOON

No. 400—COVERED SUGAR

No. 400—COVERED BUTTER

No. 400—CREAM

No. 316 HALF GAL. JUG

No. 316—CASSEROLE AND COVER

No. 316—CREAM

No. 316—PICKLE

No. 316—FOOTED JELLY AND COVER

No. 316—BUTTER AND COVER

No. 316—HANDLED NAPPY

No. 316 FOOTED JELLY

No. 316—SUGAR AND COVER

No. 316—5 IN. NAPPY

No. 316—BLOWN TUMBLER

No. 316—SPOON

No. 316—4 IN. NAPPY

No. 316—HALF GAL. JUG AND COVER

No. 316—8 IN. NAPPY

No. 400—5 IN. NAPPY

No. 400—4½ IN. DEEP COVERED NAPPY

No. 400—4½ IN. CASSEROLE AND COVER

No. 400—4½ IN. DEEP NAPPY

No. 400—8 IN. NAPPY

No. 180—9-Oz. Marmalade / Cover notched for spoon handle

No. 211—Candy Tray, 7¼ x 5⅝ x ⅞ In.

No. 320—7½ Inch Footed Candy Tray

No. 4—Insulator / Illustration full size / 3⅝ x 1¼ inches

No. 13—Optic Funnel / Quart size / No. 14—Optic Funnel / Pint size / Illustration No. 13—One-quarter size

No. 180—Orange Reamer

No. 460—Swan Dish / Capacity 12 Ounces

No. 199—Cake Cover / 9 Inches Inside Diameter

No. 209—8 Inch Oblong Candy Tray, 8 x 5 x 2 In.

No. 320—11 Oz. Flared Compot

ANTENNAE INSULATORS

Glass is acknowledged to be the best insulating material for Radio. It is impervious to moisture. Its smooth surface prevents collection of dust and has great dielectric strength.

This line has been designed to give abundant mechanical strength and highest insulating efficiency under all conditions.

No. 116—Chick Fountain and Base

LEMON AND ORANGE REAMERS

Illustrations one-half size

No. 170—Lemon Reamer / with seed catcher

No. 360—4½-Inch Nappy and Cover / Illustration one-half size

No. 215—Candy Tray, 7¼ x 3½ x ⅞ In.

No. 320—11 Oz. Straight Compot

No. 175—6½ Oz. Crimped Sundae

No. 6—Plain Funnel / Quart size / No. 12—Plain Funnel / Pint size / Illustration No. 6—One-quarter size

3½ x 1¼ inches / 4½ x 1¼ inches / 4¾ x 1⅝ inches

No. 1—Insulator / No. 3—Insulator / No. 9—Insulator / Illustration full size No. 1

No. 160—Lemon Reamer

No. 807—Child's Mug

No. 910—Cup

No. 475—Child's Mug

No. 96—Sherbet Cup

When D. C. Jenkins ran for government office he made hundreds of these cups with "D. C. JENKINS GLASS CO. KOKOMO" inscribed in the bottom.

No. 42—Sherbet Cup

No. 925—CAN

No. 209—Mug

This is Jenkins' STRAWBERRY Design

No. 10—Child's Mug

No. 40—Cup

No. 150—4 Oz. Mug

PERCOLATOR TOPS

No. 1—Pickle Dipper, 9½ in. long / with ½ in. center drain hole / Can be used with any display jars

No. 85—2-Gal. Jar and Hinge / Aluminum Cover / No. 86—5-Gal. Jar and Hinge / Aluminum Cover / Raised Flat Band for label advertisements

No. 355—1-qt. Jar / No. 356—2-qt. Jar

No. 38—8-Inch Mixing Bowl

No. 210—2-Gal. Vertical Drum Jar / and Hinge Aluminum Cover / No. 211—5-Gal. Drum Jar and / Hinge Aluminum Cover / Designed for small space

No. 290—1-qt. Jar

No. 39—9-Inch Mixing Bowl

No. 88—2-Gal. Tilted Drum Jar / and Hinge Aluminum Cover / Designed for small space

No. 77—18-oz. Jar

No. 66—14-oz. Jar

No. 44—2-Gal. Jars / With Aluminum Covers / (Priced Singly) / Two Jars in same counter space

No. 560 LINE TABLEWARE

WATER JUGS

No. 560—COVERED SUGAR

No. 560—COVERED BUTTER

No. 560—CREAM

No. 560—SPOON

55—½ gal. Ice

55—½ gal. Reg.

55—½ Gal. with Reamer Cover
(Reamer serves as cover when inverted)

"YO-YO"

No. 560—4½-IN. FOOTED JELLY
Bowl and Cover

No. 560—7½-IN. NAPPY

No. 560—4½-IN. NAPPY

No. 560—PINT COVERED JUG
Refrigerator Style

No. 560—QUART COVERED JUG
Refrigerator Style

No. 560—HALF-GAL. COVERED JUG
Refrigerator Style

220—½ gal. Jug

560—1 pt.
560—1 qt.
560—½ gal.

570—1 pt.
570—1 qt.
570—½ gal.

No. 921 LINE TABLEWARE

No. 570 LINE TABLEWARE

No. 921—SUGAR AND COVER

No. 921—BUTTER AND COVER

No. 921C—8-IN. NAPPY
No. 921C—4-IN. NAPPY

No. 570—COVERED SUGAR

No. 570—COVERED BUTTER

No. 570—CREAM

No. 570—SPOON

No. 570—4½-IN. FOOTED JELLY
Bowl and Cover

No. 570—7½-IN. NAPPY

No. 570—4½-IN. NAPPY

"HUCK FINN"

No. 921—CREAM

No. 921—SPOON

No. 921—QUART JUG
No. 921—3-PINT JUG

"YOO-HOO"

No. 570—PINT COVERED JUG
Refrigerator Style

No. 570—QUART COVERED JUG
Refrigerator Style

No. 570—HALF-GAL. COVERED JUG
Refrigerator Style

FLOWER VASES

Illustrations one-half size
For Other Vases—See Tableware Lines

No. 330—10½ In. Plain Vase
With Bird Design

No. 331—10½ In. Stippled Vase
With Bird Design

No. 310—7½ In. Vase

No. 311—7½ In. Vase

No. 312—7½ In. Vase

No. 313—7½ In. Vase

No. 330—Lamp Complete decorated with shade

No. 370—Lamp Complete decorated with shade

No. 312—Lamp Complete decorated with shade

215

Kopp

Kopp Glass of Swissvale, Pennsylvania, never made much collectible ware. But its founder, young and penniless immigrant Nicholas Kopp, happened to be brilliant with the chemistry of color and by the turn of the century had pioneered the development of several of the shades borrowed by the glass artists of a later day. Most notably he is credited with creating the first ruby glass made with selenium, the formula that gave us our Depression-era red. His company made over 40 colors but only a few lamps and lines of artistic glassware during the span of our interest, specializing rather in signal lights of every kind. Almost every traffic light you see was (still is!) made by Kopp—green, yellow, and the famous red.

No. 1210
RUBY, EMERALD or TOPAZ

TRADE MARK

RESIDENTIAL AND COMMERCIAL LIGHTING GLASSWARE AND PORTABLE LAMPS

No. 920-N
BRILLIANT UNIT

No. 909—10 x 4″
No. 910—16 x 6″

—1928 patent

—1929 patent

ALSO A LINE OF NEW CREATIONS IN KOPP COLORS IN

Table Glassware and Novelties

KOPP GLASS

SWISSVALE, PA.

—1927 ad

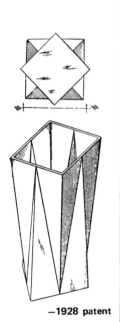

"MODERNISTIC" GLASS VASES

Newest in Gift Creations. Made in Solid Colors, Plain and Roughed Outside. Crystal, Rose, Ruby, Blue, Havana and Emerald.

These Vases also used for Portable Lamps and Pedestal Lights.

Write for Catalogues of other products — Supplement to Catalogue 31-C Modernistic lighting glassware.

Just off the press.

No. 400
Height 8½″

No. 401
Height 6½″

Lighting Units Catalogue 31-C.
Residential Lighting Glassware 32-C.
Portable Lamps, Catalogue 33-C.

—1928 ad

MODERNISTIC PORTABLE LAMP

An Up-to-Date Lamp at a Popular Price.

Modernistic in Design as well as Decoration. Furnished in five different color effects. Order a sample for inspection.

No. 1225
Total Ht. 18″
Diameter of Shade, 14″
2-Light Socket

Samples on Display at
NEW YORK OFFICE—
Dela Croix & Monroe,
225 Fifth Avenue.

CHICAGO OFFICE—
R. M. Peare Company,
17 N. Wabash Avenue.

And at our General Offices,
Swissvale, Pa.

Write for Catalogues
No. 33-C—Portable Lamps. No. 32-C—Residential Glassware. No. 34-C—Lighting Units (Just off the Press)

KOPP GLASS, INC.

2204 PALMER STREET — — SWISSVALE, PA.
Now doing the business formerly conducted by Pittsburgh Lamp, Brass & Glass Co., at Swissvale, Pa.

—1929 ad

216

Lancaster

Before this hand factory became a main subsidiary of Hocking Glass Company it was the Lancaster Glass Company of Lancaster, Ohio, built in 1908 by the man who had been the first president of Fostoria Glass Company. In 1924, the year it came under Hocking control, Lancaster was making kitchenware, cut and decorated tableware, and occasional pieces. It continued along these same lines (and with the Lancaster name until 1937) under its new management. In addition, many colored blanks during the Depression era were furnished to Standard Glass Company, also a part of Hocking, for cutting and etching. You will want to refer to the Standard chapter for a comparison of designs since the shapes were often the same. Today the factory is still in operation, still Plant #2 to Anchor Hocking Corporation.

COLOR

The popular applied (or "cold") colors decorated much of this company's ware before and even after the advent of transparent color in glass. Lancaster colors of the 20s were green, blue and canary (1925), deep pink (1926), topaz (1930), pale blue and black (1931). Gold decoration was frequently applied. In all probability other colors were made as well.

–1924 advertisement

This is one of the many attractive items in our distinctive line of finely finished blanks for cutting and decorating.

Among the other items are Sandwich Trays, Cheese & Cracker Sets, Mayonnaise Sets, Salvers, Flower Bowls, etc.

These are also furnished in attractive decorations of Coraline, Jonquil, Jade and Celeste.

Another specialty is a beautifully decorated line of Lamp Vases for mounting.

These items must be seen to be appreciated. May we have the opportunity to show them to you at our

PITTSBURGH EXHIBIT, ROOM 706, FORT PITT HOTEL

THE **LANCASTER GLASS CO.**
LANCASTER, OHIO.

No. 83—Candy Jar & Cover

CATALOG REPRINTS

Following are reprints of Lancaster sales material 1925-1931. The originals are photographs in color; pieces are in pink, green, and topaz.
DECORATIONS:
The painted-on flowers are of all colors. The flowers on the black pieces (page 222) are colored or silver. The stripes are black and red or black and yellow.

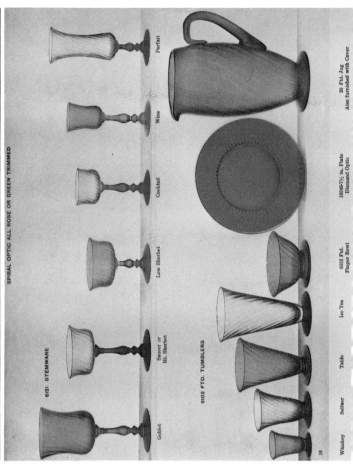

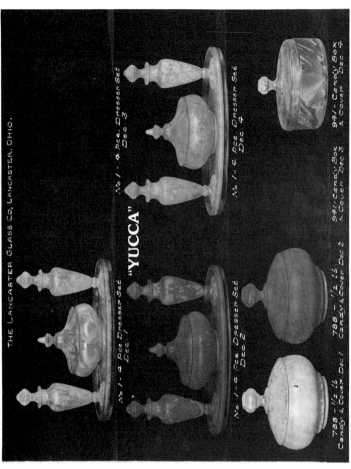

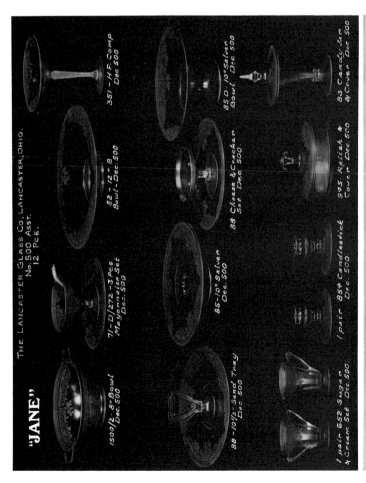

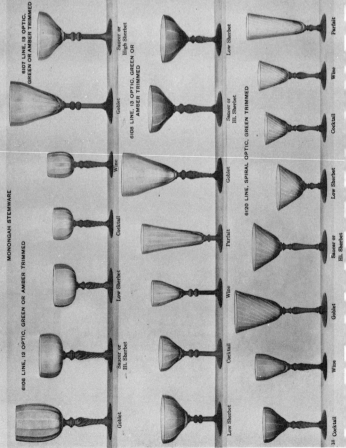

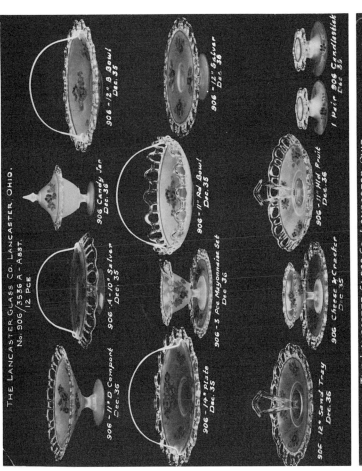

THE LANCASTER GLASS CO. LANCASTER, OHIO.
No. 906/3536 A - ASST.
12 PCE.

906-12" B Bowl
Dec. 35

906-12" Salver
Dec. 36

1 Pair 906 Candlestick
Dec. 35

906 Candy Jar
Dec. 36

906-11" Rd Bowl
Dec. 35

906-11" Hld Fruit
Dec. 36

906-11" D Compot
Dec. 36

906-A-10" Salver
Dec. 35

906-3 Pce Mayonnaise Set
Dec. 36

906 Cheese & Cracker
Dec. 35

906-11" D Compot
Dec. 36

906-14" Plate
Dec. 35

906 12" Sand Tray
Dec. 36

THE LANCASTER GLASS CO. LANCASTER, OHIO.
JUBILEE 36 PC. ASST.
DEC. 55 PINK ONLY.

607

6/2-12"

1923/4-10 1/2"

6/5

923 - 3 Pc.

620-11" D

1675/3-9 3/4"

6/2-11" D

602-11"

1675/1-9"

1923/1-9"

605-10" D

"DARLENE"

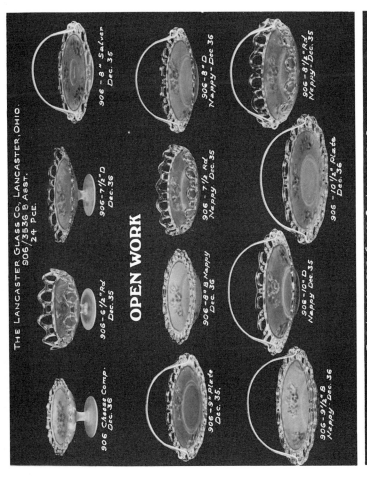

THE LANCASTER GLASS CO. LANCASTER, OHIO.
906/3536 B ASST.
24 PCE.

906-8" Salver
Dec. 35

906-8" D
Nappy-Dec. 36

906-8 1/2" Rd.
Nappy-Dec. 35

906-7 1/2" D
Dec. 36

906-7 1/2 Rd.
Nappy. Dec. 35

906-10 1/2" Plate
Dec. 36

906-6 1/2" Rd
Dec. 35

906-8" B Nappy
Dec. 36

906-10" D
Nappy Dec. 35

OPEN WORK

906 Cheese Comp.
Dec. 36

906-9" Plate
Dec. 35.

906-9 1/2" B
Nappy-Dec. 36

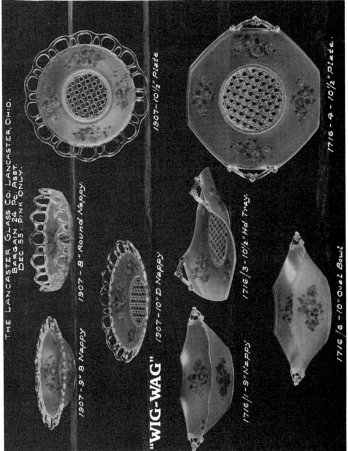

THE LANCASTER GLASS CO. LANCASTER, OHIO.
BARGAIN 24 PC. ASST.
DEC. 55. PINK ONLY.

1907-10 1/2" Plate

1716/4 - 10 1/2" Plate.

1907 - 8 " Round Nappy.

1907 - 10" D Nappy

1716/3-10 1/2" Hd Tray.

1907-9" B Nappy

1716/1 - 9" Nappy

1716/6 - 10" Oval Bowl

"WIG-WAG"

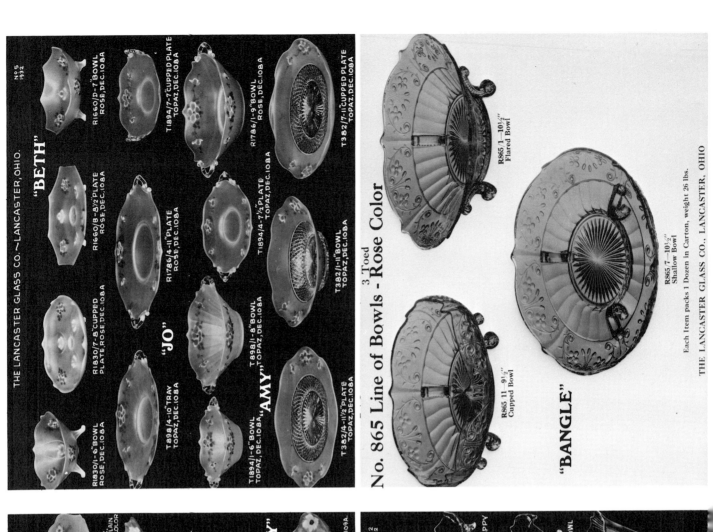

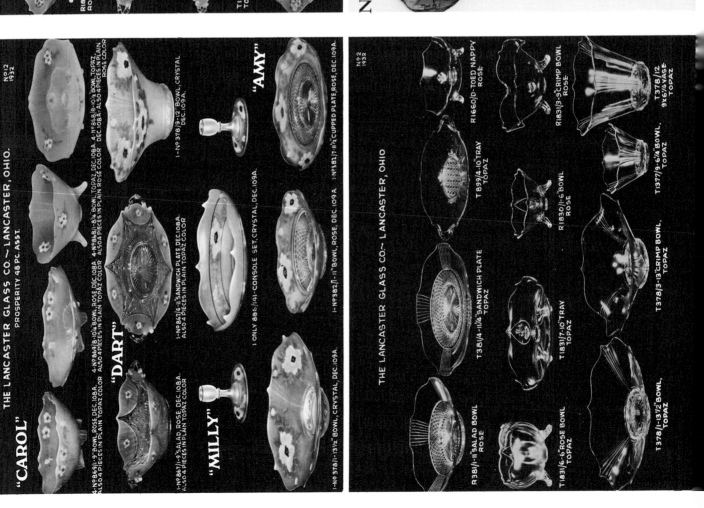

No. 865 Line of Bowls - Rose Color

3 Toed

"BANGLE"

R865/1—10½" Flared Bowl

R865 7—10½" Shallow Bowl

R865 11—9½" Cupped Bowl

Each Item packs 1 Dozen in Carton, weight 26 lbs.

THE LANCASTER GLASS CO., LANCASTER, OHIO.

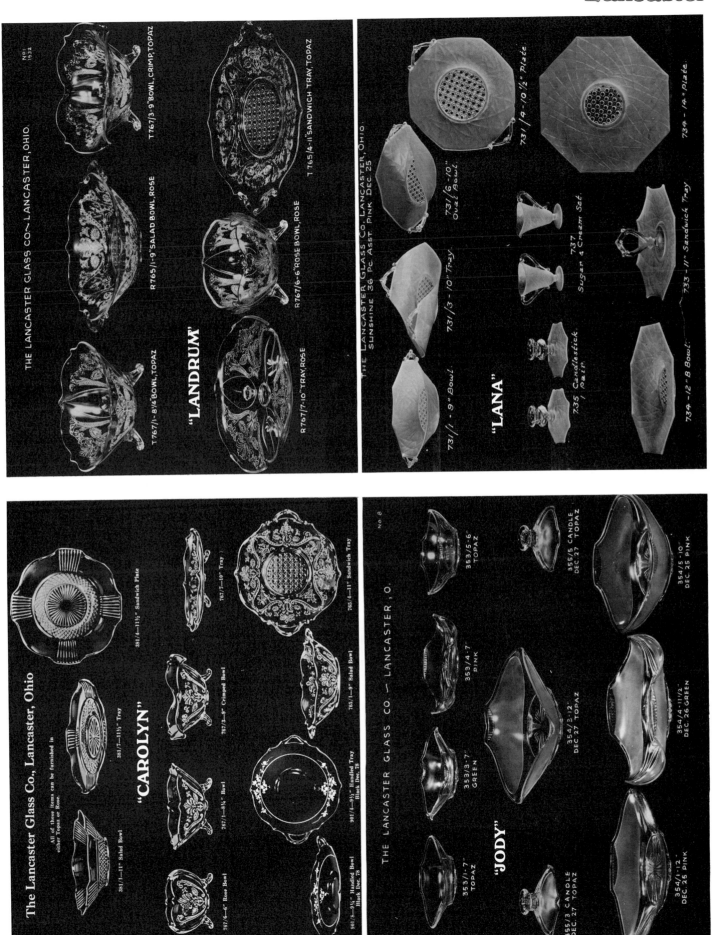

Lancaster

THE LANCASTER GLASS CO~ LANCASTER, OHIO.

T767/1-8¼" BOWL, TOPAZ
T767/3-9"BOWL, CRIMP, TOPAZ
R765/1-9" SALAD BOWL, ROSE
T765/4-11 SANDWICH TRAY, TOPAZ
R767/6-6"ROSE BOWL, ROSE
R767/7-10"TRAY, ROSE

"LANDRUM"

THE LANCASTER GLASS CO. LANCASTER, OHIO. SUNSHINE 36 PC. ASST. PINK DEC. 25

731/4-10½" Plate.
734-14" Plate.
731/6-10" Oval Bowl.
731/3-10" Tray.
737 Sugar & Cream Set.
731/1-9" Bowl.
735 Candlestick / Pair.
733-11" Sandwich Tray.
734-12" B Bowl.
734-12" B Bowl.

"LANA"

The Lancaster Glass Co., Lancaster, Ohio

All of these items can be furnished in either Topaz or Rose.

381/1-11" Salad Bowl
381/—11½" Tray
381/—11½" Sandwich Plate
767/7-10" Tray
767/3-9" Crimped Bowl
765/4-11" Sandwich Tray
765/1-9" Salad Bowl
767/6-6" Rose Bowl
767/1-8¼" Bowl
901/4-9½" Handled Bowl Black Dec. 78
901/8-9½" Handled Tray Black Dec. 78

"CAROLYN"

THE LANCASTER GLASS CO. ~ LANCASTER, O.

353/5-6" TOPAZ
355/5 CANDLE DEC. 27 TOPAZ
354/5-10" DEC. 25 PINK
353/4-7" PINK
353/3-7" GREEN
354/3-12" DEC. 27 TOPAZ
354/4-11½" DEC. 26 GREEN
353/1-7" TOPAZ
355/3 CANDLE DEC. 27 TOPAZ
354/1-12" DEC. 25 PINK

"JODY"

221

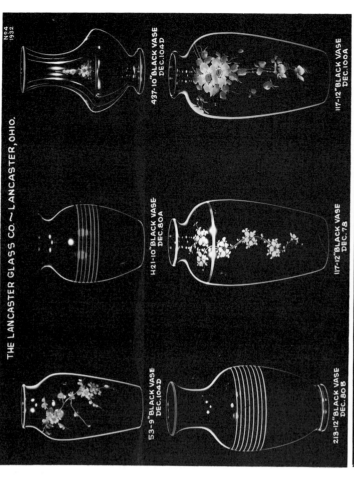

No4 1932

THE LANCASTER GLASS CO. ~ LANCASTER, OHIO.

53-9" BLACK VASE DEC.104D

H21-10" BLACK VASE DEC.80A

437-10" BLACK VASE DEC.104D

213-12" BLACK VASE DEC.80B

117-12" BLACK VASE DEC.78

117-12" BLACK VASE DEC.100A

No5 1932

THE LANCASTER GLASS CO. ~ LANCASTER, OHIO.

SALT PEPPER FLOUR SUGAR

BLACK SHAKER SET, No533, SILVER DECORATION

A B C

COOKIE JAR SET, No174, DECORATION No125, A,B &C.

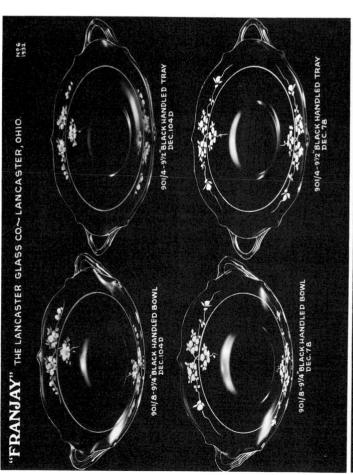

"FRANJAY" THE LANCASTER GLASS CO. ~ LANCASTER, OHIO.

No6 1932

90I/4-9 1/2" BLACK HANDLED TRAY DEC.104D

90I/4-9 1/2" BLACK HANDLED TRAY DEC.78

90I/8-9 1/4" BLACK HANDLED BOWL DEC.104D

90I/8-9 1/4" BLACK HANDLED BOWL DEC.78

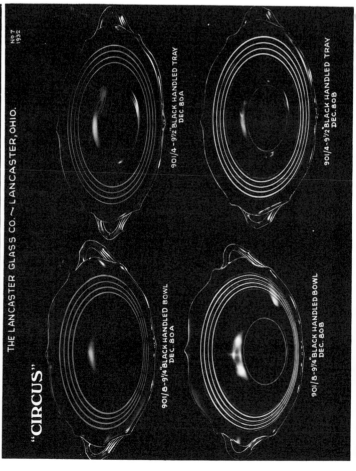

"CIRCUS" THE LANCASTER GLASS CO. ~ LANCASTER, OHIO.

No7 1932

90I/4-9 1/2" BLACK HANDLED TRAY DEC.80A

90I/4-9 1/2" BLACK HANDLED TRAY DEC.80B

90I/8-9 1/4" BLACK HANDLED BOWL DEC.80A

90I/8-9 1/4" BLACK HANDLED BOWL DEC.80B

UBILEE DOUBLE LUNCHEON SET

HIS SET is made of *Topaz* glass, the newest and richest creation of modern glass-making. It is elaborately decorated with an exquisite floral aving. A set that will be the pride of the most exacting hostess . . .

A SERVICE to excite the admiration of your most critical guests. It consists of Eight 8¾″ Luncheon Plates-Eight 7″ Salad Plates-Eight Cups-Eight Saucers-Eight Water Goblets-Two Sugars-Two Creamers and Two beautiful 11″ Sandwich or Cake Trays.

GENUINE CUT GLASSWARE
19 Piece Luncheon Set
AN ACCEPTABLE SERVICE FOR THE CHOICEST HOME

Four 8½ in. Salad Plates
Four Footed Tumblers

One 13½ in. Sandwich or Salad Tray
One Sugar—One Creamer

Four Cups
Four Saucers

TOPAZ - CUT 1200

JUBILEE

895/1 - 9 IN. HANDLED FRUIT

889/890/181 3 PIECE MAYONNAISE SET

879 SUGAR

895/4 - 11 IN. SANDWICH PLATE

879 CREAMER

885 - 11 IN. HANDLED SANDWICH TRAY

832/858 CHEESE AND CRACKER SET

"PATRICK"

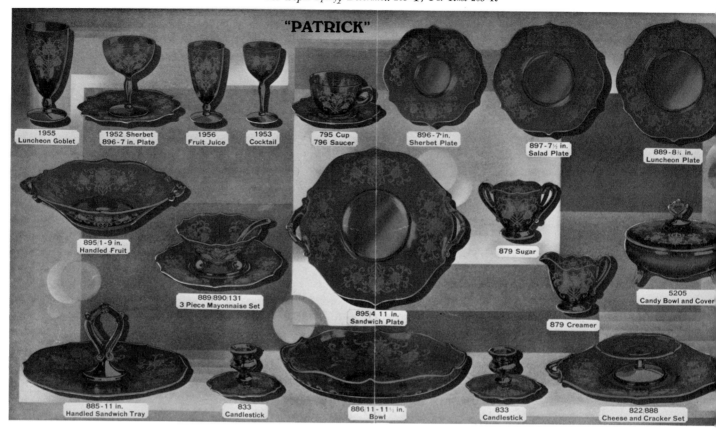

1955
Luncheon Goblet

1952 Sherbet
896-7 in. Plate

1956
Fruit Juice

1953
Cocktail

795 Cup
796 Saucer

896-7 in.
Sherbet Plate

897-7½ in.
Salad Plate

889-8¾ in.
Luncheon Plate

895/1-9 in.
Handled Fruit

889.890.131
3 Piece Mayonnaise Set

895.4 11 in.
Sandwich Plate

879 Sugar

879 Creamer

5205
Candy Bowl and Cover

885-11 in.
Handled Sandwich Tray

833
Candlestick

886.11-11½ in.
Bowl

833
Candlestick

822.888
Cheese and Cracker Set

No. 450/11—2-PIECE DISPLAY STAND
CRYSTAL BOWL—BLACK BASE
(DIAM. OF BOWL—19 INCHES)

Packs one Complete Unit to Individual Re-shipping Carton—Wt. 18 Lbs.

THE LANCASTER GLASS COMPANY—LANCASTER, OHIO

A Beautiful Oil Lamp with Parchment Sh:
STYLE—ORIGINALITY—QUALITY—APPEAL

No. 686-F Oil Lamp with 16½ in. Shade, Chimney, Burner and Wick
Rose Glass Base Complete with Green or Rose Shades

PACKS SIX BASES TO RESHIPPING CARTON

SHADES AND FITTINGS PACK SIX TO SEPARATE C/

THE LANCASTER GLASS CO.

LANCASTER,

THE NEW TUBULAR PEDESTAL AQUARIUM

SPECIFICATIONS

Crystal Glass
Height 30 inches
Diameter of bowl 9½ inches
Diameter of base 7 inches
Ornamental castle included
Each Aquarium packed in an individual reshipping carton, weight 13 pounds
Low center of gravity — will not upset easily
Holds over twice the usual amount of water — takes *less* floor space
Water need be changed but half as often as in ordinary globes. Fish only require half the usual care.

Here's the quick-turnover, big-profit item you have been looking for. Put it in your window and it sells itself; show it to your customers and they take it home. As a leader in department or furniture stores, as a unique attraction in flower and pet shops, it is in a class by itself.

To your customer it offers a beautiful addition to the furnishings in the home, something of appeal to everybody—children and grown-ups. It's a constant source of delight . . . . a thing of beauty that adds distinction anywhere.

PATENT APPLIED FOR

No. 287 Lamp with 16½ inch Shade, Cap, Socket, ½ Plug and Cord

1933's LAMP SENSATION

In 3 Colors - Jade Green - Rust - Black

THE LANCASTER GLASS COMPANY
LANCASTER, OHIO

Two close-ups of "SPHINX"

"SPHINX"

This design is found on green and yellow Lancaster blanks. A detail is drawn.

Libbey

New England Glass Company, established in 1818 in Boston, whose wares may today be seen in America's museums, is the prestigious parent of Libbey glass. The famous old firm moved to Toledo, Ohio in 1888 to be nearer a better fuel source, and in 1892 it was officially renamed the Libbey Glass Company for the family which had headed it for many years.

The move brought on a financial setback for the company, but the invention of a lightbulb-making machine and a unique all-glass display at the Chicago Exposition in 1893, which won world-wide attention for the company, brought Libbey back again. In 1916 the corporate title was changed to Libbey Glass Manufacturing Company.

The tradition of brilliant cut crystal wares was continued to some extent through the first decades of this century, but to survive Libbey found it had to develop other means of support. By the 20s the company had an entirely new look, one which insured success during these years. Now, in addition to its cut lines and artwares such as amberina, pomona, and peachblow (Libbey also made the yellow-and-green Maize pieces), it offered wares in lower price and quality ranges to better suit the real glass market of the time. It also became a major supplier to hotels and restaurants (in 1925 it assumed the Nonik Glassware Corporation, a major tumbler manufacturer) and this business carried the firm through the 20s and depression.

In 1933 Libbey made a bid to re-establish its reputation for finer wares. A. Douglas Nash came from his Corona factory to head the design department and created magnificent cuttings and artistic occasional pieces. In this year too the H. C. Fry Company was bought by Libbey.

In 1935 the Libbey organization was purchased by Owens-Illinois Glass Company of Toledo, at that time the "world's largest producers of glass containers", and has continued as a division of that company, while retaining the Libbey name, to the present. Libbey tumblers are still in household use all over the country.

COLOR

Libbey made all the characteristic Depression-era colors during its time—pink, green, amber, topaz, cobalt blue, ruby, and most others. But judging from trade journal write-ups and advertisements it was tumblers, hotel ware and then the fancier occasional pieces emphasized at Libbey, and not lines of tableware which might be collected today.

2635 4½ oz. 2600 12 oz. 2610 9 oz. 2c03 14 oz.   2903 14 oz.   2916 8 oz. 2908 10 oz. 2933 5 oz.   8401 7 oz.   8401 2 oz. 8401 5 oz.

SAFEDGE TUMBLERS

To a carefully selected and standardized group of table, room and beverage tumblers, all made with the patented Safedge features and sold under a chip-resisting guarantee, has been included a complete range of practical sizes and straight shapes embodying the no-nest feature. ›› The addition of the no-nest feature makes for an extremely dur-

able thin-blown glassware item and provides additional economic possibilities when these glasses are not in service and are necessarily stored on shelves or in cabinets. ›› Libbey Safedge tumblers are made in two grades of ware: The higher priced quality grade of lead; and a standard fine grade of lime ware

Libbey
COLORED GLASS

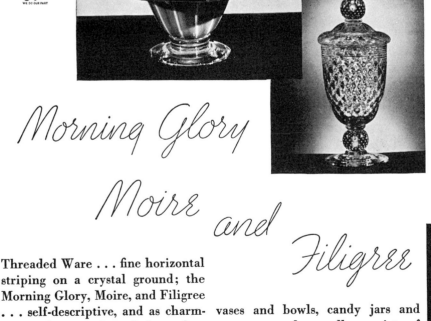

Morning Glory
Moire and
Filigree

Threaded Ware ... fine horizontal striping on a crystal ground; the Morning Glory, Moire, and Filigree ... self-descriptive, and as charming as they sound; and the sunken and relief designs, in opalescent and pastel tints.

All these patterns come in delightful gift pieces: cocktail sets,

vases and bowls, candy jars and comports, and an endless variety of glasses, jugs, and pitchers. And there's a ray of sunshine in the price list too. This holiday line is reasonably marked

—1933 advertisement

Liberty Works

This Egg Harbor, New Jersey firm began in 1903 as the Liberty Cut Glass Works, cutting and decorating fine crystal wares imported from Europe. Finished pieces were often exported back again—it's been said the company cut glass for Kaisers and other heads of state—and a continental, as well as national, reputation was claimed.

Sometime over the next decade much of this identity was dropped, along with part of its name; a new Liberty Works began making some of its own glass and came on strong with variety and color right at the time of the Depression. Extensive lines of just about everything—tableware, stemware, cut, etched, & decorated (the works, you might say)—were being made.

But Liberty clearly liked to do things its own way, and these wares were marketed as unconventionally as possible. It made the 'specialty ensemble' concept its own; in 1930, 27-piece Breakfast Sets (featuring egg cups and cereal bowls), Waffle Sets (with covered batter and syrup jugs) and Whist Sets were waved before the buyer. This scramble to have the latest thing on the market—the determination to be Trend-setter—gave Liberty Works its character, and even the trade journal press found it all remarkable.

About 1932 a bad fire damaged much of the plant, and in the middle of the hard times Liberty did not manage to rebuild.

COLOR

Liberty put out almost every color known to the Depression years. Pink, green, amber, and pale blue are mentioned in late 20s advertisements; in 1930 cobalt blue, red amber, and unusual two-tone effects such as ebony, pink, or green in combination with amber were being shown. Topaz was brought on in 1931. But several ads from the period say simply "Liberty lines available in all popular colors".

GLASS JUG OR SIMILAR ARTICLE

Filed May 21, 1926

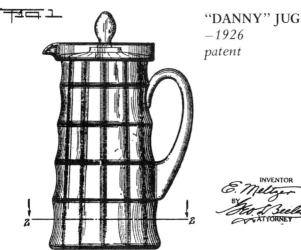

"DANNY" JUG
—1926
patent

INVENTOR
E. Meltzer
BY
Geo L Beeler
ATTORNEY

"SUE" CHEESE DISH   —1929 advertisement

BREAKFAST SETS
IN GLASSWARE TOO!

With all the promise of equal popularity to our glass luncheon sets, we introduce a twenty-four-piece breakfast set comprising a service for four.

CAN BE HAD IN ROSE OR GREEN GLASS

Cups and Saucers   Double Egg Cups
8″ Plates   Sugar and Creamer
Fruit Nappies   Salt and Pepper

THE LIBERTY WORKS

"EGG HARBOR" Line
—1929 advertisement

"CRACKERJACK"
—1929 advertisement

Featuring Two Seasonable Items

Ice Pail 124/4, strap handle and tongs
Ice Tub 98/107, with tongs

They are Crackerjacks

Full Fire Polished, Nicely Cut

Big Dollar Value

LIBERTY WORKS
THE
EGG HARBOR, N.J.

SOMETHING NEW IN GLASS

One of our smart fall presentations—a new Cookie Jar with combined floral and lattice cutting, equipped with a nickel handle with embossed design. May be had in rose or green.

THE LIBERTY WORKS

229

LIBERTY'S FAMOUS BAMBOO OPTIC LUNCHEON SETS

Luncheon Sets of glassware are becoming more and more popular. LIBERTY may be partly responsible for this. Among our excellent numbers is the set illustrated, which may be had in 15, 21 and 27 piece compositions. Made in full fire-polished glass in pink or green.

Illustrated above is the new No. 95 8-piece flower set from the Liberty Works which is shown at their New York showroom, 10 West 23rd street. This consists of a satin finished pot, saucer, and flower block with four green leaves to match and a tulip in assorted colors of red, yellow and orchid. Below are illustrated further new good things from the same factory. The square salad plate shown on the left is one of their newest shapes.

It features a pleasing optic and is very attractively priced. The large handled platter and round plate introduce a new ice cream set which the factory has just introduced. The platter is 12 inches in width and comes with six matching plates in optic in rose and green. These are all splendid numbers for the summer trade, and are very popularly priced.

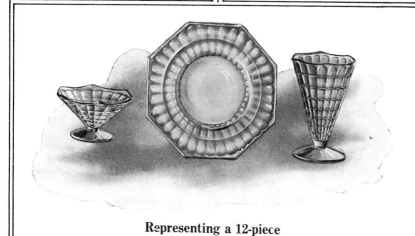

Representing a 12-piece

WHIST   SET

In Octagon Bamboo Optic

"TRUMAN" *tableware line*
—1930 trade journal write-up

"PAULA" CONSOLE SET
*decorated cobalt blue, ebony,
& red amber; 1930 advertisement*

"ROBIN" SALAD SET
*etched pink, green, amber,
cobalt blue, red amber; 1930 ad*

Above are two new arrivals at the Liberty Works showroom, 10 West 23rd street. These are items from their No. 174/25 line of stemware which features a light cut flower and leaf motif that is simple yet very pretty.

"LAWRENCE" cut line
—1930 trade journal article

American Pioneer

LIBERTY'S NEWEST
OFFERING IN POPULAR
PRICED CONSOLE SETS

"COLLINS" CONSOLE SET
*pink, green & light blue;
1930 advertisement*

AMERICAN PIONEER

*a large and popular
tableware line introduced in 1931*

(see more pieces in color section)

Was the Outstanding
Sensation of the Pittsburgh Show

A LIBERTY CREATION

The Luncheon Set as pictured here is featured in services for 4, 6 or 8 persons in addition to which our American Pioneer line may also be had in Salad Sets, Ice Pails, Old Style Footed Vases, Covered Urns, etc. Each piece will carry an embossed label worded "American Pioneer, by Liberty." A feature of this design is that the Hobnail effect has been relieved by panels and colonial flutes. The glass itself is of unusual brilliancy and offers a color selection of Green, Rose or Crystal.

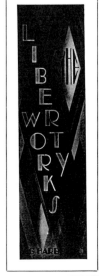

Lotus

The Lotus Glass Company of Barnesville, Ohio is unique to these chapters in that no glass was ever made there! Instead these craftsmen were extremely well known as glass decorators—they bought blanks from other factories and cut, etched, applied color, or encrusted them with gold or silver.

Lotus designs were original and its lines often popular enough to stay on the market several years. Many smaller decorating shops were in operation during the Depression era, but so significant was the Lotus market through this period it has earned a place here alongside the glassmakers of its time.

The decorating career began with the company's incorporation in 1912 and has remained steadily productive—with no major changes in leadership or in operations—to the present day. In the 20s and 30s, fine handmade blanks in all colors were obtained from the factories of Fostoria, Cambridge, Heisey, Paden City, Duncan and Miller, Bryce, Central, and others; and devotees will readily find these companies' famous shapes in the pages of Lotus to follow. Most often borrowed was stemware, but dinnerware and occasional pieces were also bought blank and transfigured into the Lotus product.

The finishers applied a variety of techniques. Cuttings, both light and heavy, were done, and deep plate etchings. Some wares were iridized and some hand painted. Perhaps the most characteristic Lotus treatment over the years has been its banding with 24 K gold or sterling silver. These trims were often added to black glass in the Depression era, but you will find it also on amethyst, canary, pink, green, topaz, amber, ruby, Steigel green, Ritz blue—almost every color of the time.

These gold and silver bands are still predominant in the Lotus lines of today, lines that due to fine glass quality and excellent finishings rank with the best on the popular market.

Silver on Black

Quality stands out in this "Call of the Wild" decoration on handsome black. It is a beautiful design and executed beautifully in silver deposit of quality.

In shape, decoration and quality, LOTUS wares are the acme of dependability. They are profitable, too, and many stores find it pays to keep ample stocks of LOTUS wares.

There is a wide range of pieces available in the "Call of the Wild" decoration in silver deposit.

LOTUS GLASS CO.
BARNESVILLE, OHIO

Lotus GLASSWARE *for every purpose.*
A wide range in shapes, colors and decorations. Complete matched patterns. Rose, Green, Amber, Crystal and Black.....

DECORATED IN GOLD AND SILVER

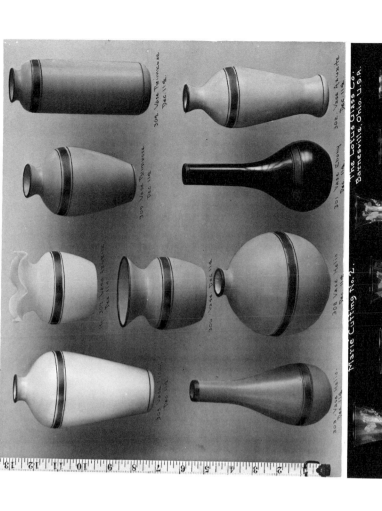

CATALOG REPRINTS

On the pages to follow are selected reprints from Lotus sales material showing its decorations on colored glass from 1925 to 1932. You will find these decorations on other blanks, and these blanks with other decorations or etchings.

The original Lotus photographs are in color—green, pink, amber, and topaz. Most pattern names are official, but some are superimposed by me.

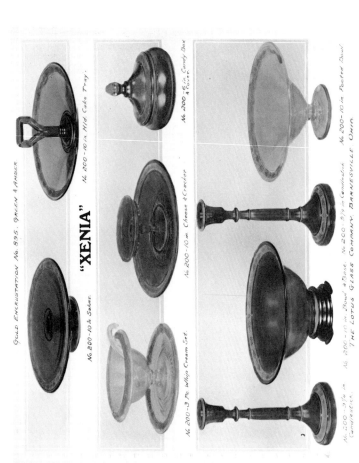

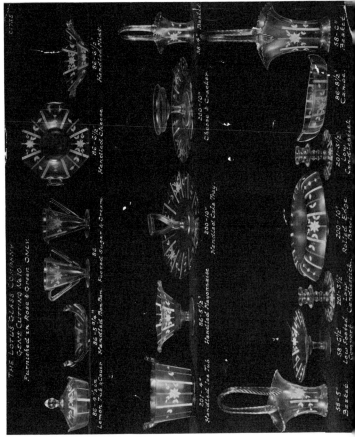

234

Colors—
Rose
Amber

Featuring
Special Sale Items

Cutting
No. 9

No. 201—3½ Inch Low Candlestick

No. 200—10 Inch Rolled Edge Bowl

No. 201—3½ Inch Low Candlestick

No. 200—10 Inch Handled Cake Plate

No. 200—3-Piece Mavonaise Set

No. 200—10 Inch Cheese and Cracker

Colors
Rose and
Green

Featuring
Special Sale Items

Good $ Numbers
For
Afternoon Teas
Euchre—Bridge
Favor Parties, Etc.

New Octagonal Assortment

No. 701—36 Piece Octagon Assortment

Single Assortment—One Barrel .... $24.00 per assortment.
Five Barrel Lots or over .... $21.60 per assortment.

What the assortment consists of and what you get:

6—only No. 701—10 in. Cheese and Crackers ...... 3 Green 3 Rose
6—only No. 701—10 in. Hld. Sandwich Plate ...... 3 "   3 "
6—only No. 701—3 Piece Whipped Cream Set ...... 3 "   3 "
6—only No. 701—3 Section Covered Relish ...... 3 "   3 "
6—pairs No. 701—4¾ in. Low Candlesticks ...... 3 Prs. "   3 Prs. "
6—only No. 701—12 in. Rolled Edge Bowls ...... 3 "   3 "
36 Pc. Asst.   Asst. comes in two colors only Rose and Green.

See other side of folder for individual prices on the above items.

23—Goblet (Optic)
Mitre Polished
Cutting No. 15

Mitre Polished
CUTTING No. 15

Rose and Green   16 Rib Optic

No.		Per Doz.
23—9 oz.	Goblet	$6.00
23—5½ oz.	High Sherbet	6.00
23—5½ oz.	Low Sherbet	6.00
23—5 oz.	Cafe Parfait	6.00
23—3½ oz.	Cocktail	5.80
23—2½ oz.	Wine	5.80
23—¾ oz.	Cordial	5.80
23—2½ oz.	Ftd. Tumbler	5.80
23—5 oz.	Ftd. Tumbler	3.20
23—9 oz.	Ftd. Tumbler	6.00
23—12 oz.	Ft. Ice Tea	6.00
840—12 oz.	Ice Tea	3.60
840—9 oz.	Table Tumbler	3.20
840—8 oz.	Tall Tumbler	3.20
840—5 oz.	Tumbler	3.20
840—2½ oz.	Whiskey	3.00
105—3 pt.	Tankard Jug	15.60
109—4 pt.	Cov. Ice Tea Jug	16.80
21	Cup and Saucer	15.00
60—6 in.	Plate	10.80
60—7½ in.	Plate	13.20
60—8 in.	Plate	14.40
60—9 in.	Plate	16.80

Keystone

Gene Cutting No. 10

STEMWARE ITEMS

Rose and Green Stem
and Foot
(OPTIC)

No.		Doz.
24—9 oz.	Goblet	$4.00
24—5½ oz.	High Sherbet	4.00
24—5½ oz.	Low Sherbet	4.00
24—3½ oz.	Oyster Cocktail	3.90
24—2 oz.	Wines	3.90
24—3½ oz.	Cocktail	3.90
24—12 oz.	Ftd. Ice Tea	4.00
24—10 oz.	Ftd. Table Tumbler	4.00
24—7 oz.	Ftd. Tumbler	3.90
24—2½ oz.	Ftd. Tumbler	3.90
24—3 pt.	Jug	21.00
24—1 qt.	Decanter	18.00
21—	Cup & Saucer	8.00
60—6 in.	Plate	5.40
60—7½ in.	Plate	6.60
60—8 in.	Plate	7.20

The Lotus Glass Co.
Barnesville, Ohio

205-12½ in.
Flared Bowl

200-10 in.
11td. Cake.

204-4½ in. Hld.
Ice Tub Oblong

204-12¾ in. Fltd. Fruit
Bowl. Decoration 730.

201-11 in. 2 Hld.
Sandwich. Dec 731.

Decoration 732.

205-12½ in.
6 Toe Flared Bowl

200-6½ in.
Tall Candle.

200-10 in.
Cheese Cracker.

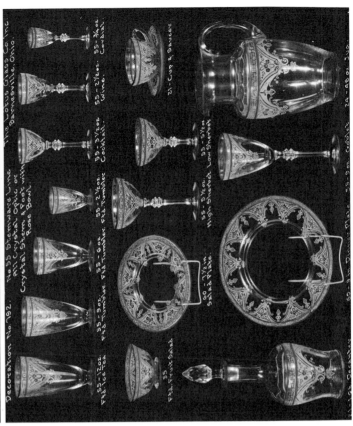

The Lotus Glass Co. Inc.
Barnesville, Ohio.

55-¾oz.
Cordial.

21-Cup & Saucer.

55-2½oz.
Wine.

55-3½oz.
Cocktail.

55-5½oz.
High Sherbet.

55-5½oz.
Low Sherbet.

No 55 Stemware Line
All Crystal Optic or
Crystal Stem & Foot with
Rose Bowl.

Fltd.55-12oz.
Ftd. Ice Tea.

55-9oz.
Ftd. Tumbler

55-6oz.
Ftd. Tumbler

55-2½oz.
Ftd. Tumbler

60-7½ in.
Salad Plate

Decoration No. 792.

55
Ftd. Fruit Salad.

60-8½ in. Dinner Plate

55-9 oz. Goblet

74-48¾ Jug

The Lotus Glass Co.
Barnesville, Ohio

"SOPHIA"

201-7 in.
Tall Comport.

201-3½ in.
Low Candle.

200-3 Pc.
Cream Set.
Whipped

Decoration 732.

201-12 in. Hld.
Pastry

201-13 in. Flared.
Bowl.

201-11 in. 2 Hld.
Celery Tray.

204-9 in. Tall Vase
3 Ftd.

201-6 in. 3 Sect.
Covered Relish

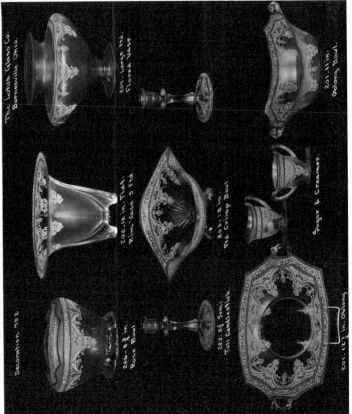

The Lotus Glass Co.
Barnesville, Ohio.

201-Large Ftd.
Flared Vase

201-11 in.
Oblong Bowl.

202-12 in. Flat.
Rim Vase 3 Ftd.

203-12 in.
Ftd. Crimp Bowl

Sugar & Creamer.

205-8½ in.
Rose Bowl.

203-5½ Semi.
Tall Candlestick.

201-12½ in. Oblong

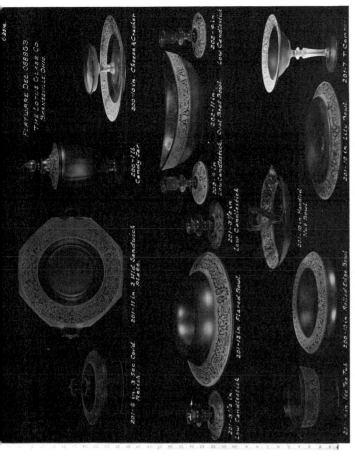

GRECIAN GOLD

The Lotus Glass Co., Barnesville, Ohio.

Dec. 663

200-10 Wld. Nut Bowl.

201-3½ Low Candle.

202-3¾ Low Candle.

Tall Comport

200-10 Cheese & Cracker.

201-7 Tall Comport

201-13 Fld. Bowl

201-4 Hld. Ice Tub

200-Whip Cream Set

201-6 Cold Relish

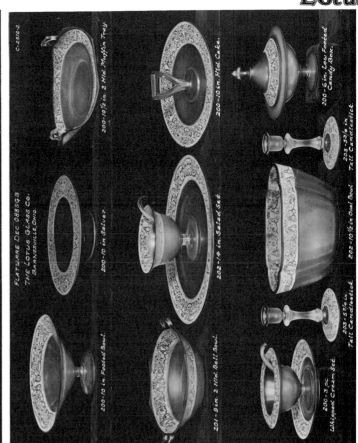

FLATWARE Dec. 0889G.3
THE LOTUS GLASS CO.
BARNESVILLE, OHIO.

C-2516.

200-10in Cheese & Cracker

200-1lb Candy Jar.

202-4in. Low Candlestick.

202-11in. Oval Seat Bowl.

201-6in Ice Tub

201-3in. 3 Sec. Cond. Relish.

201-11in 2 Hld. Sandwich Plate.

200-10in Rolled Edge Bowl.

201-13in Flared Bowl.

201-3½ in. Low Candlestick

201-3½ in. Low Candlestick

201-10 in Handled Nut Bowl.

201-7in. Comport

201-10 in Lily Bowl.

202-7 in. Low Candlestick.

The Lotus Glass Co., Barnesville, Ohio.

Decoration 885

206 Fld. Bowl.

203 Tall Candlestick.

203 R.E. Bowl.

203 Rose Bowl.

203 Crimp Bowl.

203 Tall Candlestick.

201-10½ Hld. Muffin.

205 R.E. Bowl.

203 Flared Bowl.

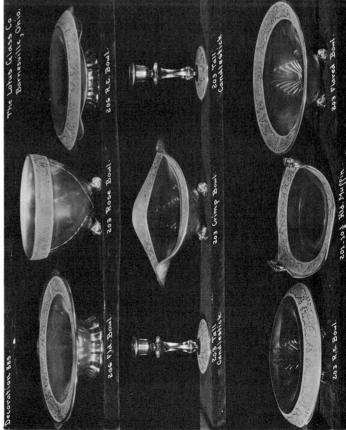

FLATWARE Dec. 088SG.3
THE LOTUS GLASS CO.
BARNESVILLE, OHIO.

C-2562

200-10½ in. 2 Hld. Muffin Tray.

200-10in. Hld. Cake.

200-6in. Low Footed Candy Boat.

200-10 in. Salver.

202-14 in. Salad Set.

202-10½ in Oval Bowl.

203-5⅞ in. Tall Candlestick.

200-10 in. Footed Bowl.

201-9 in. 2 Hld. Bell Bowl.

200-3 oz. Whipped Cream Set.

202-6⅝ in. Tall Candlestick.

Fuchsia Gold Decoration No. 905   The Lotus Glass Co.
Barnesville, Ohio.

FUCHSIA

201-10 Hld. Nut Bowl. 200 Whip Cream Set. 201-7 Tall Compart.

201-6 Sec.
Cov. Relish   200-10 Hld. Cake. 204-2 Hld.
                                        Obl. Ice Tub.

201-3½
Low Candle   205-12½
              6-Toe Bowl.

200-10
Cheese & Cracker   2-Hld. Muffin   201-11-2 Hld. Sandwich   201-9
                                                               2-Hld. Bell Bowl.

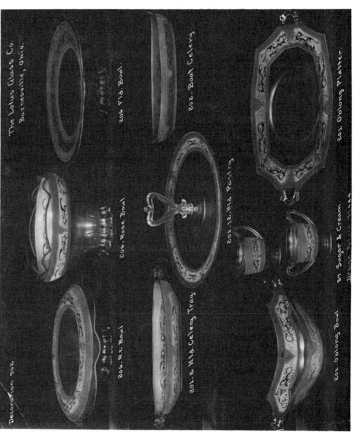

Fuchsia Etching No. 0905   Optic Crystal.
The Lotus Glass Co.
Barnesville, Ohio.

81
Sugar & Cream.

200-3 pc.
Whip Cream Set.

60-6 in.
Salad Plate.   201-6 in.
                Cov. Candy Box.   97-4 pint
                                   Jug.

60-7½ in.
Salad Plate.

7G-9oz. 7G-5oz. 7G-3oz. 7G-12oz. 7G-10oz. 21
Goblet   Shaped   Low   Cocktail   Ftd.   Cup & Saucer
                  Sherbet   Ice Tea

201-3½ in. 200-10 in. Hld. Cake. 205-12 in.
Low Candle.   6-Toe Bowl.

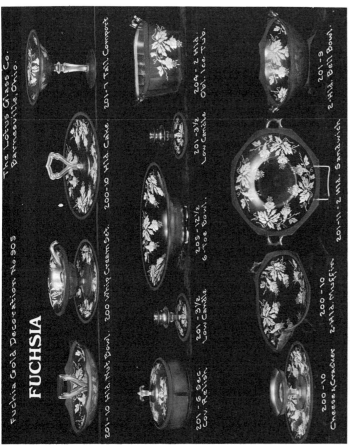

THE LOTUS GLASS CO.
BARNESVILLE, OHIO.

DECORATION No. 902.

200-10 in. Rolled Edge Bowl.   201-10½ in. 2 Hld. Muffin Tray.   201-10 in. Lily Bowl.

201-3½ in.
Low Candlestick.

201-13 in. Flared Bowl.   201-3½ in.
                           Low Candlestick.

"PARSON"

4 in. Crystal
Flower Block.

201-3 in. 2 Hld. Ball Bowl.   200-10 in. Cheese & Cracker.   201-11 in. 2 Hld. Sandwich Plate.

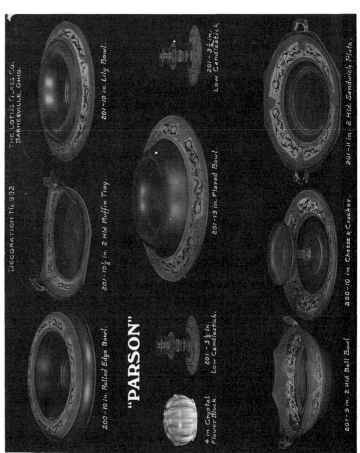

The Lotus Glass Co.
Barnesville, Ohio.

206 Ftd. Bowl.   202-Boat Celery.

206 Rose Bowl.

201-2 Hld. Celery Tray   201-12 Hld. Pastry.

206 R.E. Bowl.

201-Oblong Bowl   81 Sugar & Cream.   201 Oblong Platter.

Decoration 902.

238

REVERE

The Lotus Glass Co.
Barnesville, Ohio.

109 Line.

24-3¾ Whiskey.

24-7 Ftd. Tumbler.

22 Tumblers Same Shape as above Only all Rose.

24-10 Ftd. Tumbler.

24-12 Ftd. Ice Tea.

24 Wine.

24 Cocktail.

24-Low Sherbet.

24 Line Rose or Green Stem & Foot.

24-H Sherbet.

24-9 Goblet.

22 Fruit Salad.

24-1 Qt. Decanter.

24 Jug.

Design Patent Applied For.

21 Cup & Saucer.

60-7½- Plate.

81 Sugar & Cream.

22 Oyster Cocktail.

22. Wine. Cocktail.

22-H Sherbet.

22 Goblet.

22 Line Rose Only.

239

The Lotus Glass Co.
Barnesville, Ohio.

18 Cordial. — 18 Wine. — 18 Cocktail. — 18 H. Sherbet. — 18 H. Sherbet. — 18 Goblet. — 10 Goblet
18 Fruit Salad. — 21 Cup & Saucer. — 18-2½ Ftd. Whiskey. — 18 6 Ftd. Tumbler. — 18-10 Ftd. Tumbler. — 18-12 Ftd. Ice Tea.
18-4 Jug. Design Patent 75,974 — 18-1 Decanter. — 60-8 Salad Plate. La Furiste

No. 0907 Plate Etching (La Furiste)
STEMWARE LINE
Modern Trend Design   (Design Patent 75,974)

Furnished in Rose, Green, Amber and Crystal

No.			
18—	9	oz.	Goblet................................... (optic)
18—	6½	oz.	High Sherbet.......................... (optic)
18—	6½	oz.	Low Sherbet........................... (optic)
18—	3½	oz.	Cocktail................................ (optic)
18—	2¾	oz.	Wine.................................... (optic)
18—	1½	oz.	Cordial................................. (optic)
18—			Fruit Salad............................. (optic)
21			Cup and Saucer...................... (optic)
18—	12	oz.	Footed Ice Tea........................ (optic)
18—	10	oz.	Footed Tumbler....................... (optic)
18—	6	oz.	Footed Tumbler....................... (optic)
18—	2½	oz.	Footed Tumbler....................... (optic)
18—	4	pt.	Jug...................................... (optic)
18—	1	qt.	Decanter................................ (optic)
60—	6	in.	Bread and Butter Plate............. (optic)
60—	7½	in.	Salad Plate............................ (optic)
60—	8	in.	Salad Plate............................ (optic)
60—	9	in.	Dinner Plate........................... (optic)
60—	12	in.	Service Plate.......................... (optic)

The Lotus Glass Co.
Barnesville, Ohio.

206 R.E. Bowl. — 201-1 Tall Comporte. — 200-10 Hd. Cake
206 Rose Bowl. — 201-12 Hd. Pastry
206 Fld. Bowl. — 200-6 Covd. Relish. — 200-3 Piece Whip Cream Set. — 201 Hd. Ice Tub

Etching No. 0907
(La Furiste)
Modern Trend Design
(Design Patent 75,974)

Furnished in Rose, Green, Amber

No.		
206—	12½ x 3½	Flared Bowl.....................
206—	8¾ x 3½	Rose Bowl.....................
206—	12 x 3½	Rolled Edge Bowl..............
201—	6 in.	Three Section Covered Relish..
210—	12 in.	Handled Pastry................
201—		Tall Comport....................
201—	4	Two Handled Ice Tub...........
200—	3	pc. Whip Cream................
200—	10 in.	Handled Cake..................

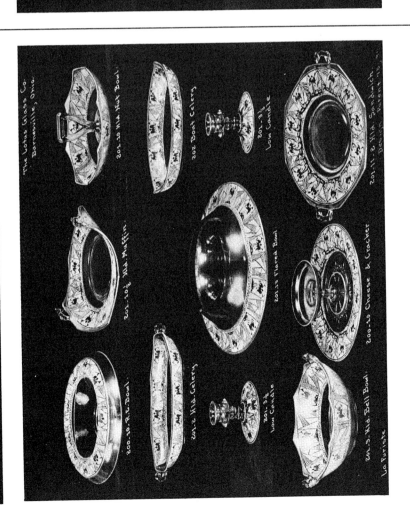

Etching No. 0907
(La Furiste)

Modern Trend Design
(Design Patent 75,974)

Furnished in Rose, Green, Amber and Crystal

No.
203—12   in. Three Footed Flared Bowl
203—7¾ x 5½ in. Three Footed Rose Bowl
203—11¼ in. Three Footed Rolled Edge Bowl
203—12   in. Three Footed Crimp Bowl
201—13   in. Semi Tall Candle
203—5½ in. Oblong Platter
201—12½ x 10 in. Oblong Bowl
201—11 x 8½ in. Oblong Bowl
87—   Sugar and Cream

Gold Band on Inner and Outer Edge of Plate

Etched Border Guaranteed—22 Karat

Furnished in Rose, Green, Amber and Crystal

Etching No. 0907
(La Furiste)

Modern Trend Design
(Design Patent 75,974)

Furnished in Rose, Green, Amber and Crystal

No.
200—10   in. Rolled Edge Bowl
201—10½ in. Two Handled Muffin
201—10   in. Handled Nut Bowl
210—12¼—4½ Two Handled Celery
201—13   in. Flared Bowl
202—10½—4½ in. Boat Celery
201—3½ in. Low Candlestick
201—9   in. Handled Bell Bowl
201—10   in. Cheese and Cracker
201—11   in. Two Handled Sandwich

Wide Gold Encrusted Border—Guaranteed 22 Karat

Furnished in Rose, Green, Amber and Crystal

Call of the Wild.

The Lotus Glass Co.
Barnesville, Ohio.

5050

6550

9550

6050

7150

7650

6450

6950

7550

EBONY GLASSWARE
POPPY DESIGN

6 IN. BULB BOWL.

5¾ IN. ASH TRAY &
CIGARETTE BOX.

7 IN. CARD TRAY.

4 IN. FLOWER BLOCK
3½ & 5 IN.

6 IN. CHOCOLATE BOX.

7½ IN. HI. FTD. COMPORT.

10 IN. CHEESE & CRACKER.

8½ IN. LOW FTD. COMPORT.

THE LOTUS CUT GLASS CO.

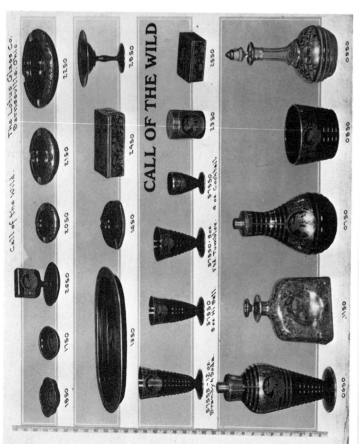

Call of the Wild.

The Lotus Glass Co.
Barnesville, Ohio.

2250

2850

0850

1650

2050

1750

2650

1850

2150

2450

2350

0650

0750

1950

CALL OF THE WILD

57550-8oz.

57550
Ftd. Tumbler.

57750
4 oz. Cocktail.

2350

57555-12 oz.
Cranberry Soda.

57550-12 oz.
Box Hi. Ball.

1750

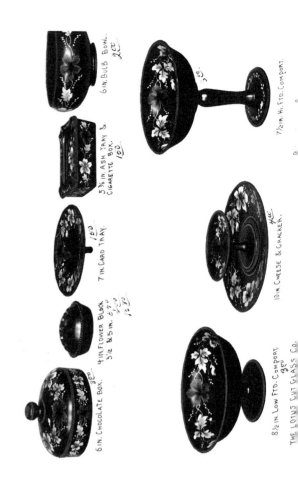

Call of the Wild.

The Lotus Glass Co.
Barnesville, Ohio.

7450 - 12½ in.

2950 - 6 in.

6850 - 5½ in.

7250 - 8¾ in.

6950

7350 - 12 in.

6850 - 5½ in.

3050 - 8 in.

9150 - 6 in.

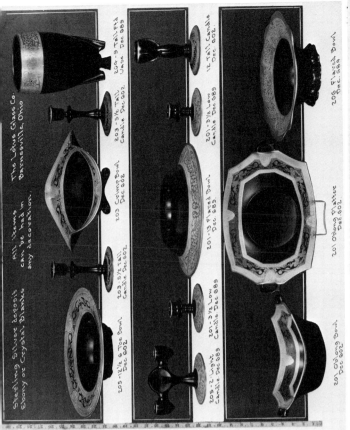

EBONY SILVER LOLA

EBONY
SILVER LOLA

243

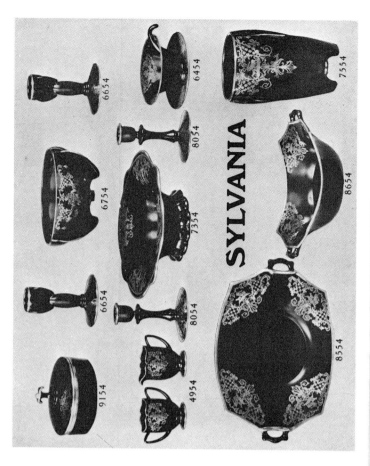

SYLVANIA

6654
6454
7554
8054
8654
6754
7354
8054
6654
9154
4954
8554

"McGUIRE"

Etching No. 1001
Square Foot Stemware Line.

The Lotus Glass Co. Inc.
Barnesville, Ohio, U.S.A.

450 — Sugar & Cream.

450 — 9 in.
Divided Plate.

450 — 7 in.
Salad Plate.

450 — 6 in.
Salad Plate.

450 - 3 oz.
Ftd. Cordial.

450 - 3 oz.
Ftd. Sherbet.

450 - 3½ oz.
Ftd. Cocktail.

450 - 8 oz.
Ftd. Tumbler.

450 - 5 oz.
Ftd. Wine.

450 — 3 oz.
Cup Sherry.

201 — 6 in. 3 Sec.
Covered Candy Box.

205 - 12 in. 6 Toe Console Bowl.
201 - 3½ in. Low Candle.

7254
9554
9854
7154
7454
6554
9554
8954
7654
9754
8854

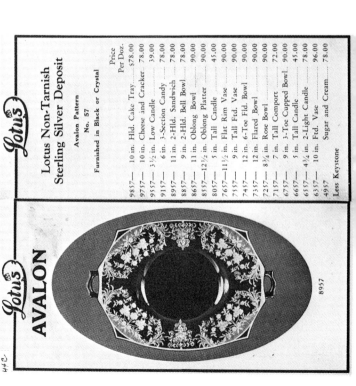

Lotus

Lotus Non-Tarnish
Sterling Silver Deposit

Avalon Pattern
No. 57

Furnished in Black or Crystal

		Price Per Doz.
9857 —	10 in. Hld. Cake Tray	$78.00
9757 —	10 in. Cheese and Cracker	78.00
9557 —	3½ in. Low Candle	39.00
9157 —	6 in. 3-Section Candy	78.00
8957 —	11 in. 2-Hld. Sandwich	78.00
8857 —	9 in. 2-Hld. Bell Bowl	78.00
8657 —	11 in. Oblong Bowl	90.00
8557 —	12½ in. Oblong Platter	90.00
8057 —	5 in. Tall Candle	45.00
7657 —	11½ in. Flat Rim Vase	90.00
7557 —	9 in. Tall Ftd. Vase	90.00
7457 —	12 in. 6-Toe Fld. Bowl	90.00
7357 —	12 in. Flared Bowl	90.00
7257 —	8¾ in. Rose Bowl	90.00
7157 —	7 in. Tall Comport	72.00
6757 —	9 in. 3-Toe Cupped Bowl	90.00
6657 —	5 in. Tall Candle	45.00
6557 —	4¾ in. 2-Light Candle	78.00
6357 —	10 in. Frd. Vase	96.00
4957	Sugar and Cream	78.00

Less Keystone

Lotus

AVALON

8957

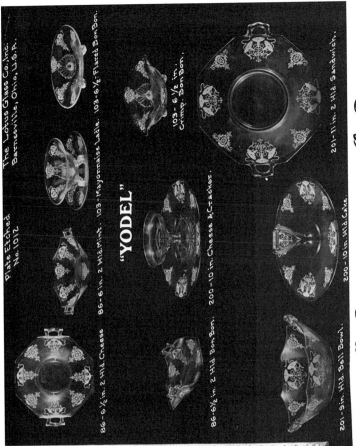

The Lotus Glass Co. Inc.
Barnesville, Ohio, U.S.A.

Plate Etched No. 1012

"YODEL"

86 - 6½ in. 2 Hld. Cheese
86 - 6 in. 2 Hld. Mint.
103 - Mayonnaise Ladle.
103 - 6½ - Flared Bon Bon.
103 - 6½ in. Crimp. Bon Bon.

200 - 10 in. Cheese & Cracker.
201 - 11 in. 2 Hld. Sandwich.
200 - 10 in. Hld. Cake.

86 - 6½ in. 2 Hld. Bon Bon.
201 - 9 in. Hld. Bell Bowl.

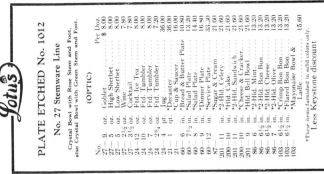

PLATE ETCHED No. 1012

No. 27 Stemware Line

Crystal Bowl with Rose Stem and Foot,
also Crystal Bowl with Green Stem and Foot.

(OPTIC)

No.			Per Doz.
27	9 oz.	Goblet	$ 8.00
27	5 oz.	High Sherbet	8.00
27	5 oz.	Low Sherbet	8.00
27	2½ oz.	Wine	7.80
27	3½ oz.	Cocktail	7.80
24	12 oz.	Ftd. Ice Tea	8.00
24	10 oz.	Ftd. Tumbler	8.00
24	7 oz.	Ftd. Tumbler	7.20
24	2¾ oz.	Ftd. Tumbler	7.20
24	4 pt.	Jug	36.00
24	1 qt.	Decanter	36.00
21		*Cup & Saucer	16.00
60	7½ in.	*Bread & Butter Plate	10.80
60	8 in.	*Salad Plate	13.20
60	9 in.	*Dinner Plate	14.40
60	12 in.	*Service Plate	16.80
87		Sugar & Cream	33.30
200	11 in.	*Hld. Celery	21.60
201	11 in.	*Hld. Cake	21.60
201	10 in.	*2 Hld. Sandwich	21.60
201	9 in.	*Cheese & Cracker	21.60
88		*Hld. Bell Bowl	21.60
88	6½ in.	*2 Hld. Mint	13.20
88	6½ in.	*2 Hld. Bon Bon	13.20
80	7 in.	*2 Hld. Cheese	13.20
103		*2 Hld. Olive	13.20
103	6½ in.	*Crimp Bon Bon	13.20
103	6½ in.	*Flared Bon Bon	13.20
103		*Mayonaise Bowl & Ladle	15.60

*These items furnished in solid colors only.

Less Keystone discount.

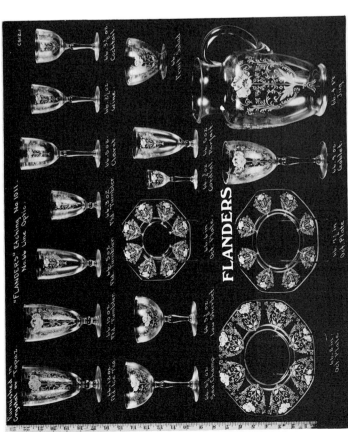

The Lotus Glass Co. Inc.
Barnesville, Ohio, U.S.A.

"FLANDERS" Etching No. 1011.
Noble Line Optic.

Furnished in Crystal or Topaz.

12 ½ oz. Cocktail

No. 2 oz. Wine

No. 5 oz. Claret

No. 3 oz. Cocktail Tumbler

No. 10 oz. Ftd. Tumbler

No. 12 oz. Ftd. Iced Tea

No. 9 oz. Goblet

No. 3½ oz. Cocktail

No. 6 oz. Fruit Salad

No. 1 Qt. Jug

FLANDERS

No. 11 in. Oct. Plate

No. 8½ in. Oct. Plate

No. 5 oz. Low Sherbet

No. 5 oz. High Sherbet

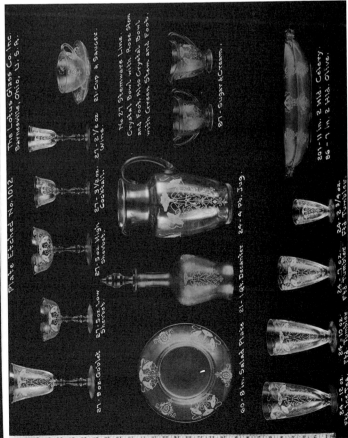

Plate Etched No. 1012.

No. 27 Stemware Line.
Crystal Bowl with Rose Stem
and Foot. Also Crystal Bowl
with Green Stem and Foot.

27 - 9 oz. Goblet.
27 - 5 oz. High Sherbet.
27 - 5 oz. Low Sherbet.
60 - 8 in. Salad Plate.
24 - 10 oz. Ftd. Tumbler.
27 - 2½ oz. Wine.
27 - 3½ oz. Cocktail
21 - 1 Qt. Decanter.
24 - 4 Pt. Jug.
24 - 2 3/4 oz. Ftd. Tumbler.
21 - Cup & Saucer.
87 - Sugar & Cream.
200 - 11 in. 2 Hld. Celery.
86 - 7 in. 2 Hld. Olive.

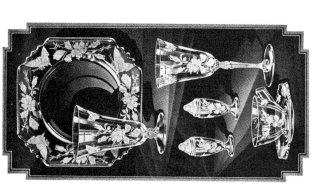

(BUTTERFLY) Etching No. 1014
Stemware & Flatware

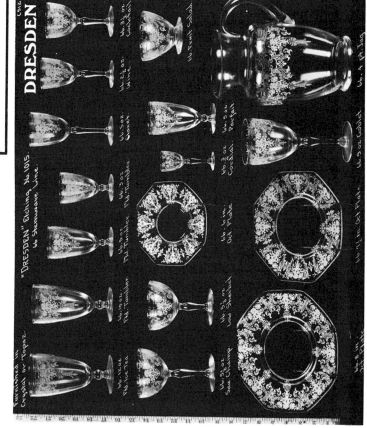

DRESDEN

"DRESDEN" Etching No. 1015
Stemware Line

Furnished in
Crystal or Topaz.

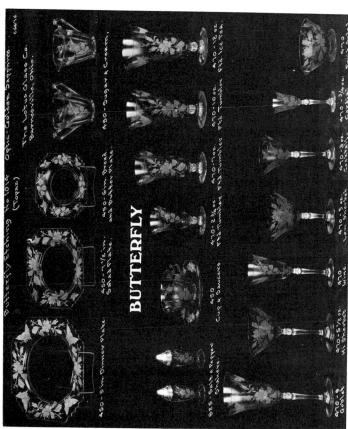

BUTTERFLY

Butterfly Etching No. 1014 Optic-Golden Sunset
(Topaz)

The Lotus Glass Co.
Barnesville, Ohio.

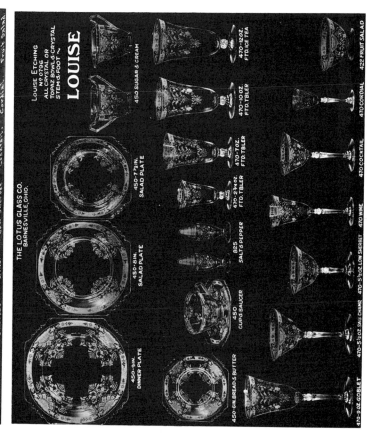

LOUISE

Louise Etching
No. 0796
ALL CRYSTAL OR
TOPAZ BOWL & CRYSTAL
STEM & FOOT

THE LOTUS GLASS CO.
BARNESVILLE, OHIO.

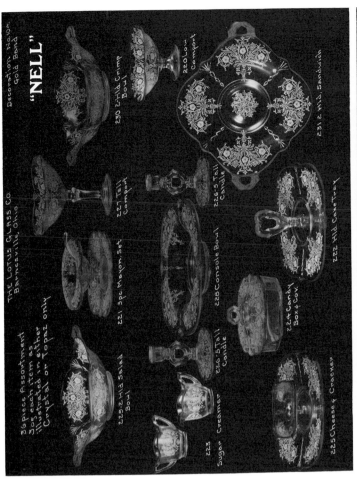

THE LOTUS GLASS CO. Barnesville, Ohio

Decoration No.19A. Gold Band

"NELL"

36 piece Assortment 3 of each item as illustrated in either Crystal or Topaz only

230 2 Hld. Crimp Bowl

220 Low Comport

227 Tall Comport

226-5 Tall Candle

231 2 Hld. Sandwich

221 3 pc. Mayon. Set

228 Console Bowl

222 Hld. Cake Tray

229 2 Hld. Salad Bowl

226-5 Tall Candle

223 Sugar Creamer

224 Candy Box & Cov.

225 Cheese & Cracker

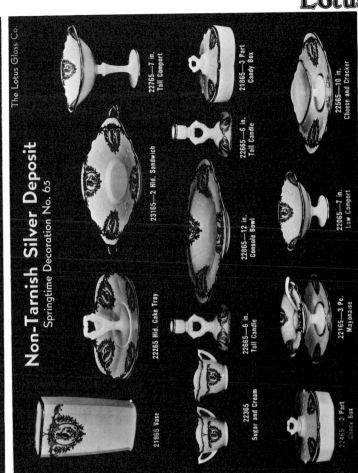

The Lotus Glass Co.

Non-Tarnish Silver Deposit
Springtime Decoration No. 65

22765—7 in. Tall Comport

22665—6 in. Tall Candle

21865—3 Part Candy Box

23165—2 Hld. Sandwich

22865—12 in. Console Bowl

22565—10 in. Cheese and Cracker

22265 Hld. Cake Tray

22665—6 in. Tall Candle

22065—7 in. Low Comport

21965 Vase

22365 Sugar and Cream

22165—3 Pc. Mayonaise

22465—2 Part Candy Box

THE LOTUS GLASS CO. Barnesville, Ohio

Cutting No.19

"WANDA"

36 piece Assortment 3 of each item as illustrated in either Rose or Topaz only

230-2 Hld. Crimp Bowl

220 Low Comport

227 Tall Comport

226-5 Tall Candle

231-2 Hld. Sandwich

221 3 Pc. Mayon. Set

225 Console Bowl

222 Hld. Cake Tray

229-2 Hld. Salad Bowl

226-5 Tall Candle

223 Sugar Creamer

224 Candy Box Cov.

225 Cheese & Cracker

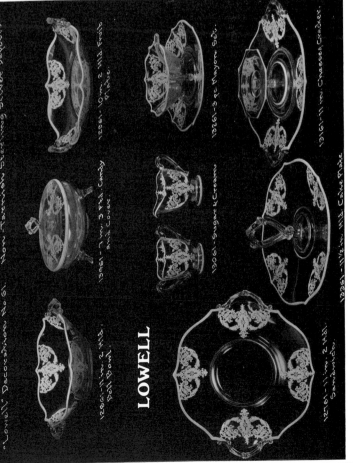

"Lowell" Decoration No. 61. Non-Tarnish Sterling Silver Deposit

13261—10 in. 2 Hld. Fruit Plate

13261—3 pc. Mayon. Set

13261—11 in. Cheese, Cracker.

13261—7 in. 3 Ftd. Candy and Cover

13061—Sugar & Cream

13261—11 in. 2 Hld. Bon Bowl.

13261—11½ in. Hld. Cake Plate

LOWELL

13261—11½ in. 2 Hld. Sandwich Cov.

Louie

Louie Glass Company and its affiliates, Weston Glass and West Virginia Specialty Company, handmade quality lines of tableware (featuring stemware, refreshment sets, and drinking accessories but including plates) during the Depression. Colors were topaz, pink, green, Royal blue, black, and ruby, often in combination with crystal. Under new management but still the old Louie name, the Weston, West Virginia factory continues to make glassware today.

"BRENNER" Stemware and "SEMPER" Refreshment Set from 1931 ad; topaz, pink, green

TOPAZ
—By Louie

Refreshment Sets from 1936 ad (counterclockwise from upper left):
"GROUCHO"
"HARPO"
"CHICO"
"ZEPPO"

Refreshment Sets In Louie Blue

Year's best color—Royal Blue, crystal handles. Other crystal & color combinations. All hand blown.

LOUIE GLASS CO. ————— **WEST VIRGINIA GLASS SPECIALTY CO.**
WESTON, WEST VIRGINIA

249

Macbeth-Evans

Two already renowned glass firms, that of Macbeth ("first successful producers of optical glass in America") and that of Evans ("the largest lamp chimney manufacturers in the world"), merged in 1899. Macbeth-Evans Glass Company went on to make its new name several times prominent in the glass history of the next century.

The purpose of the combine was to build a major new company around a just-patented invention, the glass-blowing machine. This early mechanization was a first step on the way to a new leadership in the trade. In two decades Macbeth, by expanding its facilities, its automation, and its product ideas, had become one of the largest suppliers of glass for illumination, science, and industry. Factories in Marion, Bethevan, and Elwood Indiana, and Toledo Ohio, assisted the main works at Charleroi, Pennsylvania.

For a time most famous for lamp chimneys, shades and globes, the company had eyes for other markets as well and in the mid-20s introduced its first water sets and tumblers. These and other miscellaneous table items were tried and proved in crystal and colors, and the first complete mold-etched tableware line in colored glass was created in 1930. Other major lines followed and the rest is Depression Glass history. Macbeth's successful new venture into machine-made colored glass gave us many of our most desired patterns and colors today.

In 1937 the firm was bought by Corning Glass Works of Corning, New York, but operations continued with the name Macbeth-Evans Division into the 40s. Crystal, and decorated items such as jugs and tumblers were big at this time and in 1939 new lines of dinnerware were created out of Chinex, an opaque white meant to compete with china. It too is collectible now.

The old Macbeth plant is still in Charleroi. At present it is making Corningware under the name of that illustrious company.

COLOR

Color surfaced in the Macbeth lines in the late 20s. Records show pink and Emerald being made in 1928. Topaz was done briefly in 1931 and at one point some amber was tried, for we find isolated pieces of it from time to time. Ruby and Ritz blue were the big innovations for the mid-30s as were the fired-on red, green, yellow and blue decorations and the gold or platinum trims.

The white translucent Monax color dates back prior to the 20s when it was developed as an ideal glass for illumination. The company was widely congratulated for it; it was said that the street lamps in every American city and town were topped with Monax globes. Along in the 30s Macbeth apparently couldn't resist using its favorite creation in some of the tableware lines–thus came about some of our favorites as well! Cremax, Ivrene, and Denax were 30s' variations on the Monax theme.

The major Macbeth-Evans patterns already presented in Book 1 will be reviewed on the next few pages for purposes of update. We will take them in the approximate order they were first made.

REMEMBER: Macbeth used its famous trademark only in its advertising, but Corning pressed the glassblower in some of the glassware made after 1936.

"DOGWOOD"

"DOGWOOD" was introduced in 1930, not 1928, and production continued until 1934. Pink with gold trim was also made, as were experimental pieces in amber. Items not shown in Book 1 are pictured below.

The 8" jug has two handle styles, one plain and the other ribbed. Two styles of 10-oz tumbler measure 4" and 4½". The molded tumbler shown below is definitely Macbeth's and carries the "DOGWOOD" mold number in old catalogs. Why is the platter so scarce? The mold was defective, and never replaced.

See the fat jug in the color section.

Molded "DOGWOOD" tumbler; tidbit server from 1931 trade journal.

Additional Monax "DOGWOOD": 8½" bowl, 12" salver, cup & saucer.

"THISTLE"

At this writing no cream or sugar has yet been found (we have no official listing for this pattern), but a 13" cake plate has been. "THISTLE" was also made in crystal.

"THISTLE" cake plate

S-PATTERN 6" plate in Monax.

S-PATTERN

This pattern has turned up in other colors—red, which was made in 1934-35, green, and Monax (the 6" bread and butter)—but only in pieces. Fired-on colors were made, and also some gold trim. Add to the Book 1 list the 80 oz jug with straight sides.

PETALWARE

The shakers shown with this set in Book 1 are in fact part of Hazel Atlas' "Newport".

PETALWARE was made in an all-over, fired-on red, blue, yellow, or green; a place setting in each color makes a luncheon set. The 8" bowl and the 2½" mustard attached to a 4¼" plate are found in Ritz blue.

Lamp with PETALWARE shade; other style shade; the mustard server.

Light fixture with original PETALWARE shades. These shades were made in several shapes for various lamp companies.

CORNING *Monax* PASTELS

EXQUISITE COLORED PASTEL BANDS ON RICH MONAX DINNERWARE WITH SUBTLE IRIDESCENT UNDERTONE AND FAMOUS CORNING CHIP-RESISTANT TUMBLERS

17 PIECE MONAX B-432 ASSORTMENT No. 723

This Eye Appealing Assortment Contains:

- 4 Cups
- 4 Saucers
- 4—9¼ in. Dinner Plates
- 1—11 in. Serving Plate
- 4 Tall Decorated Beverage Glasses

SET NO.	Pieces in Set	Packed Carton	Weight per Set
723 B-352	17	1 Set	11 lbs.

MACBETH-EVANS DIVISION
CORNING GLASS WORKS • CHARLEROI • PENNSYLVANIA

CORNING MONAX PASTELS: *Monax PETALWARE with pink (or red), blue, and green bands; 1939 catalog.*

CORNING *Regency* PETALWARE

Seventeen-piece *Regency* Petalware Luncheon Set (shown above) consists of: 4 cups, 4 saucers, 4—8″ salad plates, 4 gold decorated 9 oz. tall tumblers and 1—11″ salver.

Fifteen-piece *Regency* Petalware Luncheon Set consists of: 4 cups, 4 saucers, 4—8″ salad plates, 1 cream pitcher, 1 sugar bowl, 1—11″ salver.

A real profit producer! This Corning Regency Luncheon Set is perfect for parties, has *tested* appeal. Thin, lustrous, translucent, its pattern in genuine 22-carat gold, this is a service fit for a queen . . . yet priced to fit the housewife's budget.

SET NO.	PCS. IN SET	STD. PKG.	APPROX. SHIPPING WT.
28650 B-374 Gold	17	1 Set	11 Lbs.
28920 B-374 Gold	15	1 Set	10 Lbs.

Macbeth-Evans Division **CORNING GLASS WORKS** Charleroi, Pennsylvania

CORNING REGENCY PETALWARE: *Monax with gold decoration; 1939 catalog.*

CORNING *Monax* PASTELS

Distinctive Beauty That Captivates the Eye

MONAX PASTEL BANDED FRUIT AND DESSERT SET

7 PIECE MONAX B-432 ASSORTMENT No. 58

Contains: 1—9 in. Bowl and 6—6 in. Dessert Dishes

SET NO.	Pieces in Set	Packed Carton	Sets per Case	Weight per Case
58-B432	7	1 Set	8 Sets	38 Lbs.

MONAX PASTEL BANDED CAKE AND ICE CREAM SET

7 PIECE MONAX B-432 ASSORTMENT No. 729

Contains: 1—11 in. Salver and 6 Footed Sherbets

SET NO.	Pieces in Set	Packed Carton	Sets per Case	Weight per Case
729-B432	7	1 Set	8 Sets	38 Lbs.

MACBETH-EVANS DIVISION
CORNING GLASS WORKS • CHARLEROI • PENNSYLVANIA

Corning *Coronet*

22K GOLD DECORATED PETALWARE LUNCHEON SETS

Seventeen piece Coronet Petalware Luncheon set (illustrated above) consists of: 4 cups, 4 saucers, 4-8″ salad plates, 4 gold decorated 9 oz. tall tumblers, and 1-11″ salver. . . . *Fifteen piece* Coronet Petalware Luncheon set consists of 4 cups, 4 saucers, 4-8″ salad plates, 1 cream pitcher, 1 sugar bowl, and 1-11″ salver.

This beautiful decoration in genuine 22 karat gold applied to Corning's exclusive Petalware makes a luncheon service that will appeal to any woman! Expensive looking but moderately priced, these sets produce excellent volume and real profits.

SET NO.	PCS. IN SET	STD. PKG.	APPROX. SHIPPING WT.
28650 B-578	17	1 set	11
28920 B-578	15	1 set	10

by Corning

MACBETH-EVANS DIVISION
CORNING GLASS WORKS
CHARLEROI · PENNSYLVANIA

CORNING CORONET PETALWARE: *Monax and Ivrene with gold decoration; 1939 catalog.*

CORNING IVRENE PASTELS

17 PIECE *Ivrene* ASSORTMENT No. 650 B-339

CONTAINS 4 Cups 4—8-in. Plates 4 Tall Beverage Glasses
          4 Saucers 1—11-in. Serving Plate

Set No.	Pieces in Set	Packed Carton	Weight per Set
650 B-339	17	1 Set	11 lbs.

Also Available with Gold Band Decoration

17 PIECE ASST. No. 650-GOLD—CONTAINS

4 Cups 4 Tall Beverage Glasses
4 Saucers 1—11-in. Serving Dish
          4—8-in. Plates

Set No.	Pieces in Set	Packed	Weight per Set
650 Gold Banded	17	1 Set	11 lbs.

MACBETH-EVANS DIVISION
CORNING GLASS WORKS • CHARLEROI • PENNSYLVANIA

CORNING IVRENE PASTELS: Ivrene PETALWARE with yellow, green, and blue bands; 1939 catalog.

FLORETTE PETALWARE: Monax with red and green decoration; 1948 catalog.

Hand Painted FLORETTE PETALWARE

MADE BY THE MAKERS OF PYREX WARE

12" Salver
9¼" Dinner Plate
Creamer
Sugar
Cup and Saucer
9" Bowl
6" Dessert Dish
6" Bread and Butter Plate

MACBETH-EVANS DIVISION
CORNING GLASS WORKS • CHARLEROI • PENNSYLVANIA

(con't) FLORETTE listing:

Florette Cup
Florette Saucer
Florette Dinner Plate (9¼")
Florette Cereal Dish (6")
Florette Bread & Butter Plate (6")
Florette Bowl (9")
Florette Salver (12")
Florette Sugar
Florette Creamer

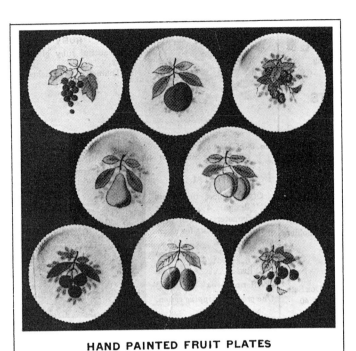

HAND PAINTED FRUIT PLATES

Snow white in color with eight different fruits, hand painted in natural colors.
Sufficiently fired to withstand salad acids.

Hand painted PETALWARE: late 40s.

"AMERICAN SWEETHEART"

Additions to Book I: Monax with gold, platinum, or smoky black trim; 56 oz and 80 oz pitchers in pink; a lazy-susan-type, 15½" plate on metal stand, found with gold rim. Monax sherbets usually have both pattern and ribbing on the outside, but some have pattern on the inside and ribbing on the outside. Cremax pieces keep showing up, usually the 9" bowl and 6" nappy.

The AMERICAN SWEETHEART lampshade comes in Denax ("a semi-indirect glass of high reflecting opacity toned with green, light blue, or pink with tan overtone, or with a delicate two-tone effect of ivory and pink which transmits a softly suffused peach glow" as an early catalog describes it). The shade alone is shown below, and an original lamp—quite a prize!—can be seen in the color section.

The Monax shakers are super rare, and so is the sugar cover pictured below. Two styles of knob have been noted on the sugar cover.

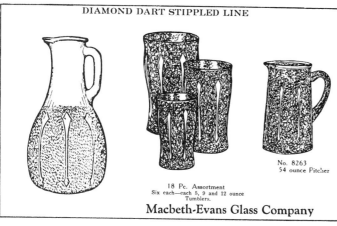

DIAMOND DART STIPPLED LINE

No. 8263
54 ounce Pitcher

18 Pc. Assortment
Six each—each 5, 9 and 12 ounce
Tumblers.

Macbeth-Evans Glass Company

DIAMOND DART

This pattern was made in Emerald green and crystal in 1928. You will probably find other pieces.

A
Quality
Shape

. . . for
Quantity
Sales

In Green or Pink

The high quality design of this new Macbeth Iced Tea Set assures its wide-spread acceptance as a real bargain . . . Classically styled, it possesses distinctive charm and appealing smartness. The popularity of its shape will be matched by the popularity of its price. Quantity production makes possible an amazingly low cost.

The set can be had as illustrated, for use as an Iced Tea Set, or with table tumblers for use as a Water Set . . . All tumblers have the patented Macbeth CHIP PROOF edge—an additional selling feature at no higher cost. The set is available in lovely tints of Green or Pink. Write now for price and package information. Act quickly to assure early delivery. MACBETH-EVANS GLASS COMPANY · Charleroi, Penna.

Macbeth

Sept. 20, 1927.

E. R. WORCESTER
GLASS JUG
Filed June 8 1927

Evan R. Worcester.
INVENTOR

"DIXIE"

*Water Set
in pink & green;
1931 advertisement*

"SPINDLE" JUG
1927 patent

"MacHOB"

The only pieces of Macbeth's H pattern to be shown in the company catalogs are these photographed below—the 5-, 9-, and 12-oz tumblers and the 75-oz jug. They were made in pink, crystal and Monax beginning in 1928.

CRYSTAL LEAF

The CRYSTAL LEAF line includes the 8½" jug in photo below; tumblers (5, 9 & 12-oz); and tankard jug and 2-piece nite set drawn at right. Pink, green, crystal; 1928.

254

LAMP BASES AND VASES

No. 8156
Moire Rose

No. 8154
Moire Rose

No. 8199
Moire Rose

No. 8157
Moire Rose

No. 8150
Moire Rose

No. 8156
Moire Gold

No. 8154
Moire Gold

No. 8199
Moire Gold

No. 8157
Moire Gold

No. 8150
Moire Gold

No. 8156
Moire Green

No. 8154
Moire Green

No. 8199
Moire Green

No. 8157
Moire Green

No. 8150
Moire Green

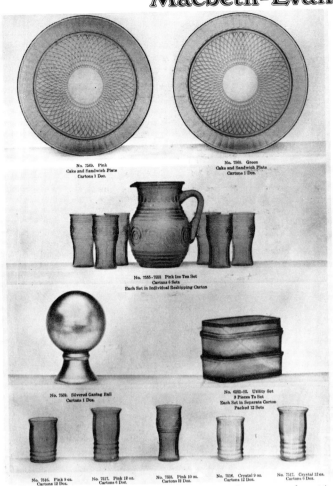

No. 7569. Pink
Cake and Sandwich Plate
Cartons 1 Doz.

No. 7569. Green
Cake and Sandwich Plate
Cartons 1 Doz.

No. 7555-7558 Pink Ice Tea Set
Cartons 6 Sets
Each Set in Individual Reshipping Carton

No. 7569. Silvered Gazing Ball
Cartons 1 Doz.

No. 6282-83. Utility Set
3 Pieces To Set
Each Set in Separate Carton
Packed 12 Sets

No. 7516. Pink 9 oz.
Cartons 12 Doz.

No. 7517. Pink 12 oz.
Cartons 6 Doz.

No. 7558. Pink 10 oz.
Cartons 12 Doz.

No. 7516. Crystal 9 oz.
Cartons 12 Doz.

No. 7517. Crystal 12 oz.
Cartons 6 Doz.

"DIAMOND LATTICE" *plates (#51 Book 1);*
"RINGED TARGET" *ice tea set (#205 Book 1).*

No. 7075. Green

No. 7070. Green
9 ounce

No. 7555-7558
Emerald Green
Water Crackled
Ice Tea Set

No. 7555-7507
Emerald Green
Water Crackled
Ice Tea Set

No. 7048-8 oz.
Emerald Green

No. 7069-12 oz.
Emerald Green

No. 7506-5 oz.
Emerald Green

No. 7506-8 oz.
Emerald Green

No. 7507-12 oz.
Emerald Green

No. 7552-7068.
No. 7552-8254.
Emerald Green
Crystal
Wide Optic
Ice Tea Set

No. 7555-7067.
No. 7552-8249.
Emerald Green
Crystal
Wide Optic
Water Set

No. 7077. Green

No. 7068. Green
10 ounce

"YANKEE" *water set; bottom* **"DIXIE"** *water set;*
also in ruby.

"SCRABBLE" *ice tea sets & tumblers; bottom row*
"SQUIRT" *water sets.*

ROLY POLY tumblers *(12, 5, & 2½-oz)* and
HOSTESS *pitcher and the cocktail shaker were all
made in 1932 in Ritz blue and Ruby red, plain or
with platinum band. Pitcher and shaker also come
crystal; pitcher also comes Monax.*

"SCRABBLE"

*Sketch of crackled
pattern on preceding page*

No. 7507 ICE TEA, 12 Ounce

No. 7541-A.   Ash Tray
Crystal or Pink

No. 7541-A.   Ash Tray Set
Crystal or Pink

No. 7535.   Coaster
Crystal or Pink

No. 10020.   Crystal
Shur-Out Ash Tray

No. 5818.   Electric Shade (2¼″ fitter)
See price list for colors

—*1932 catalog page*

"FANFARE" *6″ plate and*
"APRIL" *design 4″ sherbet
(detail of* "APRIL" *at right)
are found in pale pink and
are strongly believed to be
Macbeth products.*

*The next few pages carry reprints of Corning-
Macbeth's 1939 concept in opaque dinner-
ware: the* CLASSIC, OXFORD, *and* SHEF-
FIELD *patterns in the ivory color called
Chinex; the cream-colored Cremax* "PIE-
CRUST" *pattern; and their decorations. Pro-
duction ceased in 1942.*

256

6¼" Plate

Covered Utility Dish

7" Bowl

7½" Coupe Soup

Sherbet

9" Bowl

6" Dessert Dish

9¾" Dinner Plate

Cup and Saucer

Creamer and Sugar

CLASSIC *from 1939 brochure*

"Where can I buy it?"
SAY 7 OUT OF 10 WORLD'S FAIR VISITORS
When they see the Chinex Dinnerware Exhibit at the Glass Center

VISIT THE
GLASS CENTER
1939
NEW YORK WORLD'S FAIR

IS there a market for CHINEX, the new Corning Dinnerware? Just ask the thousands of housewives who have seen it at the New York World's Fair!

These women are literally amazed at the quality appearance and "feel" of this new dinnerware that combines all the beauty of fine china with extra strength and low cost. They like the fact that it is non-porous, washes easily, will not "craze", and is hard to chip.

CHINEX, styled by foremost American designers, is available in three distinctive patterns, Classic, Oxford and Sheffield. Rich in grace and beauty, its ivory tint harmonizes perfectly with all table settings.

Better get in on the profits! Make CHINEX the style leader of *your* dinnerware department. See it at the Fair for yourself, or write direct for prices, samples and full details.

CORNING GLASS WORKS, CHARLEROI, PA.

Also available in
Oxford and Sheffield Patterns

OXFORD   SHEFFIELD

CHINEX in Classic Pattern, is available in single pieces, or in 15, 32 and 44 piece sets. In Oxford and Sheffield patterns, it is available singly or in 18 piece sets.

CORNING *means* Research in Glass

CORNING *Ivex* DINNERWARE
CLASSIC PATTERN · PRINCESS DECORATION

12" SALVER   SUGAR AND CREAMER   9¼" DINNER PLATE

6" DESSERT DISH

SHERBET   7" BOWL   CUP AND SAUCER

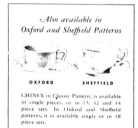

6¼" BREAD AND BUTTER PLATE   7½" COUPE SOUP   COVERED UTILITY DISH   9" BOWL

Corning Ivex Dinnerware · CLASSIC PATTERN · *Bouquet Decoration*

9¼" Dinner Plate

6¼" Bread and Butter Plate

7" Bowl

Cup and Saucer

9" Bowl

6" Dessert Dish

Sherbet

12" Salver

Sugar and Creamer

Covered Utility Dish

7½" Coupe Soup

258   *More CLASSIC from 1939 brochures*

Macbeth-Evans

Smart New CREMAX *Dinnerware* *Amazing New* CREMAX *Dinnerware*

STYLED FOR BEAUTY! • PRICED FOR VOLUME SALES!

Combines the Beauty of China With the Strength and Low Cost of Glass

Rich Ivory Color . . . Always Popular . . . Desired by Every Housewife

9″ BOWL

Description
9″ Cremax Bowl
12″ Cremax Salver

12″ SALVER

16 Piece Assortment No. 712 contains:
4 Cremax Cups   4 Cremax Dinner Plates
4 Cremax Saucers   4 Cremax Cereal Dishes

Description
16 Piece Asst. No. 712

16 PIECE ASSORTMENT NO. 712

20 Piece Assortment No. 692 contains:
4 Cremax Cups   4 Cremax Dinner Plates
4 Cremax Saucers   4 Cremax Cereal Dishes
4 Cremax Bread and Butter Plates

32 Piece Assortment No. 747 contains:
6 Cremax Cups   6 Cremax Bread and
6 Cremax Saucers   Butter Plates
6 Cremax Dinner   1 Cremax 9″ Bowl
   Plates   1 Cremax 12″ Salver
6 Cremax Cereal
   Dishes

Description	Standard Carton	Approx. Shipping Wgt. Per Carton
20 Piece Asst. No. 692	1 Set	12 Lbs.
32 Piece Asst. No. 747	1 Set	20 Lbs.

20 PIECE ASSORTMENT NO. 692

MACBETH-EVANS DIVISION • CORNING GLASS WORKS • CHARLEROI, PENNSYLVANIA

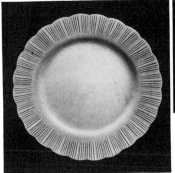

9¼″ DINNER PLATE

Description	Pcs. Per Carton	Wgt. Per Carton
Cremax Cup	6 Doz.	31 Lbs.
Cremax Saucer	6 Doz.	25 Lbs.
Cremax 9¼″ Dinner Plate	2 Doz.	28 Lbs.

CUP AND SAUCER

No Other Dinnerware Offers So Much Value For So Little Money

5⅞″ CEREAL OR DESSERT DISH

Description	Pcs. Per Carton	Wgt. Per Carton
Cremax 5⅞″ Cereal Dish	6 Doz.	24 Lbs.
Cremax 6¼″ Bread and Butter	6 Doz.	23 Lbs.

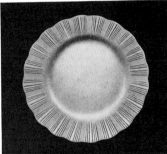

6¼″ BREAD AND BUTTER PLATE

**MACBETH-EVANS DIVISION
CORNING GLASS WORKS • CHARLEROI, PENNSYLVANIA**

Twenty-piece Cremax Starter Set, No. 28692 (shown above), consists of: 4 cups, 4 saucers, 4–9¼″ dinner plates, 4–6″ desserts, and 4 bread-and-butter plates. (For packing data, see other side.)

Cremax ware is built for VOLUME sales. Successfully merchandised all over the country, it washes easily . . . resists crazing, cracking and chipping . . . stays in service for years. Its delicate creamy tone blends into any color scheme . . . gives a "lift" to any table setting. Perfect for every-day, practical use.

MACBETH-EVANS DIVISION

Corning GLASS WORKS

CHARLEROI · PENNSYLVANIA

Cremax Cup
Cremax Saucer
Cremax Dinner
Cremax 6″ Dessert
Cremax B & B Plate

5″ Bowl
Coupe Soup
Sugar
Creamer
Sherbet
7″ Bowl
Demi-Tasse
6″ Dessert

Cremax Sherbet
Cremax Coupe Soup
Cremax Creamer
Cremax Sugar
Cremax 5″ Bowl

Cremax 7″ Bowl
Cremax 9″ Bowl
Cremax 12″ Salver
Cremax Demi-tasse Cup
Cremax Demi-tasse Saucer
Cremax Cup and Saucer

MACBETH-EVANS DIVISION · CORNING GLASS WORKS · CHARLEROI · PENNSYLVANIA

Cremax "PIE-CRUST" *from 1939 brochure; made also by a Corning plant in Canada in opaque light blue with "Pyrex made in Canada" on back.*

CREMAX *Bordette*

- 6" Dessert Dish
- 7½" Coupe Soup
- 6" Bread and Butter Plate
- 9¼" Dinner Plate
- Demi-Tasse
- 9" Bowl
- Cup and Saucer
- Sugar Bowl
- Creamer
- 12" Salver

Corning-Ivex Dinnerware ★ Cremax Pattern
RAINBOW DECORATION

- Cup and Saucer
- 12" Salver
- 9¼" Dinner Plate
- 6" Bread and Butter Plate
- 9" Bowl
- 6" Dessert Dish

SINGLE PIECES, BULK-PACKED

No.	Description	Color	Std. Pkg.	Approx. Shpg. Wt.	Price
27015	Bordette Cup	Specify*	6 doz.	25 lbs.	
27016	Bordette Saucer	Specify*	6 doz.	24 lbs.	
27012	Bordette Dinner	Specify*	3 doz.	30 lbs.	
27024	Bordette 6" Dessert	Specify*	2 doz.	10 lbs.	
27023	Bordette B & B Plate	Specify*	2 doz.	8 lbs.	
27063	Bordette Coupe Soup	Specify*	2 doz.	18 lbs.	
27076	Bordette Creamer	Green only	2 doz.	12 lbs.	
27077	Bordette Sugar	Green only	2 doz.	13 lbs.	
27064	Bordette 9" Bowl	Green only	1 doz.	16 lbs.	
27065	Bordette 12" Salver	Pink only	1 doz.	22 lbs.	
27067	Bordette Demi-tasse Cup	Specify*	6 doz.	16 lbs.	
27068	Bordette Demi-tasse Saucer	Specify*	6 doz.	14 lbs.	

*Specify one color: pink, green, blue, or yellow.

SETS

No.	Description	Std. Pkg.	Approx. Shpg. Wt.	Price
28806-A	Bordette 17 piece	1 set	10 lbs.	
28747-A	Bordette 32 piece	1 set	20 lbs.	

Corning Rainbow Colors are: PINK or GREEN. Please specify color when ordering.

Description	Standard Carton	Approx. Shipping Weight Per Carton	Price	Description	Standard Carton	Approx. Shipping Weight Per Carton	Price
Cremax Rainbow Cup	6 Doz.	26 Lbs.		Cremax Rainbow 6" Bread and Butter Plate	6 Doz.	25 Lbs.	
Cremax Rainbow Saucer	6 Doz.	25 Lbs.		Cremax Rainbow 9" Bowl	1 Doz.	19 Lbs.	
Cremax Rainbow 9¼" Dinner Plate	2 Doz.	23 Lbs.		Cremax Rainbow 12" Salver	1 Doz.	17 Lbs.	
Cremax Rainbow 6" Dessert Dish	6 Doz.	32 Lbs.		Cremax Rainbow 32-Pc. Set (Pink or Green) Asst. 747	1 "	20 Lbs.	

(BORDETTE borders fired-on dark; RAINBOW borders pastels)

Cremax Cup   Cremax Saucer

Cremax Bread and Butter Plate (6¼")

Cremax Cereal or Dessert Dish (5⅝")

Cremax Dinner Plate (9¼")

CREMAX
TABLE WARE
Windsor Pattern

ITEM	DESCRIPTION	STD. PKG.	APPROX. WEIGHT
Cup	Windsor Brown	6 Doz.	27 Lbs.
Saucer	Windsor Brown	6 Doz.	24 Lbs.
9¼" Dinner Plate	Windsor Brown	2 Doz.	21 Lbs.
5⅝" Cereal (Dessert)	Windsor Brown	6 Doz.	29 Lbs.
6¼" B & B Plate	Windsor Brown	6 Doz.	25 Lbs.

CREMAX
TABLE WARE
Available Plain Not Decorated as follows:

ITEM	DESCRIPTION	STD. PKG.	APPROX. WEIGHT
Cup	Plain	6 Doz.	27 Lbs.
Saucer	Plain	6 Doz.	24 Lbs.
9¼" Dinner Plate	Plain	2 Doz.	21 Lbs.
5⅝" Cereal (Dessert)	Plain	6 Doz.	29 Lbs.
6¼" B & B Plate	Plain	6 Doz.	25 Lbs.

Tableware
Cremax

Art. No. 20598—20 pc.
Art. No. 20599—32 pc.
Art. No. 20600—Open Stock
B. L. Page 1510

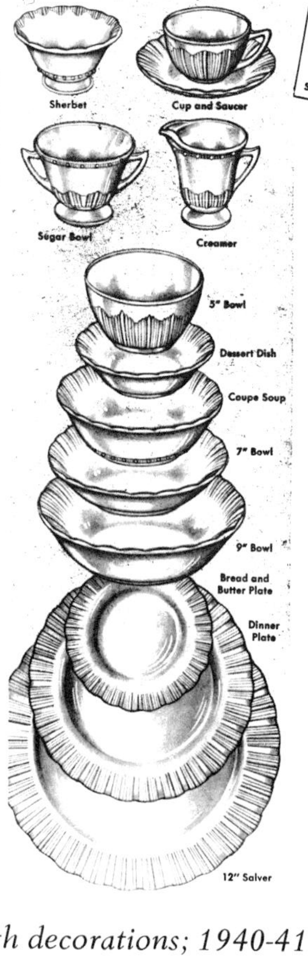

- Sherbet
- Cup and Saucer
- Sugar Bowl
- Creamer
- 5" Bowl
- Dessert Dish
- Coupe Soup
- 7" Bowl
- 9" Bowl
- Bread and Butter Plate
- Dinner Plate
- 12" Salver

BY CORNING
Makers of PYREX Brand Ware

This smart ware is made of Corning Cremax, a new material that resists chipping and "spider-web" crazing. Washes easily . . stays in service for years. Its delicate creamy tone blends into any color scheme.

Princess
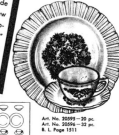
Art. No. 20595—20 pc.
Art. No. 20596—32 pc.
B. L. Page 1511

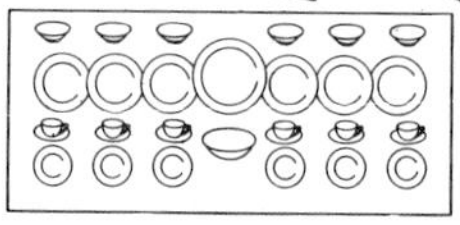

Flora

Art. No. 6626—24 pc.
Art. No. 6627—40 pc.
B. L. Page 1515

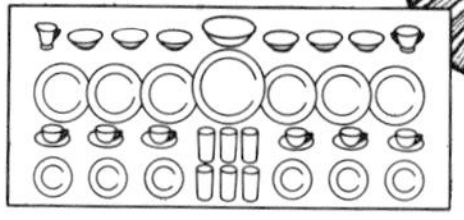

Bordette
Art. No. 6622—24 pc.
Art. No. 6623—38 pc.
B. L. Page 1514

CORNING OXFORD PATTERN TABLEWARE

12" Salver

9¾" Dinner Plate

Cup and Saucer

6" Dessert Dish

6" Bread and Butter Plate

7½" Coupe Soup

9" Bowl

Description	Standard Carton	Approx. Shipping Wgt. per Carton
27013 Oxford Cup	6 Doz.	25 Lbs.
27014 Oxford Saucer	6 Doz.	24 Lbs.
27018 Oxford Dinner Plate	3 Doz.	30 Lbs.
27037 Oxford 6" Dessert Dish	6 Doz.	28 Lbs.
27039 Oxford Bread & Butter Plate	6 Doz.	25 Lbs.
27040 Oxford Coupe Soup	2 Doz.	18 Lbs.
27076 Oxford Creamer (not illustrated)	2 Doz.	12 Lbs.
27077 Oxford Sugar (not illustrated)	2 Doz.	13 Lbs.
27041 Oxford 9" Bowl	1 Doz.	16 Lbs.
27042 Oxford 12" Salver	1 Doz.	22 Lbs.

CORNING GLASS WORKS · MACBETH-EVANS DIVISION · CHARLEROI · PENNSYLVANIA

Macbeth-Evans
Corning Ivex Dinnerware Sets
OXFORD PATTERN · BORDETTE DECORATION

17-PIECE OXFORD BORDETTE, COLOR GROUP A, ASST. NO. 760

Service for 4 Contains: 4 Cups, 4 Saucers, 4–9¾" Dinner Plates, 4–9 oz. Tumblers, 1–12" Salver

(Color Assortment as above)

12-PIECE OXFORD BORDETTE, COLOR GROUP A, ASST. NO. 638

Service for 4 Contains: 4 Cups, 4 Saucers, 4 Dinner Plates

(Color Assortment as above)

32-PIECE OXFORD BORDETTE PINK (or Green) DINNER ASST. NO. 745

Contains: 6 Cups, 6 Saucers, 6–9¾" Dinner Plates, 6–6" Dessert Dishes, 6–6" Bread and Butter Plates, 1–9" Bowl, 1–12" Salver

(All Pink, or All Green only)

Description	Standard Carton	Approx. Shipping Weight per Carton
12-Piece Set Oxford Bordette, Group A, Asst. No. 638	1 Set	8 Lbs.
17-Piece Set Oxford Bordette, Group A, Asst. No. 760	1 Set	10 Lbs.
32-Piece Set Oxford Bordette, Asst. No. 745 Pink or Green	1 Set	20 Lbs.

MACBETH-EVANS DIVISION · CORNING GLASS WORKS · CHARLEROI · PENNSYLVANIA

CORNING Ivex DINNERWARE
OXFORD PATTERN · ROSE DECORATION

12" Salver

9¾" Dinner Plate

7½" Coupe Soup

6" Bread and Butter Plate

Cup and Saucer

6" Dessert Dish

9" Bowl

Description	Standard Carton	Approx. Shipping Wgt. per Carton
Oxford Rose Cup	4 Doz.	20 Lbs.
Oxford Rose Saucer	4 Doz.	17 Lbs.
Oxford Rose 9¾" Dinner Plate	2 Doz.	23 Lbs.
Oxford Rose 6" Dessert Dish	4 Doz.	19 Lbs.
Oxford Rose 6" Bread and Butter Plate	4 Doz.	19 Lbs.
Oxford Rose 7½" Coupe Soup	2 Doz.	18 Lbs.
Oxford Rose 9" Bowl	1 Doz.	19 Lbs.
Oxford Rose 12" Salver	1 Doz.	17 Lbs.

MACBETH-EVANS DIVISION · CORNING GLASS WORKS · CHARLEROI · PENNSYLVANIA

The New OXFORD Pattern
B-399 RED BAND DECORATION
ASSORTMENT No. 708
20 PIECE "STARTER" SET

Smart Color Note Adds New Sales Appeal

OXFORD DINNERWARE HAS ALL THESE IMPORTANT FEATURES:

- *Beautiful Design* • *Rich Ivory Color* • *Smartly Styled* • *Non-Porous*
- *Combines the beauty of high priced China with the strength and low cost of Glass*

20 PIECE OXFORD B—399 RED BAND ASSORTMENT No. 708

Service for 4 CONTAINS			
• 4 Cups	• 4—9¾ in. Dinner Plates	• 4—No. 199 Tall 9 oz.
• 4 Saucers	• 4—5¾ in. Dessert Dishes	Beverage Glasses

Set No.	Pieces in Set	Packed Carton	Weight Per Set
708 B–399	20	1 Set	13 Lbs.

MACBETH-EVANS DIVISION
CORNING GLASS WORKS · CHARLEROI, PENNSYLVANIA

OXFORD from 1940-41 brochures

The SHEFFIELD Pattern

CREATED by a great American designer, pre-tested for popular appeal before actual production, Corning scores another hit with this new Sheffield pattern in famous Chinex dinnerware.

SHEFFIELD *from 1939 brochure*

UTILITY CUPS

TINTED AND PLAIN IVORIAN

Fast selling, profit making Utility Cups—of Ivorian in 4 tinted decorations and plain. Standard package, 3 doz. in shipping carton. Approximate shipping weight, 6 lbs.

27098—Tinted Pink

27098—Tinted Blue

27098—Plain

27098—Tinted Green

27098—Tinted Red

"SWAN-SONG" *Flower bowl, 2-2/3" x 4½" oblong;* "BIANCA" *Flower vase, 3-1/8" tall. Heavy opaque white, made c. 1936.*

UTILITY TRAYS

TINTED AND PLAIN IVORIAN

UTILITY TRAYS for serving bread, biscuits, salads and delicacies; also for centerpieces, miniature gardens and plants. Standard package, 1 doz. Approximate shipping weight, 19 lbs.

29628—Tinted Pink

29628—Plain

29628—Tinted Green

MACBETH-EVANS DIVISION • CORNING GLASS WORKS • CHARLEROI, PENNSYLVANIA

—1940 brochure

McKee

McKee history threads its remarkable glass pattern through one hundred years and more. The date 1853 marks the beginning of the famous pressed tableware career under the McKee and Bros. banner; 1888 the year the factory moved from Pittsburgh to the little Pennsylvania community thereafter known as Jeannette for the wife of McKee's founder.

Here the pots and furnaces have undergone name changes once, twice, and again. The first was in 1903 when the firm was reorganized. It was called the McKee Glass Company at that time and remained as such until 1951 when it changed hands and became the McKee Division of the Thatcher Glass Company. Then in 1961 Jeannette Glass Corporation—the other well-known glass producer of the area—bought the McKee Division. The next year Jeannette moved into the McKee factory where it makes glass today.

In these many years of activity the factory brought forth glass products of almost every description—the servicable, the decorative; for the office and for the home; for the table, kitchen, and playroom. Even glass for industry and illumination was made in later years.

Other books emphasize many of the opaque wares and crystal pressed patterns which shone through the last century and early this one.* Here we will look to see how the color years were spent.

For the most part McKee's Depression-era wares were made by hand (automatic methods gradually being introduced by the 40s) but the lines were usually priced at moderate levels. Occasional pieces ranging from the unassuming to the arty—inkwells and 'hair receivers' shown alongside lovely console bowls and other gift items—were offered throughout the 20s and 30s. Much kitchenware was always made, most notably the huge Glasbake line which was first marketed in the 'teens. Scores of new pieces were added to it for two decades.

Tableware lines in colors started with crackled glass in the early 20s and soon such popular older patterns as Aztec and Rock Crystal Flower were being cast in hue. Perhaps most familiar to us collectors are the colorful opaque wares which were made from 1930 to 1940, and there is a reason for this. McKee, like many other companies, was hard hit by the Crash and its production sharply curtailed. The unique opaques—dinnerware lines, kitchenware, child's sets, and even the Sunkist reamers—took such strong hold with the public that the company was boosted from its low.

COLOR

Not surprisingly we find McKee wading deep into color at the very brink of the 20s. Advertisements in 1923 tell us that Jade yellow, Jap blue, and amethyst, sometimes satin finished or combined with black bases, were then on the scene. Blue, amber, canary, and green were introduced later that year; Sky blue and Grass green in 1925; Rose pink in 1926; ruby and orchid in 1927; and Jade, Ritz blue, black, and more black feet in 1930.

Topaz appeared in 1931; that year too the opaques Seville yellow, Skokie green, Chalaine blue, and Old Rose (tan) were introduced in kitchen items. The opaques French Ivory and Poudre Blue came out in 1933 and 1936 respectively, often sporting bands of painted color. Finally, a white opal ware was made, plain and decorated, from 1937 to 1942 and again after the War.

*Vicki and Mike Gross' paperback, THAT COLLECTIBLE McKEE (1973, privately published) shows many lines in color and Sandra Stout's McKEE GLASS (1972, Trojan Press) features some of the earlier lines.

We often find the McKee circle trademark in the glassware of this period, but not always.

ROCK CRYSTAL FLOWER

ROCK CRYSTAL FLOWER was McKee's big crystal line when color made its first appearance. The pattern was cast in Jade yellow, Jap blue to start, then in blue, amber, canary, light green, medium green, and rose pink. Finally, ruby was made 1930-31. Here is an early ad (1922) and on the pages to follow are pages from a catalog showing many pieces (but not all) of the large line. The lamp can be seen in the color section.

ANNOUNCING
Two Distinct New McKEE Lines and Many Additions to Standard Lines

ROCK CRYSTAL 4 PIECE CONSOLE SET, SATIN FINISH

McKEE SATIN FINISHED GLASSWARE

This new line of Colored Glass is our latest addition.

It comes in two colors, Jap-Blue and Jade Yellow. The Satin Finish, together with the delicate Rock Crystal Flower Pattern, produces a very new and pleasing effect.

Many different pieces, such as Compotes, Console Sets, Nappies, Candlesticks, Water Sets, Stemware, Vases, Ice Tea and Grape Juice Sets, etc., in assorted sizes and shapes are included in this line.

* * * * * * * * * * * * * * * * *

No. 352—OPTIC TUBE CAKE PAN
Design Patent No. 58,201.

The latest improvement in Glasbake Transparent Cooking and Serving Ware.

Optic or Fluted Pattern   Utility Plus Beauty

The inside flute is the added attraction on this line, being an entirely new feature and making it very attractive. Beside improving the appearance of the cooking utensil this Distinctive pattern makes a beautiful Table Service enhancing the beauty of the dining table.

VIRGINIA LUNCH PLATE

One of the many new items of our manufacture intended for Light Cutting and Decorating. We will have on display many new articles for this particular class of trade such as Lunch Plates, Candlesticks, Sugar and Creams, Jugs, Candy Boxes, Compotes, etc., all genuine pot glass full fire polished and bearing all the qualities of excellence and durability that can be acquired through superior workmanship.

Early American ROCK CRYSTAL

USEFUL PIECES OF
EARLY AMERICAN ROCK CRYSTAL
IN ATTRACTIVELY DECORATED
DESIGN

½ gal. Squat Jug

1 qt. Squat Jug

12" Vase with square top

16 oz. Candy Jar and Cover

7" Candy Box and Cover

5" Finger Bowl
7" Plate P.E.

7" Round Bowl S.E.
8"   "   "   S.E.
9"   "   "   S.E.
10½" "   "   S.E.
For salads and preserved fruits

7 oz. Cup and Saucer

10 oz. Footed Berry Sugar and Cover
10 oz. Footed Berry Sugar, no Cover

9 oz. Footed Berry Cream

6 oz. Oil D.S.
6 oz. Oil G.S.

8½" Tall Candlestick

12½" Ftd. Center Bowl
For raw fruit or table decoration

2 Lite Candelabra
3 Lite Candelabra

4" Nappy S.E.
4½" Nappy S.E.
5" Nappy S.E.
For individual fruits
and sauces

Salt or Pepper

5½" Low Candlestick

7" Pickle or Spoon Tray

5" Ftd. Jelly S.E.

7½" Salad Plate S.E.
7½"   "   " P.E.
8½"   "   " S.E.
8½"   "   " P.E.

9" Cake Plate S.E.
10½"   "   " S.E.
11½"   "   " S.E.

7½" Bon Bon S.E.

10½" Dinner Plate S.E.
6" Bread and Butter Plate S.E.

13" Roll Tray

11½" 2 Part Relish

S. E. indicates scalloped edge; P. E. indicates plain edge.

14" 6 Part Relish

12" Oblong Large Celery Tray

2½ Oz.
Whiskey Tumbler

5 Oz.
Tomato Juice

9 Oz. No. 2
Concave Tumbler

12 Oz. No. 2
Concave Iced Tea

12 Oz. Iced No. 1 St.
Tea or High Ball

9 Oz. No. 1
Straight Tumbler

3½ Oz. Ftd.
Sherbet or Egg

6 Oz. Low Ftd.
Sundae

3½ Oz. Low Ftd.
Parfait

7½ Oz. Low Ftd.
Goblet
8 Oz. Low Ftd.
Goblet

11 Oz. Low Ftd.
Iced Tea

5 Oz. Old
Fashioned Whiskey

1 Oz. Ftd.
Cordial

3½ Oz. Ftd.
Cocktail

2 Oz. Small Ftd.
Wine
3 Oz. Large Ftd.
Wine

6 Oz. Ftd. Champagne
or tall Sundae

8 Oz. Large Ftd.
Goblet

"GLENDALE" Comport
blue, canary, amethyst; 1923 ad

Remainder of items this page are from 1925 advertisements. Most were offered in blue, canary, amber, green, and amethyst.

—1924 ad

"WIGGLE" *Water Set*

"HANSEN"
Sanitary Dispenser

"THOMAS" *Keg Set*

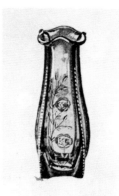

GLASBAKE
Bake Dish

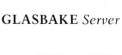

GLASBAKE *Server*

MAYFLOWER
Lamp

APOLLO
Rose Vase

Betty Jane Set
(copyright)

GLASBAKE

Only a few of the many items constituting the large and long-running **GLASBAKE** *line of kitchen and playware are illustrated.*

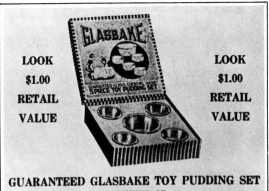

LOOK
$1.00
RETAIL
VALUE

LOOK
$1.00
RETAIL
VALUE

GUARANTEED GLASBAKE TOY PUDDING SET
CONSISTING OF
**ONE ONE-HALF PINT ROUND PUDDING DISH
AND FOUR THREE-OUNCE ROUND BAKERS**

12" vase in transparent or opaque colors; 1931

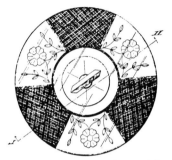

"CUNNINGHAM"—*1928 patent*

Rebecca
Two Handled Vase

TWO PIECE BRIDGE SET

Blue Crackled Satin Finish Ware

FINE AMERICAN
GLASSWARE
for
Light Cutting and Decorating

McKee furnished blanks of all colors to many other companies for finishing.

A New Decanter Set
That Is Useful for Many Occasions

The Life Saver
Eight-Piece Decanter Set
[All That the Name Implies]

Sold in the Following Transparent Colors:
Rose Pink, Green, Blue, Amber,
Canary or Crystal
Packed One to a Reshipping Carton

Special at $5.00 each List   No Packing Charge

McKEE GLASS CO.
Established 1853
Jeannette, Pennsylvania

—*1927 brochure*

Danse De Lumiere
Lamps
Adapted for Boudoir and Console Table
A Real Work of Art

Wired Complete with Bulb and Reflector
Packed Inividually in a Reshipping Carton
The Attractive Colors of
Green, Rose Pink, Canary, Blue,
Amber or Crystal
In the Delicate Satin Finish

Special at $5.00 each List   No Package Charge

SCALLOP EDGE

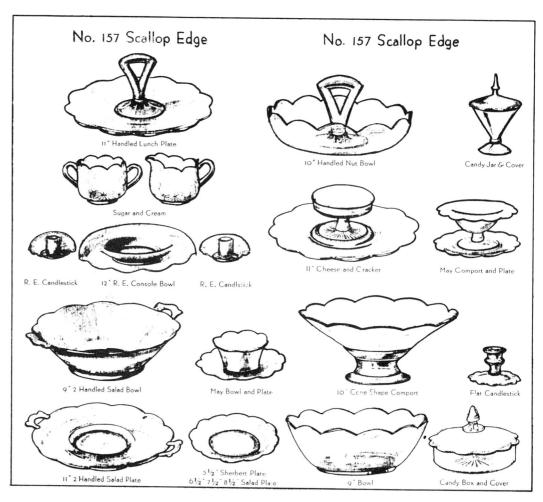

Both these lines were made in pink and green. These shapes were used as blanks for many etched patterns.

No. 157 Scallop Edge

No. 157 Scallop Edge

11" Handled Lunch Plate

Sugar and Cream

R. E. Candlestick

12" R. E. Console Bowl

R. E. Candlstick

9" 2 Handled Salad Bowl

May Bowl and Plate

11" 2 Handled Salad Plate

5½" Sherbert Plate
6½" 7½" 8½" Salad Plate

10" Handled Nut Bowl

Candy Jar & Cover

11" Cheese and Cracker

May Comport and Plate

10" Cone Shape Comport

Flat Candlestick

9" Bowl

Candy Box and Cover

OCTAGON EDGE

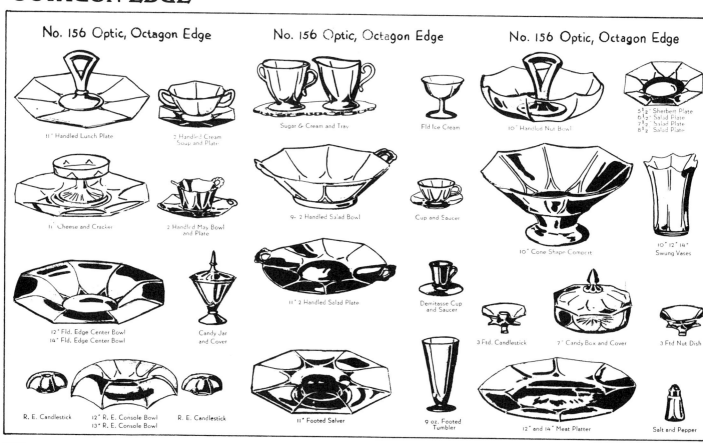

No. 156 Optic, Octagon Edge

No. 156 Optic, Octagon Edge

No. 156 Optic, Octagon Edge

11" Handled Lunch Plate

2 Handled Cream Soup and Plate

11" Cheese and Cracker

2 Handled May Bowl and Plate

12" Fld. Edge Center Bowl
14" Fld. Edge Center Bowl

Candy Jar and Cover

R. E. Candlestick

12" R. E. Console Bowl
13" R. E. Console Bowl

R. E. Candlestick

Sugar & Cream and Tray

9- 2 Handled Salad Bowl

11" 2 Handled Salad Plate

11" Footed Salver

Fld Ice Cream

Cup and Saucer

Demitasse Cup and Saucer

9 oz. Footed Tumbler

10" Handled Nut Bowl

5½" Sherbert Plate
6½" Salad Plate
7½" Salad Plate
8½" Salad Plate

10" Cone Shape Comport

10" 12" 14" Swung Vases

3 Ftd. Candlestick

7" Candy Box and Cover

3 Ftd Nut Dish

12" and 14" Meat Platter

Salt and Pepper

BROCADE

as shown in pink and green in a 1930 company brochure

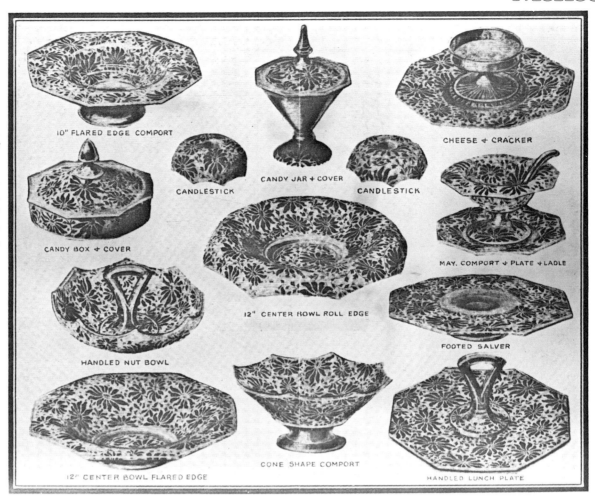

10" FLARED EDGE COMPORT

CANDLESTICK

CANDY JAR + COVER

CANDLESTICK

CHEESE + CRACKER

CANDY BOX + COVER

MAY. COMPORT + PLATE + LADLE

HANDLED NUT BOWL

12" CENTER BOWL ROLL EDGE

FOOTED SALVER

12" CENTER BOWL FLARED EDGE

CONE SHAPE COMPORT

HANDLED LUNCH PLATE

CLICO

—1930 ad

Thos. G. Jones, New York representative of the Mc-Kee Glass Co., Jeannette, Pa., has a most seasonable summer offering in the popular Lenox pattern from this factory as shown at the right. This is to be had in stemware and other table pieces and novelties in colors of rose pink, ritz blue, green and crystal. It is now on view at his showroom in the Fifth Avenue Building.

LENOX *from 1930 trade journal report*

"SARAH"
Three sizes in transparent and opaque colors; 1931

Above are two new lines of glassware. The crystal is the pressed George Washington Cherry line of the McKee Glass Co. It is entirely new in Colonial design. The ruby and crystal combination is from the Bryce Brothers Co. and illustrates line No. 720, a new shape in stemware.

—1930 trade journal report

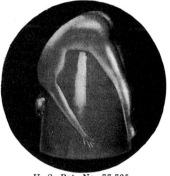
—1932 ad

"AUTUMN" was shown in 1934; it was made in French Ivory and Jade Green.

"FLOWER BAND" is a 1934 line made in Jade Green, Poudre Blue and French Ivory.

TOP ROW: **AUTUMN** *Console Set, 8½" bowl, 4" candleholder;* **FLOWER BAND** *9½" bowl, 3½" tumbler.*

ROWS 2 & 3 all **LAUREL:** *Child's 6" plate (sometimes scalloped), cup & saucer, 2½" cream & sugar (child's set also comes red/orange/green trimmed or fired-on scottie dog). 5" tumbler; 5¾" poudre blue plate "Fifty years forward 1888-1938 Jeannette McKee Celebration"; 3-7/8" wine; cheese cover on 9" plate; 2nd-style cream & sugar.*

LAUREL PATTERN TABLEWARE
New French Ivory Glass Dinnerware

LAUREL

(#238 Book I)
The original advertisement is shown. Additional pieces are photographed above and a detail is shown below.

TOM & JERRY SETS
Made in Ivory, White Opal, & black w/ red, green, gold, or black trim.
Bowls 11'' diameter. Beaded edge earlier (late 30s); smooth later (50s).

SLED SCENE
TOM & JERRY w/ scroll
TOM & JERRY w/o scroll

"KIDDIE KARNIVAL"
7'' child's dish & cup

The kitchen items pictured below were first made in opaque Skokie green, Chalaine blue, Seville yellow, and Old Rose. Later they were made in Jade green, French Ivory, Poudre blue, and White Opal. You may find them with stripes or dots in fired-on green, red, blue, yellow, or black, or with a fired-on sailboat motif. Most carry the McK circle mark.

UTILITY SET
48-oz; comes Cereal, Tea, Coffee, Flour, Sugar

CADDY SET
28-oz; comes Coffee, Tea, Sugar, Cereal

SHAKER SET
Comes Salt, Pepper, Sugar, Flour.

ART NUDE VASE & LAMP
8½''; pink, green, frosted; jade, black

SOUVENIR SHAKER 4¾''

TUMBLER 3¾''

BOWL 4¼''

SHALLOW BAKER
7'' x 4¾''

BOTTOMS UP
tumbler and coaster; also made in black, dark ivory, pink, green, crystal, & satin finish

BOWL 8½''

BUTTERDISH 1 lb.

SNACK TRAY

McKEE GLASS

No. 55 Casserole and Cover and No. 12 Chrome Tray

Louvre

McKee DeLuxe Refrigerator Glassware

ONE OF THE LATEST ITEMS.

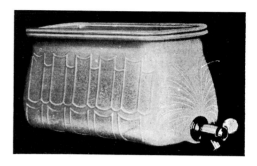

One Gallon Water Jar and Cover

Jade Green or Crystal   Packed one in a carton

It is not necessary to take water jar from the refrigerator in order to use it.

Also complete line of Refrigerator Food Storage dishes with covers and all sizes of defrosting trays.

McKEE GLASS COMPANY

ESTABLISHED 1853

JEANNETTE, PA.

"BIG JUG" Water Jar from 1933 ad

LOUVRE from 1937 advertisement; decorative bird and flower motifs in crystal satin and frosted satin.

BEACON INNOVATION
This catalog page dates to the mid-20s, but we're finding pieces of McKee's BEACON INNOVATION as well as other early lines in the company colors including Jade and opal. See the AZTEC pink punch bowl in the color section.

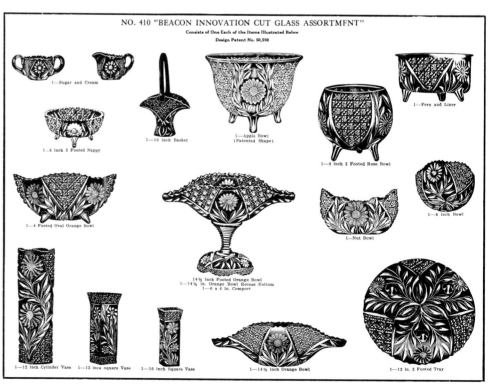

NO. 410 "BEACON INNOVATION CUT GLASS ASSORTMENT"
Consists of One Each of the Items Illustrated Below
Design Patent No. 50,590

1—Sugar and Cream

1—10 inch Basket

1—Apple Bowl (Patented Shape)

1—Fern and Liner

1—8 inch 3 Footed Nappy

1—8 inch 3 Footed Rose Bowl

1—4 Footed Oval Orange Bowl

1—8 inch Bowl

1—Nut Bowl

14½ inch Footed Orange Bowl
1—14½ in. Orange Bowl Recess Bottom
1—6 x 6 in. Comport

1—12 inch Cylinder Vase

1—12 inch square Vase

1—10 inch Square Vase

1—14½ inch Orange Bowl

1—12 in. 3 Footed Tray

274

Monongah

The Monongah Glass Company, located at Fairmont, West Virginia, was incorporated in 1903 and by the 20s it was one of the largest manufacturers of pressed and blown tumblers and stemware in the country. In the latter 20s a few lines of tableware in colors—pink, green, and amber, almost always fused with crystal and often trimmed with gold or platinum trim—were being made by hand in limited amounts for a quality market.

When Monongah came under the direction of Hocking Glass Company during the Depression many of its molds were distributed to other of the Hocking hand plants—most often Lancaster, and you'll want to refer to that chapter to see other Monongah patterns as they were later made by this Hocking subsidiary.

Another Monongah creation, the Springtime pattern, was later the inspiration for one of Hocking's favorite dinnerware lines. Springtime as originated by Monongah was crystal glass, plate-etched and pressed by hand, then hand-finished with a gold trim. So little was made it is rarely seen today. But Hocking went on to have the motif copied almost exactly and new molds made to produce it by machine-made, mold-etched techniques. Made in great quantities and vastly popular, Cameo, as the 'copy' was called, has made the dancing girl immortal to us.

For the duration of the Depression era the Monongah factory was redirected to the goals of Hocking, and its wares were made in the colors associated with that company. The old plant is a part of Anchor-Hocking today.

CATALOG REPRINT

On the following pages a company catalog circa 1927 is reprinted. Included are crystal lines, some with gold trim, lines in color, and crystal lines with color trims. Official information is retained on the original; some is superimposed by me.

DOUBLE PROCESS PLATE ETCHED AND GOLD BAND DECORATION No. 270

— SPRINGTIME —

24 CARAT ROMAN GOLD

OPTIC BLANKS

SPRINGTIME

No. 8, Sugar

No. 8, Cream

No. 41, 26 oz. Decanter Cut Stopper, Cut 61

No. 7806, 1½ oz. Individual Almond

No. 7806, 9 oz. Footed Almond

No. 7806, 6 in. Confection Stand

— S P R I N G T I M E —

24 CARAT ROMAN GOLD OPTIC BLANKS

No. 7811, Finger Bowl

No. 10340, 6½ in. Plate, Plain
Can also furnish in 8½ in. Size

No. 7851, 5½ oz. Parfait

No. 7845, 9 oz.
Goblet

No. 7845, 5½ oz.
High Footed Sherbet

No. 7845, 5½ oz.
Low Footed Sherbet

No. 7845, 4 oz.
Claret

No. 7845, 2½ oz.
Wine

No. 7845, 2¾ oz.
Cocktail

No. 7845, ¾ oz.
Brandy

— S P R I N G T I M E —

24 CARAT ROMAN GOLD OPTIC BLANKS

No. 9011, 13 oz.
Handled Ice Tea

No. 9011, 13 oz.
Ice Tea

No. 9011, 10 oz.
Ice Tea

No. 9011, 9 oz.
Water

No. 9011, 8 oz.
Water

No. 9011, 7 oz.
Ginger Ale

No. 9011, 5 oz.
Grape Juice

No. 9011, 2½ oz.
Whiskey

No. 8-6½, 60 oz. Water Jug

No. 92-6, 60 oz. Ice Tea
No. 92-4, 30 oz. Grape Juice

No. 91-6, 50 oz. Water Jug

276

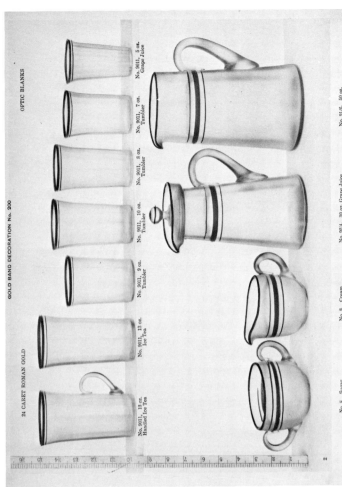

"ROSELAND"

ETCHED "800" DESIGN, OPTIC

GOLD BAND DECORATION No. 200

24 CARET ROMAN GOLD

OPTIC BLANKS

No. 9011, 5 oz. Grape Juice
No. 9011, 7 oz. Tumbler
No. 9011, 8 oz. Tumbler
No. 9011, 10 oz. Tumbler
No. 9011, 9 oz. Tumbler
No. 9011, 13 oz. Ice Tea
No. 9011, 13 oz. Handled Ice Tea

No. 91/6, 50 oz. Water Jug.

No. 92/4, 30 oz. Grape Juice
No. 92/6, 60 oz. Ice Tea

No. 8, Cream
No. 8, Sugar

7811-10 oz. Goblet
7814-6½ oz. Saucer or Hi. Sherbet
7814-3½ oz. Sherbet
7814-3½ oz. Cocktail
7815-6½ oz. Sherbet
7815-6 oz. Saucer or Hi. Sherbet
9011-5 oz.
9011-9 oz.

7050-6 oz. Parfait
7915-30 oz. Grape Fruit
7806 Finger Bowl
10310-6½ in. Plate
10310-7 in. Plate

91-7 Jug, 67 oz.

Also furnish Wine, Brandy, 13 oz. Ice Tea, Oil, Decanter, Sugar and Cream Set.

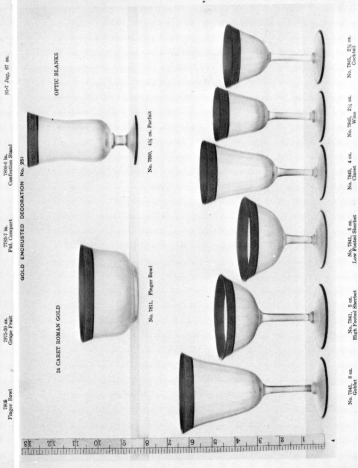

6141, STEMWARE AND FOOTED TUMBLERS, 13 OPTIC GREEN

"KEY BLOCK"

6141, STEMWARE AND FOOTED TUMBLERS, 13 OPTIC ROSEPINK

12 oz. Ice Tea
9 oz. Table
4½ oz. Seltzer
1½ oz. Whiskey
Parfait
2½ oz. Wine
3 oz. Cocktail
5½ oz. Low Sherbet
6 oz. Saucer or Hi. Sherbet
10 oz. Goblet

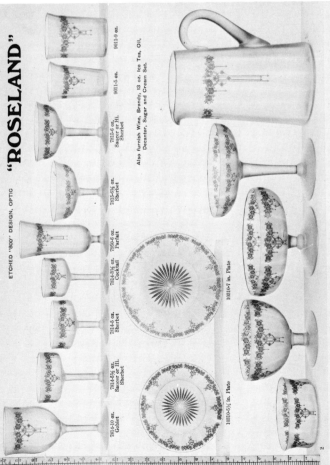

OPTIC BLANKS

GOLD ENCRUSTED DECORATION No. 251

24 CARET ROMAN GOLD

No. 7950, 4½ oz. Parfait
No. 7811, Finger Bowl

7806-6 in. Confection Stand
7785-7 in. Ftd. Comport

No. 7841, 8 oz. Goblet
No. 7841, 5 oz. High Footed Sherbet
No. 7841, 5 oz. Low Footed Sherbet
No. 7841, 4 oz. Claret
No. 7845, 2½ oz. Wine
No. 7845, 2½ oz. Cocktail

277

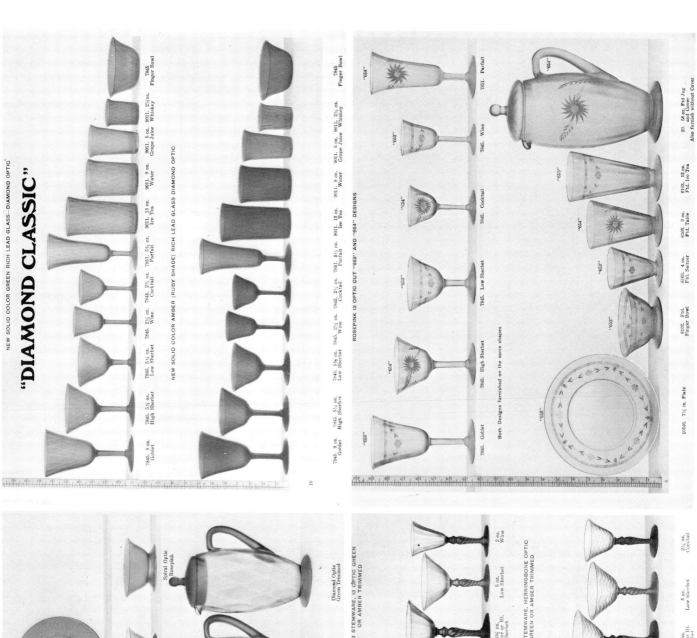

"DIAMOND CLASSIC"

NEW SOLID COLOR GREEN RICH LEAD GLASS—DIAMOND OPTIC

7845. 9 oz. Goblet • 7845. 5½ oz. High Sherbet • 7845. 5¼ oz. Low Sherbet • 7845. 2½ oz. Wine • 7845. 2½ oz. Cocktail • 7861. 6½ oz. Parfait • 9011. 13 oz. Ice Tea • 9011. 9 oz. Water • 9011. 5 oz. Grape Juice • 9011. 2½ oz. Whiskey • 7845. Finger Bowl

NEW SOLID COLOR AMBER (RUBY SHADE) RICH LEAD GLASS DIAMOND OPTIC

7845. 9 oz. Goblet • 7845. 5½ oz. High Sherbet • 7845. 5¼ oz. Low Sherbet • 7845. 2½ oz. Wine • 7845. 2½ oz. Cocktail • 7861. 6½ oz. Parfait • 9011. 13 oz. Ice Tea • 9011. 9 oz. Water • 9011. 5 oz. Grape Juice • 9011. 2½ oz. Whiskey • 7845. Finger Bowl

"653" • "654"

7845. 9 oz. Goblet • 7845. High Sherbet • 7845. Low Sherbet • 7845. Cocktail • 7845. Wine • 7851. Parfait

ROSEPINK 13 OPTIC CUT "653" AND "654" DESIGNS

Both Designs furnished on the same shapes

10340. 7½ in. Plate • 6103. Ftd. Finger Bowl • 6103. 4 oz. Ftd. Seltzer • 6103. 9 oz. Ftd. Table • 6103. 12 oz. Ftd. Ice Tea • 20. 58 oz. Ftd Jug and Cover Also furnish without Cover

10

9

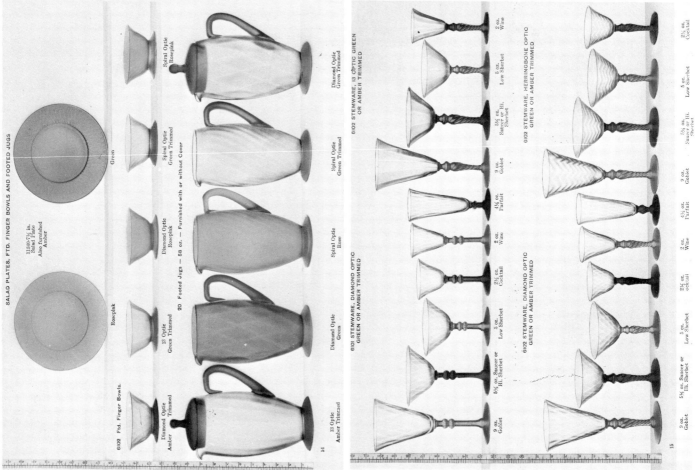

SALAD PLATES, FTD. FINGER BOWLS AND FOOTED JUGS

11340-7½ in. Salad Plate Also furnished Amber

Green • Rosepink

6102 Ftd. Finger Bowls.

Diamond Optic Amber Trimmed • 13 Optic Amber Trimmed • Spiral Optic Rosepink • Diamond Optic Rosepink • Spiral Optic Green Trimmed • Diamond Optic Green • Spiral Optic Green Trimmed • Diamond Optic Green Trimmed

20 Footed Jugs — 58 oz. — Furnished with or without Cover

6101 STEMWARE, DIAMOND OPTIC GREEN OR AMBER TRIMMED

6102 STEMWARE, DIAMOND OPTIC GREEN OR AMBER TRIMMED

6102 STEMWARE, HERRINGBONE OPTIC GREEN OR AMBER TRIMMED

6102 STEMWARE, 13 OPTIC GREEN OR AMBER TRIMMED

9 oz. Goblet • 5¾ oz. Saucer or Hl. Sherbet • 5 oz. Low Sherbet • 2¼ oz. cocktail • 2 oz. Wine • 4¾ oz. Parfait • 9 oz. Goblet • 5¾ oz. Saucer or Hl. Sherbet • 5 oz. Low Sherbet • 2 oz. Wine • 2½ oz. Cocktail

14

15

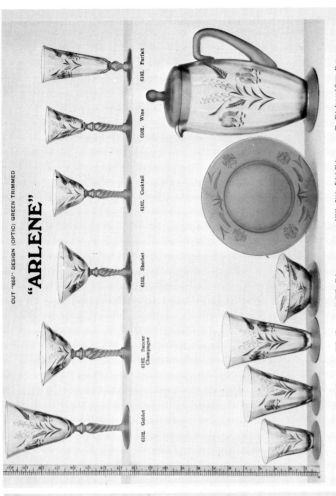

"ARLENE"

CUT "655" DESIGN (OPTIC) GREEN TRIMMED

| 6102. Parfait | 6102. Wine | 6102. Cocktail | 6102. Sherbet | 6102. Saucer Champagne | 6102. Goblet |

20. Ftd. Jug and Cover, 58 oz. Also furnish without Cover | 7½ in. Salad Plate (All Green) | 6102. Ftd. Finger Bowl | 6102. 12 oz. Ftd. Ice Tea | 6102. 9 oz. Ftd. Table | 6102. 4 oz. Ftd. Seltzer

"VIDA"

OPTIC ETCHED "808" DESIGN, AMBER TRIMMED

| 6102 Parfait | 6102 Wine | 6102 Cocktail | 6102 Low Sherbet | 6102 Saucer or Hi. Sherbet | 6102 Goblet |

10840. 7½ in. Salad Plate (All Amber) | 6102 Ftd. Finger Bowl | 20 Ftd. Jug Also with Cover | 6102. 12 oz. | 6102. 9 oz. | 6102. 4 oz.

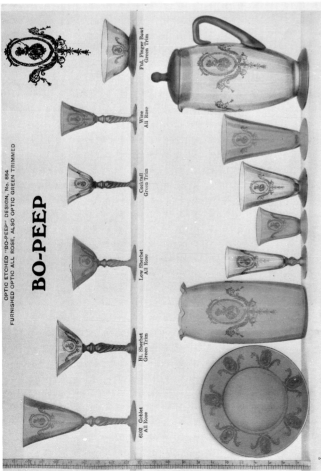

BO-PEEP

OPTIC ETCHED "BO-PEEP" DESIGN, No. 664
FURNISHED OPTIC ALL ROSE, ALSO OPTIC GREEN TRIMMED

| Ftd. Finger Bowl Green Trim | Wine All Rose | Cocktail Green Trim | Low Sherbet All Rose | Hi. Sherbet Green Trim | 6102 Goblet All Rose |

20 Ftd. Jug and Cover Green Trim Also furnish without Cover | Ftd. Ice Tea All Rose | Ftd. Table Green Trim | Ftd. Seltzer All Rose | Parfait Green Trim | 0713-9 in. Vase All Rose | 10840-7½ in. Salad Plate All Green

"MAXWELL"

CUT "680" DESIGN (OPTIC), AMBER TRIMMED

| 6120. Wine | 6120. Cocktail | 6120. Sherbet | 6120. Saucer Champagne | 6120. Goblet Also furnish Parfait. |

20. Ftd. Jug and Cover, 58 oz. Also furnish without Cover | 6103. 12 oz. Ftd. Ice Tea | 6103. 9 oz. Ftd. Table | 6103. 4 oz. Ftd. Seltzer | 6102. Ftd. Finger Bowl | 10840. 7½ in. Salad Plate (All Amber)

Morgantown

A Morgantown Glass Works was founded in Morgantown, West Virginia in the late 19th Century, but when the company was reorganized in 1903 it became the Economy Tumbler Company. Under this name it operated until 1929, when the title Morgantown Glass Works was assumed again.

For many years blown tumblers of all kinds formed the major part of the factory's output. "Economy Tumblers—Just What The Name Implies!" ran its slogan. As the demand grew for a more general line of glassware for the home, however, so did the Economy lines expand to include a wide variety of tableware items. These included pressed patterns as well as blown, and later cut and etched wares in many colors and decorations. Hundreds of blanks were sent to other companies for finishing.

Quality in the case of this organization rose along with quantity, and the more diversified—and highly regarded—its lines became, the more advisable it seemed to shed the 'economy tumbler' image. By degrees the name was changed; in 1924 the corporate title was updated to Economy Glass Company, its wares marketed under an "Old Morgantown" label. In 1929 the name Morgantown Glass Works was borrowed from the past, and the new face was complete.

The firm continued in the 30s to develop new lines and colors which were always in the front lines of the trade. In recent history further reorganization created the Morgantown Glassware Guild; then Fostoria Glass Company owned the factory for a while, retaining the Morgantown name. But the factory was bought out in 1972 and at present manufactures primarily lamp globes as the Bailey Glass Company.

COLOR

A trade journal of 1923 makes the statement that "Economy was the first to introduce quality ware in colors." Certainly the lines were swept with color that year—combinations of white translucent and True green, Moonstone, Jade, Pomona green, black, and iridescents. Amber and amethyst were introduced in 1925; in 1926 combinations of yellow and black, red and black, pink and magenta, Rose and the new shade Rose Amber were featured. 1927 brought a dark amber; 1928, blue, and many crystal-and-color combinations. Black was shown with crystal in 1929, and that year too Ritz blue was brought on. In 1931 Steigel green, topaz and ruby are widely advertised, and though almost all the colors enjoyed long runs these latter four were the most widely advertised through the 30s.

The lines this page were manufactured by the Economy Glass Company
under the Old Morgantown label. Colors given were those first advertised;
later these patterns, as well as some on pages to follow,
were variously made in other company colors.

"KRINKLE"
—1924 ad

PALM OPTIC *dinnerware line
pink, green; 1929 trade report*

"PRIMROSE LANE"
pink, green; 1929 trade report

MARILYN *dinnerware line
pink, green; 1929 trade report*

"SQUARE"
—1928 patent

**PINEAPPLE
OPTIC** *—1929 trade journal write-up*

❖ ❖ ❖ ❖

Among the new lines of blown glassware for the table introduced this year by the Economy Glass Co., of Morgantown, W. Va., is the No. 7644 luncheon service. The service includes all the items of stemware, footed tumblers and salad plates to match.

The shape is heightened in attractiveness by the pineapple optic design of the bowls which also is carried out on the edge of the salad plate. The shape is graceful, but at the same time most practical. It is made in both rose and green transparent glass.

❖ ❖ ❖ ❖

ART MODERNE
—1929 trade journal write-up

The items available in this design include most everything usable in blown stemware and footed tumblers. The shape is made in rose and green transparent glass, in quality crystal and in a most attractive combina-

tion of black stem and foot with crystal bowl. A variety of cuttings and etchings are available for decoration.

The illustration of the "Art Moderne" line herewith was made by the Economy Glass Co. to be supplied to the merchandising trade. Illustrations are available from the company in two sizes. The one herewith is the smaller one. The larger is twice the size.

❖ ❖ ❖ ❖

281

"BUTTON" – *1929 trade journal*

❖ ❖ ❖ ❖

Ritz Blue bowls on crystal stems have made the No. 7643 stemware line from the Morgantown Glass Works, Morgantown, W. Va., a very popular one. The shape also can be

had in other colors with crystal or in transparent color only.

Featuring the shape is the peculiar design of the stem with the large "button" which supplies a radiant and brilliant touch. The line is made in low stems and represents a departure from the vogue of long stems.

"MORGANA" – *1929 trade journal*

Attractive combinations of etching and gold work on stemware have been found to be regular and steady sellers by many stores and shops. One contribution of the Morgantown Glass Works, Morgantown, W. Va., which succeeded the Economy Glass Co. on July 1, is the No. 7577 stemware line illustrated.

The etching is a wave line motif and combines daintily

with the gold line and the design of the shape. Brought out in October, 1928, the shape and design has been an excellent retailer at a moderate price. The decoration is applied to crystal, green and rose blanks, supplying a selection for varied requirements.

SIMPLICITY
tableware, pink, green

"WILLOW"
stemware, pink, green

OLD ENGLISH
–1930 ad

Stemware ~ STYLED TO SELL!

There's power in this Old Morgantown style to lure dollars from today's most money-conscious customer. The designer borrowed the shape of the bowls from the Old English Rummers of the 18th century. Here is graceful simplicity in an ideal shape for displaying the vigorous colors of Steigel Green, Ritz Blue and Ruby. The Crystal golf ball stem adds a scintillating note. This is one of Old Morgantown's finest lines of stemware.

Left to right—No. 7678 Luncheon Goblet, Tall Parfait, Wine, 10 oz. Sherbet, Goblet.

PEACOCK OPTIC
Shown in pink & green in 1929 trade journal, left; water set at right from 1930 ad.

282

"Witch Ball" and- "Ivy Ball"

7643

64   64

Tempting *Tumblers* for Critical Trade

Line No. 7603½ includes five sizes of footed tumblers: 9 oz. Water; 12 oz. Iced Tea; 5 oz. Orange Juice; 5½ oz. Sundae or Sherbet; 2½ oz. Cocktail—with your choice of Rose, Green or Crystal bowls.

To match the shape and color of these footed tumblers, tall stemware items are also available in line No. 7603½.

The No. 64-6″ Witch Ball vase shown above is Peacock Optic, made in all pastel colors with Crystal foot.

THIS is a line that makes people stop, look and buy. It's dainty and different. Crystal bowls, delicately blown, rest lightly on feet of Jade—a pleasing color which adds life and brightness . . . an especial attraction to those who are no longer intrigued by conventional black trimming.

A trio of vases..

odd enough to bewitch the roving eye of the shopper . . . practical enough to gratify her sense of utility. No. 64—6″ Witch Ball Vase has round or Italian foot in crystal. No. 7643—4″ Ivy Ball Vase has stem and base in crystal. Bowls are in contrasting black, pastel, green, rose, topaz, jade or ruby—or in crystal.

D. King Irwin, 200 Fifth avenue, has some lovely items on display from the Morgantown Glass Works, several of which are shown on this page. Above reading from left to right is their No. 59 vase. No. 18 9-inch bowl and No. 11½ 10-inch vase. These smart numbers are made in Stiegel green, Ritz blue and ruby, and are part of a line that goes with the Morgantown stemware in similar colors. Just at the left are two stemware selections, the 9-oz goblet (No. 0677) and 6 oz. saucer champagne. These show the Cressey cutting and are in full crystal. The No. 514 square jug is shown below. This features a black handle and also is made in Stiegel green, Ritz blue and ruby. The 12-oz. tumbler is their No. 606 made in colors to match. The Chateau cutting is shown on the 9-oz. goblet at the lower right which is also made in full crystal.

DUCAL
crystal & black

SUPERBA
crystal & black

SAN TOY
topaz & crystal

FAIRWIN
crystal & black

There's Magic in *these Stems*

Shoppers become "Crystal gazers" when they see this delicately blown (cased) stemware on display. Even the salespeople never quite get over their wonder at the way the Ritz-Blue filament so mysteriously illuminates these daintily fluted Crystal stems. If you want to speed up your sales tempo, display "Fairwin" before the Holidays.

Stemware illustrated is the 7673 line, with Ritz-Blue "cased" stems, Crystal wide optic bowls, with etching "Fairwin." All pieces essential for a complete service are available.

MORGANTOWN GLASS WORKS
Morgantown, W. Va.

Old Morgantown
GLASSWARE

"LITTLE KING"   SPARTA   "TINKLE"

Verve . . . life . . . color—modern liquor sets that fairly tinkle with allurement. There sits the decanter (like a pert little king with a sparkling crystal crown) surrounded by six brilliant glasses with their bands of gleaming platinum. The platinum stays bright, for it's applied in a technique known only to master craftsmen in Old Morgantown.

The Last Word in LIQUOR SETS

No. 1-9051 in Ritz Blue or Black, with Crystal stopper and bright Platinum decoration No. 12.

No. 10½-9051 in Ritz Blue or Black with Crystal stopper and platinum decoration "Sparta". Or in Rose, Green, Ritz Blue or Black without decoration.

No. 2-9051 in Ritz Blue or Black, with bright Platinum decoration No. 12. Or in Rose, Green Peacock Optic, Ritz Blue or Black plain, without decoration.

MORGANTOWN GLASS WORKS
MORGANTOWN, W. VA.

—1931 advertisement

New and Unusual Vases
FOR THE SEASON OF FLOWERS

76
75   73   77

Blown rose bowls and vases in black, ruby, Ritz blue, Steigel green, and crystal; 1932 ad

NEW—STYLISH—INEXPENSIVE GOBLETS

These are splendid values to stock for immediate turnover. Whether you merely glance at the Goblets, or whether you examine them critically, you get the impression of much higher quality than their retail prices would imply. Note how exquisitely the blown Crystal bowls are either cut or etched. Read the descriptions below.

Top left: 7690 Crystal Goblet, cut "Carlos," has a brilliant, cut stem. Elaborate, but in good, popular style.

Left center: 7660 Crystal Goblet, deep-etched "American Beauty," has an engraved stem. In keeping with the popular taste in etched designs.

Right center: 7684 Crystal Goblet with etching No. 796 is our Yale shape. A distinctive creation which has been greatly admired.

Top right: 7604½ Rock Crystal Goblet, cut "Dawn," has a cut stem. An artistic design at a popular retail price.

Bottom left: 7688 Crystal Goblet, with etching No. 791, is in early-American style. Its low shape meets the newer demands for lower goblets.

Bottom right: 7682 Crystal Goblet, cut "Mt. Vernon," is of the early-American type in shape and decoration.

(These and other new lines for 1932 are now being shown by our sales offices and our traveling representatives.)

Old Morgantown GLASSWARE
MORGANTOWN GLASS WORKS
Morgantown, W. Va.

—1932 ad

285

SPARTA
Royal blue w/ crystal; 1932

Vases!

—SPLENDID NEW DESIGNS FOR QUICK TURNOVER

ANYONE who has an eye for beauty will become enamored of these Vases. Fashioned delicately from blown glass . . . then daintily embellished . . . these charming works of art need only to be displayed to be desired. A retail price range of $2.50 to $5.00 should turn them over rapidly. If we were you, we'd lose no time in making an immediate selection. You'll find no better, easier numbers to sell this season.

DANCING GIRL
crys w/black foot; pink, green; 1932

"MEDALLION"
1934 trade journal report

(A) *Symmetrical!* 78-10½" Vase has a Crystal golf-ball stem and base. Retails $2.50 to $5.00, depending on color of bowl—Crystal, Ritz Blue, Black, Stiegel Green, or Ruby.

(B) *Patrician!* 79-11" Vase has a Crystal golf-ball stem and base. Retails $2.50 to $5.00, depending on color of bowl—Crystal, Ritz Blue, Black, Stiegel Green, or Ruby.

(C) *Dainty!* 75-6" Vase, with etching "Floret." A Crystal Vase to retail for $2.50.

(D) *Utilitarian!* 57-8" Flip Vase, cut and etched "Trellis." A brilliant effect of polished etching and cutting on a Crystal blank. May be retailed for $3.50.

(E) *Magical!* 7688-4" Ivy Ball Vase with cutting No. 542. The conventional, polished cutting is in harmony with the design of the Crystal blank. An interesting gift item to sell for $2.50.

(F) *Smart!* 7643½-24" Brandy Vase. Done in alternate bands of black and white enamel on Crystal. Quite suitable for short-stemmed flowers and quite saleable at $2.50.

FAUN
crystal w/ antique gold; 1932 ad

MORGANTOWN GLASS WORKS
MORGANTOWN, W. VA.

Old Morgantown
GLASSWARE

"RADIANT RUBY"
complete line stemware ruby w/crystal base —1935 ad

286

—1932 ad

"SOMMERSET"
AN "OLD MORGANTOWN" BEVERAGE SET

For serving of iced beverages in summer weather, the Morgantown Glass Works, Morgantown, W. Va., offers the graceful shape illustrated here. Both the pitcher and the matching tumblers flare at the top and taper to a crystal foot. The set is made in the "Old Morgantown" colors of Ritz Blue, Ruby, Black and Stiegel Green and also can be

had in all-crystal. The handle for the color-glass pitchers is in crystal. The Stiegel Green color is being favored because it is cool-looking and out of the ordinary. The set may be retailed from $5 upward for seven pieces, the price varying with the color.

—1932 trade journal

More Beverage Sets in company colors:
"LANGSTON" *(right)*
"HUGHES" *(below l.)*
"MILLAY" *(below r.)*

7625—12 oz. Footed Ice Tea
37—48 oz. Footed Jug
606—Tumbler Dished Sides
9069—12 oz. Footed Tumbler
544 Square Jug Dished Sides
49—54 oz. Footed Jug

"MELON" Beverage Set
Colors and opal w/ colors;
1932 ad

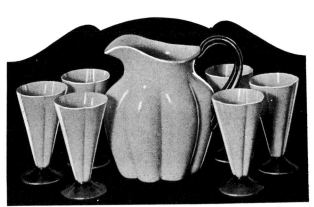

Bridge Ensembles
Octagon and Square

Hostesses who crave individuality for their bridge luncheons will be enthusiastic purchasers of this glass —dashing in shape and color contrasts of Ebony with Crystal. Unadorned by etching or cutting, these ensembles depend entirely upon their distinctive lines for beauty. Matched sets come in two shapes—octagonal or the embellished square. 1519-8¼" Salad Plate, 7659 ½-12 oz. Iced Tea and 1520 Cup with Square Saucer illustrated show the charming variation of the square shape. Note how the shape of the Saucer resembles a delicately curling leaf, conventionalized. The octagon shape is shown here in 1517-8" Salad Plate, 1518 Cup with Octagon Saucer, and 09069 ½-12 oz. Iced Tea with Octagon Foot.

Morgantown's **BRIDGE SET**
Ebony with crystal; 1932

A Summer Sales "Natural"

. . . this clever, modernly styled refreshment set by Old Morgantown will be one of your fastest moving items this summer . . . an easy means of hot-weather profits. The set includes the capacious No. 546 Pitcher (54 oz.) and six 9090 Tumblers (12 oz.) . . . furnished in all-Crystal or with the body of the Pitcher in Blue, Green or Ruby with a Crystal handle; or the body of the Pitcher may be Crystal with a colored handle. Packed one dozen sets in a barrel or each set in an individual carton. Make your order large enough to take care of the heavy seasonal demand.

 Morgantown Glass Works
MORGANTOWN, W. VA.

"MR. NATURAL" *—1937 ad*

New Martinsville

The brand new New Martinsville Glass Manufacturing Company took its name from the West Virginia town in which it was built and struck up furnaces in 1901. Glassmen there were bold with idea and color from the word 'go'. Area historians recall that a brilliant opal glass was formulated in the first years which was cast into colorful lines of decorative ware right alongside the plainer, utilitarian lines in crystal common to the time.*

Surviving company catalogs begin somewhat after this early issue, apparently, and show only pressed crystal tablewares and flashed-on ruby or gold decorations. But with the Twenties came an early intrigue with color and novel design that boosted the image of New Martinsville as innovator. In these years there was always something remarkable in its line-up; trade journals credit the company with the first all-glass floor lamp in 1925 ("It may be looked upon as a stretch of the imagination") and with popularizing the vanity set in 1926. And every year new smoker- and liquor-sets were brashly promoted despite the prohibitory times.

New Martinsville passed into the Thirties along these same lines, adding more new colors, tableware patterns, cuttings and etchings before making an early return to crystal. The organization was given a change of face in 1944, when it was bought out and renamed Viking Glass Company to set forth a new and better post-Depressionary mood.

The word 'go' is still a favorite one around the New Martinsville factory today, and its wares (still largely handmade) continue to be among the most original on the market. Look for the Viking label (and that of Rainbow Art Glass, its subsidiary) on gift glass items — you'll find it often.

COLOR

As early as 1923 New Martinsville made color offerings in wine, blue, amber, and black glass. Canary and amethyst were brought on in 1924; green in 1925 (it was called Emerald in 1926). By this time almost every item in the company's extensive ensemble of occasional pieces could be had in all colors.

Peach Melba was announced amid much fanfare in 1926—this was pink, later called Rose. Several "cold" and fired-on colors decorated the familiar New Martinsville shapes in this year, too. Alice Blue, a medium hue, was new for 1928. Then in 1931 a square-shaped dinnerware was shown in Jade, plain (a soft whitish green) and in combination with black.

Steigel green was the sole initiate between then and 1933, the year ruby, Ritz blue, and Evergreen (a dark green) were announced. At this date most all colors were still in production, but by 1935 the trend back to crystal was clearly visible in this house. Only pink, Ritz blue, and ruby lasted until 1942.

After the war years Viking turned once again to color for inspiration, and it's been color ever since. A few of the old shades have been revived—recently ruby, amethyst, blue, green, and even a lime that resembles the original Canary— and cast primarily in new molds. A very few old molds have been brought out; in 1973, for example, you could buy a couple of pieces of Radiance in ruby.

*THE NEW MARTINSVILLE GLASS STORY by Everett and Addie Miller (Richardson Publishing Co., 1972) shows many of the earlier items for those interested.

United States Patent Design for powder puff box or similar article, 1924

SUGAR AND CREAM BRIDGE SET
Advertised in amber, green, blue, amethyst in 1925.

"GENE" LIQUOR SET
1¾ oz glasses; advertised in amber, green, blue, amethyst in 1925.

No. 149-3 Candy Jar

NEW cone shaped half pound candy jar that meets a popular demand. Useful and very attractive. A high class piece of glassware with finished cover and foot. Made in crystal, blue, canary, amber and amethyst.

THE NEW MARTINSVILLE GLASS MFG. CO.

NEW MARTINSVILLE, W. VA.

"DAVIDA" Cutting, 1924 advertisement

No. 160-10 Console Set

NEW CONSOLE SET that lends itself to several uses. Consists of two No. 10 10-inch candlesticks, new style 10-inch bowl and 13-inch plate. Bowl can rest on plate or, if desired, can remain on the buffet holding fruit while the plate is being used for some other purpose.

Furnished in crystal and colors — blue, green, amber and amethyst.

THE NEW MARTINSVILLE GLASS MFG. CO.

NEW MARTINSVILLE, W. VA.

"PATTI" Console Set, 1925 advertisement

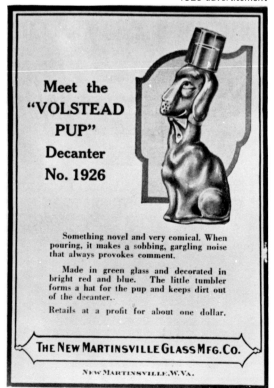

290

No. 149-4 CIGARET HOLDER
Decorated or Plain

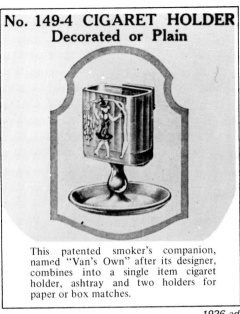

This patented smoker's companion, named "Van's Own" after its designer, combines into a single item cigaret holder, ashtray and two holders for paper or box matches.

—1926 ad

CATALOG REPRINT

Following is a reprint of a company catalog dating from about 1926. The items are shown in all the company's colors of that year—green, blue, amber, and amethyst—and some have painted-on designs.

No. 10-10 Console Set—Amber Packs 1½ Doz. Sets to Bbl.

No. 10-21 Console Set—Blue Packs 1½ Doz. Sets to Bbl.

Salad Sets

No. 160-8 Plate—Green

No. 728—7½ Plate—Amber

No. 160-12 Bowl and Plate—Green Packs 1½ Doz. Sets to Bbl.

No. 728-12 Bowl and Plate—Amber Packs 1½ Doz. Sets to Bbl.

Relish Dishes

No. 10. 5 Part Relish Dish and Liner—Amber Packs 2 Doz. to Tre.

No. 10. 5 Part Relish Dish and Liner—Amethyst Packs 2 Doz. to Tre.

Candy Jars and Boxes

No. 149-2 One lb. Candy Jar and Cover—Amber Packs 4½ Doz. to Bbl.

No. 10 1½ lb. Candy Box and Cover—Blue Packs 4 Doz. to Bbl.

No. 149-3 ½ lb. Candy Jar and Cover—Amber Packs 5½ Doz. to Bbl.

No. 149-8 ½ lb. Candy Jar and Cover—Amethyst Packs 5½ Doz. to Bbl.

No. 10 1½ lb. Candy Box and Cover—Amber Packs 4 Doz. to Bbl.

No. 149-8 ½ lb. Candy Jar and Cover—Green Packs 5½ Doz. to Bbl.

Queen Anne Dresser Sets
Packs 6 Doz. Sets to Bbl.

No. 10-2. Amber

No. 10-2. Green

No. 10-2. Blue.

No. 10-2. Amethyst

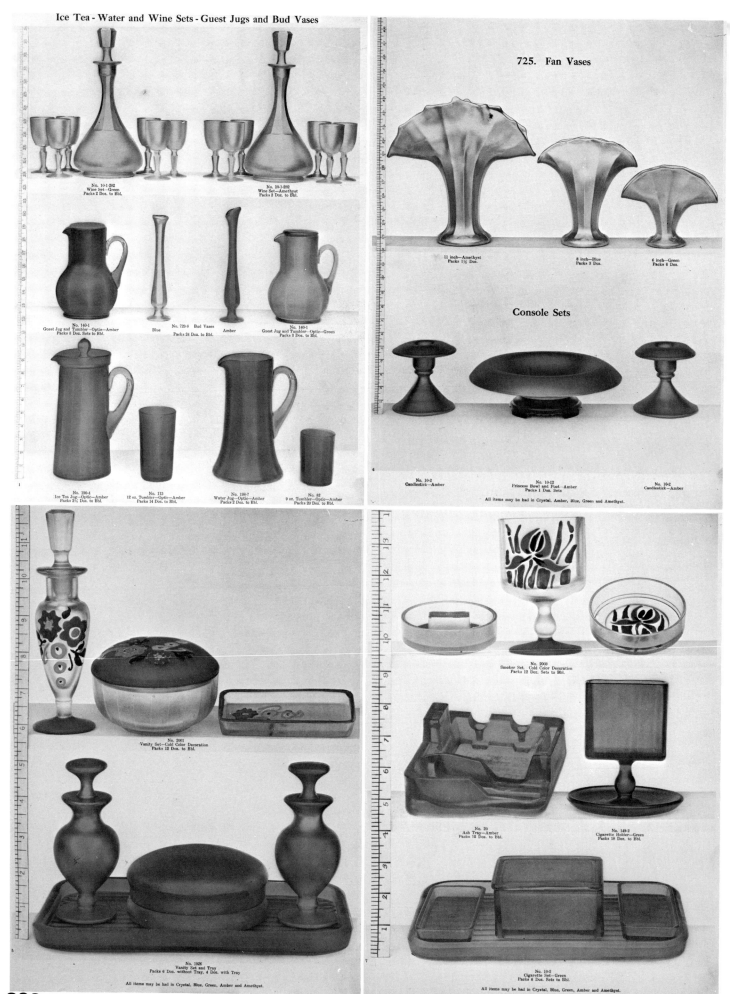

Ice Tea - Water and Wine Sets - Guest Jugs and Bud Vases

No. 10-1-282
Wine Set—Green
Packs 2 Doz. to Bbl.

No. 10-1-282
Wine Set—Amethyst
Packs 2 Doz. to Bbl.

No. 140-1
Guest Jug and Tumbler—Optic—Amber
Packs 3 Doz. Sets to Bbl.

Blue

No. 729-8 Bud Vases
Packs 24 Doz. to Bbl.

Amber

No. 140-1
Guest Jug and Tumbler—Optic—Green
Packs 3 Doz. to Bbl.

No. 190-4
Ice Tea Jug—Optic—Amber
Packs 2½ Doz. to Bbl.

No. 113
12 oz. Tumbler—Optic—Amber
Packs 14 Doz. to Bbl.

No. 198-7
Water Jug—Optic—Amber
Packs 2 Doz. to Bbl.

No. 82
9 oz. Tumbler—Optic—Amber
Packs 20 Doz. to Bbl.

725. Fan Vases

11 inch—Amethyst
Packs 1½ Doz.

8 inch—Blue
Packs 3 Doz.

6 inch—Green
Packs 6 Doz.

Console Sets

No. 10-2
Candlestick—Amber

No. 10-12
Princess Bowl and Foot—Amber
Packs 1 Doz. Sets

No. 10-2
Candlestick—Amber

All items may be had in Crystal, Amber, Blue, Green and Amethyst.

No. 2001
Vanity Set—Cold Color Decoration
Packs 12 Doz. to Bbl.

No. 1926
Vanity Set and Tray
Packs 6 Doz. without Tray, 4 Doz. with Tray

All items may be had in Crystal, Blue, Green, Amber and Amethyst.

No. 2003
Smoker Set, Cold Color Decoration
Packs 12 Doz. Sets to Bbl.

No. 20
Ash Tray—Amber
Packs 12 Doz. to Bbl.

No. 149-2
Cigarette Holder—Green
Packs 18 Doz. to Bbl.

No. 10-2
Cigarette Set—Green
Packs 6 Doz. Sets to Bbl.

All items may be had in Crystal, Blue, Green, Amber and Amethyst.

Smoker Articles---Candlesticks

No. 728
Ash Tray—Amethyst
Packs 50 Doz. to Bbl.

No. 10-3
3 inch Candlestick—Amber
Packs 15 Doz. to Bbl.

No. 728
Match Stand—Green
Packs 50 Doz. to Bbl.

No. 10
4 inch Hld. Candlestick—Green
Packs 15 Doz. to Bbl.

No. 725
Tabacco Jar with Ash Tray Cov.—Amethyst
Packs 4½ Doz. to Bbl.

No. 725
Cigarette Jar with Ash Tray Cov.—Blue
Packs 12 Doz. to Bbl.

No. 2001. 3 Piece Vanity Set.

No. 1928/2001. 3 Piece Vanity Set.

No. 728/3006. Guest Set.

No. 511/3055. 10" inch Bud Vase

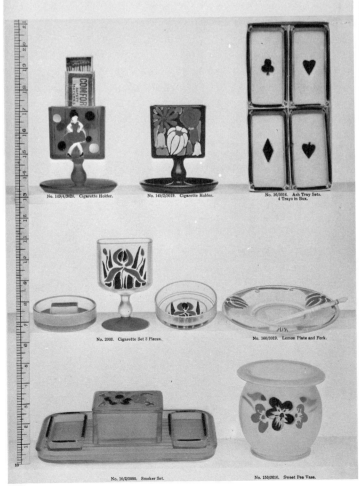

No. 149/4/3020. Cigarette Holder.

No. 149/2/3019. Cigarette Holder.

No. 10/3016. Ash Tray Sets.
4 Trays in Box.

No. 2002. Cigarette Set 3 Pieces.

No. 160/3019. Lemon Plate and Fork.

No. 10/2/3000. Smoker Set.

No. 150/3010. Sweet Pea Vase.

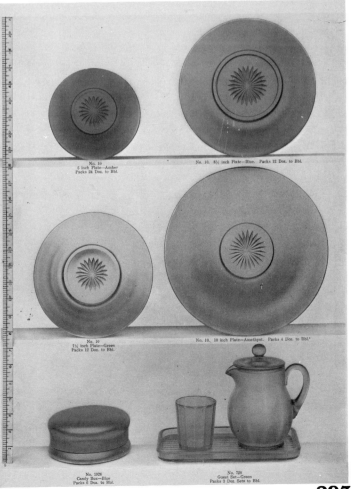

No. 10
5 inch Plate—Amber
Packs 24 Doz. to Bbl.

No. 10. 8½ inch Plate—Blue. Packs 12 Doz. to Bbl.

No. 10
7½ inch Plate—Green
Packs 12 Doz. to Bbl.

No. 10. 10 inch Plate—Amethyst. Packs 4 Doz. to Bbl.

No. 1928
Candy Box—Blue
Packs 6 Doz. to Bbl.

No. 728
Guest Set—Green
Packs 3 Doz. Sets to Bbl.

"GENEVA" *Vanity Set from 1932 advertisement*

"OSCAR" *Refreshment Set from 1935 advertisement*

"MICHAEL" *Liquor Service, 1933 ad*

"JUDY" *Vanity Set and* "SWEETHEART" *Lamp, 1933 ad*

"MOONDROPS"

New Martinsville's big line for 1932 was an immediate hit and many pieces were added in subsequent years. Luncheon and dinner sets, vanity sets, and an assortment of tumblers and decanters were made in crystal, green, Ritz blue, amber, rose, ruby, jade and Evergreen. More than one style of some pieces were made; two kinds of stopper were used with the decanter, the butterdish and cocktail shaker came with metal covers, and one version of the cocktail shaker has a handle.

The company sometimes advertised this as their #37 (Georgian) line, but we have so many Georgians by other makes that the conventional name "MOONDROPS" has proven a better one to collect by.

The wine set is pictured on the following page. You may find bowls, platters, or other pieces not illustrated here.

2-5/8" cream & sugar; 5¼" wine, metal stem & base; 4-3/8" tall sherbet; 9" decanter (dark amethyst); 9¾" oval vegetable; butter & cover; 2" high candleholder.

The cup, saucer, plate, cream, sugar, and 15" sandwich tray as illustrated in a 1933 ad

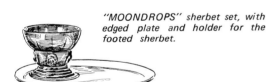

"MOONDROPS" sherbet set, with edged plate and holder for the footed sherbet.

extraordinary

Entirely new is the handsome wine set illustrated. It is our No. 37/3. We call attention to the low stemmed glasses of three-ounce capacity. The decanter is of unique design and is featured by a most attractive ground-in stopper.

"MOONDROPS" *Wine Set from 1933 advertisement*

Something New

FOUR PIECE VANITY SET
in crystal, and crystal with jade
or bright green covers and stoppers.
These retail at $1 each
— great promotional items!

"LEOTA" *Vanity Set from 1933 advertisement*

"MORNING DOVE" *Vase from 1934 advertisement*

"ROBERTO" *Liquor Service from 1934 advertisement*

SELLS FOR ONE DOLLAR
AT A
PROFIT

Here's the new No. 101 nine-inch vase, made in all our beautiful colors and crystal. It is suitable to take large bunches of short or long stemmed flowers and it is an ideal dollar retailer.

The top measures seven inches in diameter. The entire vase is finely finished. It has an exceptional appearance and is a real work of art which you can turn over profitably for $1.00.

NEW MARTINSVILLE GLASS MFG. CO.
NEW MARTINSVILLE, W. VA.

LIQUOR SERVICE

This liquor service is particularly recommended for those customers of yours who are "hard to please." The set carries a rich-looking deep plate etched design and you may have your choice of crystal or colors.

NEW MARTINSVILLE GLASS MFG. CO.

—1935 ad

THE HOSTMASTER

No. 38 Bar Bottle and Bitters Bottles, many-sized tumblers and No. 11 Jigger. This line is a reproduction of a very early pattern and is surprisingly moderate in price.

NEW MARTINSVILLE

GLASS MFG. CO.

NEW MARTINSVILLE, W. VA.

NEW WAFFLE SET

Modern 5-piece Waffle Set with batter jug and syrup jug (both covered) on handled tray. Flat covers on jugs make them serviceable for refrigerator use also. Available in crystal and all colors except ruby. Packed in individual shipping cartons and priced to retail at $1.00, you'll find these sets a profitable item for your department. Order a selection of this No. 2 Waffle Set today!

NEW MARTINSVILLE GLASS MFG. CO.
NEW MARTINSVILLE, W. VA.

—1934 ad

COCKTAILS, SIR?

"SIR COCKTAIL" —1936 ad

"With pleasure," you'll say, when you see this handsome set bring in handsome profits. And at irresistibly moderate retail prices.

It's our new No. 125 Cocktail Set, shown here in an unusually attractive deep etching. Available also in crystal, colors and ruby without etching. Furnished complete with heavy chrome plated tops. It's a leading set, at a very attractive price.

NEW MARTINSVILLE GLASS MFG. CO.
NEW MARTINSVILLE, W. VA.

"COZY CORDIAL" Set from 1936 ad

A Cozy Cordial

— 1930 trade journal.

Among the new items from the New Martinsville Glass Mfg. Co., New Martinsville, W. Va., is this book end showing the figure of a police dog. Made in various colors.

CATALOG REPRINT

On the following pages are selected reprints from an undated company catalog. Most of the items illustrated in it were made for several years in the New Martinsville colors of the 30s.

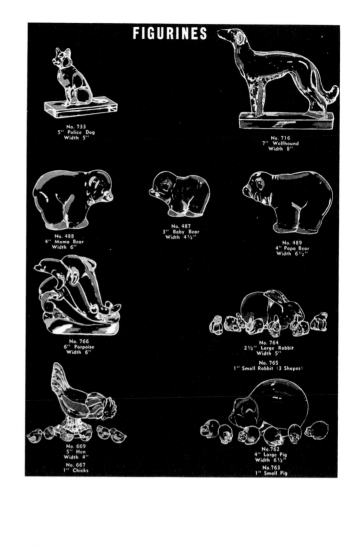

FIGURINES

No. 733
5" Police Dog
Width 5"

No. 716
7" Wolfhound
Width 8"

No. 488
4" Mama Bear
Width 6"

No. 487
3" Baby Bear
Width 4½"

No. 489
4" Papa Bear
Width 6½"

No. 766
6" Porpoise
Width 6"

No. 764
2½" Large Rabbit
Width 5"

No. 765
1" Small Rabbit (3 Shapes)

No. 669
5" Hen
Width 4"

No. 667
1" Chicks

No. 762
4" Large Pig
Width 6½"

No. 763
1" Small Pig

FIGURINES

No. 761
8" Pelican
Width 5"

No. 435
4½" Baby Seal
Width 3½"

No. 452
7" Seal
Width 5"

No. 670
5½" Squirrel W/Base
Width 6"

No. 668
7½" Rooster
Width 7½"

No. 674
4½" Squirrel No/Base
Width 6"

CARTS

No. 508
Cigarette Cart
Width 5"

No. 737
Wheelbarrow
Width 7½"

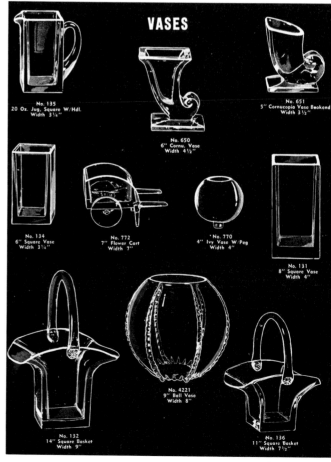

VASES

No. 135
20 Oz. Jug, Square W/Hdl.
Width 3¼"

No. 650
6" Cornu. Vase
Width 4½"

No. 651
5" Cornucopia Vase Bookend
Width 3½"

No. 134
6" Square Vase
Width 3¼"

No. 772
7" Flower Cart
Width 7"

No. 770
4" Ivy Vase W/Peg
Width 4"

No. 131
8" Square Vase
Width 4"

No. 4221
9" Ball Vase
Width 8"

No. 132
14" Square Basket
Width 9"

No. 136
11" Square Basket
Width 7½"

MISCELLANEOUS ITEMS

36 8" 3 Compt. Relish   38 9" 3 Compt. Relish   2019 6" 2 hdl. Jelly

105 7 pc. Cigarette Set

125 Cocktail

125 One qt. Cocktail Shaker

15 8 pc. Wine Set

112 7 pc. Cordial Set   606 7 pc. Cordial Set   111 7 pc. Cordial Set

28 4 pc. Vanity Set   18/2 4 pc. Vanity Set

MISCELLANEOUS ITEMS

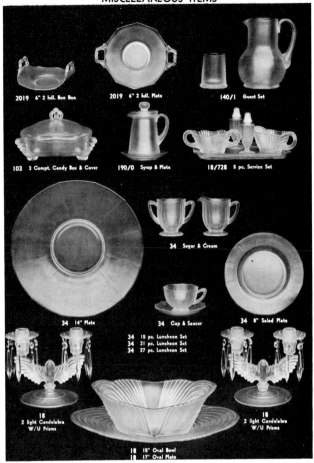

2019 6" 2 hdl. Bon Bon   2019 6" 2 hdl. Plate   140/1 Guest Set

103 3 Compt. Candy Box & Cover   190/0 Syrup & Plate   18/728 5 pc. Service Set

34 Sugar & Cream

34 14" Plate   34 Cup & Saucer   34 8" Salad Plate

34 15 pc. Luncheon Set
34 21 pc. Luncheon Set
34 27 pc. Luncheon Set

18 2 light Candelabra W/U Prisms   18 2 light Candelabra W/U Prisms

18 15" Oval Bowl
18 17" Oval Plate

JANICE PATTERN

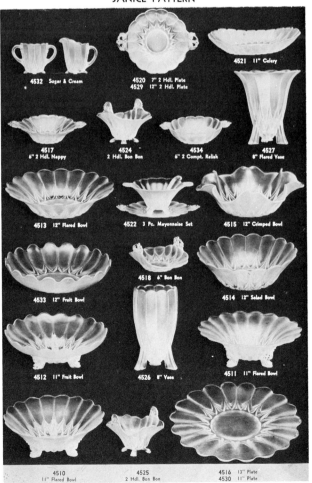

4532 Sugar & Cream

4520 7" 2 Hdl. Plate
4529 12" 2 Hdl. Plate

4521 11" Celery

4517 6" 2 Hdl. Nappy   4524 2 Hdl. Bon Bon   4534 6" 2 Compt. Relish   4527 8" Flared Vase

4513 12" Flared Bowl   4522 3 Pc. Mayonnaise Set   4515 12" Crimped Bowl

4518 6" Bon Bon

4533 12" Fruit Bowl   4514 12" Salad Bowl

4512 11" Fruit Bowl   4526 8" Vase   4511 11" Flared Bowl

4510 11" Flared Bowl   4525 2 Hdl. Bon Bon   4516 13" Plate
4530 11" Plate

ETCHED No. 30 PATTERN

4536 2 light Candlestick   4554 5" Candlestick   42 10" Celery

4460 12" Fruit Bowl   18 Single Hurricane Candlestick   4462 12" 2 Hdl. Plate

4459 12" Flared Bowl   4463 11" Salad Bowl

4461 14" Plate   4464 13" Plate

42 3 pc. Mayonnaise Set 4252 6" Crimped Compote 4251 6" Compote 4248 6" Ftd. Bon Bon

4236 5" Ftd. Mint or Compote 4246 6" Flared Bon Bon 4247 6" Crimped Bon Bon 4242 6" Crimped Bon Bon

42 5 pc. Service Set 4233 6" Covered Bon Bon 42 5 pc. Condiment Set

4253 8" Ftd. Salver 42 10" Flared Bowl 4220 10" Crimped Bowl

4214 8" Candlestick W/U Prisms 18 2 light Candelabra W/U Prisms 42 2 light Candlestick

4212 12" Crimped Bowl 4211 12" Crimped Bowl

4219 10" Ftd. Bowl, Crimped 4221 9" Ball Vase 4218 10" Ftd. Bowl, Flared

4250 7" Pickle 42 3 compt. Candy Box & Cover 42 10" Celery

42 Sugar 42 Cream

42 14" Plate 42 Cup & Saucer 42 8" Salad Plate

42 15 pc. Luncheon Set
42 21 pc. Luncheon Set
42 27 pc. Luncheon Set

42 4 pint Jug 42 9 oz. Tumbler 4232 10" Crimped Vase also made in 12" 42 10" Flared Vase also made in 12"

LINE No. 42

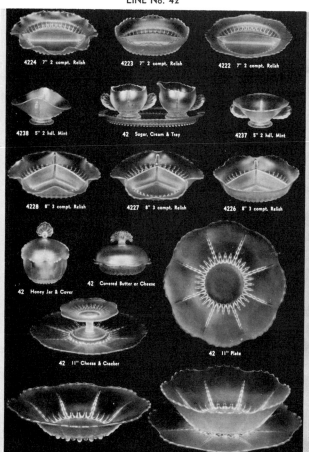

4224 7" 2 compt. Relish 4223 7" 2 compt. Relish 4222 7" 2 compt. Relish

4238 5" 2 hdl. Mint 42 Sugar, Cream & Tray 4237 5" 2 hdl. Mint

4228 8" 3 compt. Relish 4227 8" 3 compt. Relish 4226 8" 3 compt. Relish

42 Honey Jar & Cover 42 Covered Butter or Cheese 42 11" Plate

42 11" Cheese & Cracker

4213 12" Flared Bowl 42 12" Flared Fruit Bowl
42 14" Plate

ETCHED No. 26 PATTERN

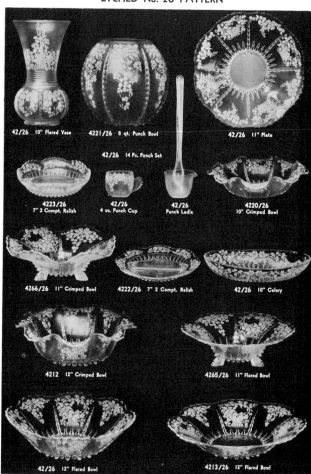

42/26 10" Flared Vase 4221/26 5 qt. Punch Bowl 42/26 11" Plate

42/26 14 Pc. Punch Set

4223/26 7" 2 Compt. Relish 42/26 4 oz. Punch Cup 42/26 Punch Ladle 4220/26 10" Crimped Bowl

4266/26 11" Crimped Bowl 4222/26 7" 2 Compt. Relish 42/26 10" Celery

4212 12" Crimped Bowl 4265/26 11" Flared Bowl

42/26 12" Flared Bowl 4213/26 12" Flared Bowl

Paden City

Paden City Glass Manufacturing Company started shop in 1916. The factory, located in Paden City, West Virginia, made mostly pressed tableware at first, in the usual crystal concepts, with vases and lamps as sidelines. Much hotel and restaurant ware was made for a time, and kitchenware. But gradually the departments specialized their techniques in cutting, etching, and decorating, and the company grew into a more sophisticated line of wares.

Paden City came into its own in the 20s when it began expressing itself with color. For many years the lines were bright with it; in 1931 a trade journal reports that wine sets by this firm were being offered in two dozen different color combinations. In addition to large assortments of occasional pieces (vanity sets and large serving pieces were favorite offerings) several lines of colored dinnerware were made. These patterns, especially those intricately etched on the familiar Paden City #300 shapes, were not made in quantity—and are all the more sought after by today's collectors because of it.

In its maturity the company reached a high level of quality production; its lines were extensive, its variety marked. Paden City had always been a hand house, often fine-blowing its tumblers and stemware, but in 1949 underwent a redesigning by new management which involved the automation of the factory. Unfortunately this new direction was not well taken, and operations came to a permanent halt in 1951.

Paden City was showing black glass in 1923 along with its crystal. Blue, green, amber, and a Mulberry color were displayed in 1924; pink, often advertised as Cheriglo, began about 1925. Other colors may well have been in production in the latter 20s also.

Golden Glow, the topaz, was introduced in 1931; Royal blue and ruby in 1932; amethyst in 1933. Black is again in the line-up in the 30s, and Forest green and a Ceylon blue are advertised in 1936. Paden City is one of the few Depression-era companies to advertise its dark blue, at least sometimes, by the name Cobalt blue. This was in 1936.

This page is a compilation of items advertised by Paden City between 1924 and 1928. All were listed in the company colors given in the ad below.

**"FLAPPER"
GUEST SET**
in crystal & colors

NEW CREATIONS IN GLASSWARE

A large line of new and original items made in the beautiful colors of Amber, Green, Blue and Mulberry with artistic patterns in cut and Deep Plate Etchings.

Manufacturers of crystal and colored glassware for the Restaurant, Hotel, Soda Fountain and Department Store.

Staple articles with pleasing shapes in pressed and blown ware for the Cutter and Decorator.

**PADEN CITY GLASS
MFG. COMPANY**
PADEN CITY, W. VA.

**"PARTY LINE"
ICE TEA SET**
*in crystal & colors;
more next page*

**"SPEAKEASY"
COCKTAIL SHAKER**
in crystal & colors

**"SHEBA"
CONSOLE SET**
in crystal & colors

**"SHEIK"
REFRESHMENT SET**
in crystal & colors

**"VAMP"
DRESSER SET**
in crystal & colors

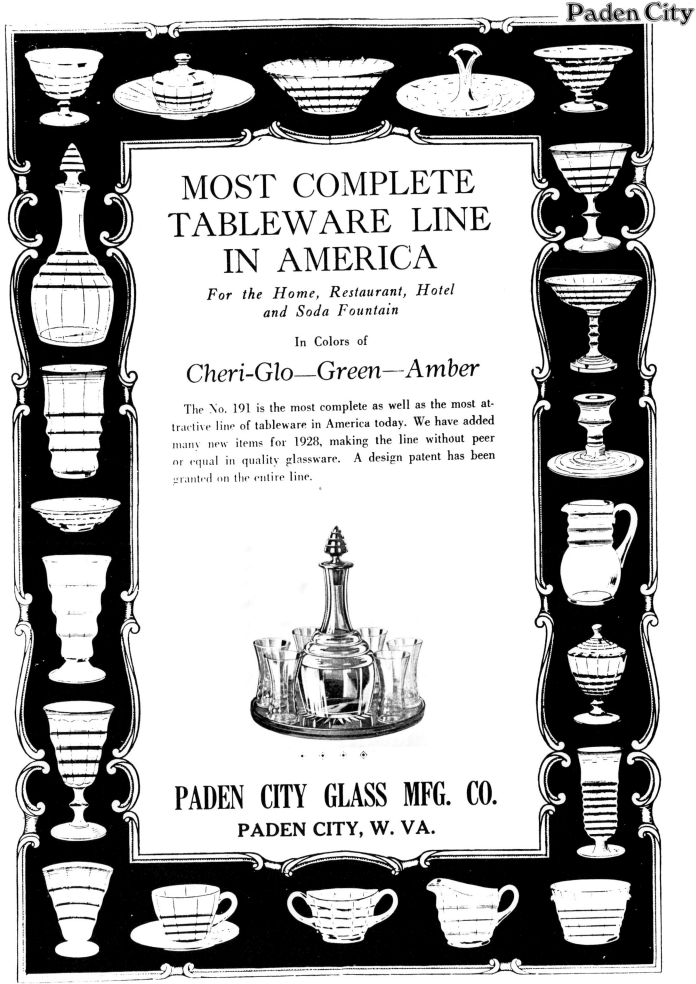

MOST COMPLETE TABLEWARE LINE IN AMERICA

For the Home, Restaurant, Hotel and Soda Fountain

In Colors of

Cheri-Glo—Green—Amber

The No. 191 is the most complete as well as the most attractive line of tableware in America today. We have added many new items for 1928, making the line without peer or equal in quality glassware. A design patent has been granted on the entire line.

PADEN CITY GLASS MFG. CO.
PADEN CITY, W. VA.

"PARTY" LINE *from 1928 advertisement*

SEE PADEN CITY'S NEW LINE

Line No. 300, illustrated in part, is absolutely new and complete. The shapes are entrancing and follow the same lines throughout in proper proportion.

The new No. 300 line is ideal for cutting and decorating of all kinds. Available in Cheri-Glo, Green, Amber and Crystal.

#300 LINE

Paden City's #300 line was introduced in 1928 and was so well received that new pieces, in virtually all the company colors, were added for several years.

This was also the factory's favorite shape for etchings, and on the next few pages more of the #300 line can be seen bearing the different etched motifs.

"PEACOCK AND ROSE"

One of the most popular Paden City etchings was the "PEACOCK AND ROSE" *(detail drawn). Several pieces are photographed at right; others are reprinted below from a 1928 ad. You may find colors in addition to Cheri-glo, green, amber, and blue, and you may find pieces besides these:*

Comport, footed, 6½" tall
Sandwich Tray, 10", hnld.
Sugar & Creamer Set, 4"
Bowl, Footed, 8½" tall
Cake Plate, 11" footed
Mayonnaise Set, 3-piece
Relish Dish & Cover, 6¼",
 3-part
Vase, 10"

Candy Box & Cover,
 7", footed
Fruit Bowl, 8½", hnld.
Fruit Bowl, 10½"
Ice Bucket, 5¾"
Console Bowl, 11",
 rolled edge
Candlesticks, 5" across,
 rolled top (pair)

"ORCHID" vase, 8¼" and "DELILAH BIRD" (detail right) vase, 6½", candleholder 3½" are shown on top row. Both issued 1929 in Paden City colors. More pieces probable.

"LELA BIRD"

The "LELA BIRD" etching, begun in 1929, was done in the company colors. Photographed at left (bottom row) is the 10" vase, 7" jug, and 5" vase.

More "LELA BIRD" below: 6½" comport; 4" cream & sugar; 7"x8"x4½" high fruit bowl; 3-pce. mayonnaise set; 10" sandwich tray; 5" candlestick; 11" footed cake plate. Other pieces made.

DDING to the popularity of Etched Tableware is our new No. 515 Plate Etching. It is a real decoration. Shown here is the No. 515 Etching on our attractive No. 300 line.

PADEN CITY GLASS MANUFACTURING CO.

—1929 advertisement

"NORA BIRD"

This 1929 etching on the #300 blank, and the other etchings this page, were probably made in the Paden City colors of Cheri-glo, green, amber and blue. Pieces pictured above include the 3" tumbler, 4¾" footed tumbler; 4" tumbler; cup & saucer; 8" plate; second-style 4" cream and sugar. Additional pieces were made. A detail is drawn at right.

"CUPID"

You will probably find this 1929 etching on more pieces than the 10" plate and 4¼" cream and sugar pictured below.

"CALIFORNIA POPPY"

12" vase bearing —1929 etching

ROCK CRYSTAL CUTTINGS

"LAZY DAISY"

*—1929
advertisement*

NOT A FLASH
NOT A GLARE
BUT

Real Rock Crystal

Prompt Deliveries Assured.

Numerous other cuttings, etchings on display in our salesrooms for early Fall delivery.

D. King Irwin, 200 Fifth Ave., New York.
Tinker Bros., 17 N. Wabash Av., Chicago

Write us direct for further information, prices, etc.

Paden City Glass Mfg. Co.
PADEN CITY, W. VA

A Smashing Hit!

Paden City's No. 994 Line.

Consider this illustration and know why.

**"POPEYE
& OLIVE"**

—1932 ad

It Will Sell, and How

Buyers at the Pittsburgh Exhibit were on the alert for new wares—distinctive new wares. They saw our No. 994 (its a beauty, really) and they bought. It is a knockout in our new Ruby.

Our New No. 991 line (illustrated in the January issue of this journal) also gained scores of friends. Quality pressed glass in attractive shades of Ruby, Royal Blue, Cheriglo, Amber, Topaz and Green and Crystal make the Paden City line outstanding for 1932. Let us tell you about it or see our agents.

"PENNY" LINE

—1932 ad

In our new No. 991 line, we present ware with a far-reaching appeal. Light enough for the home table, it is sturdy enough for hotels and restaurants. In fact, an ideal line. The ring design is reminiscent of our very popular and famous No. 191 line.

The new line is made in Crystal Green, Cheriglo, Amber, Ruby and Royal Blue. With it, we will show a new line of tableware for the decorator and cutter as well as a number of new novelties.

"WOTTA" LINE

—1933 ad

This is a popular line for 1933 which is different. It is our No. 881 and it has a universal appeal where good value at a fair price is desired. "Wotta" line it is. Available in a variety of colors including Crystal, Green, Ebony, Cheriglo, Amber, Amethyst, Royal Blue, Topaz and Ruby.

ROUND RELISH *and* WINGED RELISH *from 1934 ad*

—1936 ad

BATTER SETS
IN GRAND STYLE—FOR GRAND SALES

Here's an exceptional little set you'll find packed with action. It brings new fashion to the homely art of waffle baking—and it brings new sales to you. Well-styled crystal batter and syrup jugs are decorated with fine cuttings while the covers and tray provide pleasing contrast in black. Order now for quick action.

PADEN CITY GLASS MFG. CO.
PADEN CITY, W. VA.

You'll Relish Your Visit
TO THE PADEN CITY GLASSWARE DISPLAY

"SUN SET" *(top) and* "MOON SET" *vanities from 1936 ad.*

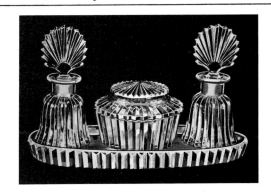

★ NEW VANITY SETS FOR NEW SALES

Vanity Sets are headed for their most popular season in years. Be prepared for the demand. Offer this leader in style and in price, and you'll get volume business. This No. 215 Vanity Set may be had in Crystal, or Crystal base with stoppers and cover in Amber, Cobalt Blue, Black, Forest Green or Ruby. It is also furnished with mirror tray in place of tray shown, if desired. A splendid set at a thrifty price. Write for prices and samples today!

PADEN CITY GLASS MFG. COMPANY
PADEN CITY, WEST VIRGINIA

"ARISTOCRAT" *Liquor Service from 1934 ad*

• The Class of All Glass •

Stepping far ahead of the field to take the "Mixing World" by storm is this aristocratic drinking service. Its rich appearance belies its moderate cost. Shown are 6-oz. Old Fashioned, 23-oz. Bar Bottle with ground stopper, 12-oz. whisky and soda, and chromium topped cocktail shaker. These may be had in Crystal, Amber, Ritz Blue, Cheriglo and Ruby.

PADEN CITY GLASS MFG. CO.
PADEN CITY   W. VA.

Seneca

The group of German immigrants who found each other and then founded the Seneca Glass Company in 1891 named their organization after a tribe of American Indians! The first factory was in Fostoria, Ohio (the one originally owned by Fostoria Glass Company, as a matter of fact) but soon facilities were built anew in Morgantown, West Virginia.

Here Seneca got off to a fresh start and began a long tradition of fine cut and blown crystal ranging from the simple to the exclusive. By the 20s it liked to bill itself "The Old Reliable" for quality tumblers and stemware, and indeed many a hotel, famous and otherwise, was furnished its signature crystal by Seneca.

At this hand house the lines of rock crystal were featured even during the Depression era, but many assortments were made in a variety of colors for the popular market. Green, Ambrosa, pink, burgundy, Royal blue, Florentine green, Amberina, Ocean blue, Azure blue and Cobalt blue were some of the colors advertised over the period.

Even today the time-honored glasshouse—led by one of the original founding families—continues to make hundreds of cut and blown patterns of classical design, often for special clients, and colorful lines of casual ware for the modern home as well.

"GERMANA"
cut line
—1930 ad

STREAMLINE
TUMBLER
—1932 ad

The Seneca Glass Co. has brought out this new shape in a combination crystal bowl with colored stem and foot, especially suitable for novelty items, such as the brandy, cordial, and cocktail glasses illustrated. Six colors are available, a light and a dark green, a light and a dark blue, amber, and amethyst.

"BAUBLES"
glassware line,
1931 trade journal

Tall and slim, these 16-ounce glasses for long, summer drinks are made by the Seneca Glass Company and come in six different colors—ruby, Florentine green, Royal blue, Ocean blue, burgundy, and amber — with square, crystal feet.

"SLIM"
glassware line,
also comes 5-oz and 10-oz,
in Wildrose and Emerald;
1932 trade journal

STEMLESS STEMWARE
IN
CRYSTAL AND BLACK

"ALLEGHENY"
Beverage Set
—1931 advertisement

CANDLEWICK
stemware line
—1936 advertisement

No. 903. GOBLET

No. 903
SAU. CHAMP.

No. 903. SHERBET

No. 903.
COCKTAIL

No. 903. CORDIAL

No. 903. WINE

No. 903. PARFAIT

No. 903. 9 oz. Ftd.
TUMBLER

No. 903. 12 oz.
HIGH BALL

No. 903
FINGER BOWL

No. 16. CREAM

No. 16. SUGAR

No. 903. 9 oz.
HIGH BALL

No. 903. 8" BUD VASE

No. 900. COVERED JUG

No. 30. 8" PLATE

No. 903. WINE SET

No. 920. 10" VASE

No. 30. CANDLESTICK

No. 1. 12" CONSOLE BOWL

No. 30. CANDLESTICK

No. 925. 10" VASE

No. 492. GOBLET
Optic, Cut 286

No. 482. GOBLET
Optic, Cut 259

No. 492. GOBLET
Optic, Cut 261

No. 482. GOBLET
Optic, Cut 218

No. 515. GOBLET
Optic, Cut 374

No. 475. GOBLET
Optic, Cut 258

No. 499. GOBLET
Optic, Cut 371

No. 492. GOBLET
Optic, Cut 300

No. 903. GOBLET
Plain, Cut 338

No. 492. GOBLET
Optic, Cut 308

No. 482. GOBLET
Optic, Cut 64

*The **NAOMI** blue & crystal line (top) and some of the many Seneca cuttings, from mid-30s company catalog.*

L.E. Smith

Around the origins of this company revolves a curious tale.

Lewis E. Smith, the story goes, was an occupational drifter out of work more often than in it. He was something of a gourmet cook, however, and while working a stint as chef in Mt. Pleasant, Pennsylvania in 1907 he came up with his own special recipe for mustard, which he decided to market.

Now the plot (not to mention the soup) thickens. Nearby stood an abandoned glass factory, so Smith got the bright idea to adopt it and manufacture his own containers for the mustard. This he did, whereupon he became so absorbed in the concepts of glass making that in no time at all lines of Smith glass were on the popular market. For a man starting from scratch he cooked up quite a business by 1911, or so they say, before he up and left, all of a sudden, for some other new kitchen. Whatever became of the mustard idea, they don't say.

In his brief career as glassmaker, he is said to have invented the glass top for percolators, the modern-style juice reamer, the first glass mixing bowl, and other kitchen implements—no doubt a throwback to his salad days!

The firm has been in other hands since, but the subsequent owners never changed the name because "it was always such an easy name to spell."

Besides the cooking articles, the factory at first made fruit jars, tableware, novelties, and some of initial automobile lenses. 20s and 30s production centered around black glass items, colorful occasional pieces and dinnerware lines—and always included the company's special patented fishbowl.

Through the years the Smith product has been largely hand-crafted, and many lines still are today. At present the firm continues to make assortments of table- and giftwares for a national market.

COLOR

Smith's color broke out all at once in the mid-20s: green, amber, canary, amethyst, and blue in 1926; pink in the following year. We remember the company best, though, for its black glass production which began in the late 20s and continued for several years. It was perhaps the largest body of black glass sold by any company at that time, and we find much of it to collect today.

LEMON JUICER AND CUP

UNIVERSAL
PERCOLATOR
TOP

NO. 3
WALL SAFETY
MATCH

SANITARY SUGAR BOWL

Some unique items from a mid-20s catalog. The aquarium was widely advertised for many years.

GLASS SANITARY DRINKING FOUNTAIN
FOR CHICKS OR FOWLS

Height 7 inches; Width of Base 6½ inches; Capacity 1 quart

THE Cleanest and Best Fountain made. Transparent—water in sight—easily filled. Shows at a glance whether or not chicks are getting clean water, and how much there is of it. Owing to its rounding top chicks cannot roost on it, which prevents getting droppings in the water. Is more sanitary and keeps the water cool longer in warm weather than founts made of tin or galvanized iron. New and superior to any metal or earthen fountain.

NINE INCH CRUCIFIX
CANDLE STICK
GOLD DECORATED

FIVE INCH
CRUCIFIX
CANDLE STICK
GOLD DECORATED

Smart and Useful!
THE L. E. SMITH GLASS CO.
Offers their new
King-Fish Aquarium
Practical $\left(\begin{smallmatrix}\text{Patent}\\\text{Applied for}\end{smallmatrix}\right)$ Sanitary

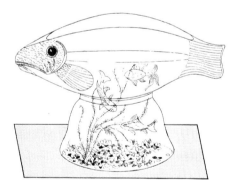

Fish Are Happy Swimming In This Large Roomy Bowl

Size 15 in. long, 10 in. high — Opening at Top 5x11 in.

Colors: GREEN OR CRYSTAL

SANITARY BUTTER CONTAINER

HOLDS ONE POUND PRINT OF BUTTER
A REFRIGERATOR NECESSITY

314

Manufactured by **L. E. SMITH GLASS COMPANY, Mount Pleasant, Pa.**

No. 1937 Jumbo Soda
8 in. high,
3 in. diameter at top.

No. 1940 Parfait
5¼ in. high,
2¼ in. diameter at top.

No. 1938 Tulip Sundae
5⅝ in. high
4 in. diameter at top.

No. 1945 Tulip Sundae
6 in. high,
4 in. diameter at top.

Smith's Sanitary Sugar Pour
Illustrated Half Size

No. 1939 Low Sundae
3 in. high,
4 in. diameter at top.

No. 1942 Banana Split
2¼ in. high,
7¼ in. diameter at top.

No. 1946 Napkin Holder
4 in. by 2¼ in.
4¼ in high.

No. 509 Ash Tray
5 in. diameter.

No. 1000 Ash Tray
5 in diameter.

No. 503 Ash Tray
6½ in. diameter.

"SODA SHOP" —*mid-20s brochure*

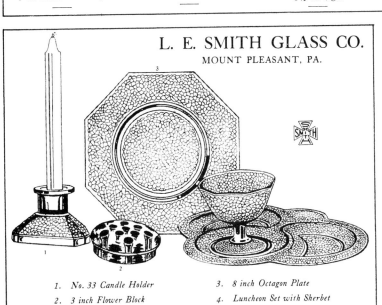

L. E. SMITH GLASS CO.
MOUNT PLEASANT, PA.

1. No. 33 Candle Holder
2. 3 inch Flower Block
3. 8 inch Octagon Plate
4. Luncheon Set with Sherbet

MADE IN CRYSTAL, CANARY AND AMBER

"BY CRACKY"

Besides the colors listed in this late-20s brochure, the pattern was made in green. More pieces are shown on the next page.

"HOMESTEAD"

In the early 30s Smith made "HOMESTEAD" in pink, green, amber and black. The cup and saucer are #193 in Book I, and other pieces are 8" and 11½" plates, 9" grill plate, cream & sugar, 4½" tumbler, sherbet on tray.

L. E. SMITH GLASS CO., Mount Pleasant, Pa.

NO. 707 40-PIECE DINNER SET

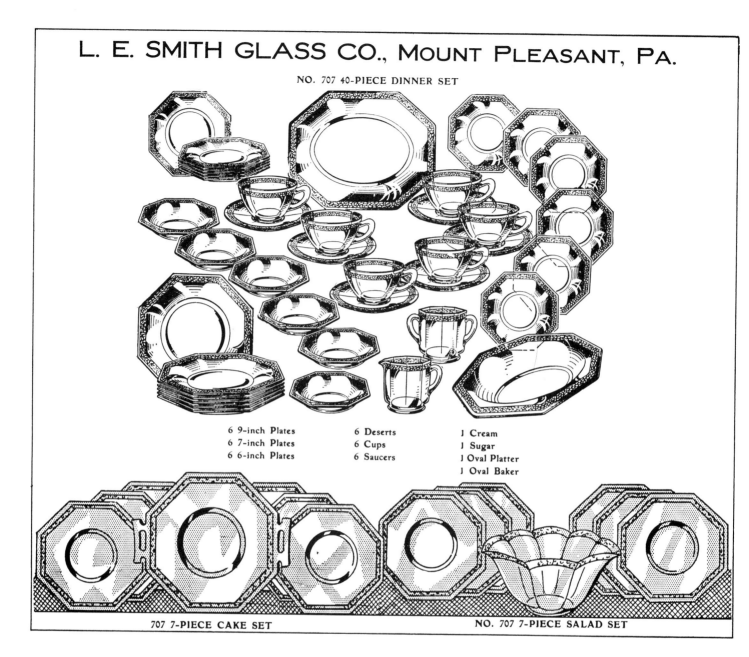

6 9-inch Plates	6 Deserts	1 Cream
6 7-inch Plates	6 Cups	1 Sugar
6 6-inch Plates	6 Saucers	1 Oval Platter
		1 Oval Baker

707 7-PIECE CAKE SET **NO. 707 7-PIECE SALAD SET**

"MELBA"

Made in pink, green, amethyst, and black in the early 30s, "MELBA" is shown above as it was presented in a company brochure (the vegetable bowl is 9½", the handled serving plate is 9" and is also found with the ship motif in the center). Then, in the photo below, the line is shown again with the candleholder and 10½" ruffled bowl included. Pieces #78 in Book I also have the "MELBA" design.

No. 100. 12 inch Oct. Bowl and Base.

No. 105. Candy Jar.

2 Piece Luncheon Set.

More pieces in the "BY CRACKY" and "ROMANESQUE" lines are on this page from a company catalog, along with other items.

No. 100 Octagon Plate.

Footed Cake Plate.

Octagon Crackled Plate.

No. 100. Round Plate.

No. 91. Cake Plate.

Round Crackled Plate.

No. 88. Sherbet.
Octagon or Round.

Tea Cup.

No. 30. Candy Box.

No. 110
Candleholder.

No. 77. Violet Bowl
and Flower Block.

No. 133
Candleholder.

No. 100. Fan Vase.

· THE ABOVE ITEMS ARE MADE IN AMBER, GREEN, CANARY AND CRYSTAL.

"ROMANESQUE"

This tableware line was made in canary, pink, green, amber and crystal in the late 20s. Here is the listing of pieces so far: plates, both octagonal and round; 10½" console bowl on base; candleholders; sherbet; 7½" fan vase; and the handled cake plate with ship motif.

27 PIECES

8—8" PLATES
8—6" SAUCERS
8—TEA CUPS
1—CREAM
1—SUGAR
1 TWO-HANDLED CAKE PLATE

The above Sets can be had with Early American Crystal Creamers, Sugars and Cups or Illuminated as above with all Black Creamers, Sugars, and Cups.

"DO-SI-DO"

This line was offered all black or mixed black-with-crystal. The original ad (about 1930) mixed things up even further, didn't it?

"MOUNT PLEASANT"

At least part of the "MOUNT PLEASANT" pattern is pictured here; it was made in black, blue, pink, and amber in the early 30s. There are two styles of candlestick; other pieces include the cream & sugar, salt & pepper-on-a-tray set, handled bowl footed nappy, and 8" plate. A ruffled console bowl (not shown) with a 4" flower block inside is another piece. This line was variously decorated, as were most Smith black items, usually in silver.

NO. 1—COOKIE JAR
BLACK GLASS WITH FANCY DECORATION

NO. 3—COOKIE JAR
CAPACITY—NINE POUNDS
BLACK GLASS WITH FANCY DECORATIONS

NO. 4 COOKIE JAR
BLACK GLASS WITH FANCY DECORATION

L. E. SMITH GLASS COMPANY

These are loose pages of an early but undated L. E. Smith sales catalog.

SILVER-ON-BLACK ASS'T

FLORAL ASS'T

No. 2. 3 Footed Fern Bowl
White Dresden Dec.
Packed 4 doz.
Wt. 50 lbs.

No. 525. 3 Footed Flared Bon Bon Dish
White Dresden Dec.
Packed 3 doz.
Wt. 35 lbs.

No. 525. 3 Footed Triangle Bowl
White Dresden Dec.
Packed 3 doz.
Wt. 35 lbs.

No. 635. Footed Square Mayonnaise Bowl
White Dresden Dec.
Packed 3 doz.
Wt. 35 lbs.

No. 505 Salt and Pepper Shaker
White Dresden Dec.
Packed 6 doz.
Wt. 15 lbs.

No. 93. 11½" Fancy Crystal Relish Dish
Packed 3 doz., Wt. 45 lbs.

Most all Smith items made in black were made in blue as well, and sometimes in opaque white. This page is from an early 30s catalog.

No. 600. Double Candlestick Holder
Black or Blue
Packed 4 doz., Wt. 55 lbs.

No. 2400. 2 Handled Footed Fruit Bowl
Black or Blue
Packed 2 doz., Wt. 65 lbs.

No. 1022. 3 Footed Console Bowl
Black or Blue
Packed 2 doz., Wt. 55 lbs.

No. 49. Crimped Top 2 Handled Footed Vase
Black with Silver Dec.
Packed 4 doz.
Wt. 45 lbs.

No. 102. Fancy 2 Handled Vase
Black with Silver Dec.
Packed 4 doz.
Wt. 60 lbs.

No. 1900. Flared Top 2 Handled Footed Vase
Black or Blue
Packed 2 doz.
Wt. 50 lbs.

No. 432/5. Fancy Crimped Top 2 Handled Footed Vase
Black or Blue
Packed 2 doz.
Wt. 33 lbs.

No. 433. Fancy Crimped Top 2 Handled Footed Vase
Black or Blue
Packed 2 doz.
Wt. 40 lbs.

No. 85. Hobnail Footed Ivy Ball

No. 1. 3 Footed Fern Bowl

No. 2400. 2 Handled Footed Bon Bon Dish

No. 1000 Cockerel Ash Tray

No. 1000 Scotty Dog Ash Tray

No. 66. Flower Pot and Saucer
Black with Silver Dec.

L. E. SMITH GLASS COMPANY

No. 3/10
SWAN DISH

No. 15/10
SWAN DISH

No. 50/10
5¾" BULB BOWL

No. 805/10
CANDLESTICK

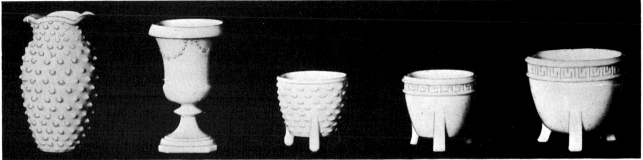

No. 99/10
HOBNAIL VASE

No. 800/10
FOOTED URN VASE

No. 2—H/10
FERN BOWL

No. 2/10
FERN BOWL

No. 1/10
5¼" FERN BOWL

No. 405/10
WINDOW BOX
7¾" x 3½" x 3½"

No. 9/10
WINDOW BOX
7⅛" x 3⅛" x 2¾"

No. 525—H/10
TRIANGLE BOWL

No. 77/10
VIOLET BOWL AND BLOCK

No. 710/4
6" VASE
Silver Bands

No. 303/4
4" FLOWER POT
Silver Decorated

No. 67/4
4" FLOWER POT
Silver Decorated

No. 66/4
4" FLOWER POT
Silver Bands

No. 201/4
3" FLOWER POT

No. 301/4 Saucer to Match

No. 67/4 Saucer to Match

No. 66/4 Saucer to Match

No. 201/4 Saucer to Match

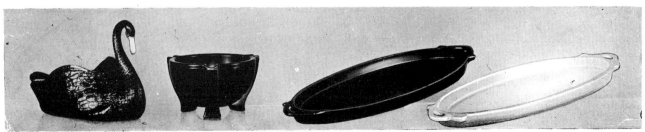

No. 3/4
SWAN DISH
Silver Decorated

No. 90/4
ASH TRAY

No. 65/4
COCKTAIL TRAY
15" x 6"

No. 65
CRYSTAL COCKTAIL TRAY
15" x 6"

—about 1930

SPECIAL LISTING

No. 1/4
5¼" FERN BOWL
Silver Bands

No. 2/4
FERN BOWL
Silver Bands

No. 2—H/4
FERN BOWL

No. 77—H/4
VIOLET BOWL AND BLOCK

No. 4/4
FLOWER BLOCK

No. 600/4
5¾" x 4½"
TWIN CANDLE HOLDER

No. 1022/4
9" CONSOLE BOWL

No. 600/4
5¾" x 4½"
TWIN CANDLE HOLDER

No. 805/4
CANDLE HOLDER

No. 27/4
CANDLESTICK
Silver Bands

No. 99—H/4
8" VASE

No. 800/4
7½" FOOTED
URN VASE

No. 433/4—F
7" VASE

No. 433/4—C
7" VASE

No. 102/4
6¼" VASE
Silver Bands

No. 1620/4
ASH TRAY

No. 1000/4
5" ASH TRAY
Silver Decorated

No. 1000/4
5" ASH TRAY
Silver Decorated

No. 1000—P
5" ASH TRAY

No. 365/4
3" ASH TRAY
Rooster or dog decoration
Silver Decorated

No. 405/4
WINDOW BOX
7¾" x 3½" x 3½"

No. 9/4
WINDOW BOX
7⅛" x 3⅛" x 2¾"

No. 50/4
5¾" BULB BOWL

No. 525—H/4
TRIANGLE BOWL

—early 30s catalog pages

No. 505
One Handled Sandwich Tray
10″ Diameter

No. 505
Two Handled Salad Bowl
8″ Diameter—3½″ High

No. 505
One Handled Nut
8¼″ Diameter

No. 505
Two Handled Salad Tray
10½″ Diameter

No. 309
Flared Console Bowl
12½″ Diameter

No. 309
Cupped Bowl
8¼″ Diameter—5½″ High

No. 327
Cupped Bowl
6¼″ Diameter—5″ High

No. 404
Window Box and Block
8″ Long—3¾″ Wide—3¾″ Hi

No. 515
Footed Nut Bowl
9″ Diameter

No. 1
Fern Bowl
6¼″ Diameter—5½″ High

No. 515
Footed Cake
10½″ Diameter

No. 515
Footed Cupped Bowl
7″ Diameter—3¾″ High

No. 1000
Flared Vase
11″ Diameter—6″ High

No. 1000
Cupped Vase
6½″ Diameter—7¾″ High

No. 1000
Fan Vase
10″ Diameter—8″ High

No. 1931
Vase
4½″ Diameter—7¾″ High

THE L. E. SMITH GLASS COMPANY · Mount Pleasant, Pa.

No. 309/38.   3-piece Crimped Console Set, Crystal
Packed 1 set to carton

No. 982.   3-piece Console Set, Crystal
Packed 1 set to carton

No. 982.   7-piece Console Set, Crystal
Packed 1 set to carton

No. 1/18.   3-piece Console Set, Crystal with Prisms
Packed 1 set to carton

No. 1/308.   3-piece Console Set, Crystal with Prisms
Packed 1 set to carton

—catalog page about 1930

"WIG-WAM"

*Drawing of
console bowl pattern
from preceding page;
see also in color section.*

No. 208 ROOSTER
9″ High

—1935 brochure

PUT PUNCH INTO YOUR SELLING

Dollar Items Will Do It—We Have Them

Quality and Price. Seven-Piece Dresser Set.

CRYSTAL and color combinations in Colonial design are extremely popular. Here is a seven-piece dresser set to meet that demand at $1. A retailer of real merit. The pebbled surface is unusually attractive. The set consists of tray, powder box and cover and two bottles, each with ground-in stopper. Available in crystal and black, crystal and green and crystal and pink. Packed one set to a carton and 12 sets to the shipping case. No repacking necessary.

Another exceptional Dollar Retailer which has seasonal appeal is the vase shown to the right. Made in smooth finish black glass with decorations, hand applied, in fired silver. It is 10 inches high and most appealing in design. Packed six to the carton.

Our line includes many other items to retail most profitably at $1. Ask us about them.

▼

L. E. SMITH
GLASS COMPANY

MOUNT PLEASANT, PENNA.

Quality and Price. No. 905 Vase, 10 Inches

"PUNCH" Dresser Set, 1932 ad

The
L.E. SMITH
Glass Company

Manufacturers of Pressed Glassware
MOUNT PLEASANT, PA.
Telephones 2341 — 2919

Black Silver Decorated Items

No. 49. Crimped Black Silver Dec. Vase
Carton 4 dozen, 40 lbs.

No. 432. Crimped Black Silver Dec. Vase
Carton 1 dozen, 35 lbs.

No. 1000. Black Ash Tray
w/ Silver Dec. "Scotty"
Carton 6 dozen, 40 lbs.

No. 1000. Black Ash Tray
w/ Silver Dec. "Cockerel"
Carton 6 dozen, 40 lbs.

No. 2. Black 3-Footed Jardiniere
Carton 4 dozen, 55 lbs.

4″ Black Flower Block
Carton 6 dozen, 75 lbs.

No. 1. Black 3-Footed Jardiniere
Carton 1½ dozen, 45 lbs.

12 oz. Crystal Polished Bottom Beer Mug
Carton 8 dozen, 50 lbs.

—early 30s catalog

325

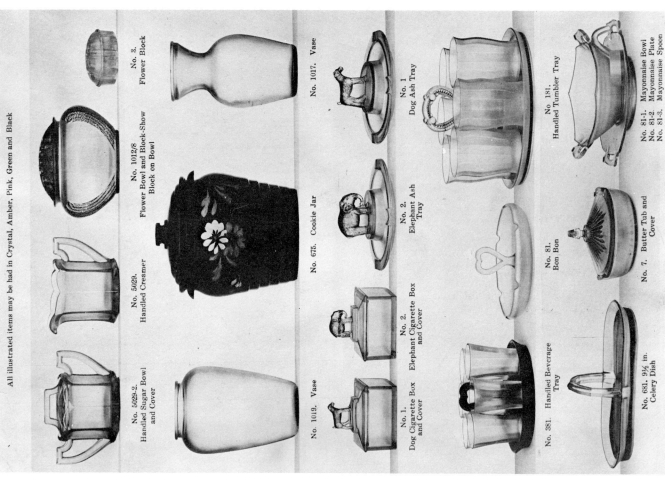

All illustrated items may be had in Crystal, Amber, Pink, Green and Black

No. 3.
Flower Block

No. 1012/8
Flower Bowl and Block-Show
Block on Bowl

No. 1017. Vase

No. 1
Dog Ash Tray

No 181.
Handled Tumbler Tray

Mayonnaise Bowl
Mayonnaise Plate
Mayonnaise Spoon

No. 5029.
Handled Creamer

No. 675. Cookie Jar

No. 2.
Elephant Ash
Tray

No. 81.
Bon Bon

No. 81-1.
No. 81-2.
No. 81-3.

No. 5029-2.
Handled Sugar Bowl
and Cover

No. 2.
Elephant Cigarette Box
and Cover

No. 7.
Butter Tub and
Cover

No. 1019. Vase

No. 1.
Dog Cigarette Box
and Cover

No. 381. Handled Beverage
Tray

No. 681. 9½ in.
Celery Dish

GREENSBURG GLASS WORKS

GREENSBURG, PENNSYLVANIA

All illustrated items may be had in Crystal, Amber, Pink, Green and Black.

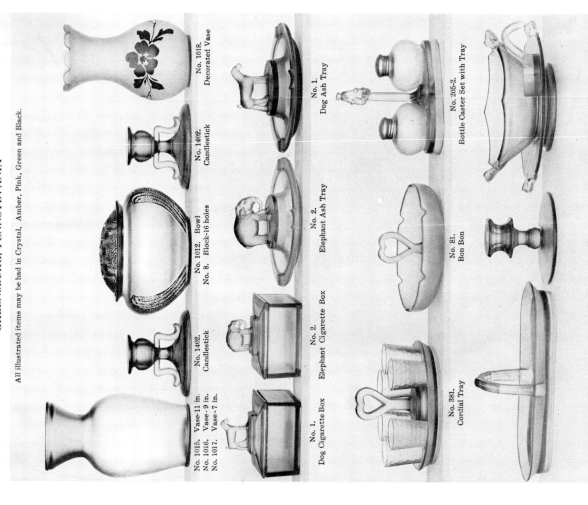

No. 1018.
Decorated Vase

No. 1402.
Candlestick

No. 1
Dog Ash Tray

No. 205-2.
Bottle Caster Set with Tray

No. 81-1. Mayonnaise Bowl
No. 81-2. Mayonnaise Plate
No. 81-3. Mayonnaise Ladle

No. 1012. Bowl
No. 8. Block-16 holes

No. 2.
Elephant Ash Tray

No. 81.
Bon Bon

No. 1002.
Candlesticks

No. 1015. Vase-11 in.
No. 1016. Vase- 9 in.
No. 1017. Vase- 7 in.

No. 1402.
Candlestick

No. 2.
Elephant Cigarette Box

No. 1.
Dog Cigarette Box

No. 381.
Cordial Tray

No. 681-9½ in.
Celery Dish

Greensburg was acquired by Smith during the period so its wares will be included here.

326

Standard

Standard Glass Manufacturing Company—with two plants at Bremen and Canal Winchester near Lancaster, Ohio—came into being as a subsidiary of Hocking Glass Company when Hocking's big "Black Cat" Plant #1 burned to the ground in 1924. It and Lancaster Glass Company, another main branch of Hocking acquired at the same time, were immediately employed to fill the orders while a major new plant was being built.

Afterwards Standard's Depression-era activity was directed, as was Lancaster's, to cutting and etching fanciful designs onto handmade colored ware, while the main Hocking effort at the new plant expanded the potential of machine-made glass. A comparison will show that the blanks used at both subsidiaries were for the most part the same, and the sales of both were handled by Hocking. Yet it seems convenient for our purposes to group the designs by these different factories into respective chapters.

Standard's two old plants have been known simply as Plants #11 and #12 of Anchor Hocking Corporation since 1940, and continue as such today.

COLOR

The same colors were in evidence at all the Hocking hand plants at about the same time: green, blue, and canary in 1925; deep rose pink in 1926; topaz in 1930; pale blue and black in 1931. Quite possibly short runs of other colors were made here through the years.

19 PIECE MARTHA WASHINGTON LUNCHEON SET

TOPAZ CUT 89
Try to match this value in any other gift item at double the price

The Gift Supreme

FOUR SALAD PLATES
FOUR CUPS
FOUR SAUCERS
FOUR FOOTED TUMBLERS
ONE SUGAR
ONE CREAMER
ONE SANDWICH PLATE

Each Set Packed in an Individual Carton Weight 16 lbs.

THE STANDARD GLASS MFG. CO.   LANCASTER, OHIO

MARTHA WASHINGTON
Pink, topaz: 1930 brochure

CATALOG REPRINTS
The following pages are reprints of company sales material from 1925 to 1932. You may find colors besides those listed.

327

The Standard Glass Mfg. Co., Lancaster, Ohio

729—6" Plate Cut 230

33—Sherbet Cut 230
729—6" Plate Cut 230

G25—Shaker
Chome N. T.
Cut 23

131—High Ftd. Sherbet
729—6" Plate

65—21½ oz.
Beverage Cut 6

61—9 oz.
Tumbler Cut 6

68—12 oz.
Ice Tea Cut 6

69—15 oz.
Ice Tea Cut 6

G305—5 oz.
Fruit Juice
Cut 6

G308—10 oz.
Tumbler Cut 6

G306—13 oz.
Ice Tea Cut 6

G280—80 oz. Jug Cut 23

G34—56 oz. Jug Cut 23

54—56 oz. Jug

CRYSTAL CUT 92

740—8" Plate

188—15 oz.
Ftd. Ice Tea

181—10 oz.
Ftd. Tumbler

142—9½ oz.
Tall Goblet

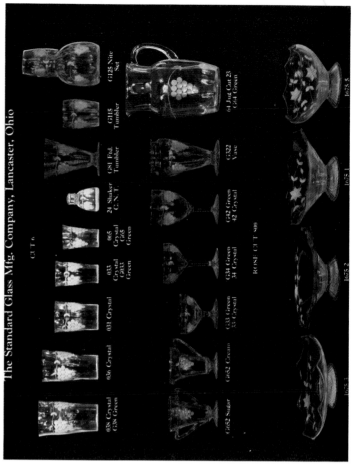

The Standard Glass Mfg. Company, Lancaster, Ohio

CUT 6

038 Crystal
G38 Green

G62 Sugar

036 Crystal

G62 Cream

031 Crystal

G33 Green
34 Crystal

033
Crystal
G33
Green

065
Crystal
G65
Green

G34 Green
34 Crystal

24 Shaker
C.N.T.

081 Ftd.
Tumbler

G42 Green
42 Crystal

G115
Tumbler

G322
Vase

G125 Nite
Set

64 Jug Cut 23
G64 Green

ROSE CUT 800

1075.5

1075.1

1075.2

1075.3

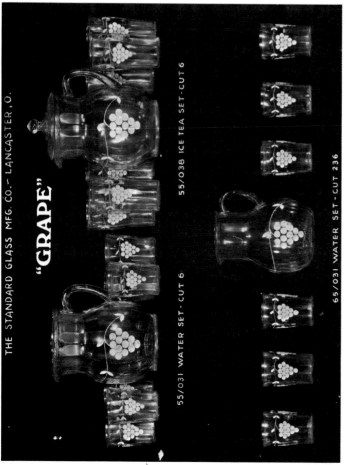

THE STANDARD GLASS MFG. CO. ~ LANCASTER, O.

"GRAPE"

55/038 ICE TEA SET - CUT 6

55/031 WATER SET - CUT 6

65/031 WATER SET - CUT 236

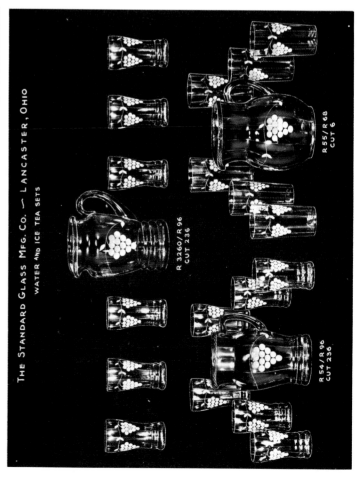

THE STANDARD GLASS MFG. CO. ~ LANCASTER, OHIO

WATER AND ICE TEA SETS

R 3260/R 96
CUT 236

R 55/R 68
CUT 6

R 54/R 96
CUT 236.

328

THE STANDARD GLASS MFG. CO., LANCASTER, O.
ROSE—CUT 6
"GRAPE"

R-23—SALT
CHROME NIC. TOP

R-23—PEPPER
CHROME NIC. TOP

R-42
GOBLET

R-33—SHERBET
R-729—6" PLATE

R-88
FTD. ICE TEA

R-53
SUGAR

R-53
CREAM

R-32
COCKTAIL

R-80
FTD. FRUIT JUICE

R-34
SUNDAE

R-81
FTD. TUMBLER

R 740
8" PLATE

THE STANDARD GLASS MFG. CO., LANCASTER, OHIO
TOPAZ—CUT 6

T-303—5 OZ. FRUIT JUICE

T-306—10 OZ. TUMBLER

T-308—12 OZ. ICE TEA

T-181—10 OZ. FOOTED TUMBLER

T-53 SUGAR

T-53 CREAMER

T-112—9 OZ. BARREL TUMBLER

T-134 HIGH SHERBET
T-729—6" PLATE

T-54—57 OZ. JUG

T-179—CUP
T-729—SAUCER

T-729—6" PLATE

T-23 SHAKERS CHROME N.T.

T-740—6" PLATE

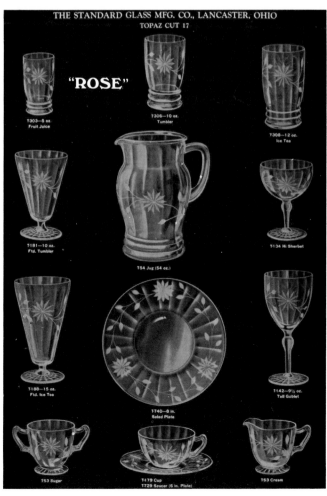

THE STANDARD GLASS MFG. CO., LANCASTER, OHIO
TOPAZ CUT 17
"ROSE"

T303—5 oz. Fruit Juice

T306—10 oz. Tumbler

T308—12 oz. Ice Tea

T181—10 oz. Ftd. Tumbler

T54 Jug (54 oz.)

T134 Hi Sherbet

T188—15 oz. Ftd. Ice Tea

T740—8 in. Salad Plate

T142—9½ oz. Tall Goblet

T53 Sugar

T179 Cup
T729 Saucer (6 in. Plate)

T53 Cream

CUT 3001

3511—6 oz. 3512—7 oz. 3513—8 oz. 3514—10 oz. 3515—12 oz.

CUT 2

3353—5 oz. 3351—9 oz. 3356—13 oz. 3358—15 oz. R720/1—Bowl Cut 400

CUT 6

3305—2½ oz. 3303—5 oz. 3301—9 oz. 3306—12 oz. 22 Footed Sherbet
131—6 Sherbet Plate

THE STANDARD GLASS MFG. CO.
LANCASTER, OHIO

G380-G309 ICE TEA SET
CUT 236

ONE 80-OUNCE JUG
SIX 15-OUNCE ICE TEAS

Packed Each Set in Chip Carton,
6 Chips to Outer Reshipper
Weight 35 Pounds

THE STANDARD GLASS MFG. CO., LANCASTER, OHIO

3

No. 380 Crystal Assortment
Cut 38

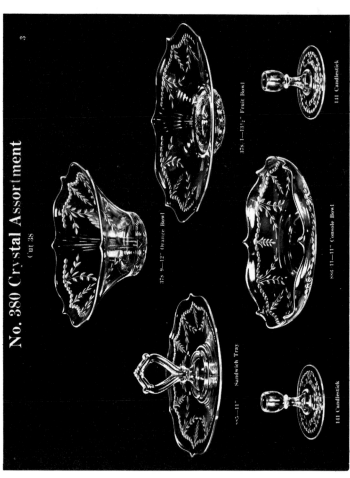

378   9—12″ Orange Bowl

378 4—13½″ Fruit Bowl

886   11—11″ Console Bowl

—5—11″ Sandwich Tray

141 Candlestick

141 Candlestick

5

G300/3—17 Piece
Refreshment Set
Green Cut 6

Composition
One G380—80 oz. Jug
Eight G308—12 oz. Ice Teas
Eight G303—5 oz. Fruit Juice Glasses

THE STANDARD GLASS MFG. CO., LANCASTER, OHIO

"GREAT NORTHERN PRODUCTS CO. ~ CHICAGO, ILL."
GENUINE ROCK CRYSTAL
CUT 7

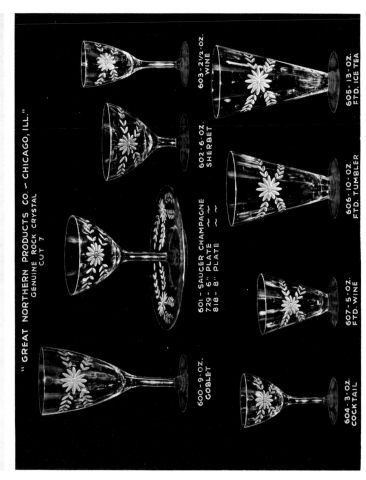

603 - 2½ - OZ.
WINE

605 - 13 - OZ.
FTD. ICE TEA

602 - 6 - OZ.
SHERBET

606 - 10 - OZ.
FTD. TUMBLER

501 - SAUCER CHAMPAGNE
729 - 6″ PLATE ~ ~
818 - 8″ PLATE ~ ~

607 - 5 - OZ.
FTD. WINE

600 - 9 - OZ.
GOBLET

604 - 3 - OZ.
COCKTAIL

330

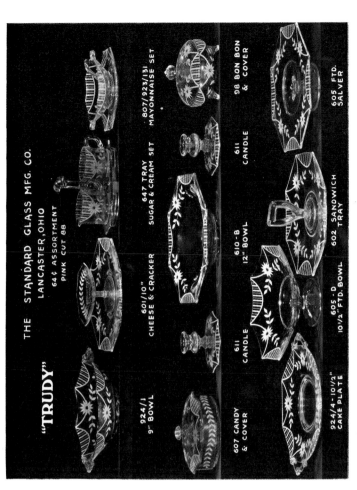

THE STANDARD GLASS MFG. CO.~ LANCASTER, OHIO.
"TRUDY"

64¢ ASSORTMENT
PINK CUT 88

924/I
9" BOWL

601/10"
CHEESE & CRACKER

647 TRAY
SUGAR & CREAM SET

807/923/131
MAYONNAISE SET

98 BON BON
& COVER

607 CANDY
& COVER

611
CANDLE

610-B
12" BOWL

611
CANDLE

605 FTD.
SALVER

602 SANDWICH
TRAY

924/4 - 10½"
CAKE PLATE

605 - D
10½" FTD. BOWL

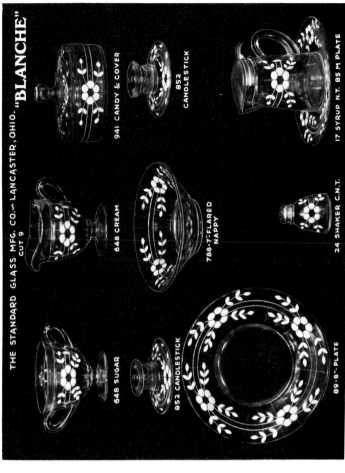

THE STANDARD GLASS MFG. CO.~ LANCASTER, OHIO. "BLANCHE"
CUT 9

941 CANDY & COVER

852
CANDLESTICK

17 SYRUP N.T. 85 M PLATE

648 CREAM

788-7" FLARED
NAPPY

24 SHAKER C.N.T.

648 SUGAR

852 CANDLESTICK

89-8" PLATE

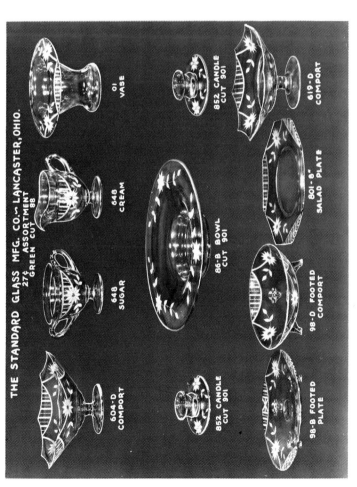

THE STANDARD GLASS MFG. CO.~ LANCASTER, OHIO.
27¢ ASSORTMENT
GREEN CUT 88

604-D
COMPORT

648
SUGAR

648
CREAM

01
VASE

852 CANDLE
CUT 901

86-B BOWL
CUT 901

852 CANDLE
CUT 901

98-D FOOTED
PLATE

98-D FOOTED
COMPORT

801-6"
SALAD PLATE

619-D
COMPORT

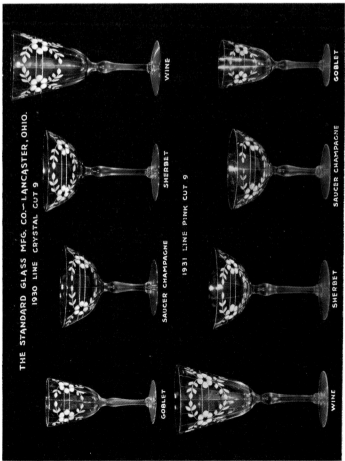

THE STANDARD GLASS MFG. CO.~ LANCASTER, OHIO.
1930 LINE CRYSTAL CUT 9

WINE

GOBLET

SHERBET

SAUCER CHAMPAGNE

SAUCER CHAMPAGNE

1931 LINE PINK CUT 9

SHERBET

GOBLET

WINE

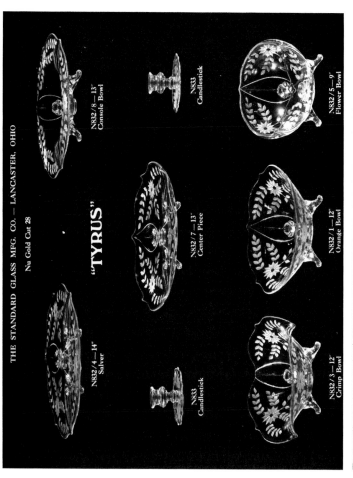

THE STANDARD GLASS MFG. CO. — LANCASTER, OHIO

Nu Gold Cut 28

"TYRUS"

N832/8—13" Console Bowl

N833 Candlestick

N832/5—9" Flower Bowl

N832/7—13" Center Piece

N832/1—12" Orange Bowl

N832/4—14" Salver

N833 Candlestick

N832/3—12" Crimp Bowl

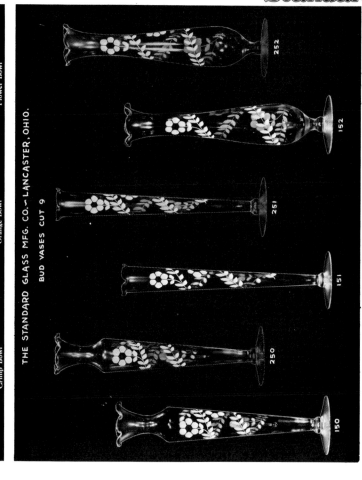

THE STANDARD GLASS MFG. CO.— LANCASTER, OHIO.

BUD VASES CUT 9

252 · 152 · 251 · 151 · 250 · 150

"FAITH" No. 2000 Topaz Assortment

Cut 200

T832/4—13½" Cake Stand

T879—3 Pce. Tray, Sugar and Cream Set

T833 Candlestick

T832/7—13" Sandwich Plate

T893—13" Sandwich Tray

T832/11—12" Console Bowl

T832/1—11" Orange Bowl

T833 Candlestick

THE STANDARD GLASS MFG. CO., LANCASTER, OHIO

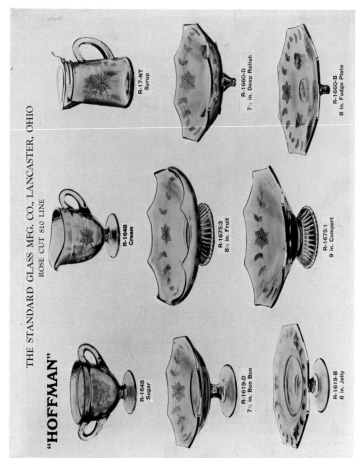

THE STANDARD GLASS MFG. CO., LANCASTER, OHIO

ROSE CUT 810 LINE

"HOFFMAN"

R-17-NT Syrup

R-1660-D 7½ in. Deep Relish

R-1660-B 8 in. Fudge Plate

R-1648 Cream

R-1675-3 8½ in. Fruit

R-1675-1 9 in. Comport

R-1648 Sugar

R-1619-D 7½ in. Bon Bon

R-1619-B 8 in. Jelly

332

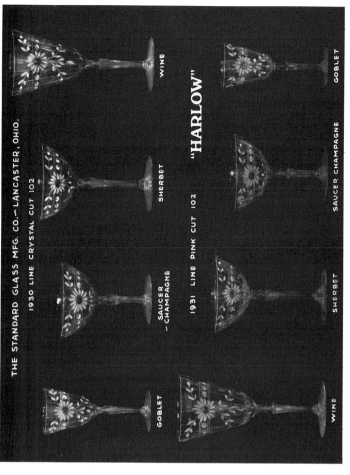

THE STANDARD GLASS MFG. CO. — LANCASTER, OHIO.

1930 LINE CRYSTAL CUT 102

1931 LINE PINK CUT 102

"HARLOW"

WINE

GOBLET

SHERBET

SAUCER ~ CHAMPAGNE

SHERBET

SAUCER CHAMPAGNE

GOBLET

WINE

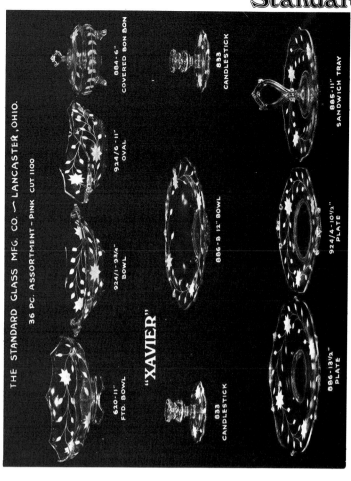

THE STANDARD GLASS MFG. CO. — LANCASTER, OHIO.

36 PC. ASSORTMENT ~ PINK CUT 1100

"XAVIER"

884 · 6" COVERED BON BON

833 CANDLESTICK

885 · 11" SANDWICH TRAY

924/6 · 11" OVAL

886 · B 12" BOWL

924/4 · 10½" PLATE

924/1 · 9¾" BOWL

620 · 11" FTD. BOWL

833 CANDLESTICK

886 · 13½" PLATE

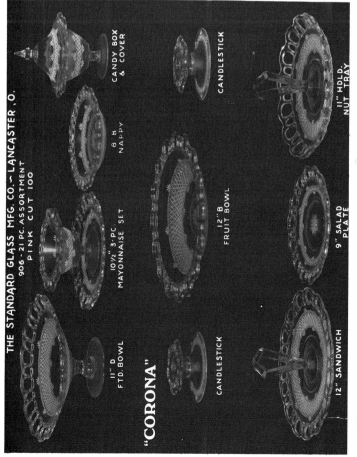

THE STANDARD GLASS MFG. CO. — LANCASTER, O.

906 · 21 PC. ASSORTMENT
PINK CUT 100

"CORONA"

CANDY BOX & COVER

8 B NAPPY

11" HDLD. NUT TRAY

CANDLESTICK

10½" 3 · PC. MAYONNAISE SET

12" B FRUIT BOWL

9" SALAD PLATE

11" D FTD. BOWL

CANDLESTICK

12" SANDWICH

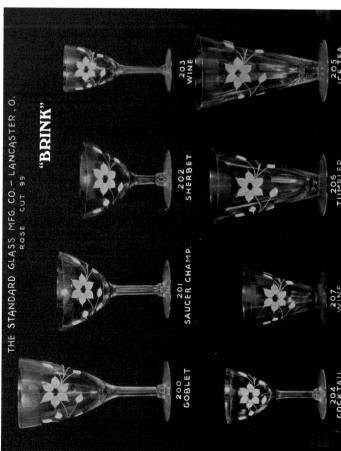

THE STANDARD GLASS MFG. CO. — LANCASTER, O.

ROSE CUT 99

"BRINK"

200 GOBLET

201 SAUCER CHAMP.

202 SHERBET

203 WINE

204 COCKTAIL

207 WINE

206 TUMBLER

205 ICE TEA

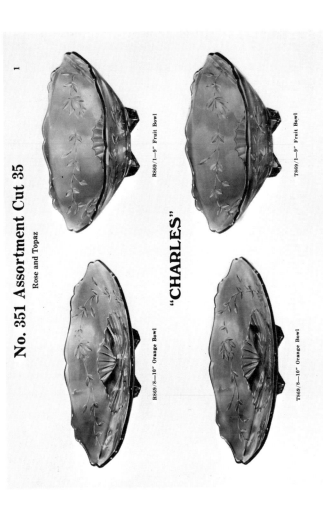

No. 351 Assortment Cut 35
Rose and Topaz

"CHARLES"

R869/1—9" Fruit Bowl

T869/1—9" Fruit Bowl

R869/8—10" Orange Bowl

T869/8—10" Orange Bowl

THE STANDARD GLASS MFG. CO., LANCASTER, OHIO

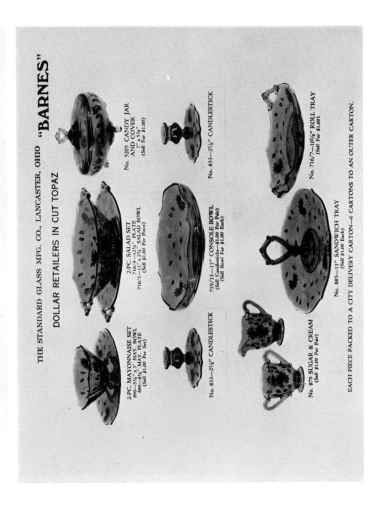

"BARNES"

DOLLAR RETAILERS IN CUT TOPAZ

THE STANDARD GLASS MFG. CO., LANCASTER, OHIO

No. 5205 CANDY JAR
AND COVER
(Sell For $1.00)

2-PC. SALAD SET
716/4—12½" PLATE
716/1—11 x 2¼ SALAD BOWL
(Sell $1.00 Per Piece)

No. 833—2½" CANDLESTICK

No. 716/7—10¼" ROLL TRAY
(Sell For $1.00)

2-PC. MAYONNAISE SET
890—3¾ x 3" MAY. BOWL
889—8½" MAY. PLATE
(Sell $1.00 Per Set)

719/11—11" CONSOLE BOWL
(Sell Bowl For $1.00 Each)
(Sell Candlesticks—$1.00 Per Pair)

No. 833—2½" CANDLESTICK

No. 879 SUGAR & CREAM
(Sell $1.00 Per Pair)

No. 885—11" SANDWICH TRAY
(Sell $1.00 Each)

EACH PIECE PACKED TO A CITY DELIVERY CARTON—6 CARTONS TO AN OUTER CARTON.

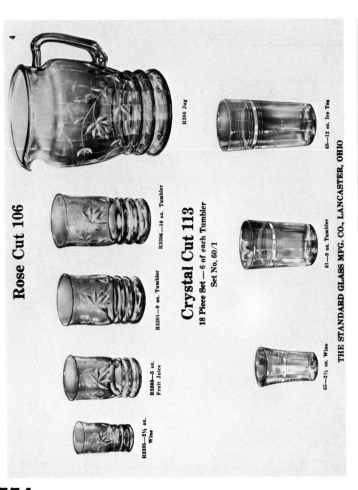

Rose Cut 106

R3305—2½ oz. Wine

R3303—5 oz. Fruit Juice

R3301—9 oz. Tumbler

R3306—10 oz. Tumbler

R380 Jug

Crystal Cut 113
18 Piece Set — 6 of each Tumbler
Set No. 60/1

65—2½ oz. Wine

61—9 oz. Tumbler

63—12 oz. Ice Tea

THE STANDARD GLASS MFG. CO., LANCASTER, OHIO

"YUMMY"

THE STANDARD GLASS MFG. CO., LANCASTER, OHIO

FLOWER, FRUIT AND CANDLE SET
378/10—4¾" VASE
378/7—13½" TRAY
833—2½" CANDLESTICK
(This 4-Piece Set Packs in a Reshipping Carton)

378/1—13" x 4"

378/1—13½" x 3¾"

378/9—11" x 4½"

EACH PIECE PACKED TO A CITY DELIVERY CARTON—6 CARTONS TO AN OUTER CARTON.

THE STANDARD GLASS MFG. CO., LANCASTER, O.
ROSE—CUT 600

"BEADLES"

R-1831/1—9" - 3 TOED BOWL

R-1831/7—9½" - 3 TOED FRUIT

R-1831/3—8½" - 3 TOED CRIMP

R-1675/1—9" FOOTED FRUIT

R-1675/3—9" FOOTED COMPORT

R-1675/5—7" FOOTED ROSE BOWL

THE STANDARD GLASS MFG. CO., LANCASTER, O.
PINK—CUT 28

832/1
12" FOOTED ORANGE BOWL

832/5
9" FOOTED FLOWER BOWL

"TWINKLE"

832/3
12" FOOTED CRIMP BOWL

832/4
14" FOOTED SALVER

832/7
13" FOOTED CENTER PIECE

832/8
13" CONSOLE BOWL

THE STANDARD GLASS MFG. CO., LANCASTER, O.
TOPAZ—CUT 77
"PAULINE"

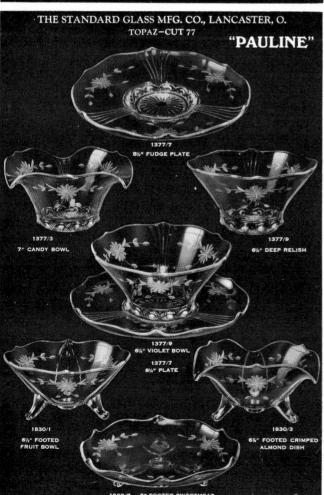

1377/7
8¼" FUDGE PLATE

1377/3
7" CANDY BOWL

1377/9
6¼" DEEP RELISH

1377/9
6¼" VIOLET BOWL

1377/7
8¼" PLATE

1830/1
6½" FOOTED FRUIT BOWL

1830/3
6¾" FOOTED CRIMPED ALMOND DISH

1830/7 8" FOOTED SWEETMEAT

THE STANDARD GLASS MFG. CO., LANCASTER, O.
ROSE—CUT 1200

"TAT"

R-1931—SHERBET
R-729—6" PLATE

R-1931 GOBLET

R-1931—SAUCER CHAMPAGNE

R-1931 WINE

R-1931 FTD. FRUIT JUICE

R-1931 FTD. TUMBLER

R-1931 FTD. ICE TEA

R-740—8" PLATE

BUD VASES ROSE—CUT 1200

BUD VASE CUT 58

R-250

R-252

R-251

59

U.S. Glass

To pin down all the dates and glass descriptions pertinent to the United States Glass Company would not be easy, for this unique firm was formed by the coming together of no less than 18 different glass factories in 1891. This was a particularly rough period in glassmaking history, and all these companies had one purpose in mind—to survive it with a combined strength.

A good idea, but with head office at Pittsburgh and body in 18 various parts over Ohio, West Virginia, and Pennsylvania, the effort was about as coordinated as an octopus trying to put a jigsaw puzzle together before the tide rushed in. All in all, one of the greatest fizzles ever charted in the glass industry!

After the combine, each limb for the most part continued to make the pressed tableware, novelties, or whatever else it had been making. Two factories were built anew and these (the automatic facility at Gas City, Indiana and the hand operation at Tiffin, Ohio) along with the Glassport, Pennsylvania and Pittsburgh plants, proved to be the important ones.

Other of the factories were lost along the way to strikes or other pressures; some (like the Duncan in Pittsburgh, which went on to become Duncan and Miller) simply dropped out, intent on a better way. Most of those managing to survive the organizational difficulties of this oversized company eventually went broke or were sold when the Depression collected its pieces of silver.

At the Tiffin plant quality ware was the goal from the beginning, and in the 20s blown stemware and delicately pressed dinnerware lines with light cutting or etching, or simply plain, were made in crystal and most all colors.

At the Gas City and Glassport functions, lines of machine-made kitchenware, dinnerware and table items were produced in canary, green, amber, pink, and black through the early 30s.

In Pittsburgh the facilities for decorating were among the most advanced any-where, and hand-decorated and painted lamps, comports, and stemware, in colored glass as well as crystal, drew much attention from the trade.

In 1938 main offices were moved to Tiffin. By then, only that and the Pittsburgh plant were left to carry on; by 1951, only Tiffin was. This it has done, more or less successfully, ever since, surviving several more crises, transfers of ownership and changes of face through the years.

In 1955 the old Duncan and Miller molds were acquired and many were produced, in crystal and new colors, by the "Duncan and Miller Division" of the United States Glass Company, Tiffin, Ohio. At one point in the 60s the business was barely kept alive by an individual who operated the molds and presses out of a garage. Continental Can owned it briefly between 1966 and 1969. The Interpace Corporation has owned it since 1969—and today the old factory is still producing crystal "by Tiffin". Its handcrafted stemware and gift items are often seen at the crest of current glass waves.

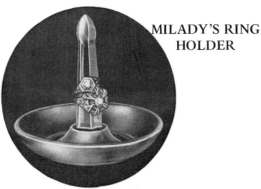

MILADY'S RING HOLDER

1922; satin finish blue, canary, black

The U. S. Glass items on this page were being advertised in these colors in 1924. You may find them in other colors.

COLOGNES
red, emerald, canary, lt. blue; also satin finish

STIPPLE: *in green; jug also comes* **CRACQUELLED** *(see below) in blue and canary.*

CENTER SERVER
satin finish jasper, amethyst, blue, canary

CHEESE AND CRACKER STAND
several colors and decorations

CRAQUEL: *crystal with green trim*

in green

satin finish blue, black, and canary

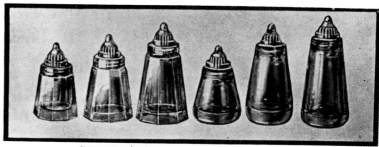

SLICK *shakers, made entirely of glass crystal or colored tops*

ECHEL

satin & brilliant finishes combined with gold bands

TAPESTRY
crystal w/ blue trim

BOUDOIR LAMP

satin finish green, blue, canary

VANITY SET
colognes and powder box in blue and amber

Stippled Glassware

At Popular Prices and With a Fall Appeal.

Made in Blue, Green, Amber and Canary.

No. 15328 Stippled Conic Candy Jar and Cover. Will retail at about $1.00.

No. 15328 Stippled 10" Cheese and Cracker. Will retail at about $1.50.

No. 15328 Stippled Handled Cake Plate. Will retail at about $1.00.

SMOKER'S TRAY: *black, green, blue; satin finish*

LEEDS: *green, red, blue; also satin finish; black bases*

FISH BOWL
blue, amber, canary

GLASS SALAD SET: *amber, green*

The U. S. Glass items this page were being advertised in these colors in 1925. You may find other colors.

"FLOWER GARDEN WITH BUTTERFLIES"

"FLOWER GARDEN WITH BUTTERFLIES" was a major tableware line made by U.S. Glass in 1925 and several years subsequent.

It was first advertised in Canary, green, blue, and amber; later it was made in pink and blue-green. We don't have the official listing but many pieces besides those shown here were offered.

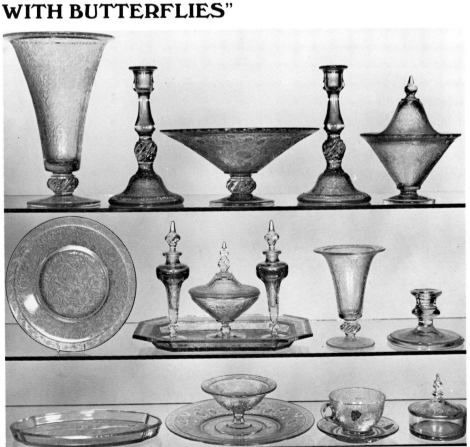

ROW 1: *10" vase, 8" candlesticks, 10" console bowl, 8" tall candy dish & cover*
ROW 2: *8" plate, dresser set (7½" colognes on 11¾"x7¾" tray), 6" vase, 3¼" candlestick*
ROW 3: *5½"x10" tray, cheese & cracker set (10" plate), cup & saucer, flat powder jar & cover*

THE PARAKEET TWINS *above and the* **PARROT** *decoration at right are somewhat different motifs. Birds are in colors; the* **PARROT** *was advertised as 20 pieces in light green satin glass.*

The U. S. Glass items on this page were being advertised in these colors in 1926. Other colors may show up as well.

wall vase, candy jar, candleholder

ENGLISH LAMP
blue, green, amber

No. 9389—3 in. Long

GALLEON: *ashtrays 3",*
6" in blue, green, amber

340

The U. S. Glass items on this page were being advertised in these colors in 1926. Other colors may show up as well.

BEE HIVE *line*
pink, crystal w/green, amber trim

"ELYSIUM" bulb box: satin finish blue, green, amber, black

United States Glass Company
Pittsburgh, Pa.

PRESENTS

KIMBERLY DECORATION
on Black or Ruby Glass

CONSOLE SET

Hand-blocked and relief-etched on the finest pot glass. Tapering satined diamonds, with clear glass dividing bands, form a pleasing decoration, adaptable to any and all furnishings.

Console Bowls and Sets
Flower Bowls and Vases
Candlesticks—Candy Boxes
Cigarette Boxes—Dresser Sets
are just a few of the thirty
or more articles in this line.

CLASSIC SIMPLICITY

In the transparent colors, Amber, Green, Blue and Canary, bright spots are made in the boudoir, while the same colors, in the satin finish, appeal to those buyers who prefer softer tones.

UNITED STATES GLASS COMPANY
PITTSBURGH, PENNSYLVANIA.

Consult our nearest Sales Representative or write us direct

THE SHIELD OF A GREAT NAME IS YOUR PROTECTION

ETCHED "PSYCHE"

on
FIRE POLISHED
LEAD BLOWN CRYSTAL
POT GLASS
With GREEN TRIM

Plates—6, 8 and 10 in.
(all green)
Sugar Bowls
Cream Pitchers
Bon Bons
Bud Vases

PSYCHE
a complete line of tableware in green and crystal w/green trim.

The 016 Optic Tableware Line carries a compelling appeal to those who discriminate between good and best.

Footed items are Jugs, with and without covers, Table and Iced Tea Tumblers, Oyster Cocktails and Finger Bowls.

In the Stemware are Goblets, Cafe Parfaits, Saucer Champagnes, Wines and Cocktails.

PATENT APPLIED FOR

UNITED STATES GLASS COMPANY
PITTSBURGH, PA.

A full line of samples can be seen at our Sales and Display Rooms, or color plates are yours for the asking.

MILADY *dresser set; amber, blue, green, canary; also satin finish; and ivory*

The U. S. Glass items on this page were being advertised in these colors in 1926. Other colors may show up as well.

"TWIRL" *Beverage Set*

THE SANTA CLAUS LAMP

DECORATED

NO. 7562

SANTA LAMP

TORCHIERE
pink, green; satin finish with satin black trim

HELIO *decoration applied to under surface; gold scroll on upper. In rose-pink satinware.*

FLANDERS *dinnerware: pink, pink w/ crystal trim*

The items this page were being advertised in these colors in 1927. You may see other colors as well.

WALL VASE: *blue, green, canary; also satin finish*

"TOP O' THE MORNING" *sets: green*

SANDWICH OR CAKE PLATE

pink, green, canary, amber

"DINER" *dinner line green, amber, pink*

Announcing
The smart new OCTAGON bridge set

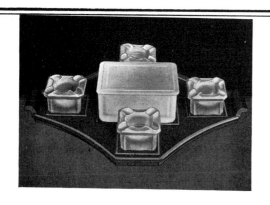

Offered in 1928 by Tiffin in several colors.

"UPSY DAISY" CONSOLE
several colors; 1929

"POPPY" VASE
(#185 Book I)
*black satin and
painted red & green
in this 1930 ad;
also in pink, green,
blue, canary*

"UNCLE SAM" COCKTAIL SET
*several colors,
1929 ad*

*No. 16256—Bath Salt
with cover. Made in
black, black satin, green
and pink. Useful as a
vase without cover. Can
be had that way, too.*

*No. R9557 Candy Jar and
Cover. Crystal with foot and
cover in black. It is beautiful
Tiffinware at its best. Decorated with the popular "Byzan-
tine" etching. Stemware to
match also attractive.*

*Here are two items from the
310½ Tableware line in the
popular "Rosemary" etching.
They are a footed mint wafer
and a footed marmalade. Made
in both pink and green. The
line includes many other attractive items.*

SYLVAN *etching
on stemware line;
several colors;
1929 ad*

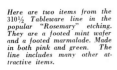

—1930 advertisement

No. 8135—Six-piece Refrigerator Set

No. 6494—Five-piece Kitchen Set

IT'S
U. S. KITCHENWARE

Crystal and Transparent Colors

UNITED STATES
GLASS CO.

PITTSBURGH, PA.

Sales Offices in all Principal Cities

No. 6493—Five-piece Kitchen Set

No. 8196—Five-piece Mixing Bowl Set

(NOTE: "TIC-TAC-TOE" ice bucket; "ACORN" salver (detail next page); SLICK reamer, batter bowl.)

(NOTE: Bowl set; "STAG" ashtray; "KING TUT" 3-ft bowl; "SHAGGY DAISY" cake plate detail next page.)

—pink, green; 1930 advertisements

U. S. ITEMS IN GREEN

SLICK CUP
  Bottom motif same as plate center bottom row; marked

SNOWFLAKE MEASURING JUG
  5 cup, 2½ pt; has ledge for reamer

SLICK MEASURING CUP
  2 cup capacity

U. S. MIXING BOWL
  9", part of set 5", 7"; marked

SLICK BATTER
  Or utility jug; marked

"JUMBO" MIXING BOWL
  6½" deep, 7" diam., 2-spout

"BIMBO" MIXING BOWL
  4½" deep, 8½" diam.; has 9" plate cover;

SLICK PLATE
  9", matches cup top row; marked

"SCROLL" PLATE (#186 Book 1)
  8½", also found in pink and black

Detail from "ACORN" salver shown preceding page.

Detail from "WALLFLOWER" utility plate (#47, Book I) pictured below.

Detail from "SHAGGY ROSE" cake plate pictured below

Drawing of "SHAGGY DAISY" cake plate (#48 Book 1), shown preceding page; 1930 patent

Detail from "ROSE BURR" cake plate pictured below.

Detail from "POPPY-COCKLEBURR" refrigerator dish pictured below.

"ROSE BURR" Utility or Cake Plate 9½", pink, green; **"WALLFLOWER"** Utility Plate 5½" (7½" is #47 Book 1), pink, green; **"SHAGGY ROSE"** Cake Plate 10" pink, green, black; **"POPPY-COCKLEBURR"** Refrigerator Dish & Cover 6½ x 6½", green.

trade journal brief

"BRILLE" cutting
in crystal and black

"BURNISH"
gold decoration
on black bowl

HOT CAKES
PLATE AND COVER
(below right)

—*1930 ad*

SLICK
condiment
holder
—*1928 patent*

Detail from "EVE"
dresser set shown below

Detail from "ROSE & THORN"
(#110 in Book I)
shown below.

ROW 1: "EVE" Cosmetic Set, pink (detail above). "ROSE & THORN" Bowl, 11" and nappy 5", pink, green, black (detail above). "TENDRIL" Plate, 9¾" pink, green, black. "TITA" Water Set, 8" jug, 5-1/8" tumbler, green.
ROW 2: "DONNA" Bowl, 11" pink, green, black. "BOWMAN" Console Set, 10½" reversible bowl, 1½" candlesticks, green. "PEEP-HOLE" Bowl, 11" pink, green, black. PARAMOUNT SERVICE (inscribed) Napkin Holder, 5" tall, pink.

Grotesque animal figures in black are made by the United States Glass Co., Pittsburgh. The cat shown is made in several sizes and several postures, all of them amusing and arresting.

Various figures have been and are used in decorating glassware. The ash tray shows a moose in relief. From the United States Glass Co., Pittsburgh, Pa.

Items as they were described in a 1930 trade journal. Offered in several colors. Clockwise from cat:

U. S. CAT
U. S. MOOSE
U. S. BRIDGE SET
"U. S. BIG CHIEF"
U. S. LOVEBIRD LAMP
U. S. PARROT LAMP

The New U. S. Bridge Set

Another form of the use of birds in all glass lamps is represented by the parrot done in natural colors. This lamp is from the United States Glass Co., Pittsburgh, Pa.

Among the all glass lamps are several in which bird figures are used. The pair of love birds on a stump shown are from the United States Glass Co., Pittsburgh.

This design can be had on a great variety of pieces in both Rose Pink and Green glass. The pieces include a complete line of stemware, plates, footed tumblers, finger bowl, sugar and cream set, coffee cup and saucer, jugs, comports, center piece set, bud vases and other items.

❉ ❉ ❉ ❉

New Sales Items For 1931

"LARIETTE"

This tableware line was advertised in 1931 as made in the U. S. Glass popular colors. You may find additional pieces to this set.

PRIMO

(#168 Book I)

U. S. Glass' PRIMO was a major table-ware line in 1932. Besides the Mandarin Yellow advertised, the pattern was made in green.

Pieces shown immediately below are plate, cup & saucer, cream & sugar, and large and small nappies. Additional pieces are photographed below.

Detail showing **PRIMO** *design*

UNITED STATES GLASS COMPANY

PITTSBURGH

Sales Offices in all Principal Cities

This is one assortment in the strikingly new "Primo" table glass in Mandarin Yellow. Various sets and assortments can be made up. Moderately priced and a complete line.

PRIMO 7¾" nappy, coaster ashtray with 5¾" footed tumbler, 3-footed cake plate, and sherbet.

PARADE
*Liquor Set
—1935 ad*

A LIQUEUR SET
in Tiffin . . .

Clear hand-made crystal with just the necessary trimming in the attractive, popular cobalt blue.

A gift item--A piece of finer saleable merchandise --An effective display for an alive department--This Tiffin Liqueur Set has been fittingly christened *Parade* by its makers, the United States Glass Company.

Van Deman

The Frank L. Van Deman & Son merchandising concern operated at 39 West 23rd St., New York City during the Depression Era. The reason for its inclusion in these chapters is that Van Deman is responsible for the Black Forest line of tableware which was widely advertised and sold from 1929 to 1931, and is popularly collected today. Probably the ware was made for Van Deman by special contract with some American glass factory, or even imported. The line was large—plates, cups & saucers, sugar & cream, fruit bowls, cake plate, comport, candlesticks, and more—and often embellished.

After the success of Black Forest, the company brought out another pattern hand decorated on ebony glass (shown right). This assortment included salad and nut bowls, cake and sandwich trays, handled bonbons, and card trays.

"BAGHEERA" Bowl
—1930 trade report

BLACK FOREST DEEP PLATE ETCHED GLASSWARE

BLACK FOREST
Deep Plate Etched Ebony Glassware
has met such a popular reception
that we have now brought it out
with two rich new treatments,
viz., with Burnished White Gold Bands;
also with complete borders in
White Gold Encrustation
in a full range of Tableware.

No. 532—14 inch Console Bowl

No. 531—Candlestick

No. 529—Sugar and Cream Set

No. 526—11-inch Cake

No. 525—Covered Candy Box

No. 527—9-inch Hld Bowl

The Black Glassware that the Stylish Store Presents. Sold at Moderate Prices in Open Stock or Sets by the better stores and shops everywhere.

FRANK L. VAN DEMAN & SON
39 WEST 23RD STREET   NEW YORK CITY

Vineland

Long after the Vineland Flint Glass Works proper had become well known in the field of chemical and scientific glassware (it was begun in 1887 in Vineland, New Jersey) the company took a different tack and made an entirely new and widely respected name for itself in the Depression-era period. Its owner specially created the Durand Art Glass Division in 1924 and, with the help of expert craftsmen, brought forth artistic pieces in cased, hammered, and spun glass (brilliant lamp shades and bases were a specialty) which were almost as greatly sought after then as they are by collectors now. Tragically, Mr. Durand was killed in 1931 and his factory closed shortly thereafter.

Besides these highly styled and extravagantly colored giftwares ("even the storeroom of this factory is a veritable riot of color in itself" marvels a trade reporter just a year after it opened), the Division also hand-made more popularly priced tableware, stemware (and lamps such as the "vanity sticks" pictured below) in the transparent colors of the day—rose, green, amber, and probably others. Unfortunately no catalogs have yet come to light that we might identify more of Vineland's collectible wares.

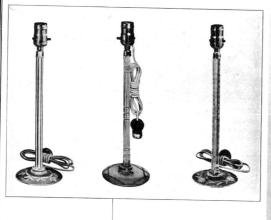

Vanity Sticks, left to right:
"POLA"
"PICKFORD"
"KEATON"
"CHAPLIN"

-1929 ad

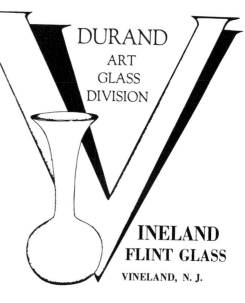

Westmoreland

The "Westmoreland Specialty Company" first began making glass at Grapeville, Pennsylvania in 1890. Glass was its main product, but interestingly the company in its earliest years also processed vinegar, mustard, baking powder and other condiments to fill its glass containers. During WW I glass items filled with candy were made, and sold via newsstands and dime stores across the country. These attracted so much attention that Westmoreland was deluged with requests for all kinds of outlandish "specialties" it couldn't begin to make — no wonder it was decided to drop the "Specialty" from its name!

The factory wanted to concentrate on its glassware, which was from the outset a handmade product of very high quality. Decorations and reproductions became the specialty then. In the early 20s Westmoreland's capacity doubled and the decorating facility became one of the largest anywhere. In other departments Early American patterns — The Hobnails, the Dolphins, etc. — were recreated and a career of milk glass production begun that has been successful to the present day. Color came in vogue, and several large lines of tableware were issued through the Depression years in patterns which are still popular with collectors today.

The well-known Grapeville plant is one of the few hand houses surviving to the present. Color, decorations, and clearly marked reproduction glass continue to figure predominantly into the lovely lines. Look in any giftshop window and chances are you'll find Westmoreland.

COLOR

The color splash at Westmoreland came as early and as big as it did anywhere. By 1923 the lines were suffused with many color effects — fired-on solids, fancy decorations, black and white satined glass — and attracted much attention from the trade. The first transparent color was apparently amber in 1924; green and blue came in 1925 and Rose (sometimes called 'Roselin') in 1926. These colors were made until the 30s.

Crystal-and-black glass combinations were offered to the 1929 market; crystal-and-topaz and decorations on black and topaz, were for 1930. A deep blue called Belgian blue, and an opalescent blue Moonstone, came out in 1931. By 1935 this company, like so many other hand houses, had returned to a largely crystal production. Later, in the 40s, 50s, and 60s, black and ruby were issued, and an amber, Golden Sunset, was used for some of the old patterns in the 60s.

ENGLISH HOBNAIL

Made in amber and crystal in 1925; in blue, green, crystal and Rose in 1926 to 1931. A partial line was made with crystal bowls and black stems from 1929 to 1931. Some topaz was made in 1930 and in 1931, #555 Square ENGLISH HOBNAIL Design was offered in Belgian Blue, and Moonstone.

In the early Sixties (not Fifties as in Book I) certain pieces were cast in Golden Sunset, an amber hard to distinguish from the 1925 amber; and in the late Sixties pieces were made with a flashed red trim.

The crystal has been made from the late Twenties to the Seventies. Also in the Seventies, footed salt dips were made in new colors such as peach, light blue, dark blue, etc. and some of these are frosted.

I have reprinted here all the pieces I have ever found catalogued; you may find others. Note that the pattern was made with either round, square, or hexagon-shaped bases, and compare ENGLISH HOBNAIL to its close cousin, Waterford.

WESTMORELAND GLASS

FOR 1926

We are featuring reproductions of the old Sandwich glass which is enjoying a popular vogue and these will be shown in high grade Crystal and beautiful shades of Amber, Green and Blue.

WESTMORELAND GLASS CO.
GRAPEVILLE, PA.

In early ads Westmoreland referred to its #555 as "a Sandwich reproduction". Later the company advertised it as ENGLISH HOBNAIL.

555/5oz. Toilet Bottle

555 Cig. Jar and Cover

555 Marmalade and Cover (Notched)

555 Ftd. Sugar and Cream Set

555/5oz. Bridge Goblet

555/8oz. Goblet

555 H. F. Sherbet

500 L. F. Sherbet

555/5oz. Ginger Ale

ENGLISH HOBNAIL reprinted from company catalog c. 1924.

Quart Jug

One-Half Gallon Jug

Tumbler

Ice Tea, Straight

Ice Tea, Belled

½-lb. Candy Jar

8" Plate

8½" Plate

10" Plate

12" Flange Bowl

11" Bell Bowl

14" Plate

11" R. E. Bowl

12" Flared Bowl

555 Ftd. S. & P. SPT

555 4½" Finger Bowl

555 Ind. Footed Nut (Cut Full Size)

555 6½" Grapefruit

555 6½" F. B. Plate

555 6" Puff Box and Cover Also made in 5"

555 Cup and Saucer

7½" Bell Nappy

6½" Square Nappy

9" Bell Nappy

8" Bell Nappy

555 5½" Plate

8" Cupped Nappy

4½" Nappy

6½" Round Nappy

7" Round Nappy

8" Round Nappy

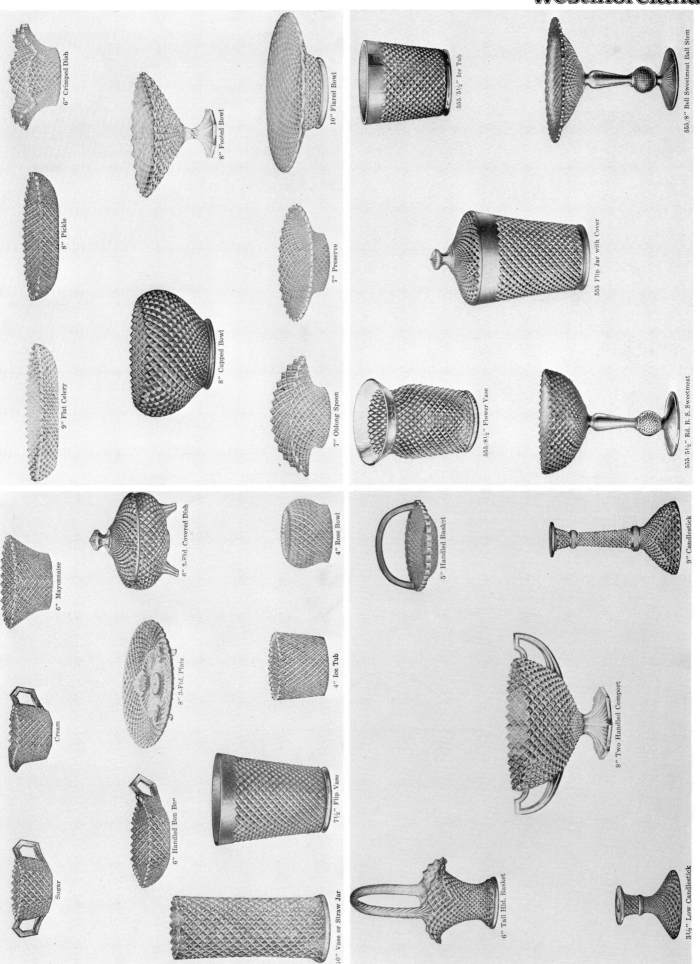

6" Crimped Dish

8" Footed Bowl

10" Flared Bowl

555 5½" Ice Tub

555/8" Bell Sweetmeat Ball Stem

8" Pickle

7" Preserve

555 Flip Jar with Cover

9" Flat Celery

8" Cupped Bowl

7" Oblong Spoon

555 8½" Flower Vase

555 5½" Rd. B. S. Sweetmeat

6" Mayonnaise

6" 3-Ftd. Covered Dish

4" Rose Bowl

5" Handled Basket

9" Candlestick

Cream

8" 3-Ftd. Plate

4" Ice Tub

8" Two Handled Comport

Sugar

6" Handled Bon Bon

7½" Flip Vase

10" Vase or Straw Jar

6" Tall Hld. Basket

3½" Low Candlestick

This page reprint is Westmoreland's ENGLISH HOBNAIL reissue in crystal in the 60s. Many of these pieces, even though they did not appear in the early catalog reprinted on the preceding pages, were made in the 30s in pink, blue, green, and amber.

555/12½ oz. Ice Tea, ftd.
555/9 oz. Tumbler, ftd.
555/7 oz. Tumbler, ftd.
555 Parfait
555 Sherbet High foot.
555 Sherbet Low foot.
555/3 oz. Cocktail
555/8 oz. Goblet

555/5 oz. Claret
555/2 oz. Wine
555 Cardial
555 Old Fashioned Cocktail
1½ oz. Whiskey, Also 3 oz.
555/5 oz. Ginger Ale
555/8 oz. Tumbler
555/10 oz. Ice Tea
555/12 oz. Ice Tea

555/2 oz. Oil
555/6 oz. Oil
555/6 oz. Oil-Vinegar Comb.
555/20 oz. Decanter
555/1 qt. Jug Also in ½ Gal.
555/38 oz. Jug. Also 23 oz., 60 oz.

555/10" Plate
555/8" Plate Also 6½", 5½"
555/7" Pie Plate
555/1/8½" Plate Plain Edge.
555/6½" Plate, Depressed Center

555 Cream Soup 555 Cream Soup plate
555 Cup & Saucer
555/4½" Finger Bowl 555/6½" Finger Bowl, Plate

555/8" Relish, 3 part
555/6" Mayo
555/6" Nappy, Square
555/10½" Grill Plate, 3 part

555/8" Nappy, Round
555/6" Nappy, Round
555/5" Nappy, Round
555/4½" Nappy, Round
55⅝/5½" Nappy, Bell

555/7½" Nappy, Bell

555/11" Bowl, Bell
555/12" Bowl, Flared

555/5" Compote, Round, footed
555/6" Honey, footed
555/12" Bowl, Oval Crimped Also in 10"
555/½ lb. Candy and Cover

555/2/11 oz. Ice Tea, ftd.
555/2/9 oz. Tumbler, ftd.
555/2/7 oz. Tumbler, ftd.
555/2/5 oz. Ginger Ale
555/2/8 oz. Goblet
555/2/3 oz. Cocktail
555/2 Sherbet, Low
555/2 Sherbet, High

555/2/2 oz. Wine
555/2 Cardial
555/2 Oyster Cocktail
555/2 Mustard
555/2 Salt and Pepper
555/2 Cream and Sugar, footed

555/2/5" Compote, Round
555/2/5½" Compote, Bell
555/2/6" Honey, ftd.
555/2/5½" Candlestick
555/2/4½" Nappy, Sq.
555/2 Finger Bowl, footed

555/2 Cup and Saucer
555 Finger Bowl 555/2/6" Sq. Plate
555/2/6" Cheese and Cover. Also 8¾"

555/2/10" Square Plate
555/2/4½" Ash Tray, Sq.
555/2/8¾" Square Plate
555/2/6" Square Plate
555/2/6½" Flower Holder, footed
555/2/6½" Ivy Ball, Crimp Top, ftd.

555/4½x2½" Cigarette Box & Cover
High Hat
Low Hat
555/4½" Ash Tray.
555 Ind. Nut, ftd.
3" Ash Tray
555 3" Coaster

555/6½" Grapefruit
555/6½" Bon Bon, H'ld.
555/8" Pickle
555/6" Crimped Dish

555/6" Rose Bowl
4" Rose Bowl
555/8"/6 Pt. Bowl, Also in 7"
555/2-Lite Candelabra
555/6" Basket, Tall Handled.

555/6" Three-Footed Covered Dish
555 Marmalade and Cover
555/3½" Candlestick
555/9½" Bowl, Round, Crimped

555/12" Celery, Also 9"

555/14" Torte Plate, Also in 20½"
555/15 Piece Punch Set

BOOK 2 PATTERNS

Some of the items shown on the next few pages will reappear in the catalog reprint later this chapter. The ads are given to show how, when, and in what colors they were originally introduced.

Westmoreland Specialty Co.

GRAPEVILLE, PA.

Manufacturers of High Grade Glassware—Plain, Cut and Decorated —For Gift Shops, Florists and Table Use.

U. S. HAT
In Plain Crystal or Decorated White and Blue.

SOLDIER HAT
In Plain Crystal or Decorated in Khaki Color with Colored Cords.

STRAW HATS
In Plain Opal or Decorated Straw Color with Black Band.

The above Novelties suitable for Souvenirs. The U. S. Hat particularly good for Campaign purposes.

U.S. HAT—SOLDIER HAT—STRAW HAT
These ashtrays disguised as hats (fooled me!) were popular novelties for several years says a trade journal; this ad is from 1924

Westmoreland Specialty Co.

GRAPEVILLE, PA.

crystal, amber   blue, green

TRADE EXTRA W QUALITY MARK

"ORPHAN ANNIE" *Breakfast Set*
consisting of 39 pieces from 1925 advertisement

Westmoreland's uncommon contribution to the pickle jar market never failed to bring comment from the trade journal scouts.

Our forefathers in the Eastern states must have loved pickles if the reproductions of old pickle jars made by the Westmoreland Glass Co., of Grapeville, Pa., are any criterion. These pickle jars have embossed flowers and have a rim at the top. They are made in thin glass in crystal, amber, blue, green, and Roselin. The colors are clear, making the jars transparent.

These reproductions come in heights of 9, 12, and 15 inches. The colors are clear, making the jars transparent. They are also used as flower vases and make most acceptable bases for lamps.

Vases of good size always are good retail items and in the shape and design of this one from the Westmoreland Glass Co., Grapeville, Pa., they are certain to attract attention. The vase comes in various transparent colors in glass and is the No. 106.

Pickled tink, aren't they?

Here's what they had to say about the 1926 jar, the 1929 jar (middle) and the 1927 jar.

A very new find for the vase collection is this old fashioned pickle jar vase. The person who first introduced roses as a decoration for pickle jars—when they really were pickle jars—must have been blessed with a sense of humor, or else he totally lacked one. Anyway, we have no quarrel with him for they make an exceedingly attractive rose vase decoration.

This jar comes in two sizes, 13" high and 15" high. It comes in a greenish glass.

"LAZY SUSAN"
*as she is
introduced in a
1926 trade report*

If you do not know "Lazy Susan", we are glad to make the introduction. Her serviceability as a table centerpiece is not indicated by the name which ap- plies more to those who make use of the article than to the article itself. "Lazy Susan" is a very large footed plate, either eigtheeen or twenty inches in di- ameter, which sets on a base which has a rim to keep the large pieces from slipping off. The article is used as a centerpiece for fruits or flowers. The name derives from the fact that the large plate can be turn- ed around on the base as an axis without too much reaching and stretching. This movability makes everything on it within easy reach. The plate is made in the form of a large leaf and can be had in blue, green, amber or roselin glass. The Westmoreland Glass Co., Grapeville, Pa., are the makers of "Lazy Susan."

ARTISTIC GLASSWARES

No. 1058—Handled Sugar and Cream

This is a fruit design pressed in the glass. It can be had in colors, including Roselin, Green and Amber, as well as in crystal. A special matt finish brings out the design in marked relief.

WESTMORELAND GLASS CO.
GRAPEVILLE, PA.

DELLA ROBBIA
*from 1928 advertisement
more pieces in catalog reprint to follow*

WESTMORELAND'S DOLPHIN CONSOLE
*as presented in a 1925 advertisement
in crystal, amber, blue, and green*

"WOOLWORTH"

(#89 in Book 1)

A Westmoreland spokesman says this tableware line was made specially for Woolworth stores in the early 30s. It comes in pink, green, blue, & crystal. Refer to Book 1 for the plates (one plain, one scalloped) and the cream & sugar. Shown here are the 5½" basket, 8" round nappy, 6" square nappy, and the 5½" handled nappy.

Article reprinted from 1927 trade journal

No. 1904 DICE LAMP

No. 1905 WATER LAMP

Water Lamps For Vari-Colored Water And Glass Lamps In Colors As Well

TABLE and boudoir lamps with glass bases have become a feature of every lamp display and the variety of bases to be had only is limited by the imagination and resource of the glass and lamp manufacturers. The glass bases for the so-called "water-lamps" have been very popular as have the smaller glass bases in reproduction of Colonial and Early American styles.

Glass bases are available in all the colors of glass and the use of colored water inside the crystal bases offers a wide range of combinations and contrasts between the base and the shade.

In order to depict some of the types of glass bases available, we are illustrating a number of these productions as made by the Westmoreland Glass Co., of Grapeville, Pa., which is known for the variety in color and form of its productions. There should be and probably is a shape of glass base for any desired effect or for use with any type of shade, whether it be of glass or parchment or silk.

The illustrations show the lamps with electric socket attached, just as they are shipped from the factory. The bases shown are made in crystal, amber, green, blue and "Roselin" or pink glass.

Illustrated on this page are two unusual designs, which, while odd, have certain appeal. The No. 1905 water lamp is an unusual shape. It has a rather wide base and is in two seeming portions. The top of the base is pressed in all around, giving the base the appearance of a squash. The base is all in one piece and, of course, will hold water or any other material.

In connection with the water lamps, it may be expected that alert manufacturers and distributors will see the possibilities of placing other than a liquid in the base or of decorating the inside of the lamp with material corresponding to the shade. Certainly, there are possibilities in that direction.

A most unusual conception is the No. 1904 design, which is called a dice lamp. The base is in the form of a large dice of glass. It is patterned after a dice and is made of opal or white glass with the dice marks brought out with black enamel. It really makes a giant dice.

These five shapes in water lamps offer some choice and indicate the possibilities for this form of lamp base. While they may be called "Lamps" they actually are supplied only as bases with the electric socket affixed.

Also illustrated are some of the Early American types of bases, the only point of similarity between them and the others being the fact that they are made of glass. These also are made in several colors and crystal such as amber, green, blue and "Roselin."

The Dolphin base is similar to productions of the famed Sandwich works and other American factories of a century or more ago. Fish and animals of many kinds then were used as a motif in glassware design. In this design the Dolphin is a part of the base, resting upon the foot proper and holding what once was used for holding the oil.

Also Early American in conception is the No. 555, which

No. 1049/2 DOLPHIN LAMP

No. 1049/1 DOLPHIN LAMP

No. 1900 WATER LAMP

No. 1901 WATER LAMP

No. 1902 WATER LAMP

No. 1903 WATER LAMP

No. 1505

No. 1017

No. 555

No. 185

is in hobnail design. This is quite effective in green and "Roselin" with the points of the rough-surfaced portion acting as light reflectors. The lamp could be used as an oil burner, but is quite effective with the electric attachment and, probably, much more efficient.

The No. 185 is Colonial in design. It is marked by wide panels in three sections each. In each section the center is hollowed out. In each panel, there are three sections of different size. The base is elaborate and also in paneled effect.

The variety of designs and shapes possible in glass water lamps and in other forms of glass bases for lamps is indicated by the illustrations here. No attempt is made to illustrate all of the many shapes being produced, but a number of designs are shown in the hope of giving lamp merchandisers a conception of the real possibilities.

Undoubtedly the forthcoming Pittsburgh Exhibit will find many manufacturers with something new in shapes and designs for lamp bases. There also probably will be all-glass lamps as well as glass shades. The colorful glass shade still is being made, but not in as large quantities as formerly. Whether the glass shade will return to its former popularity and glory depends entirely upon the whims of fashion, but in the past several years the glass shade has been in apparent eclipse while the glass base has come into comparative popularity.

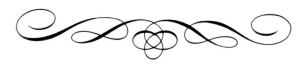

**All lamps furnished with adapters or without.
Made in Crystal, Roselin, Amber, Green, & Blue Glass**

1917/9″ Lamp with Fixtures

1918 9″ Lamp with Fixtures

1707/8″ Spiral Lamp with Fixtures
(Also made in 12″)

1911 Lamp with Fixtures

1921 Lotus Lamp with Fixtures

TRUE REPRODUCTION
LAMPS

by

WESTMORELAND GLASS CO.
GRAPEVILLE, PENNA.

Handmade Glassware Since 1889

No. 185 Lamp — From the days of "Moby Dick" and the whaling ships of New Bedford comes this reproduction of the old whale oil lamp - appropriate for colonial settings.

1955 Lamp
with Fixtures

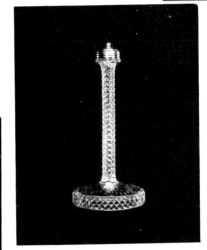

555/8″ Vanity Lamp
Opal and Crystal

555/9″ Candlestick Lamp

With and without hole in bottom. Opal and Crystal.

1920 Lamp

Crystal fount with opal base. Also antique blue base and black. (Can also be had with red and blue founts).

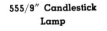

300/8″ Lamp

With and without hole in bottom. Crystal.

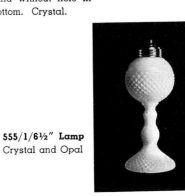

555/1/6½″ Lamp
Crystal and Opal

1920 Lamp—In an old fashioned parlor when great grandmother was a girl you would find this two-piece lamp, a crystal fount and milk glass base, joined by a hand spun brass collar, black base supplied if desired; extremely good with old maple.

An early 40s brochure shows these in crystal & opal; they were made earlier in pink, green, and blue.

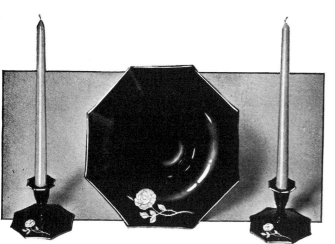

As an attractive server for nuts, sweetmeats and table delicacies this little swan is most useful. Made in various colors and finishes in glass by the Westmoreland Glass Co., Grapeville, Pa.

The combination of hen on a nest has been used for many years. It is made in several sizes and in some sections is used as a container and server for egg dishes. Made in natural colors by the Westmoreland Glass Co., Grapeville, Pa.

A handy container in representation of a camel at rest. Useful for cigarettes or sweetmeats. This is one of the numerous items from the Westmoreland Glass Co., Grapeville, Pa.

*"OCTAVIA ROSE" Console Set
black with silver decoration
from 1930 advertisement*

1820/8″ Hld. Tea Tray

1801 Cheese Tray and Cover

1820/10″ Bridge Service Tray

1820/3 Pce. Ind. Salt and Pepper Set

1820/12″ Hld. Service Tray

Novelty items made in colors; 1930

A WATERFORD REPRODUCTION BY WESTMORELAND

"CAMEO DIAMOND"

*a tableware line introduced
in this 1930 ad; more
pieces in catalog reprint following*

WATERFORD

*This 1931 advertisement lists WATERFORD in pink,
and crystal in combination with black or amber feet;
in the 60s this pattern was reissued
with fired-on red trim*

5" Nappy, Heart

Mint

6" Nappy, Cupped

Candy, Crimped

12½" Urn

Candy, Covered

Sugar / Cream

Compote, Crimped

12" Cake Salver

12" Celery

8" Nappy, Heart

12" Bowl, Lipped

13" Bowl, Turned Edge

10" Bowl, Cupped

14" Plate

6" Candlestick

12" Bowl, Bell Footed

6" Candlestick

10 oz. Goblet

Sherbet

2 oz. Wine

12 oz. Ice Tea, Footed

8½" Plate

Our No. 1932 Wakefield Crystal Goblet Is One of Many Items.

WAKEFIELD

Pieces of this large line were being made as early as 1933, the year this advertisement (left) appeared. The reprint above, however, is from a company brochure from the 50s when it was advertised under the name "Waterford". In the 60s it was reissued with fired-on red trim.

PRINCESS FEATHER

Each year new pieces were added to this popular line which was made in pink, blue (aqua), green, and crystal. #201 was named PRINCESS FEATHER in 1939 ads; in the 60s it was reissued in Golden Sunset and illustrated in the tablesetting at right.

CATALOG REPRINT

The following page reprints of a 1924 catalog show the beginning of Westmoreland's color era. You will find these items in amber, green, Roselin and the early blue; you may also find them in crystal and in additional pieces since these lines were carried for several years through the next crystal era.

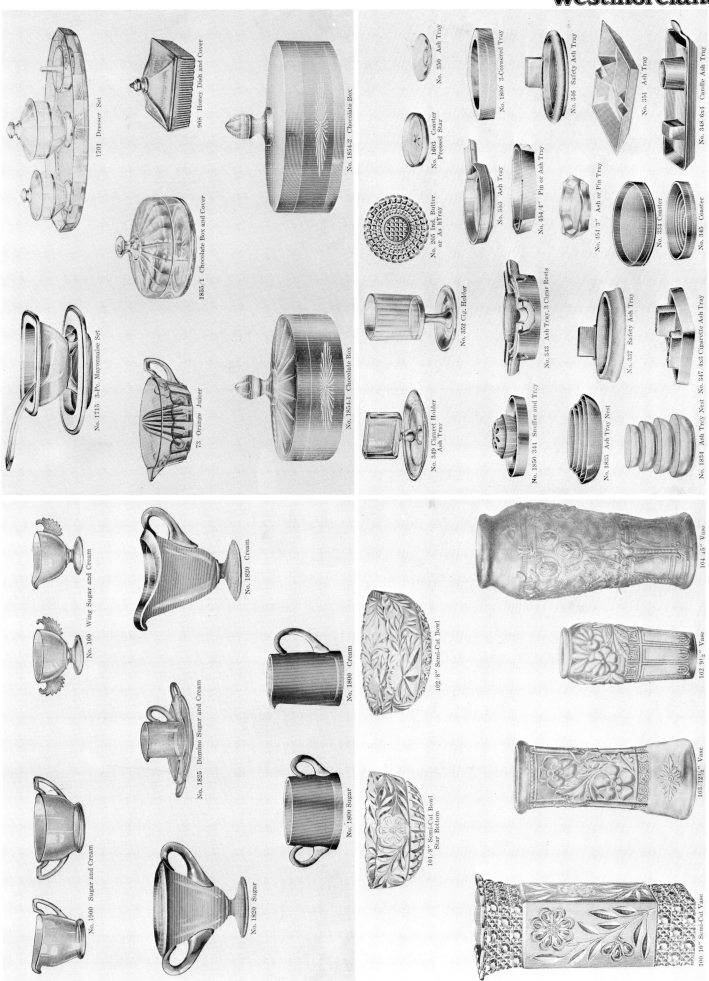

1701 Dresser Set

908 Honey Dish and Cover

No. 1854-2 Chocolate Box

1855/1 Chocolate Box and Cover

No. 1715 3-Pc. Mayonnaise Set

73 Orange Juicer

No. 1854-1 Chocolate Box

No. 350 Ash Tray

No. 1603 Coaster Pressed Star

No. 1800 3-Cornered Tray

No. 346 Safety Ash Tray

No. 351 Ash Tray

No. 348 6x4 Candle Ash Tray

No. 205 Ind. Butter or As hTray

No. 362 Ash Tray

No. 454/4" Pin or Ash Tray

No. 454 3" Ash or Pin Tray

No. 334 Coaster

No. 345 Coaster

No. 352 Cig. Holder

No. 343 Ash Tray, 3 Cigar Rests

No. 327 Safety Ash Tray

No. 347 4x3 Cigarette Ash Tray

No. 349 Cigaret Holder Ash Tray

No. 1850/344 Snuffer and Tray

No. 1834 Ash Tray Nest

No. 1835 Ash Tray Nest

No. 100 Wing Sugar and Cream

No. 1820 Cream

No. 1825 Domino Sugar and Cream

No. 1800 Cream

No. 1900 Sugar and Cream

No. 1800 Sugar

No. 1820 Sugar

No. 102/8" Semi-Cut Bowl

No. 101/8" Semi-Cut Bowl Star Bottom

No. 104/15" Vase

No. 102/9½" Vase

No. 103/12½" Vase

No. 100/10" Semi-Cut Vase

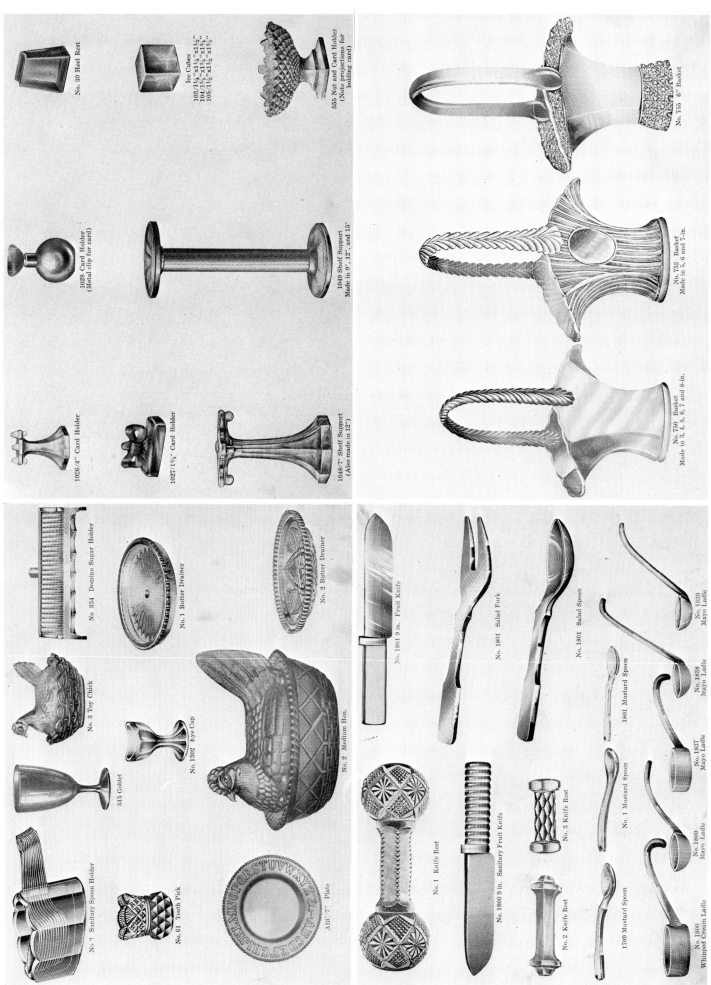

No. 30 Heel Rest

Ice Cubes
103/1¼"x1¼"x1¼"
104/1¾"x1¾"x1¾"
105/1½"x1½"x1¾"

555 Nut and Card Holder
(Note projections for holding card)

1028 Card Holder
(Metal clip for card)

1049 Shelf Support
Made in 9", 12", and 15"

1026/4" Card Holder

1027/1¾" Card Holder

1048/7" Shelf Support
(Also made in 12")

No. 755 6" Basket

No. 752 Basket
Made in 5, 6 and 7-in.

No. 750 Basket
Made in 3, 4, 5, 6, 7 and 8-in.

No 334 Domino Sugar Holder

No. 1 Butter Drainer

No. 2 Butter Drainer

No. 3 Toy Chick

No. 1302 Eye Cup

No. 2 Medium Hen.

515 Goblet

No. 1 Sanitary Spoon Holder

No. 61 Tooth Pick

ABC 7" Plate

No. 1801 9 in. Fruit Knife

No. 1801 Salad Fork

No. 1801 Salad Spoon

No. 1839 Mayo Ladle

1801 Mustard Spoon

No. 1838 Mayo Ladle

No. 1 Knife Rest

No. 1800 9 in. Sanitary Fruit Knife

No. 3 Knife Rest

No. 1 Mustard Spoon

No. 1837 Mayo Ladle

No. 2 Knife Rest

1709 Mustard Spoon

No. 1800 Mayo Ladle

No. 1800 Whipped Cream Ladle

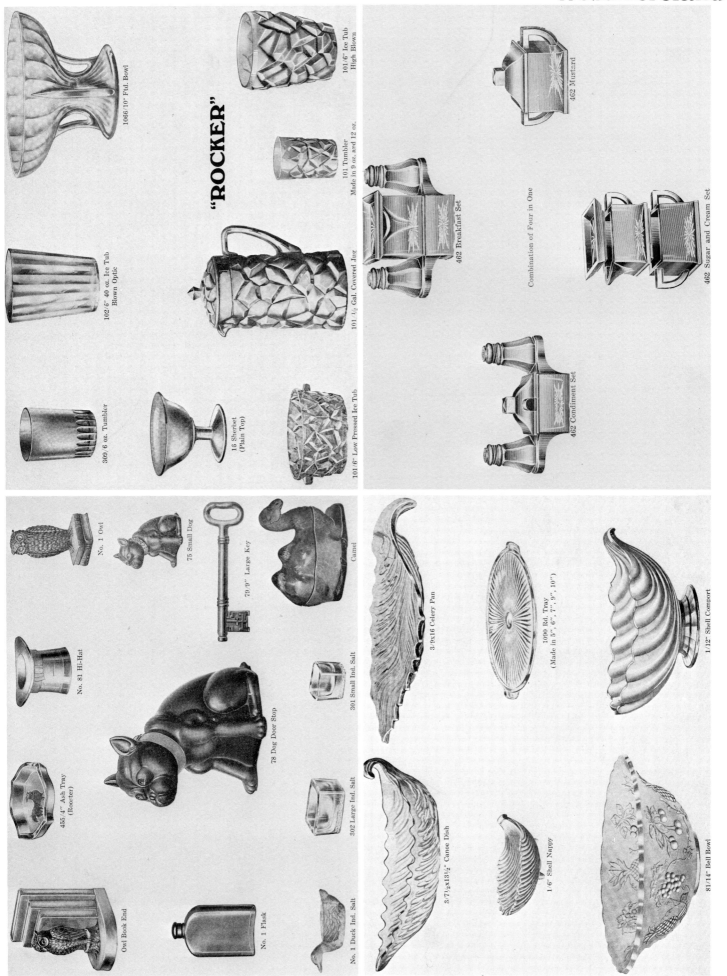

1066/10" Ftd. Bowl

101/6" Ice Tub
High Blown

"ROCKER"

101 Tumbler
Made in 9 oz. and 12 oz.

102/6" 40 oz. Ice Tub
Blown Optic

101 1/2 Gal. Covered Jug

309/6 oz. Tumbler

16 Sherbet
(Plain Top)

101/6" Low Pressed Ice Tub

462 Mustard

462 Breakfast Set

Combination of Four in One

462 Sugar and Cream Set

462 Condiment Set

No. 1 Owl

75 Small Dog

79/9" Large Key

Camel

No. 81 Hi-Hat

301 Small Ind. Salt

455/4" Ash Tray
(Rooster)

78 Dog Door Stop

302 Large Ind. Salt

Owl Book End

No. 1 Flask

No. 1 Duck Ind. Salt

3/9x16 Celery Pan

1090 Rd. Tray
(Made in 5", 6", 7", 9", 10")

1/12" Shell Comport

3/7 1/2 x13 1/2" Canoe Dish

1/6" Shell Nappy

8 1/14" Bell Bowl

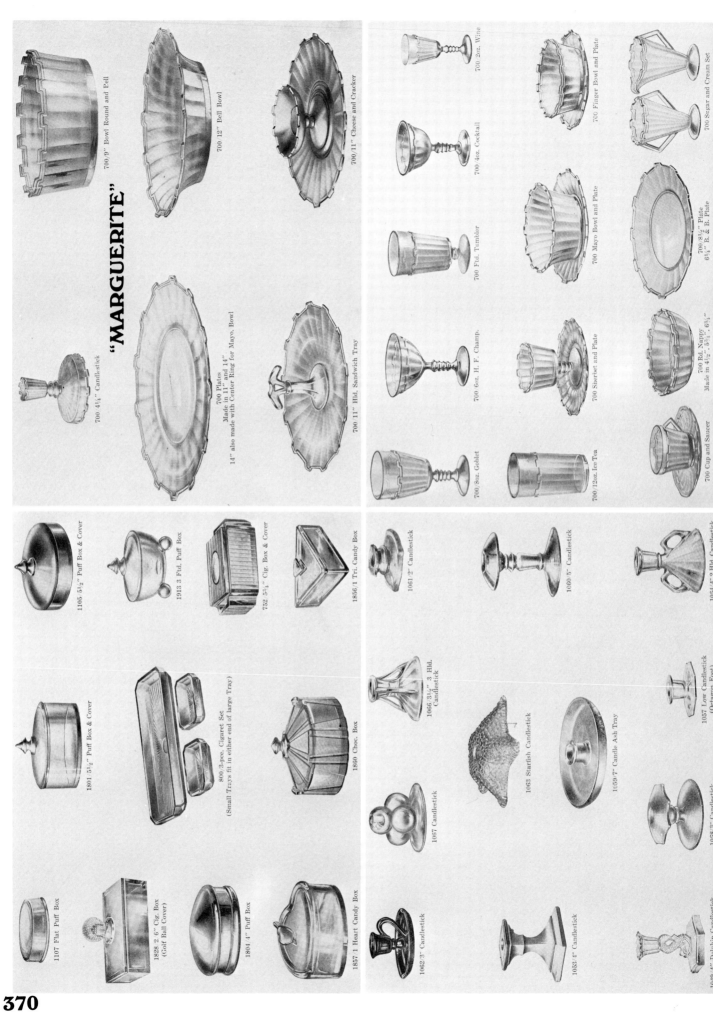

"MARGUERITE"

700 9" Bowl Round and Bell

700 12" Bell Bowl

700 11" Cheese and Cracker

700 4¼" Candlestick

700 Plates
Made in 11" and 14"
14" also made with Center Ring for Mayo. Bowl

700 11" Hd. Sandwich Tray

700 2oz. Wine

700 4oz. Cocktail

700 Ftd. Tumbler

700 6oz. H. F. Champ.

700 8oz. Goblet

700 Finger Bowl and Plate

700 Mayo Bowl and Plate

700 Sherbet and Plate

700 12oz. Ice Tea

700 Sugar and Cream Set

700 8½" Plate
6¼" B. & B. Plate

700 Rd. Nappy
Made in 4½", 5¼", 6¾"

700 Cup and Saucer

1105 5¼" Puff Box & Cover

1913 3 Ftd. Puff Box

752 5¼" Cig. Box & Cover

1856 1 Tri. Candy Box

1801 5½" Puff Box & Cover

800 3-pee. Cigaret Set
(Small Trays fit in either end of large Tray)

1860 Choc. Box

1107 Flat Puff Box

1828 2 6" Cig. Box
(Golf Ball Cover)

1804 4" Puff Box

1857 1 Heart Candy Box

1061 2" Candlestick

1060 5" Candlestick

1054 4" 2 Hd. Candlestick

1066 3½" 3 Hd.
Candlestick

1063 Starfish Candlestick

1059 7" Candle Ash Tray

1057 Low Candlestick
(Octagon Foot)

1067 Candlestick

1062 3" Candlestick

1053 4" Candlestick

1058 3" Candlestick

1049 4" Dolphin Candlestick

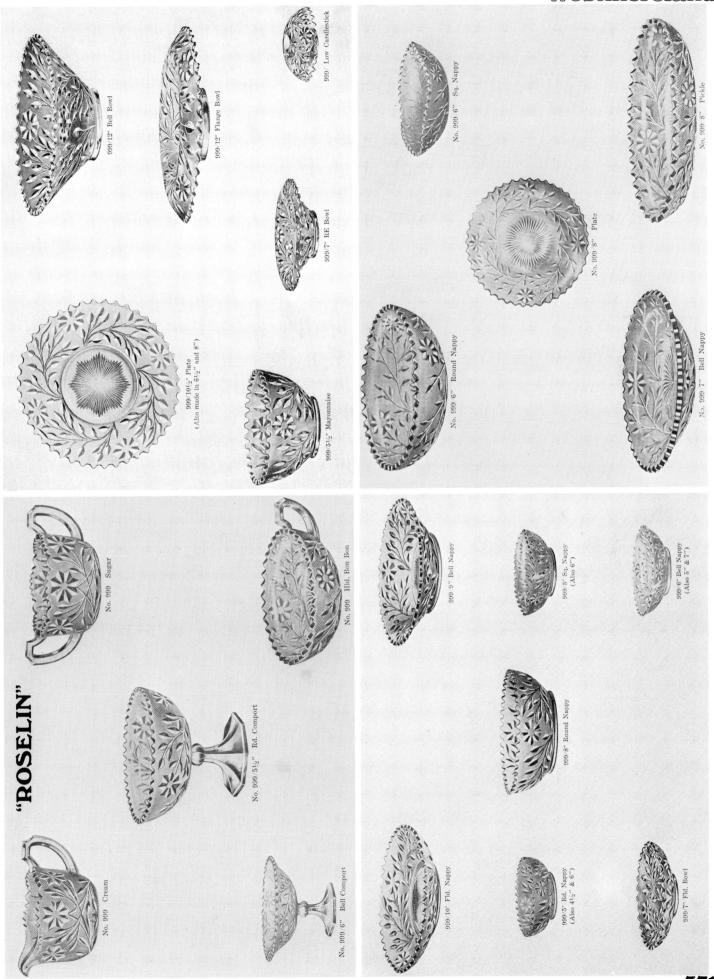

999/12" Bell Bowl

999/12" Flange Bowl

999/ Low Candlestick

999/7" RE Bowl

999/10½" Plate
(Also made in 6½" and 8")

999/5½" Mayonnaise

No. 999 6" Sq. Nappy

No. 999 8" Pickle

No. 999 8" Plate

No. 999 6" Round Nappy

No. 999 7" Bell Nappy

"ROSELIN"

No. 999 Sugar

No. 999 Hld. Bon Bon

No. 999 Cream

No. 999/5½" Rd. Comport

No. 999/6" Bell Comport

999/9" Bell Nappy

999/5" Sq. Nappy
(Also 6")

999/6" Bell Nappy
(Also 5" & 7")

999/8" Round Nappy

999/10" Fld. Nappy

999/5" Rd. Nappy
(Also 4½" & 6")

999/7" Fld. Bowl

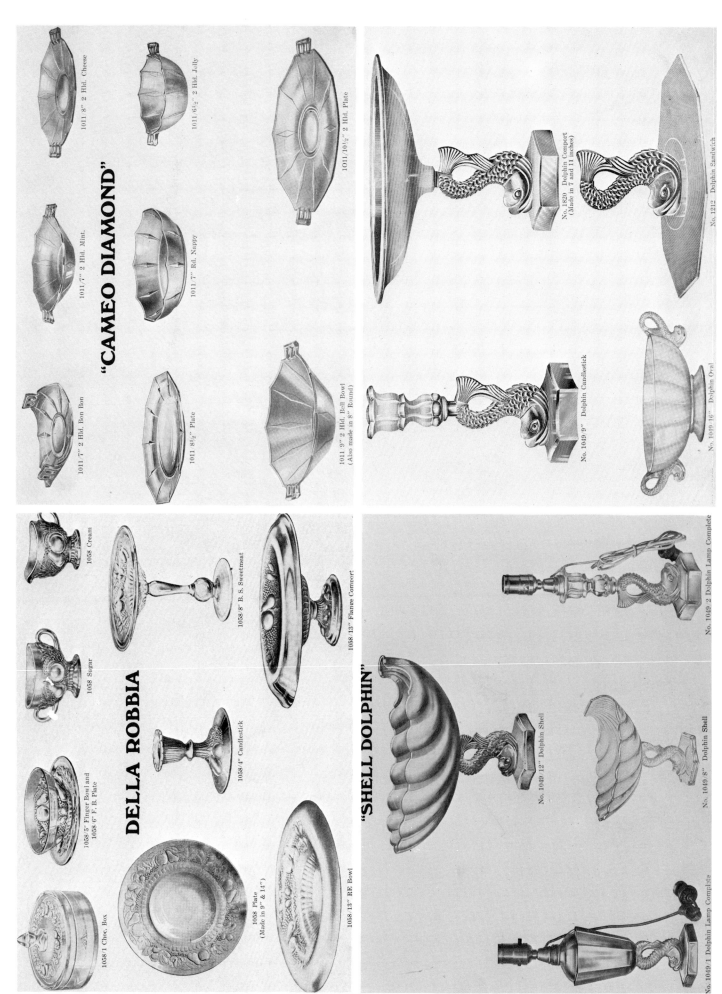

"CAMEO DIAMOND"

1011 8" 2 Hld. Cheese

1011 6½" 2 Hld. Jelly

1011/10½" 2 Hld. Plate

1011 7" 2 Hld. Mint.

1011 7" Rd. Nappy

1011 7" 2 Hld. Bon Bon

1011 8½" Plate

1011 9" 2 Hld. Bell Bowl
(Also made in 8" Round)

No. 1820 Dolphin Comport
(Made in 7 and 11 inches)

No. 1212 Dolphin Sandwich

No. 1049 9" Dolphin Candlestick

No. 1049 16" Dolphin Oval

DELLA ROBBIA

1058 Cream

1058 Sugar

1058/5" Finger Bowl and
1058 6" F. B. Plate

1058/1 Choc. Box

1058/3" Sweetmeat

1058/13" Flange Comport

1058 4" Candlestick

1058 Plate
(Made in 9" & 14")

1058 13" RE Bowl

"SHELL DOLPHIN"

No. 1049 2 Dolphin Lamp Complete

No. 1049 12" Dolphin Shell

No. 1049 8" Dolphin Shell

No. 1049 1 Dolphin Lamp Complete

1211 Ftd. Mayo

1211 /½oz. Cologne

1211 Open Soap

1211 /10x6¼" Tray

1211 /5½" Cigar Tray

1211 Toothbrush Holder

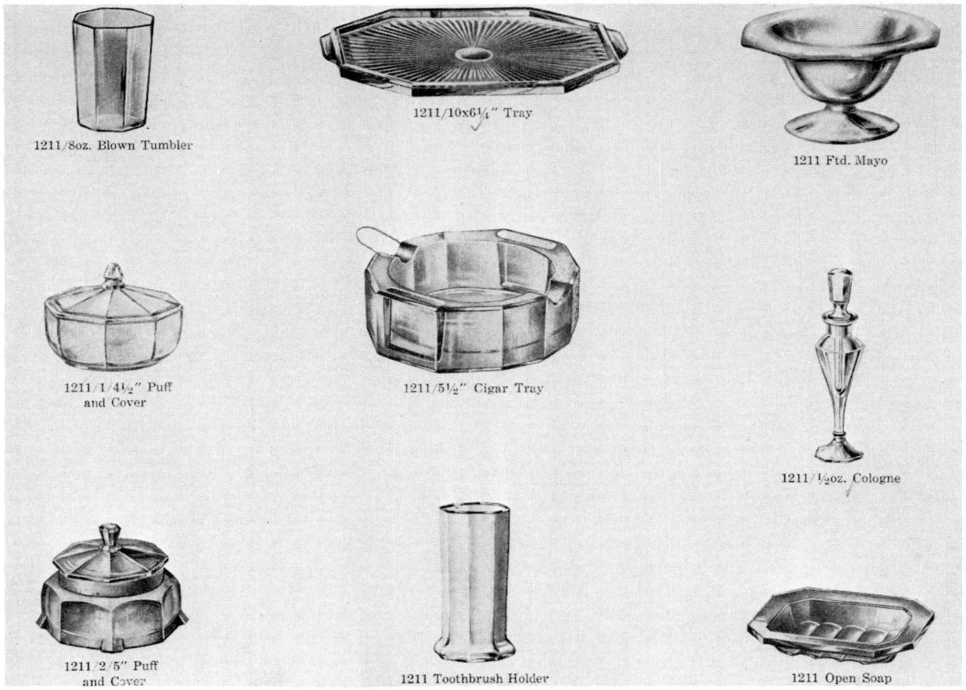

1211 /8oz. Blown Tumbler

1211 / 4½" Puff and Cover

1211 /2 5" Puff and Cover

1211 8" 3-Footed Plate

1211 Bread and Butter Plate

1211 1lb Candy Jar

1211/13" 8-Part Relish with Cocktail Center

1211 6" Butter Ball

1211 / 1 Candy Box

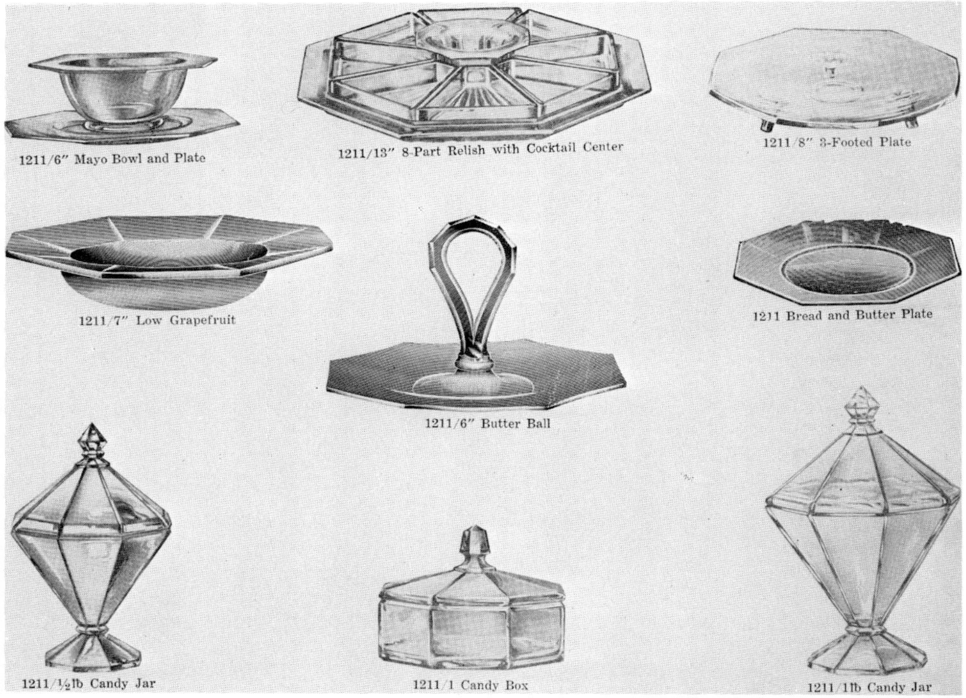

1211 6" Mayo Bowl and Plate

1211 7" Low Grapefruit

1211 ½lb Candy Jar

1211 Cup and Saucer

1211 /7½" Ftd. Sweetmeat RE and SE

1211 Cream

1211 Custard Cup

1211 5x6 Ice Tub with Metal Hld.

1211 Sugar

"DOREEN"

1211 7" 2 Hld. Mint

1211 7" 2 Hld. Bon Bon

1211 6½" 2 Hld. Jelly

1211 8" 2 Hld. Cheese

1211 /4" 2 Hld. Candlestick

1211/13" 2 Hld. Sandwich Plate

1211/13" 2 Hld. L. F. Comport

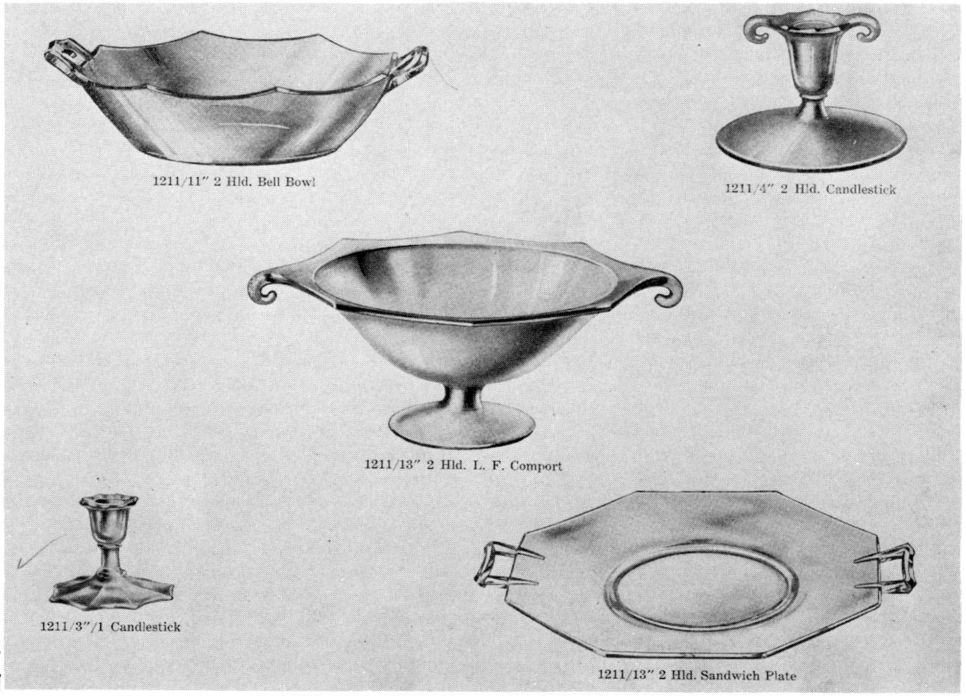

1211/11" 2 Hld. Bell Bowl

1211 /3" /1 Candlestick

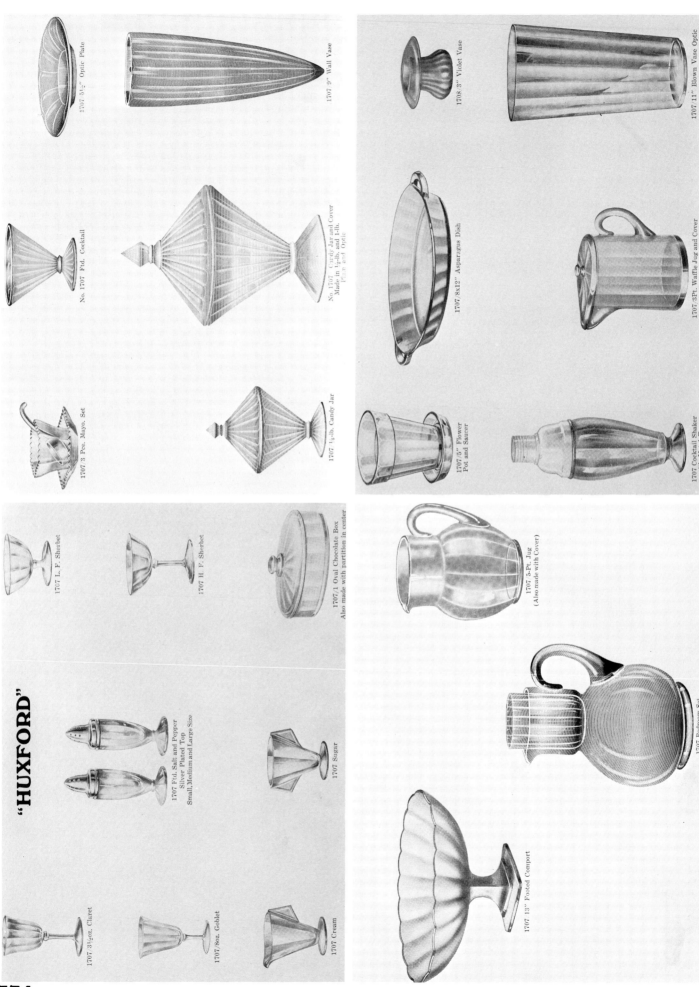

"HUXFORD"

1707 3½-oz. Claret

1707 8-oz. Goblet

1707 Cream

1707 L. F. Sherbet

1707 H. F. Sherbet

1707 Ftd. Salt and Pepper
Silver Plated Top
Small, Medium and Large Size

1707 Sugar

1707/1 Oval Chocolate Box
Also made with partition in center

1707 3½-oz. Optic Plate

1707 9" Wall Vase

No. 1707 Ftd. Cocktail

No. 1707 Candy Jar and Cover
Made in 1½-lb. and 1-lb.
Plain and Optic

1707 3 Pce. Mayo. Set

1707 ¼-lb. Candy Jar

1708 3" Violet Vase

1707 11" Blown Vase Optic
(Also made in 8" and 9")

1707 8x12" Asparagus Dish

1707 3-Pt. Waffle Jug and Cover

1707/5" Flower
Pot and Saucer

1707 Cocktail Shaker
with Metal Top

1707 5-Pt. Jug
(Also made with Cover)

1707 Bedroom Set

1707 13" Footed Comport

1855 1 oz. Cologne Tri. Foot & Stopper

200 Icicle Sugar & Cream Set

200 6" Icicle Ice Tub

176 Tumbler

1930 Shaker SPT

1800 5" Nappy Also made in 5½" & 6"

1899 Grapefruit & Liner

1709 8" Vase Also made "Umbrella" style with handle in center

300 Covered Jar

1931 Shaker 2 B Top

1803 2½ oz. M. C. Cocktail

15 Cocktail Shaker with Silver Plated Top

1930 9" Bowl

1803 3½" Coaster

3000 Flower Pot

1708 7" Fld. Vase

74 2-Pce. Orange Juicer

1930 3" Candlestick

1707 13" 3 Ftd. RE Bowl

1707, 6 6x7 Lipped Ice Bucket with Metal Handle

1707, 10½x13½ SE Oval

1707, 2 6x4½ Low Ice Tub with Metal Handle

1707 11½" 3 Ftd. Cupped Bowl

1707 5x6 High Ice Tub with Metal Handle Also other sizes

1900, 3¼" Coaster

1900/7 2-Part Cov'd Dish

1900/2 Hld. Cream Soup Set

1900/8½" H. F. Sweetmeat SE

1900 Combination Puff and Powder Box

1900/7" RE Bowl and Stand

1900/8½" H. F. Sweetmeat RE

1900/1 Puff Box (3½) 1900/2 Puff Box (4¼")

1900/8" L. F. Comport

1900/7½" H. F. Comport

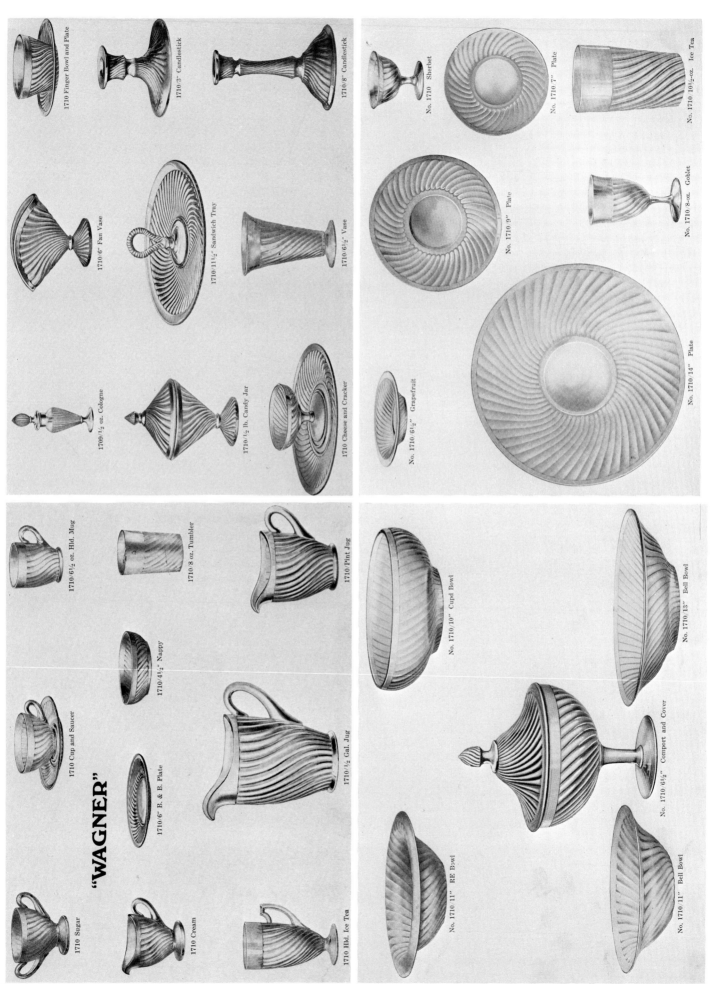

1710 Finger Bowl and Plate

1710·3″ Candlestick

1710·8″ Candlestick

1710·6″ Fan Vase

1710·11½″ Sandwich Tray

1710·6½″ Vase

1709·½ oz. Cologne

1710·½ lb. Candy Jar

1710 Cheese and Cracker

No. 1710 Sherbet

No. 1710·7″ Plate

No. 1710·10½·oz. Ice Tea

No. 1710·9″ Plate

No. 1710·8·oz. Goblet

No. 1710·6½″ Grapefruit

No. 1710·14″ Plate

1710·6½ oz. Hld. Mug

1710·8 oz. Tumbler

1710 Pint Jug

1710/4½″ Nappy

"WAGNER"

1710 Cup and Saucer

1710·6″ B. & B. Plate

1710·½ Gal. Jug

1710 Sugar

1710 Cream

1710 Hld. Ice Tea

No. 1710·10″ Cupd Bowl

No. 1710·13″ Bell Bowl

No. 1710·6½″ Comport and Cover

No. 1710·11″ RE Bowl

No. 1710·11″ Bell Bowl

376

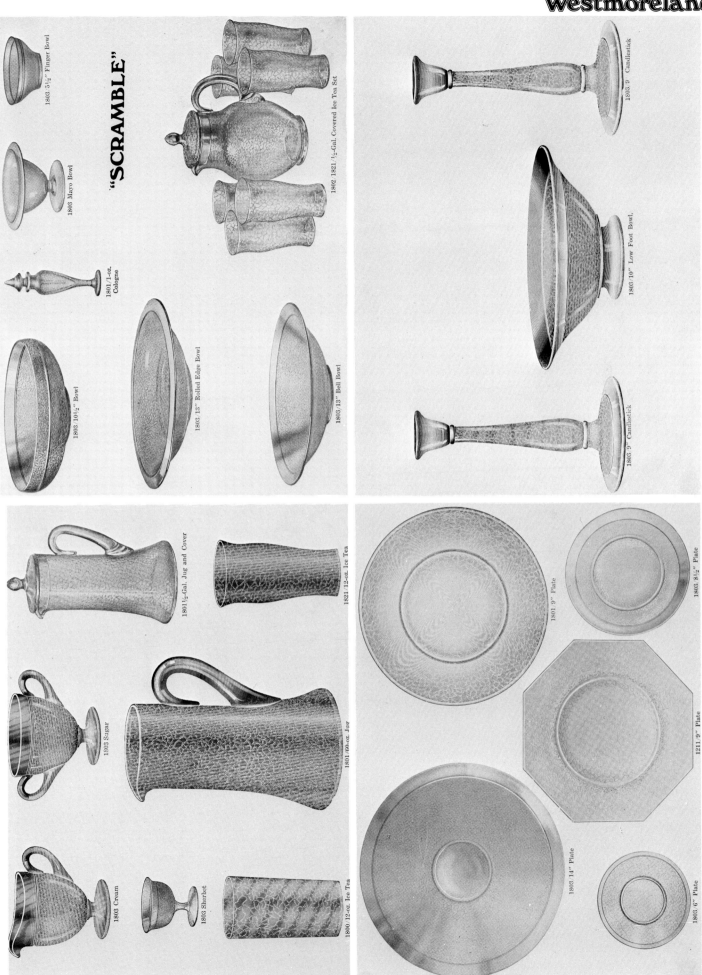

"SCRAMBLE"

1803 5½" Finger Bowl

1803 Mayo Bowl

1801/1-oz. Cologne

1802 1821 ½-Gal. Covered Ice Tea Set

1803 10½" Bowl

1803/13" Rolled Edge Bowl

1803/13" Bell Bowl

1803/9" Candlestick

1803/10" Low Foot Bowl,

1803/9" Candlestick

1801½-Gal. Jug and Cover

1821/12-oz. Ice Tea

1803 Sugar

1801/60-oz. Jug

1803 Cream

1803 Sherbet

1800/12-oz. Ice Tea

1801/9" Plate

1803/8½" Plate

1211/9" Plate

1803/14" Plate

1803/6" Plate

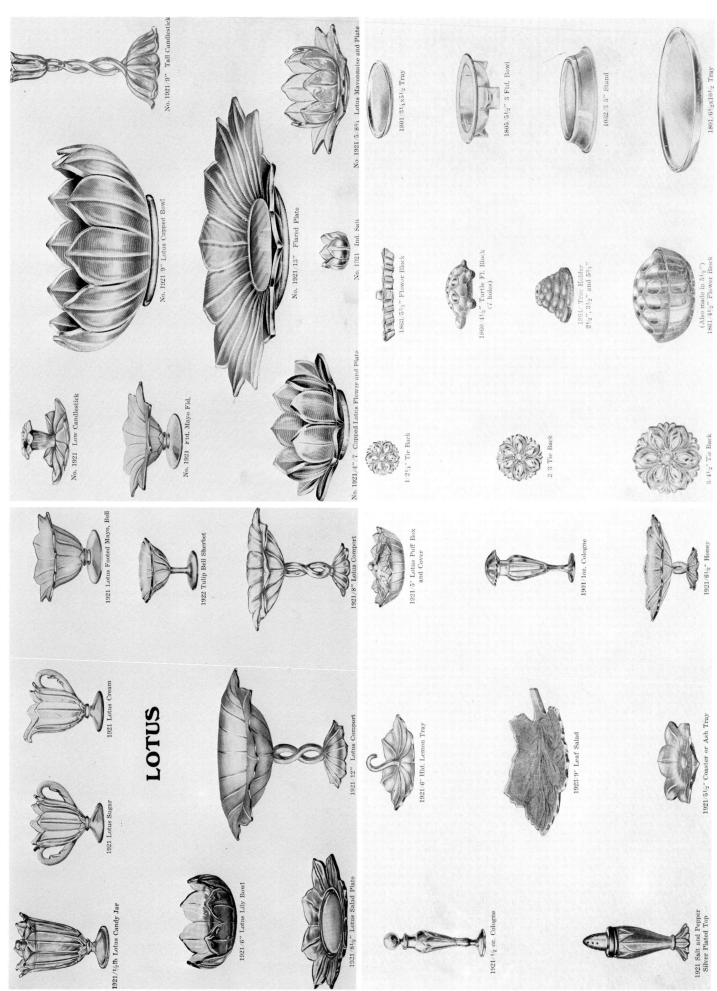

LOTUS

No. 1921 9" Tall Candlestick

No. 1921 5.8¼ Lotus Mayonnaise and Plate

No. 1921 9" Lotus Cupped Bowl

No. 1921 13" Flared Plate

No. 1921 Ind. Salt

No. 1921 Low Candlestick

No. 1921 Ftd. Mayo Fld.

No. 1921/4" 7 Cupped Lotus Flower and Plate

1921 Lotus Footed Mayo, Bell

1922 Tulip Bell Sherbet

1921/8" Lotus Comport

1921 Lotus Cream

1921 Lotus Sugar

1921/1½lb. Lotus Candy Jar

1921 6" Lotus Lily Bowl

1921 8½" Lotus Salad Plate

1921 12" Lotus Comport

1801 3¼x5½ Tray

1805 5½" 3 Ftd. Bowl

1082 3 5" Stand

1801 6½x10½ Tray

1863 5½" Flower Block

1860 4½" Turtle Fl. Block (7 holes)

1854 Tree Holder 2½", 3½" and 5¼"

1861 4½" Flower Block
(Also made in 5½")

1 2¾" Tie Back

2 3 Tie Back

3 4½" Tie Back

1921 5" Lotus Puff Box and Cover

1901 1oz. Cologne

1921/6½" Honey

1921 6" Hld. Lemon Tray

1923 9" Leaf Salad

1921/5½" Coaster or Ash Tray

1921/½ oz. Cologne

1921 Salt and Pepper Silver Plated Top

378

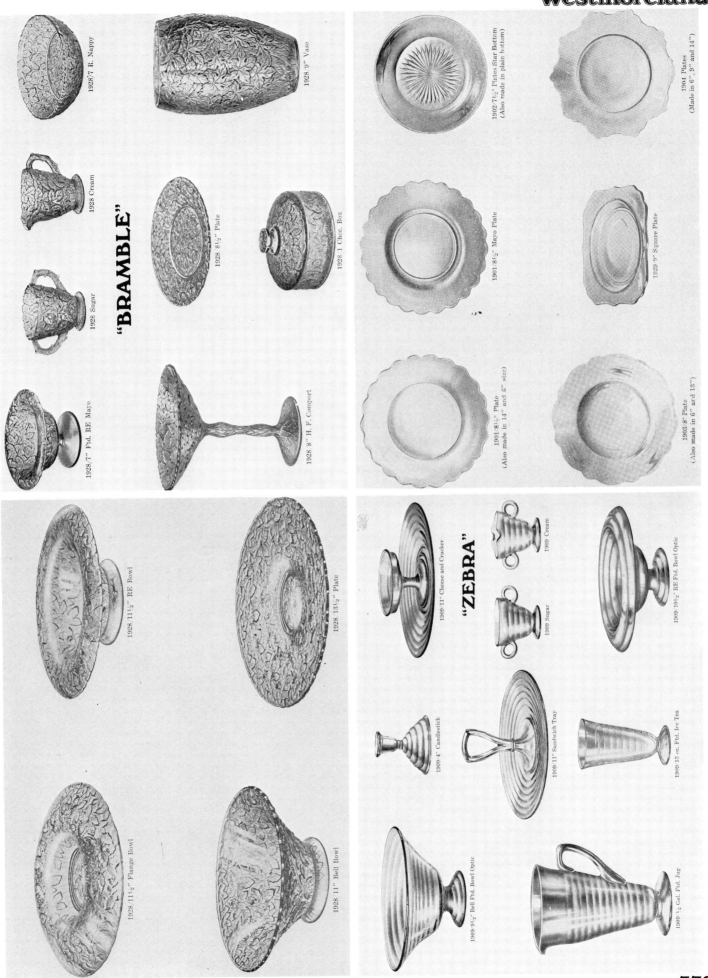

"BRAMBLE"

1928/7 R. Nappy

1928 /9" Vase

1928 Cream

1928 Sugar

1928 8½" Plate

1928 1 Choc. Box

1928/7 Ftd. RE Mayo

1928 8" H. F. Comport

1928 /11½" RE Bowl

1928 13½" Plate

1928/11½" Flange Bowl

1928 11" Bell Bowl

1902 7½" Plates Star Bottom
(Also made in plain bottom)

1904 Plates
(Made in 6", 9" and 14")

1901 8½" Mayo Plate

1929 9" Square Plate

1901/8½" Plate
(Also made in 14" and 6" size)

1903 8" Plate
(Also made in 6" and 13")

"ZEBRA"

1909/11" Cheese and Cracker

1909 Cream

1909 Sugar

1909 10½" RE Ftd. Bowl Optic

1909 4" Candlestick

1909/11" Sandwich Tray

1909 12 oz. Ftd. Ice Tea

1909 9½" Bell Ftd. Bowl Optic

1909 ½ Gal. Ftd. Jug

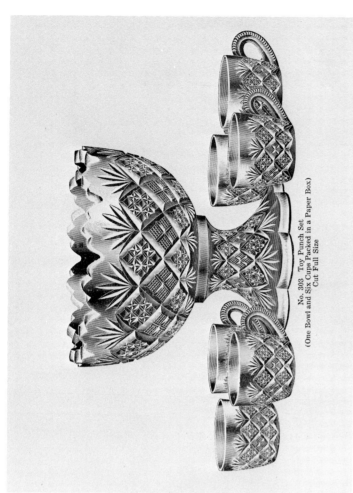

No. 303　Toy Punch Set
(One Bowl and Six Cups Packed in a Paper Box)
Cut Full Size

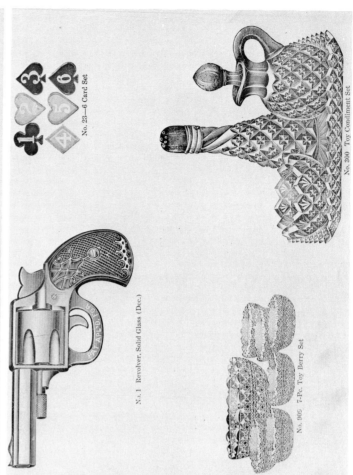

No. 23—6 Card Set

No. 1　Revolver, Solid Glass (Dec.)

No. 300　Toy Condiment Set

No. 305　7-Pc. Toy Berry Set

No. 299　Cream

No. 299　Spoon

Toy 4-Pc. Set
(1 Set to Paper Box)

"THUMBELINA"

No. 299　Butter

No. 299　Sugar

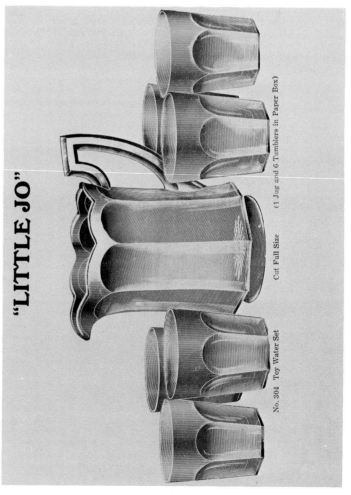

"LITTLE JO"

Cut Full Size

(1 Jug and 6 Tumblers in Paper Box)

No. 304　Toy Water Set

"XYZ"

Grouped together in the next few pages are some of the many glass companies which were active during the period of our interest, but which cannot be better covered at this time. There are still others which cannot even be mentioned for lack of space.

This chapter can only give examples of these factories' wares; perhaps it best serves us by illustrating how very much remains to be seen of colored glassware from the Depression Era.

TULIP

The **DELL GLASS COMPANY** *of Mill-ville, N.J., which was in operation during the 30s, made this line which includes, besides the 6" plate, cup & saucer and creamer pictured here, a wine decanter, tumblers, 6" nappy, and other pieces. Colors are green, amber, amethyst, blue, and crystal.*

OWENS-ILLINOIS GLASS CO. *of Toledo, Ohio, chiefly a maker of containers (1929 to the present), made interesting shakers and bottles during our period, often in dark green and marked like the items shown.*

OWENS SHAKER 4¼" (larger canisters made); 2-QT WATER BOTTLE *Patented Sept. 15, 1931* inscribed; 7-UP BOTTLE.

"RUFF N' READY" RANGE SET (#279 Book 1) This set correctly belongs to Owens-Illinois, it is 10 pieces complete (small sugar not shown). Dark green.

STEUBEN GLASS WORKS
of Corning, New York,
—crown prince among glasshouses—
began its brilliant production
in 1903; in 1918 it became a
division of Corning Glass Works.
Still today it represents
the very highest achievement
in American glasswork.
Besides the many
2- and 3- layer, cased- and
sculptured-glass creations,
Steuben colors of the Depression Era
included ruby, amber, topaz,
Alexandrite, jade, heliotrope, blue,
yellow, rose, dark blue, cinammon,
Calcite Aurene, Ivorene, and more.
Many lines of this period
—ice tea sets, candlesticks, bowls,
and vases—were popularly priced.
A 1931 trade journal featured
this ivory and black display.
Further reference: Robert Rockwell's

1968 "Frederick Carder and His Steuben Glass" and Paul Gardner's "Glass of Frederick Carder" (Crown, 1972).

HOUZE GLASS CO. of Pt. Marion, Pa., has been making utilitarian glass products for years (gear shift balls and glass eyes for taxidermists are only a few of their lines). But during the 20s and 30s the company did make lamps and bases like the one shown here (often with the trademark 'Houzex' in the base) in such transparent, satin-finished, and opaque colors as Coralex (pink), baby blue, opal blue, Moonstone, Nile green, Jadine, Canary, and Veined Onyx. The lamps were made for national stores such as Woolworth's.

A. Douglas Nash began his **CORONA ART GLASS COMPANY** *in Long Island in 1929 and wrought many beautiful pieces there before going to work for Libbey Glass Company about 1933.*

This art line blends combinations of subtle color into crystal, such as Beryl-Peridot (pale amber-green) on crystal foot. The large line includes table pieces, vases, flasks, compotes, and even aquariums. From 1931 trade feature.

CHINTZ

A new departure in American glass, not pressed—not blown. New, smart shapes and designs styled for the present trend, but most important of all made by a NEW and DIFFERENT PROCESS for table glassware, resulting in a HARD BRILLIANCE in finish never before attained.

Eight different patterns in crystal and five colors—cobalt blue, aquamarine, green, wine, amber, afford a wide range from which to choose.

MISSISSIPPI GLASS CO.

"STRIPPLE" *by the* MISSISSIPPI GLASS CO. *from a 1927 advertisement.*

"VERLYS OF AMERICA" *of Newark, Ohio, is a branch of the French Holoplane Co., makers of Verlys in France. The American product is similar but less expensive. The first year opened, 1935, sixteen patterns were made in smoky topaz, blue, amber, and opalescent. Besides the LES CHARDONS (Thistles) and LES PAPILLONS (Butterflies) patterns pictured here, motifs of fish, ducks, shells, pine cones, and flowers were used.*

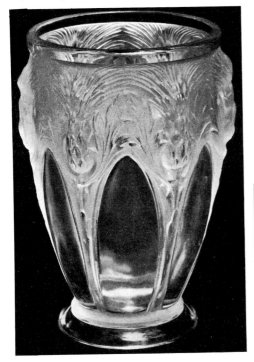

H. NORTHWOOD CO.
WHEELING, W. VA.

NEW ITEMS IN COLORED GLASS
Console sets in blue, topaz, russet iridescent, and chinese red. Candlesticks have hollow foot.

The well-known NORTHWOOD *company made many items in transparent colors, as well as its famous iridescent effects, before it was sold in 1926.*

Twelve Piece Assortment
Bison Decorating Co.
may be had in ten different designs

DECORATING COMPANIES

*Many firms large and small specialized in adding their
own decorations to "blanks" (plain patterns) which
they bought from other factories. Ads this page show
some of the varieties of decorating.*

"NEW VOGUE" —1930 advertisement

A new liquor set from the Germania line of E. Torlotting, Inc., is shown above. In addition to this ebony set this line may also be had in a number of other solid colors as well as crystal in combination with colors. It is reasonable in price, extremely good looking and brand new.

"ESSEN"—1932 trade report

PREMIER WATER SET in green mould crackled glass, 9" jug, 4¾" glasses. Embodying the usually high-priced cone-shaped footed jug and tumblers for the first time at a popular price. May be retailed at $1.19 or lower if you choose.

GEO. BORGFELDT & CO.
NEW YORK, NEW YORK

—1926 ad

IMPORTED GLASS—*Colored glassware was being made abroad during this time period as well, and firms such as these did a competitive business with imported glass.*

THE MARY RYAN ORGANIZATION

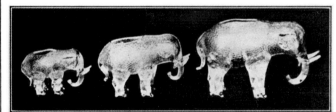

CRYSTAL,
GREEN
and
AMBER.

PEBBLED ELEPHANTS

MYRAN TURTLE

—1926 ad

Now, when warmer weather turns the thoughts of the hostess to glassware more than ever, this interesting pattern known as the Floradora is introduced. It is from the show-

FLORADORA —1929 trade report

"SWEDA" —1933 trade report

rooms of Graham & Zenger, Inc., 104 Fifth avenue, and may be had in green, amber or amethyst. It is an importation of exceptional merit for the design is not only unique but represents excellent craftsmanship.

There are a lot of smart new beverage sets, one of which is shown here, in the Germania line of E. Torlotting, Inc. These are stocked and come in colors of Swedish blue, sea green and amber. They offer a good quality glass that will retail for $2.59 and, of course, are only one of a fine and varied selection of new lines this firm have for 1933.

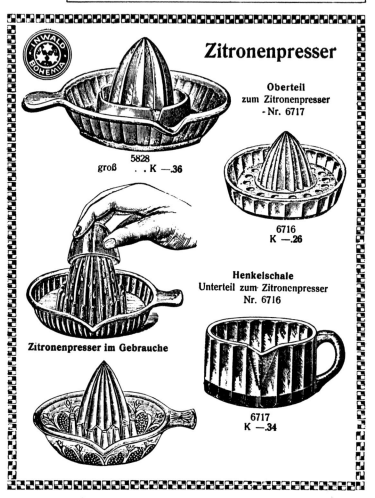

A glass company had in its files this flyer illustrating a variety of German reamer concepts of the period.

SPICER STUDIO *made extensive lines of lustred ware in the 20s; transparent colors in the Depression years.*

POTOMAC GLASS CO. *of Cumberland, Md. (1904-1929) made colored tableware; this candlestick from a 20s patent.*

The Spicer Studios, 532 East Market street, Akron, O., makes this honey jar in the form of a bee-hive with a detachable top. It comes in Amber, blue, Amethyst or iridescent rainbow and sells for $6.75 a doz.

—1927 ad

Something New in Two-Tone Stemware

Spicer glass from the Spicer Studios, Akron, Ohio, is well known by this time throughout the trade as one of the most striking and original iridescent lines to be found. It comes

in amber, rose or green, or in combinations of colors, and the entire line comprises some fifty items. The sugar and creamer featured here are typical—both possessed of a quaintness and an appeal that is noteworthy.

We are featuring refreshment sets and blown stemware in two-tone combinations. Our new lustre effects also are worthy of your attention.

McDONALD GLASS WORKS, INC.
McDonald, Penna.

Three of the many lines of stemware, often optic in design, offered by McDONALD GLASS WORKS in combinations of pink/green & crystal.

—two 1929 trade journal reports

A beautiful collection of blown glassware in four gorgeous iridescent colors. Hundreds of shapes, popular for beauty and price.

SPICER STUDIO
532 E. Market St.   Akron, Ohio

Flashing iridescence in blown glassware of quality. An exceptional line of distinct appeal.

Four beautiful colors— Amber, Amethyst, Blue and Rainbow in many very delicate shapes.

SPICER STUDIO

—1926 ad

The Unknowns

It won't surprise anyone that, even after years of research, many patterns and pieces remain mysteries in the boundless world of colored glassware of the Depression Era.

Will we ever find the identity of these challengers? Will the real manufacturers ever stand up? For some, perhaps. But I believe that for many, the secret will be lost forever, hidden beneath the dust of glass history too fragile to last the long years through.

I don't mind so much, really. Those of us who like to fish, after all, are hooked on the fishing itself—it's the one that got away, the ones still swimming around out there, that hold our interest. It's the same for us collectors of glass, and us collectors of glass history. Much of the intrigue is the search itself. So it really doesn't bother me so much to include these pages of Unknowns (and there are, of course, many more than these which must wait for still another publication). Some of these riddles I've been trying to solve for years—but I'll wave the white flag for now. Peace.

If I could just find out who made that #@% STRAWBERRY!*

"CARAVAN"

"MOONDANCE"

"INTO THE MYSTIC"

4¼" ASHTRAYS
*in green;
sketch of etched
centers*

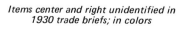

"DOMINO" Smoker Set
Pink, green, ruby, dark blue, topaz

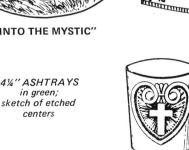

"ST. DOMINIC'S" Candle Tumbler

*Items center and right unidentified in
1930 trade briefs; in colors*

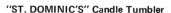

"CYPRUS OWL"
Combination Pitcher & Tumbler

**"ASTRAL
OWL"
Bookend**

"BELFAST TURTLE"

The Greatest Mystery of Them All — what company made the patterns on this page (and our "STRAWBERRY" on page 390)? So many characteristics in common—colors very close, same-style handles, butterbottoms all alike (7", plain rim, starred base) and interchangeable, only tableware pieces made, and all advertised in the late 20s with no maker given— yet in all my research I have not found the company who made them!

"UNKNOWN SWIRL"
butterdish & cover, sugar & cover, creamer, 4¾" tumbler, 5¾"x2" dish & cover, 8" plate; in green

"FLORAL AND DIAMOND BAND"

(#155 in Book 1)
Pink, green, black, medium blue.
ROW 1:
butterdish & cover, sugar & cover, creamer, small sugar
ROW 2:
4", 5" tumblers, 8" jug, 8¼" plate
NOT SHOWN:
4½", 8" nappies, 4" comport, sherbet

"AUNT POLLY"

Pink, green, medium blue, iridescent amber.
ROW 1:
butterdish & cover, sherbet & sherbet plate, 5¼" handled comport, 3¾", 9-oz tumbler
ROW 2:
7¼" pickle dish, sugar (cover not shown), creamer, 4-3/8" nappy, (7-7/8" nappy not shown)
ROW 3:
6½" footed tumbler, 8" jug, 8" plate

NOT SHOWN:
salt & pepper, oval vegetable 8-3/8"

389

This popular line—a major pattern in Book 1—is further confusing because all the pieces made with strawberries were also made with cherries only. So, we'll call one

"STRAWBERRY" and the other one "CHERRY-BERRY"

Large covered sugar, 5½"
Butterdish, 7" bottom
    with plain rim
Jug, 7¾"

Pieces in addition to
    those in Book 1
    pictured here

Jug, 7¾"

The "FRUITS" family.

The first two pieces shown, 8" and 4" nappies, match the FRUITS pattern shown as a major line in Book 1. The second two, the 4¼" tumbler and 7" jug with cherries only, are more-or-less related, as are the 4" and 4¼" tumblers on the right with small etched grapes.
    All come in green and all are being collected as part of one family, if not exactly matching, under the FRUITS label.

"ROXANA" is also a major pattern of Book 1, with additional pieces shown here: 4½x2½" bowls, topaz and opaque white; 6" nappy, 5" nappy, and 5½" saucer.

S & R OVENWARE (inscribed), 10½x5″ and 6¼x4¾″, crystal (detail). *DIAMOND CRYSTAL SHAKER SALT 7½″* Mixing Bowl and *T & S HANDMAID* 2-Cup Measure, both inscribed and green.

STRAW HOLDER, 9½″ green, metal cover.
MISSION GRAPEFRUIT Dispenser, 12½″ green, pink. Paper label says *Real fruit juice, Sweetened. Property of Mission Dry Corporation, Ltd.*
NESBITTS Dispenser, 9″ pink. Inscribed in glass *Property of Nesbitts for our syrups only C. A. Look, Los Angeles.*

"SIMPLETON" Plate
6″ green
DUCHESS Sherbet
crystal; metal holder
(see detail)
"SUNDANCE" Tumbler
4″ topaz, green, pink
"DRIP-DROP" Cup & Saucer
light blue; other
pieces in this line

GREEN KITCHEN GADGETS
4-cup Measuring Cup, 7″. ICE CRUSHER, 10½″ with 4¼″ square CRISSCROSS bowl. METAL JUICER usually found w/green bowl. D & B BEATER BOWL, 5½″, 32-oz. VIDRIO Electric Beater, 4½″. "BLOCK FROSTED" Ice Bowl, 5½″.

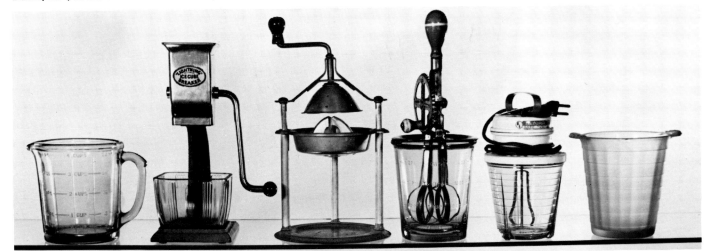

"TRICIA"

This unidentified line comes in pink and light green, and sometimes the pieces have an etching. Shown: Plates, 6½" and 8"; sherbet; sugar & cover; creamer.

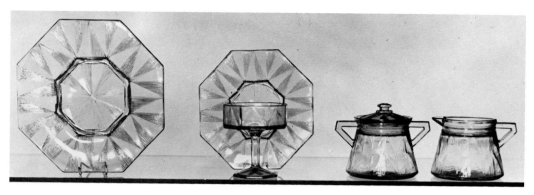

"HOBLIGHT" Light Fixture, pink. We find many light fixtures from the 30s made, like this one, from a large bowl mold with a small hole in the center for a metal rod.

"FAVE" Vase, 7", green

"MY PET" Powder Jar & cover, pink

"ORNATE" Vase, 10¼" pink, green

"CHARADE"

Made in dark blue, amethyst, and pink. Known pieces so far are the 8" plate, cup & saucer, cream & sugar, and the 10" sandwich server.

"HUNT Plate", 8" topaz (see detail).

"COLUMBUS Plate", 8" amber.

"DOILY Plate", 8¼" crystal, green.

"ROSANNA Plate", 8¾" crystal.

"STAR WHEEL Plate", 8" pink.

"STAR FLOWER Plate", 9¾" green.

"CONSTELLATION Plate", 8" pink.

"STAR WHIRL Plate", 8-3/8" green.

"OLLIE MAY"
Dresser Set
6" candlestick, 11½" tray,
3-5/8" ring holder, 3-5/8" dish,
3-5/8" dish & cover, 4½" powder
dish & cover, pink.

"EBB" shaker
pink, green

"FLO" Shaker
also with glass handle
pink, green

ROW 1:
"ZIPPER RIB" cheese &
cracker, 8¼" plate w/indent
for cheese dish, pink.
"ADAM'S RIB" handled tumbler, 5", cream & sugar on
8½x6¾" tray, green.

ROW 2:
"SHORT RIB" 3-part candy
dish, 7"; metal cover, catalin
handle; dark blue, burgundy.
"STANDING RIB" cocktail
shaker, 11" including chrome
top, and 4½" cocktail with
metal base; dark blue.
"PRIME RIB" bowl, 9" with
metal base; dark blue, burgundy.

ROW 1:
"KRACKLE" Keg Set,
7¾" tall, green, six
tumblers.
"SHIRLEY" Water Set,
4½" tumbler, 8½"
jug, pink.
"AUSTIN" Water Jug,
8" green (detail).

ROW 2:
"FRANCES" Vase, 7¾"
pink (more pieces
probable).
"COPE" Cake Stand,
6-5/8" tall, green.
"MITCHELL" Vase, 9"
green.
"LITTLE TY" Jug, 5½"
pink.

ROW 1: "SNAPPY" Server, 10" pink. "DROOPY ROSE" Tumbler, 6-1/8" green (1st detail). "MAIZY DAISY" Mug, 3½" pink (2nd detail). HUMPTY DUMPTY—TOM TOM Mug, 3½" green (detail). "KIPLING" Dish, 6" amber w/green plastic base (detail).

ROW 2: "ADELE" Nappy, 8¼" green, 8-pt star in bottom. "AGGY" Nappy, 9" pink. "ADDY" Comport, 5¾" pink (could be late). "ABBY" Nappy, 7" pink.

VARIOUS AND ASSORTED "SWIRLS": 10" platter, 8" jug, butterdish, 10" cake plate.

ROW 1:
"SHARI" Dresser set, 7" base 4½" tall (detail). "FANNY BRICE" Rose Bowl, 7" pink. "FROLIC" Dresser Tray, 10x5¾" frosted pink.
Row 2: "FERN" Coaster, 4-5/8" pink. "FROND" Ashtray, 4-5/8" pink. "MAGGIE BOWL", 5" amber, dk. blue, green. "NANCY DREW" Nappy, 5¾" pink. "STAR" Coaster, 4-3/8" pink.

ROW 1: ODD RED PIECES
Cup & saucer, 8¼'' plate,
2¾'' high creamer

ROW 2: "MILDRED"
2½'' high cream & sugar,
8½'' plate, cup & saucer
Pink, red

ROW 1:
   "COCKLESHELL" Berry Set, 8'', 4½'' nappies, pink. "MARYMONT" Berry Set, 4½'' ruffled nappy, 4¼'', 7¼'' nappies, pink, green (detail)
ROW 2:
   "CONCORD" Berry Set, 7¼'', 4½'' nappies, green. "LEXINGTON" Console set, 11'' bowl, 6'' candlestick, pink.

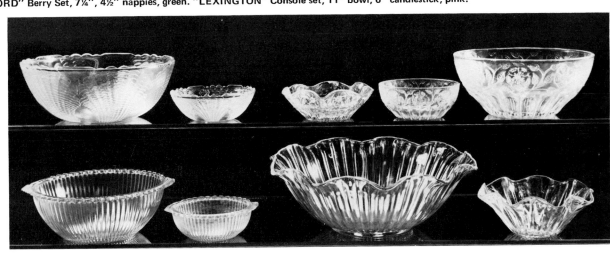

ROW 1: "ANITA" Chicken waterer, 5½'' pink. "Johanna" Bird feeder, 3¼'' green. "PARKER" Shaving mug, 3½'' pink. TOOTHBRUSH holder,
   6½'' frosted pink. "WOODPECKER" vases, 8'' green & black.
ROW 2: "SCOTTIE" Blotter, 3½'' opaque green, black, blue, amber, pink, green (also other animals). SPONGE Holder, 3-1/8''x1-5/8'' green.
   CRACKLE BALL, 3¼'' green. "LIL' FISH", 2-5/8'' green.
ROWS 3 & 4: DRAWER PULL, 4-1/8'' green. "CUTIE" Tie for curtains, 6'' green, pink. Curtain Ring, 4'' pink, green. "DOWNY" Curtain holder,
   4'' pink, green. GLASS KNIVES (top) 9-1/8'' pink, 8½'' green, 9-1/8'' crystal (see drawing of same, in same order l. to r.).

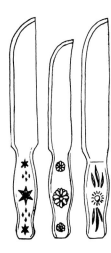

ROW 1:
"SWAN LAKE" Console Set, 6½"
candlesticks, 10" bowl, pink, green.
"THRUSH" 6¼" tumbler, 3¼"
high comport, green.

ROW 2:
BOTTLE SET, 6x8" tray, 5½"
high bottle, lt. green. "EVA" Jar &
Cover, 4" high, oval, pink, green
(see detail above). "TOPSY" Jar &
Cover, 3½" high, pink. TROUGH,
2½x5" pink, green. "HOLDEN"
Set, 3" tumblers, 6" diameter
holder, pink.

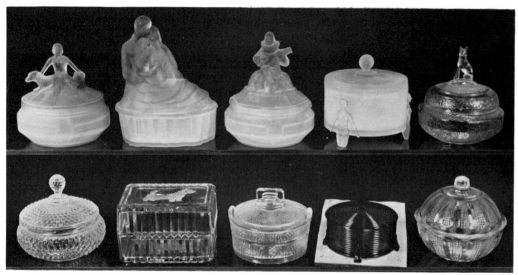

Powder Jars & Covers

(all dimensions vertical)

"ANNETTE", 4¾" pink frost
"LOVERS", 6", pink frost
"MINSTREL", 5¼", green frost
"FLAPPERS", 4-1/8", pink frost
"MASCOT", 4½" green
"HOBNAIL", 4-1/8" pink & crystal
"BOWSER", 5x3¾x3", pink
"BARK", 3¼", pink, green
"SPINNER", 2½", dk. blue-green
"DIAMOND PANEL" (#156 Book I)
   4", pink, green

ROW 1: "FEATHER" Tumbler 3¾", 4½", dk. blue (detail below). "CHEERI-O" Cocktail
Shaker, 10" dk. red, recipe cards on side in holder "Copyright 1934". "JOSEPH" Cocktail 3½"
dk. blue, metal base. "RING OF RINGS" Decanter 10", tumbler 3", dk. blue. "MICKEY"
Cream & Sugar, 2½" dk. blue. "CLEOPATRA" Sherbet in metal holder, dk. blue (detail at
left). ROW 2: "ALTON" Set, 8½" sq. tray, 4" sq. inserts, dk. blue. "VALENTI" Relish,
13x8" dk. blue, metal holder, has ribbed sides, prism bottom. "KRAFT" Cheese Dish, 5" base,
dk. blue, red, or green w/crystal cover.

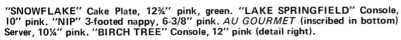

"SNOWFLAKE" Cake Plate, 12¾" pink, green. "LAKE SPRINGFIELD" Console, 10" pink. "NIP" 3-footed nappy, 6-3/8" pink. *AU GOURMET* (inscribed in bottom) Server, 10¼" pink. "BIRCH TREE" Console, 12" pink (detail right).

OPAQUE GREEN MISCELLANEOUS

"JENNIFER" Centerpiece,
8½x5¾x4½" tall
"CLINK" Shaker, 5½"
"PLAIN" Tumbler, 5½" ground
bottom
"HOWARD" Cruet, 6¾"
"MARION" Bird Bath Dish,
2-5/8" base
"RICHIE" Dolphin bowl, 6"
"CLINTON" Vase, 7"
HALL'S WATER DISPENSER,
10½x5x5" tall

BLACK GLASS MISCELLANEOUS
ROW 1: "BRUNO" Vase, 5", 7" also green, (detail below). "MOWGLI" Line, 3¾", 9-oz tumbler, 8½" plate, cup & saucer. "EBON" Soda, 5½" (holds disposable paper cup?). "NADA" Cup & Saucer.
ROW 2: "SIMON" Cream & Sugar, 2¾". "EDAL" Manicure Set, tray 7x4½". "SHERMAN" Candlestick, 3¾". "TRIAD" Candlestick, 2½". "SAMPSON" Candlestick, 4".

397

ADVERTISING ITEMS

ROW 1:
Clark's Teaberry Gum, 3¼" high, canary. *Little Deb Toys*, 3" crystal. MOBIL ashtray, 5" black glass w/red metal horse. *Mission* 4" tumbler, crystal. GEORGE WASHINGTON tumbler, 4½" green with *1732 – 1932* under cameo.

ROW 2:
Centennial Celebration 1834 – 1934, 7½" plate on one of Imperial's patterns.   Two plates, 8-3/8" (hobnail) and 8" (swirl) with *Urban's Liberty Flour, George Urban Milling Co. Buffalo, N.Y.*, pink.

ROW 3: (all ashtrays)
The General Tire 3½" pink. *Goodrich Silvertown* 4¾" blue-green. *Pennsylvania Tires* 3½" pink. *Macbeth-Evans Charleroi Pa.* glassblower, 3¼" pink. *Anchor Hocking Glass Corp. 38 Years of Progress 1905 – 1943*, 4" crystal. *Best Wishes from Baxter Careful Launderers Dry Cleaners*, 3¼" pink.

LAMPS

Electric glass lamps of all descriptions and colors were made in the 20s and 30s. Only a few are shown here. Others may be found in the company chapters.

ROW 1:
"CELESTIAL" 11" green, also in opaque green w/white stars & moons. "SPOOL" 12½" pink. "OLD CAFE" 11½" Royal Ruby, base is the 7¼" vase upside down, Anchor Hocking. "TARA GIRL" 12", comes in frosted-on pink, blue, white; this shade plastic, you may find glass or silk; girl 6"; similar lamps carry Houze Glass Co. label. LAMP BASE, 8½" green with screws for electric light socket; Indiana Glass Co. "ZELDA" 7" pink, hobnail bowl & floral base. "DIAMOND" 9" pink.

ROW 2:
"FREDEE" Lamp base, 4½" pink, green, crystal. "SOUTHERN BELLE", base 5", shade 4", pink painted on crystal, similar to Houze Glass Co. lamps. "BLACK BEAUTY", 7½" black diamond motif w/partial wood stem. "HOBNAIL", 6" pink. "FITZGERALD" 7½" amethyst. "SEA DOLPHIN" 7" pink. "BLACK ELEPHANT", base 3", shade 5" green satin.